Time Longer Than Rope

Time Longer Than Rope

A Century of African American Activism, 1850–1950

EDITED BY

Charles M. Payne and Adam Green

New York University Press

NEW YORK AND LONDON

NEW YORK UNIVERSITY PRESS
New York and London
www.nyupress.org

Library of Congress Cataloging-in-Publication Data
Time longer than rope : a century of African American activism,
1850–1950 / edited by Charles M. Payne and Adam Green.
p.   cm.
Includes bibliographical references.
ISBN 0-8147-6702-8 (cloth : alk. paper)
ISBN 0-8147-6703-6 (pbk. : alk. paper)
1. African Americans—Civil rights—Southern States—History—19th
century. 2. African Americans—Civil rights—Southern
States—History—20th century. 3. African Americans—Social
conditions—To 1964. 4. African American political activists—Southern
States—History. 5. African American civil rights workers—Southern
States—History. 6. Civil rights movements—Southern States—
History—19th century. 7. Civil rights movements—Southern States—
History—20th century. 8. Southern States—Race relations.
9. Southern States—History—1865–1951.   I. Payne, Charles M.
II. Green, Adam, 1963–
E185.61.T497   2003
323.1'196073075'09034—dc21   2003009492

New York University Press books are printed on acid-free paper,
and their binding materials are chosen for strength and durability.

Manufactured in the United States of America

10 9 8 7 6 5 4 3 2 1

Contents

Introduction

> The American Negroes are the only people in the history
> of the world, so far as I know, that ever became free with-
> out any effort of their own. . . . They twanged banjoes
> around the railroad stations, sang melodious spirituals,
> and believed that some Yankee would come along and
> give each of them forty acres and a mule.
>
> —W. E. Woodward, *Meet General Grant* (1938)

Historical analysis of African American activism has certainly improved since Woodward's day, but less than one might suppose. Though they might take issue with the suggestion, until very recently most American scholars discussed African American agency in ways that were little more than dignified versions of Woodward's caricature. Popular thought, including some African American popular thought, all too often has proceeded from similar assumptions. Younger Black Americans, for example, sometimes seem to think that struggle began with Martin Luther King and Malcolm X and that prior to them Blacks did little to challenge their oppression.

Scholars know better, but even in scholarly work on the modern Civil Rights Era one finds reluctance to acknowledge the depth of African Americans' activist initiative. What Julian Bond, among others, calls the Master Narrative of the civil rights movement, a history framed around Dr. King, the Kennedys, and the redemptive days of Montgomery and Memphis, highlights national spokesmen and power brokers, rendering the mass of Black people invisible, as if they were off somewhere engaging in the contemporary equivalent of strumming banjoes.[1] Though it makes a dramatic and even inspiring story, the Narrative does so by refusing to take seriously "ordinary" people whose years of persistent struggle often made the big events possible. Delivered from the wilderness of Jim Crow law and custom, Black folk's scripted role becomes that of the rescued survivors.

Seen in this light, the dignity of suffering and the power of eloquent witness are the core lessons of the civil rights struggles, rather than the birth of modern movement practice and the radicalization of the very idea of citizenship. Romantic notions of consensus across the color line obscure the real difficulties activists had in sustaining cross-racial alliances. Faith in the rule of law and the power of the national conscience displaces a historical record in which some activists who placed their confidence in the national sense of fair play paid for that with their lives while others grew angry and desperate. This kind of normative history automatically marginalizes radicalism. If we are such a morally responsive society, militant response is hardly justified. The Narrative consistently underestimates how arduous and uncertain it has been—and remains—to remake a nation anew, as the nonracist society its founders in fact never intended it to be, and how much of that burden has been borne by the least privileged Americans.

The easy triumphalism of the Master Narrative, of course, rings false to many of those who took part in the struggles of the 1950s and 1960s. As the work of reconstructing the Civil Rights Era in public memory has been taken up by this group witness, the story has become less one of the heroism of a few and more one of mass activism. Over the last decade or more, a new generation of scholars has joined this debate, overturning virtually every tenet of the traditional story of the modern movement. That scholarship has led to more emphasis on local movements and local leaders, on women, and on the historically creative roles that non-elites can play under the appropriate structural circumstances.[2] Even our basic conception of what constitutes opposition has been transformed by the application to twentieth-century struggles of the idea of "everyday resistance."[3]

The growing interest in the ordinary roots of extraordinary change has begun to define study of earlier periods as well. The essays included in this volume extend this revision, demonstrating over and over again the depth and breadth of Black oppositional spirit and activity. The sections in which they appear are organized roughly by chronology. There are some significant points of disagreement among them but there are also some very important unifying themes.

The quest for economic justice is arguably the first and most significant of these themes. Several of these essays show that Black responses to economic exploitation and labor abuse have defined some of the most challenging, imaginative—and underappreciated—campaigns to better Black life conditions. Nan Woodruff's essay on Arkansas's Elaine Massacre of 1919, for example, shows how tenant farmers throughout the Mississippi/ Arkansas delta pursued an energetic campaign to reform labor practices and increase compensation, the spark for one of the most profound examples of racist atrocity during the twentieth century. Greta de Jong and Michael Honey examine efforts later in the twentieth century to organize sharecroppers in rural Louisiana and factory workers in Memphis, respectively, pointing out, among other things, the important—though not determinative—role of white leftist organizers in fostering the birth and growth of the Louisiana Farmers' Union and the southern Congress of Industrial Organizations, while also demonstrating how each community's legacy of labor activism demanded a more material orientation from subsequent local antidiscrimination campaigns during the 1960s. It may be common now to separate the civil rights struggle from labor struggle, but Paul Ortiz demonstrates conclusively that such a separation was completely alien to the thinking of Black activists in early-twentieth-century Florida and to the people who were oppressing them. These essays do more than place Black workers at the center of the Black activist tradition. They establish, in distinct yet linked ways, how local economies of sugar, cotton, and rice, steel and mining, and machine manufacture informed the course of activist struggles in a given community and among particular groups of Black workers.

No matter how demeaning the job, workers may be able to redefine it, to find value where the broader society denies it. Michael Honey's analysis of the oral narratives of Black workers in twentieth-century Memphis foregrounds how their artisan-like sense of the dignity of their work, far from constituting a concession to the terms of their oppression, could constitute the psychic cornerstone on which those workers raised challenges to the material deprivation of their lives. One is reminded here of the famous first-person narrative of Alabama tenant farmer and Sharecroppers' Union member Nate Shaw, whose sense of himself as "an overaverage man," derived in part from his expertise in so many different lines of work, consistently informed his willingness to challenge the supremacist presumptions of his white neighbors. Seen in this light, the spaces and institutions of worker unity and workplace justice take on new importance within the development of black activism, as important to the broader movement as the Black church and press have been seen to be in more traditional accounts.

Too, Black labor's priority as a social concern often defined lines of political affiliation not only for whites, but also Black elites, as Brian Kelly's analysis of turn-of-the-century Birmingham shows.

This last observation illuminates another theme linking these pieces as a group: their stress on the everyday nature of Black political concerns and organizing. That everyday life for Black folk was invariably politicized, as historians of the post-emancipation period have noted, characterizes most depictions of Black experience, from Ida Wells to Malcolm X. The inverse formulation—that everyday life constitutes the core substance of Black politics—is less readily acknowledged. Yet it is precisely the interplay between everyday conditions and motivating ideas that these essays illuminate so well—Paul Ortiz's discussion of "nonpolitical" lodges and mutual benefit associations and their crucial role in the political mobilization of Black Floridians; Elsa Barkley Brown and David Cecelski's depiction of the fervent yet precarious process of community formation in Richmond, Virginia and Wilmington, North Carolina following emancipation; and Thavolia Glymph's analysis of community celebrations during the same period. Mundane activities like church meetings and outdoor sermons, freedom jubilees and holiday drill marches all served as rehearsals for more ambitious expressions of struggle and engagement. Barkley Brown's essay captures, as few others have before it, how an everyday interpretation of Black politics clarifies in particular the role played by Black women in articulating group concerns, providing effective checks on leadership's tendency to define community in self-serving terms, and transforming the ballot into a representation of collective interest rather than individual preference. Similarly, Cecelski points out that the contraband camps of slave refugees accompanying Union soldiers behind southern lines during the Civil War have generally been overlooked as important sites of social and political formation for the freedmen. If traditional scholarship tends to marginalize militance, more recent scholarship often romanticizes it. Glymph's essay normalizes it, finding a recognition of the need for armed self-defense deeply rooted in the ordinary rituals of local communities, even if it was not clearly reflected by the pronouncements of national spokespersons.

The term "activism" hardly conjures up the issue of how people construct their past, but several articles here—in particular those by Glymph, Barkley Brown, Ortiz, and Scott Sandage—make a persuasive case for the centrality of "memory-work." The ability of a community to control the images of its past can be a vital form of social capital. An alternative understanding of the past can help people envision alternative futures and the steps that lead there. Many of the essays here emphasize the decades of self-education, of building community by building shared memories, that then informed stands against oppressive conditions. Indeed, a case could be made that when the movement downplays these more mundane elements of struggle in favor of its more dramatic expressions, it undermines its own long-term viability. At the same time, "memory-work" often involves a constant reinvention of the idea of America itself, exemplified by Scott Sandage's analysis of the changing meaning of the Lincoln Memorial.

Yet the power of group memory has at times imposed strict limits on the political imaginations of Blacks and other Americans. For Charise Cheney, the long memory of U.S. Blacks and the hunger for respect engendered by that memory encouraged an ongoing conservation of masculinity, so that both classical and modern phases of black nationalism as cultural practice revolve around aggressive—and often reflexive—invocations of manhood. Converging with recent work in the field of political science, Cheney presents the masculinist bias in various iterations of nationalist culture and insurgency as a "linked fate" approach: one in which unity of outlook and agenda among blacks is presumed rather than achieved, and alternative conceptions of the root conditions of racial oppression are dismissed as unhelpful distraction.[4] Peter Wood takes up the question of how slavery itself is remembered in classroom and popular history, arguing that much discourse on race and racial activism, past and present, amounts to a trivialization of the American racial experience. We hide the reality even as we study it exhaustively.

Trivialization can take flattering forms. If students of Black struggle have had to overcome the deeply rooted stereotype of Black passivity, there has also been a tendency, from the other side, to find heroic resistance in all social and political acts, to the point where oppositional activity seems natural, even omnipresent.[5] Indeed, some of the relatively new, bottom-up history is really not so different from the scholarship it is critiquing as its authors suppose. A number of articles here, Cheney's most explicitly, suggest that critics of the Master Narrative may reject some aspects of it only to uncritically embrace other aspects.

Rigid conceptions of the boundaries of racial community are one source of uncritical thinking. A central element of conveying a sense of a redeemed future is acknowledging the real breadth of the very idea of "Black community." Works produced by the past generation of scholars have foregrounded how attention to sexuality, diasporic roots, ethnicity, class, and in particular gender require a much broader conception of what is meant by Black community than had been habit in both scholarly and popular writings. The essays in the collection build on this crucial intervention. Indeed, they attest in strikingly uniform fashion to the need to think expansively about the parameters of black group experience and aspiration, by addressing in diverse ways the question of how to represent the indigenous base for a given campaign or struggle. Ula Taylor's groundbreaking examination of the role of Amy Ashwood Garvey and Amy Jacques Garvey in the rise of the Universal Negro Improvement Association, to cite one example, demonstrates how even when women are, in some senses, treated as being outside the political community, their work can still help create and sustain that community. Similarly, negotiation of class differences is as central a problem for scholars as for activists. Taken collectively, the essays implicitly warn against any of the either-or formulations that have dominated much of this discourse. Does the Black middle class consist of the "house Negroes" that Malcolm X derided, supporting the social systems that oppress all Black people; or are they the Talented Tenth, providing the leadership the larger struggle has to have? Brian Kelly finds elements of the Black middle class in Birmingham as corrupt and self-serving as anything E. Franklin Frazier ever described, but Caroline Emmons and Wim Roefs remind us that from the same social strata came much of the post–World War II leadership that changed the South, often at great cost to themselves, similar to what Ortiz found in Florida decades earlier. Here again, these essays provide grounds for wondering whether a significant part of the variation in response to class privilege is a function of how different actors construct the racial past.

Winston James is centrally concerned with the issue of how African Americans understand the nature of their "community." Whether African Americans should organize on the basis of racial oppression or on the basis of their exploitation as workers is a question that has at least 150 years of debate behind it. If the measure of victory is the ability to appeal to the Black masses, then the nationalist position has ordinarily trumped the socialist one. But even as he explains that, James demonstrates that the socialist position has greatly enriched the activist discourse.

Several other authors, including Glymph, Ortiz, Barkley Brown, and Cecelski, are concerned with the issue of exactly how Blacks forge solidarity among themselves on a day-to-day basis. This contrasts with the more common stance among scholars of taking Black-on-Black relationships for granted and focusing on Black-white interaction, be it good or bad. Compare, for example, the number of books written about the integrated experience of Mississippi's Freedom Summer with the number written about the mostly Black period of organizing that preceded it. For different reasons, radicals—especially Marxists—and more conservative scholars can end up portraying interracial cooperation as a vital and, again, a natural part of the movement. The essays by de Jong, Honey, James, K'Meyer, and Kelly suggest that there have indeed been moments at which interracial cooperation has been crucial, but they may be both powerful and fragile.

Sandage's essay offers the most explicit development of the idea of America, as much as Africa, as invented tradition. Rejecting official representations of the Lincoln Memorial as a shrine to sectional reconciliation, Blacks worked to make the shrine a memorial to Emancipation, an act of popular historical revision that long predated the similar turn in formal scholarship. This argument resonates with many if not most of the pieces in this collection—from Barkley Brown and Cecelski to Emmons and Ortiz—in recognizing the ambition and ingenuity of Black folk in conceptualizing their own sense of place in this country. Everyday rituals of democratic practice like parades and drill teams, party organizing, and election law reform come together as a fundamental field of engagement and struggle. The quest for authorized status within the national polity—often presumed an acquiescent form of Black group struggle—now appears imaginative and ambitious in ways often attributed to approaches seeking "ways out" through either emigration or extraterritorial notions of group solidarity and affinity. Several of the essays here that do not foreground electoral politics—such as Honey, de Jong, and K'Meyer—consider extrapolitical institutions, from labor unions to federal assistance programs to civic associations and fraternal organizations, as crucial stages for articulation of Black struggle and intervention.

In sum, these renegotiations of formal public roles for Black people make clear the dynamic nature of African Americans' relationship to their adoptive, though all too often unwelcoming, home. We feel that this suggests that the idea of critical citizenship (the phrase is Adam Green's), the belief that Blacks realized full public participation in this country to the extent that they acutely noted its hypocrisies or outrages concerning themselves or others—how they "read" America, as vernacular usage would have it—undergirds many of the essays, and much of Black conception and practice of social struggle in this country. Certainly nineteenth-century activists like Frederick Douglass, Sojourner Truth, and Ida B. Wells anticipated, through their efforts, the observation of W.E.B. Du Bois that

Blacks' unique powers of "second sight" enabled and obliged them to a unique role in this country, and in the realization of the ideal of developed egalitarian politics globally. Blacks' progressive comprehension of their own citizenship was critical, then, in two senses: as evidence of their own ingenious use of formal political resources to generate searching comment upon their own unacceptable circumstances and as realization of the most ambitious, enduring, and transformative tradition of public dissent that this country has known. Students of modern citizenship generally would do well to note this aspect of African American political thought and activity, for it constitutes a singularly robust example of utopian outlook and commitment—an element often identified as crucial to any comprehensive manifestation of civic affinity and public trust—in recent U.S. history.[6]

NOTES

1. Following Bond, we can think of the master narrative as saying something like:

Traditionally, relationships between the races in the South were oppressive. Many Southerners were very prejudiced against Blacks. In 1954, the Supreme Court decided this was wrong. Inspired by the Court, courageous Americans, Black and white, took protest to the street, in the form of sit-ins, bus boycotts, and Freedom Rides. The protest movement, led by the brilliant and eloquent Reverend Martin Luther King Jr., aided by a sympathetic Federal government, most notably the Kennedy brothers and a born-again Lyndon Johnson, was able to make America understand racial discrimination as a moral issue. Once Americans understood that discrimination was wrong, they quickly moved to remove racial prejudice and discrimination from American life, as evidenced by the Civil Rights Acts of 1964 and 1965. Dr. King was tragically slain in 1968. Fortunately, by that time the country had been changed, changed for the better in some fundamental ways. The movement was a remarkable victory for all Americans. By the 1970s, southern states where Blacks could not have voted ten years earlier were sending African Americans to Congress. Inexplicably, just as the civil rights victories were piling up, many Black Americans, under the banner of Black Power, turned their backs on American society.

2. Connie Curry, *Silver Rights* (Athens: University of Georgia Press, 1995); John Dittmer, *Local People: The Struggle for Civil Rights in Mississippi* (Urbana: University of Illinois Press, 1994); Adam Fairclough, *Race and Democracy: The Civil Rights*

Struggle in Louisiana, 1915–1972 (Athens: University of Georgia Press, 1995); Cynthia Fleming, *Soon We Will Not Cry: The Liberation of Ruby Doris Smith Robinson* (Lanham, Md.: Rowman & Littlefield, 1998); Vincent Harding, *Hope and History: Why We Must Share the Story of the Movement* (New York: Orbis, 1990); Robin Kelley, *Race Rebels: Culture, Politics and the Black Working Class* (New York: Free Press, 1996); Aldon Morris, *The Origins of the Civil Rights Movement: Black Communities Organizing for Change* (New York: Free Press, 1984); Robert Moses and Charles E. Cobb, *Radical Equations—Math Literacy and Civil Rights* (Boston: Beacon Press, 2001); Charles Payne, *I've Got the Light of Freedom: The Organizing Tradition and the Mississippi Freedom Struggle* (Berkeley: University of California Press, 1995); Rural Organizing and Cultural Center, *Minds Stayed on Freedom: The Civil Rights Struggle in the Rural South—an Oral History* (Boulder, Colo.: Westview Press, 1991); Timothy B. Tyson, *Radio Free Dixie: Robert F. Williams & the Roots of Black Power* (Chapel Hill: University of North Carolina Press, 1999).

3. E.g., Kelley, *Race Rebels.*

4. Michael Dawson, *Behind the Mule: Race and Class in African American Politics* (Princeton, N.J.: Princeton University Press, 1994); Cathy Cohen, *The Boundaries of Blackness: AIDS and the Breakdown of Black Politics* (Chicago: University of Chicago Press, 1999).

5. James C. Scott, *Weapons of the Weak: Everyday Forms of Peasant Resistance* (New Haven, Conn.: Yale University Press, 1985), and *Domination and the Arts of Resistance: Hidden Transcripts* (New Haven, Conn.: Yale University Press, 1990).

6. See especially John Rawls, *The Law of Peoples* (Cambridge: Harvard University Press, 1999), Introduction and part I.

Slavery, Memory, and the Democratic Impulse

Americans are often profoundly uncomfortable at any discussion of slavery—confused or shamed, angered or defensive—and we ought not to be surprised when people devise ways to buffer themselves from uncomfortable social realities. Peter Wood, reminiscent of George Orwell, reminds us that language itself is among the most readily available buffers; we construct a language that helps us to not see. We say "plantation" when we mean "slave labor camp," "discrimination" when we mean "white supremacy," "segregation" when we mean "racism," and "civil rights for Negroes" when we mean a movement that raised profound questions about the adequacy of American institutions. We see less of what is relevant in the present because we deny so much of what mattered in the past. A society that can convince itself that plantation life was genteel is unlikely to think clearly about Black Power or affirmative action (and may not recognize a stolen election when it sees one).

One of the most powerful current manifestations of denial in popular culture is the idea that all the problems are in the past; racism names a problem our parents had.[1] In academe, the translation would be "Race isn't real; it's just a social construct." Of course, masculinity is "just" a social construct, too, but there seems to be much less confusion about its continuing importance in structuring life-chances.

Debates about the long-term impact of slavery continue in this confused atmosphere. Although it may not affect popular discourse, scholars can now say with great confidence that slavery did not destroy the Black family nor emasculate Black men.[2] Perhaps one of the things it did do was leave African Americans with a particularly acute hunger for respect, even as compared to other marginalized groups. In practice, in a society where masculinity is one of the most pervasive markers of human worth, it is easy to see how that translates into an acute need to demonstrate "manhood." An 1863 Union recruiting broadside is explicit:

> If we would be regarded men, if we would forever silence the tongue of Calumny, of Prejudice and Hate, let us Rise Now and Fly to Arms! We have seen what Valor and Heroism our Brothers displayed at Port Hudson and Milliken's Bend, though they are just from the galling, poisoning grasp of Slavery, they have startled the World by the most exalted heroism. If they have proved themselves heroes, cannot WE PROVE OURSELVES MEN?[3]

Proving their manhood on the battlefield, Black soldiers were making a statement about the collective worth of the race. David Cecelski gives us a complex rendering of one of these men. Cecelski's portrait of Abraham Galloway, like the essay by Elsa Barkley Brown that follows it, recalls the intense energy with which Black freedmen during and after the Civil War fashioned viable public cultures, and both scholars emphasize how indebted these projects were to rituals and institutions rooted in communal memory and feeling.

Galloway's story shows how a Black civil culture first emerged in the contraband camps with experiments in collective expression and debate. What even Du Bois described as "homeless and helpless hordes" proved capable of radical initiative, a further example of the imaginative and rigorous manner in which the former slaves rehearsed their own ideas of freedom in preparation for the unknown trials of the future.

The popular idea that African American leadership is virtually synonymous with church leadership probably has elements of condescension built into it, but it certainly lacks historical specificity. Like other complex struggles, the African American struggle found leadership in different places at different times. According to Nell Painter, in the late nineteenth century, "As nightriders assassinated political organizers or forced them into exile or inactivity, the growing ranks of preachers inherited the Black public arena by default."[4] Prior to that, in the decades immediately after slavery, Black communities tended to select their leaders from among those they saw as having contributed to their freedom, Civil War veterans like Abraham Galloway. In proportion to population, more Blacks than whites participated in the Civil War. The white supremacists of the last century successfully drew the veil of forgetfulness over the militancy and radicalism that many Civil War veterans embodied, at least in the white community. The nation may choose to reconstruct the war as a struggle among white men, but Black people in the late nineteenth and early twentieth century cherished the men and women who had fought for their freedom.

That the church has played a central role in the freedom struggle (and, perhaps, spirituality an even more central one) is not in question. The problem is that when we reduce Black leadership to clerical leadership, we give the movement a more middle-class cast than is historically justifiable. Since we do not ordinarily think of church leadership as being very militant, clerical reductionism may obscure the breadth and depth of militant feeling in Black communities. Similarly, casting a few individuals, no matter how talented, as the voices of the people can mute the angriest—and, arguably, the clearest—voices. Treating Douglass, Du Bois, and Washington as the voices of turn-of-the-century Black America introduces class and gender biases into our thinking, obviously, but there is also an ideological bias. Thavolia Glymph reminds us that if we turn to local communities, some of the voices there happen to be more militant than the familiar national voices. When Douglass is worrying about which racist to support for the White House, local leaders are trying to organize self-defense clubs.

This is syptomatic of a recurring problem. The racial militancy of the Black Power period in the late 1960s surprised most Americans, but only because they had not paid sufficient attention to similar voices, from A. Philip Randolph to Robert Williams, earlier. Similarly, Garvey may seem like a sharp break from the past but only because we know so little about the voices coming from local communities in the years before Garvey.

Militancy can be obscured by our tendency to listen to more consensus-oriented voices. On the other hand, when militancy becomes the focus of study, it has the potential to obscure less dramatic forms of struggle, including memory work. Glymph gives such work a central place in her analysis, as do the articles that follow by Ortiz and Sandage. Glymph describes a campaign of popular education among Blacks, using community celebrations as "schools of citizenship and [for] the training of a new group in the struggle," as the *Atlanta Daily Worker* put it. As assiduously as white southerners constructed a public history centered on the Lost Cause, African Americans constructed a history of the Won Cause, a history that celebrated their own role in the winning of freedom and the remaking of America.

There is always tension between the will to remember and the will to forget. As some white people deny history, some Black people "disremember," a term Glymph takes from slave narratives, where it seems to connote the false consciousness of those who forget the struggles of the past. (In contemporary terms, Black people refer to some of their number as having "forgotten where they came from.") We know that there were communities where Emancipation Day was being celebrated through the 1950s, but clearly such celebrations had ceased to be central rituals of community self-definition some time prior to that. It is a reasonable guess that some kind of major shift in the configuration of African-American historical memory took place between the two world wars, coincident with the decline of self-contained rural and small-town communities, with increased urbanization and exposure to mass culture, and, significantly, with the passing of the last generation of Black people for whom slavery was a living memory. Instead of acquiring a sense of the past from grandparents who had lived it, African Americans were getting it from *Gone with the Wind.* Whatever the moment, it follows from the analysis developed by Glymph and Ortiz particularly, that the point at which significant numbers of African Americans came to think of slavery as something shameful and of the Civil War as a moment when African Americans were acted upon or acted on behalf of should be thought of as one of the great watersheds, a moment of possibilities foreclosed.

A recent survey of college seniors found that only 30 percent of them could correctly identify the term "Reconstruction," which speaks volumes about the amount of historical information Americans can bring to bear on contemporary racial discourse.[5] Scholars of Reconstruction have their own lacunae. As we noted earlier, the question of how ex-slaves related to one another on a daily basis is only beginning to get the attention it deserves, presumably as a consequence of our continued predilection for the "race relations" paradigm, with its tendency to ignore questions about how Blacks interacted among themselves. The authors in this section make that a focal concern. Elsa Barkley Brown, looking at late-nineteenth-century Richmond, uncovers among freed people a striking degree of moral and intellectual agency, an ability to imagine an egalitarian civic order that their former masters could scarcely have conceived.[6] Black Richmonders were doing more than simply demanding entry into a white civil society; they were living their lives in a way that challenged the underlying values of American society, shaping an egalitarian civic culture that crossed lines of gender, class, and age. We are accustomed to thinking of call-and-response as a distinctive feature of African-American culture expression, but Brown urges us to think of it as a way of reducing the traditional distance between speaker and audience, a part of the egalitarian style of newly freed slaves, a style that also included the validation of emotion and personal experience—not just book-learning—as part of public expression, the participation of women and children in public life, the sanctioning of a group presence in activities where the wider society expected individual participation, and even the practice of "lining" hymns so that the illiterate could take part in church singing.

Barkley Brown points us to some important questions. How widespread were the democratic sentiments she describes? How were they expressed in daily popular culture, as opposed to civic behavior? Does the process of their erosion as described in Richmond apply elsewhere? Are there parallels to be drawn between the way Black men embraced patriarchy at the end of the nineteenth century and the way white men were embracing race? As Black political space is increasingly narrowed, do Black men compensate by drawing the cloak of masculinity even more tightly around themselves? How do we think with more specificity about the links between the contemporary devaluation of women's issues in some parts of African-American popular culture and the precedents set at the end of the nineteenth century? Whatever the full answer to the latter, it seems certain that Barkley Brown is right when she says that the result of the tendency to equate "manhood rights" with the welfare of all Black people was a dumbing down of Black civic discourse, another foreclosing of possibility.

NOTES

1. Richard Morin, "Misperceptions Cloud Whites' View of Blacks," *Washington Post*, 10 July 2001.

2. Herbert Gutman, *The Black Family in Slavery and Freedom* (New York: Pantheon, 1976); Stewart Tolnay, *The Bottom Rung: African American Family Life on Southern Farms* (Urbana: University of Illinois Press, 1999).

3. Frederick Douglass and others, *Men of Color to Arms! To Arms!* Recruitment broadside, Philadelphia, 1863. Gilder Lehrman Institute of American History.

4. Nell Painter, *Exodusters: Black Migration to Kansas after Reconstruction* (New York: Knopf, 1976).

5. Scott Veale, "History 101: Snoop Doggy Roosevelt," *New York Times,* 2 July 2000.

6. See also Painter, *Exodusters,* 14.

Chapter 1

Slave Labor Camps in Early America
Overcoming Denial and Discovering the Gulag

Peter H. Wood

> There, sir, stop.
> Let us not burden our remembrance with
> A heaviness that's gone.
> > —Prospero, in *The Tempest*[1]

> If you suppress any part of the story, it comes back later,
> with force and violence.
> > —Elie Wiesel[2]

We live in a nation in denial. For all our openness to controversy and our fascination with violence, we Americans are still unable to grasp the full depth of the huge collective wound that predated the country's founding and that haunted its infant and adolescent years. In the past decade, our society has slowly become more sensitive to child abuse within families and to the lasting effects that prolonged and arbitrary mistreatment can have upon all concerned. But this growing sensitivity to individual abuse, and to its impact upon later generations, has not yet been matched by an increased awareness of the collective long-term trauma represented by race slavery. Why would we expect the nation's power structure even to acknowledge, much less come to terms with, such a dark and formative chapter in our collective family history? After all, as several eminent academics have recently reminded us, "nations need to control national memory, because nations keep their shape by shaping their citizens' understanding of the past." But, as these scholars go on to point out, in actual practice this process, for better or worse, depends heavily upon individual historians. For "it is the historians who do research on the past, write the histories, and teach the nation's youth. It is they who lock up and unlock memory. . . . Whether democratic leaders like it or not, historians fashion the nation's collective self-understanding. . . ."[3]

In the United States this complicated interplay between political leaders and professional historians has existed in some form since at least the second quarter of the nineteenth century, when American history first came into its own as a full-time vocation. In an era when political leaders were imposing "gag laws" and allowing censorship of the U.S. mail in order to prevent open discussion of the volatile slavery issue, many historians followed the same course, emphasizing God's "manifest destiny" for Europeans in America and ignoring slavery altogether.[4] For example, in John Frost's popular book, *A History of America*, published in 1837, the controversial subject went virtually unmentioned.[5] After 1850 some writers would follow the lead of Harriet Beecher Stowe in criticizing the institution, but many others would follow the example of South Carolina's John C. Calhoun in praising slavery as a positive American institution endorsed by George Washington himself.[6]

When the dust from a prolonged Civil War and a hopeful but unrealized Reconstruction had finally settled, slavery times—too repugnant for most black Americans to dwell upon—became a source of veritable nostalgia for much of the society. "Jefferson's slaves thought that no one could be better than their master," mused a popular elementary history text in 1902. "He was always kind to them, and they were ready to do anything for him."[7] Colonial Williamsburg, reconstructed by John D. Rockefeller Jr. in the 1920s, marketed the gentility of planters and the satisfaction of their unpaid workers in the Old South,[8] as did Margaret Mitchell's *Gone With the Wind* a decade later. The publication and "docudramatization" of Alex Haley's *Roots* in the mid-1970s surprised a generation of Americans raised on *Gone With the Wind*, just as the films *Glory!* in 1989 and *Amistad* in 1997 have surprised a generation which felt *Roots* had shown them all that they needed to know about enslavement.

Still, for historians during the past thirty years to speak of "inequality in early America" has commonly been criticized as an act of exaggeration, presentism, or alarmist hyperbole. Mainstream writers have preferred to emphasize the significant fact that most European immigrants, sooner or later, found themselves better off in the New World than in the Old World.[9] So long as nearly half a million Africans could be factored out of

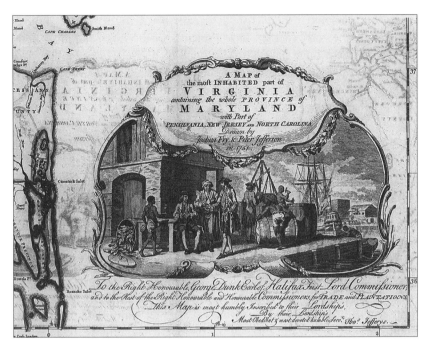

Fig. 1. Joshua Fry and Peter Jefferson, A Map of the Inhabited Part of Virginia (London, 1751). Cartouche. Courtesy of the Henry E. Huntington Library and Art Gallery, San Marino, California.

the equation entirely, then all of England's Atlantic settlements, even the Chesapeake colonies, could appear models of equity and harmony where, according to one scholar, "conspicuous social issues were nonexistent" and where "conscious divisions, within the society" or "any obvious . . . class antagonism" proved difficult to discern. "Of all the colonies in the mid-eighteenth century," Gordon Wood wrote in the *William and Mary Quarterly* in 1966, "Virginia seems the most settled, the most lacking in obvious social tensions."[10]

"Obvious to whom?" one might ask, for the evidence available to us often appears ambiguous. Consider a document from that very time and place: the often-reprinted cartouche from a mid-eighteenth-century map of the Chesapeake region (fig. 1). It depicts eight men in a dockside scene where casks of tobacco are being loaded aboard a British ship. Four well-dressed individuals, obviously white, count the year's cargo, tally its value, negotiate its shipment, and consume a symbolic pipeful of tobacco. The other four persons in the picture are clearly black and enslaved. Three of them pack the tobacco they have grown into the hogsheads they have made, roll these huge barrels to the dock to be weighed, and then row them to the waiting ship, while a forth individual serves spirits to the planter, the factor, and the captain, so that the three entrepreneurs can drink to their mutual success.

The picture is a virtual metaphor for the fundamental divisions within Virginia society, and any of the four black men could certainly have offered testimony that "conspicuous social issues" were far from "nonexistent" in the Tidewater. But if class antagonism existed on Chesapeake docks, it is not easy to discern in this traditional depiction. The artists have done everything in their power to obscure it. The map was made in the 1750s by Joshua Fry, professor of mathematics at William and Mary College, and Peter Jefferson, Virginia Burgess, surveyor, and planter.[11] Needless-to-say, we know a tremendous amount concerning the Virginia gentry at the center of this picture (and increasingly about their spouses as well).[12] They are the people who drafted the colonial map, so to speak, who are featured on it, and who used it for their gain. We know far less about the workers on the edges of the picture, though thanks to a generation of scholarship we certainly grasp more than we once did.

After decades of concerted scholarship, however, the heart of the enslavement experience and its deepest moral and social implications still seem to elude us. This is especially true in the classroom, where even our best books and articles, lectures, and films too often continue to fall short of the mark. (Some readers will resist the view that, despite all our efforts, we have so far failed rather significantly in conveying the deep realities of hereditary enslavement.) What follows is a brief speculation on the dilemmas of teaching about the most extreme long-term inequities of early America. The word *inequality*, when applied to our colonial past, is far from an exaggeration; it is actually a euphemism, which continues to understate and disguise shocking conditions that even now most Americans do not seem fully able to acknowledge.

If racism has proved more tenacious in modern America than many anticipated, this is due in part to the fact that racial enslavement was far worse than most Americans have understood. We have remained in denial, despite the best efforts of singular writers across several centuries to convey the full degradation of this "peculiar institution" and its links to pervasive racism. David Walker, the African American born in North Carolina who published *An Appeal to the Colored Citizens of the World* in 1829, was one such individual. "Treat us like men, and there is no danger but we will all live in peace and happiness together," he told the white readers of his fiery pamphlet. But to continue the forced incarceration of several million people would prove futile and dangerous. "We must and shall be free I say, in spite of you," he warned. "You may do your best to keep us in wretchedness and misery, to enrich you and your children; but God will deliver us from under you. And wo, wo, will be to you if we have to obtain our freedom by fighting." Historian Peter Hinks, in a fascinating recent study, makes clear that Walker repeatedly "returned to the theme that whites were simply incapable of facing honestly and fully the horror of their actions against blacks."[13]

Angelina Grimké, a white contemporary of Walker's who grew up in Charleston, South Carolina, also tried to overcome denial, by confronting Northerners with the phenomenon of people being "chained and driven like criminals, and incarcerated in the great prison-house of the South." "Slavery exerts a most deadly influence over the morals of our country," she wrote, "not only over that portion of it where it actually exists as 'a domestic institution,' but like the miasma of some pestilential pool, it spreads its desolating influence far beyond its own boundaries." She was outraged at the society's willingness to continue "drinking the waters of that river of pollution," oblivious to its dire consequences for all Americans. "But this is not all," she told a northern audience in the 1830s, protesting the way in which legalized enslavement fed the nation's racial prejudices:

> . . . our people have erected a false standard by which to judge men's character. Because in the slaveholding States colored men are plundered and kept in abject ignorance, are treated with disdain and scorn, so here, too, in profound deference to the South, we refuse to eat, or ride, or walk, or associate, or open our institutions of learning, or even our zoological institutions to people of color, unless they visit them in the capacity of *servants*, of menials in humble attendance upon the Anglo-American. Who ever heard of a more wicked absurdity in a Republican country?[14]

A few historians have been equally frank in each succeeding generation, but not until the 1960s did the effort to challenge America's persistent denial regarding enslavement take on renewed force. In 1959, Stanley Elkins had drawn upon early studies of Nazi concentration camps to suggest that American slavery constituted a similarly arbitrary and irrational institution. But this effort to compare the brutal Middle Passage and enslavement with the horrors perpetrated during World War II backfired in unfortunate ways; his discussion of how brutal treatment can traumatize and infantilize whole groups seemed to reinforce a stereotype of African Americans as hapless and helpless victims.[15] Following Elkins's assessment of slavery as a dehumanizing "total institution," fellow historians penned assertions that emphasized this dubious stance. For example, Richard Hofstadter (in a volume on early America published posthumously in 1971) summarized the arrival of slaves in the New World:

> To Africans, stunned by the long ordeal of the Middle Passage, the auctions could only have marked a decrescendo in fright and depression. . . . But as one tries to imagine the mental state of the newly arrived Africans, one must think of people still sick, depleted, and depressed by the ordeal of the voyage, the terror of the unknown, the sight of deaths and suicides, and the experience of total helplessness in the hands of others. What they had been and known receded rapidly, and the course of their experience tended to reduce their African identity to the withered husks of dead memories.[16]

After rediscovering the harshness of Atlantic slavery, some liberal historians of the 1960s seemed to end up precisely where their racist predecessors had stood when they had written about Africa itself. To the earlier scholars, Africa had been an unknown dark continent with no culture worth remembering, and its exiles had been docile by nature. To the later contingent, Africa, although a viable world, had been blotted out for slaves by the trauma of the Middle Passage. Though avowedly "sympathetic" to the black experience, certain writers from the Civil Rights era agreed that enslaved newcomers, their "African identity" reduced to a withered husk, could only have fallen into a passive acceptance of their fate.[17] Approaching the problem of enslavement from almost opposite directions, these two groups of writers had ended up in the same tobacco field.

An outcry of dismay was certainly in order, and we have spent much of the past thirty years examining continuities with Africa, reassessing "the weapons of the weak," cataloguing acts of resistance, searching out signs of unbroken cultural strength, and applauding forms of family life that endured through enslavement. Such work is far from over, especially given the overwhelming ignorance of Africa with which most Americans, black and white, began the reassessment. But having exposed the shortcomings in various arguments that stressed total discontinuity from Africa and passivity in the face of oppression, we may have freed ourselves to revisit, with more openness, the deep and troubling question of the high human costs of long-term, hereditary racial enslavement.

Inevitably, the resistance to such a re-examination is strong, especially if the reassessment proceeds from the premise that the central story is more harrowing than all but a few have dared to portray it. What will become of the fragile and ultimately untenable "balance" that now exists in most U.S. history texts between the best insights of the new black history and the most tenacious clichés of the earlier Southern history? What will become of the expanding new industry of "heritage tourism" now taking hold in the South, a business premised on the idea of balancing and reconciling inherently contradictory images of the region's past? During the 1996 Olympics, for example, the world was repeatedly invited to "come see Atlanta, birthplace of Margaret Mitchell and Martin Luther King!"

It is important to note that resistance to re-examining slavery comes from all quarters. Many, perhaps most, African Americans shy away from revisiting a chapter in our history so filled with pain and so frequently misconstrued by mainstream scholars. Conversely, many European Americans rightly suspect that further study might move the guilt away from a small category of "bad planters" personified by Simon Legree and implicate generations of Christian believers, North and South, rich and poor.[18] If African and European descendants have their reasons for ongoing denial, numerous modern migrants from Asia, Latin America, and the Middle East feel skeptical about revisiting remote chapters of Atlantic history in which they feel they have only an indirect and uncertain stake. Finally, and most importantly, all these groups and their leaders retain in different ways a deep commitment to the national mythology of freedom and opportunity; a long, clear look at our much-denied secret could shake, or even shatter, that commitment. Perhaps more than anything else, "this tying of national identity to the achievement of equality and liberty has prevented the custodians of national history from publicly coming to terms with the import of slavery and its legacy of racial prejudices."[19]

If slavery seemed too close for many people to discuss clearly in the 1870s (much as the Holocaust remained too close for most persons in the 1950s), in recent times enslavement sometimes feels excessively far away. These days my students, both black and white, often peg their primary sense of racial injustice in America on the fact that buses, schools, lunch counters, and rest rooms were once segregated. When activist Dick Gregory spoke on the Duke University campus in 1997, I was struck by his answer to a question about progress in race relations. "People say what a bad time it is to be black in America," Gregory replied. "Trust me—try Biloxi, Mississippi in 1942." In other words, the far worse situation of African-Americans in 1842 or 1742 is less frequently invoked these days. For many Americans, though certainly not for Gregory, slavery remains some distant and brief aberration, unworthy of concern and therefore long forgotten.[20]

All over the world—in Russia and Bosnia, Rwanda and South Africa, Argentina and Guatemala, Japan and Cambodia, Germany and Switzerland—people are facing similar decisions about when and whether and how closely to examine the darkest chapters of their national past. But each of these countries must wrestle with some unique twentieth-century chapter of "family abuse" writ large, while America's midnight of legalized hereditary bondage is a seventeenth-, eighteenth-, and nineteenth-century chapter. If our own long nightmare of "soul-murder" (to use historian Nell Painter's powerful term) seems relatively remote in time, does that make it any easier to examine? Still, the topic seems painfully hard to raise and confront at both the local and the national level, since we cling so tenaciously to a myth that the United States is exceptional in every way, unblemished by the deep scars that afflict other, more obviously dysfunctional national families.

Would a tougher re-examination of enslavement resonate with those members of our dysfunctional national family who currently refuse to acknowledge that slavery has any enduring significance? The character played by Sean Penn in the film *Dead Man Walking* comes to mind: the rough, slightly likable racist on death row who is caught up in hating and dismissing blacks, people whom he categorizes as "sitting on the porch whining about slavery." One need not visit prison cells or Hollywood sound lots to find these smoldering antagonisms; mutual resentments pervade our schools and places of work. If Americans were able to re-view slavery in a prolonged and sustained manner, such a renewed effort might well stem from, and then help to alleviate, the deep racial malaise that lingers in the United States. For societies, as for individuals, the act of remembering, acknowledging, and reliving the pain of terrible experiences can lead to awareness and empathy. Only then can grieving, reconciliation, and rebirth follow.

When I first presented a draft of this essay to a conference at the Huntington Library in early 1997, President Clinton had just delivered his second inaugural address, speaking on the Martin Luther King Holiday and urging the improvement of race relations in America. I could still hear the voice of one young African-American, interviewed at the Million Man March in Washington in 1996, who had commented wistfully, "I just wish they would say they were sorry." So I began to ruminate on themes of atonement and apology. Can public or official apologies also be heartfelt and cathartic? Can it ever be too late to apologize? Must useful apologies be asked for and accepted, or can they simply be given? My speculations about how these complex social interactions work are as personal and anecdotal as the next person's, especially since we live in a society that has very few forms of meaningful public contrition. I always watch with great interest and a good deal of cultural envy when prominent figures in Japanese business or politics make public and personalized apologies regarding misdeeds for which they or their predecessors are somehow responsible. Wondering if such things could ever happen here, and marveling at the groundswell of fascination with the newly-opened Holocaust Museum, I was prompted to include the following paragraph in my 1997 remarks about the reconsideration of slavery:

> Forthright public leadership from the top in such matters would make a tremendous difference, of course, though the thought of such initiative seems an idle pipe dream in the current age. Imagine if the southern-born president and vice president declared a National Day of Atonement for Slavery, as some of their earliest predecessors used to do with serious social matters. . . . Imagine if the Federal Congress . . . could undertake to put a Slavery Museum on the Mall, not far from the tremendously popular and undoubtedly healing Holocaust Museum. I for one would support either gesture, and many others besides, but I am not holding my breath.

After my talk, several fellow historians took issue with such proposals, characterizing them as impractical or diversionary and asserting that they would only cause rancorous cultural divisions. Perhaps they were correct. Several months later, emboldened by the success of his apology for the U.S. government's role in the notorious syphilis experiments at Tuskegee, President Clinton floated the idea of an official apology for generations of government-sanctioned racial enslavement. Immediately (as my colleagues had predicted), a barrage of criticism rained down upon this modest proposal from all sides. Pundits suggested that such an action was too large or too little, too early or too late, too broad or too narrow, too crudely symbolic or not symbolic enough. Made cautious by these initial outbursts, the president soon retreated from the idea, saying through his press secretary that such an apology might be considered by his Presidential Commission on Racism.

A subsequent resolution in the Congress did not fare much better during the summer of 1997. Democrat Tony Hall of Ohio and Republican Dave Weldon of Florida introduced House Concurrent Resolution 96, which consisted of a single sentence: "Resolved by the House of Representatives (the Senate concurring), That the Congress apologizes to African-Americans whose ancestors suffered as slaves under the Constitution and laws of the United States until 1865." House Speaker Newt Gingrich, perhaps because his Georgia district might feel implicated in any such apology, was swift to distance himself from the proposal: "Any American, I hope, feels badly about slavery," he observed. "I also feel badly about genocide in Rwanda."[21] Clearly, even such a simple resolution remained highly controversial, and at one level I had to concede to my skeptical friends that their intuitions of trouble had been well founded. In the next breath, however, I had to ask whether the shrill tone and contradictory elements of the flare-up might not in fact confirm my suspicion of a society in lingering denial regarding a deep trauma that has been more repressed than healed.

Whatever steps, symbolic or otherwise, elected officials may choose to take, the creative task of reconciliation and understanding ultimately falls back on concerned sectors of the public, and one such sector is professors of American history with an interest in—I shall use the euphemism—inequality. As a member of that community, let me offer two related suggestions for ways by which teachers of enslavement might revitalize the discussion of what William Dusinberre, in the title of his excellent 1996 book, has called *Them Dark Days*.[22] The first proposal concerns terminology, since, as Shakespeare pointed out nearly four centuries ago, how we name things has a major hold over how we understand them. "You taught me language, and my profit on't / Is, I know how to curse," Caliban, the New World slave, exclaims to his European master, Prospero, in Act I of *The Tempest*. "The red plague rid you / For learning me your language!"[23]

I have no doubt that Caliban would support and Prospero would vigorously oppose the suggestion, intimated in my title, to substitute the term *slave labor camp* for the word *plantation*. I am sick of seeing glossy magazine ads for "plantation tours" that will introduce us to the elegant living of olden times. Examples abound. Consider an issue of *Carologue*, a history magazine published in Charleston, which contains a full-page color ad for a numbered edition of a "coffee-table" historical atlas of Carolina's tidal rice plantations. The cost is $100, some of which will benefit Ducks Unlimited. "They harnessed the moon and turned the marshes into fields of gold," reads the headline over a dreamy picture of a low-country vista, complete with Spanish moss. "Travel back down South Carolina's Ashepoo, Combahee and Edisto Rivers to the rice plantations that made South Carolina an economic force in a young nation. The planters there grew Carolina Gold—a variety of rice that bestowed great wealth and lavish lifestyles on a few and set the course for the history of the Palmetto State."[24] For me, the useful description in recent decades of the American plantation as a "factory in the field" was only an appropriate first step toward accurately describing what the written records have amply put before us. I would be both surprised and pleased to see *slave labor camp* become an occasional synonym for *plantation*. As Richard Wright once observed, English speakers have traditionally suffered from "a genius for calling things by the wrong names."[25] We need to alter our benign terminology.

My second suggestion is that we make far greater use of comparative modern-day materials. Even as our knowledge of the institution expands steadily, our capacity to empathize—to get inside the process from the perspective of the individual African American who endured it—does not increase accordingly. In part, this is because the task is so formidable; the weight of the burden, the intensity of the storm, is almost too enormous to fathom. But it is also because "them dark days" are long past, and our primary sources are severely limited. How fortunate we are to have Olaudah Equiano's *Travels* and Frederick Douglass's *Life* and an expanding array of slave narratives.[26] And yet, how much more engaged we could become with access to thousands of additional first-hand accounts. What if we possessed tapes and transcribed interviews several generations older than the useful Works Progress Administration slave narratives? Imagine if we had hours of real-time film footage and videotapes of participants, situations, and events, allowing us to make an "Eyes on the Prize" series for the eighteenth century.[27]

In 1996, when the television program *20/20* ran a story on current slavery in Sudan, American viewers encountered women whose leg irons had only recently been removed, and whose ankles were still scarred from the shackles. The century that recently came to an end had no shortage of mass bondage and exploitation in a multitude of forms, and much of it has been documented with cameras and described vividly by survivors. The Holocaust itself, so recent and so imperfectly understood when Stanley Elkins wrote, has been examined from many different angles since his book appeared.[28] Anyone watching the endless deportation trains in Claude Lanzmann's epic 1985 documentary, *Shoah*, while keeping in mind the agonizing one-way flow of the Middle Passage, cannot help but gain new insights into the long-lasting and evil banality of the Atlantic slave trade, as well as the Jewish Holocaust.[29] Sadly, there is no shortage of contemporary evidence with which to "compare and contrast" American enslavement; we have numerous depressing and inspiring situations from which to choose.

In selecting one particular modern saga that students of enslavement could pursue further, in the classroom and beyond, my own choice at present would be the labor camps established in Russia by Josef Stalin.[30] Westerners have had some sense of the "Gulag Archipelago" since the works of Aleksandr Solzhenitsyn and Eugenia Ginzburg were first translated in the mid-1970s,[31] but only with the demise of Soviet Communism in the 1980s did firsthand testimony become more widely accessible and verifiable. In 1988, *New York Times* editor A. M. Rosenthal became one of the first foreigners to tour an operating Russian labor camp when he visited Perm 35,[32] and the following year a few Russian and Western historians were given access to the NKVD archives.[33] By 1992 the Felix Travel Agency in Moscow was offering a "Gulag Camp Tour" taking visitors to work camps in Siberia, and by 1995 former prisoners were returning to visit the labor camps where they had once been confined.[34] Additional books and articles are beginning to appear on the experience of the camps and on the social and political atmosphere in which they were created and sustained.[35]

Obviously, there is no simple parallel between eighteenth-and nineteenth-century America and twentieth-century Russia, for differences abound, both large and small: private property versus state labor, regional variety versus bureaucratic sameness, agricultural work versus industry and mining, hereditary bondage versus political incarceration, hot versus cold. The American experience lasted longer and had a larger generational aspect; the Soviet experience involved a higher annual death rate and a greater number of people. The Siberian gulag absorbed more deportees in two generations than all the slave labor camps of the New World absorbed in four centuries. There were roughly seven million persons in Stalin's work camps at the height of the Great Purge in 1938 and roughly twelve million by the time of his death in 1953.[36] Indeed, recent estimates of the number who *died* in the Gulag Archipelago, "somewhere between 12 million and 20 million people over 74 years,"[37] mirror generally the uncertain modern estimates of total Africans deported to the Americas by the entire European slave trade.

But there is still much to be learned from such a comparison, primarily because we have access to first-hand accounts by survivors—resources that remain all too scarce and fragmentary for American enslavement—now that the rich and tantalizing WPA interviews from the 1930s have been widely examined and explored.[38] When the Polish writer Ryszard Kapuściński, one of the great journalists of our era, visited the sites of former labor camps in Siberia several years ago he summarized the physical conditions in terms that journalist Frederick Law Olmsted might have used in touring the nineteenth-century South: "Everywhere, in Vorkuta, in Norilsk, in Magadan, one is struck by the squalor of the camp world, by its extreme shabby poverty, its clumsy, careless provisionality, slovenliness, and primitivism. It is a world stitched together from patches and rags, nailed together with rusted nails driven in with an ordinary ax, tied together with a burlap rope, secured with a piece of old wire."[39]

It is not only the sparse and depressing outer world of enslavement that can be recaptured through these twentieth-century narratives; it is the inner pain and resolution that can be examined as well. In his amazing book entitled *The Long Walk*, written in the 1950s about experiences in the 1940s, another Polish writer, Slavomir Rawicz, tells a tale of capture, deportation, deprivation, labor, and escape that sheds revealing light on the psychological experience of enslavement.[40] Like Equiano and Douglass, he is one of the strong and lucky ones who manages to escape his chains and tell his story. In the process, he helps us think realistically about how large heterogeneous groups adapt to brutal treatment, perverse illogic, and the death of hope—whom to trust and whom to avoid, whom to help and whom to abandon, when to submit and when to resist? His vivid account also reminds us of inner thoughts and feelings—the agonizing, Proustian recollection of a freshly baked cake, the life-giving force of a sarcastic joke shared among suffering sojourners.[41]

Similarly Hilda Vitzthum, in her memoir of ten years in a Soviet labor camp, recounts emotional thoughts for which we have few first-hand equivalents in the recollections of American slaves. Vitzthum recalls how, even in the darkest situations, she drew strength from encounters with nature—"moments that briefly diverted us from the despair of our situation." Thrown aboard a prison transport ship, she underwent a harrowing journey suggestive of the Middle Passage. But despite the shear weariness that overcame her each evening, she "always enjoyed the sight of the glittering stars and the shining moon" before falling asleep at night. Arriving as a stranger at a new slave labor camp, she was "suddenly overwhelmed by the total misery of this compound. . . . What an accursed, puked-on bit of earth! . . . I felt the absolute absurdity, the utter inhumanity of the situation. . . . What all did not go through my head! My whole life passed by my mind's eye." But even as she saw herself "sliding more and more deeply" into "the abyss," she found a token of hope in the natural world.

> At that moment all these depressing thoughts and images dominated me with such intensity that I was overcome with deep despair, and my hopes, already weak, seemed to perish utterly. But some spark of defiance must still have remained in my heart. How else could I have noticed the little daisy that had sprouted from this scarred and trampled earth? Instinctively I bent down and loosened the earth around it so that people could see it more readily and not crush it. Had I not just asked myself if there was any purpose in living any longer, since the chance of survival was again reduced and I had nothing but the worst to look forward to? Had this plain little flower, which had grown despite the thousands of footsteps that daily tramped by, become a symbol for me?[42]

For Vitzthum, whose husband had died in the gulag, the tiny daisy foretold an upturn in her bitter fortunes. "I would probably soon have forgotten this little flower," she writes, "had it not formed part of my introduction to a fine human being, such as existed in all camps." A strange man offered her much needed words of encouragement, and this kindred spirit became her partner. "Something that had been completely buried in me came to life again," Vitzthum recalls. "With this day a new chapter had begun in my camp life."[43] Eugenia Ginzburg relates a similar story from her gulag experience, overcoming hesitations to write about the man who shared her tribulations. "The main thing," she remarks, "is that I wanted to show through his image that the victim of inhumanity can remain the bearer of all that is good, of forbearance, and of brotherly feelings toward his fellow man."[44]

Nothing is harder to recreate within the long annals of American enslavement than the complex human dynamics, both depressing and uplifting, that exist within the confines of the slave labor camp experience. We have come a long way in our studies of American slavery, but we have a long way to go. Indeed, only by coming this far can we catch our breath, take stock, and realize that some of the toughest research and most difficult and important discussions still lie ahead. Southern plantations, when one looks beyond the carefully maintained elegance and cultivation of the big house, were in fact privately owned slave labor camps, sanctioned by the powers of the state, that persisted for generations, and we may gain insight into those who endured or were crushed under this perverse regime by examining the rapidly expanding record of modern enslavement. Perhaps then Americans can look at the "decorative" Jefferson-Fry cartouche and, instead of seeing "the elegant living of olden times," see a world of perpetual exploitation and incessant degradation built upon racist ideology and overwhelming physical force.

NOTES

1. William Shakespeare, *The Tempest* (act five, scene one).

2. Quoted in Lance Morrow, "The Justice of the Calculator," *Time,* February 24, 1997, 45.

3. Joyce Appleby, Lynn Hunt, Margaret Jacob, *Telling the Truth about History* (New York, 1994), 154–55. The authors are invoking Mary Douglas. They go on to remind us that "to speak of the nation as an institution working assiduously to forget experiences incompatible with its righteous self-image is to fudge the issue of whose experiences must be forgotten and for which groups' benefit" (p. 155).

4. An excellent essay by Inga Clendinnen discusses the parallel issue of how indigenous cultures were being portrayed by prominent historians in the decade of the Mexican War and the Oregon Trail. She observes that Spain's original "Mexican Conquest as a model for European-native relations was reanimated for the English-speaking world through the marvelously dramatic *History of the Conquest of Mexico* written by W. H. Prescott in the early 1840s, a bestseller in those glorious days when History still taught lessons. The lesson that great history taught was that Europeans will triumph over natives, however formidable the apparent odds, because of cultural superiority." It is hard to dispute her assertion that, for the most part, "Historians are the camp followers of the imperialists." Inga Clendinnen, "'Fierce and Unnatural Cruelty': Cortes and the Conquest of Mexico," in *New World Encounters,* ed. Stephen Greenblatt (Berkeley, 1993), 12, 18.

5. John Frost, *A History of the United States* (Philadelphia, 1837).

6. In his final speech to the U.S. Senate in 1850, Calhoun chastised Northerners for "invoking the name of the illustrious Southerner whose mortal remains repose on the western bank of the Potomac. He was one of us—a slaveholder and a planter. We have studied his history, and find nothing in it to justify submission to wrong." *Congressional Globe,* 31 Cong., I Sess. (March 4, 1850): 454.

7. Once, when Jefferson returned from a long trip to France, the jaunty text continues, "the negroes went to meet his carriage. They walked several miles down the road; when they caught sight of the carriage, they shouted and sang with delight. They would gladly have taken out the horses and drawn it up the steep hill. When Jefferson reached Monticello and got out, the negroes took him in their arms, and, laughing and crying for joy, they carried him into the house. Perhaps no king ever got such a welcome as that; for that welcome was not bought with money: it came from the heart." D. H. Montgomery, *The Beginner's American History* (Boston, 1902), 165–66.

8. Richard Handler and Eric Gambler, *The New History in an Old Museum: Creating the Past at Colonial Williamsburg* (Durham, N.C., 1997), especially chapter 5.

9. Unable to see American slavery clearly or take it seriously, scholars of the so-called "consensus school" during the Cold War era were quick to generalize. One wrote in 1959, in an assertion that was commonplace for the time: "All historians would agree that, in comparison with Europe, the United States was a relatively classless society." Marcus Cunliffe, *The Nation Takes Shape, 1789–1837* (Chicago, 1959), 168.

10. Gordon S. Wood, "Rhetoric and Reality in the American Revolution," *William and Mary Quarterly*, 3d ser., 23 (January 1966): 27. Robert E. Brown and B. Katherine Brown, *Virginia, 1705–1786: Democracy or Aristocracy?* (East Lansing, 1964) had appeared two years earlier. The assertion that "tranquility . . . distinguished the politics of Virginia" is repeated in Robert Middlekauff, *The Glorious Cause: the American Revolution, 1763–1789* (New York, 1982): 39–40. For a discerning fresh look at some of Virginia's actual inequalities and why they have long been underestimated, see Holly Brewer, "Entailing Aristocracy in Colonial Virginia: 'Ancient Feudal Restraints' and Revolutionary Reform," *William and Mary Quarterly*, 3d ser., 54 (April 1997): 307–46, and Woody Holton, *Forced Founders: Indians, Debtors, Slaves, and the Making of the American Revolution in Virginia* (Chapel Hill, N.C., 1999).

11. Until his early death at age 49, Peter Jefferson was known not only for his civic energy in Virginia's gentry community but for his physical strength. According to lore, this huge man could "head," or pull upright, two hogsheads of tobacco at one time, though each weighed more than 500 pounds. Eye witnesses said he once pulled down a small outbuilding with a rope, when three slaves were unable to complete the task. Scholars who seek to explain how Thomas Jefferson reconciled a fierce commitment to independence with a willingness to own slaves need only examine the contradictions of this revered father. "A cardinal maxim" of Peter Jefferson was "Never ask another to do for you what you can do for yourself," and yet the master of Shadwell Plantation controlled sixty enslaved Africans at the time of his death. Fawn M. Brodie, *Thomas Jefferson: An Intimate Portrait* (New York, 1974), chapter 1.

12. The obvious absence of women from this representation of mercantile soci-

ety in the Chesapeake prompts another discussion. Clearly, contemporary representations of the region's women exist in which the dynamics of class and race were represented in a similar manner. See Kathleen M. Brown, *Good Wives, Nasty Wenches, and Anxious Patriarchs: Gender, Race, and Power in Colonial Virginia* (Chapel Hill, N.C., 1996).

13. David Walker, *An Appeal to the Colored Citizens of the World* (Boston, 1829), 69–70. Peter P. Hinks, *To Awaken My Afflicted Brethren: David Walker and the Problem of Antebellum Slave Resistance* (University Park, Pa., 1997), 210.

14. Angelina Grimké, *An Appeal to the Women of the Nominally Free States*, second edition, issued by an Anti-slavery Convention of American Women (Boston, 1838), 13–16, 19–23.

15. Stanley M. Elkins, *Slavery: A Problem in American Institutional and Intellectual Life* (Chicago, 1959).

16. Richard Hofstadter, *America at 1750: A Social Portrait* (New York, 1971), 90.

17. I recall vividly an evening when Professor Elkins visited Princeton University in the early 1970s and spoke to students interested in Black Studies. I was working in the Firestone Library, completing work on a study of early enslavement called *Black Majority*, and I attended the talk. When he finished his remarks and the questioning had reached a stalemate, I spoke up from the back of the room, saying that I had recently come across a significant act of slave resistance, then virtually unknown, in Stono, South Carolina, in 1739. As I sketched the details of the Stono Rebellion, a black undergraduate in front of me spun around and exclaimed with enthusiasm, "Hey, man, where did you come from?" Serious researchers into eighteenth-century enslavement in the deep South were still rare and surprising creatures.

18. In the wake of Daniel Jonah Goldhagen's controversial volume, *Hitler's Willing Executioners: Ordinary Germans and the Holocaust* (New York, 1996), it is possible to imagine an equally provocative volume about the U.S. entitled *Columbia's Willing Exploiters: Ordinary Americans and African Enslavement*. Though unfavorably received in America, Goldhagen's book was swiftly translated into a dozen languages, and the author received the 1997 Democracy Prize of the *Journal for German and International Politics* in Bonn. The journal praised Goldhagen for providing a generation of young Germans with answers "which, as a rule, parents and grandparents had denied them," adding that "the answers of German historiography have until now not been able to fill the gap." *Harvard University Gazette*, January 9, 1997. Could the same be said of the American historiography of enslavement?

19. Appleby, Hunt, Jacob, *Telling the Truth about History*, 296.

20. Alex Gordon, "Activist blazes trail with pointed humor," *Duke Chronicle* (February 17, 1997): 5. Dick Gregory knows this long history all too well, of course, and has written about it effectively in *No More Lies: The Myth and Reality of American History* (New York, 1971).

21. "Apology for Slavery," *Poverty and Race*, vol. 6, no. 4 (July/August 1997): 4.

22. William Dusinberre, *Them Dark Days: Slavery in the American Rice Swamps* (New York, 1996).

23. William Shakespeare, *The Tempest*, act one, scene two, lines 363–65.

24. *Carologue* (summer 1997), inside back cover.

25. Richard Wright, *White Man, Listen!* (1957; reprint New York, 1995), 57.

26. *Equiano's Travels: The Interesting Narrative of the Life of Olaudah Equiano or Gustavus Vassa, the African*, abridged and ed. Paul Edwards (London, 1996); *Life and Times of Frederick Douglass: His Early Life as a Slave, His Escape from Bondage and His Complete History, Written by Himself* (New York, 1962). Also see, for example, William Henry Singleton, *Recollections of My Slavery Days*, published as four newspaper articles in 1922 and now available as a book, with an excellent introduction and annotations by Katherine Mellen Charron and David S. Cecelski, from the North Carolina Department of Archives and History (Raleigh, 1999).

27. Such materials can only be imagined, but interesting steps in this direction include the six-hour PBS television series on enslavement, "Africans in America" (1998), and Ira Berlin, Marc Favreau, and Steven F. Miller, eds., *Remembering Slavery: African Americans Talk about Their Personal Experiences of Slavery and Emancipation* (New York, 1998) [a book and audiotape set].

28. See, for example, Terrence Des Pres, *The Survivor: An Anatomy of Life in the Death Camps* (New York, 1976); Elie Wiesel, *Night*, trans. Stella Rodway (New York, 1982); Lawrence L. Langer, *Holocaust Testimonies: The Ruins of Memory* (New Haven, Conn., 1991); Christopher Browning, *Ordinary Men: Batallion 101* (San Francisco, 1991); Hilene Flanzbaum, *The Americanization of the Holocaust* (Baltimore, 1999). There are now more than 3,300 books in print in English relating to the Jewish Holocaust.

29. Claude Lanzmann, *Shoah, An Oral History of the Holocaust: The Complete Text of the Film* (New York, 1985). See also Annette Insdorf, *Indelible Shadows: Film and the Holocaust* (New York, 1983); Jeffrey Shandler, *While America Watches: Televising the Holocaust* (New York, 1999). For a strongly worded restatement of the place of the slave trade in Atlantic History, see the brief but important Forward by Cornel West on "The Ignoble Paradox of Western Modernity" in Madeleine Burnside, *Spirits of the Passage: the Transatlantic Slave Trade in the Seventeenth Century* (New York, 1997), 8–10.

30. In 1987 Peter Kolchin showed us that there is much to be learned from comparing American slavery and Russian serfdom. But a great deal has changed in the years since then, and we are now beginning to learn about more recent forms of "unfree" Russian labor. Peter Kolchin, *Unfree Labor: American Slavery and Russian Serfdom* (Cambridge, MA, 1987).

31. Aleksandr I. Solzhenitsyn, *Gulag Archipelago, 1918–1956: An Experiment in Literary Investigation*, 3 vols. (New York, 1974–78); Eugenia Ginzburg, *Journey into the Whirlwind* (New York, 1975); *Within the Whirlwind* (New York, 1981).

32. A. M. Rosenthal, "Into the Heart of the Gulag," *Reader's Digest*, April 1989:

71–76. See also Jean-Pierre Vaudon, "Last Days of the Gulag?" *National Geographic* 177, no. 3 (March 1990): 40–47.

33. Karen J. Winkler, "Opening a Window on Life in Soviet Labor Camps," *The Chronicle of Higher Education*, October 30, 1991, A8; R. W. Davies, "Forced Labor under Stalin: The Archive Revelations," *New Left Review* 214 (November-December 1995): 62–81.

34. Deborah Stead, "The Gulag Tour: It Ain't Club Med," *Business Week*, November 16, 1992, 148; Andrew Nagorski, "Back to the Gulag," *Newsweek*, September 25, 1995, 46–48. Gulag is the Russian acronym for the official name of Stalin's vast system of labor camps. For moving recent descriptions of Magadan, "the Soviet Union's equivalent to Auschwitz," see Colin Thubron, *In Siberia* (New York, 1999), chapter 9; and Anna Reid, *The Shaman's Coat: A Native History of Siberia* (New York, 2002).

35. See, for example, Irena Ratushinskaya, "En Route to the Gulag," *Commentary* 86, no. 3 (September 1988): 35–41; Leona Toker, "Awaiting Translation: Lev Konson's Gulag Stories," *Judaism: A Quarterly Journal of Jewish Life and Thought*, 45:1 (winter 1995): 119–28; Véronique Garros, Natalia Korenevskaya, and Thomas Lahusen, eds., *Intimacy and Terror: Soviet Diaries of the 1930s* (New York, 1995); Robert W. Thurston, *Life and Terror in Stalin's Russia, 1934–1941* (New Haven, CT, 1996); Tzvetan Todorov, *Facing the Extreme: Moral Life in the Concentration Camps* (New York, 1996); Janusz Bardach and Kathleen Gleeson, *Man is Wolf to Man: Surviving the Gulag* (Berkeley, 1998): Tzvetan Todorov, *Voices from the Gulag: Life and Death in Communist Bulgaria* (University Park, PA, 1999).

36. Mike Edwards, "The Gulag Remembered," *National Geographic* 177, no. 3 (March 1990): 48–49.

37. Nagorski, "Back to the Gulag," 46.

38. Hopefully, we shall one day have first-hand accounts for the extensive "Laogai gulag" of forced labor in China. Chinese human rights activist Harry Wu, speaking at a luncheon in his honor, sponsored by The Independent Institute, in Oakland California, March 27, 1996, discussed

> . . . the laogai camp system, of which we have identified 1,100 camps. It is also an integral part of the national economy. Its importance is illustrated by some basic facts: one third of China's tea is produced in laogai camps; 60 percent of China's rubber vulcanizing chemicals are produced in a single laogai camp in Shanghai; . . . one of the largest and earliest exporters of hand tools is a camp in Shanghai; an unknown but significant amount of China's cotton crop is grown by prisoners. I could go on and on and on.
>
> Sometimes people ask me, "What are you fighting for?" And my answer is quite simple. I want to see the word *laogai* in every dictionary in every language in the world. I want to see the laogai ended. Before 1974, *gulag* did not appear in any dictionary. Today it does. This single word conveys the

meaning of Soviet political violence and its labor camp system. *Laogai* also deserves to become a word in our dictionary. (Harry Wu, "The Outlook for China, Human Rights: The Laogai Gulag," *Vital Speeches*, 62, no. 17 [June 15, 1996]: 522)

39. Ryszard Kapuściński, *Imperium* (New York, 1995), 211.

40. Slavomir Rawicz, *The Long Walk: The True Story of a Trek to Freedom* (New York, 1984); originally published as *The Long Walk: A Gamble for Life* (New York, 1956).

41. Rawicz, *The Long Walk*, 32–34. Slavomir Rawicz became a runaway slave. He escaped from Camp 303 on the Lena River near the Arctic Circle in the dead of winter, with five companions and a stolen ax; they trekked south across Siberia, Mongolia, the Gobi Desert, and the Himalayan Mountains. It took an entire year for the survivors in the party to reach northern India.

42. Hilda Vitzthum, *Torn Out by the Roots: The Recollections of a Former Communist* (Lincoln, Nebraska, 1993), 153–54, 184–85.

43. Ibid., 186.

44. Ginzburg, *Within the Whirlwind*, 122. For an overview, see Anne Applebaum, *Gulag: A History* (New York, 2003).

Chapter 2

Abraham H. Galloway
Wilmington's Lost Prophet and the Rise of Black Radicalism in the American South

David S. Cecelski

In the spring of 1863, a recruiting agent for the Union army walked the streets of New Bern, North Carolina, looking for Abraham H. Galloway. The seaport was usually a town of 5,500 inhabitants, but at that moment it was overflowing with thousands of fugitive slaves who had escaped from the Confederacy. The setting was one of excess in all things: hardship, disarray, fear, heartbreak, joy. Federal troops crowded into colonial homes and antebellum manors. Downtown buildings lay in charred ruins: retreating Confederates had burned some of them, and a Union general torched the others after snipers shot at his sentries. The Confederates had fled so quickly that they left doors banging in the wind, family portraits in front yards, a piano in the middle of a street. The murmur of sawmills could be heard across the Trent River, the sound of the former slaves building a new city. The days clattered noisily by, and even the stillness of evening was broken by short bursts of ecstasy: slave sisters reunited after a lifetime apart or a slave family that had survived a journey of 150 miles. No one breathed easy. New Bern was a sliver of sanctuary for African Americans in the slave South, and the Confederate army could have recaptured the city at any time.[1]

Edward W. Kinsley, the recruiting agent, had not come to New Bern with the intention of looking for Galloway. He had arrived there as an emissary of Governor John Albion Andrew of Massachusetts, an abolitionist leader seeking to recruit an African American regiment. Kinsley had expected the former slaves to throng into the army's ranks; instead, they avoided him nearly to a man. "Something was wrong," he realized, "and it did not take [me] long to find out the trouble." All pointed him to one individual, the man whom the slave refugees considered their leader. "Among the blacks," he learned, "was a man of more than ordinary ability, a coal black negro named Abraham Galloway."[2]

In 1863 Galloway was only twenty-six years old, a prodigy who had already lived three men's lives. Born into enslavement by the Cape Fear River, Galloway had grown up in Wilmington. He had become a fugitive slave, an abolitionist leader, a Union spy. He was tall, strong, and handsome, with long wavy hair and flashing eyes. He was not, as Kinsley remembered, "coal black," but light-skinned. He consented to see Kinsley but even after several meetings refused to help recruit former slaves into the Union army. Then, for unknown reasons, Galloway changed his mind. He sent a message to Kinsley to meet him at the home of a black leader named Mary Ann Starkey. When the New England abolitionist arrived that night at midnight, somebody blindfolded him and led him into an attic room. When the blindfold came off, as Kinsley later recounted, "he could see by the dim light of the candle that the room was nearly filled with blacks, and right in front of him stood Abraham Galloway and another huge negro, both armed with revolvers."[3]

That night the convocation of liberated slaves did not mince words. If the Union intended to make the war a crusade for black freedom, then Kinsley would find no shortage of recruits in New Bern. But if the Federal army planned to use black men like chattel and wage a war merely for the preservation of the Union, that was another story. Kinsley had to know that Galloway was serving the Union army—wild rumors of his exploits as a Union spy were whispered on every street corner—and must have wondered, was Galloway really willing to hurt the Union cause by withholding black troops or was this merely a negotiating tactic to improve the lot of black soldiers and their families? Galloway and his lieutenants did not let Kinsley know, and we will probably never know either. Instead, they bluntly listed their demands: equal pay, provisions for black soldiers' families, schooling for soldiers' children, and assurances that the Union would force the Confederacy to treat captured blacks as prisoners of war rather than execute them as traitors.

Kinsley later described the next few moments as the most harrowing of his life. Galloway had not brought him to that dark attic to negotiate terms, but to guarantee them. Holding a revolver to Kinsley's head, he compelled the Union recruiter to swear a personal oath that the Federal army would meet these conditions. After Kinsley did so, the former slaves released him into the night air. "The next day," he remembered later, "the word went forth, and the blacks came to the recruiting station by [the] hundreds and a brigade was soon formed."[4] The more than 5,000 African Americans eventually recruited in New Bern, most of them former slaves, became the core of the 35th, 36th, and 37th Regiments, United States Colored Troops, known originally as the African Brigade.[5]

Rarely have we glimpsed what the tens of thousands of black Southerners who found asylum in Federal territory during the Civil War did with their new freedom. Instead, historians have tended to see the "freedpeople," or "contrabands" (as the Union army called blacks under Federal occupation), either as if through the eyes of so many New England missionaries, as downtrodden, helpless souls entirely reliant on white goodwill, or, just as misleadingly, as patriotic "good soldiers" blindly devoted to the Union cause and serving unquestionably under the terms and conditions that Union commanders offered them. This scene in New Bern hints at a different story: instead of docility, we see militancy; instead of unquestioning loyalty to the Union cause, we see former slaves attempting to shape the Union cause; instead of imbibing the politics of white abolitionists or Republicans, we see black Carolinians charting their own political course; instead of the contrabands looking to Northern blacks for political guidance, we glimpse a new politics emerging out of the struggle against slavery in the South.

For all of the story's broader implications about the former slaves and the Civil War, the center of its intrigue is Kinsley's portrayal of that "man of more than ordinary ability . . . named Abraham Galloway." The young black leader comes to mind particularly now, as we contemplate the various meanings of the Wilmington "race riot" a hundred years ago. Galloway spent most of his life in Wilmington, but he has been utterly forgotten there, as elsewhere. He became arguably the most important black leader in North Carolina during the Civil War and Reconstruction. Yet, except for brief entries in a few biographical dictionaries and short passages in broader scholarly works about Reconstruction, this mercurial figure has received little notice, having never been the subject of a book, a journal article, or a magazine feature.[6] The white supremacists of 1898 drew a veil of forgetfulness over the black militancy and political radicalism that Galloway embodied. They revised the history of the Civil War and Reconstruction into a fable of "Negro domination" and black sexual predation. In the history books they replaced black radicals such as Galloway with images of shiftless, deferential, and primitive blacks, so unable to recognize their own best interests that they needed white guidance at every step.[7] Galloway and the black insurgents who followed in his footsteps were purged from the Southern past, victims of the white supremacists of the post-Reconstruction generation no less than those who died in Wilmington in 1898. Galloway, son of Wilmington, personified a different path into the twentieth century, a democratic politics that was sown in slavery, grew into first light during the Civil War, and flowered in Reconstruction. Here, then, is the story of Abraham H. Galloway: slave, fugitive, abolitionist, Union spy, special agent, leader of the freedpeople, women's suffragist, state senator.

Galloway was born on 13 February 1837 in Smithville (later Southport), the seat of Brunswick County, North Carolina, twenty-five miles south of Wilmington at the mouth of the Cape Fear River.[8] His mother, Hester Hankins, was a slave born in 1820.[9] His father, John Wesley Galloway, the son of a Brunswick County planter, was white.[10] Relatively little is known about Abraham's mother: she was likely, but not certainly, owned by planter William Hankins of Town Creek, and she married Amos Galloway, one of John Wesley's slaves, in or about 1846.[11] As we will see later, she and her son remained close throughout his life. Not surprisingly, the life of Abraham's father is better documented. The Galloways included some of the wealthiest planters and merchants in Brunswick County, but John Wesley was only a small farmer, later a ship's pilot and, sometime after 1850, captain of the federal lightship off Frying Pan Shoals. He seems to have shared the aristocratic values of his wealthier cousins, but he never owned much property beyond four African Americans.[12] The circumstances of his relationship with Abraham's mother are altogether murky. We know only that Abraham later recalled that John Wesley "recognized me as his son and protected me as far as he was allowed so to do."[13]

A well-off railroad mechanic in Wilmington named Marsden Milton Hankins owned Galloway from infancy.[14] How the mulatto child came into the Hankins household is not clear; Hankins may have owned Abraham's mother, or, if she was owned by John Wesley Galloway, Abraham may have been sold for discretion's sake when John Wesley first married in 1839. Galloway later recalled that Hankins "was a man of very good disposition who always said he would sell before he would use a whip." His wife Mary Ann evidently was not so even-tempered; Galloway remembered her as a "very mean woman" who "would whip contrary to his orders."[15] Trained as a brickmason, young Galloway was hiring out his own time be-

fore his twentieth birthday, a common practice for slave artisans in antebellum Wilmington. Hankins, a skilled laborer himself, could not super-
vise a slave closely. He left Galloway to seek out brickmasonry jobs when,
where, and how he pleased so long as the slave continued to bring into the
Hankins household a steady $15.00 a month.[16]

In 1857 Galloway escaped from Wilmington. He later explained that he
fled the port city because he could no longer earn the $15.00 a month that
Hankins required of him. This may seem a rather uncompelling motivation for such a risky undertaking, especially if we take his word that Hankins was not a malicious master. But if the failure to earn money might lead
to Galloway's sale in the local slave market—a fate that could have ma-
rooned him on one of the rice fields or turpentine orchards of the Lower
Cape Fear—then it makes sense. No matter his gentle nature, Hankins
clearly saw Galloway primarily as a financial investment—and every in-
vestor sometimes has to cut his losses. At any rate, Galloway and a friend, a
slave named Richard Eden, found a schooner captain willing to conceal
them among the turpentine barrels in his cargo hold.[17]

An abolitionist underground of free and slave residents of Wilmington
helped fugitive slaves to escape by ship throughout the 1850s.[18] The seaport's political leaders seemed to find solace in blaming free black sailors
from ports outside of the South for such antislavery activity. "They are of
course," wrote the *Wilmington Aurora*'s editor, "all of them, from the very
nature of their position, abolitionists."[19] Local whites seemed reluctant to
acknowledge subversive elements within the local slave community. Typically, when copies of David Walker's *Appeal to the Free Citizens of the World*
—one of the primary documents in American antislavery thought—appeared in Wilmington in 1830, the town's leaders struck out brutally at
black sailors, but they apparently did not consider the fact that Walker
had been born and raised a free black in Wilmington. Though Walker had
traveled extensively after leaving the South, his call for armed resistance
to slavery had its roots in the intellectual culture of African Americans in
the Cape Fear. Sustained by strong linkages to maritime black communities across the Western Hemisphere, this intellectual culture was grounded
in the egalitarian ideals of the Enlightenment, an evangelical theology
that stressed the "natural rights" of all peoples before God, and a particular brand of abolitionism born of African American slavery. Slave literacy had been outlawed in North Carolina in 1830, but this political vision
was preserved among a predominately illiterate people in song, sermon,
and saying, eventually, with David Walker and others, to make its way

onto the page at first flush of formal learning.[20] Galloway left Wilmington, as Walker had, with a political vision far more defiantly egalitarian than that of most of the abolitionists he would meet north of the Mason-Dixon Line.

Galloway arrived in Philadelphia in June of 1857. Perhaps with the help of black sailors, he and Eden reached the Vigilance Committee of Philadelphia. They met with William Still, an African American coal merchant who was the committee's executive secretary, and they were soon forwarded to its contacts in Canada in order to evade the fugitive slave laws of the United States. On 20 July 1857, Eden wrote one of the committee's directors that he and Galloway had arrived in Kingston, Ontario, in "good health" and that Galloway had found employment, presumably as a brick-mason, at $1.75 a day.[21] Over the next four years, Galloway immersed himself in the abolitionist movement and quite likely in aiding other African Americans to flee the South. As the nearest part of Canada for most fugitive slaves who fled the South, Ontario had a large African American community with a strong stake in the abolitionist cause. The black fugitives founded relief societies, newspapers, political groups, and even secret militias that supported the "Underground Railroad" in the United States and helped black refugees get established in Canada.[22] Galloway seems to have devoted himself to the abolitionist cause in a serious way. Several newspaper reports later indicated that he left Canada and gave antislavery speeches in the United States and was especially active in the abolitionist movement in Ohio, which, if true, he did at risk of being prosecuted under the Fugitive Slave Act of 1850.[23] During these years, Galloway also built extensive ties among the abolitionist leaders of Boston, though the exact character of his relationship with the Bird Club and other Boston antislavery groups remains uncertain.

Whatever else Galloway accomplished in the abolitionist movement or the Underground Railroad, he convinced George L. Stearns, the Boston industrialist who bankrolled John Brown's military raids in Kansas and sponsored the 54th Regiment, Massachusetts Volunteers (the black regiment featured in the 1989 movie *Glory*), that he would serve the Union army well as a spy. This is the single most compelling reason for believing that Galloway was involved in covert activities in the abolitionist movement. Stearns was a serious man who recruited thousands of black soldiers from Maine to Texas, and Galloway would have made a fine Union enlistee. By the outbreak of the Civil War, however, Stearns had seen something in Galloway that suggested a far more decisive role.[24]

Galloway returned south at the beginning of the Civil War. Stearns had brought the young mulatto to the attention of a Boston acquaintance, Colonel Edward A. Wild, who evidently introduced Galloway to General Benjamin F. Butler at Fortress Monroe, Virginia. Galloway was soon recruited into the Union's secret service under Butler. Working out of Fortress Monroe, Galloway undertook special missions in the coastal portions of Virginia and North Carolina that had been captured by Federal troops during General Ambrose E. Burnside's campaign of 1861–62.[25] We will probably never know more than a hint of what Galloway did in his capacity as an intelligence agent for the Union army. Mystery shrouds much of his life, and none more than his service under Butler.[26] He reportedly answered directly to Butler and was said to "possess the fullest confidence of the commanding General."[27] It is quite likely that Galloway returned to North Carolina even prior to the Federal occupation; a Union corporal stationed in the occupied seaport of Beaufort, North Carolina, later noted in his diary that Galloway was "in the detective service of Gen. Butler" and had scouted marine landings for Union troops, presumably during the Burnside campaign.[28] That is quite plausible. Union commanders depended heavily on local slaves to identify landing sites during the Burnside expedition. Somebody had to recruit the slave pilots or somehow elicit the necessary piloting knowledge from African American watermen. One report indicated that Galloway also investigated claims of Union sympathy among Confederate prisoners of war near Norfolk and recruited white Unionists into a military regiment.[29]

Galloway began working out of New Bern soon after its capture by Federal forces in March 1862. The colonial-era port became the headquarters of the Federal regiments in North Carolina and the Union blockading fleet. During the remainder of the war, the Union kept a precarious hold on the city, using it as a base for military raids into eastern North Carolina and for a nasty war with Confederate guerrillas. Thousands of runaway slaves poured into the city. One can only imagine the different ways that Galloway might have been, as a Northern journalist later wrote of him, "of some service to the Union army." The slaves who flocked to New Bern brought with them a wealth of information about the Confederacy that had to be culled. Guides for reconnaissance missions and raids into the state's interior had to be recruited, as did spies willing to move across Confederate lines on espionage and intelligence-gathering missions. Familiar with the terrain, Confederate defenses, and local slave communities, the former slaves were especially well situated to perform these challenging tasks. "Upwards of fifty volunteers of the best and most courageous," wrote Vincent Colyer, superintendent of Negro affairs in New Bern in 1862–63, "were kept constantly employed on the perilous but important duty of spies, scouts, and guides." Colyer reported that the black operatives "were invaluable and almost indispensable. They frequently went from thirty to three hundred miles within the enemy's lines; visiting his principal camps and most important posts, and bringing us back important and reliable information."[30] More than likely, Galloway was the chief intelligence agent working among the fugitive slaves in North Carolina. He worked closely with the Union commanding officers in New Bern, including Brigadier General Edward A. Wild (promoted from colonel in 1863), Brigadier General John J. Peck, and Major General John C. Foster.[31]

Whatever duties Galloway carried out as a spy for the Union army, they gave him a unique vantage point to organize among the great crowds of former slaves congregating behind Federal lines. As soon as New Bern had fallen in March 1862, the city was, in Burnside's words, "overrun with fugitives from the surrounding towns and plantations." Hundreds, then thousands, of African American men, women, and children fled from bondage in Confederate territory to freedom in New Bern. "It would be utterly impossible . . . to keep them outside of our lines," an overwrought Burnside reported to the secretary of war, "as they find their way to us through woods and swamps from every side."[32] Situated in New Bern, Galloway built strong contacts among the fugitives there as well as among the smaller, outlying contraband camps in Beaufort, Plymouth, and Washington and on Roanoke Island. In these camps congregated the most ardent radicals, the most incorrigible troublemakers, the most militant artisans, the most defiant slave preachers—in short, the black Carolinians who had most ardently dared to defy or deceive slavery. Inevitably, these insurgents saw the nature of power in the slave South with the clarity characteristic of outlaws. They saw its inherent violence, its paternalist veneer, its pathological foundations in ideas of racial purity, sexual domination, and social hierarchy. They bore scars that they had acquired the hard way, as they negotiated plantation discipline and eluded slave patrols and the Home Guard. It was no accident that Galloway emerged as a leader among this self-selected assembly of liberated slaves. Many, including Galloway himself, moved back and forth between occupied and Confederate territory, venturing into the latter even as far as Wilmington, working as Union agents or searching for families and friends still in bondage. Out of New Bern's contraband camps, then, black men and women extended lifelines

deep into Confederate territory, expanding and informing the radical political culture that was emerging in New Bern.

By the spring of 1863, Galloway had become more than a Union spy. He
had become the most important political leader among the more than
10,000 former slaves who resided in the contraband camps and seaports
occupied by the Federal army. The liberated slaves had erected their largest
shanty towns along the outskirts of New Bern. Out of those roughhewn
villages arose a great revival of African American political culture, a ferment comparable in ways to the black freedom movement that would
come a century later. Unfettered by slavery, the black multitude exulted in
the free expression of worship, family life, even music. Moreover, they
looked to politics both as a weapon against their outlandishly racist treatment by the Union occupying forces and as a tool to shape their destiny
after the Civil War.[33] They organized schools, relief societies, self-help associations, and churches, including St. Peter's, the first African Methodist
Episcopal Zion church in the South.[34] These institutions became corner-
stones of black political life.

Confronted by the dangers of Confederate guerrillas and the depreda-
tions of Union soldiers, they also organized a black militia. William H.
Singleton, the only black veteran who wrote a memoir of the New Bern
occupation, indicated that the refugees had been drilling on their own
during the early spring of 1862, well before President Lincoln permitted
African Americans to serve in the army. Singleton suggests, in fact, that
this militia formed the heart of the black brigades recruited in New Bern
in the summer of 1863. If that is true, then on the night that Galloway negotiated the terms of black enlistment, he had a stronger hand than merely
the revolver aimed at Edward Kinsley's head; he had a fighting force of at
least several hundred black soldiers anxiously waiting to join the fray.[35]
The fact that hundreds of black men showed up almost instantly at a word
from their leader certainly suggests a high degree of existing organization.
Galloway had also clearly begun to mark an independent political course
that placed his first loyalty to the former slaves, not the Union army.

This was the milieu in which Galloway grew into political prominence.
No matter how much his radical politics had been shaped by his own
life in slavery, in the abolitionist movement, or as a Union spy, Galloway
was home. He was of this society, knew its people, knew its horrors. He
could scarcely help but play a leadership role in the black political movements emerging within New Bern, and he developed a close relationship
to the black women organizing support for the slave refugees. He worked

especially closely with Mary Ann Starkey, at whose home Edward Kinsley met Galloway that night. Starkey had turned her home into a meeting place for a small adult "reading school" and a Bible school class. She also led a black women's relief society that solicited funds and supplies among both the former slaves and Northern abolitionists for refugee families and, later, for black soldiers.[36]

Working with black groups like Mary Ann Starkey's relief society and William Singleton's militia, Galloway seems to have discovered a new maturity. Prior to this moment, the twenty-six-year-old had lived the kind of rebel's life that required talents for subterfuge: guile, restraint, dissemblance, patience, the ability to act boldly but carefully under pressure and in solitude. These gifts served Galloway well as a fugitive, an abolitionist, and a spy. Now Galloway developed a genius for politics. He became a grassroots organizer, a coalition builder, and an inspiring orator. As a secret agent and political leader, he seemed to pop up everywhere in Federal territory—and he struck quite a figure. He was already renowned for a severe sense of honor and a fearless readiness to defend it, a trait that could only have endeared him to former slaves, for whom honor had always been a white man's prerogative. Galloway may already have gotten into the habit that he developed later of always carrying a pistol where people could see it in his belt. Yet he could not have seemed reckless or foolhardy. For all his bravado, there was a disarming quiet about Galloway; patience, tact, and wariness had helped him to survive too many dangers not to be a part of him. Still, he laughed loud and often, and he must have had a sweet side, for everywhere the young man went black Carolinians crowded around him as if he were a prophet.[37]

The recruitment of North Carolina's former slaves into the Union army began in May of 1863. In the seaport of Beaufort, thirty-five miles east of New Bern, a Confederate sympathizer named James Rumley groused in his diary that "the black traitors are gathering in considerable numbers" to join the army. Rumley described the "horror, or the fiery indignation that burns in [the Rebels'] bosoms . . . when they think of their husbands and brothers and sons who may fall at the hands of the black savages."[38] Galloway did nothing to allay such Confederate hostility. Prior to President Lincoln's approval for former slaves to join the Union army, Galloway had made black military service the issue about which he was most outspoken. He not only recruited black soldiers when the time came, but he also articulated a political rationale for armed struggle that unnerved die-hard Rebels such as Rumley. At black political rallies held during the Federal occupation, Galloway argued that the former slaves would fight harder and better than white Union soldiers. At one point, he was quoted as saying that although McClellan "failed to take Richmond with 200,000 white soldiers, Butler would soon take it *with twenty thousand negroes*."[39]

More fervently, Galloway contended that the black regiments would compel a victorious Union to grant the former slaves both freedom and political equality—that is, the right to vote, serve on juries, and run for elected office, all issues around which no political consensus had yet been reached, even in the North. Galloway's linkage of military service and political equality reflected a growing accord among African American leaders. "Once let the black man get upon his person the brass letters U.S., let him get an eagle on his button and a musket on his shoulder and bullets in his pocket," Frederick Douglass had said, "and there is no power on earth which can deny that he has earned the right to citizenship in the United States."[40] Galloway shared Douglass's conviction. During a speech at a rally celebrating the first anniversary of the Emancipation Proclamation, Galloway told Beaufort's freed men and women, as James Rumley remembered it, "that their race would have not only their personal freedom, but political equality, and if this should be refused them at the ballot box[,] they would have it at the cartridge box!"[41]

With more than 50,000 blacks fighting in the Union army by the end of 1863, Galloway shifted his priorities toward the achievement of black political equality after the Civil War.[42] He was still seen frequently among the liberated slaves in North Carolina: he moved to Beaufort and married Martha Ann Dixon, the eighteen-year-old daughter of two former slaves, on 29 December 1863.[43] He was active with pro-Union political groups and local organizations that defended the rights of black soldiers in Beaufort and New Bern. He spoke frequently at the black churches that had become the heart of political education and community organizing in the contraband camps, as well as at the mass rallies held by the freedpeople on Independence Day and the anniversary of Emancipation Day. He assisted Union officers in recruiting black soldiers in Beaufort and New Bern, and probably over a much wider area.[44] Brigadier General Wild referred to him at this point not as a Union spy but as his "confidential recruiting agent," a term that suggests that Galloway was recruiting former slaves for special missions, presumably in Confederate territory. Galloway's contacts among slaves even in the most heavily fortified cities of the Confederacy were extensive by the fall of 1863. Their extent can be measured by his success that November, in Wild's words, at "manag[ing] to get his *mother* sent out of

Wilmington, N.C." Wilmington was one of the most heavily guarded cities in the Confederacy, yet Galloway somehow arranged for his slave mother to escape to New Bern. Three Union generals—Wild, Peck, and Foster—felt so beholden to Galloway that they promised their former spy and "confidential recruiting agent" that they would play a part in getting his mother from New Bern to the home of one of Galloway's contacts in Boston. "I would like to do all I can for Galloway, who has served his country well," Wild wrote Edward Kinsley on 30 November 1863.[45]

The scope of Galloway's political leadership grew as he represented the liberated slave communities of North Carolina at the national level. In May of 1864, he was part of a five-man delegation of black leaders who met with President Lincoln to urge him to endorse suffrage for all African Americans. He also began to travel extensively to Boston and New York, where he met with abolitionist leaders about the political fate of former slaves after the war.[46] In addition, Galloway was one of 144 black leaders who answered the call to "the strong men of our people" and attended the National Convention of Colored Citizens of the United States, on 4 October 1864, in Syracuse, New York. Presided over by Frederick Douglass, the convention was the most important gathering of American black leaders during the Civil War. Skeptical of the commitment to racial equality in both the Democratic and Republican Parties, the convention delegates articulated a black political agenda that called for the abolition of slavery, the end of racial discrimination, and political equality.[47] They also founded the National Equal Rights League and pledged themselves to organize state chapters to advocate political equality. Though his political organizing in the freedpeople's camps must have tailed off at the end of 1864—many of his most militant lieutenants were fighting with Grant in Virginia, and a yellow fever epidemic had swept New Bern and Beaufort—Galloway had organized a state chapter and five local chapters of the Equal Rights League in North Carolina by January 1865.[48]

New Bern and Beaufort remained the central points for black political organizing in North Carolina immediately after the Civil War. New Bern and its adjacent freedpeople's camp, James City, were especially important. The Federal forces had compelled the state's other contraband camps to disband and return the lands on which they were situated to their antebellum owners, but the former slaves in James City had refused to surrender their new homes. They and other black residents of the Federal occupation area had developed political, educational, and religious institutions that gave them a long head start in confronting postwar life. For all its hardships (or perhaps because of its hardships), the Federal occupation had been a very effective "rehearsal for Reconstruction," to borrow the title of Willie Lee Rose's landmark study of black freedpeople in South Carolina.[49] While former slaves elsewhere struggled to disentangle themselves from the web of slavery, fitfully trying out new rights and testing their new limits for the first time, the freedpeople whom Galloway had helped to politicize during the Federal occupation of the North Carolina coast moved steadfastly to make an impact on Reconstruction politics. Galloway remained in the thick of this political ferment, exhibiting, as one journalist said, an "exceedingly radical and Jacobinical spirit" that resonated deeply among African Americans.[50] When, in 1865, more than 2,000 former slaves celebrated the Fourth of July with a Beaufort parade organized by the Salmon P. Chase Equal Rights League, Galloway delivered the keynote address, calling for "all equal rights before the law, and nothing more."[51]

Not surprisingly, a few weeks later, on 28 August, Galloway emerged, as a correspondent for the *New York Times* put it, as the "leading spirit" of a mass meeting of New Bern's black citizens, organized to shape a political agenda for the postwar era. It was the first such gathering of former slaves held in the South. In a long keynote address, Galloway called for voting rights and public schooling. "We want to be an educated people and an intelligent people," he told the crowd. In a double-edged declaration that echoed his words of two years before, he also declared that "if the negro knows how to use the cartridge box, he knows how to use the ballot box."[52]

Beyond endorsing black suffrage, the mass meeting in New Bern addressed the white backlash against the freedpeople and the violent, undemocratic nature of the postwar society that had emerged during Presidential Reconstruction. The black New Bernians, led by Galloway, resolved "that the many atrocities committed upon our people in almost every section of our country . . . clearly demonstrate the immense prejudice and hatred on the part of our former owners toward us." They protested "the enforcement of the old code of slave laws that prohibits us from the privileges of schools, that deny us the right to control our families, that reject our testimony in courts of justice, that after keeping us at work without pay till their crops are laid by and then driving us off, [refuse] longer to give us food and shelter." In great detail, the delegates described white terrorism—"whipping, thumb-screwing and not infrequently murdering us in cold blood"—against blacks who challenged the antebellum racial code.

"In our judgement," they concluded, with something more than a measure of understatement, North Carolina "comes far short of being a republican form of government and needs to be remodeled."[53]

The New Bern assembly appointed Galloway and two other men, John Randolph and George W. Price, to head the call for a statewide freedpeople's convention in Raleigh on 29 September. The organizers appealed to the state's black citizens soon thereafter with newspaper announcements under the banner: "Freedmen of North Carolina, Arouse!" The three New Bern leaders instructed black Carolinians to assemble in every township to "speak their views" and to organize district meetings where delegates would be nominated to the freedpeople's convention in Raleigh.[54] On the same day that Governor William Holden called to order a state constitutional convention dominated by the antebellum aristocracy, Galloway called to order 117 black delegates representing 42 counties at an African Methodist Episcopal church in Raleigh. Few dressed so finely as their white counterparts across town, some had passed the collection plate to obtain a railroad ticket, and many had slipped out of their hometowns quietly in order to avoid violence at the hands of local white conservatives.[55] While the white conservatives drafted the so-called Black Codes to bar African Americans from political life, the black delegates articulated a profoundly more democratic vision of Southern society. They demanded the full rights of citizenship, public schools, equal protection under the law, regulation of working hours, and the abolition of all laws "which make unjust discriminations on account of race or color."[56]

The black delegates represented a wide range of political views, from strident nationalists to fearful accommodationists, but the more radical delegates from New Bern, Beaufort, and Roanoke Island dominated the convention in large part because they had refined their political ideology and gained practical experience in political argument and strategy during the years of Federal occupation. Several black leaders from the Federal occupation shone with special brilliance in Raleigh. The Reverend James W. Hood, an AME Zion leader in New Bern, was elected chairman of the convocation, for instance. His moderate willingness to appeal to white goodwill and his cautious advice for the freedpeople to move slowly carried a great deal of influence. But none of the delegates made a deeper impression on the black participants or white observers than Galloway. "Perhaps the most remarkable person among the delegates," a Northern journalist, John Richard Dennett, observed, was "a light-yellow man whose features seemed to indicate that there was a cross of Indian blood in his veins." In

Dennett's description of Galloway one can imagine why white conservatives found the former slave so unsettling and why he held so powerful an appeal for so many freedpeople. The ex-slaves had been born into a Southern society that upheld white supremacy and tried to deny the existence of interracial sex, that associated blackness with ugliness, that compelled black men to carry themselves with great deference, and punished any black who dared to challenge a white man's superior intelligence. Politically and personally, Galloway would have none of it. "His hair was long and black and very curly," Dennett wrote.

> He appeared to be vain of its beauty as he tossed it carelessly off his forehead, or suffered it to fall heavily and half conceal his eyes. These were twinkly and slippery, and nearly always half shut, for he laughed much, and then they partly closed of themselves, and at other times he had a way of watching from under his dropped lids. He was a well-shaped man, but it was hardly to be discovered as he lolled in his seat, or from the insufferably lazy manner of his walking. When he spoke, however, he stood erect, using forcible and graceful gestures. His voice was powerful, and, though an illiterate man, his speaking was effective.

We can hear Dennett trying to fit Galloway into an antebellum racial stereotype—"the insufferably lazy manner of his walking," his "slippery" eyes —but neither Galloway's force of will nor Dennett's grudging admiration allows him to do it. "His power of sarcasm and brutal invective," Dennett conceded, "and the personal influence given him by his fearlessness and audacity, always secured him a hearing."[57] Galloway's defiance of white authority alarmed more cautious black delegates, and the freedpeople's convention as a whole struck a more conciliatory posture when they presented their demands to the white convention. But few would forget Galloway or fail to tell stories about him when they returned to homes besieged by white terror. He may have frightened them, for they knew how white conservatives might react to such an insurgent, but he also gave voice to the vision of freedom born in bondage.

Galloway left New Bern for Wilmington late in 1866 or early in 1867. He may have moved to rejoin his mother—she probably returned to Wilmington soon after the Civil War (she was definitely there by 1870)—or he may have returned home because he recognized that Wilmington would again become the capital of African American political life in North

Carolina.[58] Wilmington was the state's largest city and had a majority-black population; its large number of black artisans and maritime laborers formed the core of a politically militant class that would have attracted Galloway. By 3 January 1866, the North Carolina office of the Equal Rights League had also conspicuously opened in downtown Wilmington. Galloway's relocation to Wilmington and the opening of the Equal Rights League's office may not have been unrelated.[59]

Galloway tried to give his life a semblance of normalcy in Wilmington. He and his wife went about raising their two sons and attended St. Paul's Episcopal Church, while he joined the Masons. Reconstruction was not an ordinary time, however, and a quiet life was not his destiny. The Wilmington that Galloway returned to was in the throes of a violent conflict over the shape of postwar society. Nothing was guaranteed—certainly not the freedpeople's right to vote, to own land, to receive schooling, to earn decent wages, to enjoy the normal privileges of civil society, and to have equal protection under the law. These issues were all being worked out on the streets of towns like Wilmington just as surely as in the halls of the U.S. Congress. Every encounter between a black person and a white person was fraught with danger. "They perceive insolence in a tone, a glance, a gesture, or failure to yield enough by two or three inches in meeting on the sidewalk," a visitor noted of Wilmington's white citizens.[60] Cape Fear conservatives sought to reestablish their antebellum power at the same time that blacks sought to assert their new rights of freedom and citizenship. The talents for covert organizing and self-defense that Galloway had honed as a runaway slave, a fugitive abolitionist, and a Union spy would be put to good use in Reconstruction Wilmington.

By the beginning of 1866, conservatives had regained power in Wilmington, in large part due to Union military commanders who sympathized more with the Cape Fear aristocrats than with former slaves. "The true soldiers, whether they wore the gray or the blue are now united in their opposition . . . to negro government and negro equality," gloated a local newspaper, adding, "Blood is thicker than water."[61] Nightriders and white militias brutally beat, killed, and otherwise terrorized African Americans who dared to act like free citizens, and they strove to reimpose control over the freedpeople's lives—including control over whom they worked for, what wages they commanded, where they lived, and how they raised their children. The presence of black troops among the Federal occupying force in Wilmington had momentarily restrained conservative violence, but Union commanders showed a lack of resolve in supporting the black troops, even refusing to intervene when Confederate militia groups targeted them. Increasingly, the black troops realized that they were on their own in postwar Wilmington. They mutinied against their white officers in September 1865, and in February 1866 they laid siege to the city jail in order to halt the public whipping of black prisoners convicted in a trial in which the conservative judge had not allowed black testimony. After that, Union commanders withdrew all black troops from the Lower Cape Fear and replaced them with white soldiers.[62] White terror reigned throughout the Cape Fear. "The fact is," a freedman reported, "it's the first notion with a great many of these people, [that] if a Negro says anything or does anything that they don't like, [they] take a gun and put a bullet into him."[63] Not far from Wilmington, in Duplin County, a police captain named J. N. Stallings gave orders to shoot without trial blacks who had been accused of minor theft.[64]

With passage of the Reconstruction Acts by the Radical Congress of 1867, Wilmington blacks gained a crucial new political opportunity. The Reconstruction Acts restored federal military authority in the South and required states in the former Confederacy to pass a constitution that guaranteed universal male suffrage before they could be readmitted to the Union. The acts also opened the polls to black voters while banning from political life any antebellum officeholder who had taken an oath to uphold the U.S. Constitution but sided with the Confederacy. Galloway was soon looking toward the constitutional convention that would occur in Raleigh early in 1868. On 4 September 1867, he addressed a mass meeting of the state's Republican Party at Tucker Hall in Raleigh, delivering a conciliatory address aimed at building broad, biracial support for the Republicans. He exhorted his audience to "go everywhere there is a black man or a poor white man and tell him the true condition of the Republican Party."[65] Later that month, "after loud calls for 'Galloway,'" he addressed a torchlit procession of black citizens from the top of Wilmington's market house. "My people stand here tonight fettered, bound hand [and] foot by a Constitution that recognizes them as chattel," Galloway exclaimed.[66] That fall he was elected one of thirteen delegates from seven Cape Fear counties to serve at the constitutional convention.

Galloway was, in the words of historian W. McKee Evans, one of "a small group of active delegates who largely dominated the life of the convention."[67] During the constitutional convention, which ran from January to March of 1868, Galloway served on the judiciary committee, and alongside white reformer Albion Tourgée on the committee for local government. As one of only 13 blacks among the 120 persons elected to the constitutional convention, however, he felt a special responsibility to represent the political concerns of the state's African American population. At one point, on 20 February, Galloway explained his support for the popular election of the judiciary by saying, in a reporter's paraphrase, that "the Judiciary in New Hanover was a bastard, born in sin and secession." "In their eyes, it was a crime to be a black or a loyal man," he continued, and he denounced conservative judges who had allegedly imprisoned blacks solely to keep them from voting.[68] At another point, Galloway vehemently opposed public support of a railroad that, in his words, "did not employ a single colored man," and he also refused to support a YMCA request to use the convention hall unless "no distinction be made between the races."[69]

Galloway routinely endured arguments about black inferiority from conservative delegates and their newspaper editors, as he would later in the state senate. Every day that he spent in Raleigh, he heard comments such as the *Sentinel*'s, that true North Carolinians would blush "that a set of apes and hybrids should be holding a brutal carnival in her halls of legislation."[70] Much to their dismay, conservative delegates discovered that such remarks inspired Galloway's most cutting rhetoric. Following one harangue on the unfitness of blacks for suffrage, Galloway responded by saying "that the best blood in Brunswick County flowed in [my] veins," a reference to his own mixed-race heritage, "and if [I] could do it, in justice to the African race, [I] would lance [my]self and let it out."[71] Despite the rancor, conservatives were a small minority at the constitutional convention. On 16 March 1868, the delegates signed a new state constitution that introduced universal male suffrage, removed all religious and property qualifications for officeholding, endorsed the popular election of county officials, increased public school support, and made the state's penal code more humane.[72]

When he returned to Wilmington, Galloway discovered that the conservatives had launched a vicious campaign to intimidate black voters from ratifying the new constitution or electing Radical leaders in the upcoming April election. Galloway himself was running for the state senate, in the first election in which blacks were eligible to hold state office. Under the leadership of Colonel Roger Moore, one of the Cape Fear's most celebrated aristocrats, the Ku Klux Klan attempted to frighten blacks away from the polls. Klan terrorism prevailed in other parts of North Carolina but collided with a stubborn militancy among African Americans in Wilmington. Black men patrolled the city's streets, firing their guns in the air and wielding fence rails to intimidate Klansmen. Shots and scuffles shattered the evening quiet on the downtown streets repeatedly on the nights between 18 and 21 April in 1868, and while exactly what happened in the darkness is unknown, after that the Ku Klux Klan was never a force in Wilmington during Reconstruction.[73] Even without documentary proof, one feels confidant that Galloway was not sitting quietly at home with his family. In the spring 1868 election the Republicans carried two-thirds of the electorate in New Hanover County, and voters chose Galloway to represent New Hanover and Brunswick Counties in the state senate. That fall, he was also voted the first black elector to a presidential convention in North Carolina history.[74]

Galloway realized that armed self-defense was crucial to political survival in Wilmington. Conservative leaders held him in contempt, Democratic editors parodied him mercilessly, and the threat of assassination followed his every step. Wherever he went in the port city, Galloway conspicuously wore a pistol in his belt, a noteworthy symbol of defiance only two years after Wilmington conservatives had organized house searches to disarm the black population. The rise of the Republican Party helped to back up Galloway's lone firearm. Later in 1868, a local militia, one of several organized by Wilmington blacks to defend themselves against white terrorists, elected Galloway their commander. Led most commonly by Union veterans, the black militias—like their ubiquitous white counterparts—supposedly existed to fight off foreign invasion or to quell insurrections, but they acted during Reconstruction as a military wing of the Republican Party.[75] Nobody understood better than former slaves and Union veterans that a constitution was only as strong as the military power available to defend it. The Klan would rage out of control in the Carolina Piedmont from 1868 to 1870 but remained prudently quiet in Wilmington.[76]

Galloway was one of three black senators, joined by seventeen black representatives, in the North Carolina General Assembly of 1868. He was only thirty-one years old, poor, and still could not read or write.[77] He was, however, an extraordinary orator and an influential legislator. He was an intelligent, ferocious debater, the kind of man whose biting sense of humor and sharp eye for hypocrisy inspired most of the senate conservatives to steer away from a direct argument with him. Few of his fellow senators had ever been compelled to confront a black man as an equal, much less a black man as fearless and battle-tested as Galloway. The *Wilmington Daily Journal*, a Democratic newspaper that was apparently still squeamish about Galloway's mixed-race parentage, once referred to him as "the pugilistic 'Indian Senator.'"[78] On one occasion, after a white senator from Craven County had insulted him in the midst of a floor debate over the racial makeup of New Bern's city council, Galloway declared "that he would hold the Senator from Craven responsible for his language, outside of this Hall; and . . . that, if hereafter, the Senator from Craven insulted him, he would prove to him the blood of a true Southron."[79] That was by no means the only incident in which Galloway reminded conservative Democrats that he was at least as aristocratic by birth as them. He not only claimed to be "a true Southron," but he also brazenly touted his parentage by a black woman and a white man.[80] No senate floor debate could examine the "color line" or anti-black laws without Galloway taunting his Democratic colleagues for their hypocrisy in language that reminded them that they were ultimately talking about family. Repeatedly, when a conservative called black men sexual predators posing threats to "white womanhood," Galloway reminded the senators how commonly white men pursued black women—and, knowing Galloway, he was probably well enough acquainted with the conservative Democrats' private lives to make more than a few of them nervous with a wink or a whisper. No wonder Galloway attracted venomous editorials in Democratic newspapers. The *Wilmington Journal* referred to Galloway's flaunting of his "bastardy" as "disgusting vulgarity [that is] a disgrace to any civilized community." Another time, the *Daily Journal*'s editors could barely bring themselves to acknowledge Galloway's having mentioned his parentage and interracial sex, referring obliquely to "some indelicate remarks [by Galloway] in regard to . . . white men mingling with negroes which we omit for the sake of decency."[81]

The codifying of a new color line occupied the senate repeatedly during Galloway's first term. This was true even with respect to the conduct of the General Assembly itself. On 8 July 1868, as a typical example, Galloway successfully amended a proposal to segregate the senate galleries by race to allow for a middle section that could be occupied voluntarily by blacks and whites.[82] Such a racial "middle ground" would become unthinkable after the Wilmington massacre of 1898, but for a generation black activists such as Galloway drew a more fluid boundary between black and white North Carolinians. It required constant diligence, however, as can be seen from a floor debate over racial segregation in public schools on 26 February 1869. When a Senator Love introduced an amendment requiring that no black teacher be employed in a school that had white students, a Senator Hayes, with Galloway's support, moved to amend Love's amendment to say, "or employ white teachers to serve in any school wherein colored children are to be instructed." This second amendment unnerved conservatives, who feared the political implications of black control over black schooling. To make the point stronger, Galloway moved next to amend Love and Hayes's amendment, facetiously adding a provision "that no white Democrat should teach any colored girl." Ruled out of order, Galloway had won the day if not the war. The full senate rejected Love's amendment and later created a state board of education and the first statewide system of public schooling. Yet not even white Republicans supported the call by Galloway and his fellow black legislators for racially integrated public schools or for equal funding of black schools.[83]

Much of Galloway's brief senate career addressed the most fundamental rights of the freed men and women. He voted for the Fourteenth and Fifteenth Amendments to the U.S. Constitution, introduced a successful bill to help former slaves hold onto land and homes given them while in bondage, and supported several measures to curtail the Ku Klux Klan, including a bill to create a state militia to combat white terrorism. Galloway strongly supported Governor Holden's ill-fated attempts to crack down on the Ku Klux Klan in the Piedmont, where by mid-1870 at least 260 KKK terrorist acts had been documented. He also pushed to guarantee that blacks serve on juries, a right granted by the 1868 constitution, but one that Galloway contended was often ignored by county commissioners.[84]

More than any other elected leader in North Carolina, Galloway also fought for women's rights. The rights of women had become an important political issue in the Reconstruction South, with Radicals and suffragists briefly finding common cause in an advocacy of universal suffrage. Black Southerners supported women's suffrage far more strongly than whites, perhaps a sign of the relatively higher status that black women had held in slave families and of a more collective sensibility toward voting among the ex-slaves.[85] Twice Galloway introduced bills to amend the state's constitution to allow women's suffrage, once in 1868 and again in 1869. Outraged by an 1868 state supreme court ruling that men had a right to beat their wives, he sought unsuccessfully to force the senate judiciary committee to report a bill against domestic violence. He also supported a bill that gave women a greater right to sign deeds, and another to protect married women from willful abandonment or neglect by their husbands.[86] Women's suffrage and many of the other pioneering women's rights measures advocated by Galloway would not become law in North Carolina for half a century.

With respect to his support for women's suffrage, as for most issues for which he fought, we should resist the temptation to see Galloway as ahead of his time. The fiery young activist had emerged out of a politically vibrant slave culture deeply committed to egalitarian democracy and communitarian values in the Cape Fear. His years as a fugitive slave, Northern abolitionist, and Union spy had strengthened his commitment to the African American men and women among whom he had grown up. He had also been deeply influenced by his experience in the freedpeople's camps of North Carolina. Galloway embodied the black radicalism that emerged in the Cape Fear during Reconstruction, but he did not invent it; this tradition grew from a collective experience. To his credit, he found within himself the strength of spirit and the raw courage to carry that collective vision of racial justice and political equality out into a world that was not ready for it.

Galloway died unexpectedly of fever and jaundice on 1 September 1870 at his mother's home in Wilmington.[87] He was only thirty-three years old. He had just been reelected to the state senate, still held together a fragile biracial coalition in the local Republican Party, and had recently survived an assassination attempt.[88] He died on the cusp of a conservative resurgence that would prevail across North Carolina between 1870 and 1877. Racial violence, official corruption, and the Republican Party's own internal divisions paved the way for the Democratic triumph. Compared to the rest of North Carolina, however, Wilmington remained a stronghold of African American political power and working-class militancy. W. McKee Evans has argued, in fact, that the unique ability of Wilmington Republicans to maintain significant numbers of black policemen and militia units preserved the relative peace of Cape Fear society from 1868 to 1877. At one point, in 1875, the *Wilmington Journal* even alleged that "there are now nearly, or quite as many negro [militia] companies in this city, as there are white companies throughout the limits of North Carolina."[89] This was an exaggeration, but it does suggest that Wilmington blacks continued to embrace the political militancy personified by Galloway long after his death.

Though he died a pauper, an estimated 6,000 mourners gathered at Galloway's funeral on 3 September 1870. They came from every Wilmington neighborhood and from the countryside for many miles around. The funeral procession stretched half a mile through a downtown Wilmington draped with American flags at half-mast. The Masons in their finery, the black firemen's brigades, the political and fraternal societies, a hundred carriages, and throngs of people on horseback and on foot marched down Market Street to St. Paul's Episcopal Church. The multitude could not fit into the church and crowded the streets nearby. One newspaper called it the largest funeral in the state's history.[90] As the vast mass of black men, women, and children accompanied Galloway's coffin to the cemetery, they could not possibly have imagined that his life would so quickly seem like a half-forgotten dream. Indeed, Galloway's story is a familiar saga, and one that cuts across the ages. It is the oft-told story of the rebel hero who lives a life so deeply unreconciled to tyranny that it inspires even the most down-trodden and despised to suspect, at least for a brief instant, that freedom and justice may not be just a dream. That we have forgotten him says as much about our day as his.

NOTES

1. The broad picture that I have drawn of occupied New Bern and the specific incidents that I have mentioned are derived from a variety of primary and secondary sources. See John Barrett, *The Civil War in North Carolina* (Chapel Hill: University of North Carolina Press, 1963), 93–113; Joe A. Mobley, *James City: A Black Community in North Carolina, 1863–1900* (Raleigh: North Carolina Department of Cultural Resources, Division of Archives and History, 1981), 1–25; and David Cecelski, "A Thousand Aspirations," *Southern Exposure* 18, no. 1 (Spring 1990): 22–25. Among the most interesting of the many published reminiscences and diaries written by Union soldiers in New Bern, see W. P. Derby, *Bearing Arms in the Twenty-seventh Massachusetts Regiment of Volunteer Infantry during the Civil War, 1861–1865* (Boston: Wright & Potter, 1883), esp. 94–95; James A. Emmerton, *A Record of the Twenty-third Regiment Mass. Vol. Infantry in the War of the Rebellion, 1861–1865 . . .* (Boston: William Ware & Co., 1886); "Corporal" [Z. T. Haines], *Letters from the Forty-fourth Regiment M.V.M.: A Record of the Experience of a Nine Months Regiment in the Department of North Carolina in 1862–3* (Boston: Herald Job Office, 1863); Vincent Colyer, *Report of the Services Rendered by the Freed People to the United States Army, in North Carolina, in the Spring of 1862, After the Battle of New Bern* (New York: Vincent Colyer, 1864); J. Waldo Denny, *Wearing the Blue in the 25th Mass. Volunteer Infantry* (Worcester, Mass.: Putnam & Davis, 1879); Thomas Kirwan, *Soldiering in North Carolina* (Boston: n.p., 1864); John J. Wyeth, *Leaves from a Diary, Written While Serving in Co. #44 Mass. From September, 1862, to June, 1863* (Boston: L. F. Lawrence & Co., 1878); J. Madison Drake, *The History of the Ninth New Jersey Veteran Vols.* (Elizabeth, N.J.: Journal Printing House, 1889); Herbert E. Valentine, *Story of Co. F, 23d Massachusetts Volunteers in the War for the Union, 1861–1865* (Boston: W. B. Clarke & Co., 1896); D. L. Day, *My Diary of Rambles with the 25 Mass. Volunteer Infantry, with Burnside's Coast Division: 18th Army Corp and Army of the James* (Milford, Mass.: King and Billings, 1884); and Albert

W. Mann, *History of the Forty-fifth Regiment Massachusetts Volunteer Militia* (Jamaica Plain, Mass.: 1908.)

2. Mann, *History of the Forty-fifth Regiment*, 446–49.

3. Ibid.

4. Ibid., 301–2, 446–49. Kinsley later related this story to a reunion of the 45th Regiment, Massachusetts Volunteer Infantry, which had been stationed in New Bern in 1863. The essential parts of Kinsley's story—including his role in the recruitment of African American soldiers in New Bern, his acquaintance with Galloway and Starkey, Galloway's involvement in Union recruitment despite his devotion to independent black organizing, and Starkey and Galloway's having worked together—are confirmed in a series of letters among Kinsley, Brigadier General Edward A. Wild, and Mary Ann Starkey in the Edward W. Kinsley Papers, 1862–89, Special Collections Library, Duke University, Durham, N.C. (hereafter, DU).

5. For an excellent overview of the recruitment of the African Brigade in New Bern, and for references to more general works on the recruitment of black soldiers into the Union army, see Richard Reid, "Raising the African Brigade: Early Black Recruitment in Civil War North Carolina," *North Carolina Historical Review* 70, no. 3 (July 1993): 266–97.

6. The few published works that discuss Galloway refer mainly to his political life during Reconstruction. See W. McKee Evans, *Ballots and Fence Rails: Reconstruction on the Lower Cape Fear* (Chapel Hill: University of North Carolina Press, 1966), 87–91; Leonard Bernstein, "The Participation of Negro Delegates in the Constitutional Convention of 1868 in North Carolina," *Journal of Negro History* 34, no. 4 (October 1949); Elizabeth Balanoff, "Negro Legislators in the North Carolina General Assembly, July, 1868–February, 1872," *North Carolina Historical Review* 49, no. 1 (January 1972): 23–24, 27; William S. Powell, ed., *Dictionary of North Carolina Biography* (Chapel Hill: University of North Carolina Press, 1979–96), 2:271–72; and Eric Foner, *Freedom's Lawmakers: A Directory of Black Officeholders during Reconstruction* (New York: Oxford University Press, 1993), 81–82.

7. For background on this literature of the "Age of Reaction" in North Carolina, see David S. Cecelski, "Oldest Living Confederate Chaplain Tells All? Or, James B. Avirett and the Rise and Fall of the Rich Lands," *Southern Cultures* 3, no. 4 (Winter 1997/98), 5–24.

8. *New National Era*, 4 September 1870.

9. Martha A. Little deposition, 22 September 1927, Celie Galloway Pension Application File (1927), U.S. Department of the Interior: Bureau of Pensions, Veterans Administration Hospital, Winston-Salem, North Carolina (hereafter, VA); 15 October 1866 entry, New Hanover County: Record of Cohabitation, 1866–68, North Carolina State Archives, Raleigh (hereafter, NCSA); Ninth Federal Census: New Hanover County, North Carolina, Population Schedule, 1870, National Archives, Washington, D.C (hereafter, NA). In 1927 Celie Galloway, the widow of another Abraham (or Abram) Galloway, also of Brunswick County, applied for veterans

benefits based on her husband's military service in the Union army. To establish that her husband was not the better-known Abraham H. Galloway, the subject of this essay, her attorney visited Beaufort, North Carolina, to take depositions from the surviving family of Abraham H. Galloway in order to ascertain details about his personal appearance, military career, and death that would distinguish the two men and justify the widow's claims for pension benefits. The attorney interviewed Abraham H. Galloway's widow, Martha Ann Little, who still lived in her native Beaufort; she had remarried in 1887.

10. William Still, *The Underground Railroad: A Record of Facts, Authentic Narratives, Letters, etc., Narrating the Hardships, Hair-Breadth Escapes, and Death Struggles of the Slaves in their Efforts for Freedom* (Philadelphia: Porter & Coates, 1872), 150–52; Petition of Lewis A. Galloway for Division of Negroes (March 1837), Lewis A. Galloway Estate Record, Brunswick County Estate Records, NCSA; Lewis Galloway Will (1826), Brunswick County Wills, 1765–1912, NCSA.

11. William Hankins is the only member of the Hankins family in Brunswick County or New Hanover County who owned slaves in 1850. In that year, he owned twenty-four slaves, including two female slaves of Hester's age. The 1850 census does not list slaves by name, only by age and gender. Seventh Federal Census: Brunswick County, North Carolina, Population and Slave Schedules, 1850, and New Hanover County, Population and Slave Schedules, 1850, NA.

Amos Galloway belonged to Lewis Galloway at the time of his death in 1826 and was apportioned to his son John Wesley legally by 1837 and in practice some time before that date. Amos and Hester Hankins considered themselves married as of April 1846, though it is doubtful that they shared a household at that time. They were living together in Wilmington as of the 1870 federal census. See Petition of Lewis A. Galloway for Division of Negroes (March 1837), Lewis Galloway Estate Record, Brunswick County Estate Records, NCSA; 15 October 1866 entry, New Hanover County Record of Cohabitation, 1866–68, NCSA; Ninth Federal Census: New Hanover County, North Carolina, Population Schedule, 1870, NA.

12. Sixth, Seventh, and Eighth Federal Censuses: Brunswick County, North Carolina, Population and Slave Schedules for 1840, 1850, and 1860, NA; Seventh and Eighth Federal Censuses: New Hanover County, North Carolina, Population and Slave Schedules for 1850 and 1860, NA; John W. Galloway (1864), Brunswick County Estate Records, NCSA; John W. Galloway died at the age of fifty-three of yellow fever, evidently while serving in the Confederate coast guard in Bermuda on 27 September 1864. See *Wilmington Daily Journal*, 15 October 1864. Cited in Helen Moore Sammons, *Marriage and Death Notices from Wilmington, North Carolina Newspapers, 1860–1865* (Wilmington, N.C.: North Carolina Room, New Hanover County Public Library, 1987), 76.

13. Quoted in Still, *Underground Railroad*, 150–52.

14. William Still indicates that a Milton Hawkins owned Galloway, but the deposition of Galloway's wife and the listings of a locomotive mechanic named

Milton Hankins in the 1860 and 1870 federal censuses confirm his owner as Milton Hankins. The mistake was presumably a typographical error. See Martha A. Little deposition, Celie Galloway pension file, VA; Still, *Underground Railroad*, 150–52; Eighth and Ninth Federal Censuses: New Hanover County, North Carolina, Population Schedules for 1860 and 1870.

15. Still, *Underground Railroad*, 150–52; Fugitive Slave Ledger, William Still Papers, Historical Society of Philadelphia, Philadelphia, Pa.; *Wilmington Daily Journal*, 20 July 1869.

16. Still *Underground Railroad*, 150–52. For background on slave life in antebellum Wilmington, see esp. Peter P. Hinks, *To Awaken My Afflicted Brethren: David Walker and the Problem of Antebellum Slave Resistance* (University Park, Pa.: Pennsylvania State University Press, 1997), 1–21; David S. Cecelski, "The Shores of Freedom: The Maritime Underground Railroad in North Carolina, 1800–1861," *North Carolina Historical Review* 71, no. 2 (April 1994): 174–206; Alan D. Watson, *Wilmington: Port of North Carolina* (Columbia, S.C.: University of South Carolina Press, 1992), 46–52; and James Howard Brewer, "Legislation Designed to Control Slavery in Wilmington and Fayetteville," *North Carolina Historical Review* 30, no. 2 (April 1953): 155–66. There are also two indispensable autobiographies written by former slaves who grew up in Wilmington. See Rev. William H. Robinson, *From Log Cabin to the Pulpit; or, Fifteen Years in Slavery*, 3rd ed. (Eau Claire, Wis.: James H. Tifft, 1913), and Thomas H. Jones, *The Experience of Thomas H. Jones, Who Was A Slave for Forty-Three Years* (Boston: Bazin & Chandler, 1862).

17. Still, *Underground Railroad*, 150–52.

18. For a detailed examination of slave runaways and maritime culture in antebellum Wilmington, see Cecelski, "The Shores of Freedom," 174–206.

19. Guion Griffis Johnson, *Ante-Bellum North Carolina: A Social History* (Chapel Hill: University of North Carolina Press, 1937), 577–78.

20. Hinks, *To Awaken My Afflicted Brethren*, 1–21, 173–236; Julius S. Scott, "The Common Wind: Currents of Afro-American Communication in the Era of the Haitian Revolution" (Ph.D. diss., Duke University, 1986); W. Jeffrey Bolster, *Black Jacks: African American Seamen in the Age of Sail* (Cambridge: Harvard University Press, 1997), esp. 190–214; David Walker, *Appeal to the Colored Citizens of the World, But in Particular, and Very Expressly, to Those of the United States of America*, rev. ed. with intro. by Sean Wilentz (New York: Hill & Wang, 1995).

21. Still, *Underground Railroad*, 151–52.

22. David G. Hill, *The Freedom-Seekers: Blacks in Early Canada* (Agincourt: Book Society of Canada Ltd., 1981), 24–61; Ken Alexander and Aris Glaze, *Towards Freedom: The African-Canadian Experience* (Toronto: Umbrella Press, 1996), 51.

23. The abolitionist movement in Ohio seems a likely field for Galloway's labors. Secret, militant black abolitionist groups with strong ties to Canada operated out of Ohio throughout the 1850s, among them a military group known as the

Liberators that had close ties to John Brown. There is some evidence that these clandestine groups served the Union army in an intelligence capacity in the early stages of the Civil War, which, if true, makes it an enticing possibility that it was from one of these groups that Galloway was recruited into the spy service. See Richard Hinton, *John Brown and His Men* (New York: Funk & Wagnalls, 1894), 171–75, and William Cheek and Aimee Cheek, *John Mercer Langston and the Fight for Black Freedom, 1829–65* (Urbana: University of Illinois Press, 1989), 350–52.

24. Wild to Kinsley, 30 November 1863, Edward W. Kinsley Papers, DU; *National Cyclopaedia of American Biography* (New York: James T. White & Co., 1898), 8:231; Frank P. Stearns, *The Life and Times of George Luther Stearns* (Philadelphia: J. B. Lippincott Co., 1907), esp. 276–320; Charles E. Heller, *Portrait of an Abolitionist: A Biography of George Luther Stearns, 1809–1867* (Westport, Conn.: Greenwood Press, 1996), 123–59.

25. Wild to Kinsley, 30 November 1863, Edward W. Kinsley Papers, DU; *New National Era*, 4 September 1870.

26. Union military records occasionally refer to spying activities, but no official records have yet been found that discuss Galloway's duties as an intelligence agent. The following National Archives records have been consulted for mention of Galloway without success: RG 110, Scouts, Guides, Spies, and Detectives; Secret Service Accounts; RG 109, Union Provost Marshal's Files of Papers Relating to Citizens or Business Firms (M345); RG 92, index to scouts in Reports of Persons and Articles Hired and the index to Quartermaster Claims; RG 59, Letters of Application and Recommendation During the Administrations of Abraham Lincoln and Andrew Johnson; RG 94, indexes to Letters Received by the Adjutant General's Office, 1861–65 (M725); and General Information Index.

27. *Raleigh Weekly Standard*, 7 September 1870.

28. Edmund Cleveland diary, 24 November 1864, Southern Historical Collection, University of North Carolina Library, Chapel Hill.

29. *New National Era*, 22 September 1870.

30. Colyer, *Report of the Services Rendered by the Freed People*, 9–10. Colyer describes a number of intelligence missions conducted by former slaves in Confederate territory. See pp. 10–22.

31. Wild to Kinsley, 30 November 1863, Edward W. Kinsley Papers, DU.

32. Gen. Ambrose E. Burnside to Hon. E. M. Stanton, Secretary of War, 21 March 1862, U.S. War Department, *The War of the Rebellion: A Compilation of the Official Records of the Union and Confederate Armies* (Washington, D.C.: Government Printing Office, 1880–1901), ser. 1, vol. 9, 199–200.

33. The racist conduct of the Union army is one of the strongest themes in both the private papers and published works by Federal soldiers stationed in North Carolina during the Civil War. See, among many others, Arthur M. Schlesinger, ed., "Letter of a Blue Bluejacket," *New England Quarterly* I, no. 4 (October

1928), 562, 565; Emmerton, *A Record of the Twenty-Third Regiment, Mass. Vol. Infantry*, 135–36; James Rumley diary, 15 August 1863, 17 August 1864, Levi W. Pigott Papers, NCSA.

34. See esp. Colyer, *Report of the Services Rendered*, 29–51; Mobley, *James City*, 5–13, 29–46; Cecelski, "A Thousand Aspirations," 22–25.

35. William H. Singleton, *Recollections of My Slavery Days* (New York: n.p., 1922), 8–9. Copy in the New York Public Library, New York, N.Y.

36. Andrew J. Wolbrook to Edward W. Kinsley, 3 September 1863, and Wolbrook to Kinsley, 12 September 1863, Edward W. Kinsley Papers, DU. Starkey and Galloway worked closely throughout the Civil War, and Starkey clearly held Galloway in great esteem. After the war, however, the two seem to have had at least a momentary falling out over financial matters. See Mary Ann Starkey to Edward W. Kinsley, 27 July 1865, Edward W. Kinsley Papers, DU.

37. Evans, *Ballots and Fence Rails*, 111–12; John Richard Dennett, *The South As It Is: 1865–1866*, ed. Henry M. Christman (New York: Viking, 1965), 151–53.

38. Rumley diary, 30 May, 1, 18 June 1863, Levi W. Pigott Papers, NCSA.

39. Ibid., 1 January 1864; *Proceedings of the National Convention of the Colored Citizens of the United States, 1864*, reprinted in Herbert Aptheker, ed., *A Documentary History of the Negro People in the United States* (New York: Citadel Press, 1951), 1:511–13.

40. Aptheker, *Documentary History*, 1:522–23.

41. Rumley diary, 1 January 1864, Levi W. Pigott Papers, NCSA.

42. The Lincoln administration first considered the use of black troops in mid-1862. "Limited and unauthorized" use of black troops had actually occurred in at least Kansas, Louisiana, and South Carolina before August 1862, when the War Department finally authorized the recruitment of the first slave regiment—the 1st South Carolina Volunteers, recruited from the occupied portion of the Sea Islands—into the Union army. In September 1862, Lincoln issued a "Preliminary Proclamation of Emancipation" that stated that as of 1 January 1863 slaves in the Confederate states would be "forever free." Once the proclamation went into effect, blacks were recruited on a mass scale. Six months later, thirty black regiments had been organized. More than 186,000 blacks enlisted in the Union army, and roughly one-third of them would eventually be listed as dead or missing. See Leon F. Litwack, *Been in the Storm So Long: The Aftermath of Slavery* (New York: Knopf, 1979), 69–71, 98.

43. Galloway married Martha Ann Dixon at the Beaufort home of her parents, Napoleon and Massie Dixon. Martha A. Little deposition, Celie Galloway pension file, VA; Marriage Register: Carteret County, N.C., 1850–1981, NCSA; Eighth Federal Census: Carteret County, N.C., Population and Slave Schedules, 1860.

44. Rumley diary, 4 August 1863, Levi W. Pigott Papers, NCSA; Cleveland diary, 24 November 1864, Southern Historical Collection, University of North Carolina Library, Chapel Hill.

45. Wild to Kinsley, 30 November 1863, Edward W. Kinsley Papers, DU. In this letter, Wild refers to Galloway's Boston contact as a "Mr. Stevenson of 7 Hull St." This was presumably John Hubbard Stephenson (1820–88) of 9 Hull Street, of the millinery firm of Stephenson & Plympton. He is not known to have been a part of the city's abolitionist movement. See *Boston Directory* (Boston: George Adams, 1862) and *Boston Evening Transcript*, 22 December 1888.

46. *North Carolina Times* (Raleigh, N.C.), 21 May 1864; Mary Ann Starkey to Edward W. Kinsley, 21 May 1864, Edward W. Kinsley Papers, DU.

47. *The Liberator*, 9 September 1864, reprinted in Aptheker, *Documentary History*, 1:511, 516.

48. Horace James, *Annual Report of the Superintendent of Negro Affairs in North Carolina, 1864, With an Appendix, Containing the History and Management of the Freedmen in this Department up to June 1st, 1865* (Boston: W. P. Brown, n.d.), 6–18; *Old North State* (Beaufort, N.C.), 7 January 1865; John Niven, ed., *The Salmon P. Chase Papers*, vol. 1, *Journals, 1829–1872* (Kent, Ohio: Kent State University Press, 1993), 542–44.

49. Willie Lee Rose, *Rehearsal for Reconstruction: The Port Royal Experiment* (Indianapolis: Bobbs-Merrill, 1964).

50. Sidney Andrews, *The South Since the War; As Shown by Fourteen Weeks of Travel and Observation in Georgia and the Carolinas* (Boston: Ticknor & Fields, 1866), 125.

51. Roberta Sue Alexander, *North Carolina Faces the Freedmen: Race Relations during Presidential Reconstruction, 1865–67* (Durham, N.C.: Duke University Press, 1985), 16; Rumley diary, 4 July 1865, Levi W. Pigott Papers, NCSA.

52. *New York Times*, 17 September 1865.

53. Ibid.

54. *Wilmington Herald*, 8 September 1865.

55. Evans, *Ballots and Fence Rails*, 87–91.

56. Aptheker, ed., *Documentary History*, 1:546.

57. Dennett, *The South As It Is*, 151–53.

58. *New National Era*, 22 September 1870. Galloway is not listed in the city directories of New Bern or Wilmington in 1865–66. See Frank D. Smaw Jr., *Smaw's Wilmington Directory* (Wilmington, N.C.: Frank D. Smaw Jr., ca. 1866), and R. A. Shotwell, *New Bern Mercantile and Manufacturers' Business Directory and North Carolina Farmers Reference Book* (New Bern, N.C.: W. I. Vestal, 1866).

59. Evans, *Ballots and Fence Rails*, 93.

60. Dennett, *The South As It Is*, 42.

61. Quoted in Litwack, *Been in the Storm So Long*, 271.

62. Evans, *Ballots and Fence Rails*, 64–81; Litwack, *Been in the Storm So Long*, 289.

63. Dennett, *The South As It Is*, 110.

64. Evans, *Ballots and Fence Rails*, 83–85.

65. *Tri-Weekly Standard* (Raleigh, N.C.), 7 September 1867.

66. Wilmington *Evening Star*, 25 September 1867; *New National Era*, 22 September 1870.

67. Evans, *Ballots and Fence Rails*, 95–97.

68. *Wilmington Journal*, 21 February 1868.

69. *The Standard* (Raleigh, N.C.), 25 January, 17 February 1868, cited in Bernstein, "The Participation of Negro Delegates," 399, 407.

70. Quoted in Evans, *Ballots and Fence Rails*, 98.

71. *Wilmington Weekly Journal*, 28 February 1868.

72. Evans, *Ballots and Fence Rails*, 95–97.

73. Ibid., 98–102.

74. Linda Gunter, "Abraham H. Galloway: First Black Elector," *North Carolina African-American Historical and Genealogical Society Quarterly* (Fall 1990): 9–10.

75. *The Christian Recorder*, 24 September 1870. For background on the black militias in the Reconstruction South, see Otis A. Singletary, *Negro Militia and Reconstruction* (Austin: University of Texas Press, 1957).

76. Allen W. Trelease, *White Terror: The Ku Klux Klan Conspiracy and Southern Reconstruction* (Baton Rouge: Louisiana State University Press, 1971), 189–225; Evans, *Ballots and Fence Rails*, 101–2, 145–48; William C. Harris, *William Woods Holden: Firebrand of North Carolina Politics* (Baton Rouge: Louisiana State University Press, 1987), 287–307.

77. Balanoff, "Negro Legislators," 23–24, 27.

78. *Wilmington Daily Journal*, 20 July 1869.

79. *Wilmington Weekly Journal*, 2 April 1869.

80. See, for example, *New York Times*, 17 September 1865.

81. *Wilmington Daily Journal*, 20 July 1869; *Wilmington Journal*, 4 August 1870, Bill Reaves Collection, New Hanover County Public Library, Wilmington, N.C. (hereafter, NHCPL).

82. *Senate and House Journals, 1868*, 41–42.

83. *Senate and House Journals, 1869*, 360–61; Balanoff, "Negro Legislators," 34–36.

84. Balanoff, "Negro Legislators," 41–42, 44–48; *North Carolina Standard* (Raleigh, N.C.), 21 January 1868, 10 February 1870; *Laws of North Carolina, 1868–69–70*, chap. 77; A. H. Galloway George Z. French, and J.S.W. Eagles to Governor Holden, 10 August 1869, Governors Letter Book 60, NCSA.

85. For an informative discussion of the collective outlook on voting held by Reconstruction blacks, see Elsa Barkley Brown, "Negotiating and Transforming the Public Sphere: African American Political Life in the Transition from Slavery to Freedom," *Public Culture* 7 (1994): 107–46.

86. *Senate and House Journals, 1868–1869*, 209, 223, 648; *1869–70*, 466; *Wilmington Journal*, February 1869, Bill Reaves Collection, NHCPL; Balanoff, "Negro Legislators," 42–44.

87. Galloway grew ill so suddenly that his wife and two young sons, John L. and

Abraham Jr., were not able to return from a trip to New Bern before his death. "Widow's Declaration of Pension for Martha A. Little," 29 January 1894, Celie Galloway pension file, VA.

88. *Raleigh Weekly Standard*, 7 September 1870; *Wilmington Daily Journal*, 2–4, 10 September 1870, 23 April 1871, Bill Reaves Collection, NHCPL; *The Christian Recorder*, 24 September 1870.

89. Evans, *Ballots and Fence Rails*, 137–41.

90. *The Christian Recorder*, 24 September 1870; *Wilmington Journal*, 2–4 September 1870, Bill Reaves Collection, NHCPL; *Raleigh Weekly Standard*, 17 September 1870.

Chapter 3

Negotiating and Transforming the Public Sphere

African American Political Life in the Transition from Slavery to Freedom

Elsa Barkley Brown

On April 15, 1880, Margaret Osborne, Jane Green, Susan Washington, Molly Branch, Susan Gray, Mary A. Soach and "over two hundred other prominent sisters of the church" petitioned the Richmond, Virginia, First African Baptist Church's business meeting to allow women to vote on the pastor:

> We the sisters of the church feeling that we are interested in the welfare of the same and also working hard to finish the house and have been working by night and day. . . . We know you have adopted a law in the church that the business must be done by the male members. We don't desire to alter that law, nor do we desire to have anything to do with the business of the church, we only ask to have a vote in electing or dismissing him. We whose names are attached to this petition ask you to grant us this privilege.[1]

The circumstances surrounding these women's petition suggest the kinds of changes taking place internally in late-nineteenth- and early-twentieth-century black Richmond and other southern black communities. In the immediate post–Civil War era women had voted in mass meetings and Republican Party conventions held at First African, thus contradicting gender-based assumptions within the larger society about politics, political engagement and appropriate forms of political behavior. Now, women sitting in the same church were petitioning for the right to vote in an internal community institution, couching the petition in terms designed to minimize the request and avoid a challenge to men's authority and position.

Scholars' assumptions of an unbroken line of exclusion of African American women from formal political associations in the late-nineteenth century has obscured fundamental changes in the political understandings within African American communities in the transition from slavery to freedom. Women in First African and in other arenas were seeking in the late-nineteenth century not a new authority but rather a lost authority, one they now often sought to justify on a distinctively female basis. As these women petitioned for their rights within the church and as other women formed voluntary associations in turn-of-the-century Richmond they were not, as often depicted in the scholarly literature emerging into the political arena through such actions. Rather these women were attempting to retain space they traditionally had held in the immediate post-emancipation period. This essay explores the processes of public discourse within Richmond and other southern black communities and the factors which led to increasingly more clearly gendered and class spaces within those communities to understand why women by the 1880s and 1890s needed to create their own pulpits from which to speak—to restore their voices to the community. This exploration suggests how the ideas, process, meanings and practice of freedom changed within late-nineteenth-century southern African American communities and what the implications of those changes may be for our visions of freedom and for the possibilities of African American community in the late-twentieth century.

After emancipation, African American men, women and children, as part of black communities throughout the South struggled to define on their own terms the meaning of freedom and in the process to construct communities of struggle. Much of the literature on Reconstruction portrays freed African Americans as rapidly and readily adopting a gendered private-public dichotomy.[2] Much of the literature on the nineteenth-century public sphere constructs a masculine liberal bourgeois public with a female counterpublic.[3] This essay, focusing on the civic geography of post–Civil War black Richmond suggests the problematic of applying such generalizations to African American life in the late-nineteenth century South. In the immediate post-emancipation era black Richmonders enacted their understandings of democratic political discourse through mass meetings attended and participated in (including voting) by men, women and children and through mass participation in Republican Party conventions. They carried these notions of political participation into the state Capitol engaging from the gallery in the debates on the constitutional convention floor.

Central to African Americans' construction of a fully democratic notion of political discourse was the church as a foundation of the black public sphere.[4] In the post-slavery era, church buildings also served as meeting halls and auditoriums as well as educational and recreational facilities, employment and social service bureaus and bulletin boards. First African, especially, with a seating capacity of nearly 4000, was the site of large political gatherings. Schools such as Richmond Theological Seminary and Richmond Colored High and Normal School held their annual commencement exercises at First African Baptist, allowing these events to become community celebrations. Other groups, such as the Temperance Union were regularly granted the church for their meetings or rallies. As a political space occupied by men, women and children, literate and nonliterate, ex-slave and formerly free, church members and nonmembers, the availability and use of First African for mass meetings enabled the construction of political concerns in democratic space. This is not to suggest that official versions and spokespersons were not produced, but these official versions were the product of a fairly egalitarian discourse and, therefore, represented the conditions of black Richmonders of differing classes, ages and genders. Within black Richmonders' construction of the public sphere, the forms of discourse varied from the prayer to the stump speech to the testimonies regarding outrages against freedpeople to shouted interventions from the galleries into the debates on the legislative floor. By the very nature of their participation—the inclusion of women and children, the engagement through prayer, the disregard of formal rules for speakers and audience, the engagement from the galleries in the formal legislative sessions—Afro-Richmonders challenged liberal bourgeois notions of rational discourse. Many white observers considered their unorthodox political engagements to be signs of their unfamiliarity and perhaps unreadiness for politics.[5]

In the decades following emancipation as black Richmonders struggled to achieve even a measured amount of freedom, the black public sphere emerged as more fractured and perhaps less democratic at the end of the nineteenth century, yet even then it retained strong elements of a democratic agenda. This essay examines the changing constructions of political space and community discourse in the post-emancipation era.

Envisioning Freedom

In April 1865, when Union troops marched into Richmond, jubilant African American men, women and children poured into the streets and crowded into their churches to dance, kiss, hug, pray, sing and shout. They assembled in First African, Third Street African Methodist, Ebenezer and Second African not merely because of the need to thank God for their deliverance but also because the churches were the only institutional spaces, and in the case of First African certainly the largest space, owned by African Americans themselves.[6] As the process of reconstruction unfolded, black Richmonders continued to meet regularly in their churches, now not merely to rejoice. If Afro-Richmonders had thought freedom would accompany emancipation, the events of the first few weeks and months of Union occupation quickly disabused them of such ideas. Throughout the summer and fall of 1865 black Richmonders reported numerous violations of their rights. Among them were pass and curfew regulations designed to curtail black mobility and force African American men and women out of the city to labor in the rural areas. Pass and curfew violators (800 in the first week of June) were detained in bullpens-one for women and children, a separate one for men-away from and often unknown to family members. Black Richmonders also detailed numerous incidents of disrespectful treatment, verbal abuse, physical assault and torture. "Many poor women" told "tales of their frights and robberies"; vendors told of goods destroyed by military police. Private homes were not immune to the intrusions of civilian and military white men. One couple was confronted by soldiers, one of whom stood over them in bed "threatening to blow out their brains if they moved" while others "pillage[d] the house of money, watches, underclothing, etc."[7] Many spoke of the sexual abuse of black women: "gobbling up of the most likely looking negro women, thrown into the cells, robbed and ravished at the will of the guard." Men and women in the vicinity of the jail testified "to hearing women scream frightfully almost every night."[8]

The regular meetings in the African churches, originally ones of jubilation, quickly became the basis for constructing a discourse about freedom and organizing large-scale mass protest. On June 10, 1865 over 3000 assembled at First African to hear the report of the investigating committee which had conducted hearings and gathered the evidence and depositions necessary to present black Richmonders' case directly to Governor Francis

H. Pierpoint and to the "chief head of all authority," the President of the United States. The protest memorial drawn up during the meeting was ratified at meetings in each of the other churches and money was raised through church collections to send six representatives (one from each church in Richmond and one from First Baptist, Manchester) to Washington. On Friday, June 16, these delegates delivered the mass meeting's protest directly to President Andrew Johnson:[9] "Mr. President: We have been appointed a committee by a public meeting of the colored people of Richmond, Va., to make known . . . the wrongs, as we conceive them to be, by which we are sorely oppressed." In their memorial, as in their meetings, black Richmonders recounted not merely the abuses but they also used their individual stories to construct a collective history and to combat the idea of being "idle negroes" unprepared for freedom.[10]

> We represent a population of more than 20,000 colored people, including Richmond and Manchester, . . . more than 6,000 of our people are members in good standing of Christian churches, and nearly our whole population constantly attend divine services. Among us there are at least 2,000 men who are worth $200 to $500; 200 who have property valued at from $1,000 to $5,000, and a number who are worth from $5,000 to $20,000. . . . The law of Slavery severely punished those who taught us to read and write, but, not withstanding this, 3,000 of us can read, and at least 2,000 can read and write, and a large number of us are engaged in useful and profitable employment on our own account.

The community they described was one based in a collective ethos; it was not merely their industry but also their responsibility which was the basis on which they claimed their rights.

> None of our people are in the alms-house, and when we were slaves the aged and infirm who were turned away from the homes of hard masters, who had been enriched by their toil, our benevolent societies supported while they lived, and buried when they died. and comparatively few of us have found it necessary to ask for Government rations, which have been so bountifully bestowed upon the unrepentant Rebels of Richmond.

They reminded Johnson of the efforts black men and women in Richmond had taken to support the Union forces against the Confederacy.

During the whole of the Slaveholders' Rebellion we have been true and loyal to the United States Government; . . . We have given aid and comfort to the soldiers of Freedom (for which several of our people, of both sexes, have been severely punished by stripes and imprisonment. We have been their pilots and their scouts, and have safely conducted them through many perilous adventures.

They declared themselves the loyal citizens of the United States, those the federal government should be supporting. And finally they invoked the religious destiny that emancipation had reaffirmed, reminding the President of a "motto once inscribed over the portals of an Egyptian temple, 'Know all ye who exercise power, that God hates injustice!'"[11]

Mindful of others' versions of their history, standing and entitlements, black Richmonders also moved to have their own story widely circulated. When local white newspapers refused to publish their account, they had it published in the *New York Tribune*.[12] Throughout 1865 and 1866 black Richmonders continued to meet regularly in mass meetings where men, women and children collectively participated in constructing and announcing their own story of community and freedom.[13] The story told in those mass meetings, published in northern white newspapers, carried in protest to Union officials, was also carried into the streets as black Richmonders inserted themselves in the preexisting national political traditions and at the same time widened those traditions. John O'Brien has noted that in the immediate aftermath of emancipation, black Richmonders developed their own political calendar, celebrating four civic holidays: January 1; George Washington's birthday; April 3 (emancipation day); and July 4.[14] White Richmonders were horrified as they watched former slaves claim civic holidays and traditions they believed to be the historical possession of white Americans and occupy spaces, like Capitol Square, which had formerly been reserved for white residents.[15]

The underlying values and assumptions that would pervade much of black people's political struggles in the city were forged in slavery and war and in the weeks following emancipation. Military regulations which limited black mobility and made finding and reunifying family members even more difficult placed the economic interests of white men and women above the material and social interests of African Americans. The bullpens, which detained many away from their families, and the raids on black homes, which made all space public and subject to the interests of the state, obliterated any possible distinctions between public and private spheres. Demanding passes and evidence of employment denied black Richmonders the right to act and to be treated not as economic units and/or property but as social beings and family members. The difficulty of finding decent housing at affordable prices further impeded freedpeople's efforts to bring their families together. All of these obstacles to and expectations of family life were part of what Eric Foner speaks of as the "'politicization' of everyday life."[16]

These political issues underpinned Afro-Richmonders' petition to Johnson and would continue to underpin their political struggles in late-nineteenth century Richmond. Even as they fashioned individual stories into a collective history, black Richmonders could and did differ on the means by which they might secure freedom—vigorously debating issues such as the necessity of confiscation.[17] But they also understood freedom as a collective struggle. When they entered the formal political arena through Republican party politics in 1867 this understanding was the foundation for their initial engagement with issues of suffrage and democracy. As Julie Saville has observed for South Carolina, freedpeople in Richmond "were not so much converted to the Republican party as they were prepared to convert the Republican party to themselves."[18] The post–Civil War southern black public sphere was forged in jubilation and struggle as African American men, women and children claimed their own history and set forth their own political ideals.

All the resources of black Richmonders became elements in their political struggles. The *Richmond Whig*, intending to ridicule the inappropriateness of freepeople's behaviors and assumptions, highlighted the politicized nature of all aspects of black life during Reconstruction; the freedpeople's "mass meetings, committee meetings, and meetings of the different societies all have political significance. The superstitions of the colored people are availed on, and religion and Radicalism are all jumbled together. Every night they have meetings and musterings, harangues and sermons, singing and praying—all looking to political results."[19] Similarly the *Richmond Dispatch* reported an 1867 Republican meeting which began with "Harris, colored" offering "the most remarkable" prayer" we have ever heard. It was frequently interrupted by laughter and manifestations of applause":

> Oh, Lord God, bless our enemies—bless President Johnson. We would not even have him sent to hell. Come, oh come, good Lord, and touch his

heart even while I am talking with you here to-night. [Amen.] Show him the error of his ways. Have mercy upon our "Moses," [Sarcastic. Great laughter and amens.] who, like Esau, has sold his birthright for a morsel of pottage—took us in the wilderness and left us there. Come down upon him, oh Lord, with thy blessing. God bless us in our meeting to-night, and help us in what we do. God forbid that we should choose any Conservative that has the spirit of the devil in his heart, and whose feet take hold on hell. God bless our friend—true and tried—Mr. Hunnicut, who has stood a great many sorrows and I think he can stand a great many more. [Laughter.] Bless our judge, Mr. Underwood, who is down here among us, and don't let anything harm a hair of his head.[20]

What the *Whig* and the *Dispatch* captured was a political culture in which the wide range of institutional and noninstitutional resources of individuals and the community as a whole became the basis for defining, claiming and securing freedom in post-emancipation Richmond. The church provided more than physical space, financial resources and a communication network; it also provided a cultural base that validated emotion and experience as ways of knowing, and drew on a collective call and response, encouraging the active participation of all.[21]

Virginia's rejection of the Fourteenth Amendment brought the state under the Reconstruction Act of 1867; a constitutional convention became prerequisite for full restoration to the Union. Black men, enfranchised for the delegate selection and ratification ballots, were to have their first opportunity to engage in the political parties and legislative chambers of the state. The struggles in which they had engaged in the two years since emancipation influenced the manner of black Richmonders' initial participation in the formal political arena of conventions and voting. On August 1, 1867, the day the Republican state convention opened in Richmond to adopt a platform for the upcoming state constitutional convention, thousands of African American men, women and children absented themselves from their employment and joined the delegates at the convention site, First African Baptist Church.[22] Tobacco factories, lacking a major portion of their workers, were forced to close for the day.

This pattern persisted whenever a major issue came before the state and city Republican conventions held during the summer and fall of 1867, or the state constitutional convention which convened in Richmond from December 1867 to March 1868. A *New York Times* reporter estimated that "the entire colored population of Richmond" attended the October 1867 local Republican convention where delegates to the state constitutional convention were nominated. Noting that female domestic servants were a large portion of those in attendance, the correspondent reported: "as is usual on such occasions, families which employ servants were forced to cook their own dinners, or content themselves with a cold lunch. Not only had Sambo gone to the Convention, but Dinah was there also."[23]

These men and women did not absent themselves from work just to be onlookers at the proceedings, but to be active participants. They assumed as equal a right to be present and participate as the delegates themselves, a fact they made abundantly clear at the August 1867 Republican state convention. Having begun to arrive four hours before the opening session, African American men and women had filled the meeting place long before the delegates arrived. Having showed up to speak for themselves, they did not assume delegates had priority—in discussion or in seating. Disgusted at the scene, as well as unable to find a seat, the conservative white Republican delegates removed to the Capitol Square to convene an outdoor session. That was quite acceptable to the several thousand additional African American men and women who, unable to squeeze into the church, were now still able to participate in the important discussions and to vote down the proposals of the conservative faction.[24]

Black men, women and children were also active participants throughout the state constitutional convention. A *New York Times* reporter commented on the tendency for the galleries to be crowded "with the 'unprivileged,' and altogether black." At issue was not just these men and women's presence but also their behavior. White women, for example, certainly on occasion sat in the convention's gallery as visitors silently observing the proceedings; these African Americans, however, participated from the gallery, loudly engaging in the debates. At points of heated controversy, black delegates turned to the crowds as they made their addresses on the convention floor, obviously soliciting and relying upon mass participation. Outside the convention hours, mass meetings were held to discuss and vote on the major issues. At these gatherings vote was either by voice or rising and men, women and children voted. These meetings were not mock assemblies; they were important gatherings at which the community made plans for freedom. The most radical black Republican faction argued that the major convention issues should actually be settled at these mass meetings with delegates merely casting the community's vote on the convention floor. Though this did not occur, black delegates were no doubt influenced by both the mass meetings and the African American presence in the galleries, both of which included women.[25]

Black Richmonders were operating in two separate political arenas: an internal one and an external one. While these arenas were related, they each proceeded from different assumptions, had different purposes, and therefore operated according to different rules. Within the internal political process women were enfranchised and participated in all public forums —the parades, rallies, mass meetings and the conventions themselves.[26] Richmond was not atypical in this regard.[27]

It was the state constitutional convention, however, which would decide African American women's and men's status in the political process external to the African American community. When the Virginia convention began its deliberation regarding the franchise, Thomas Bayne, a black delegate from Norfolk, argued the inherent link between freedom and suffrage, and contended that those who opposed universal suffrage were actually opposing the freedom of African American people. In rejoinder, E. L. Gibson, a Conservative white delegate, enunciated several principles of republican representative government. Contending that "a man might be free and still not have the right to vote," Gibson explained the fallacy of assuming that this civil right was an inherent corollary to freedom: if the right were inherent then it would belong to both sexes and to all from "the first moment of existence" and to foreigners immediately. This was "an absurdity too egregious to be contemplated."[28] And yet, this "absurd" notion of political rights was what was in practice in the Richmond black community—males and females voted without regard to age, the thousands of rural migrants who came into Richmond suffered no waiting period but immediately possessed the full rights of the community. What was absurd to Gibson and most white men—Republican or Democrat—was obviously quite rational to many black Richmonders. Two very different conceptions of freedom and public participation in the political process were in place.

In the end only men obtained the legal franchise. The impact of this decision is neither inconsequential nor fully definitive. African American women were by law excluded from the formal political arena external to their community. Yet this does not mean that they were not active in that arena; witness Richmond women's participation in the Republican and the constitutional conventions. Southern black men and women debated the issue of women's suffrage in both the external and internal political arenas.

In Nansemond County, Virginia, for example, the mass meetings resolved that women should be granted the legal franchise; in Richmond, while a number of participants in a mass meeting supported female suffrage, the majority opinion swung against it.[29] But the meaning of that decision was not as straightforward as it may seem. The debate as to whether women should be given the vote in the external political arena occurred in internal political arena mass meetings where women participated and voted not just before and during, but also after the negative decision regarding legal enfranchisement. This maintained the status quo in the external community; ironically enough, the status quo in the internal community was maintained as well—women continued to have the vote. African American men and women clearly operated within two distinct political systems.

Focusing on formal disfranchisement obscures women's continued participation in the external political arena. In Richmond and throughout the South exclusion from legal enfranchisement did not prevent African American women from shaping the vote and the political decisions. Throughout the late 1860s and 1870s women continued to participate in political meetings in large numbers and to organize political societies. Some like the Rising Daughters of Liberty and the Daughters of the Union Victory in Richmond or the United Daughters of Liberty organized by coal miners' wives living outside Manchester had all-female memberships. Others, like the 2000 member National Political Aid Society, the Union League of Richmond and the Union Equal Rights League of Manchester had male and female members. Even though white Republicans made efforts to exclude them from further participation in political meetings by the late 1860s, African American women in Virginia, South Carolina, Louisiana and elsewhere were still attending these meetings in the 1870s.

Women's presence at these meetings was anything but passive. In the violent political atmosphere of the last years of Reconstruction, they had an especially important and dangerous role. In South Carolina, for example, while the men participated in the meeting, the women guarded the guns— thus serving in part as the protectors of the meeting. For those women and men who lived in outlying areas of Richmond and attended outdoor meetings, political participation was a particularly dangerous matter, a fact they clearly recognized. Meetings were guarded by posted sentinels with guns who questioned the intent of any suspicious people, usually white men, coming to the meeting. A reporter for the *Richmond Daily Dispatch* described one such encounter when he attempted to cover a political meeting of fifty women and twenty-five men.[30]

Women as well as men took election day off from work and went to the polls. Fraud, intimidation and violence became the order of election days. White newspapers and politicians threatened loss of jobs, homes and lives. Afro-Richmonders countered with a group presence. Often even those living within the city and short distances from the polling places went early, even the night before, and camped out at the polls, hoping that their early presence would require the acceptance of their vote and that the group presence would provide protection from violence and intimidation. In the highly charged political atmosphere of late-nineteenth-century Richmond it was no small matter for these women and men to participate in political meetings and show up at the election sites. The reasons for the group presence at the polls were varied. African American women in Virginia, Mississippi, South Carolina and elsewhere understood themselves to have a vital stake in African American men's franchise. The fact that only men had been granted the vote did not at all mean that only men should exercise the vote. Women throughout the South initiated sanctions against men who voted Democratic; some went along to the polls to insure a properly cast ballot. As increasing white fraud made black men's voting more difficult, early arrival at the polls was partly intended to counter such efforts.

Although election days in Richmond were not as violent as they were elsewhere throughout Virginia and other parts of the South, guns were used to intimidate and defraud. It is also probable that in Richmond, as elsewhere throughout the South, when black men went to camp out overnight at the polls, households feared leaving women and children unprotected at home. Thus the women's presence, just as the group presence of the men, may have been a sign of the need for collective protection. If Richmond women were at all like their sisters in South Carolina and Danville, they may have carried weapons with them—to protect themselves and/or help protect the male voters.[31] Women and children's presence reflects their excitement about the franchise but also their understanding of the dangers involved in voting. The necessity for a group presence at the polls reinforced the sense of collective enfranchisement. Women's presence at the polls was both a negative sanction and a positive expression of the degree to which they understood the men's franchise to be a new political opportunity for themselves as well as their children.

In the dangerous political atmosphere of the late-nineteenth century, the vote took on a sacred and collective character. Black men and women in Richmond, as throughout the South, initiated sanctions against those black men perceived as violating the collective good by supporting the Conservative forces. Black Democrats were subject to the severest exclusion: disciplined within or quite often expelled from their churches and mutual benefit societies; denied board and lodging with black families. Additionally, mobs jeered, jostled and sometimes beat black Democrats or rescued those who were arrested for such acts. Women were often reported to be in the forefront of this activity. Similarly, black women were said to have "exercised a positive influence upon some men who were inclined to hesitate or be indifferent" during the early 1880s Readjuster campaigns.[32]

All of this suggests that African American women and men understood the vote as a collective, not an individual possession; and furthermore, that African American women, unable to cast a separate vote, viewed African American men's vote as equally theirs. They believed that franchise should be cast in the best interest of both. This is not the nineteenth century patriarchal notion that men voted on behalf of their wives and children. By that assumption women had no individual wills; rather men operated in women's best interest because women were assumed to have no right of input. African American women assumed the political rights that came with being a member of the community even though they were denied the political rights they thought should come with being citizens of the state.

To justify their political participation Richmond and other southern black women in the immediate post–Civil War period did not need to rely on arguments of superior female morality or public motherhood. Their own cultural, economic and political traditions provided rationale enough. An understanding of collective autonomy was the basis on which African Americans reconstructed families, developed communal institutions, constructed schools and engaged in formal politics after emancipation. The participation of women and children in the external and internal political arenas was part of a larger political worldview of ex-slaves and free men and women, a worldview fundamentally shaped by an understanding that freedom, in reality, would accrue to each of them individually only when it was acquired by all of them collectively. Such a worldview contrasted sharply with the "possessive individualism" of liberal democracy.[33] This sense of suffrage as a collective, not an individual possession was the foundation for much of African American women's political activities in the post–Civil War era.[34] Within these understandings the boundary lines between men's and women's political behavior were less clearly drawn and active participation in the political arenas—internal or external—seldom required a retreat into womanhood or manhood as its justification.

Even in the organization of militia units, post-emancipation black Richmonders, at least for a time, rejected the liberal bourgeois ideal of a solely male civic domain. By 1886 black men had organized three militia companies. By the late 1870s black women had also organized a militia company, although apparently only for ceremonial purposes; it reportedly was active only before and during emancipation celebrations. Its members conducted preparatory drills on Broad Street, one of Richmond's main thoroughfares. Frank Anthony, the man who prepared and drilled the women's company, demanded military precision and observance of regular military commands.[35] Unlike the men participating in the militias, who came from working-class, artisan, business and professional backgrounds, the women were probably working-class. Although they served no self-defense role, their drilling in Richmond streets and marching in parades challenged ideas and assumptions about appropriate public behavior held by both white southerners and white Unionists. The women's unit not only challenged, as did the men's, the idea of black subservience, but also suggested wholly new forms and meanings of respectable female behavior. There is no evidence concerning how long this women's unit survived or the causes of its demise. We can speculate that, besides horrifying whites, such a unit may have also become unacceptable to a number of black Richmonders. Increasingly, concerns about respectable behavior were connected to the public behavior of the working class and of women. This black women's militia, however, suggests the fluidity of gender notions in the early years of emancipation. The brevity of its appearance suggests how questions of public behavior became integral within black Richmond, just as they had been within the larger society. Yet for a time the actions of these women declared that perhaps no area of political participation or public ceremony was strictly a male domain.

Renegotiating Public Life

The 1880 First African women's petition followed three contentious church meetings, some lasting until two or three o'clock in the morning, at which the congregants considered dismissing and/or excluding the pastor, the

Reverend James H. Holmes. This discussion was initiated at an April fifth meeting where two women were charged with fighting about the pastor. The April sixth meeting considered charges of "unchristian conduct" on the part of Holmes; those men present voted to exclude Holmes. A meeting on April eleventh endorsed a protest signed by all but two of the deacons against the earlier proceedings. The protest charged the anti-Holmes faction with trying to "dispose of the deacons, take charge of prayer meetings, the Sunday school and revolutionize things generally." The discussions which ensued over the next two months split the congregation; the May and June church business meetings were "disorderly" and "boisterous." Holmes and the deacons called in the mayor, city court judge, and chief of police to support the pastor and the police to remove or arrest those members of the congregation designated as "rebellious." After the anti-Holmes faction was removed from the church, the June meeting expelled forty-six men for "rebelliously attempting to overthrow and seize upon the church government." It also excluded the two women initially charged, one for fighting and the other for tattling; exonerated Holmes "from all false" accusations; and thanked the civil officers who attended the meeting and restored order. Only after these actions did the church consider the women's petition which had been presented in the midst of the controversy more than two months earlier.[36]

First African's records do not adequately reveal the nature of gender relations within the church in the late 1860s and 1870s. We do know that the pre–Civil War sex-segregated seating patterns were abandoned by Richmond black Baptist churches immediately after the Civil War and that by the late 1860s women "not only had a voice, but voted in the business meetings" of Ebenezer Baptist Church.[37] Women who voted in political meetings held in First African in the 1860s and 1870s may have carried this participation over to church business meetings. Often in the immediate post–Civil War period, business and political meetings were not clearly distinguishable.

The petition of the women of First African makes clear, however, that by the early 1880s, while women attended and apparently participated in church meetings, the men had "adopted a law in the church that the business must be done by the male members." Whether Margaret Osborne, Jane Green, and others thought that their voices and interests were being inadequately represented, even ignored by the deacons, or wanted to add their voices to those, including the deacons, who were struggling to retain Holmes and control of First African, these women understood that they would have to defend their own rights. The women argued their right to decide on the pastor, justifying their petition by both their work on behalf of the church and the importance of their economic support to the church's ongoing activities and to the pastor's salary. Not until after the matter of Holmes's exclusion was settled were the petitioners granted their request. Since they apparently remained within First African, the petitioners' organization probably indicates that they were not among those dissatisfied with Holmes. It does suggest, however, their dissatisfaction with church procedure and the place of women in church polity. Still, the petition was conservative and the women denied any intention to demand full voting rights in church matters. The petition was not taken as a challenge to church authority, as were the actions of the anti-Holmes faction. When brought up for a vote in the June meeting, the women's petition was adopted by a vote of 413 to 16.[38]

The women's petition and the vote in favor of it suggest the tenuous and ambiguous position that women had come to occupy both within First African and within the internal political arena more generally. They participated actively in church meetings but the authority for that participation and the question of limiting women's role resurfaced throughout the late-nineteenth century. In the 1890s the women of First African would again have to demand their rights, this time against challenges to their very presence at church meetings, when a deacon sought to prohibit women from even attending First African business meetings. The women protested and the church responded quickly by requiring the deacon to apologize to the women and assure them that they were welcome at the meetings. The degree of women's participation and decision-making powers, however, remained ambiguous. In 1901–1902 during another crisis period in First African, a number of men sought to blame the problems on women. John Mitchell, Jr., a member of First African and editor of the *Richmond Planet*, cited the active participation of women ("ladies who knew nothing of the machinery at work or the deep laid plans on foot") and children ("Sunday School scholars from 8 years of age upward") in church affairs, suggesting that they did not comprehend the proceedings and had been easily misled or manipulated by male factions. Deacon J. C. Farley cited women's active participation in church meetings as the problem, reminding the congregation that "it was the rule of the church" that women were only allowed to vote on the pastor but had extended their participation far past that. And the new minister, the Reverend W. T. Johnson, admonished the women, saying that "the brethren could almost fight in the church meeting and when they went out they would shake hands and laugh and talk. But the sisters would talk about it going up Broad St. and everybody would know what they had done."

First African women rejected these assessments of their church's problems. A significant number walked out rather than have their participation censured; those who remained reportedly refused to be silent but continually "talked out in the meeting." Sister Margaret Hewlett later sought out the editor of the *Richmond Planet* to voice her opposition to the men's denunciation of women's roles and to make clear that the women thought the church's problems lay in the male leadership, saying specifically "the deacons were the cause of all the trouble anyway."[39]

In the early 1890s the *Virginia Baptist* publicized its belief that women, in exceeding their proper places in the church by attempting to preach, and in the community by their "deplorable" efforts to "exercise the right of suffrage," would lose their "womanliness."[40] The complexity of gender relations within the African American community was such that at the same time First African was debating women's attendance at church meetings and the *Virginia Baptist* was advocating a severely restricted women's role, other women such as Alice Kemp were known throughout the community as the authors of prominent male ministers' sermons and women such as the Reverend Mrs. Carter were establishing their reputations as "soul-stirring" preachers. The *Richmond Planet* reported these women's activities without fanfare, as if they were commonplace. The debate over women's roles also had become commonplace. The Reverend Anthony Binga, pastor of First Baptist (Manchester), noted the debate in his sermon on Church Polity; Binga supported women teaching Sunday School, participating in prayer-meetings and voting "on any subject pertaining to the interest of the church" including the pastor; but he interpreted the Bible as forbidding women "throwing off that modesty that should adorn her sex, and taking man's place in the pulpit." The subject received community-wide attention in June 1895 when Ebenezer Baptist Church staged a debate between the ministers of Second Baptist (Manchester) and Mount Carmel, judged by other ministers from Fourth Baptist, First African, First Baptist (Manchester) and others on the subject, "Resolved that a woman has every right and privilege that a man has in the christian church."[41]

The debates within First African and other churches over women's roles were part of a series of political struggles within black Richmond in the late-nineteenth and early-twentieth centuries. As formal political gains, initially secured, began to recede and economic promise became less certain and less surely tied to political advancement, the political struggles over relationships between the working-class and the newly emergent middle-class, between men and women, between literate and nonliterate, increasingly became issues among Afro-Richmonders. Briefly examining how the sites of public discourse changed and how discussions regarding qualifications for and nature of individual participation developed suggests the degree to which debates over space and relationships represented important changes in many black Richmonders' assumptions about freedom itself.

The authority of the church in personal and civil matters decreased over the late-nineteenth and early-twentieth centuries. The church quietly acknowledged these changes without directly confronting the issue of its changed authority. The use of civil authorities to resolve the church dispute, especially since individual members continued to face censure if they relied on civil rather than church sanctions in a dispute with another member, suggests the degree to which First African tried to maintain its traditional authority over its members while acknowledging the limitations of its powers. First African turned outside not only itself but also the black community by inviting the intervention of the mayor, police chief and judge.[42] The decreasing authority of the church, however, accompanied a shrinking sphere of influence and activity for the church and the development of secular institutions and structures to take over, compete for, or share functions traditionally connected to the church as institution and structure. The changing church axis suggests important developments in the structures, nature and understandings of community in black Richmond.

After the Reverend James Holmes and the deacons of First African survived the 1880 challenge to their leadership, one of their first actions was to establish a regulation that church business meetings be closed to all but members. They had argued that it was outside agitators who had instigated and sustained the disorder and opposition. While this reflects concerns about internal church business, the closing off of the church was reflected in other central ways which potentially had more far-reaching consequences, and suggests the particularization of interests, concerns and functions of internal community institutions, and the changed nature of internal community politics. Having completed, at considerable expense, their new edifice, First African worried about avoiding damage and excess wear and tear. In November 1882 the church adopted regulations designed to eliminate the crowds of people attending weddings in the church by requiring guest lists and tickets, and to deny entirely the use of the main auditorium with the largest capacity for "programmes, closing of public schools, political meetings or feasts." In February 1883 when the Acme Lyceum requested use of the main auditorium for a lecture by Frederick Douglass, the church, following its new regulations, refused to grant the request, although it did offer as substitute the use of its smaller lecture room. That same year it denied the use of the church for the Colored High and Normal closing. The paucity of facilities available to black Richmonders meant that these activities now had to be held in much smaller facilities and the possibilities for the large mass meetings which First African had previously hosted were now reduced. Political meetings and other activities moved to other, smaller church sites or to some of the new halls being erected by some of the societies and businessmen. The latter, however, were more expensive to obtain since their rental was a major source of revenue for the group or individual owner; it also often particularized the meeting or occasion to a specific segment of the community. Without the large facility of First African, graduations and school closings could no longer be the traditional community-wide mass celebrations. Denied the use of First African and barred from the Richmond Theatre where the white high school students had their graduation, the 1883 Colored High and Normal graduation class held their exercises in a small classroom where very few could attend.[43]

First African did not initiate and was not singly responsible for the changing nature of Republican Party participation, but its actions reinforced the narrower sense of party politics that white Republicans had already tried to enforce. Disturbed at black influence over Republican meetings, beginning in 1870 white Republican officials had taken steps to limit popular participation and influence in party deliberations. First they moved the party conventions from First African to the United States courtroom, a facility which held many fewer people and was removed from the black community; then they closed the gallery, thus allowing none but official delegates to attend and participate. In such a setting they were able to adopt a more conservative platform. Black Republicans had continued, however, to hold mass meetings, often when dissatisfied with the official Republican deliberations. When they were dissatisfied with Republican nominees for municipal office that came from the 1870 closed party convention, for example, black Republicans agreed to convene their own sessions and make their own nominations.[44]

In increasingly delimiting the church's use, distinguishing more clearly between sacred and secular activities as when it began to disallow certain kinds of entertainments in its facilities or on its behalf, and attempting to reserve the church for what was now designated as the "sacred," First African contributed to the increasing segmentation of black Richmond.[45] With the loss of the largest capacity structure some black Richmonders recognized the need to reestablish a community space. Edward A. Randolph, founder and first editor of the *Richmond Planet*, used Acme Literary Association meetings to argue regularly throughout 1883 and 1884 for the construction of a hall, a public meeting place within the community. His call was reinforced when the Choral Association was denied use of the Richmond Theatre and had to have its production in a small mutual benefit society hall, an inadequate facility for such a production. The construction of a large auditorium on the top floor of the Grand Fountain, United Order of True Reformers' bank and office building when it opened in 1890 was an effort to provide that space. It could hold larger gatherings than the other halls and most churches but still had only a small percentage of the seating capacity of First African.[46] A mass meeting on the scale common in the 1860s and 1870s could be held only outside the community and the facilities for such were often closed to African Americans.

As political meetings moved to private halls rather than church buildings, they became less mass meetings not only in the numerical sense; they also became more gatherings of an exclusive group of party regulars. This signaled not only a change in the role of the church but also a change in the nature of politics in black Richmond. The emerging format gave business and professional men, especially, greater control over the formal political process. First African's prohibitions against mass meetings, school closings, and other programs did not last long; the need and desire of members and other Afro-Richmonders for a space which could truly contain a community-wide activity eventually led members to ignore their prohibition. But instituting the prohibition had not only significantly affected community activities in the early 1880s; it also meant that, even after strict enforcement was curtailed, decisions about using the church for graduation exercises, political meetings and other activities were now subjects of debate. Afro-Richmonders could no longer assume the church as a community meeting place; instead they had to argue such. The church remained an important community institution, but it increasingly shared power with both civil authorities and other community institutions such as mutual benefit and fraternal societies.

The efforts by white Republican officials to limit popular decision-making and the decreased accessibility of First African as a community-wide meeting place affected a politics which had been based in mass participation. Mass meetings were still held throughout the late-nineteenth century, but they were now less regular. These changes were exacerbated by the struggle to retain the vote and office-holding and the necessity, therefore, to counter various tactics of both white Republicans and Democrats. The fraudulent tactics employed to eliminate black voters, for example, led some black Republicans, like John Mitchell, who continued to argue against literacy qualifications for voting, in the 1890s to encourage nonliterate black men to abstain from voting. Difficulty with many of the election officials' questions and with the ballots could not only delay the line but also the nonliterate voter's rights and/or ballot would more likely be challenged.

Mitchell thought it important to get those least likely to be challenged or disqualified, and most capable of correctly marking the ballots, through the lines first before polls closed on them. While Mitchell argued for a temporary change in practice—not perspective—regarding the right of all to vote, his and other prominent black Republicans' prioritizing of the literate voter significantly changed the makeup of the presumed electorate.

As the divisions between black and white Republicans became deeper in the 1890s, Mitchell and other black Republicans began to hold small Republican caucuses in selected homes, in essence attempting to control ward conventions by predetermining nominees and issues. The ward conventions themselves were often held in halls rather than the larger churches. The organization in 1898 of a Central Republican League which would oversee black Republican activities through sub-Leagues in all the city's wards reinforced the narrowing party politics framework. Republican Party decision-making was now more clearly limited to Party regulars; the mass of black voters and other election activists were expected to support these channels of decision-making.[47] These changes, consistent with democratic politics and republican representative government as practiced in late-nineteenth century United States, served to limit the power and influence of most black Richmonders in the electoral arena. If many black men abandoned electoral politics even before formal disfranchisement, it was in large measure due to the effectiveness of the extra-legal disfranchisement efforts of white men. The exclusion from real decision-making power within the Republican Party and, in this respect within the community, was also decisive.

The increasingly limited notion of political decision-makers which these changes encouraged is also evident in other ways. In 1896 during a factional dispute among black Republicans, John Mitchell challenged the decisions made in one meeting by noting that a substantial portion of those attending and participating were not even "legal voters," that is they were women. Although he espoused feminine dress and comportment, Mitchell supported women's rights and championed Dr. Sarah G. Jones's success as a physician as evidence of women's equality. He also endorsed women's suffrage while advising black women to understand the racism of the white women's suffrage movement and not to align themselves with it. Despite these personal convictions, Mitchell could dismiss or minimize opposing factions by a reference to the participation of women, suggesting the ways in which the meanings and understandings of politics, of appropriate political actors and even of the ownership of the franchise had changed in the late-nineteenth century.[48]

Questions of qualifications for participation in the external political arena and internal community institutions were now frequent. During the conflictual 1901 business meeting at First African, for example, John Mitchell, Jr., questioned his opponents' right to participate even though they were all church members by pointing out their unfamiliarity with parliamentary procedure or their inelegant ways of speaking. The women, who were the targets of much of Mitchell's challenge, refused to accept these as criteria for their participation and even denigrated what he put forth as his formal qualifications by talking out when he got up to speak, saying derisively, "Don't he look pretty."[49] Questions of formal education had already affected the congregation in fundamental ways, most obviously in the late-nineteenth century debate over song, a debate which represented a significant change in the basis of collective consciousness.

The antiphonal nature of the traditional church service at First African and many black churches reinforced a sense of community. The services included spontaneous verbal and nonverbal interaction between minister and prayer, speaker and congregation thus allowing for the active participation of everyone in the worship service. It was this cultural discourse that was carried over into the political meetings. One important element that bound the congregation together was song; as Lawrence Levine has noted, through their collective song churchgoers "meld[ed] individual consciousness into the group consciousness."[50] However, the practice of lining hymns which was basic to collective song was one which white visitors often referred to when they described what they perceived as the unrefined black church services. Some black churchgoers saw the elimination of this practice as part of the work of uplifting the religious style and uplifting the race. But with the elimination of this practice, those unable to read and follow the lyrics in a song book were now unable to participate, to be fully a part of the community, the collective. It was the equivalent of being deprived of a voice, all the more significant in an oral culture. Daniel Webster Davis, a member of First African and pastor of Second Baptist (Manchester) as well as public school teacher, suggested such in his poem, "De Linin' Ub De Hymns":

> Dar's a mighty row in Zion, an' de debbil's gittin' high,
> . . . .
> 'Twuz 'bout a berry leetle thing—de linin' ub a hymn.
> De young folks say 'tain't stylish to lin' um out no mo';
> Dat dey's got edikashun, an' dey wants us all to know
> Dey likes to hab dar singin'-books a-holin' fore dar eyes,
> An' sing de hymns right straight along 'to manshuns in de skies.'
> . . . .
> An' ef de ol' folks will kumplain 'cause dey is ol' an' blin',
> An' slabry's chain don' kep' dem back frum larnin' how to read—
> Dat dey mus' take a corner seat, an' let de young folks lead.
> . . . .
> We don' edikate our boys an' gals, an' would do de same again;
> . . . .
> De sarmon's highfalutin', an' de church am mighty fin';
> De ol'-time groans an' shouts an' moans am passin' out ub sight—
> Edikashun changed all dat, an' we belebe it right,
> We should serb God wid 'telligence; fur dis one thing I plead:
> Jes' lebe a leetle place in church fur dem ez kin not read.[51]

The debates about women's roles in the church and in the more formal political arenas, like the debate over lining the hymns, were part of widespread discussions about the nature of community, of participation and of freedom.

The proliferation of scholarly works centered on the flowering of black women's political activity in the late-nineteenth and early-twentieth centuries[52] has perhaps left the impression that this was the inaugural moment or even height of black women's participation in politics. Overt or not, the suggestion seems to be that black women came to political prominence as (because) black men lost political power.[53] In much of this scholarship the reasons for black women's "emergence" are usually tied to external factors. For example, the development of black women's clubs in the late-nineteenth century and their important roles in the political struggles of the twentieth century most often have been seen by historians as the result of the increasing development of such entities in the larger society and as reaction to vitriolic attacks on the morality of black women. Such a perspective explains this important political force solely in terms of external dynamics, but external factors alone cannot account for this development.[54] The internal political arena, which in the immediate post–Civil War era was grounded in the notion of a collective voice which gave men, women and children a platform and allowed them all participation, came increasingly in the late-nineteenth century to be shaped by a narrowing notion of politics and appropriate political behavior.

While mass meetings continued to be held, the more regular forums for political discussions were literary societies, ward meetings, mutual benefit society and fraternal society meetings, women's clubs, labor organizations, newspapers, street corners, kitchens, washtubs and saloons. In the development of literary societies as a primary venue for public discussion, one can see the class and gender assumptions that by the turn-of-the-century came to be central to the political organization of black Richmond. While some, as the Langston Literary Association, had male members only, most of the literary societies founded in the 1880s and 1890s had middle-class and working-class men and women members. Despite the inclusive nature of the membership and often of the officers, the form of discussion which developed privileged middle-class males. Unlike mass meetings where many people might take the floor in planned and unplanned expositions and attendees might freely interrupt or talk back to speakers, thus allowing and building mass participation, literary forums announced discussion topics in advance; charged individual members, apparently almost always male, to prepare a paper on the subject; and designated specific, also male, members to reply.

The discussions that then ensued were open to all present but the structure privileged those familiar with the conventions of formal debate. Women, who served as officers and attended in large numbers, may have joined in the discussion but their official roles were designated as the cultural arm of the forum—reading poetry, singing songs, often with political content appropriate to the occasion. The questions under consideration at the meetings often betrayed the class bias of the forum. Even when the discussions centered on some aspect of working-class life and behavior, the conversation was conducted by middle-class men. The purpose of the forums, as articulated by the Acme Literary Society, suggested the passive observer/learner position that most were expected to take: to hold "discussions, lectures, and to consider questions of vital importance to our people, so that the masses of them may be drawn out to be entertained, enlightened, and instructed thereby."[55] Given the exclusionary nature of the discussion in these literary forums, even though welcoming a wide audience, it is understandable that far more working-class black men and women saw the Knights of Labor as their principal political vehicle in the late 1880s.[56]

In the changing circumstances of the late-nineteenth century, working-class men and women and middle-class women were increasingly disfranchised within the black community, just as middle-class black men were increasingly disfranchised in the larger society. Men and women, working-class and middle-class, at the turn-of-the-century were struggling to move back to a political authority they once had—internally and externally. As they did so they each often justified such authority along distinctively gendered and class-based lines.

African American men countered the image of themselves as uncivilized, beastly rapists—an image white southerners used to justify disfranchisement, segregation and violence—with efforts to demonstrate their own manhood and to define white males as uncivilized and savage.[57] While white Richmonders told stories of black barbarity, John Mitchell, Jr., inverted the tale. The *Richmond Planet*, for example, repeatedly focused on the sexual perversions of white men with cases of rape and incest and spoke of white men in terms designed to suggest their barbarism: "Southern white folks have gone to roasting Negroes, we presume the next step will be to eat them."[58] In the process of unmanning white males, however, Mitchell and others developed a narrative of endangered black women. Urban areas, once sites of opportunity for women, became sexually dangerous places for the unprotected female, easy prey to deceitful and barbarous white males.[59] Black men's political rights were essential so that they could do as men should—protect their communities, homes, families, women. The focus on manhood could, initially, be the venue for discussing domestic violence as well. For example, the Reverend Anthony Binga, sermonizing against physical abuse of one's wife drew on the discourse of manhood: "I have never seen a man whip his wife. I mean a *man*. Everyone who wears a hat or a coat is not a *man*. I mean a *man*." And the members of First African took as a serious issue of concern the case of a husband who had infected his wife with syphilis.[60] Concurrent with the narrative of sexual danger in the city and the larger society was an implied corollary narrative of protection within one's own community. Thus the discourse on manhood could keep the concern with violence against women in the public discussion while at the same time setting the stage for issues of domestic abuse and other forms of intraracial violence, which could be evidence of the uncivility of black men, to be silenced as politically dangerous.

In drawing on the new narrative of endangered women, middle-class black women, increasingly disfranchised by the connections between manhood and citizenship in the new political discourse, turned the focus from themselves and on to the working class, enabling middle-class women to project themselves as the protectors of their less fortunate sisters. In this manner they reinserted themselves into a public political role.[61] Autonomous women's organizations, such as the Richmond Women's League (later the Richmond Mothers' Club) or women's divisions within other organizations such as the Standing Committee on Domestic Economy of the Hampton Negro Conference, developed to serve these functions. These associations promulgated class-specific ideas of respectability, in part justifying their public role through the need to impart such protective measures to working-class women. Specific constructions of womanhood, as manhood, thus became central to the arguments for political rights. Through discussions of manhood and womanhood, middle-class men and women constructed themselves as respectable and entitled, and sought to use such constructions to throw a mantle of protection over their working-class brothers and sisters. By increasingly claiming sexual violence as a women's issue, middle-class black women claimed a political/public space for themselves but they also contributed to an emerging tendency to divert issues of sexual violence to a lesser plane and to see them as the specific interest of women, not bound up in the general concerns and struggle for freedom. This set the stage for the masculine conception of liberation struggle which would emerge in the twentieth century.[62]

Collective History/Collective Memory

In July 1895 three black women—Mary Abernathy, Pokey Barnes and her mother, Mary Barnes—were convicted in Lunenberg County, Virginia, of murdering a white woman. When the women were moved to the state penitentiary in Richmond their case became a cause célèbre in the black community there. For over a year black men and women in Richmond struggled to keep the Lunenberg women from being hanged or returned to Lunenberg County for a retrial, fearing that a return to Lunenberg would mean death, the women lynched at the hands of an angry white mob. The community succeeded and the three women were eventually released.[63]

The organization of black Richmonders in defense of these women partly illustrates the increasingly gendered nature of internal community politics. Men and women were portrayed as having decidedly different roles in the defense; one avenue of defense was to draw on ideas of motherhood in defending these three women; and the Lunenberg women's release called forth very particular discussions of respectability and womanhood. John Mitchell, Jr., portrayed himself as the militant defender of the women. Women, led by schoolteacher Rosa Dixon Bowser, organized the Richmond Women's League for the purposes of raising funds for the women's defense, visiting them in jail and supporting their husbands and families. Through her column in the *Woman's Era* and her participation in the National Federation of Afro-American Women, Bowser, as did Mitchell, brought the case to national attention. The front page stories in Mitchell's *Planet* emphasized the Lunenberg women as mothers, especially reporting on Mary Abernathy's pregnancy and the birth of her child in her jail cell. While the pictures and stories during the fourteen-month struggle for their release portrayed the women as simply clad, barefoot, farm women the announcement of Pokey Barnes's final victory was accompanied by a photograph of her now transformed into a true Victorian woman with elegant balloon-sleeved dress, a symbol of respectable womanhood. Later descriptions of Barnes, on speaking engagements, emphasized her dress: "a neat fitting, changeable silk gown and . . . a black felt hat, trimmed with black velvet and ostrich plumes." Mitchell emphasized the importance of this transformation: "The picture showing what Pokey Barnes looked like when brought to Richmond the first time and what she appears to-day will be a startling revelation to the public and will fill with amazement the conservative people everywhere when they realize what a terrible blunder the execution of this young woman would have been." He thus suggested that it was her ability to be a respectable woman (signified superficially by a class-based standard of dress) which was the justification for his and others' protection of her.

But the year-long discussion of these women's fates (the front page of nearly every issue of the Richmond Planet from July 1895 through early fall 1896 was devoted to these cases and included pictures of the women and sketches of their cabins) occurred alongside stories about lynchings or near lynchings of black men. Importantly, therefore, when black Richmonders spoke of lynching in the late-nineteenth century, they had no reason to assume the victim as male. When a freed Pokey Barnes rode as "mascot" in the 1896 Jackson Ward election rally parade, the idea of Mitchell and other black men as defenders was reinforced. But also affirmed was the underlying understanding that violence, including state repression, was a real threat to African American women as much as men. This meant that the reconstruction of clearly delineated notions of womanhood and manhood as the basis for political activism remained relatively ambiguous in late-nineteenth century black Richmond. But issues of class and gender were increasingly evident, as when Pokey Barnes and Mitchell accepted public speaking engagements—ones in which she was clearly expected to be the silent symbol of oppression and he the vocal proponent of resistance. Barnes, countering that assumption, set forth her own understandings of her role and qualifications, contradicting the class and gender assumptions of Mitchell and of those who invited them: "she said that she was not an educated lecturer and did not have any D.D.'s or M.D.'s to her name, but she was simply Pokey Barnes, c.s. (common sense)." Her two-hour lecture on her ordeal, while giving credit to Mitchell, established herself as not only victim but also heroine.[64]

The rescue of the Lunenberg women by black Richmonders brought women's struggles to the fore of black rights and reaffirmed violence against women as part of their collective history and struggle. At the same time black Richmonders struggled to create a new category of womanhood that would be respected and protected, and of middle-class womanhood and manhood that could protect.[65] The plight of the Lunenberg women reaffirmed the collective history of black men and women at the same time as it invigorated increasingly distinct political vehicles for middle-class black men and women.

Just as disfranchisement, segregation, lynching and other violence denied the privileges of masculinity to African American men; segregation, lynching, sexual violence and accusations of immorality denied the protections of womanhood to African American women. Increasingly black women relied on constructing not only a respectable womanhood but, in large measure, an invisible womanhood. Hoping that a desexualized persona might provide the protection to themselves and their communities that seemed otherwise unobtainable, many black women carefully covered up all public suggestions of sexuality, even of sexual abuse. In the process issues specific to black women were increasingly eliminated from public discussion and collective memory.[66] In the late-twentieth century therefore many African Americans have come to link a history of repression and racial violence exclusively to challenges to black masculinity and thus to establish a notion of freedom and black liberation which bifurcates public discussion and privileges men's history and experiences. In 1991 when Supreme Court justice nominee Clarence Thomas challenged his questioners by calling the Senate Judiciary Committee hearings a "high-tech lynching," black Americans were divided in their response. Some men and women supported his analysis; others opposed either Thomas's analogy or his right to, in using such, assume the mantle of black manhood that he had so often rejected. Few people, however, questioned the assumption basic to Thomas's analogy that lynching and other forms of violence had historically been a masculine experience. Similarly, when black people across the country responded to the video of Los Angeles policemen's brutal beating of Rodney King, a narrative of state repression against black men followed.[67] The masculine focus is most evident in the widespread public discussion of "endangered" black men. While, appropriately focusing attention on the physical, economic and social violence which surrounds and engulfs many black men in the late-twentieth century United States, much of this discussion trivializes, or ignores the violence of many black women's lives—as victims of rape and other forms of sexual abuse, murder, drugs and alcohol, poverty and the devastation of AIDS. Seldom are discussions of rape and domestic violence included in summits on black-on-black crime. The masculinization of race progress which this implies often has some black leaders, looking to ways to improve the lot of men, not only omitting women from the picture but often even accepting the violence against women. What else can explain how Mike Tyson, even before he was charged with the rape of an eighteen-year-old black woman, would have been projected by ministers of the National Baptist Convention as a role model for young black men? By what standards would a man who had already publically acknowledged that he enjoyed brutalizing women have been put forward as a role model—unless rescuing black men from poverty and inner-city death at any price, including violence against women, was the standard by which the good of the race was being defined?

Such is the long term consequence of political strategies developed in the late-nineteenth century to empower black men and black women. Understandable and necessary in their day, they served to maintain a democratic agenda even as black political life became more divided. Eventually, however, the experiences of men were remembered as central to African American's struggles but the experiences of women, including the physical violence—lynchings, rapes, sexual and other forms of physical abuse as employees in white homes, domestic abuse—as well as the economic and social violence which has so permeated the history of black women in the United States, were not as vividly and importantly retained in our memory. We give life and validity to our constructions of race, community and politics by giving those constructions a history. Those who construct masculine notions of blackness and race progress and who claim only some forms of violence as central to African American liberation struggles are claiming/remembering a particular history. African American collective memory in the late-twentieth century often appears partial, distorted and dismembered. The definitions and issues of political struggle which can come from that partial memory are limited. Before we can construct truly participatory discussions around a fully democratic agenda where the history and struggles of women and men are raised as issues of general interest necessary to the liberation of all, we have some powerful lot of re-remembering to do.[68]

NOTES

1. Petition of Mrs. Margaret Osborne, et al. To the deacons and members of the First Baptist Church, April 15, 1880, recorded in First African Baptist Church, Richmond City, Minutes, Book II, June 27, 1880 (microfilm), Archives, Virginia State Library and Archives, Richmond, Virginia (hereafter cited as FABC).

2. The idea of the immediate adoption of a gendered public-private dichotomy pervades much of the historical literature on post–Civil War black communities. It is most directly argued by Jacqueline Jones: "the vitality of the political process, tainted though it was by virulent racial prejudice and violence, provided black men with a public forum distinct from the private sphere inhabited by their womenfolk. Black men predominated in this arena because, like other groups in nineteenth-century America, they believed that males alone were responsible for—and capable of—the serious business of politicking," *Labor of Love, Labor of Sorrow: Black Women, Work, and the Family from Slavery to the Present* (New York: Basic Books, 1985), 66. But it is also an accepted tenet of otherwise rigorous analyses such as Eric Foner, *Reconstruction: America's Unfinished Revolution 1863–1877* (New York: Harper and Row, 1988), esp. 87.

3. Many recent discussions of the public sphere among U.S. scholars have orbited around the work of Jurgen Habermas whose 1962 *Strukturwandel der Offentlichkeit* was published in 1989 in English as *The Structural Transformation of the Public Sphere: An Inquiry into a Category of Bourgeois Society,* trans. Thomas Burger with assistance of Frederick Lawrence (Cambridge: MIT Press). See also, Jurgen Habermas, "The Public Sphere: An Encyclopedia Article (1964)," *New German Critique* 1 (Fall 1974): 49–55. Critics who have emphasized the masculine bias in the liberal bourgeois public sphere and posited a female counterpublic include Nancy Fraser, "Rethinking the Public Sphere: A Contribution to the Critique of Actually Existing Democracy" and Mary Ryan, "Gender and Public Access: Women's Politics in Nineteenth-Century America," both in *Habermas and the Public Sphere,* ed. Craig Calhoun (Cambridge: MIT Press, 1992), 109–142 and 259–289, respectively. See also, Nancy Fraser, "What's Critical About Critical Theory? The Case of Habermas and Gender," in Nancy Fraser, *Unruly Practices: Power, Discourse, and Gender in Contemporary Social* Theory (Minneapolis: University of Minnesota Press, 1989); Mary Ryan, *Women in Public: Between Banners and Ballots, 1825–1880* (Baltimore: John Hopkins University Press, 1990); Joan B. Landes, *Women and the Public Sphere in the Age of the French Revolution* (Ithaca: Cornell University Press, 1988); Rita Felski, *Beyond Feminist Aesthetics: Feminist Literature and Social Change* (Cambridge: Harvard University Press, 1989), 154–182. Focusing on contemporary politics, Iris Marion Young offers a critique of an ideal public sphere in which the universal citizen is not only masculine but also white and bourgeois, *Justice and the Politics of Difference* (Princeton: Princeton University Press, 1990).

4. For a study that conceptualizes the history of the black church in relation to Habermas's theory of the public sphere, see Evelyn Brooks Higginbotham, *Righteous Discontent: The Women's Movement in the Black Baptist Church 1880–1920* (Cambridge: Harvard University Press, 1993), esp. 7–13. Higginbotham describes "the black church not as the embodiment of ministerial authority or of any individual's private interests and pronouncements, but as a social space for discussion of public concerns" (1993:10).

5. Similar negotiations and pronouncements occurred in other post-emancipation societies. For a discussion of the ways in which British colonial officers sought to impose ideas of a liberal democratic moral and political order, with its attendant gender relations, on former slaves in the West Indies and then pronounced these ex-slaves incapable of responsible citizenship when they failed to wholly adopt such, see Thomas C. Holt, "'The Essence of the Contract': The Articulation of Race, Gender, and Political Economy in British Emancipation Policy, 1838–1866," paper presented at "The Black Public Sphere in the Reagan-Bush Era Conference," Chicago Humanities Institute, The University of Chicago, October 1993 (cited with permission of Holt).

6. The question of ownership was one of the first issues Afro-Richmonders ad-

dressed, as antebellum law had required the titles be in the names of white male supervising committees although the black congregants had themselves bought and paid for the buildings. Through a series of struggles black churchgoers had by the end of 1866 obtained titles to all of their church buildings. See *New York Tribune*, June 17, 1865; Peter Randolph, *From Slave Cabin to Pulpit* (Boston: Earle, 1893), 94–95; John Thomas O'Brien, Jr., "From Bondage to Citizenship: The Richmond Black Community, 1865–1867" (Ph.D. diss., University of Rochester, 1974), 273–275.

7. Statement of Jenny Scott, wife of Ned Scott, colored, June 8, 1865; Statement of Richard Adams, colored, June 8, 1865; Statement of Nelson E. Hamilton, June 9, 1865; Statement of Lewis Harris, June 9, 1865; Statement of Wm. Ferguson, June 9, 1865; Statement of Albert Brooks, colored, June 10, 1865; Statement of Thomas Lucas, colored, June 12, 1865; Statement of Washington Hutchinson, Summer 1865; Statement of Edward Davenport, n.d.; Statement of Bernard H. Roberts, n.d.; Statement of Albert Williams, n.d.; Statement of Thos. J. Wayer, n.d.; Statement of Harry R. Jones, n.d.; Statement of Wellington Booker, n.d.; Statement of Stephen Jones, n.d.; Statement of John Oliver of Mass., n.d.; Wm. M. Davis to Col. O. Brown, June 9, 1865, all in Records of the Assistant Commissioner for the State of Virginia. Bureau of Refugees, Freedmen and Abandoned Lands, 1865–1869, Record Group 105, M1048, reel 59, National Archives, Washington, D.C.; *New York Tribune*, June 12, 17, August 1, 8, 1865; *Richmond Times*, July 26, 1865; S.E.C. (Sarah Chase) to Mrs. May, May 25, 1865, in Henry L. Swint, ed., *Dear Ones at Home: Letters from Contraband Camps* (Nashville: Vanderbilt University Press, 1966), 159–160; Julia A. Wilbur in *The Pennsylvania Freedman's Bulletin*, I (August 1865), 52, quoted in John T. O'Brien, "Reconstruction in Richmond: White Restoration and Black Protest, April–June 1865," *Virginia Magazine of History and Biography*, 89, 3 (July 1981): 273, 275.

8. *New York Tribune*, August 1, 8, 1865. One of the most neglected areas of Reconstruction history and of African American history in general, is that of violence against women. This has led to the still prevalent assumption that black women were less likely to be victims of racial violence and the generalization that this reflects the fact that black women were less threatening than black men. Historian W. Fitzhugh Brundage, for example, concludes that black women had "greater leeway" to "voice their opinions and anger without suffering extralegal violence themselves," *Lynching in the New South: Georgia and Virginia, 1880–1930* (Urbana: University of Illinois Press, 1993), 80–81, 322–323n. This reflects both the emphasis on lynching as the major form of racial violence, and the limited historical attention to the black women who were lynched (at least fifteen between 1889 and 1898; at least seventy-six between 1882 and 1927). Even those ostensibly attuned to issues of gender and sexuality still assume that "the greatest violence was reserved for black men"; see, for example, Martha Hodes, "The Sexualization of Reconstruction Politics: White Women and Black Men in the South after the Civil War," *Journal of*

the History of Sexuality 3 (January 1993): 404. Yet the evidence from Richmond and elsewhere suggests that the extent of violence against black women is greater than previously recognized, even greater than reported at the time. One North Carolina man, Essic Harris, giving testimony to the Senate committee investigating Ku Klux Klan terror, reported the rape of black women was so frequent as to be "an old saying by now." Essic Harris testimony, July 1, 1871, in U.S. Congress, *Testimony Taken by the Joint Select Committee to Inquire into the Condition of Affairs in the Late Insurrectionary States* Vol.: *North Carolina* (Washington: GPO, 1872), 100. Only recently have historians begun to uncover and analyze sexual violence against black women as an integral part of Reconstruction history. See for example, the dissertation-in-progress by Hannah Rosen, University of Chicago, which examines the rapes connected with the 1866 Memphis race riot. See also, Catherine Clinton, "Reconstructing Freedwomen," *Divided Houses: Gender and the Civil War*, eds. Catherine Clinton and Nina Silber (New York: Oxford University Press, 1992), chapter 17.

9. *New York Tribune*, June 12, 17, 1865.

10. *The Richmond Times* (May 24, 1865), in refusing to publish black Richmonders' statements of protest, reasoned that they were mistaken in believing that they were all oppressed by the military and civilian officials; only the "idle negroes" were targets of military restrictions and inspections. Throughout the early months of emancipation both white southerners and white Unionists defined freedpeople's mobility in search of family or better jobs and in expression of their new found freedom as evidence of an unwillingness to work. Similarly, those who chose to vend goods on city streets rather than signing work contracts with white employers were seen as lazy or idle. See, O'Brien, "From Bondage to Citizenship," 117–131; see also various communications among the military command reprinted in U.S. War Department, *The War of the Rebellion: A Compilation of the Official Records of the Union and Confederate Armies*, Series I, Volume XLV, Part III-*Correspondence*, Etc. (Washington: GPO, 1894), 835, 932–933, 1005–1006, 1091, 1094–1095, 1107–1108, 11311132.

11. *New York Tribune*, June 17, 1865.

12. Black Richmonders were countering the very different image of their community put forth not only by white southerners but also by Union officers. Major-General H. W. Halleck, for example, emphasized the goodwill between Rebel and Union soldiers, both "brave and honest men, although differing in opinion and action"; justified the military restrictions on African Americans; and reported a lack of marriage relationships among African Americans "and the consequent irresponsibility of the parents for the care and support of their offspring." He argued that "colored females," especially, needed legal restrictions, supervision and suitable punishments, because "being released from the restraints imposed by their former masters and mistresses, . . naturally fall into dissolute habits." H. W. Halleck, Major-General, Commanding, Headquarters Military Division of the James, Richmond, Va. to Hon. E. M. Stanton, Secretary of War, June 26, 1865, in U.S. War

Department, *The War of the Rebellion*, 1295–1297. Halleck was one of the Union officers who was reassigned to a different command as a result of the June protest.

13. O'Brien details these meetings in "From Bondage to Citizenship," chapters 6–9.

14. O'Brien, "From Bondage to Citizenship," 326.

15. See, for example, *Richmond Enquirer*, February 23, 1866; Richmond Dispatch, July 6, 1866; *Richmond Times*, July 6, 1866.

16. Foner, *Reconstruction*, 122.

17. *Richmond Dispatch*, April 19, 1867; *New York Times*, April 19, 1867.

18. Julie Saville, "A Measure of Freedom: From Slave to Wage Laborer in South Carolina, 1860–1868" (Ph.D. diss., Yale University, 1986), 273.

19. *Richmond Whig*, April 1, 1867.

20. *Richmond Dispatch*, October 5, 1867.

21. Aldon Morris makes a similar argument regarding the church and the modern civil rights movement, emphasizing the ways in which the church served as a physical, financial and cultural resource, with its sermons, songs, testimonies and prayers becoming political resources in the mobilization of participants and in the construction and communication of political ideology. *The Origins of the Civil Rights Movement: Black Communities Organizing for Change* (New York: Free Press, 1984). See also, Robin D.G. Kelley, "'Comrades, Praise Gawd for Lenin and Them!': Ideology and Culture Among Black Communists in Alabama, 1930–1935," *Science and Society* 52, 1 (Spring 1988): 59–82; Brenda McCallum, "Songs of Work and Songs of Worship: Sanctifying Black Unionism in the Southern City of Steel," *New York Folkore* 14, 1 & 2 (1988): 9–33. For an argument that eliminating emotions and aesthetics from acceptable forms of public discourse becomes a means to eliminate particular groups of people from active participation in public life, see Iris Marion Young, "Impartiality and the Civic Public: Some Implications of Feminist Critiques of Moral and Political Theory," in *Feminism as Critique: On the Politics of Gender*, ed. Seyla Benhabib and Drucilla Cornell (Minneapolis: University of Minnesota Press, 1987), 56–76.

22. The following discussion of collective enfranchisement as the basis for black women's political activism in the post–Civil War era is drawn from Elsa Barkley Brown, "To Catch the Vision of Freedom: Reconstructing Southern Black Women's Political History, 1865–1880." in *To Be a Citizen*, ed. Arlene Avakian, Joyce Berkman, John Bracey, Bettye Collier-Thomas, and Ann Gordon (Amherst: University of Massachusetts Press, forthcoming).

23. *Richmond Dispatch*, August 1, 2, September 30, October 9, 1867; *New York Times*, August 1, 2, 6, October 18, 1867. My discussion of these events follows closely Peter J. Rachleff, *Black Labor in the South: Richmond, Virginia, 1865–1890* (Philadelphia: Temple University Press, 1984), 45–46. See also Richard L. Morton, *The Negro in Virginia Politics, 1865–1902*, Publications of the University of Virginia Phelps-Stokes Fellowship Papers Number Four (Charlottesville: University of Virginia

Press, 1919), 40–43. Similar reports issued from other areas throughout the South, causing one chronicler to report that "the Southern ballot-box" was as much "the vexation of housekeepers" as it was of farmers, businessmen, statesmen or others: "Elections were preceded by political meetings, often incendiary in character, which all one's servants must attend." Election day itself could also be a problem. As one Tennessean reported in 1867, "Negro women went [to the polls], too; my wife was her own cook and chambermaid," Myrta Lockett Avary, *Dixie After the War: An Exposition of Social Conditions Existing in the South, During the Twelve Years Succeeding the Fall of Richmond* (New York: Doubleday, Page and Co., 1906; reprint, New York: Negro Universities Press, 1969), 282–284. See also, Susan Bradford Eppes for similar occurrences in Florida. *Through Some Eventful Years* ([1926] reprint ed., Gainesville: University of Florida Press, 1968).

   24. *Richmond Dispatch*, August 1, 2, 1867; *New York Times*, August 2, 6, 1867; see also Rachleff, *Black Labor in the South*, 45; Morton, *Negro in Virginia Politics*, 40–43.

   25. The October 1867 city Republican ward meetings and nominating convention adopted the practice common in the black community's mass meetings: a voice or standing vote which enfranchised men, women, and children. See, for example, the October eighth Second Ward meeting for delegate selection: "All who favored Mr. Washburne were first requested to rise, and forty were found on the floor, including women." *Richmond Dispatch*, September 20, October 9, 1867; January 2, 4, 14, 23, 24, February 15, 25, April 3, 8, 25, 1868; *New York Times*, August 6, October 15, 18, 1867; January 11, 1868; Rachleff, *Black Labor in the South*, 45–49; Avary, *Dixie After the War*, 229–231, 254. The issue of children's participation is an interesting one, suggestive of the means by which personal experience rather than societal norms shaped ex-slaves' vision of politics. A similarly telling example was in the initial proposal of the African National Congress that the new South African constitution set the voting age at fourteen, a testament to those young people, as those in Soweto, who experienced the ravages of apartheid and whose fight against it helped bring about the political negotiations to secure African political rights and self-determination.

   26. Compare black women's active participation in Richmond's formal politics—internal and external—in the first decades after the Civil War to Michael McGerr's assessment that nineteenth-century "women were allowed into the male political realm only to play typical feminine roles-to cook, sew, and cheer for men and to symbolize virtue and beauty. Men denied women the central experiences of the popular style: not only the ballot but also the experience of mass mobilization." McGerr's analysis fails to acknowledge the racial basis of his study, i.e., it is an assessment of white women's political participation, Michael McGerr, "Political Style and Women's Power, 1830–1930." *Journal of American History* 77 (December 1990): 864–885. esp. 867. My analysis also differs substantially from Mary P. Ryan. *Women in Public*. Ryan gives only cursory attention to African Americans but finds black women's political expression in the Civil War and Reconstruction eras re-

stricted "with particular severity" and "buried beneath the surface of the public sphere," see, 146–147. 156, passim.

27. For women's participation in political parades in Louisville, Kentucky, Mobile, Alabama, and Charleston, South Carolina, see Herbert G. Gutman, *The Black Family in Slavery and Freedom*, 380; *Liberator*, July 21, 1865 and *New York Daily Tribune*, April 4, 1865. both reprinted in *The Trouble They Seen: Black People Tell the Story of Reconstruction*, ed. Dorothy Sterling (Garden City, New York: Doubleday, 1976), 2–4. In other areas of Virginia besides Richmond and in South Carolina and Louisiana men and women participated in the political meetings. See, for example, Vincent Harding, *There Is A River: The Black Struggle for Freedom in America* (New York: Harcourt Brace Jovanovich, 1981), 294–297; Rupert Sargent Holland, ed., *Letters and Diary of Laura M. Towne Written from the Sea Islands of South Carolina 1862–1884* (Cambridge: Riverside Press, 1912; reprint ed., New York: Negro Universities Press, 1969), 183; Testimony of John H. Burch given before a Senate committee appointed to investigate the exodus of black men and women from Louisiana, Senate Report 693, 46th Congress, 2nd Session, part 2, 232–233 reprinted in *A Documentary History of the Negro People in the United States*, 2 vols., ed. Herbert Apetheker (New York: Citadel Press, 1951), 2: 721–722; Thomas Holt, *Black Over White: Negro Political Leadership in South Carolina during Reconstruction* (Urbana: University of Illinois Press. 1977), 34–35. Graphic artists recognized the participation of women as a regular feature of parades, mass meetings, and conventions as evidenced by their illustrations. See "The Celebration of Emancipation Day in Charleston" from *Leslie's Illustrated Newspaper* reprinted in Francis Butler Simkins and Robert Hilliard Woody, *South Carolina During Reconstruction* (Chapel Hill: University of North Carolina Press, 1932; reprint ed., Gloucester, Mass.: Peter Smith, 1966), facing 364; "Electioneering at the South," *Harper's Weekly*, July 25, 1868 reprinted in Foner, *Reconstruction*, fol. 386; "Colored People's Convention in Session" reprinted in Sterling, *The Trouble They Seen*, 65.

28. *New York Times*, January 11, 22, 1868; *The Debates and Proceedings of the Constitutional Convention of the State of Virginia, Assembled at the City of Richmond* (Richmond, 1868), 505–507, 524–527.

29. *Richmond Dispatch*, June 18, 1867; Rachleff, *Black Labor in the South*, 48.

30. Rachleff, *Black Labor in the South*, 31–32; *Richmond Daily Dispatch*, May 10, 1867; *New Nation*, November 22, 29, December 6, 1866; Holt, *Black Over White*, 35: Avary, *Dixie After the War*.

31. Barkley Brown, "To Catch the Vision of Freedom"; *Richmond Enquirer*, October 22, 1867; *Richmond Whig*, October 19, 1867; Robert E. Martin, "Negro Disfranchisement in Virginia," *The Howard University Studies in the Social Sciences*, I (Washington, D.C., 1938), 65–79; *Richmond Afro-American*, December 2, 1962; Mrs. Violet Keeling's testimony before Senate investigating committee, February 18, 1884, Senate Report No. 579, 48th Congress, 1st Session, reprinted in Apetheker, *Documentary History*, 2: 739–741.

32. Barkley Brown, "To Catch the Vision of Freedom"; Howard N. Rabinowitz, *Race Relations in the Urban South, 1865–1880* (New York: Oxford University Press, 1978), 222; Alrutheus Ambush Taylor, *The Negro in the Reconstruction of Virginia* (Washington, D.C.: The Association for the Study of Negro Life and History, 1926), 181, 269; Michael B. Chesson, "Richmond's Black Councilmen, 1871–96," in *Southern Black Leaders of the Reconstruction Era*, ed. Howard N. Rabinowitz (Urbana: University of Illinois Press, 1982), 219n; Peter J. Rachleff, "Black, White and Gray: Working-Class Activism in Richmond, Virginia, 1865–1890" (Ph.D. diss., University of Pittsburgh, 1981), 473, 488n; *Richmond Dispatch*, October 25, 26, 1872; September 14, 1874; Avary, *Dixie After the War*, 285–286, 347; Thomas J. Evans, Alexander Sands, N. A. Sturdivant, et al., Richmond, to Major-General Schofield, October 31, 1867, reprinted in *Documents of the Constitutional Convention of the State of Virginia* (Richmond, Va.: Office of the New Nation, 1867), 22–23; John H. Gilmer to Gen. Schofield reprinted in *New York Times*, October 30, 1867; *New York Times*, November 3, 1867; Wendell P. Dabney, "Rough autobiographical sketch of his boyhood years" (typescript, n.d.), 98–99, microfilm copy in Wendell P. Dabney Papers, Cincinnati Historical Society, Cincinnati, Ohio; Proceedings before Military Commissioner, City of Richmond, 26 October 1867 in the case of Winston Jackson filed as G-423 1867 Letters Received, ser. 5068, 1st Reconstruction Military District, Records of the U.S. Army Continental Commands, Record Group 393. Pt. 1, National Archives [SS-1049] (bracketed numbers refer to files in the Freedmen and Southern Society Project, University of Maryland; I thank Leslie S. Rowland, project director, for facilitating my access to these files); George F. Bragg, Jr., Baltimore, Maryland, to Dr. Woodson, August 26, 1926, reprinted in "Communications," *Journal of Negro History* XI (1926), 677.

33. See Thomas C. Holt, "'An Empire over the Mind': Emancipation, Race, and Ideology in the British West Indies and the American South," in *Region, Race, and Reconstruction: Essays in Honor of C. Vann Woodward*, ed. J. Morgan Kousser and James M. McPherson (New York: Oxford University Press, 1982), 283–314; also David Montgomery, *The American Civil War and the Meanings of Freedom: An Inaugural Lecture delivered before the University of Oxford on 24 February 1987* (Oxford: Clarendon Press, 1987), 11–13.

34. This is not to suggest that African American women did not desire the vote nor that they did not often disagree with the actions taken by some black men. One should, however, be careful about imposing presentist notions of gender equality on these women. Clearly for them the question was not an abstract notion of individual gender equality but rather one of community. That such a vision might become over time a lead into a patriarchal conception of gender roles is not a reason to dismiss the equity of its inception.

35. Dabney, "Rough autobiographical sketch," 17–18.

36. FABC, II, April 5, 6, 11, May 3, June 27, 1880.

37. First African minutes for 1841–1859 and 1875–1930, are available at First

African and on microfilm in Archives, Virginia State Library. The Civil War and immediate post-emancipation minutes apparently have not survived. Peter Randolph, who came to Richmond from Massachusetts within weeks of emancipation and became the first black man elected pastor of Ebenezer Baptist, attributed both the change in seating patterns and the formal inclusion of women as voters in church business meetings to his own progressivism. Whether or not he initiated such measures, it is unlikely either change would have been effected without wide acceptance within the congregation. Randolph, *From Slave Cabin to Pulpit*, 89.

38. FABC, II, June 27, 1880.

39. FABC, III, November 7, 20, 1899; *Richmond Planet*, July 6, 20, August 10, 31, 1901, March 8, 15, 1902. Similar debates must have occurred in Ebenezer Baptist Church as well. In approving the conduct of business at Ebenezer, Mitchell noted that "only the male members were permitted to vote" on the appointment of a new pastor, *Richmond Planet*, September 14, 1901. These debates over gender roles within black churches occurred on congregational and denominational levels. For studies which examine these debates at the state and/or national level, see, for example, Higginbotham, *Righteous Discontent*; Glenda Gilmore, "Gender and Jim Crow: Women and the Politics of White Supremacy in North Carolina, 1896–1920" (Ph.D. diss., University of North Carolina, Chapel Hill, 1992); Cheryl Townsend Gilkes, "Together and in Harness': Women's Traditions in the Sanctified Church," *Signs: Journal of Women in Culture and Society* 10 (Summer 1985): 678–699.

40. *Virginia Baptist* cited in *Woman's Era* 1 (September 1894): 8.

41. *Richmond Planet*, July 26, 1890; June 8, 1895; September 17, 24, November 19, 1898; September 9, 1899; Anthony Binga, Jr., *Sermons on Several Occasions*, I (Richmond, 1889), 9799. Both Kemp and Carter were Baptist. A few women also conducted services in the Methodist church. Evangelist Annie E. Brown, for example, conducted two weeks of revival services at Leigh Street Methodist Episcopal Church in 1900, *Richmond Planet*, April 28, 1900. Even when one "female preacher . . . took up station" outside a Manchester barbershop and preached against the male members, claiming they were leading the young down to perdition," the *Planet's* Manchester correspondent did not denounce her right to preach but rather suggested that if she "is called to preach the gospel, and is sanctified, as some say, why not organize a church of sanctification," rather than stand on street corners issuing "broad and uncalled for" attacks upon other ministers, *Richmond Planet*, December 12, 1896.

42. In July 1880 a council representing nine Richmond black Baptist churches censured First African for having called the police. "The First African Baptist Church. Richmond, Virginia, to the Messengers & Churches in General Ecclesiastical Council Assembled," in FABC, II, following April 3, 1881 minutes. For late-nineteenth-century disciplinary procedures with regard to members who got civil warrants against other members, see for example, FABC, II, January 7, October 6, 1884; February 3, 1890.

43. FABC, II, June 27, November 6, 1882; February 5, April 2, 1883. Wendell P. Dabney, a member of that 1883 graduating class, remembered the students as having met in early June and "determined not to go to any church. That we would go to the Richmond Theatre or no where." He calls this "the first school strike by Negro pupils on record in the United States!" First African had, however, already denied the use of its facilities because of its new regulation. There is some evidence that, subsequent to the students' action, other black churches may have supported the young people by denying their facilities as well. Dabney, "Rough autobiographical sketch of his boyhood years," 107–109; Wendell P. Dabney, *Maggie L. Walker and the I. O. of Saint Luke: The Woman and Her Work* (Cincinnati: Dabney Publishing Co., 1927), 32–33. *New York Globe*, June 23, 1883.

44. Rachleff, "Black, White, and Gray," 307–309.

45. See, for example, the discussion of the reconfiguration of leisure space, including the barring of cakewalks and other dancing from the church, in Elsa Barkley Brown and Gregg D. Kimball, "Mapping the Terrain of Black Richmond," *Journal of Urban History* (forthcoming).

46. *New York Globe*, October 1883–January 1884. Estimates of the True Reformers' auditorium's seating capacity range from 900 to 1,500 to 2,000. Nearly 4,000 people had been able to attend the March 1867 mass meeting held in First African in support of the Federal Sherman Bill. With their new edifices erected in 1890, Sixth Mount Zion and Sharon Baptist Churches had seating capacity of 1,400 and 1,200 respectively; most churches seated far fewer. Rachleff, *Black Labor in the South*, 40; *Richmond Planet*, March 14, May 31, 1890.

47. For information on the Central Republican League, see *Richmond Planet*, August-September 1898; *Richmond Evening Leader*, August 6, 16, 24, 27, 30, September 1, 28, October 12, 1898: *Richmond Times*, August 3, September 3, 11, 1898; *Richmond Dispatch*, September 14, 1898.

48. *Richmond Planet*, January 26, 1895; October 17, 1896. Similarly, when black Republican men formed the Negro Protective Association in 1898 to organize to retain their vote and political influence, one of the most controversial discussions concerned whether to allow a women's auxiliary, the main purpose of which would be to raise monies for electoral activities. Because of heated opposition the proposal was abandoned. *Proceedings of the Negro Protective Association of Virginia, Held Tuesday, May 18th, 1897, in the True Reformers' Hall, Richmond, Va.*

49. *Richmond Planet*, July 6, 1901.

50. Lawrence Levine, *Black Culture and Black Consciousness: Afro-American Folk Thought from Slavery to Freedom* (New York: Oxford University Press, 1977).

51. Daniel Webster Davis, "De Linin' Ub De Hymns," *'Weh Down Souf and Other Poems* (Cleveland: The Helman-Taylor Company, 1897), 54–56.

52. The scholarly emphasis on this latter period is not merely a reflection of available sources. It also reflects the conceptual paradigms that have guided the investigation of black women's politics: a focus on the national level, often with min-

imal attention to different patterns within the North and the South; the acceptance of what Suzanne Lebsock has called the "consensus . . . that for women the standard form of political participation" in the nineteenth century "was the voluntary association"; an emphasis on autonomous women's organizations; and a focus on excavating political (and feminist) texts. This scholarly emphasis has produced a number of insightful works about the period; among them are Higginbotham, *Righteous Discontent;* Gilmore, *"Gender and Jim Crow";* Hazel V. Carby, *Reconstructing Womanhood: The Emergence of the Afro-American Woman Novelist* (New York: Oxford University Press, 1987); Claudia Tate, *Domestic Allegories of Political Desire: The Black Heroine's Text at the Turn of the Century* (New York: Oxford University Press, 1992). Quote is from Suzanne Lebsock, "Women and American Politics, 1880–1920," in *Women, Politics, and Change,* ed. Louise A. Tilly and Patricia Gurin (New York: Russell Sage Foundation, 1990), 36.

53. Seeing the 1880–1920 period as "the greatest political age for women (including black women)," Suzanne Lebsock raises the question "what does it signify" that such occurred at "the worst" age for black people; "an age of disfranchisement and increasing legal discrimination," "Women and American Politics," 59, 37. Glenda Gilmore, in an otherwise thoughtful and nuanced study, contends that black women in North Carolina gained political prominence at the turn of the century as (because) black men vanished from politics—either leaving the state altogether or sequestering themselves in a nonpolitical world, "Gender and Jim Crow," chapter 5. It is an idea, however, that is often unstated but implicit in much literature which imagines black women's turn-of-the-century club movement as their initial emergence into politics. Such a narrative contributes to the fiction that black women were safer in the Jim Crow South than were black men.

54. I am indebted to Stephanie J. Shaw for making the point that it was internal community dynamics more so than external factors which gave rise to the black women's clubs in the late nineteenth century. See, Stephanie J. Shaw, "Black Club Women and the Creation of the National Association of Colored Women," *Journal of Women's History* 3 (1991): 10–25. In the end, my analysis of what those internal factors were differs somewhat from Shaw's; she attributes their rise to migration and the resultant presence of a newly migrated group within the community in the 1890s, who sought to recreate in these communities the associational life they had left in their home communities.

55. *New York Globe,* 1883 and 1884, *passim;* Acme quote is June 23. 1883; *Richmond Planet,* July 26, 1890: January 12, 1895: 1890–1895, *passim.*

56. For a discussion of black Richmonders' participation in the Knights of Labor, see Rachleff, *Black Labor in the South,* chapters 7–12.

57. Efforts to demonstrate manhood increasingly took on class and status dimensions. For an example of this, see the discussion of black militias and the military ritual taken on by black fraternal orders such as the Knights of Pythias, in Barkley Brown and Kimball, "Mapping the Terrain."

58. See for example, *Richmond Planet*, June 11, 1891; February 24, September 22, 1900; February 16, 1901; October 25, November 1, December 20, 1902. Ida Wells-Barnett, in her struggle against the violence aimed at black women and black men, also challenged the links between white supremacy and manliness. For a discussion of Wells-Barnett's writings in this regard, see Gail Bederman, "'Civilization,' the Decline of Middle-Class Manliness, and Ida B. Well's Antilynching Campaign (1892–94)," *Radical History Review* 52 (Winter 1992): 5–30. Similarly, Frances Ellen Watkins Harper and Anna Julia Cooper associated Anglo-Saxon "imperialism with unrestrained patriarchal power," depicting white males as bestial devourers "of lands and peoples." Hazel V. Carby, "'On the Threshold of Woman's Era': Lynching, Empire, and Sexuality in Black Feminist Theory," *Critical Inquiry* 12 (Autumn 1985): 265.

59. The idea of sexual danger had been a part of the Reconstruction era discourse, as evidenced in the mass indignation meetings and testimonies. Then, however, it was constructed as a matter of general interest, part of the general discussion of repression of African Americans. Now a more clearly gendered discourse developed where violence against men was linked to state repression and the struggle against it to freedom and violence against women became a matter of specific interest, increasingly eliminated from the general discussions.

60. First African also excluded men found to have physically abused their wives. Binga, "Duty of Husband to Wife," in Binga, *Sermons on Several Occasions*, 1, 304–305 (emphasis in original); FABC. II, August 6, September 3, November 5, 1883, April 7, 1884. Ultimately the members of First African were at a loss as to how to deal with the sexually transmitted disease but the persistence of the church's efforts to take it up suggests the degree to which some members considered this a serious issue.

61. It is important to note the constructed nature of this narrative. Suzanne Lebsock has taken the development of women's clubs with these concerns as possible evidence of the increased instances of exploitation of women, "Women and American Politics," 45. I suggest that the exploitation is not increased or even of greater concern, but that the venues for expressing and acting on that concern and the ideology through which this happens—both the narrative of endangerment and the narrative of protection—are the new, changed phenomenon. While the emphasis on motherhood and womanly virtues which undergirded the ideology of middle-class women as protectors may resonate with much of the work on middle-class white women's political activism in this period, it is important to bear in mind two distinctions: African American women's prior history of inclusion, not exclusion, shaped their discourse of womanhood and their construction of gender roles; they did so not in concert with ideas in the larger society but in opposition as white Americans continued to deny African Americans the privileges of manhood or the protections of womanhood, reinforcing the commonality rather than the separateness of men's and women's roles.

62. James Oliver Horton and Lois E. Horton suggest that a masculine conception of liberation, based on violence as an emancipatory tool available principally to men, developed within African American political rhetoric in the North in the antebellum period. "Violence, Protest, and Identity: Black Manhood in Antebellum America," in James Oliver Horton, *Free People of Color: Inside the African American Community* (Washington, D.C.: Smithsonian Institution Press, 1993), chapter 4.

63. Abernathy's and the Barneses' trials, incarceration, retrials, and eventual releases can be followed in the *Richmond Planet*, July 1895–October 1896; *Richmond Times*, July 23, 1895; *Richmond Dispatch*, September 13–19, October 2, 23, November 8, 9, 12, 14, 16, 21, 23, 24, 27, 28, 1895; July 5, 1896. For Bowser's discussion of the formation of the Women's League to protect the Lunenberg women, see *Woman's Era*, October and November 1895; Charles Wesley, *History of the National Association of Colored Women*. The first photographs of the women in the *Planet* appear August 3, 1895. The first picture of "Mary Abernathy and Her Babe" was published February 15, 1896. The post-release photograph of Pokey Barnes and Mitchell's comment regarding it appeared June 27, 1896. For a description of Barnes's attire, see March 6, 1897. Discussions of the case can be found in Brundage, *Lynching in the New South*: and Samuel N. Pincus, *The Virginia Supreme Court, Blacks and the Law 1870–1902* (New York: Garland Publishing, 1990), chapter 11. Brundage emphasizes the role of Governor O'Ferrall, and Samuel Pincus emphasizes the legal maneuverings which prevented the women's certain lynching. While emphasizing the importance of Mitchell's stands against lynching, Ann Alexander dismisses the prolonged front page coverage of the Lunenberg case in the *Richmond Planet* as mere sensationalism. "Black Protest in the New South: John Mitchell, Jr., (1863–1929) and the *Richmond Planet*" (Ph.D. diss., Duke University, 1973), 152–153. Yet it is certain that it was the continuous efforts of black men and women in Richmond which created the climate of protection for Pokey Barnes, Mary Abernathy and Mary Barnes, keeping their cases in the public eye, encouraging government and judicial officials to intervene, and providing the financial resources necessary to acquire a team of prominent white men as defense attorneys and advocates for the Lunenberg women. Pamela Henry has pointed to the focus on motherhood as a central point of the *Planet's* defensive strategy and suggested the futility of such a strategy in an era when black women were denied the protections of Victorian womanhood. Pamela J. Henry, "Crime, Punishment and African American Women in the South, 1880–1940," paper for Research Seminar in African American Women's History, University of Michigan, Fall 1992 (cited by permission of Henry). I am uncomfortably cognizant of the fact that my narrative also, for the most part, silences Mary Abernathy and Pokey and Mary Barnes. This reflects my primary interest in understanding what this case illuminates about black Richmond. Abernathy and the Barneses, their lives and their cases, are certainly worthy of investigation in their own right: Suzanne Lebsock is currently undertaking such a study.

64. *Richmond Planet*, March 6, 1897.

65. The narrative of class and gender, protectors and protected, was not uncontested. For example, the women of the Independent Order of Saint Luke offered a counternarrative which emphasized the possibilities of urban life not only for the middle class but importantly the possibilities of urban life for single, working-class black women who, through their collective efforts, could be their own protectors. Still further, they suggested that women—working-class and middle-class—through their political and economic resources, could become men's protectors. Reinterpreting the standards for "race men" to require support for women's rights, they thus reinserted women's condition and rights as a barometer of freedom and progress. Some aspects of the Saint Lukes' ideas regarding the relationship between the well-being of women and the well-being of men and of the community as a whole are traced in Elsa Barkley Brown, "Womanist Consciousness: Maggie Lena Walker and the Independent Order of Saint Luke," *Signs: Journal of Women in Culture and Society* 14, 3 (Spring 1989): 610–633.

66. It is important to understand this desexualization of black women as not merely a middle-class phenomenon imposed on working-class women. Many working-class women resisted and forged their own notions of sexuality and respectability. But many working-class women also, independent of the middle class and from their own experiences, embraced a desexualized image. Who better than a domestic worker faced with the sexual exploitation of her employer might hope that invisibility would provide protection? Histories which deal with respectability, sexuality, and politics in all its complexity in black women's lives have yet to be written. For beginning discussions see Darlene Clark Hine, "Rape and the Culture of Dissemblance: Preliminary Thoughts on the Inner Lives of Black Midwestern Women," *Signs: Journal of Women in Culture and Society* 14 (Summer 1989): 919–920; Elsa Barkley Brown, "'What Has Happened Here': The Politics of Difference in Women's History and Feminist Politics," *Feminist Studies* 18 (Summer 1992): 295–312; Paula Giddings, "The Last Taboo," in *Race-ing Justice, En-gendering Power: Essays on Anita Hill, Clarence Thomas, and the Construction of Social Reality*, ed. Toni Morrison (New York: Pantheon Books, 1992), 441–463.

67. Bytches With Problems, "Wanted," is one effort by young black women to democratize the discussion of repressive violence: focusing on the often sexualized nature of police brutality against black women, they remind us that such is often less likely to be included in statistics or acknowledged in the public discussion. *The Bytches* (Noface Records, 1991).

68. Elsa Barkley Brown, "Imaging Lynching: African American Women, Communities of Struggle, and Collective Memory," in *African American Women Speak Out: Responses to Anita Hill-Clarence Thomas*, ed. Geneva Smitherman (Detroit: Wayne State University Press, forthcoming).

Chapter 4

"Liberty Dearly Bought"
The Making of Civil War Memory in Afro-American Communities in the South

Thavolia Glymph

The great leaders of the Israelites, Moses and Joshua, were very solicitous to implant in the minds of the people a perpetual remembrance of God's kindness. They therefore marked the stations and stages in their progress with monumental circumstances and objects. They erected monuments, built alters, and anointed pillars to be memorials of some remarkable transaction. It is our duty to use every possible means of turning the past into lessons of solemn admonitions.
—Reverend C. T. Walker[1]

The chief witness in Reconstruction, the emancipated slave himself, has been largely barred from the court.
—W.E.B. Du Bois[2]

For every reification is a forgetting. . . .
—Theodor W. Adorno[3]

Frederick Douglass spent a good part of the last three decades of his life working to keep before the nation a memory of the Civil War and its legacy that paid tribute to the war's revolutionary spirit. He wrote and spoke endlessly on the importance of remembering the contribution of black soldiers to Union victory and emancipation. He castigated the increasingly popular understanding of the war as a fight between two equally noble positions. In a battle between slavery and freedom Douglass (along with many others) believed the only noble position had been that on the side of freedom. Douglass early on denounced any reunion of North and South that in his view rewarded Southern treason, and he continued to do so throughout his life. Yet, by the end of his life in 1895 Douglass seemed to be speaking to the wind, his work to "somehow save the legacy of the Civil War for blacks" dishonored by the resurrected claim that the Civil War was a white man's war. Douglass's faith in "a new generation of black leaders" who would take up his work and go "forth to do battle for America's memory of their freedom" seemed mightily trumped by the faith of white Americans that the war's legacy would be saved for white people alone.[4] And it perhaps would have been but for the work of former slaves and their descendants, particularly in the South.

For the vast majority of former slaves and their descendants the legacy of the Civil War would be saved not in Rochester or Boston but in the shotgun houses and tenant and sharecropper shacks, schools, churches, and lodges of the southern countryside. In decorating the graves of Union dead buried in the South, coming together to celebrate freedom, sending their children into dilapidated and unheated schoolhouses to learn reading and writing along with the history of their people, the former slaves worked as hard as Douglass to preserve a memory of the war and thus a political legacy.

Yet scholars have largely ignored the struggle of former slaves—the principal bearers of the story of the Civil War's transformation into a war for freedom—to remember and give meaning to the Civil War. We know a great deal about the construction of Civil War memory among white Americans and to some lesser extent among Afro-Americans in the North. We know almost nothing about its construction in southern Afro-American communities. Studies of the Civil War and Civil War memory continue to be framed with little reference to or acknowledgment of the contributions of ordinary Afro-Americans.[5] Scholarly focus on two of the giants in the field of Afro-American memory—Douglass and W.E.B. Du Bois—has immensely increased our knowledge and understanding of the story. It has also, perhaps inadvertently, blinkered that understanding. This essay explores both how this has happened and how we might alternatively look at the question of black people's memories of the Civil War and freedom. Was the "indelible memory" forged by Du Bois, or Douglass before him, a memory shared by those on whose behalf it was forged?

The portraits of Douglass as "America's principal symbol of a people's journey from slavery to freedom," working "to forge an African-American counter-memory," and of Du Bois as "a self-conscious creator of black counter-memory," attempting "to forge a place for blacks in the national memory" are not altogether inaccurate.[6] Du Bois's work, historian David Blight writes, "combined the beauty and power of nature, the sweep of history in epic proportions, and the painful ruck of the freedmen's daily lives to forge an indelible memory, a memory that countered the romance of the Lost Cause and national reunion."[7] Both men stood among the first rank of those Americans who objected to the growing acceptance of the narrative construction of the war, uncomplicated by matters of treason, slavery, or emancipation, that came to dominate scholarship and popular culture in the late nineteenth and early twentieth centuries. Yet one suspects that both men would have objected to a revision of the story of the Civil War, freedom, and the creation and preservation of Afro-American Civil War memory that did not call to testify, in Du Bois's words, the "chief witness."[8]

In the postwar struggle "to sustain an ideological interpretation of the Civil War," Douglass certainly faced an uphill battle. He did not, however, fight it with only a "small band of old abolitionists and reformers" at his side.[9] And if in the end, as Blight concludes, Douglass lost his battle for Civil War memory despite his magisterial testimony in its behalf, it was not the case (as historians seem to thus conclude) that the war itself was lost. In the end, in the struggle to "save the legacy of the Civil War," the work of Douglass and northern neo-abolitionists was minuscule compared to that of the masses of former slaves themselves. The work of former slaves and their descendants in the creation of black Civil War memory and the ideas that guided them—ideas verified in their everyday lives—is the larger, missing, and perhaps most instructive story.

Beyond the "small band of old abolitionists and reformers" and the "new generation of black leaders" mobilized to follow in Douglass's footsteps were hundreds of thousands of former slaves and their descendants. Though Douglass made no special effort to mobilize them, the success of his mission ultimately depended on them. For the former slaves in the South, remembering the war and placing emancipation chronologically in the time line of the Afro-American diaspora were political as well as cultural imperatives. The strategies and tactics they employed promoted politicization on several fronts from matters of self-defense and education to political economy. In the late nineteenth and early twentieth centuries, southern Afro-Americans participated in the making of a distinct Civil War memory.

Afro-Southerners shared the view of northern black leaders like Douglass and a dwindling number of white liberal reformers that emancipation constituted a signal event in American history which should be kept in the forefront of the nation's historical memory. But where Douglass, for example, appeared particularly concerned to reach the northern white reform audience, hoping to spur it to take on as a political, if not social, challenge the resurgence of white supremacy in the nation, former slaves and their descendants appear to have been more convinced of the efficacy of their own agency.[10] There is, thus, on the one hand the crucial matter of "seeing" black people's memory-work, and on the other the need to find a language with which to talk about it. As an analytical device, the concept of counternarrative, while broadly useful as a means to understand the ways in which Afro-Americans contested racism, is far less so as a method for understanding the process by which a counternarrative comes to be, particularly among the non-elite. It thus serves poorly the goal of understanding the intellectual world and work of the largely poor and illiterate, rural and working-class southern black population.[11]

Civil War memory among black Southerners developed as a political tool, as part of the larger struggle for autonomy, a key component of the complicated task of molding a class consciousness among former slaves. Emancipation was an empowering legacy. And the story of emancipation black people in the South came to know and remember and to pass on diverged as sharply and in as important ways from that of northern black intellectuals as it did from that of white southerners. Civil War memory was fractured from the outset, composed by different parties whose agendas and perceptions of the past differed. It would seem a mistake, though, to attempt its analysis within the discursive vocabulary of "dominant" and "counter" memories popularized in recent decades.

We still know little about the processes by which slaves, and later freedpeople, came to understand the world beyond the plantations and farms on which most spent their entire lives; how they came to see and link individual experiences of injustice and inequality to larger injustices experienced as a community; or how they came to connect these experiences to broader social movements. How, in other words, they forged a sense of themselves as a community of Afro-Americans. We know little about how they came to see and understand the role memory played in such matters.

For decades following the Civil War, black people met annually to celebrate freedom, to proclaim *to each other* the progress they had made, and to outline the struggles that remained. Each occasion, one contemporary noted, provided an opportunity to "speak of the great day that brought personal liberty to our race in the nation," a time "when we tell the country in plain terms that the freedom which came to us at that day shall be preserved even if its preservation required the sacrificing of our lives; that we intend to contest every inch of ground until we secure all the rights of freemen and American citizens."[12] From 1865 into at least the middle of the twentieth century, Emancipation Day celebrations, as the *Atlanta Daily Worker* proclaimed in 1955, were "schools of citizenship" for "the training of a new group in the struggle for the realization of first-class citizenship."[13] Church anniversaries and other gatherings often served the same goal. Speeches with such titles as "Why We Celebrate," "Woman, Her Work and Influence," and "Our Duty as Citizens" proclaimed their didactic purposes.

At the end of the nineteenth century, at a time when white Americans—North and South—were being called to remember the Civil War as a noble endeavor, former slaves gathered at Emancipation and Independence Day celebrations, church anniversaries, and political rallies to cheer a far different interpretation of the war, a far more radical vision of its meaning.[14] By the hundreds and thousands, sharecroppers and tenant farmers, many of whom had traveled long distances, came together with rural and urban day laborers, skilled mechanics, teachers, domestic servants, ministers, and timber and railroad workers to attend the celebrations. The geographical reach of these gatherings, extending into back country and rural areas, helped to transform individual memories into a collective community historical memory.

The 1888 centennial celebration of the founding of Afro-Baptism in Georgia attracted Afro-Americans to Savannah from throughout the state. Many would have come from the much smaller (in comparison to First Baptist) church prayer houses that dotted the rural landscape. Several small prayer houses prospered within a few miles of the city of Savannah. The Sand Fly Station and Zion Hill, each six miles from the city, claimed thirteen and sixty-five members, respectively. Four miles distant from the city stood the Thunderbolt Society, with 125 members. The Dittmersville Society, two and a half miles away, claimed fifty members. At least five other states—Florida, Tennessee, Pennsylvania, Alabama, and South Carolina—were also represented at the celebration. The small town of Salem,

Virginia hosted an 1893 emancipation celebration that began with a mile-long parade that included two brass bands, five thousand horsemen, and nine hundred pedestrians.[15] To the consternation of planters and other employers of black labor, often no labor could be had on these days.[16] While there would have been pleasure enough to be found in seeing distant family members and friends, in making new acquaintances, and in the bounty of well-spread tables, the principal focus remained the business of recalling the arrival of freedom. These celebrations often ran for several days, with each day's program featuring several speakers who might each speak for hours. The Bishop William H. Heard, an ex-slave, recalled such an occasion where the speaker was the noted Henry M. Turner. Turner spoke for two hours and Heard remembered being "so impressed with the pictures and historic facts he presented of the Race in past ages, and of the men of the present, that my life is largely what it is because of the impression made at this meeting."[17]

Just as the process of creating historical memory among ordinary people is poorly understood, so too is the significance of such memory-work. Outside of their own circles, the memories of ex-slaves have gone largely unacknowledged. Yet the lack of public or official recognition does not mean that they were indiscernible any more than it means that they constitute a "counter-memory." Black people's Civil War memory shaped the white South's own memory and the precise ways in which southern history came to be produced. The Lost Cause movement stands as an explicit rejoinder to the memory-work of black southerners, not the other way around.[18]

In remembering slavery and the Civil War, black people grounded and voiced a political and class consciousness. Even in the face of the removal of federal guarantees to the protection of their freedom and civil rights and of the rampant racist violence that paved the way for the reestablishment of political rights, public civic space and public speech as preeminently white preserves, Afro-Americans continued to narrate stories that braced their lives and communities. They continued to proclaim the centrality of emancipation to their lives and to define for themselves its meaning. Grassroots Afro-American memory-work aimed to brace black people, to move them forward. The importance black people attached to remembering can be traced partly in the disdain they expressed for "disremembering." As countless slave narratives from the 1920s and 1930s make clear, "disremembering" was considered a conscious act of community betrayal, a deliberate act of false consciousness. One may have a lapse in memory or remember wrongly, but one may not "disremember." In Afro-American communities, to be accused of disremembering was to be accused of having acted in seeming disregard of the history of slavery and racism and, in particular, of the freedom struggles of black people. Such a person, as the character "Uncle Albert" asserts in Alice Walker's short story, "Elethia," was someone "who seriously disremembered his past."[19] Racist repression considerably changed the political, social, and economic landscape of the South by the end of the nineteenth century. But like the work of subjugating southern black labor, the complementary work of silencing black people proved a never-ending labor—requiring constant vigilance, the invention of new tools, the retooling of old ones.

In doing their own memory-work, black southerners did not rely on a Douglassian nor, later in the twentieth century, a Du Boisian articulation of a usable past. Former slaves and their descendants acted on the belief that they had a stake in how the war and emancipation were remembered. Most probably knew little or nothing of Douglass's efforts to "save the legacy of the Civil War for blacks" and most would not have been considered by Du Bois capable of leading themselves. Though he believed that the ex-slave, the "chief witness," should be called to testify, Du Bois nevertheless on some level distrusted the black masses, "the lowest of their people," as opposed to men and women more like himself who to him represented "thinking" and "intelligent" black folks.[20] The chief witnesses believed otherwise and constructed at their own hands a usable past. Each year local chapters of the Colored Women's Corps in the South decorated the graves of some forty to fifty thousand Union dead—black and white. Members of the tiny Marche, Arkansas local chapter of the Colored Women's Corps walked three miles into the woods to hold their meetings in the face of threats to burn down their meeting hall.[21] Corps members organized and held Memorial Day programs and participated in Sabbath memorial services. In New Bern, North Carolina, Lucinda J. Keyes, the widow of an Afro-American Civil War veteran, formed a boys' brigade to the Grand Army of the Republic. The Robert G. Shaw Post #3 in Savannah, like many black women's detached corps, helped to underwrite the cost of Memorial Day programs.[22] In engaging in such activities, black people memorialized the Civil War even as they embodied the ongoing process by which memory-work is done. In the process, they created an Afro-American Civil War memory.

Stories of the war and the coming of freedom told and retold in the southern countryside, in shotgun houses, tenant and sharecropper shacks, at Emancipation Day celebrations, church anniversaries, grave decoration days, and in black schools formed the central components of the project of remembering. George Washington Albright remembered with pride that his "first job in the fight for the rights of my people was to tell them they were free, to keep them informed and in readiness to assist the Union armies whenever the opportunity came." Elizabeth Russell recalled with pride how as a child she was entrusted with the task of alerting slaves on neighboring plantations to news of the war and emancipation.[23] Black soldiers were also remembered as central to the fight for freedom and Union. Albright's reminiscence, for example, includes an account of his father's wartime flight from slavery and service as a soldier. Still, Albright recalled the war mostly as a people's struggle. But while central to the making of Civil War memory among former slaves, black soldiers did not in the minds of black people occupy that central ground alone.

Ex-slave narratives more often than not positioned ordinary people at the center of that struggle. Slaves who ran away, or who by other means slowed the pace of plantation labor, or who spread the story of the Emancipation Proclamation, the First Confiscation Act, and other measures that bit by bit opened the path to freedom, were all important actors in the drama of emancipation and in the construction of Civil War memory in southern black communities. That was Albright's point, it seems, in noting that the effectiveness of the "underground information service" depended almost wholly on the slaves working in "dead secrecy" as they carried "the news to one another."[24] Albright likely told this story of slave agency many times before it was recorded by the WPA in the 1930s. Importantly, he would have told it in his own community, where it would have become part of the lore of slavery, war, and freedom. The story of war and emancipation black people told and passed on thus diverged in significant ways from the memory of the war molded by Frederick Douglass. A crucial divide distinguished their understanding of the genesis of the war, why it was important to remember the conflict, and for whom it was important.

Against a growing army of North-South reunionist purveyors of Civil War memory, Frederick Douglass continued to view the war and postwar Memorial Day celebrations through a moral lens. Memorial Day celebrations captured the war's "moral character," its "eternal principles."[25] At speaking engagements in the North and Upper South, he recalled the political and moral divide that had led to war and asked Americans to remember its human cost in lives lost on the battlefield. In emphasizing a moral victory—even ironically, one that could be secured only by force of arms—Douglass hoped to arm northerners for the fight against late-nineteenth-century white supremacy. Douglass pleaded the case for black Civil War memory as a kind of salvation, a balm that would both heal racial wounds and legitimize black people's claims to citizenship. The audience for such talk, of course, became thinner and thinner in the North. Yet, in the South, a more straightforward and radical message found a growing audience. Had Douglass taken his message to the deep South, he might very well have faced a more skeptical, even hostile audience, whose constitution he likely would not have anticipated.[26]

Emancipation Day speakers in the South faced audiences of former slaves *expecting* to hear a distinctly different message. Holding to a different understanding of the war, black southerners—preeminently rural and working-class—embraced and passed on a different historical memory. There was little talk among them of the war's high "moral character" and precarious support for the idea that the war had been waged as a contest "between freedom and African slavery." The latter notion was roundly criticized in black southern communities by speakers who reminded the former slaves and their children that freedom had "only entered as a war measure."[27] This understanding of the war did not lessen the meaning of freedom or black people's joy at its arrival. It did recommend an ideological interpretation and framing of the war with important consequences for the making of black Civil War memory and Afro-American history.

The one hundredth joint anniversary celebration in 1888 of the founding of Savannah's First African Baptist Church—hailed as the "*Grand Mother Church of Negro Baptists*"—and Afro-Methodism in Georgia addressed these questions directly. The celebration was one of the most important events in the lives of black people throughout Georgia and the larger Afro-Baptist world. The thousands gathered would have spilled out from the church grounds at Franklin Square and onto the Savannah River waterfront. One participant remembered it as "a feast of good things."[28] The remarks of the scheduled speakers would have been greatly anticipated. The Rev. C. T. Walker devoted a portion of his sermon to the "history of my people," with particular attention to emancipation. Freedom, he emphasized, had come from the hands of God. "Some attribute their freedom to Abraham Lincoln and the Union Armies," Walker preached, "but we received our liberty, like Israel of Old, from the great God of heaven and earth."[29] This idea was quite different from Douglass's notion of the war's moral character, which Douglass saw as proceeding much less directly from God and more directly from the hearts of good men and women.

Speaking before the same audience, the Rev. Emanuel King Love, pastor of the five-thousand-member First African Baptist Church, drove home Walker's message. The freedom of black people, Love reminded the audience assembled before him, was "a liberty dearly bought." The accounting, he insisted, must include those who had died in slavery along with those who had lost their lives during the war. Like Walker, Love admonished those who believed that freedom was a gift from President Lincoln. For, he stated, Lincoln had received "more honor than I candidly believe he deserves." He urged remembrance instead of "the means which God used in our emancipation.[30]

> Our people have learned to think that Abraham Lincoln was the greatest champion of our cause. But such is not true. The thing that was uppermost in the mind of Mr. Lincoln was the salvation of the Union. So far as Mr. Lincoln was concerned the Emancipation Proclamation was purely a war measure—for he would "save the Union with or without freeing the slaves." From this single sentence it must be clear to you that our freedom was not first in Mr. Lincoln's mind.[31]

This view of Lincoln and the Union would have resonated with black people's experience of war and emancipation. As wartime fugitives, soldiers and wives, mothers, fathers and children of soldiers, as slaves separated from family members refugeed to isolated corners of the Confederacy, they had experienced firsthand the effects of the federal government's vacillation in adopting emancipation as a war aim. They had seen their own persistence contribute to—and help push—the transformation of Union policy. They were people like March Hayes, born into slavery in South Carolina in 1825, who after the war was a celebrated figure in his community, recognized not only for his leadership as a deacon in the church but also for having led slaves to freedom during the Civil War and, afterward, serving as a "valiant" soldier in the Union army.

> He was active in putting many of his race over on the Union side, where they enjoyed freedom. He was a brave soldier. In attempting to get some of his people from Savannah over on the Yankee side he encountered the enemy, who commanded him and his faithful few to halt. This command was given to the wrong man. He was willing to meet death rather than obey that command. He knew it was death to obey and could but be death

to disobey, hence the war began between them, in which he was terribly wounded. He made good his escape, however, to the Union soldiers.[32]

Escaped slaves returned to slavery by Union officers and soldiers at the beginning of the war or the wives of black soldiers for whom the federal government had little use, and for whom Union commanders held little respect, were no doubt predisposed to the argument that Lincoln was more concerned for the "salvation of the Union" than for black people's freedom. Union army camps had served as an important refuge for tens of thousands of slaves during the Civil War and in general slaves had cheered the arrival of northern soldiers. Still, the idea that the Union armies "had fought as earnestly in behalf of slavery as they had for the Union and the Constitution" conformed to the experience of many Afro-Americans.[33]

At church and Emancipation Day celebrations, Afro-Americans in the South heard their own experience of slavery and the war validated. Collectively as communities, they recalled the contributions of black soldiers who had contributed "gallons of the richest blood that ever coursed its way through the veins of man" to the cause of freedom and citizenship.[34] Collectively, they remembered slavery and those among them like Elizabeth Russell and March Hayes who had stepped into the breach when the Union army could or would not. The time had not yet come when Afro-Americans would be ashamed to speak of slavery. They spoke of it as an unmitigated evil, the antithesis of democracy and Christian belief, as a time when even the right to worship had come at tremendous cost. Welcoming the thousands who had come to celebrate the centennial of Afro-Baptism in Georgia, Rev. Love began with a statement of faith:

> Our church was planted in blood. Rev. Andrew Bryan, its founder and pastor, was whipped until his flesh was terribly torn. His blood ran freely and puddled by his lacerated body for no other crime than that he preached Jesus to Africa's sable sons and daughters enslaved in this country.[35]

Emancipation-Day and church anniversary orators in the late nineteenth century offered global perspectives on black people's historical and contemporary condition and appealed in a quite deliberate and conscious way to radical traditions in African American and European history. The rededication service of First African Baptist Church would probably have seemed incomplete without sermons that spoke to the question of black people's political condition, past and present, as well as to God's love. Comparative analyses of slavery and emancipation ground the U.S. South experience in the precolonial and post-emancipation European and Atlantic worlds. Walker's sermon, for instance, encompassed a comparative analysis of slavery and emancipation in the United States, Prussia, and Cuba. Public forums in the form of church and emancipation celebrations thus became sites for the spread of an orally based literacy and the dissemination of knowledge about the world, the history of people of African descent in the diaspora, and systems of unfree labor.[36] There were the more familiar lessons on the glories of ancient Egypt and Ethiopia and the less familiar ruminations on Russian serfdom, Cuban emancipation, "*colored martyrs*" who traversed the transatlantic world, and the contributions of black people to the economic growth of the United States.[37] If, as Elsa Barkley Brown argues, a rising black middle class turned increasingly inward on itself, to its own world of literary societies and race clubs, ordinary black people in an important sense turned ever outward.[38] The turn, as the remarks of Rev. S. A. McNeal made clear, was critically important to the construction of Afro-American memory:

> The white press was never intended to praise and elevate the negro. They do not spend their money for that purpose. The white press, if it means no ill will to the negro, it means elevation to the white, and to support the long believed theory that the negro is inferior to the white man. A press that believes that can not elevate both races.[39]

Even Douglass, the most celebrated Afro-American of his time, was not immune to criticism and attack. Love argued that the lionization of Douglass was just as harmful as that of Lincoln, though for different reasons. To his mind Lincoln had demonstrated insufficient moral courage. Douglass, on the other hand, he saw as a traitor to the race. The betrayal, Love told a large audience, lay in Douglass's decision to marry a white woman. Douglass's courageous flight from slavery, his heroic work in the abolition movement, his fight on behalf of the right of black men to enlist as soldiers in the Union forces, and his ongoing efforts after the war on behalf of black people, Love believed, were not sufficient to merit the esteem of black people in the face of his marriage to a white woman. Love stated that Douglass had "testified in this one single act that he believed his own race so inferior that the money—that he had made by mere accident and good luck to be used by great men at an opportune time, not a Negro woman in all the land was worthy to share its comforts with him."[40] Thus, amidst the clamor of white supremacy campaigns that rode slouched on the back of allegations charging black men with the rape of white women, some black speakers argued that miscegenation was "damaging to both races."[41] White men, not black, were primarily responsible for what he called "blood poisoning."[42] Indeed, James M. Townsend ridiculed the postwar obsession with miscegenation when before the war, "white men were not alarmed at the thought of 'social equality.' The best blood of the south mingled with that of the negro. . . . Much today is being said upon this subject. We lose no sleep over the question of social equality, this matter will regulate itself. . . . It is political and civil equality which is our right, and for which we will contend."[43]

In contrast to black middle-class rhetoric counseling the adoption of quiet public demeanor along with bourgeois familial patterns and domestic economies, and to the philosophy of accommodation popularized by Booker T. Washington, Emancipation-Day speakers adopted a more radical stance, telling Afro-Americans they should stay armed. Neither the rhetoric nor the application of race uplift ideology, they made clear, would protect black people from racial violence or disfranchisement. Speakers emphasized the contributions of black people to the nation's economic growth before and after the war and their contribution to Union victory. As one stated, black people had "helped to make and save" the United States and should "raise a howl" until they secured their own civil and political rights.[44] Without dignity and civil rights, the notion of middle-class respectability seemed an oxymoron.

> We have had the worst things done to us and we have pardoned the grossest insults. I deplore the fact however, that we are such cowards and so afraid to die in vindication of our virtue and rights. We can change things by true manhood I would not council violence except in self-defence. No people have much respect for cowards. . . . While life is precious, character and virtue are far more precious. We could bury any member of our race with far more grace and less regret and less loss than to have him to dishonor and disgrace the race.[45]

Insults to black womanhood especially ought not be tolerated: "If lynch law must prevail in this age as a result of advance [*sic*] civilization," argued Love, "then let the Negroes apply this law to those who destroy the virtue of their women."[46] Interestingly, the protection and defense of black women's virtue was talked about as a "manly" and "womanly" duty: black women were cast as active participants in resistance. "Whenever a colored girl spits in the face of a white scoundrel who insulted her," stated one speaker, "she elevates, dignifies, glorifies negro womanhood (great applause) and there ought to be more spitting in the face than there is."[47]

Emancipation celebrations and other public gatherings in the postbellum South created spaces for black people to remember individually and collectively and to construct their own history. They provided tutoring in the use of historical knowledge as a tool of resistance. In addition to being occasions for looking back and assessing the historical record, for linking past conditions to the present, emancipation and some religious celebrations also formed an integral part of the process by which ex-slaves achieved self-awareness and political consciousness. The "lower classes," Gramsci writes, "historically on the defensive, can only achieve self-awareness via a series of negations, via their consciousness of the identity and class limits of their enemy."[48] For slaves, the Civil War was a defining moment in this ongoing process, starkly revealing the "identity and class limits" of slaveholders.[49] The damage that was done to white supremacist ideology could not from that point on be fully repaired. In this sense, segregation, disfranchisement laws, and the Lost Cause Movement signaled a defeat for white supremacy as much as they signaled anything else.

On an individual or small-community level, slaves understood well the process of exploitation inherent in the institution of slavery. Less clear, as noted above, is the extent to which they understood or were able to place themselves within the wider political economy of slavery.[50] For most slaves, it was no doubt difficult to imagine the *world of slavery*, even acknowledging a general awareness of slavery's geography as exemplified by the fear of being sold to the deep South. For most, no doubt, the *world of slavery* consisted of the farm or plantation on which they lived and worked, and perhaps adjacent farms, plantations, or towns. They could not have known that spread across the South were millions of enslaved people like themselves. The Civil War had an enormous impact in clarifying such matters.

In countless ways, the war made the structural basis of slavery more visible and as the personal, financial, political, and social losses of slaveholders piled up, they constituted the primary exhibit. Moreover, former slaves learned an important new vocabulary. The Civil War provided a miniature, if sometimes confusing, lesson in American politics, governance, and society generally: the office of the president; the existence of a *federal* military force that claimed supremacy over slaveholders, local southern militias, and patrollers; the existence of organizations of abolitionists. In the mass meetings of church anniversaries and emancipation celebrations in the postwar era the vocabulary of freedom was enlarged, aiding in the process the ability of black people to link their particular historic circumstance to broader national and international questions and institutional structures. It was not a small matter that this new postwar vocabulary defined former masters as constituting a *class* rather than a superior race. Such language provided a different means of conceptualizing the experience of slavery and freedom but one that still embraced familiar understandings of what slavery had meant. When Emancipation Day speakers labeled former slaveholders a "master class" or spoke of the "pernicious doctrine of states' rights" and of "the insolent demands of the master class" and its "determination to rule or ruin" as "never more rampant than today," they placed on the ground an accessible language that embodied a collective experience and point of view.[51]

In the decades following the Civil War, black people's belief system, their intellectual life, was a cobbled together—though not incoherent—thing. The thinking of Ned Cobb is a case in point. Like many black people in Alabama, Cobb traveled to Tuskegee on numerous occasions to hear Booker T. Washington speak. He understood that Washington was an "important" and "noted man," "a business man as a white man would be" with a national reputation that enabled him to raise "piles of money" for Tuskegee. Cobb was nonetheless critical of Washington's role as a leader of black people. The "trouble" with Washington, he stated, was that "he didn't feel for and didn't respect his race of people enough to go rock bottom with them," "never did get to the roots of our troubles." Washington "had a lot of anything a man needed for himself, but the right main thing. . . . He should have walked out full-faced with all the courage in the world and realized, 'I was born to die. What use for me to hold everything under the cover if I know it? How come I won't tell it in favor of my race of people.'" Instead, he was "wrong-spirited."[52] He disremembered. Those who did not may have played a more significant role in southern Afro-American communities than has previously been understood or acknowledged by scholars.

A former slave, R. R. Wright was a thirty-year-old schoolteacher in 1883 when the United States Senate investigating committee on capital and labor relations arrived in Georgia. Given the subject of the investigation, questions concerning the "negro labor problem" were central to the committee's work and deliberations. Wright attended the hearings listening patiently and carefully to the testimony of several local white persons before taking the stand himself. Wright testified to a different reality. He offered the senators a global context for understanding and framing the history of the South and of racism. The senators were no doubt surprised to learn that "very nearly three-fourths of this globe is owned and inhabited by colored people," no doubt startled by Wright's assertion that "what is called the Aryan race has not originated a single great religion . . . that our methods of alphabetic writing all came from the colored race," as did, he stated, "the majority of the sciences."[53]

One would reasonably suppose that Wright's understanding of history found its way into the classes he taught. Conceivably, his students were among the throngs who took part in Emancipation Day and church celebrations in Georgia; conceivably what they learned in the classroom found support in what they heard in public forums and in their homes. To be sure, this would have all come in bits and pieces. They would somehow have to put those pieces together to form coherent ideas about the world and their place in it.

Over the past thirty years scholars have labored to uncover the history of the oppressed, the subaltern, and to better understand how subaltern voices challenge and force revisions in "master" narratives. This emphasis, important as it is, has resulted in the comparative neglect of the study of how "subordinate" voices function within the communities of the subjugated, what they mean to the subalterns themselves. Perhaps the next step is to pay closer attention to the language of ordinary people and to the resources at their disposal for the transmission of knowledge as well as culture. It has been said of historian and political activist Eric Williams that his strength lay in his ability to "[turn] history, the history of the Caribbean, into gossip, so that a story of a people's predicament seemed no longer the infinite, barren tracts of documents, dates and texts. Everything became news: slavery, colonialisation. . . . His lectures retained always the character of whisper which everyone was allowed to hear, a rumour which experience had established as truth."[54] This was also the strength of Afro-American celebrations, community and religious gatherings.

Some years ago, in a seminal essay on historical memory, Herbert G. Gutman attempted an explanation of how once vibrant political worlds become deadened, how people become "victims of a truncated and shrunken historical consciousness," "deprived of access to the historical processes that had shaped their lives, the lives of their parents, and the nation at large." Between 1910 and 1940, Gutman writes, this phenomenon embraced the entire nation as historical writing came to constitute a narrowly defined notion of what it meant—and what it took—to be an American.[55] In southern Afro-American communities, the Civil War fueled the possibilities for an expanded historical consciousness, and the memory-work of black people after the Civil War extended these possibilities further still. "Everything became news" and "everyone was allowed to hear." The whispers of freedom before and during the Civil War helped to produce a historical consciousness whose most significant mediators and translators were Afro-Americans themselves. Rooted in the soil of slavery and in the process of emancipation, Emancipation Day and other celebrations came to be an integral part of a wide-ranging campaign of popular and often radical education among black people.

The reconstitution of the power of white southerners after the Civil War was accomplished by segregation, disfranchisement, rampant violence against black southerners, and memory-work. With the end of the Civil War former masters and mistresses faced the loss of their slaves and greatly reduced material circumstances. Defeat had brought the unanticipated loss of the absolute power to make their voices heard, to define the South's past, present, and future. Instead they faced constructions of the past— memories—that did not originate with them. Eliza Andrews, in training before the war to be a mistress, recognized it at once: defeat meant having to suffer the North's "horrid newspapers" and the "lies they tell about us, while we have our mouths closed and padlocked," leaving no choice but to "figure just as our enemies choose to paint us." Similar reckonings could of course be heard across the South.[56]

But it was not just northern opinion that troubled the white South. Equally, and perhaps more, troubling was the seeming eagerness of former slaves to put forth their own interpretation of the past and to claim a voice in defining the present. The two tasks were, of course, inextricably linked. Outside the planter class itself, no other group—as northern abolitionists had always maintained—was in a better position to give damning testimony against masters, whom Frederick Douglass called slavery's "every-hour violators."[57] Former slaves stepped forward to articulate and remember the violence at the heart of slavery. They became the foremost narrators of a memory of the Civil War in which the destruction of slavery was the core point of reference, and in which Lincoln was not the great emancipator.[58]

Language and contesting memories lay at the heart of postbellum struggles. In the voices of freedpeople the planter class perceived a threat and challenge to their assumed prerogative to rule and to continue to speak for black people.[59] Struggles over the right to speak infused all others—over land, education, working hours, the reconstitution of families and personal lives, and so much more. The verbal articulation of freedom drew fierce rage. At its most fundamental level, it spoke to a historical record at odds with antebellum proslavery ideology and with postwar white supremacist ideology. Former planters were not merely seeking to recreate the old order when they included clauses in labor contract stipulating that former slaves were to address their now free labor employers as "master." Such demands arose inevitably in a situation where language had become problematic.

With the support of the federal government, white southerners soon enough regained political power and with it the power to define, produce, and control *at the public level* the history of the South that came to be inscribed in public school textbooks and symbolically embodied in monuments that still project onto the southern landscape in rejection of northern "lies" and Afro-American/southern truths. Decades-long and labor-intensive efforts involving a host of individuals and organizations—from former slaveholders and Confederate veterans' associations to female memorial associations, religious leaders, and educators—were devoted to the cause. As secretary of the North Carolina Division of the United Daughters, Rebecca Cameron in 1903 enlisted the support of the state's forty-eight chapter historians in tracking down "grandmothers, mothers, aunts in every community" in the effort to write the story of North Carolina's participation in the Civil War. In 1912, Mildred Lewis Rutherford, state historian of the Georgia Division, presented her recruits with a precise list of topics to be researched and reported. Suggestions included histories of memorial associations, the Georgia dead, war poems, tributes to faithful slaves, and a black mammy memorial. The movement led to the erection of specially commissioned statues to Confederate leaders and hundreds of mass-produced monuments to the "common soldier," all aiming, Du Bois was to declare, to "achieve the impossible by recording of Confederate soldiers: 'They died fighting for liberty!'"[60]

The memory of the Civil War composed by the white South, including and beyond the Lost Cause movement, has come to be regarded as the dominant memory against which Afro-Americans have struggled to compose a counternarrative. The work of Douglass and Du Bois is most frequently cited as proof. The voices of the masses of freedpeople have been erased from memory narratives and thus the manner in which they defined their ideological and political struggle.[61] This analysis slights two crucial points:

the attempt by the white South to defeat the memories of former slaves and the capacity of even oppressed groups to formulate and voice independent narratives that, while they must of necessity implicitly recognize and even sometimes explicitly address other narratives simultaneously in play, may also contest such narratives from a distance. From the moment of emancipation, southern whites moved to void black memory of slavery and the Civil War, initially by declaring their narratives undocumentable and "false." The attempt by Afro-Americans to redraw boundaries of race, gender, and politics were deemed "bad behavior" and "unjust."[62] Federal support for the cause of the white South bolstered this interpretation. On his tour of the South at the close of the nineteenth century, President William McKinley praised Confederate heroism. In the first decade of the twentieth century, Congress passed legislation providing federal funding for the care of Confederate graves in the North and for the return of Confederate battle flags captured by the Northern armies. It would refuse the call to appropriate funds for a national celebration of emancipation on the occasion of the fiftieth anniversary of the Battle of Gettysburg.[63]

The effort to deny the "false" ideas of black people required the construction of greater, more elaborate counter-memories. Matthew Page Andrew's *American History and Government* (1921), written (according to its publisher, J. B. Lippincott) "specifically for the use of Junior High School students," praised the Ku Klux Klan as a "remarkable organization" that had "saved the civilization of the South from perhaps almost irredeemable depths of degradation and despoliation." Only "the evil element," "the criminal or vicious classes" had any reason to fear the Klan, he writes.[64] The national call to "reunion" and the theme of "heroism" served the purpose most effectively, making invisible the Mason-Dixon line and the ideological and moral boundaries it had by 1860 come to represent. It soon became "neither wise nor patriotic to speak of all the causes of strife," and the shared public memory of Afro-Americans that spoke to the "causes of strife" was eventually dismissed as a counter-memory.[65]

The legacy was still resonant a hundred years later in the centennial celebration of the Civil War from 1961 to 1965. The war's complexity and the widely varying motives that had braced Unionist and Confederate convictions, and through four years of death and carnage transformed them, was reduced, historian John Bodnar writes, to the symbolic language of "heroism." Major General U. S. Grant III, chairman of the Centennial Commission established by a resolution of the U.S. Congress, announced that "heroism and self-sacrifice" of Confederate soldiers must be recognized because they too were Americans and because during the war they too "were heroically fighting for what they thought was right."[66] It was a far cry from the spirit of Manuel Fenollosa's 1863 "Emancipation Hymn." "Asking for a Land, for a Land united," the hymn read in part, "We forgot the slave."[67] The Civil War Centennial celebrated a "version of the past" that was "intended to connect with and ratify the present."[68] "It was still convenient," historian John Hope Franklin wrote in 1962, "to remember that slavery had been abolished and to forget that the doctrine of the superiority of the white race was as virulent as ever."[69] Or, as Du Bois put it equally bluntly, "Our histories tend to discuss American slavery so impartially that in the end nobody seems to have done wrong and everybody was right."[70]

In the history of the making of Civil War memory, the memory-work of former slaves has been forgotten or recast in the larger culture as countermemories even though the narrative memory Afro-Americans embraced more directly confronted and contended with black people's sense of their own place in the world. It helped steady them for the fight for freedom and civil rights and helped arm them to live with as much dignity as possible. It could not prevent lynching, restore the vote to black men, or of itself establish equitable educational and economic opportunities. This did not, however, make it nothing. The white South continued to control much of black people's world but black people's memories of the Civil War and emancipation pressed against that control in ways that are only beginning to be explored and understood. If Afro-American women fought attacks on their bodies by spitting in the face of the attacker or by defending themselves by some other means, they risked economic, physical, and emotional retaliation, even death. Perhaps what is important, however, is that there was a moment in the late nineteenth century when they were encouraged to take death. There were, they learned, "*colored* martyrs" who had preceded them. The memory of the Civil War black people constructed constituted for them a primary history-memory of a people and of the South. It fought disremembering.

NOTES

1. Rev. C. T. Walker, "Sermon on the Occasion of the 1888 Celebration," in Rev. E. K. Love, *History of the First African Baptist Church, From Its Organization, January 20th, 1788, to July 1st, 1888. Including the Centennial celebration, Addresses, Ser-*

mons, Etc. (Savannah, Ga.: The Morning News Print, 1888), 207. Rare Book Collection, University of North Carolina at Chapel Hill.

2. W. E. Burghardt Du Bois, *Black Reconstruction in America: An Essay Toward a History of the Part Which Black Folk Played in the Attempt to Reconstruct Democracy in America, 1860–1880* (1935; reprint Cleveland: Meridian Books, 1962), 721.

3. As quoted in Martin Jay, *Marxism and Totality: The Adventures of a Concept from Lukacs to Habermas* (Berkeley: University of California Press, 1984), 228.

4. David W. Blight, "'For Something Beyond the Battlefield': Frederick Douglass and the Struggle for the Memory of the Civil War," *Journal of American History* 75 (March 1989): 1158; David W. Blight, "W.E.B. Du Bois and the Struggle for African-American Memory," in *History and Memory in African-American Culture,* ed. Geneviève Fabre and Robert O'Meally (New York: Oxford University Press, 1994).

5. See, for example, David W. Blight, "Fifty Years of Freedom: The Memory of Emancipation at the Civil War Semicentennial, 1911–15," in *After Slavery: Emancipation and Its Discontents,* ed. Howard Temperley (London: Frank Cass, 2000), 117–34, esp. 121. In Afro-American history, the most significant shift in this paradigm in historical writing has occurred in studies of twentieth-century freedom struggles. See, for example, John Dittmer, *Local People: The Struggle for Civil Rights in Mississippi* (Urbana: University of Illinois Press, 1994); and Charles M. Payne, *I've Got the Light of Freedom: The Organizing Tradition and the Mississippi Freedom Struggle* (Berkeley: University of California Press, 1995).

In addition to the important body of work by David Blight, promising new work in the study of Afro-American memory includes Kathleen Clark, "Celebrating Freedom: Emancipation Day Celebrations and African-American Memory in the Early Reconstruction South," in *Where These Memories Grow: History, Memory, and Southern Identity,* ed. W. Fitzhugh Brundage (Chapel Hill: University of North Carolina Press, 2000), 107–32; Laurie Maffly-Kipp, "Redeeming Southern Memory: The Negro Race History, 1874–1925," in *Where These Memories Grow,* ed. Brundage, 169–89; Cecelia Elizabeth O'Leary, *To Die For: The Paradox of American Patriotism* (Princeton, N.J.: Princeton University Press, 1999); and William O. Wiggins, *O Freedom!: Afro-American Emancipation Celebrations* (Nashville: University of Tennessee Press, 1987). John Hope Franklin's "A Century of Civil War Observation," *Journal of Negro History* 47 (April 1962): 97–107, remains an indispensable starting point.

6. Blight, *Race and Reunion: The Civil War in American Memory* (Cambridge: Harvard University Press, 2001), 302; Blight, "Du Bois and the Struggle for African-American Memory," 46; Blight, "Douglass and the Memory of the Civil War," 1165. Elizabeth Rauh Bethel similarly sites the roots of Afro-American identity and memory among leading black intellectuals and abolitionists in the North. See Bethel, *The Roots of African-American Identity: Memory and History in Free Antebellum Communities* (New York: St. Martin's Press, 1997). A more recent example of the pitfalls of this sort of analysis is Laurie F. Maffly-Kipp's "Redeeming Southern Memory."

Maffly-Kipp argues that Afro-American "race historians" of the late nineteenth and early twentieth centuries were part of an "ongoing mission to ex-slaves" that sought to provide "a history, and thus a moral identity" despite the "distinctive northern disdain" they had "for what they saw as an inferior southern way of life" (Maffly-Kipp, "Redeeming Southern Memory," 170, 171, 182 respectively.)

7. Blight, "Du Bois and the Struggle for American Historical Memory," 46 and 56.

8. Du Bois, *Black Reconstruction in America*, 721.

9. Blight, "For Something Beyond the Battlefield," 1163.

10. For an excellent discussion and analysis of Douglass's overtures to the northern public, see Blight, "For Something Beyond the Battlefield," 1156–78. Some scholars have also argued for the existence of a viable alliance between Afro-Americans—particularly southerners—and white northerners. This seems at best much over-drawn. See O'Leary, *To Die For*, 6.

11. For an example of the view I am arguing against, see Blight, "Du Bois and the Struggle for African-American Memory," 50–51, where Blight writes: "Claiming the center as scholars, or singing from the margins as poets, writers about race have for generations fashioned a 'counter-memory,' a concept elucidated by Michael Foucault and several other theorists."

George Lipsitz's definition of counter-memory as "a way of remembering and forgetting that starts with the local, the immediate, and the personal" leaves open the door for the inclusion of the voices of ordinary people. "Unlike historical narratives that begin with the totality of human existence and then locate the specific actions and events within that totality," he writes, "counter-memory starts with the particular and the specific and then builds outward toward a total story. Counter-memory looks to the past for the hidden histories excluded from dominant narratives." Lipsitz, *Time Passages: Collective Memory and American Popular Culture* (Minneapolis: University of Minnesota Press, 1990), 213. Still, the term in its most common usage implies a certain illegitimacy or irregularity. It cannot thus be the real thing. It seems to me as well that the idea of a contested memory is of a quite different order from the notion of a counter-memory. I argue against the tendency to conflate what are two quite distinct notions.

12. J. Gordon Street to Magnus L. Robinson, December 16, 1890, enclosed in Papers of the Alexandria, Virginia Emancipation Celebration, January 1, 1891. While emancipation continues to be celebrated into the twenty-first century, it is no longer a community-shaping event. And among Afro-Americans today, the Civil War is not a historical moment that is claimed. The two developments are no doubt linked.

13. "The Addresses of the Emancipators," *Atlanta Daily Worker*, 4 January 1955, 5, as quoted in Wiggins, *O Freedom*, xvii. Wiggins's study, focusing on the twentieth century, provides notable evidence of the ways in which Emancipation Day celebrations functioned as grass-roots political forums. See also Clark, "Celebrat-

ing Freedom: Emancipation Day Celebrations and African-American Memory in the Early Reconstruction South," 107–32; Genevieve Fabre, "African-American Commemorative Celebrations in the Nineteenth Century," in *History and Memory in African-American Culture*, 72–91; and Karen Fields, "What One Cannot Remember Mistakenly," in *History and Memory in African-American Culture*, 150–63.

14. Clark argues, however, that disfranchisement "forced accommodations in Africa American historical memory" and "emptied [them] of much of their former significance" (125). She offers no evidence in support of this conclusion, identifying neither the accommodations made nor evidence of a diminished significance.

15. Love, *History of First African Baptist Church*, 149–52, 208, 218; Emancipation Celebration Club of Salem, Virginia, joined by Roanoke Club, January 2, 1893, Library of Congress. The Savannah celebration also began with a mile-long processional. The centrality of the smaller churches to the larger body of Black Baptists is underscored in the church history. Emancipation celebrations in the North also attracted large crowds and drew from surrounding or nearby villages and communities. See Richard White, "Civil Rights Agitation: Emancipation Days in Central New York in the 1880s," *Journal of Negro History* 78 (winter 1993): 17–19.

16. See Elsa Barkley Brown and Gregg D. Kimball, "Mapping the Terrain of Black Richmond," *Journal of Urban History* 21 (March 1995): 305, 309; Clark, "Celebrating Freedom," 110.

17. "Centennial Celebration of the Negro Baptists of Georgia . . . Programme," in Love, *History of the First African Baptist Church, From its Organization;* Reginald Hildebrand, *The Times Were Strange and Stirring: Methodist Preachers and the Crisis of Emancipation* (Durham, N.C.: Duke University Press, 1995), 56. The 1888 centennial celebration of the founding of the first Afro-American Baptist churches in Georgia lasted thirteen days, from June 6 to June 18. The program began each day at 9:00 a.m. and concluded with an 8:00 p.m. sermon.

18. It would be hard to know this though from current discussions of the Lost Cause movement which tend to ignore or summarily dismiss any connection between the construction of black Civil War memory and the Lost Cause Movement. Gaines M. Foster's valuable discussion of white southern Civil War memory is notable for the nuance of its portrayal of the movement's evolution. Foster is also notably vague about the precise content of the social tensions that he argues helped to seed the movement. The struggles of Afro-Americans figure not at all, by his account, in the construction of white southern memory. See Gaines M. Foster, *Ghosts of the Confederacy: Defeat, the Lost Cause, and the Emergence of the New South* (New York: Oxford University Press, 1987). O'Leary's work is an important exception. See, for example, O' Leary, *To Die For*, 89 and 110–49.

19. Alice Walker, "Elethia," in *You Can't Keep a Good Woman Down* (San Diego: Harcourt Brace Jovanovich, 1981), 30.

20. W.E.B. Du Bois, *The Souls of Black Folk*, in *W.E.B. Du Bois: Writings* (New York: Library of America, 1980), see esp. 478–91; quotes from 491.

21. O'Leary, *To Die For*, 87–88.

22. *Journal of the Twenty-Third National Convention of the Woman's Relief Corps: Auxiliary to the Grand Army of the Republic*, September 7th and 8th, 1905, Denver, Colorado, 57, 1153.

23. George P. Rawick, Jan Hillegas, and Ken Laurence, eds., *The American Slave: A Composite Autobiography*, Supplement, Series 1, vol. 6, Mississippi Narratives (Westport, Conn.: Greenwood Press, 1977), part 1, 8, 11, 13; Rawick, ed., *The American Slave: A Composite Autobiography*, Supplement, Series 1, vol. 5, Indiana Narratives (Westport, Conn.: Greenwood Press, 1977), 180.

24. Rawick, ed., Mississippi Narratives, Supplement, Series 1, p. 13.

25. Blight, "'For Something Beyond the Battlefield,'" 1162.

26. For an interesting discussion of Douglass's increasing detachment from the reality of Afro-American life in the South, see Angela Y. Davis, "From the Prison of Slavery to the Slavery of Prison: Frederick Douglass and the Convict Lease System," in Joy James, ed. *The Angela Y. Davis Reader* (Malden, Mass.: Blackwell Publishers, 1998), 74–95. It was only in the aftermath of a trip to South Carolina in 1888, writes Phillip Foner, that Douglass "realized how little he had known about the true conditions of his people in the South." Foner, quoted in Davis, "From the Prison," 76. My thanks to Adam Green for bringing this essay to my attention.

27. Speech of Hon. James M. Townsend, Emancipation Celebration, January 1, 1891, Alexandria, Virginia (hereafter cited as Townsend Speech).

28. By 1888 some 1,500 Afro-Baptist churches in Georgia were home to 166,429 black Baptists and 500 ordained preachers. C. T. Walker, in Love, *History of First African Baptist Church*, 207–11; for quote see Rev. S. A. McNeal, Address, "To the President and Members of the Centennial Committee of the Negro Baptists of Georgia, and of the Grand Mother Church of Negro Baptists," in Love, *History of the First African Baptist Church*, 219. For the location of the Front Street Church, see Map of Savannah, 1885, http://www.lib.utexas.edu/maps/historical/savannah_1885.jpg

29. Rev. C. T. Walker, "What God Hath Wrought Providentially," in Love, *History of the First African Baptist Church*, 212. The idea that Emancipation was the work of God represented a distinct theme that was sometimes linked by black intellectuals to African American agency and sometimes not. In the latter framework, the idea sustained probably the most conservative interpretation of emancipation: while the Lord, "the God of Battles," fought the slaveholders, slaves who "firmly believed they would live to be free" waited patiently and humbly "till God broke their chains." William J. Simmons, *Men of Mark: Eminent, Progressive and Rising* (1887; reprint, New York: Arno Press, 1968), 7. See also William E. Montgomery, *Under Their Own Vine and Fig Tree: The African-American Church in the South, 1865–1900* (Baton Rouge: Louisiana State University Press, 1993), 246–47. Douglass viewed the war as an "instrument of a higher power."

30. Rev. E. K. Love, "Oration Delivered on Emancipation Day," January 2, 1888,

Savannah Tribune, http://memory.loc.gov. Emanuel King Love was born into slavery in 1850 in Alabama. He became pastor of First African Baptist in Savannah in 1885. For biographical information on Love, see Simmons, *Men of Mark*, 481–83; and Carter G. Woodson, *The History of the Negro Church* (Washington, D.C.: The Associated Publishers, 1921), 260–65.

31. Love, "Oration Delivered on Emancipation Day."

There were of course others who preached that emancipation was largely the work of Lincoln. The contrary belief, however, remained strong into the twentieth century. In the late twentieth century, for example, a black worker testified to the persistence of this critical tradition: "Then, another thing: Abraham Lincoln—my perception of the Emancipation Proclamation—freeing the slaves—was only done to win the war." The interview was conducted in the mid-1990s. The respondent also noted that while he acknowledged George Washington as the nation's first president, he found incomprehensible the idea of Washington as the father of the country. Roy Rosenzweig and David Thelen, *The Presence of the Past: Popular Uses of History in American Life* (New York: Columbia University Press, 1998), 153.

32. Love, *History of the First African Baptist Church*, 177. The entry on Hayes also notes that he was pensioned "but not near so much as he should be."

33. Bishop Daniel Alexander Payne, *Recollections of Seventy Years* (1888; reprint, New York: Arno Press, 1969), 145, 148. Payne was free-born in Charleston, South Carolina, in 1811.

34. Hildebrand, *The Times Were Strange and Stirring*, 56.

35. Love, *History of the First African Baptist Church*, 202. See also C. T. Walker, in Love, *History of the First African Baptist Church*, 202; and William J. Walls, *The African Methodist Episcopal Zion Church: Reality of the Black Church* (Charlotte, N.C.: AME Zion Publishing House, 1974), 391. Such evidence seems to demonstrate the determination and capacity of ex-slaves to locate themselves within the history of slavery and emancipation. For a different view, see David Blight, who argues that it was "the post-generation challenging the slavery generation" to remember slavery and emancipation. See Blight, "Fifty Years of Freedom," 121.

36. Sermon by Rev. C. T. Walker, in Love, *History of the First African Baptist Church*, 210, 212. Walker's sermon on the occasion of the 100th anniversary celebration (July 1, 1888) of the First African Baptist Church of Savannah included the reading of an excerpt from W. M. Brown's *Jamaica, Past and Present*, documenting diasporic connections between Afro-Americans and black Jamaicans. These programs also featured speeches calling for the support of black writers as well as the industrial trades and entrepreneurial enterprise. Importantly, however, speakers urging industrial education were just as likely in the next sentence to offer support for a broad-based liberal arts education and emphasize the need for education on the contributions of black people to the United States from colonial times.

37. D. B. Williams, Emancipation Day Speech, January 2, 1893. Williams's remarks remind us that, contrary to the conclusion reached by Clark ("Celebrating

Freedom," 125), these celebrations remained forums for radical critiques of American society into the 1890s. George Leile, for example, "the black apostle" of Georgia and Jamaica and a former slave, was considered one of the "*colored* martyrs." On Leile, see Walker, in Love, *History of the First African Baptist Church*, A.

38. Elsa Barkley Brown, "Negotiating and Transforming the Public Sphere: African American Political Life in the Transition from Slavery to Freedom," *Public Culture 7* (1994): 107–46.

39. S. A. McNeal, in Love, *History of the First African Baptist Church*, A.

40. Love, "Oration Delivered on Emancipation Day." Historian Wilson J. Moses contends that while Douglass's marriage to Helen Pitts "has no doubt contributed to the opinion that he was antinationalistic," it was of no consequence to his standing among black people. Indeed, Moses writes, "the fact of marriage to a white woman has never invalidated the credentials of any black nationalist." See Wilson Jeremiah Moses, *The Golden Age of Black Nationalism, 1850–1925* (Hamden, Conn.: Archon Books, 1978), 84, 282 n. 3. Love's analysis tempers this assessment.

41. Love, "Oration Delivered on Emancipation Day."

42. Love, "Oration Delivered on Emancipation Day."

43. Townsend Speech.

44. Townsend Speech. Indeed, wrote one Afro-American, black people in the South should congratulate themselves for "the fact that a change in the political aspect of our national government has not dampened your ardor in keeping green and fresh the memories of our freedom and achievements." D. B. Williams to B. F. Fox, Petersburg, Virginia. http://memory.loc.gov.

45. Love, "Oration Delivered on Emancipation Day."

46. Love, "Oration Delivered on Emancipation Day."

47. Townsend Speech. The subject of Afro-American women's participation in Emancipation Day ceremonies has received the least attention from scholars. In her study cited above, Kathleen Clark argues that "African-American commemorative culture was defined and expressed in substantially gendered terms" with the programs largely controlled by men ("Celebrating Freedom," 122). Sermon-making was the most gendered aspect of the culture, but there was flexibility in other aspects of the programs. Black women routinely, for example, were given the part of reading aloud the Emancipation Proclamation. According to a male participant in twentieth-century celebrations, it was "an honor to be chosen to read the Emancipation Proclamation" (Wiggins, 117).

48. Gramsci, *Selections from the Prison Notebooks of Antonio Gramsci*, edited and translated by Quintin Hoare and Geoffrey Nowell Smith (New York: International Publishers, 1997), 273. An "understanding of the state," Gramsci also notes, "exists not only when one defends it, but also when one attacks it in order to overthrow it" (*Selections*, 275).

49. Scholars have pointed to a similar experience among southern yeomen

who during the secession crisis and Civil War, Eric Foner writes, "discovered themselves as a political class." Foner, *Reconstruction: America's Unfinished Revolution, 1863–1877* (New York: Harper and Row, 1988), 13. Alfred F. Young's study of the experience of Boston shoemaker George Robert Twelves Hewes in the American Revolution is a brilliant exploration of the process by which ordinary people gain what Young calls "a sense of citizenship and personal worth." The Revolution, Young writes, provided an "affirmation of [Hewes's] worth as a human being" and thus "a form of class consciousness." Alfred F. Young, "George Robert Twelves Hewes (1742–1840): A Boston Shoemaker and the Memory of the American Revolution," *William and Mary Quarterly* 38 (October 1981): 599. I am indebted to Lil Fenn for bringing Young's work to my attention.

50. Clearly, this would depend on individual circumstances and would have been influenced as well by such matters as geography, the nature of the crop, and demographic patterns particularly within individual slave communities and among neighboring slave communities. As many of the WPA slave narratives along with those by Douglass, Harriet Jacobs, and other fugitive slaves attest, slaves often arrived at sophisticated critiques of the race and class dimensions at the heart of American slavery prior to the Civil War. Indeed it would have been impossible to exist in the system without some critique of it.

51. Townsend Speech.

52. Theodore Rosengarten, ed., *All God's Dangers: The Life of Nate Shaw* (New York: Vintage Books, 1989), 542–43.

53. Testimony of R. R. Wright, *Report of the Committee of the Senate upon the Relations between Labor and Capital: Testimony*, vol. 4 (Washington, D.C.: Government Printing Office, 1885), 812–15. Assertions of past African and Afro-American achievements indeed were ubiquitous in Afro-American oratory in the late nineteenth and early twentieth centuries. See, for example, Hildebrand, *The Times Were Strange and Stirring*, 56.

54. Selwyn R. Cudjoe, "'Eric E. Williams Speaks': An Address," Lecture delivered at Port of Spain, Trinidad, October 23, 1993 (n.p.).

55. Herbert G. Gutman, "Historical Consciousness in Contemporary America," in *Power and Culture: Essays on the American Working Class*, ed. Ira Berlin (New York: New Press, 1987), 395–412; quotations are from 400.

56. Eliza Frances Andrews, *The War-Time Journal of a Georgia Girl, 1864–1865*, ed. Spencer Bidwell King Jr. (1908; reprint, Macon: Ardivan Press, 1960), 371. For an extended discussion of this phenomenon, see Foster, *Ghosts of the Confederacy*, and O'Leary, *To Die For*.

57. Frederick Douglass, *The Life and Times of Frederick Douglass* (1892; revised reprint, New York: Collier Books, 1962), 153–54.

58. As Gaines M. Foster demonstrates, immediately after the war white southerners had generally embraced the notion that slavery had been its primary cause,

but by the end of the nineteenth century they had essentially rejected this position. Reunion sentiment at the same time smoothed over the most difficult political issues that had engaged Northerners and Southerners before and during the war.

59. Gaines Foster argues that a similar threat from poor white southerners was effectively contained by the Lost Cause movement. See Foster, *Ghosts of the Confederacy*.

60. Rebecca Cameron to [U. D. C. Chapter Historians], September 8, 1903; Memorial Day Edition Flyer, 19 April 1912, in S. R. Cameron Files, Cameron Papers, Southern Historical Collection, Wilson Library, University of North Carolina; Du Bois, *Black Reconstruction in America*, 716.

61. A large body of interdisciplinary literature, for example, embodies the idea that the memories of former slaves (and black people and the oppressed in general) constitute counter-memories. See, for example, Lipsitz, *Time Passages*, and Michel Foucault, *Language, Counter-Memory, Practice: Selected Essays and Interviews*, ed. Donald F. Bouchard, trans. Sherry Simon (Ithaca, N.Y.: Cornell University Press, 1980).

62. W. M. Poisson to President Johnson, April 18, 1866, Records of the Assistant Commissioner, North Carolina, ser. 2452, Box 1, P-53, A-559. On the proper role ascribed to Afro-Americans in Lost Cause narratives, see Foster, *Ghosts of the Confederacy*, 136, 140.

63. See Foster, *Ghosts of the Confederacy*, 153–56; and O'Leary, *To Die For*, 200–201, 203. Foster concludes, wrongly I think, that the Lost Cause movement but negligibly concerned Afro-Americans. O'Leary, on the other hand, emphasizes the central role of racism in the construction of Lost Cause propaganda (see O'Leary, 203).

64. Matthew Page Andrews, *American History and Government* (Philadelphia: J. B. Lippincott, 1921), 361 n. 24.

65. Du Bois, *Black Reconstruction in America*, 713–14.

66. John Bodnar, *Remaking America: Public Memory, Commemoration, and Patriotism in the Twentieth Century* (Princeton, N.J.: Princeton University Press, 1992), 209–10. In general see Bodnar's insightful discussion of the Civil War Centennial, 206–26. "Ordinary foot soldiers," he writes, "were transformed into model human beings who followed their leaders and fought for the larger political structures in which they lived." Bodnar also reminds us of Robert E. Lee's reconstruction after the war as "a great and knightly *American* soldier and citizen"—not as a great Confederate soldier but as an American patriot (209–10, emphasis added). The effort by the commission to project an image of a harmonious past foundered. The American Negro Emancipation Centennial Authority of Chicago, for example, refused its premise, recalling a different past and present. The refusal of the headquarters hotel in Charleston, South Carolina, where the meeting of the national commission was scheduled in 1961, to register a black member of the New Jersey Centennial Commission because of her race led some northern and western

state delegations to threaten to leave. The meeting was moved to the Charleston Naval Base. Still southern white delegates boycotted the integrated opening luncheon and held a separate opening luncheon of the "Confederate States Convention." The state of Alabama spent $100,000 to commemorate the inauguration of Confederate president Jefferson Davis (211–13). On Frederick Douglass's opposition to an undifferentiated ideological interpretation of the war, see Blight, "'For Something Beyond the Battlefield,'" 1162.

67. Manuel Fenollosa, "Emancipation Hymn," June 1863, Library of Congress. Fenollosa's hymn was composed for and dedicated to the Salem, Massachusetts Union League.

68. Quoted in Gutman, *Power and Culture*, 402.

69. Franklin, "A Century of Civil War Observation." See also Charles S. Wesley, "The Civil War and the Negro-American," *Journal of Negro History* 47 (April 1962): 77–96.

70. Du Bois, *Black Reconstruction in America*, 714.

Part II

"As Though They Had Never Been Born"
Forgotten Movements

Our view of African American struggle in the early twentieth century has been dominated by towering figures like Du Bois and Washington and Garvey, by such major social disruptions as the Great War and the Great Migration. Even when we look beyond national leaders, when, for example, we think of the New Negro, the phrase usually evokes the growing postwar militancy in the urban North. The struggles chronicled here by Ortiz, Woodruff, and de Jong contradict or modify much of this. Like the Black populist movement, the rural (or, in the case of Ortiz, statewide) movements they look at achieved few of their manifest goals, but they still tell us much about the capacity of African Americans to keep the struggle alive under the most adverse circumstances.

St. Clair Drake and Horace Cayton described Black residents of Chicago in the 1940s as "thoroughly American in their acceptance of . . . optimistic dogmas of progress."[1] There must have been some similar streak of optimism among the leadership of pre- and post–World War I rural communities. This is not to suggest that they didn't understand how high the odds were against which they were struggling. Nevertheless, given an opening— the destabilizing effect of the war, the possibility of help from the Federal level—they were quickly able to mobilize their communities despite the planter control that seeped into virtually all areas of sharecropper life. This ability suggests some pre-existing faith in new possibilities.

A somewhat different picture emerges in some Jim Crow urban communities in the South, according to Brian Kelly. In Birmingham, Alabama —seat of New South dreams of both industrial expansion and "modernized" racial codes of paternalistic control of Black workers and client obligation among Black elites—both the militancy of mine workers and the sycophancy of the early bourgeoisie proved little match for the relentless white desire for social control. Though scholars such as Tera Hunter and

Glenda Gilmore have written compellingly about Black resistance else-where in the Urban South, even they acknowledge, as Kelly does here, that the years following the turn of the century proved a time when, paradox-ically, conditions of Jim Crow bore down with particular intensity on urban African Americans of all classes. That middle-class Black Birming-hamians linked their fate with that of local workers with condescension, rather than a spirit of cooperation, no doubt indicates that the influence of the region's most modern and ambitious industrialists ultimately proved irresistible. It also indicates, though, that Black activism in urban areas of the Jim Crow South was an oddly difficult proposition, given the con-founding aspect of the labor question for Black as well as white elites at this time and the high penalties for those seen as subversive to the emerg-ing racial order.

Harry T. Moore was an NAACP activist killed in Florida in 1951 (see the essay in this volume by Caroline Emmons). A 1999 book by Ben Green gives Moore the signal honor of being "America's first civil rights martyr."[2] The fact that such disinformation could slip through the editorial process at a major publishing house suggests again the degree to which popular understanding of African American struggle is dominated by reference to the 1960s, pushing into obscurity everything that happened before that, in-cluding the long line of martyrs who preceded Harry Moore.

Not just individuals but whole movements get lost. Paul Ortiz performs a valuable service in recovering one such movement, the 1919–20 struggle of Black Floridians for the right to vote. When we think of civil rights ac-tivist groups, we are hardly likely to think of fraternal organizations, but Afro-Floridians found "free space" for organizing in lodges, labor unions, women's clubs, mutual aid societies, and secret societies—in everyday as-sociations. Along with human and material resources, these groups helped nurture a distinctive sense of the African American past. Like Glymph, Ortiz finds that Emancipation Days and other deliberate attempts to shape a Black public memory "bolstered African American pride and claims to equality." Postwar mobilization for the right to vote may have looked rapid to outsiders, but in fact Florida Black communities had been nurturing the necessary organizational and spiritual resources over decades. In Florida, Ortiz says, the New Negro had gray hair.

While Ortiz makes a powerful case that Floridians were building pri-marily on indigenous resources, Greta de Jong and Michael Honey point to the impact of external strategies and organizers—specifically those con-

nected to the radical wing of the labor movement—in focusing mass grievances in the countryside of Louisiana and on the shop floors of Memphis.
The way indigenous and outside resources come together—or work at cross
purposes—is something we have to understand anew in every case.

On the other hand, these articles are essentially of one mind in the way
they describe the power structure—the degree to which the key issue for
whites of standing was labor control, the lengths to which whites were
willing to go in order to break Black militancy, the collusion of govern-
mental authorities at all levels, the difficulty whites had wiping out resistance completely, even after massive violence. They also paint the same
picture of the way Black communities were able to use religious belief—
not always the church, but religious belief—and of the way "nonpolitical"
organizations could be turned to political account.

Billie Holiday first sang her haunting anti-lynching melody, "Strange
Fruit," in 1939. A recent book on the song's social impact is subtitled "An
Early Cry for Civil Rights."[3] What does "early" mean in this context? Apparently, it just means prior to the movement of the 1950s and 1960s. In
fact, "Strange Fruit" wasn't an early cry for anything; it was a very late cry
for justice. This is just one example of the kind of conceptual silliness we
invite when we treat the "civil rights movement" as an omnibus term for
the fight for racial justice and center it in the mid-fifties to mid-sixties, ignoring and devaluing the struggles documented here by Woodruff, Ortiz,
de Jong, and Honey. The post–World War II movement becomes the
touchstone by which all African American struggle is judged and understood, guaranteeing that we will in fact misunderstand much of it, as, for
example, when Malcolm X is referred to as a "civil rights leader," a way of
summarizing his work that might have made him smile.

The "civil rights" terminology doesn't necessarily evoke issues of economic justice, which means there is a degree of class bias in using that
term as the all-purpose label for African American struggle. As early as the
1930s, part of the critique of the NAACP was that it was insufficiently concerned with the economic issues that mattered most to the Black masses.
The historian Adam Fairclough points out that the Depression "made the
organization's stress on individual rights appear more attuned than ever to
the interests of the black middle class." Working-class advocate A. Philip
Randolph spoke for many when he argued that the "old policy of defending Negroes rights is well-nigh bankrupt."[4] Greta de Jong notes that the
central problem of most African Americans' lives was making a living. For

the working-class populations she, Ortiz, Honey, and Woodruff are describing, we can be certain that there was no way to conceive of freedom that did not include economic well-being; but when most Americans think of the civil rights struggle they are unlikely to visualize fights over job classifications, acreage allotments, segregated union locals, and the price of hoe hands. Referring to the mid-1960s, Robert Norrell notes that while the general white public was reluctant to recognize the economic component of the freedom struggle, "Few activists ever actually separated economic objectives from the political ones except to decide which was addressed first."[5] The passage of the 1964 Civil Rights Act was certainly understood as a liberating moment by most Black Americans; but for Black women (to take one example), it may have been no more liberating than the day they walked out of Miss Ann's kitchen and into a factory job at union wages (which brought its own problems, of course, as Michael Honey demonstrates). Marginalizing the struggle for decent pay and decent treatment at work marginalizes working-class Black life. It cannot be accidental that of the two largest mass movements among African Americans, populism and the Garvey movement, one was essentially an economic appeal and the other was so to a significant degree.

Certainly, knowing the history of the Black struggle for economic justice militates against the tendency to identify the African American struggle with charismatic, clerical leadership. You don't build unions by just making good speeches and appealing to conscience. It also militates against that part of the national discourse that begins with the proposition that the civil rights revolution was won in the 1960s ("A great victory for all Americans") and then uses that as the basis for questioning Black militancy ("You people have come a long way, after all").

The irony is that the "great-victory-for-all-Americans" rhetoric is true but in ways people are unlikely to think about. It is true in the sense that the struggle of Black people to destroy occupational barriers made it easier for other excluded groups, including white women, to attack similar barriers. It is true in the sense that the movement forced the rationalization of the Southern political economy, bringing archaic social, economic, and political structures into alignment with modern economic practice, creating new job opportunities for some of the same white men who had fought the movement the longest. In popular parlance, "civil rights movement" comes to mean "something for the Blacks," obscuring the question of what it did for Americans as a whole.

"Critical citizenship" implies a struggle not for self alone but for a revisioning of the American possibility that at times encompassed all citizens. Bernice Reagon (1979) calls the modern civil rights struggle "the borning struggle" because it did so much to generate and sustain the other struggles of the 1960s. Framing it just as a movement for Blacks obscures its centrality in the postwar remaking of American democracy. Some of the angriest forms of Black political activities, even if formally separatist, may still reflect a profound citizenship. It is very clear that Garvey and Malcolm X were both fighting for the respect of white America, implying some surviving form of imagined community, of citizenship. (And it may be that one of the crucial mistakes made by Black nationalists of the 1960s and 1970s was their failure to appreciate the extent to which Black discontent was still rooted in citizenship.)

In the last chapter of *Black Reconstruction*, titled "The Propaganda of History," Du Bois asserts that the nineteenth-century efforts of Blacks and their allies constituted "the finest effort to achieve democracy for the working millions." Yet, "we discern in it no part of our labor movement, no part of our industrial triumph and no part of our religious experience."[6] In the same sense, the idea of the "civil rights movement," as popularly construed, is the language of denial, to hearken back for a moment to the Peter Wood article, a language that makes a conceptual ghetto of the subject matter, obscuring the ways in which struggles for racial justice have created a more open field for all Americans.

It wouldn't be difficult to construct a typology of racial denial by ideology. Right denial just denies the reality of oppression altogether or admits it but frames it as non-actionable: "We never did nothing to them, but if we did, it was for their own good and even if it was wrong it was a long time ago and the best thing we can do now is put all that behind us and move on." Liberal analysis affirms the problem but not its institutional and structural dimensions. "It's ignorance and prejudice, people need to be educated; it's a moral problem; race is just a social construction anyway; we just need more interracial cooperation." Left denial affirms the structural dimensions of the problem but frames them in nonracial terms—"It's an epi-phenomenon, it's really just class, race is super-structural"—with little independent analytical value.

One could find examples of all of these forms of denial among labor historians, including a questionable emphasis on interracial solidarity as a vehicle of change. In his detailed discussion of the role of race in American labor history, Herbert Hill points out the tendency to "celebrate the episodic occurrences of interracial solidarity while ignoring the overall historical pattern."[7] Obviously, from populism's early days through the CIO struggles of the 1930s through Mississippi Summer in 1964, there have been moments when interracialism pushed the movement forward. Hill is warning against the tendency to exaggerate it, to naturalize it, to underestimate the difficulties of sustaining it, as, for example, when we treat a few years of interracial cooperation in the South in the early 1960s as the real movement and treat the end of the period as a great problematic, as if Blacks and whites just ought to be able to get along.

Michael Honey, in contrast, shows us interracial solidarity in the midst of constant, sometimes agonizing racial tension. One has to wonder where a union organizer like George Holloway got the moral stamina to go on building a union for men who tried to kill him, who heaped indignities on him at every opportunity? The only comment Holloway makes about it points in the direction of looking at the kinds of communities these people came from and the collective memory developed there: "My parents taught me something. They taught me."

Whatever that was, we can wonder whether Holloway's generation was able to teach it to their own children. That is one way to think about the differences between the generation that made the transition from field to factory and the generation that followed. Honey finds that some of the latter generation did not appreciate the struggle of their elders, did not necessarily even understand their lives as having been about struggle. They thought the older people had been too humble, too willing to let white folks do anything to them. The parental generation was an object of shame, not one of veneration. Perhaps this kind of disremembrance reflects some erosion of the earlier optimism about the ultimate ability of the country to make a place for Black people. Perhaps it means that the younger generation had so thoroughly accepted masculinist conceptions of social respect that they could no longer appreciate the more communal understanding of their parents.

Hugh Mulzac, a captain of the Black Star Line, described the events that led him to Marcus Garvey's movement: the "outrageous discrimination" Blacks faced during the war; the "vicious murders and pogroms" that greeted Black troops returning from the war; the disappointment of migrants who left the South only to learn that "social abuse, debasement, the thwarting of ambition, caricature and the disparagement of their culture" were hardly strangers to the North and the "deep-seated unconcern" with which the Wilson and Harding administrations viewed it all. This is the context, according to Mulzac, that set the stage for Garvey and his Universal Negro Improvement Association, by most reckonings the largest single political organization in African American history. It is normally thought of as a model of patriarchal organization. It is instructive, then, to find Ula Taylor arguing that, at crucial moments during that organization's development, women played pivotal roles in it, sometimes by maneuvering around chauvinism, sometimes by openly confronting it. Indeed, in its earliest years the UNIA had a policy that each chapter would have both a male and a female president and vice president, anticipating the same policy in the National Black Independent Party by sixty years.

It is important to know that progressive tendencies on gender were present in the Garvey movement but hardly surprising that they were always contested. Constitutionally, the woman president of each local was required to report to her male counterpart, although Winston James reports that some locals functioned on an egalitarian basis.[8] At the 1922 Convention, James reports, a majority of the women delegates signed a set of resolutions seeking to improve the status of women in the organization "so that the Negro Women all over the world can function without restriction from men" (139). James notes that "the role of women within the UNIA declined in inverse proportion to the size of the movement" (138). Women were relatively more influential as the movement was forming, less so when it was at the height of its powers and again more so when the organization went into decline. It would not be surprising to find that James is describing a general pattern. What we know about the participation patterns of women in the Deep South in the movement of the 1960s seems roughly consistent with the idea that leadership from women is accepted while the movement is struggling but that once it has won some victories there is a regression to traditional gender patterns of leadership. The pushing of women out of public space in late-nineteenth-century Richmond described by Elsa Barkley Brown might be another example of the same pattern.

When Garvey first set foot on a Harlem stage, it was A. Philip Randolph, one of Harlem's ranking Black socialists, who had made the arrangements for the talk, an appropriate symbol of the bond, sometimes antagonistic, sometimes symbiotic, that would shape the relationship of Black nationalism and Black socialism for the rest of the century. While our images of Black socialists start with the Depression, Winston James (whose *Holding Aloft the Banner of Ethiopia* may be the closest thing we have to a diasporic theory of activism) demonstrates that African American interest in socialist alternatives has a long history. Peter Humphries is among the earliest of whom we have a record. By turns putting his faith in emigration, socialism, the Republican Party, the Democratic Party, and the Black church, Humphries captures in miniature the restless searching of many a Black activist, willing to try this weapon or that, willing explore programs and ideologies. This contrasts with the rigidity that has characterized many socialist overtures to Black Americans, from the Workingmen's Party in the nineteenth century through the Progressive Labor Party in the 1970s. However powerful their critique of exploitation, socialists have frequently underestimated how much of the fight has always been a response to the "social abuse, debasement . . . disparagement" that Mulzac spoke of. Critics derided the theatricality and pomposity of the Garvey movement, but those very features allowed Garvey to penetrate the lives of people who needed assurances of their self-worth as much as they needed better jobs. The masculinist posturing of the Black Panther Party allowed them to put a socialist agenda before young Black men, who almost certainly would not have been receptive to the usual means of Left organizing. The question, always, is how one shapes a politics that resonates with the daily life experiences of Blacks without simultaneously pandering to regressive social values. Socialists are hardly alone in their inability to answer that question.

NOTES

1. St. Clair Drake and Horace Cayton, *Black Metropolis: A Study of Negro Life in a Northern City*, vol. 2 (New York: Harper and Row, 1962), 716.

2. Ben Green, *Before His Time: The Untold Story of Harry T. Moore, America's First Civil Rights Martyr* (New York: Free Press, 1999).

3. David Margolick, *Billie Holiday, Café Society and an Early Cry for Civil Rights* (Philadelphia: Running Press, 2000).

4. Adam Fairclough, *Better Day Coming: Blacks and Equality, 1890–2000* (New York: Viking, 2001), 147, 152.

5. Robert Norrell, "The One Thing We Did Right: Reflections on the Movement," in (eds.) *New Directions in Civil Rights Studies*, ed. Armisted Robinson and Patricia Sullivan (Charlottesville: University of Virginia Press, 1991), 76.

6. W.E.B. Du Bois, *Black Reconstruction* (New York: Harcourt, Brace and Co., 1935), 727.

7. Herbert Hill, "The Problem of Race in American Labor History," *Reviews in*

American History 24 (1996) 190; see also Hill, "Lichtenstein's Fictions: Meany, Reuther and the 1964 Civil Rights Act," *New Politics* 7 (Summer 1998).

8. Winston James, *Holding Aloft the Banner of Ethiopia: Caribbean Radicalism in Early Twentieth-Century America* (London: Verso, 1998), 140.

Chapter 5

The New Negro in the American Congo
World War I and the Elaine, Arkansas Massacre of 1919

Nan Elizabeth Woodruff

The Red Summer of 1919 following World War I marked a year of violence and terror across the United States. Racial confrontations swept the nation, and not simply in the urban centers of Washington and Chicago, but throughout the hinterlands—in Omaha, Longview, Charleston, and in the plantation region of the Arkansas Delta. African Americans, emboldened by the war meant to make the world safe for democracy, returned to delta towns and villages to demand their political and economic rights. In Phillips County, Arkansas, this struggle found expression through the Progressive Farmers and Household Union, who sought to secure a just price for the sharecroppers' cotton. This legal action directly challenged planter dominance and led to an extensive massacre of African American men, women, and children.

The Elaine Massacre represented the planters' brutal response to the growing African American assertiveness and independence that stemmed from the changes wrought by World War I in the Arkansas Delta. The war created new opportunities for southern black people: thousands migrated north to find jobs in the wartime economy, leaving those behind in a stronger bargaining position; and military service abroad politicized black soldiers. Whether black workers went to Chicago, stayed in Arkansas, or went to France, their changed social and economic condition led them to press the limits of planter power and to insist upon a more just life for their families and communities.

The Arkanas Delta was a major sector of the "New South" plantation economy that emerged in the late nineteenth and early twentieth centuries.[1] Ambitious entrepreneurs from the flagging southeastern cotton region or the Midwest joined lumber and railroad companies from Chicago, Memphis, New York, and St. Louis to carve out large-scale cotton plantations worked mainly by black sharecroppers and tenant farmers. Since the 1880s, labor agents had lured black workers and families to the region with promises of tropical abundance and high wages. Instead of Eden, workers found a "hellhole" of ruthless landowners who hired on shares, forced their tenants to purchase all supplies at planter-owned commissaries, and kept them in perpetual debt regardless of the size of the harvest. It was a region notorious for peonage and brutality: planter violence underwrote the social relations that defined delta society, and the mechanisms of the government enforced and legitimated the oppression.[2]

The expansion of sharecropping and tenant farming into the Arkansas and Mississippi Delta developed simultaneously with the legal framework of segregation and disfranchisement—together, they shaped the contours of life and work in the Age of Jim Crow that stretched into the 1960s. This modern alluvial empire was characterized by a polity that defined citizenship in terms of race and that drew little distinction between the functions of the state, or government, and those of civil society.[3] Legal disfranchisement, sanctioned by the United States Supreme Court, forced African Americans to negotiate with employers for whatever they could get. Planters controlled those offices that bore directly on their interests. Wherever black people turned, they encountered a world overseen by constables and justices of the peace who arbitrarily enforced vagrancy laws, by sheriffs who engaged in peonage by providing planters with vagrants when they needed labor, by plantation managers who also served as deputies, by planters who had the power to protect their workers from arrest or to send them to the state penitentiary, and by enough lynchings to remind black people of the costs involved in defying their oppressors. To survive, workers depended on the precarious good will of employers for protection from local authorities and the courts.[4]

By removing African Americans from the realm of citizenship through segregation and disfranchisement, employers could intervene in areas of their workers' lives that in liberal democracies are the preserve of civil society. Planters extended their authority into workers' private or cultural space, into their families, homes, churches, and lodges. Through commissaries, planters determined what croppers ate, wore, or purchased for their homes, while lien laws allowed them to seize the laborers' every possession.[5] Employers built the churches and schools and paid the preachers and teachers. Most croppers received their mail through the commissary, allowing regulation of what they read and of the people with whom they corresponded. Planters even withheld mail until the crops were gathered, to ensure that workers remained on the plantation through the harvest.

There were moments, however, when developments outside the region created possibilities for black people to test the limits of planters' authority and to press forward their inclusive notions of citizenship and the attendant challenges to segregation, the sharecropping system, and disfranchisement. World War I created new economic opportunities for both men and women plantation workers, while military service abroad politicized black soldiers. Both threatened planters' dominance.

The Great Migration of southern black people formed one of the major historical developments in twentieth-century American history. As many scholars have shown, southern workers went north seeking not only economic improvement, but better education, housing, and a chance to exercise their civil rights.[6] However, some southern black people remained at home to secure the benefits of a wartime economy in the South. This was especially true in the Arkansas Delta, where hundreds of families crossed over the river from Mississippi, escaping the boll weevil and hoping to find better wages, fairer landlords, and perhaps even the opportunity of landownership in the rapidly expanding plantation economy.

Often migrants secured land rights, but the majority found a world much like the one they had left behind in Mississippi. For as the region geared up to fight the war, planters pressed their workers harder and with more help than usual from the federal government. Wartime demand for foodstuffs and cotton led to further consolidation of lands along the Arkansas side of the Mississippi River and its tributaries as lumber companies built canals and drainage ditches.[7] The labor regime required by land expansion clashed with black workers' determination to improve their working conditions. Pointing to new job options, plantation laborers who remained on the land bargained for better wages, driving them from a prewar sixty cents per hundred pounds of picked cotton to two dollars per hundredweight by 1917. Daily earnings in the companion industries of the cotton oil, compress, and lumber mills shot up from $1.25 to $2.00. In 1918, daily wages had climbed on both sides of the river to $4.50.[8]

Workers found other ways to test planter authority over labor relations. Arkansas Delta planters blamed laborers in 1917 for a slow harvest and loss of crops. "Negro farm hands," they claimed, had been "demanding and receiving weekly settlements, and upon being paid quitting work until their money was spent."[9] In Desha County, landlords blamed high wages for "irregular" work habits. "Negroes," they complained, who "used to gladly work six days in the week now work three or four and idle about the rest of the time, or work a few days at one place and quit and go to another."[10]

Rural laborers' refusal to work according to planter rules, and their determination to claim family and leisure time as their own, concerned not only employers, but also the federal government. National wartime mobilization spawned a liberal state apparatus that touched southern life in ways not experienced since Reconstruction.[11] The decentralized nature of government agencies handed authority for administering the wartime programs to the planter class, who made vital decisions through the state and local Councils of Defense, which were composed of landowners, businessmen, bankers, and agricultural extension agents. These local councils mobilized labor, aided local draft boards in securing inductees, conducted Liberty Bond drives and food conservation campaigns, instilled loyalty, and monitored communities and plantations for subversion.[12]

Such an all-encompassing mission allowed planters and local officials to further extend their power into plantation community life. Concerns centering on labor control underwrote all other aspects of the mobilization effort. People accused of sedition were often labor organizers or agents, while many draft dodgers were croppers who refused to work for low wages.[13] The U.S. Department of Agriculture required its county agents to report to the War Department on the morale of their subjects as well as their attitude toward the military and the draft. Agricultural agents thus became spies.[14] Federal wartime agencies, then, like the Committee for Public Information, the Military Intelligence Division, and Herbert Hoover's Food Administration Conservation Campaigns, by operating through a decentralized structure of local committees, handed enormous power to a regional elite that hardly needed empowering.

African Americans' commitment to the war effort worried federal and Delta civic leaders: 66 percent of those drafted in Arkansas did not answer the call.[15] Arkansas Governor Charles H. Brough argued that the failure of black men to enlist resulted not from disloyalty but from ignorance, illiteracy, and their "moving disposition."[16] A local postmaster may have been closer to the truth when he observed that many men simply left their notices in their mailboxes, hoping that "through ignorance they believed they will not be drafted."[17] Resistance to the draft throughout the Delta region as a whole was illustrated dramatically in Memphis, where three thousand African Americans tried to flee across the river to Arkansas to avoid police rounding up "recruits" for a registration day. U.S. marshals came and dragged them off the boats.[18] The "slacker" problem in the Arkansas Delta persisted throughout the war. In the summer of 1918, Phillips County draft officials blamed their low recruitment numbers on the labor agents who had recruited "hundreds upon hundreds of Negroes" to places all over the country. Thus, many "slackers" were actually employed outside the region, though none had left forwarding addresses.[19] A national draft inspector found that the Arkansas Selective Service had a "higher degree of activity ... in regard to deserters than has yet come under his observation."[20]

Another war-related irritant to planters concerned the allotments paid to black soldiers who then sent the money to their wives, sisters, parents, and grandparents. The outside income allowed family members some independence from the planters. Women in particular gained some economic latitude with this arrangement. According to one observer in Desha County, Arkansas, "the worst feature of the labor question is the domestic, or Negro women labor," who quit work due to the increasing earnings of menfolk or relatives in the military. This travesty, he continued, had undermined the war efforts of women who had worked for the Red Cross, Liberty Loan drives, and other wartime organizations. "It looks hard that the white women who are striving so hard to assist in the war should sacrifice so much and undergo so many hardships and the Negro women live in ease and idleness." Moreover, black women refused to work in other jobs they considered demeaning. For the first time, small businesses like steam laundries employed white women. To the consternation of employers, they could not compel black women to work; their independent income sheltered them from vagrancy laws.[21]

When planters in Pine Bluff complained about black women's refusal to work as domestics or to pick cotton, one black leader observed that the "labor question" was "simply the old story of the white people not being able to adjust themselves to the new order of things." Noting that the cost of living had increased 100 percent and that white people's wages had also grown dramatically, he argued that white people seemed "to think that the Negro is such a financial wizard that he can make the Wages [sic] of ten years ago" and still live with the inflationary growth in the cost of living. "Negro women have not refused to work," he insisted, when employers paid adequate wages. However, many have refused to pick cotton for seventy-five cents or a dollar per hundredweight, for that was their wage when cotton brought ten cents per pound rather than the wartime price of thirty-five cents. Instead of dodging work, black women worked in railroad shops, sawmills, and other wartime jobs for three dollars a day rather than as domestics for three dollars a week.[22] Although black women did not serve in the military, they fought their own struggles at home as they looked to consolidate opportunities previously denied them.

Local defense councils cooperated with planters in securing and retaining a labor force. Prominent black leaders went into plantation communities to instill loyalty and muster support for the war, to raise funds for Liberty Bonds, and to encourage croppers to remain on the land rather than head north.[23] Joseph A. Booker, an official of the National Negro Baptist Convention who lived in Little Rock, spoke to the association's local meeting in the Arkansas Delta counties and noted that the war allowed black people to show their usefulness and loyalty. He pleaded with people to remain on the land and also asked white leaders to provide better schools, teachers, "protection of life and property, and better pay for honest service rendered."[24]

In Phillips County, Arkansas, the Negro Business League formed "war clubs" to mobilize support for the war. However, white defense council members still sent out sixty-seven speakers each Sunday to explain the council's goals, since they could not "write a negro a letter and get any results."[25] Fraternal lodges were among the first to endorse Wilson and the war, though not without qualification. When one of the strongest organizations, the Woodmen of the Union, held its convention in Helena with fellows from both Arkansas and Mississippi attending, it proclaimed loyalty to the flag but insisted that "Lynch law does violence to organized society, civilization, and Christianity."[26] Black Arkansans' patriotism did not come without expectations.

As wages continued to rise and laborers demonstrated increasing independence, landowners looked to the federal government for assistance in securing workers. In the summer of 1918, Provost Marshal E. H. Crowder issued a "Work or Fight" order to all local exemption boards, allowing them to draft men who were not engaged in employment essential to the war. Local councils of defense helped identify "loafers" and turned them in to the local exemption board. In a sense, Crowder's order federalized local vagrancy laws that empowered constables, justices of the peace, mayors, and sheriffs to arrest whomever they deemed a vagrant. In Arkansas, justices of the peace and constables were "deriving great profit from the Work or Fight Order," by "arresting negroes and ignorant whites" and virtually "placing part of our citizens in a terrorized state of mind, because they have no understanding of the distinction between State and Federal jurisdiction and they naturally believe that a Constable or a Justice of the Peace is the embodiment of power, both State and Federal."[27] Reports from other communities found planters and businessmen applying the "work or fight" order to women, even though they did not fall under the jurisdiction of the draft boards.[28] One deputy sheriff arrested thirteen women, listing them as prostitutes, for refusing to work, while planters in Pine Bluff demanded that the order apply to black women who refused to pick cotton at planter-defined wages.[29]

Officials also restricted the leisure time of black workers. In Marked Tree, Arkansas, the defense council requested help in closing two pool rooms and several soft drink stands, hoping to then force the owners to work in the fields.[30] The Arkansas State Council recommended that local officials refuse to grant any new licenses for pool halls and attempt to persuade those current owners to change their line of business.[31] Planters were especially concerned about the traveling circuses and Negro minstrel shows that had drained workers of their money. In 1917, Arkansas had seventy circuses visit the state, prompting Governor Brough to ask the State Council to discuss ways of restricting these activities.[32]

Labor organizers added to planters' labor woes. No sooner had the war started than Arkansas defense councils found evidence of organizers working among plantation workers. In Latour, in Phillips County, two men received a $500 fine for supposedly threatening seventeen black workers with violence if they did not walk off their jobs. Since the men failed to appear for work the next day, officials assumed they had been threatened away.[33]

The Industrial Workers of the World (IWW) struck the greatest fear in employers' minds. The Arkansas State Council of Defense addressed an entire memorandum to the activities of the union in the state, instructing local councils to utilize the military intelligence committees to monitor the radical movement. Businessmen throughout the state insisted that western laborers recruited to work in the cantonments in Little Rock had brought with them the radical ideas of the Wobblies. Apparently, federal agents had warned Helena officials to place extra guards around local factories, mills, and compresses. Officials had arrested an IWW organizer in Clay County who had goals of organizing in Phillips County as well; other reports blamed the union for having caused telephone trouble in several towns and cities. According to council member C. T. Carpenter in Poinsett County, the IWW was quite active, "using a good deal of seditious language."[34]

To some planters' relief, the federal government intervened to prevent industries from poaching rural workers by organizing the U.S. Employment Service (USES) to coordinate the movement and distribution of labor throughout the country. Each county provided a quota of unskilled labor for war industries, thus preventing the development of an unfair shortage in the countryside.[35] The USES had representatives in each delta region to coordinate labor quotas. However, to many planters government agents were no different from private ones, and they therefore refused to allow any workers to leave. According to one official, unless the USES agents could operate "unmolested," recruiting efforts in the South must stop.[36] Planters were probably further outraged when they discovered that the agency intended to use rural mail carriers to distribute applications for jobs, effectively making the mail carriers farm labor agents.[37]

Faced with rising cotton-picking wages in the fall of 1918, Mississippi County planters took matters into their own hands when they met and established a wage ceiling of $1.50 per hundredweight and a five-and-a-half day work week. They urged surrounding counties to do the same. Gins refused to accept offenders' cotton and local officials arrested violators. The county council of defense enforced the plan to control the smaller farmers and sharecroppers who paid high wages to harvest their small crops early, driving the price of labor higher for the large planters. By November, wages had risen in some areas to $4 per hundredweight as some planters complained that workers refused to work for less. The local council held firm, claiming that the larger planters reaped great profits as a result of the ceiling.[38]

The massive efforts of local defense councils to control both the labor and the personal and cultural realms of their workers' lives implied that rural peoples contested not only the war but also the power relations governing them at home. A government that called upon people to participate in patriotic ceremonies and purchase war bonds even as it required field laborers to work six days a week for low wages, or that invoked "work or fight" laws, surely led African Americans to question whether the war would make the delta safe for democracy.

The politically awakened and assertive "New Negro" of the urban north, then, had followers in the plantation South. Delta leaders anxiously observed an increasingly defiant attitude among their workers. According to a member of the Arkansas State Defense Council, "We have noticed for some time, a very perceptible difference in the hitherto respectful demeanor of the colored people of this locality." While arguing that German propaganda was partly responsible for "upsetting the racial situation," the member was sure that the widespread circulation of the Chicago *Defender* was a major cause of unrest.[39]

African American servicemen provided further tension, especially when they returned home. Having offered their lives in service to the nation, the soldiers expected to have their citizenship instated: to have equal access to public accommodations, a just return on their crops, freedom to move about without fear of retribution, political participation—justice. Black veterans, however, did not control nor were they responsible for the actions of delta white people who saw their military service in Europe as a threat to the "southern way of life" rooted in segregation and disfranchisement. While walking down a sidewalk in Star City, near Pine Bluff, in early September 1919, veteran Flinton Briggs stepped aside to allow a white couple to pass by. Apparently, the white woman brushed into Briggs, scolding him that "Niggers get off the sidewalk down here." When Briggs replied that "This is a free country," the woman's escort seized and held him until others came with an automobile that carried Briggs outside of town. Unable to find a rope to hang him with, the mob took automobile chains, tied Briggs to a tree, and riddled his body with bullets.[40] Briggs's murder was the fifth lynching in Arkansas in 1919, a prelude to the wholesale massacre that happened less than a month later in nearby Phillips County, where returning veterans and their families sought, like Briggs, to claim their "free country."

In Elaine, Arkansas, black workers' determination to secure economic justice following the war clashed dramatically and brutally with delta planters' fears of returning black veterans and their concerns over labor control. Located twenty miles south of the commercial city of Helena, Elaine exemplified the rapidly expanding economy of the early twentieth-century delta. Founded in 1911, it became a small trading town for large-scale plantations and lumber companies on the White and Mississippi Rivers. For example, in 1916, Gerard B. Lambert, a native of St. Louis who owned the New York–based pharmaceutical company that made Listerine, purchased a 20,000-acre plantation that included Elaine and neighboring Lambrook. Lambert divided the land into 1,300-acre units, each with its own managers, sharecroppers, gins, houses, and commissaries.[41]

By 1919, the area surrounding Elaine still resembled a frontier, bordered by dense swamplands and forests and connected to the outside by a single line of the Missouri Pacific Railroad linking it with Helena. Its population was overwhelmingly African American. As Lambert later recalled:

> Ours was a primitive and pioneer country where racial hatred was close to the surface. Here we had a tinderbox to be set off by the slightest spark.

White men, with their families on their minds, were constantly alert for the first signs of what they considered danger to their women and children. And the Negroes knew this. If they got out of line, they realized that there would be no compromise with sudden death.[42]

In spite of planter offensives to restrain their workers, the war created economic opportunities locally that black people aimed to secure. Lumber companies in the vicinity of Elaine had raised wages to meet wartime labor demands. As men made better wages, their wives, mothers, and daughters chose to remain at home rather than to work as domestics or to pick cotton for planter-defined low wages. Some women even found employment in the lumber mills, where they earned higher wages than if they had picked cotton. And for those men and women who did remain in the fields, many talked of forming a union to press planters for decent wages.[43]

Sharecroppers, tenants, and lumber workers had managed to make enough during the war to acquire various forms of personal property; some had even become landowners. These black families also knew that wartime should have brought decent prices for their cotton and better crop settlements. As the war ended and cotton rose to more than forty cents a pound, laborers were determined to secure their share of the profits. For example, Ed Ware and his wife had cultivated 120 acres of cotton and he owned a Ford car that he drove daily to Helena as a taxi service when his crops were laid by. The Wares owned two mules, one horse, a Jersey cow, a farm wagon, all of their farm tools, a harness, eight hogs, and 135 chickens. Ed Hicks rented 100 acres from Stanley and Moore Brothers, and he and his brother farmed it in corn and cotton. He and his wife owned four mules, a wagon, and farming tools. Alfred Banks worked thirty-two acres of cotton, eight acres of corn, and one acre of truck crops. Frank Moore, just returned from the war, and his wife worked fourteen acres of cotton and five acres of corn, and they owned $678 worth of household goods. Ed Coleman, at seventy-nine years old, farmed twelve acres in cotton and six in corn. He had obtained a number of household items and owned fifteen head of hogs.[44]

Planters watched their tenants produce good crops and acquire livestock and household goods that gave them a better life. Many of the tenants traveled to Helena to buy their goods, bypassing the commissary. This acquisition of property threatened the planters' power and especially their control of the surplus brought by the war. Consequently, many landlords moved to steal both the crops and the possessions of their workers, as did

Billy Archdale, who rented a farm outside of Elaine. He had hired thirteen black families to work the land on shares for three years. By the time the crops were laid by, he had driven all but four of them away, and he refused to feed them at his commissary any longer, insisting they were deep in debt to him. He then stole their crops, furniture, chickens, and hogs. The families of Gilbert Jenkins; James and Frank Moore, who had just returned from the war; and Daisy Frazier refused to leave and made arrangements to secure their supplies elsewhere. In the face of his laborers' defiance, Archdale aimed to secure their crops and household goods, one way or another, though his chance to do so awaited the fall.[45]

Sharecroppers in other communities faced similar problems. On September 26, 1919, Ed Ware's merchants, Jackson and Longnecker, came to buy some cotton he had just ginned and offered him first 24 and then 33 cents per pound. Ware refused the price, saying he intended to take his cotton to Helena and sell it himself for the market price—at that time 44 and a half cents per pound. Warned that the merchants planned to "mob" him, Ware refused their invitation to enter their store. On September 29, Ware went to Helena and hired a prominent white Little Rock attorney, U. S. Bratton, who also had an office in Helena and was known to have represented tenants in their efforts to secure settlements, to represent his interests.[46]

A sharecropper from Mellwood had also approached Bratton's Helena office and claimed that his landlord, B. F. O'Banon, had driven him from the plantation after he had raised ninety acres of cotton. O'Banon took not only his cotton, but his possessions as well. Soon after, another cropper came from the same plantation with a similar complaint. Bratton filed suits on their behalf without any results. In late September another cropper, from Ratio, approached Bratton to ask him to represent sixty-eight men and women workers on the northern-owned Fathauer plantation, where the manager had refused to issue itemized statements of accounts and had sold their cotton without any compensation. The croppers agreed to pay a lawyer's fee and to meet in Ratio on Wednesday, October 1, with Bratton's son, O. S. Bratton, who had just returned from the war in France.[47]

Sharecroppers in the villages of Ferguson, Hoop Spur, Mellwood, Modoc, Old Town, and Ratio did more than hire a lawyer, however. In the spring of 1919, they joined the Progressive Farmers and Household Union of America with the aim of securing a fair settlement from their landlords. Tenants knew that cotton was selling for forty cents per pound and they demanded their share of the profits. The founder of the union, Robert L.

Hill, lived in neighboring Drew County. According to Hill, the union had first been organized in 1865 under an act of Congress, as the Colored Union Benevolent Association in the District of Columbia. The association's charter had a section that allowed the association to purchase and own real estate for the purposes of the organization.[48] Hill and V. E. Powell, a physician, had incorporated the organization in Winchester in 1918. According to the articles of the group's constitution, the object of the union "shall be to advance the interests of the Negro, morally and intellectually, and to make him a better citizen and a better farmer."[49]

The union's structure resembled fraternal orders like the Masons; it had a password, door words, grips, and signs for its members, and changed each every three months to insure the order's secrecy. Each lodge had a doorkeeper who refused entry to anyone who did not know the password. The union provided for a joint stock company with a capital stock of one thousand dollars. Members bought shares for a dollar each, with the aim of building at least a two-thousand-dollar base to allow the organization to invest in real estate for the order. The order elected a salaried deputy to a six-month term of office, with duties that included organizing clubs in the county for two dollars each.

The "business of this Grand Lodge," read the constitution,"shall be to further advance the cause, uniting the race into a perfect Union in various counties. And to levy special taxes on subordinate Lodges for the purpose of purchasing land." Slogans at the end of the constitution read "We Battle for the Rights of Our Race; In Union is Strength; We Champion the Moral, Material, Political, and Intellectual Interest of Our Race."[50]

On the surface, this lodge did not look like a labor union at all. It had all of the rituals of a fraternal order; it even referred to itself as a Grand Lodge, and to its locals as lodges. It also had the usual provisions of benevolent associations in that its aim was to purchase real estate, though the goal of these investments was not stated. It is entirely possible that Hill and his followers intended to form not a labor union, but a fraternal order that assisted rural peoples in purchasing land and in improving their general economic condition.

Sharecroppers, lumber workers, and farm owners in the Elaine region belonged to the Masons as well as other lodges such as the Odd Fellows and the Mosaic Templars, headquartered in Little Rock. These fraternal orders stressed social, political, and economic improvement and sent their members to meetings all over the country.[51] There is also evidence to suggest that Hill and the lodge knew of Secretary of the Interior Franklin

Lane's plan to provide returning veterans with homesteads in the cut-over lands of the Delta, acreage left after lumber companies had cleared the vast swamplands and forests and moved on to other places.[52] Thus, the union may have pursued two basic goals: assistance to croppers in purchasing land and help in obtaining a lawyer to represent them in securing the right to market their crops independent of the landlord.

When members of the Hoop Spur lodge heard that Bratton had been retained by the Ratio union, they decided to meet and discuss the possibility of retaining the attorney themselves. On the evening of Tuesday, September 30, an estimated 120 to 200 men, women, and children met in the Hoop Spur Church to discuss hiring Bratton. At eleven o'clock in the evening, according to the members present, at least five cars of armed white men drove up in front of the church and began firing into the building, killing some of the attendants. In self-defense, many lodge members fired back. Eventually, many black people fled. In the end a white man, W. A. Adkins, an agent of the Missouri Pacific Railroad, lay dead, and another, deputy sheriff Charles Pratt, was seriously wounded. One of the union guards heard a white man in the crowd yell "We are killing our own men." Ed Collins, a black trusty who had accompanied the white men, apparently fled and phoned the sheriff in Helena that black people were armed and had killed Adkins.[53]

Meanwhile, landowners from around Elaine who were not among those already at the Hoop Spur Church formed their own posse, organized into squads, and joined the pursuit of the union members as they fled the church.[54] Before pursuing the workers, however, the planters burned the Hoop Spur Church.[55] Ed Ware, secretary of the Hoop Spur union, had escaped from the church to his home for protection. After he arrived, 150 armed men stormed his house, breaking open trunks and drawers, taking all of his secretary minutes for the union and his Masonic lodge books. They also shot a friend of Ware's, an old crippled man named Charley Robinson, as he tried to flee the vigilantes. The posse then left Robinson in a bed in Ware's house for four days before he was buried.[56]

Elaine planters had immediate reinforcements, as landowners, managers, sheriffs, and veterans from all over the Mississippi and Arkansas Delta brought their guns to combat the "insurrection." Meanwhile, the Mayor of Elaine, fearing a "negro revolt," telegraphed Governor Charles H. Brough for assistance. After receiving permission from Secretary of War Newton Baker, the Governor personally escorted 583 federal troops, men who had also just returned from France, including a machine gun battalion with twelve guns.[57]

The next morning, Wednesday, October 1, black people heard from the planters that "they were coming down there and 'kill every nigger they found.'"[58] Phillips County Sheriff Frank F. Kitchens sent his own posse of 300 men, many of them members of the local American Legion who had just returned from World War I.[59] Union member and World War I veteran Frank Moore described events once the posse and vigilantes arrived. On October 2, around 11:30 a.m., Moore saw around 300 to 400 men walking with guns or riding in automobiles. As Moore and others ran to the back of his field, they saw gunmen shoot and then burn the president of the Hoop Spur lodge, Jim Miller, and his entire family. By five o'clock that evening, Moore saw "300 more white people coming on with guns, shooting, and killing men, women, and children." Moore quickly gathered all the women and children that he could and hid in the woods until federal troops arrived the next morning.[60]

The mob also seized Lula Black and her four children from their house, demanding to know if Mrs. Black belonged to the union. Confirming their suspicion, she said she belonged because "it would better the condition of the colored people; when they worked it would help them to get what they worked for." Members of the mob responded by knocking her down, pistol-whipping and kicking her, and then taking her to jail.[61] The mob moved on to Frank Hall's house, where twelve men from Mississippi armed with guns and an axe killed an elderly woman, Frances Hall, tied her clothes over her head, and threw her body in the road, where it lay exposed for several days.[62]

While the planters' posse pursued black people around Hoop Spur, O. S. Bratton was meeting in Ratio with Robert Hill and the union to plan their strategy for demanding settlements from their landlords and to collect the lawyer's fee paid in the form of checks and Liberty Bonds. During the meeting, the manager of the northern-owned Fathauer plantation rode up with a posse and accused Bratton of keeping the "negroes" out of the fields and inciting them to riot. He seized Bratton and took him to Elaine, where an angry mob accused him of being the ringleader of the insurrection. Bratton was then taken to a brick store and chained to two other union members from Ratio in an effort to further humiliate a white man who had dared to work with black people. Several men searched Bratton and waved an IWW paper in his face, claiming they had found it on his person.

After a few hours, officials moved Bratton, still chained to the other two men, to the Helena jail, where he remained until the federal troops released him.[63]

Once the army arrived with machine guns, it was only a matter of hours before enough black people had been murdered or arrested to allow local leaders to declare the end of the insurrection. The army joined with the vigilantes to comb a radius of 150 to 200 miles in search of the "insurrectionists." Men, women, and children—some estimates claim as many as a thousand—were arrested and placed in a stockade where they were interrogated by law officials and planters who identified the "trustworthy" Negroes. Eventually, most were dismissed, but the discharge was contingent upon the authorization of their planters and managers, and it was obtained at a price: the men and women had to agree to return to the fields and work on planter-defined terms. Black landowners and those who had no white person to vouch for them remained in custody.[64]

The "insurrection," as the landowners quickly renamed the legal efforts of their workers to secure justice, provided planters, businessmen, and officials the opportunity to settle scores with black people they considered too independent and prosperous. Apparently this was the case in the murder of the four Johnston brothers. Dr. D.A.E. Johnston, a prominent Helena dentist, was married to the daughter of Reverend Abraham H. Miller, one of the city's most prosperous citizens and the first black person to serve in the Arkansas State Legislature. Dr. Johnston's own father, Professor Lewis Johnston, had established several seminaries under the auspices of the Presbyterian Church, among them the Richard Allen Seminary in Pine Bluff. Dr. Johnston had studied dentistry in Chicago and had returned to establish a successful practice in Helena. He owned a major building on main street as well as a drug store. His two younger brothers, one of whom had just returned from France where he served in the Fifteenth New York Infantry, ran a local automobile business. A fourth brother, a prominent physician from Oklahoma, had recently arrived for a visit with his brothers.[65]

The four went hunting and were on their way back on October 2 when a man informed them that a riot had broken out and that they should not drive through Elaine. The Johnstons left their car and rifles and boarded a train. When the train passed through Elaine, some men boarded, took the brothers off, and placed them in a car driven by Orley A. Lilly, a Helena real estate dealer and a member of the Helena City Council. Amos Jarman, County Treasurer, a deputy U.S. attorney, and Lilly's chauffeur were also in the car. According to Jarman, "We had no handcuffs so we chained the Johnstons' feet and hands together and placed them in the rear seat." En route to Helena, Jarman saw a group of men having car trouble and he stopped to help them out. As he stepped out of the car, he claimed he heard "A commotion behind me, and, looking around, saw the larger of the Johnston brothers reach over and snatch Lilly's pistol from its scabbard and begin shooting." According to Jarman, one of the Johnstons killed Lilly, whereupon Jarman and others immediately shot and killed all four brothers. Local authorities and the newspaper did not seem amazed that the Johnston brother was able to shoot Lilly with his feet and hands chained.[66]

The Johnston brothers lay on the roadside for four days. Finally, Mrs. Eliza A. Miller, Dr. Johnston's mother-in-law, received permission to bring them to a funeral home.[67] The local newspaper announced that Dr. Johnston had killed Lilly, even though his hands were cuffed behind his back. Officials then ransacked Johnston's properties, claiming to have found more than a dozen high-powered rifles and several cases of ammunition.[68]

Other members of the black middle class in Helena also became targets of the authorities. A. R. Dupree and J. W. Jennings were jailed on October 2 for dispensing "vicious propaganda" among the Negroes of Hoop Spur and Elaine. Dupree owned a cleaning and pressing establishment and operated a jitney line in Helena; Jennings owned a drug store and managed a local black baseball team.[69]

Ultimately, 122 people were indicted in Helena on charges stemming from the "riot"; seventy-three of these were charged with murder.[70] Twelve of the union members, including Ed Ware and Frank Moore, were taken to the Helena jail, severely whipped, and shocked in an electric chair in an effort to secure confessions for the murders of the three white men who died during the "insurrection." Once the cases went to trial, it took the all-white jury only a few minutes to convict all twelve men, sentencing them to death. Many of the jurors had actually participated in suppressing the "rebellion."[71]

As federal troops withdrew, Helena leaders proclaimed the area safe and the rebellion suppressed. Prominent officials and businessmen appointed a Committee of Seven to investigate the causes of the uprising. Among its members were Sheriff Kitchens; Sebastian Straub, a local planter and acting sheriff; and a county judge; the remaining members were prominent planters and businessmen, one of whom represented the Lambert Plantation. In their view, Robert Hill had led poor illiterate sharecroppers into believing that the federal government would back their demands for better wages and land redistribution and had encouraged them to rise up and murder their landlords. The Committee claimed to have a list of planters the union members intended to murder. Local leaders also blamed the Chicago *Defender* for encouraging sharecroppers to demand better working conditions and political equality.

The Committee of Seven's report was published in major newspapers throughout the country as the most accurate account of events. The first challenge to this version came from Walter White of the National Association for the Advancement of Colored People (NAACP), who traveled to Phillips County a few days after the massacre disguised as a white reporter from Chicago. White interviewed a number of prominent participants, including Governor Brough, and reported that the planters had oppressed the sharecroppers by denying them a just return on their crops. When the croppers exercised their constitutional right and hired a lawyer, the planters repelled their efforts with the utmost force. The *Crisis* estimated that from twenty-five to fifty black people were killed, while only five white men died; the reporter claimed that the "stench of dead bodies could be smelled for two miles."[72]

The planter class was outraged when White's article appeared. Governor Brough did not even know that he had spoken to White, since the reporter had gone undercover and had passed for a white man. The leaders of Phillips County denied White's versions of the massacre, pointing to his work as another example of outside agitators coming to the delta to incite black people. The NAACP launched a successful campaign to reverse the convictions of the twelve men convicted of murder, employing a prominent black lawyer from Little Rock, Scipio Jones. Actually, two separate cases existed—one with Ed Ware and five other men, and another with Frank Moore and five men. The Arkansas Supreme Court overturned the convictions in the case that bore Ed Ware's name, arguing that the jury had failed to state the degree of murder the men were found guilty of committing. The other case, which bore Frank Moore's name, went to the U.S. Supreme Court and was overturned in 1923 in *Moore v. Dempsey*. Justice Oliver Wendell Holmes, writing for the Court, argued that the trial had been dominated by a mob spirit, that the Committee of Seven had as much as promised the convictions of the defendants if the public would not lynch them, and that their confessions were secured through electric shock. Any trial, he ruled, was void if dominated by a mob spirit, for it violated the Fourteenth Amendment right to due process.[73]

Planters were outraged when news came of the Court's ruling. Their account of the Elaine "riot" had never mentioned the murder of the Jim Miller family or the other burnings and slayings that had occurred, nor did they ever acknowledge the electric shock treatments given to defendants. Planters held to their view of events at least until the 1960s.[74]

Although Frank Moore and all of the other defendants were eventually freed, the lives of sharecroppers and tenant farmers in the Elaine area and throughout the delta grew worse, if anything. Indeed, if one account is to be believed, the slaughter of black people continued after the troops left. An anonymous letter from Wabash written to "Uncle Sam" in November 1919 said that "we as colored people of the south is having a dreadful time down here. All of the men are being taken away and lynched . . . and we wemon [sic] are left in a suffering condition being treated awful cruel." She concluded that her people "are begging for mercy." One can only imagine what "awful cruel" actually entailed for these women. The letter suggested that while men and women had gone to prison, those left behind suffered retribution on the farm.[75]

The families of the union members found no welcome when they returned to their homes. Mrs. Frank Moore had managed to escape the massacre and to hide for four weeks. After she read in the newspaper that the trouble had ended, she returned to the Archdale farm to pay what she owed and to get her furniture and clothes. Mrs. Archdale told her that she had nothing, although Mrs. Moore saw her furniture in the Archdale house. When Mrs. Moore asked the whereabouts of her husband Frank, Archdale replied that he was in the Helena jail. "Did he kill anybody?" queried Mrs. Moore. "No," she said, "but he had just come from the army and he was too bigoted." Billy Archdale then appeared and told Mrs. Moore that if she did not leave, he would "kill her, burn her up, and no one would know where she was." When she left, another landlord who was considered a leader of the mob arrested her and took her to the Helena jail. She remained there for eight days, working with fifteen other black women from three o'clock in the morning until ten at night.[76]

Mrs. Ed Ware and her daughter spent one month in prison at hard labor, sleeping on concrete floors. Officials told them when they were discharged to go back home and go to work and "never join nothing more unless they got their lawyers' or landlord's consent." When Mrs. Ware returned, however, she had nothing, though she saw some of her belongings in white people's homes.[77]

Ida B. Wells-Barnett made a clandestine trip to the Little Rock prison to visit those who had been convicted. She also spent time with the families of the accused. With their help, she collected information on the acreage and the cotton produced by thirty-four of the seventy-five prisoners. She found that the twelve men sentenced to death row had alone produced $100,000 dollars of cotton and corn in 1919. She estimated that those people arrested had produced more than a million dollars worth of cotton. Wells-Barnett concluded that the planters had killed the black people because many had refused to give up their cotton, had denied the planters' right to market it for higher prices and to settle with the croppers for far less. In the face of this defiance of authority, landowners drove the families off their land and seized the cotton. According to union member John Martin, the "white people know that they started this trouble. This union was only for a blind. We were threatened before this union was there to make us leave our crops."[78]

The wholesale massacre in Phillips County indicated how fearful planters and their allies had become of the changes wrought by the war, and it revealed their determination to destroy whatever aspirations Delta black people had, both at home and abroad. Delta leaders did not have to worry about federal intervention to end segregation and disfranchisement. However, planters could not erase the growing expectations generated among African Americans by the wartime mobilization. The use of federal troops to quell the "uprising" testified to the seriousness with which the planter class took any attempts by their workers to press their demands for political and economic rights. By sending in federal troops, they signaled to African Americans throughout the Delta that any assertions of their citizenship would be met with the utmost force. By burning the Hoop Spur Church and the president of the lodge and his family, planters sought to destroy any trace of black assertions of citizenship. And by indicting Bratton for barratry (for encouraging unwarranted complaints and lawsuits from the sharecroppers), officials made it difficult for others to provide legal representation for the croppers.

Rumors spread of potential revolts in other parts of the Delta. In January 1920, 130 troops were called into Dumas, Arkansas, when ten men forced a deputy sheriff to relinquish a man he had arrested for stealing hogs from a nearby plantation. Although the soldiers did not uncover another plot, their deployment demonstrated the continued fears regarding African American militancy.[79] Measures were taken throughout the region to outlaw the distribution of the *Crisis* and the Chicago *Defender*. Mississippi passed a law in 1920 making it a misdemeanor to "print or publish or circulate" literature favoring social equality.[80] In Arkansas, Governor Brough also moved to ban the *Defender*, while delta counties sought to ban the sale of firearms and ammunition to African Americans. And the Committee of Seven requested from the federal government more than one hundred regulation army rifles and twenty-five thousand rounds of ammunition, plus six Browning rifles with five thousand rounds of ammunition, to help preserve order.[81]

Civic leaders became especially concerned with banning fraternal orders, often referred to as secret societies. Fraternal lodges alarmed planters because they had become, as in Elaine, a locus for political activity. As affiliates of national organizations, lodges served as conveyers of outside information. Many had organized entire communities for the migration northward and some had contributed the first members to local NAACP chapters and to labor unions. Their secretive nature fueled planter anxieties in the wake of the Elaine massacre.[82] Indeed, a man whose work involved calling upon funeral homes in several southern states had written to the Department of Justice in April 1919 regarding the forming of secret African American societies in Arkansas and Mississippi. He had predicted at the time "that there would be a race war in the States within six months. . . . That race war has happened," he continued, "only it happened in Arkansas in place of Mississippi where I thought the outbreak would occur." The writer urged the Department to send investigators to determine how extensive these organizations had become.[83]

Planters tightened their control of labor during the decade following World War I. In 1922, numerous letters from the Democrat, Arkansas, NAACP chapter in St. Francis County, described the violence and terror sharecroppers experienced. "In June," wrote one cropper, "Mr. Johnson take a Iron Single Tree (the crossbar to a draft harness) and beat a man and taken his mule and hogs and chickens and household goods that he brought from Miss.," while "Mr. E. Williams, he has got all of his people starving and in debt to his day hands and won't pay them off . . . now they want to run the hands off from their crops and take them." The landowner did not pay his workers last year, according to the writer, "and now they are having high power rifles shipped out here and is trying to find out when we hold our meetings." He concluded that "they are aiming to do us as it was dun at Elaine." Other members wrote that they were prohibited from attending church services and funerals, and that men and women were driven to the fields at gunpoint. Some croppers complained that their children continued to attend classes only four months out of the year.[84]

Numerous lynchings also followed the war and the Elaine massacre. Beginning in January 1919, when an African American soldier was lynched in Memphis, Tennessee, people were tortured and burned all over the Delta. At least eighteen lynchings of men and women in Arkansas and Mississippi were reported to the NAACP in 1919, some involving the murder of more than one person. While some of the men were killed for alleged violations of white women's honor, many instances centered on crop disputes or the actions of returning veterans.[85]

Delta leaders realized African Americans had become politicized during the war. From their perspective, only massive force could restore the social order. Their ability to call in federal troops demonstrated the planters' control of the instruments of state power. Their authority was buttressed during the war by the intrusion of a liberal state apparatus that linked local authorities more directly with federal agencies, a connection that continued and was strengthened in the decades that followed. African American challenges to planter dominance now carried the additional weight of defying federal power, which created the ability to bring in federal, not state, troops. The wartime experience of African Americans in the Arkansas Delta revealed important changes that had occurred in the plantation South during the First World War and its aftermath. Wars by their nature destabilize societies by creating demands for citizen support and loyalty. President Wilson, by making the war one for democracy, raised the issue of citizenship on a national level. However, delta black people did not need a presidential decree to impress upon them their rights of citizenship. Enough former slaves had survived into the early twentieth century to remind their descendants of the meaning of the victories embedded in Emancipation and Reconstruction. Indeed, Phillips County had been occupied by union troops, and during Reconstruction and afterwards the county had elected numerous black officials.[86]

But black people in Phillips County also had their more immediate experiences to shape their views of citizenship, for they struggled daily with the planters and their minions over the just fruits of their labor, and through their lodges and churches they had developed a sense of political rights that centered on community participation. As Elsa Barkley Brown has argued for Reconstruction, African Americans saw the vote not as a male attribute but as something to be exercised collectively in the interest of the entire community. Even though disfranchisement laws denied black people the vote, they continued to think politically and to exercise their notions of politics in a collective way. And so it was with the sharecroppers at Elaine. Men, women, and children attended the union meetings and were in the Hoop Spur Church when the massacre began. Women heads of households joined the organization, as did the married women; indeed, soldiers found automatic pistols hidden in the stockings of the women they took into custody. Sharecropping was a family arrangement, and the harshness and injustice of it bore down on the family, not on individuals. Men and women went to prison, men and women were killed, men and women were beaten. And their children bore the consequences as well.

The Elaine Massacre illuminated the core of what black people defined as citizenship—justice, fairness, equity, legal representation, trial by a jury of one's peers, but above all a sense of common decency in dealing with daily transactions, working to provide families with a better existence, having the privacy of one's own home, the right to enjoy and to keep the material possessions worked for and paid for, the right to a just return on one's labor.

The Elaine Massacre did not destroy delta black people's will to fight or to survive. In the 1920s, they organized NAACP chapters all over the region, and in the remotest places. They gave money to the Dyer Anti-Lynching Bill campaign in Congress and they read of other struggles throughout the nation and the world. When the Great Depression came in the 1930s and the nation faced a new crisis, Arkansas sharecroppers and tenant farmers formed an interracial union to once again press their demands for justice.[87] And they sent their men and women to fight fascism during World War II. After the second war, however, delta black people became part of the larger regional and national struggle to end Jim Crow forever. Nor is their fight for justice over, for delta black people have continued to demand that the federal government live up to its commitment to equal justice before the law and to economic equity.

NOTES

1. For a discussion of the creation of the New South plantations on the Mississippi side of the river, see Robert L. Brandfon, *Cotton Kingdom of the New South: A History of the Yazoo Mississippi Delta from Reconstruction to the Twentieth Century* (Cambridge: Harvard University Press, 1967). For an excellent discussion of the development of the plantations in Poinsett County, Arkansas, see Jeannie M. Whayne, *A New Plantation South: Land, Labor, and Federal Favor in Twentieth Century Arkansas* (Charlottesville: University of Virginia Press, 1996). Parts of this essay appeared in an earlier article. See Nan Elizabeth Woodruff, "African American

Struggles for Citizenship in the Arkansas and Mississippi Deltas in the Age of Jim Crow," *Radical History Review* 55 (winter 1993): 33–51.

2. As Harold Woodman has argued, sharecropping was a form of wage labor that emerged after emancipation whereby the worker brought only his or her labor to the crop. The planter furnished housing, the tools needed to till the crop, feed, seed, and fertilizer, all of which was charged to the sharecropper; he also forced croppers to purchase all of their food, clothes, and necessities at his commissary. Planters thus retained a lien not only on the crop itself, but on all of the sharecroppers' possessions. Landowners also controlled the distribution and marketing of the crop. Thus, at settlement time after the crops had been gathered, planters added up the costs of production and living expenses and deducted them from the sharecroppers' share of the crop. Landowners rarely, if ever, gave their workers a fair price for their cotton, insuring their continued indebtedness. Tenant farmers theoretically retained greater control over their crops and their possessions, for they simply rented the land and paid for it either in cash or in a share of the crop. However, in the Arkansas Delta, it appears that planters made no distinction in how they treated croppers and renters—they seized and marketed the crops regardless of the contractual agreement. The workers, however, understood the agreements differently and acted accordingly. See Harold D. Woodman, *New South—New Law: The Legal Foundations of the Credit and Labor Relations in the Postbellum Agricultural South* (Baton Rouge: Louisiana State University Press, 1995).

3. I am drawing on the distinction made by Antonio Gramsci between state (or political) and civil society. According to Gramsci, civil society is composed of the educational, religious, and associational institutions, while the state or political society consists of the courts, legislature, and elections. In bourgeois democracies, the latter are theoretically separate from the former. Gramsci argued that the elaborate structure of liberal democracy—elections, legislatures, courts—created a façade of popular control and participation and served as a means through which the population's consent to be governed was obtained. However, in the plantation South, planters removed African Americans from political society, for the same people controlled both the political and the civil. See Joseph V. Femia, *Gramsci's Political Thought: Hegemony, Consciousness, and the Revolutionary Process* (Oxford: Oxford University Press, 1987), 26–29; and Antonio Gramsci, *Selections from the Prison Notebooks*, ed. and trans. Quinto Hoare and Geoffrey Nowell Smith (New York: International Publishers, 1971), 206–78. The finest application of Gramsci's work to explaining an entire society's specific historical development remains Eugene D. Genovese's *Roll, Jordan, Roll: The World the Slaves Made* (New York: Pantheon, 1974).

4. On peonage, see Pete Daniel, *The Shadow of Slavery: Peonage in the South, 1901–1969* (Urbana: University of Illinois Press, 1972); and William Cohen, *At Freedom's Edge: Black Mobility and the Southern White Quest for Racial Control, 1861–1915* (Baton Rouge: Louisiana State University Press, 1991).

5. Harold D. Woodman, "Post–Civil War Southern Agriculture and the Law," *Agricultural History* 53 (January 1919): 319–37.

6. Peter Gottlieb, *Making Their Own Way: Southern Blacks' Migration to Pittsburgh, 1916–1930* (Urbana: University of Illinois Press, 1987); James Grossman, *Land of Hope: Chicago, Black Southerners, and the Great Migration* (Chicago: University of Chicago Press, 1989); Joe William Trotter, *Black Milwaukee: The Making of an Industrial Proletariat, 1915–45* (Urbana: University of Illinois Press, 1989); idem.; *Coal, Class, and Color: Blacks in Southern West Virginia, 1915–32* (Urbana: University of Illinois Press, 1990); Neil McMillen, *Dark Journey: Black Mississippians in the Age of Jim Crow* (Urbana: University of Illinois Press, 1989). See also, U.S. Department of Labor, Division of Negro Economics, *Negro Migration in 1916–1917* (Washington, D.C., 1919); Emmett J. Scott, "Letters of Negro Migrants of 1916–1918," *Journal of Negro History* 4 (October 1919): 412–75.

7. The Northern Ohio Cooperage Company developed lands in eastern Arkansas where it had planted several thousand acres of food and feed crops. Memphis (Tennessee) *Commercial-Appeal*, April 27, 1917.

8. G. B. Ewing to Arkansas State Council of Defense, October 23, 1918, Arkansas Council of Defense Papers, Arkansas History Commission, Little Rock, Arkansas. Hereafter cited as ACD.

9. Minutes of the Arkansas State Council of Defense, January 21, 1918, ACD.

10. G. B. Ewing to Arkansas Council of Defense, October 23, 1918, ACD.

11. For the creation of wartime agencies, see David M. Kennedy, *Over Here: The First World War and American Society* (New York: Oxford University Press, 1980). For a discussion of the liberal state during this time, see Alan Dawley, *Struggles for Justice: Social Responsibility and the Liberal State* (Cambridge and London: Harvard University Press, 1991).

12. Arthur H. Fleming to Several Southern State Councils of Defense, "Organization of Negroes," July 24, 1918, RG 62, Council of National Defense, Field Division, Winterbotham Correspondence, 15-QA, Box 859, located in the Washington National Records Center, Suitland, Maryland.

13. W. H. Smith to W. E. Gifford, June 27, 1917, RG 62, Council of National Defense, State Councils, Box 665.

14. States Relations Service memorandum to County Agents, August 2, 1918, RG 16, U.S. Secretary of Agriculture Papers, Accession 234, Drawer 267, located in the National Archives, Washington, D.C.

15. Captain N. M. Cartmell, USA, who was in charge of recruiting for the District of Arkansas, said that the draft quota for Arkansas between April 1, 1917 and June 30, 1917 was 3,000. However, only 719 had reported for registration. Arkansas State Council of Defense Memorandum, n.d., RG 62, Council of National Defense, State Councils, Box 692. See also E. H. Crowder to Charles H. Brough, November 6, 1917, RG 163, U.S. Selective Service System, 1917–1919, State Files, Arkansas, Box 86, Washington National Records Center, Suitland, Maryland. Hereafter cited as SSS.

16. C. H. Brough to E. H. Crowder, November 2, 1917, RG 163, SSS, 1917–1919, State Files, Arkansas, Box 88.

17. J. W. Johnson to E. H. Crowder, November 8, 1918, RG 163, SSS, State Files, Arkansas, Box 89.

18. Memphis (Tennessee) *Commercial-Appeal*, June 6, 1917.

19. J. P. Burks to Lloyd England, July 28 and August 23, 1918, RG 163, SSS, State Files, Arkansas, Box 86.

20. T. S. Frazier, "Report of Inspection Made of State Headquarters," Little Rock, Arkansas, September 28, 1918, RG 163, SSS, State Files, Arkansas, Box 86; Helena (Arkansas) *World*, October 3, 1917.

21. G. B. Ewing to Arkansas State Council of Defense, October 3, 1918, ACD. For concerns about allotments in Mississippi, see A. M. Pepper to E. H. Crowder, August 15, 1918, RG 163, SSS, Mississippi, Box 178; for Arkansas, see J. E. Stevenson to E. H. Crowder, August 15, 1917, RG 163, SSS, Box 88.

22. J. H. McConico to John R. Shillady, October 9, 1918, NAACP Papers, Group I, Box C-417. See also Rev. W. E. Watson and W. D. Reddick, "Open Letter to the Chamber of Commerce of Pine Bluff, Arkansas, and to the Public," n.d., NAACP Papers, Group I, Box C-417. The letter was from several black leaders in Pine Bluff. The NAACP Papers are located in the Library of Congress Manuscripts Division, Washington, D.C.

23. Charles E. Sullenger to Wallace Townsend, October 2, 1918, ACD; R. B. Keating to Wallace Townsend, June 6, 1918, ACD; Arkansas State Council of Defense Minutes, September 2, 1918, RG 62, Council of National Defense, Field Division, Box 857.

24. Arkansas *Gazette*, August 4, 1917.

25. Edwin Bevens to Lloyd England, October 11, 1918, ACD.

26. Helena (Arkansas) *World*, August 30, 1917. Another large organization, the Royal Circle of Friends, also endorsed the war. Arkansas *Gazette*, September 4, 1917.

27. A. N. Meeks to Wallace Townsend, July 31, 1918, ACD.

28. John R. Shillady to Woodrow Wilson, September 25, 1918, RG 174, U.S. Secretary of Labor Papers, Chief Clerks Files, Box 18, File 8\102-E, National Archives, Washington, D.C.

29. W. R. Smith to Lloyd England, March 26, 1918, ACD.

30. L. L. Cantrell to Wallace Townsend, October 8, 1918, ACD.

31. Lloyd England to Chairmen, County Councils of Defense, August 13, 1918, ACD.

32. Minutes, Arkansas State Council of Defense, January 2, 1918, ACD.

33. Helena (Arkansas) *World*, August 30, 1917.

34. Helena *World*, July 11, November 16, 1917; Arkansas State Council of Defense Circular Letter no. 23, February 16, 1918; C. T. Carpenter to Lloyd England, July 25, 1917, ACD. McKinley quote cited in Helena *World*, August 23, 1917.

35. Lloyd England to County Councils of Defense, n.d., ACD.

36. J. B. Densmore to W. B. Wilson, May 29, 1918, RG 174, Department of Labor, 1907–42, Box 139.

37. U.S. Employment Service Bulletin, May 17, 1918, RG 174, Department of Labor, 1907–42, Box 139.

38. R. A. Nelson to State Council of Defense, October 9, 1918; Theo Rectin to U.S. Commissioner of Agriculture, October 21, 1918; A. B. Fairfield to Wallace Townsend, December 13, 1918, all in ACD.

39. D. Whipple to A. M. Briggs, July 5, 1917, RG 65, Department of Justice, Bureau of Investigations; Theodore Kornweibel, ed., *Federal Surveillance of Afro-Americans, 1917–1925: The First World War, the Red Scare, and the Garvey Movement* (Bethesda, Md.: University Publications of America, 1986), reel 9.

40. Chicago *Whip*, September 13, 1919, in NAACP Papers, Group I, Box C-350. See also "Asks Governor if He Approves of Murder," NAACP press release, NAACP Papers, Group I, Box C-350.

41. Helena *World*, October 23, 1916. Other lands were owned by the Chicago Lumber and Mill Company.

42. The population of Phillips County in 1920 was 44,530, with 32,929 African Americans. B. Boren McCool, *Union, Reaction, and Riot: A Biography of a Rural Race Riot* (Memphis, Tenn.: Bureau of Social Research, Memphis State University, June 1970), 1–2. Gerard B. Lambert, *All Out of Step: A Personal Chronicle* (New York: Doubleday, 1956), 73–74.

43. "The Causes of Two Race Riots," *The Crisis* 19 (December 1919): 57. This article, while unsigned, was probably written by Walter White, who reported that a separate union of strictly wage hands had organized to secure better wages. I have never found any additional evidence of this, but that does not mean such a union did not exist. The difficulty of securing sources on the events surrounding the massacre leads me not to discount this information.

44. Ida Wells Barnett, *The Arkansas Race Riot* (Chicago: Hume Job, 1920), 13–18.

45. Ibid., 19.

46. Ibid., 13. Also see U. S. Bratton to David Y. Thomas, September 5, 1921, David Y. Thomas Papers, Box 1:2, University of Arkansas, Fayetteville, Special Collections.

47. U. S. Bratton to Frank Burke, November 6, 1919, Arthur I. Waskow Collection, State Historical Society of Wisconsin, Madison.

48. George B. Sanger, ed., *The Statutes at Large, Treaties and Proclamations of the United States of America from December 1863 to December 1865,* vol. 13 (Bost, 1866), 535–36; Wells Barnett, *The Arkansas Race Riot,* 49.

49. Wells Barnett, 49.

50. Ibid., 48–49.

51. *History of the Mosaic Templars of America—Its Founders and Officials,* ed. A. E. Bush and P. L. Dorman (Little Rock, Ark.: Central Printing Company, 1924);

William H. Grimshaw, *Official History of Freemasonry among the Colored People in North America* (New York: Broadway Publishing Company, 1903).

52. For information on Lane's program, see the *Southern Lumberman*, November 16, 1918, 23; November 23, 1918, 26; December 21, 1918, 124. See also *The Letters of Franklin K. Lane: Personal and Political,* ed. Anne Wintermute Lane and Louise Herrick Wall (Boston: Houghton-Mifflin, 1922), 285–90.

53. Wells-Barnett, *The Arkansas Race Riot*, 10.

54. McCool, *Union, Reaction, and Riot*, 26–27.

55. Wells-Barnett, *The Arkansas Race Riot*, 10.

56. Ibid., 14, 20.

57. Ibid., 28.

58. Ibid., 17.

59. McCool, *Union, Reaction, and Riot*, 26.

60. Wells-Barnett, *The Arkansas Race Riot*, 11–18.

61. Ibid., 20–21.

62. Ibid. Bessie Ferguson wrote an account of the massacre as a master's thesis in 1927. She interviewed prominent white men who had been involved as well as some black people. While sympathetic to the planter class, Ferguson nevertheless wrote: "The negroes rightfully charge but greatly exaggerate the indiscriminate killings which took place. A party of twelve men from Mississippi equipped with eleven guns and one axe created havoc wherever they went. One instance of their brutality being the murdering of a harmless crazy negro woman, Frances Hall." Bessie Ferguson, "The Elaine Race Riot" (M.A. Thesis, George Peabody College for Teachers, August 1927), 83. I am grateful to Tom Dillard for pointing this source out to me and for kindly providing me with a copy.

63. O. S. Bratton to U. S. Bratton, November 5, 1919, NAACP Manuscripts, Waskow Papers.

64. "The Causes of Two Riots," 58–59.

65. Reverend A. H. Miller, *How I Succeeded in My Business* (n.p., n.d.). Dr. Robert Miller of Helena, Arkansas, kindly provided me with a copy of his grandfather's memoir.

66. Helena *World*, October 3, 1919.

67. Wells Barnett, *The Arkansas Race Riot*, 25–26.

68. Ibid.

69. Helena *World*, October 3, 1919.

70. Richard C. Cortner, *A Mob Intent on Death: The NAACP and the Arkansas Riot Cases* (Middletown, Conn.: Wesleyan University Press, 1988), 15.

71. Cortner, *A Mob Intent on Death*, 15–18.

72. Walter White, "Massacring Blacks in Arkansas," *Nation*, December 6, 1919, 715–16; White, "The Race Conflict in Arkansas," *Survey* (1919): 233–34; and "The Causes of Two Riots," 56–62.

73. Cortner, *A Mob Intent on Death*, 107–200. The Moore decision, according to

Cortner, had an important impact upon federal habeas corpus law, becoming a "milestone" in the modern interpretation of the due process clause in relation to the conduct of state criminal trials. It was the first in a series of decisions to liberalize the rules determining whether a state conviction may be collaterally attacked via the federal writ of habeas corpus because of alleged violations of the federal constitutional rights of the defendant (185)

74. J. W. Butts and Dorothy James interviewed some of the survivors of the "uprising" in the early 1960s and wrote an article that reflected the traditional planter view. Butts drew heavily from a scrapbook he had kept of the event. J. W. Butts and Dorothy James, "The Underlying Causes of the Elaine Riot of 1919," *Arkansas Historical Quarterly* 20 (spring 1961): 95–104.

75. "Oblige" to Uncle Sam, November 14, 1919, RG 60, General Records of the Department of Justice, Straight Numerical Files, 1904–37, Box 1284. National Archives, College Park, Maryland. I am grateful to Greta De Jong for finding and providing me with this letter.

76. Wells Barnett, *The Arkansas Race Riot*, 19–20.

77. Ibid., 20.

78. Ibid., 11, 15, 23–24.

79. Major Robert Q. Poage to Director of Military Intelligence, January 22, 1920, RG 60, Department of Justice Files, Glasser Files, *Federal Surveillance of Afro-Americans*, Reel 16.

80. McMillen, *Dark Journey*, 174.

81. Cortner, *A Mob Intent on Death*, 15.

82. For an example of a leading lodge member who belonged to the NAACP and had attended the association's anti-lynching convention, see W. L. Purifoy to John R. Shillady, May 21, 1919, NAACP Papers, Group I, Box C-3. For the role churches and fraternal orders played in the great migration, see Grossman, *Land of Hope*, 92.

83. C. T. Schade to Department of Justice, RG 65, Department of Justice, *Surveillance of Afro-Americans*, Reel 12.

84. H. L. Henderson to Joel Spingarn, August 26, 1922. See also Jim Coleman's Report, August 12, 1922; J. C. Coleman to Joel Spingarn, August 29, 1922; Lucious Holiday to Spingarn, August 11, 1922; L. B. Sanford to NAACP, June 12, 1922; Josie Coleman, Report of Chairman of Democrat Branch of NAACP, June 12, 1922; all in NAACP Papers, Group I, Box C-386.

85. For the numerous lynchings in both Arkansas and Mississippi, see NAACP Papers, Group I, Boxes C-349, 350, 360, 389. See also McMillen, *Dark Journey*, and Todd E. Lewis, "Mob Justice in the 'American Congo': Judge Lynch in Arkansas during the Decade after World War I," *Arkansas Historical Quarterly* 52 (summer 1993): 156–84.

86. Joseph M. St. Hilaire, "The Negro Delegates in the Arkansas Constitutional Convention of 1868: A Group Profile," *Arkansas Historical Quarterly* 33 (summer

1974), 38–69; Willard B. Gatewood, "Negro Legislators in Arkansas, 1891: A Document," *Arkansas Historical Quarterly* 31 (autumn 1972): 220–33.

87. For another scholar who has also made these connections between Elaine and the STFU, see M. Langley Biegert, "Legacy of Resistance: Uncovering the History of Collective Action by Black Agricultural Workers in Central East Arkansas from the 1860s to the 1930s," *Journal of Social History* (fall 1993), 73–99.

Chapter 6

Intellectual Pan-African Feminists
Amy Ashwood-Garvey and Amy Jacques-Garvey

Ula Y. Taylor

Paul Gilroy's *The Black Atlantic: Modernity and Double Consciousness* (1993) has become a foundational text for discussions of the roots and routes of black intellectual life and traditions. Gilroy's cartography, however, is limited by the fact that his theoretical, diasporic "root" is largely constructed around an elite entourage of African American men. While few would dispute the critical role of African American thinkers like W.E.B. Du Bois, Frederick Douglass, and Richard Wright in the shaping of black radical thought, it is quite problematic to position them as the exclusive progenitors of black modernity. By anchoring his text in African American life, Gilroy gives one the unsettling impression that "America is the Diaspora, and that black modernity cannot take place without it."[1]

Equally alarming is Gilroy's reluctance to offer any sustained discussion of the female intellectuals who also struggled with a "restlessness" that he attributes to "de-centered identities." The unique contributions of African-American women like Mary Church Terrell and Ida B. Wells (political journalists who wrote extensively about how their travels abroad transformed them and their understanding of the Pan-African world) are inexcusably absent from Gilroy's discussion of diasporic knowledge and black critical thought.

In an effort to expand the intellectual diaspora beyond Gilroy's male bodies and American centeredness, I would like to explore the contributions of two Jamaican women, Amy Ashwood-Garvey (1897–1969) and Amy Jacques-Garvey (1895–1973), the first and second wives of Marcus Garvey (1887–1940), leader of the Universal Negro Improvement Association (UNIA), one of the earliest Pan-African mass movements in the twentieth century, and the largest.[2] An analysis of their speeches and articles of the years from 1920 to 1945 reveals the unflinching determination of both women to make feminist issues fundamental to the global black intellectual enterprise. It is also vital to recognize that their efforts to focus attention on problems that uniquely impacted black women took place during a time when a term like "Afrocentric feminism" had not yet entered the theoretical vocabulary. What was more common then was the idea that "race" women had an additional moral obligation to be efficient housewives because their domestic responsibilities to their husbands and children were paramount in the struggle for racial progress.[3] The scholarship and activism of Jacques and Ashwood are a testament to how two women maneuvered between—and at times openly challenged—these stiflingly patriarchal ideas.

As intellectuals committed to Garveyism—a brand of Pan-African thought that Gilroy would locate under "romantic conceptions" of "race," "nation," and "people"—Ashwood and Jacques wanted to build a nation in which women had every opportunity to reach their full potential. They combined what are today viewed by most as intrinsically oppositional or incompatible forces (despite a close historical connection)—nationalism and feminism—into one theoretical construct. Their aim was to unite black women in an effort to counter both imperialism and the masculine prerogatives that kept them in a subaltern state. This political goal required a Herculean effort on their part, since, as Carol Boyce Davies points out, "Afrocentric feminism sounds like a contradiction in terms, for if it is Afro-centered then the feminine/feminism is already an appendage, an excess, easily expelled or contained within."[4] Gilroy would add that within the construction of Pan-Africanism, diasporic differences, let alone differences among Africans, were "unresolved within [this] political culture that promise[d] to bring the disparate peoples of the black Atlantic world together again."[5] But dislocations and geographic separations, along with color, religious, and cultural distinctions, were collapsed by Garveyites in an attempt to encourage people of African descent to view themselves as part of a single Pan-African family, united for the common good against their European oppressors. This intellectual construct helped to inspire a fighting spirit among the black masses and motivated women like Ashwood and Jacques to prove, as Jacques put it, "that Negro women are great thinkers as well as doers."[6]

Ashwood and Jacques were both born into respectable Jamaican families. Ashwood's father was a successful caterer and mortician, and Jacques's heritage was deeply rooted in the brown (the miscegenated population largely produced by the bodies of black women) middle class. Jacques's great-great-grandfather was the first mayor of Kingston, and her father was a manager at a cigar factory and a prosperous landowner. Both women received a formal education during a time when compulsory elementary schooling was nonexistent in Jamaica. In fact, in 1910, only approximately one quarter of the "colored" population could read and write, and this number was considerably lower for black Jamaicans.[7] Thus, the formal secondary education of Jacques and Ashwood further distinguished them from their middle-class peers. Ashwood attended the prestigious Westwood Boarding School for Girls, while Jacques was enrolled at Wolmers, the oldest existing secondary school on the island. These elite academic environments also acculturated students to the values and lifestyles of the British. In 1911, during Jacques's tenure there, Wolmers was considered as "good [as a] Girls Day school in an English town."[8]

Although Wolmers and Westwood provided the extent of their formal education, both Ashwood and Jacques were fortunate enough to have access to other learning settings and teachers who supplemented their schooling. In addition to taking private lessons in shorthand and typing, Jacques proudly stated that "the biggest influence in my life was my father."[9] After dinner on Sundays, Mr. Jacques would challenge and stimulate his daughter by making her read foreign newspapers, particularly the editorials. Sometimes she would have to write an essay on a news item or explain an article to him. Jacques recalled how this dialectical and intergenerational exchange made her "learn to think independently on world affairs and to analyze situations."[10] For her part, Ashwood was a young woman with aspirations to a theatrical career who was noted for her masterful recitations and debating skills. The most popular venues for social and intellectual engagement in Jamaica at that time were literary and debate societies, and it was there that Ashwood cultivated the ability to take a public role and assert her ideas with unwavering confidence and skill. Although neither woman went to college (which would eventually position them outside "bourgeois" intellectual circles), their formal and informal education provided them with a double learning context, both expanding their political focus beyond the island of their birth (giving them a foundation from which to grasp, assess, and analyze sophisticated liberation paradigms) and, just as importantly, socializing them to be self-confident and high-achieving.

Amy Ashwood

Amy Ashwood met Marcus Garvey in 1914 at a meeting sponsored by the East Queen Baptist Literary and Debating society.[11] The two struck up a friendship and soon decided to co-found the UNIA. Ashwood later recalled that they "planned a great Black Confraternity, under our own vine and fig tree in our own Africa."[12] Despite the published aims of the organization—which included pledges "to establish a universal confraternity among the races, to promote the spirit of race pride and love," and to "assist in civilizing the Backward tribes of Africa"—the UNIA meetings and activities in Jamaica resembled those of other middle-class "societies" at the turn of the century. They raised funds to feed the poor of Kingston on Christmas Day, distributed flowers at hospitals, and sponsored debates.[13]

For the most part, the subject matter at the UNIA forums was palatable by even the most conservative standards, but there were occasions when topics included questions like "Is the intellect of woman as highly developed as that of man?" and "Women or men: Whose influence is more felt in the world?"[14] The fact that these questions were even raised suggests that early members like Ashwood confronted serious issues about women as intellectual beings and about their roles in global affairs. In general, though, and contrary to contemporary opinion, Garvey took pains to make it clear that his association was "nonpolitical."[15] Essentially, the function of the UNIA in Jamaica was to appeal to dark-skinned middle-class people at a time when other comparable associations denied them membership.

Jamaican society was grossly stratified at that time, and although color alone did not exclusively determine class and status, it had much to do with it. Based on a racial gradation between the "African" and the "European," racial identities were divided, subdivided, and then diced. Despite the fact that no legal color bar existed, scholars have documented color discrimination against dark-skinned people in employment, particularly in public service occupations. Ashwood's biographer, Lionel Yard, comments that her dark skin positioned her to be "part of an avant-garde element that challenged the color lines drawn by past generations."[16] This was undoubtedly at least part of the reason why Ashwood was drawn to co-found an association that first and foremost did not view dark-skinned black people as offensive and unworthy, but regarded their color as a direct linkage to an honorable lineage with the potential to rise again. Therefore the "root" of Ashwood's Pan-African intellectual development was directly lodged within Afrocentric epistemology. Ashwood later wrote that on the "very day" that she learned about Africa and the slave trade, a "consciousness of race stirred to life within [her]. A burning desire to know something of the land of [her] fathers seized [her]."[17] Molefi Asante explains this desire and its subsequent search as "an uncovering of one's true self . . . the pinpointing of one's center, and . . . the clarity and focus through which black people must see the world in order to escalate."[18]

Ashwood's Africalogy would eventually take her to Ghana and its Ashanti capital, Kumasi. In 1947, after a nearly forty-year search, Ashwood's heritage was verified and the *Ashanti Pioneer* recorded her welcome-home ceremony, where it was declared that she was "of the family of Damanhene, a native of Juaben and an Ashanti."[19] During the 1920s, however, Ashwood theorized about reconnecting black diasporians to their African past not so much to take refuge within an "African genius" narrative (of which Gilroy and others are rightly critical), but as a building block toward what she believed all black diasporians were entitled to: an African national citizenship and the right to self-determination.

As a co-founder of the UNIA, Ashwood insisted that women be well integrated into the organization's structure; thus, she saw to it that the UNIA's constitution stipulated that each local division elect a male and female president and vice president. There does not seem to be any precedent for this egalitarian structure in similar organizations. Clearly, Ashwood had taken the initiative to ensure that women were not pushed to the sidelines of female auxiliaries but were an integral part of interpretive activities. In addition, she guaranteed herself a place in the parent body by being elected general secretary of the Ladies Division. In the minds of most people, secretary was a proper position for a lady, but Ashwood transformed this behind-the-scenes, low-key role into a public forum to disseminate her ideas and those of others regarding the critical steps that were needed for black autonomy.

It should be mentioned that at this time Ashwood's rhetoric did not challenge the notion of domestic roles for women. For example, at one meeting in St. Ann's Bay she delivered a message that "the future of our race and country will be assured" only through "Co-operation." Placing the success of the UNIA squarely on the shoulders of black women, she said, "To you ladies let me say that on you depends the making of our men. We want a country of good women, women whose influence in the home can be [an] influence felt for good, that influence that will inspire our men to do good and noble things."[20] However, it is important to remember that

Ashwood was only seventeen years old at the inception of the UNIA and eighteen when she gave this speech. As she matured with the organization, her budding feminist perspective, which is clearly evident in the formation of the Ladies Division, would grow to critique ideas that confined women to a familiar sphere.

Despite Ashwood's and Garvey's efforts, it was difficult to generate support for the UNIA in Jamaica, and Ashwood reports that by the time Garvey left the island for the United States in 1916, he was swimming in debt and contributors were clamoring for an account of the organization's funds.[21] When Ashwood immigrated to the United States two years later, the two again worked as a team to increase support for the UNIA. By this time, the post–World War I context offered them an optimal climate for a Pan-African movement that strategically capitalized on a variety of injustices, and they worked to shape the organization to embrace the then current tenets of African-American life: racial solidarity, moral uplift, and self-reliance. Garvey convincingly argued that it was not "humanity that was lynched, burned, jim-crowed and segregated, but Negro people." Ashwood's Harlem oratory was just as riveting. Primarily noted for her masterful recitations of Paul Laurence Dunbar poems, she also gave speeches that galvanized people to attend meetings (she went door to door from Harlem to Brooklyn generating support) and to donate money to the UNIA's commercial activities, most notably to its steamship company, the Black Star Line. Former Garveyite Arden Bryan declared that he and Ashwood alone raised $200,000 for the steamship company when they traveled to five eastern states.[22] Clearly, Ashwood was able to convince others of the merits of the UNIA, which was no longer a mere society pledged to uplift the poor and unrefined; it was now a political organization committed to reconnecting black diasporians to an imagined African homeland for their political, economic, social, and cultural well-being.

Although there were at this point many disparate elements within the movement, including the effort to build up an African Palestine (Liberia) and the presence of some members who were seeking to establish or expand their personal wealth, it was Ashwood's intellect that helped to construct the UNIA's philosophical component. Her message of an undiluted expression of racial affirmation struck a chord with disgruntled black people the world over by shrewdly combining black political and economic empowerment to end domination and exploitation. By 1919 the UNIA was a formidable movement claiming a membership of millions, with branches in the United States, Canada, Central and South America, the Caribbean, Great Britain, and Africa.[23]

On the evening of December 25, 1919, more than three thousand people witnessed Ashwood and Garvey seal their union with an elaborate wedding ceremony. Three months later, however, they were separated. Ashwood writes, "In the full glare of the limelight the Marcus Garvey I knew receded into the shadows. The public figure Garvey took his place, and we found we were unable to continue the old partnership."[24] Garvey certainly would not have been the first man to change under the pressure of leadership. It seems, though, that what happened was not so much a transformation of the man as a transformation of his expectations of Ashwood. It was one thing to be Garvey's cofounder, but another to be his wife. He wanted Ashwood to function in a way that she had never done before; he wanted her to become more subdued in her public persona and to support him in all of his undertakings, questioning neither his political nor his business decisions.

Despite Garvey's progressive anticolonial political views, in many respects he was very traditional, and his Jamaican upbringing led him to expect his wife to be a compromising helpmate. Garvey described his own mother as a "soft and good" woman who "always returned a smile for a blow." Although Garvey was critical of his father's maltreatment of his mother, he believed that women should be self-sacrificing and supportive, and he set this standard for all UNIA wives. In fact, Garvey's belief that women were to be self-sacrificing and supportive had a long history within black intellectual traditions. Gilroy points out that Martin Delany was the first black intellectual to put forth the argument that masculine power was fundamental to nationalist doctrine and that women were to be educated exclusively for motherhood.[25] The idea that a "supreme patriarch" was needed for the "integrity of the race" has since become something of a mantra for black nationalist thought. For his part, Garvey argued that his male-centered nation benefited women because it allowed them the opportunity to develop their God-given talents: making the home a haven of comfort and nurturing children, the future generation. Garvey believed in a construction of roles that allowed men and women to wield proper influence and authority over separate spheres: public and familial. But as Barbara Bair persuasively argues, these culturally constructed roles were not "separate and equal," as Ashwood had envisioned, but "separate and hierarchal."[26]

Ashwood represented a new generation of black women, and it was against her nature to submit totally and to accommodate Garvey's every need. She had a mind of her own and refused his control over it. So perhaps it is not surprising that six months after their wedding Garvey filed suit for an annulment. He had quickly come to the conclusion that his inability to control his wife was detrimental to the UNIA. Ashwood's feminine power was evidenced not only by her unwillingness to be subdued but also by her free spirit—her lifestyle resembled that of the few other women in America who were experiencing a taste of liberation during the Roaring Twenties. She frequently consumed alcohol in public and apparently never terminated her close friendships with other men. Such behavior was considered anathema to Garvey's nation, and this fact helped to set the stage for defining the social roles that were deemed suitable for women in the movement as well as the possible repercussions if one were to go against the grain.

To be sure, Ashwood did not sit meekly by and let Garvey expel her from the organization she had cofounded. She had been a good organizer and a captivating speaker who was adored by the general membership. In the end, though, she was no match for Garvey, who strategically defamed and maligned her character to all who had an interest. After their divorce in 1922, she began the extensive travels that would eventually take her all over the globe and lead her to become the "western sister" who brought a message of "feminine emancipation" to Liberia, Ghana, and Nigeria.[27] More specifically, in 1924 she became a founding member of the Nigerian Progress Union, and during the 1930s she was an active member of both the International African Service Bureau, led by George Padmore, and C.L.R. James's International African Friends of Ethiopia. During the 1940s she was active with Paul Robeson's Council on African Affairs and campaigned for Adam Clayton Powell Jr. and the Afro-Women's International Alliance in New York. Everywhere she went she spent hours in historical archives, and she wrote several unpublished manuscripts. She seemed proudest of her piece on the history of Liberia, for which Sylvia Pankhurst issued a "preview" pamphlet giving an overview of its contents and calling it a "highly interesting and informative history."[28]

Ashwood's departure from the UNIA produced the first major division within the movement, as some members were disappointed with Garvey's behavior toward her. But once Ashwood moved to England—the first step of her nomadic life—another first lady of the UNIA arrived on the scene in the person of Amy Jacques.

Amy Jacques

Amy Jacques had met Garvey in 1919, after recurring bouts with malaria had forced her to leave Jamaica for the United States. She joined the UNIA, and married Garvey in 1922, two months after he divorced Ashwood. While Ashwood was celebrated for her inspiring, motivational speeches, Jacques became recognized for her editorials. Between 1924 and 1927, Jacques served as associate editor of the UNIA's newspaper, *The Negro World*, and introduced the women's page, "Our Women and What They Think." During this period the women's sections in most newspapers consisted merely of columns highlighting the fine points of etiquette, fashion, and social events. Jacques argued that these discussions were frivolous, and she sought instead to create an open forum in which women could express their ideas and opinions on serious matters. Jacques led the way by writing 173 different editorials exclusively for the woman's page, many of which clearly challenged the patriarchy within the UNIA.

At the time Jacques was writing, African American integrationists were arguing that it was the duty of women to engage in a particular brand of community leadership, such as the social work detailed in Stephanie Shaw's research on professional black women during the era of Jim Crow and in Jacqueline Rouse's biography on Lugenia Hope Burns in Atlanta. In addition, most Pan-African intellectuals of the time were reluctant to admit that women could move beyond domestic activism and tackle political affairs, despite the recent passage of the Nineteenth Amendment. In her editorial "Women's Function in Life," Jacques addressed this issue of "whether [a] woman's place is in the home, in business, in politics or in industry." She understood that countries were different and women's status varied; however, "present day events convince us that women, lovely women if you please, are making their presence felt in every walk of life." She compared the "New Negro Woman's" function in life to that of other women in the world, commenting that women of the East (India, Egypt, Turkey) were being educated and no longer considered themselves "slaves to their husbands" but rather saw themselves as "intelligent, independent human beings [able] to assert and maintain their rights in co-partnership with their men."[29] In this piece Jacques went on to urge black women to recognize that they were part of an international sisterhood.

Jacques maintained that the woman "of today has a place in nearly all places of man's life, and where such a place is not yet properly established her voice is heard in that regard." Clearly she was not the only black woman who had a strong gender lens focused on declaring that women had the right to multiple identities and the wherewithal to engage successfully on contested terrain; the vast majority of black women's lives reflected this reality. But her assertions can be seen as exceptional when contextualized within a nationalistic political rhetoric that stipulated that racial progress was inextricably tied to men and women "functioning" within gendered spaces to guarantee masculine control. Garvey clearly wanted a patriarchal nation, and Jacques's editorials contradicted what was presumed by many of the UNIA members to be indispensable to nationhood—masculine dominance.

To make sure that her readership recognized that her position differed somewhat from Garvey's, Jacques restated in numerous editorials that women must not be denied roles as intellectuals and political activists. In the editorial "No Sex in Brains and Ability," she wrote that "some men declare that women should remain in the homes and leave professions and legislation to men, but this is an antiquated belief, and has been exploded by woman's competency in these new fields and further by the fact that their homes have not suffered by a division of their time and interest."[30] Jacques wanted her readership to understand how the familiar and public spheres were linked in a way that required women to become aware of and participate in the political world.

While editorial writing became for Jacques the training ground for testing ideas that would eventually become part of her intellectual Pan-African arsenal, the women's page was not the only place where we see her thriving as an editor. She also assembled the two volumes of *The Philosophy and Opinions of Marcus Garvey* (1923, 1925). Jacques collected Garvey's speeches and articles, the majority of which had been originally printed in the *Negro World*, and decided to publish them "so that by [Garvey's] own words he may be judged" and "not from inflated and misleading newspapers and magazine articles" about him. But Jacques clearly located herself in the editing process, saying, at one point, "I have produced what I consider two of the best speeches of my husband."[31] A line-by-line comparison of the original documents with the reprints reveals that most of her revisions were abridgments or conflations of two or more separate texts. Still, she did edit some of Garvey's writings by removing entire sections. Some of these excised passages revealed Garvey's more rebellious side. They include, but are not limited to, statements about the use of the latest artillery, explosives, and war strategy, and about retribution. In the second volume there are a few examples of Jacques softening the intensity of Garvey's words. For example, at one point she inserted the word "constitu-tional" before the word "fight," implying that black people were going to be not volatile but civil and law-abiding. This one word changed the essential message of his text from holding out the possibility of a bloody battle to offering a civil rights argument.

Jacques assembled both volumes when Garvey was attempting to gather support to fight his indictment on mail fraud. This may help to explain why she removed some of his more inflammatory statements. Not sur-prisingly, Garvey's most radical speeches are not included at all. Robert Hill points out that, unfortunately, the first volume of *The Philosophy and Opinions* "has institutionalized a distorted picture of the militant stage of the UNIA and its mass following."[32] While historians can quibble over the far-reaching impact of Jacques's editorial changes, it was undoubtedly her intellect that coalesced and disseminated what we today identify as Garveyism.

After Garvey was indicted and convicted of mail fraud, pardoned by President Harding, and later deported to Jamaica from the United States in 1927, he decided to embark on a "scientific" tour of Europe to learn first-hand of the conditions of black people there. It was at the Century Theatre in West London that Jacques gave a ringing address from the "Negro woman to the white woman of London." She raised many issues in this speech, moving back and forth from complimenting white women to criti-cizing their unwillingness to learn more about black women the "world over." Her comments reflected her ambivalence toward white women in general. On the one hand, she recognized that they were discriminated against as women in a patriarchal society: "know this, that we suffer even as you do, because the color of our skins does not make us different in our physical bodies, does not make us different in our ambitions, and in our aspirations and in our hopes. No. We hope for as much as you have hoped and longed for." At the same time, it was their whiteness that em-powered them to insult black women with the Jim Crow statement "I am sorry; we do not serve black people in here." She lambasted this position as un-Christian and appealed to the hearts of women who have a "finer conscience, or perhaps more conscious, in them than men have." "Think twice" and "remind your men" that "we are all human beings, and as chil-dren of God, we deserve equal treatment, equal fairness, and equal jus-tice in common with all humanity."[33] The English were "surprised" by Jacques's "force and conviction," but Garveyites were not. By now they were hailing her as "the Greatest Negro Woman of Our Race," unshaken in her commitment to present the cause of the black woman internationally to the European world.[34]

As World War II engulfed the globe, Jacques was confined to the island of her birth. Garvey had died in 1940, leaving her a single parent of two teenaged boys. But single motherhood did not curtail her drive to be an active intellectual force; nor did the fact that the UNIA had by now gone through a stream of national officers, had experienced countless financial setbacks, and was divided along United States-versus-Caribbean lines. As she grieved the loss of Garvey, Jacques made peace with all of his foes and moved to another intellectual level. Although still wedded to Garveyism, she was no longer concerned about membership affiliation. She wrote countless letters to black intellectuals around the world to meet her new objective: directing "Garveyism into the folds of organizations, groups, etc."[35] Her decision not to "bottle up Garveyism in one or two organizations" also freed her to view former competitors as comrades in the Pan-African struggle.[36] And it was during this period that she cultivated important intellectual exchanges with Nnamdi Azikiwe of Nigeria, Kwame Nkrumah of Ghana, W.E.B. Du Bois, and a host of other prominent thinkers. Most importantly, her copious correspondence was crucial in establishing links between prominent Africans and diasporian black people. For example, documents suggest that she introduced Du Bois to Azikiwe, who, by the way, happened to "adore Garveyism." Azikiwe argued that the philosophy, "with its elements of race pride, race consciousness, nationalism and its correlant of economic stability, appeals to the modern political enthusiast, who keeps his head clear and steers away from chauvinism or ethnocentricism; for it will aid in ameliorating various political, economic, social and other problems which affect this modern age."[37]

Given her commitment to unifying a dispersed and divergent movement, Jacques was elated when Du Bois proposed a fifth meeting of the Pan-African Congress and requested that she serve as a co-convenor. Du Bois also sought her "reaction and suggestions" on a letter he was writing to convene the Congress after the war.[38] Jacques critiqued the letter, adding that she found it regrettable that the Congress "could not be held before the war is over, so that United Africa would speak as never before."[39] After the war, she wrote, "the Nations of the world would be in a state of complacency and do not care how we burn, as long as they are no longer being bombed and blasted."[40] As the only scheduled female co-convenor, Jacques also suggested that invitations be sent to Una Marson, who "could represent the West Indian Woman," and to Ivy Tracy Timothy, who was born "of

an English mother and West Indian father, and has suffered from the inequalities meted out to English-born Colored people."[41]

Although Du Bois enlisted Jacques's help, it was George Padmore who
became the planning mastermind of the Congress, held in London in 1945.
Jacques informed Padmore that she had contacted Garveyite organizations
all over the world in order to ensure a strong representation at the meeting, and indeed, the session proved to be the most powerful gathering ever
assembled of Africans and people of African descent (African Americans
numbering the fewest, largely due to visa problems) working toward the
defeat of imperialism.

When the Congress opened in London on October 15, 1945, a Mrs. A.
Garvey was present, but unbeknownst to many, it was Amy Ashwood, not
Amy Jacques. Financial hardship had continued to loom over Jacques's
household after Garvey's death and she was unable to attend because she
"did not have a cent to go."[42] Ashwood was present at Du Bois's request.
After her divorce from Garvey, Ashwood had continued to live an adven-
turesome life, never staying in any one country more than four years at a
time.[43] But she continued to be just as dedicated as Jacques to advancing
the political interest of African peoples and standing up for women's
rights. And at the Congress, Ashwood gave a moving speech exposing the
sexist agenda of the meeting. There had only been a handful of female
delegates to the Congress, and Ashwood made sure that her voice was
heard. She said, "Very much has been written and spoken of the Negro, but
for some reason very little has been said about the black woman." Ashwood went on to say that the black woman "has been shunted into the social background to be a childbearer. This has been principally her lot." She
also expressed her concern with the fact that Jamaican women's wages
were much lower than men's, and her conviction that black men were
"largely responsible, as they do little to help the women to get improved
wages."[44] Ashwood's brief comments went to the core of socially constructed and globally held ideas about womanhood; that is, as Honor
Ford-Smith points out, "by paying lower wages for the tasks women did at
the workplace and none for the work done in the home, it justified male
privilege at the workplace and the home."[45]

The Fifth Pan-African Congress went down in history as the most important turning point in the Pan-African movement from a "passive to an
active stage," a fact that makes Ashwood's timely comments connecting
feminist concerns to a global Pan-African agenda even more powerful.
Furthermore, although Jacques could not attend, Padmore assured her

that he had read her comprehensive memorandum for African redemption, which addressed the need to create a Federation of the British West Indies and to remove the travel barriers and restrictions connected with "entering our motherland."[46] In the end, thanks in part to Jacques and Ashwood, the Congress resolutions were sophisticated, intellectual indictments of political, economic, and social imperialism.

In theory, Jacques and Ashwood would have found much common ground, but similar political and intellectual agendas do not automatically generate sincere communication and friendship. In the case of these two, their possible closeness was undoubtedly complicated by emotional tensions over their having been married to the same man. Jacques and Ashwood were notoriously hostile toward one another, and this is significant for this essay because it reveals the fallacy of a utopian black sisterhood. E. Frances White has warned against adopting the position that "accepts as unproblematic an Afro centric sisterhood across class, time and geography"; indeed, differences and tensions exist between and among black women, just as they do among members of any other group.[47]

In order to avoid the danger of oversimplifying diasporic experiences and knowledge, it is imperative that we broaden our focus to include more diverse thinkers. Jacques and Ashwood are simply two examples. Both were steadfast Pan-African intellectuals who deserve considerable attention from scholars committed to documenting the full range of historical black radical thought. Both women traveled throughout the black diaspora and Africa, and overall their analysis of the conditions of their "Pan-African family," especially the plight of women, helps us to understand that black women are not simply bodies that reproduce and pass on culture to the next generation, but astute cultivators of ideas that can help us transform the next millennium for the betterment of all peoples of African descent.

NOTES

1. Natasha Barnes, "Black Atlantic–Black America," *Research in African Literatures* 27, no. 4 (winter 1996): 106.

2. Tony Martin documents that in the early 1920s there were approximately 1,200 branches in more than forty countries with millions of active members. Tony Martin, *Race First: The Ideological and Organizational Struggles of Marcus Garvey and the Universal Negro Improvement Association* (Dover, Mass.: The Majority Press, 1986).

3. Stephanie Shaw, *What a Woman Ought to Be: Professional Black Women during the Jim Crow* Era (Chicago: University of Chicago Press, 1996).

4. Carol Boyce Davies, *Black Women Writing and Identity: Migration of the Subject* (New York: Routledge, 1994), 50.

5. Paul Gilroy, *The Black Atlantic: Modernity and Double Consciousness* (Cambridge: Harvard University Press, 1993), 34.

6. Horace Campbell, "Garveyism, Pan-Africanism and African Liberation in the Twentieth Century," in *Garvey, His World and Impact,* ed. Rupert Lewis and Patrick Bryan (Mona, Jamaica: Institute of Social and Economic Research, 1988); Amy Jacques-Garvey, "Our Page is Three Years Old," *Negro World,* 12 February 1927, 10.

7. Sir Harry S. Johnston, *The Negro in the New World* (New York: Macmillan, 1910), 270.

8. Wolmers School, Kingston, Jamaica, *Wolmers Bicentenary Souvenir 1729–1929* (Kingston, Jamaica: Committee, 1929).

9. Ida Lewis, "Mrs. Garvey Talks with Ida Lewis," *Encore,* May 1973, 68.

10. Amy Jacques Garvey, "The Role of Women in Liberation Struggles," *Massachusetts Review* (winter/spring 1971): 110. It is important to note that newspapers were considered a luxury item for the average working-class Jamaican. See "Charles S. Shirley to the Gleaner," in *Marcus Garvey Papers Vol. I,* ed. Robert A. Hill (Berkeley: University of California Press, 1983), 47–48.

11. *Marcus Garvey Pavers I,* 69.

12. Lionel M. Yard, *Biography of Amy Ashwood Garvey, 1897–1969: CoFounder of the UNIA* (Washington, D.C.: The Associated Publisher, 1990), 16.

13. *Marcus Garvey Papers I,* 80, 88.

14. Tony Martin, "Women in the Garvey Movement," in *Garvey: His Work and Impact,* ed. Rupert Lewis and Patrick Bryan (Mona, Jamaica: Institute of Social and Economic Research, 1988), 68.

15. *Marcus Garvey Papers I,* 100.

16. Yard, *Biography of Amy Ashwood Garvey,* 68.

17. Ibid., 7.

18. Molefi Asante, *Kemet, Afrocentricity and Knowledge* (Trenton, N.J.: African World Press, 1989), viii.

19. Tony Martin, "Discovering African Roots: Amy Ashwood Garvey's Pan-Africanist Journey," *Comparative Studies of South Asia, Africa and the Middle East* 17, no. 1 (1997): 125.

20. "UNIA Meeting in St. Ann's Bay," *Jamaican Times,* 13 November 1915; reprint in *Marcus Garvey Papers I,* 162–63.

21. *Marcus Garvey Papers I,* cxiii.

22. Yard, *Biography of Amy Ashwood Garvey,* 45, 55.

23. Tony Martin, *Race First: The Ideological and Organizational Struggles of Marcus Garvey and the Universal Negro Improvement Association* (Westport, Conn.: Greenwood Press, 1976), 14–16.

24. Amy Ashwood Garvey, "Marcus Garvey Chapter 11," 21, in Amy Ashwood Garvey Collection MS. 1977B, National Library of Jamaica, Kingston, Jamaica, Box V.

25. Gilroy, *The Black Atlantic,* 25–26.

26. Barbara Bair, "True Women, Real Men: Gender, Ideology, and Social Roles in the Garvey Movement," in *Gendered Domains: Rethinking Public and Private in Women's History,* ed. Dorothy O. Helly and Susan M. Reverby (Ithaca, N.Y.: Cornell University Press, 1992), 155.

27. Yard, *Biography of Amy Ashwood Garvey,* 2.

28. Ibid., 143.

29. Amy Jacques Garvey, "Women's Function in Life," *Negro World,* 12 December 1925.

30. Amy Jacques Garvey, "No Sex In Brains and Ability," *Negro World,* 27 December 1924, 8.

31. Amy Jacques Garvey, *The Philosophy and Opinions of Marcus Garvey Or, Africans for the Africans Vol. I* (Dover, Mass.: The Majority Press, 1986), preface.

32. *Marcus Garvey Papers I,* xciv.

33. "Mrs. Garvey Delivers Ringing Message to White Women of London at Great Meeting," *Negro World,* 22 September 1928.

34. "The Greatest Negro Woman of Our Race," *Negro World,* 3 November 1928, 3.

35. Amy Jacques Garvey to Mr. Geo Covington, 2 May 1946, Fisk University Papers, Box #1, File #5.

36. Amy Jacques Garvey to Mr. Blades, 14 August 1944, Fisk University Papers, Box #1, File #3.

37. Nnamdi Azikiwe, *My Odyssey: An Autobiography* (New York: Praeger Publishers, 1970), 162.

38. W.E.B. Du Bois to Amy Jacques Garvey, 8 April 1944, Du Bois Papers, Reel #56, Frame #110, Enclosure.

39. Amy Jacques Garvey to W.E.B. Du Bois, 24 April 1944, DuBois Papers, Reel #56, Frame #111.

40. Amy Jacques Garvey to Mr. Gibbons, 5 April 1944, Fisk University Papers, Box #1, File #12.

41. Amy Jacques Garvey to George Padmore, 28 July 1945, Fisk University Papers, Box #2, File #2.

42. Interview with Amy Jacques Garvey by Dabu Gizenga, 10 January 1973, Kwame Nkrumah Collection 128-1 to 128-2, Moorland Spingard Library, Howard University.

43. Tony Martin, "Amy Ashwood Garvey Wife No. 1," *Jamaican Journal* 20, no.3 (August-October 1987): 33.

44. George Padmore, ed., *History of the Fifth Pan-African Congress* (London: The Hammersmith Bookshop Ltd., 1947), 52.

45. Honor Ford-Smith, "Women and the Garvey Movement in Jamaica," in *Garvey: His Work and Impact,* ed. Rupert Lewis and Patrick Bryan (Mona, Jamaica: Institute of Social and Economic Research, 1988), 75.

46. Interview with Amy Jacques Garvey by Dabu Gizenga, 10 January 1973, Kwame Nkrumah Collection 128-1 to 128-2, Moorland Spingard Library, Howard University.

47. E. Frances White, "Africa on My Mind: Gender, Counter Discourses and African-American Nationalism," *Journal of Women's History* 2, no. 1 (spring 1990): 93.

Chapter 7

"Eat Your Bread without Butter, but Pay Your Poll Tax!"

Roots of the African American Voter Registration Movement in Florida, 1919–1920

Paul Ortiz

> In the South, the negro in politics is not tolerated—in
> other sections he must obediently follow. There are lynch-
> ings so nearly everywhere that the rule is established. . . .
> If the negro be wise he will respect the limits set for him
> as does the elephant and the tiger and the others who ac-
> cept rules and make no pretense to reason.
> —"The Color Line that Belts the Earth,"
> *The Florida Times-Union* (1904)[1]

In the final week of May, 1919, members of the Jacksonville branch of the National Alliance of Postal Employees, a union of African American railway mail clerks, gathered at the home of A. J. Gillis, a senior clerk, for their monthly meeting.[2] D. H. Dwight, the local's president, proudly recalled that the older clerks had organized the union "to help our younger brother coming into the service," after discovering that all incoming black clerks would be barred from the Railway Mail Association after 1913.[3] Dwight noted that the union had become a cornerstone of mutual aid, establishing a benefit fund that members in good standing as well as their widows and children could draw upon during hard times. Dwight's narrative of the union's history emphasized the grievance procedure that the clerks had negotiated with management as well as the patriotic service members had rendered during World War I.

After opening with a prayer, the membership discussed union business and plans for the union's national convention in Jacksonville. "And last, but not least," the secretary reported, "The committee appointed to see that each local clerk had paid his poll tax and was duly qualified as a citizen, and registered voter, they reported that every clerk, with one exception, possessed the proper credentials, and the one clerk mentioned who had just become of age, gave assurance of obtaining the necessary qualifications real soon."[4]

The clerks' union was able to call upon its members to risk the dangers of engaging in politics in the Deep South because the union had woven together personal relationships of trust and reciprocity that allowed members to survive Jim Crow.[5] In 1919 and 1920, black Floridians in thirty counties drew on similar kinds of bonds to create a statewide voter registration movement that challenged white supremacy's stranglehold on power in the Sunshine State.[6] The Florida voter registration movement was forged by African American secret societies, women's clubs, unions, churches, and other institutions that bolstered black dignity and thrived outside of Jim Crow's grasp.[7] In these groups, black Floridians cultivated the kinds of intergenerational relationships and social spaces that must exist for a social movement to emerge.[8] Older African Americans, male and female, played leading roles in local movement-building, roles usually reserved in the literature on the "New Negro" after World War I to a younger, more "militant" generation.[9]

In a skillful tactical maneuver, black Floridians used their lodges and secret societies as primary organizing vehicles to build their statewide social movement. Time and time again, this strategy confused white Democrats, Klansmen, and local sheriffs who sought to crush whoever was encouraging African Americans to vote—Bolsheviks were a favorite if elusive culprit.[10] By the time the smoke had cleared from these futile countywide searches, hundreds of black citizens had added their names to the voter rolls.[11] Florida's white supremacists cried that an "unseen hand" was threatening the survival of the one-party state and Jim Crow.

The organizing strategies that infused the Florida voter registration movement were rooted in the institutional and cultural forms African Americans developed to survive Jim Crow. In 1889, Florida native Emanuel Fortune had asserted that black southerners "should form strong organizations among themselves for mutual and effective protection in time of need. . . . The existence, the objects and the aims of these organizations should be known only to the members of them, and they should be appealed to and used at the right time and in the proper manner."[12] Black Floridians followed this advice and embarked on decades of building institutions that operated behind veils of secrecy designed to ward off the blows of white supremacy.[13]

The Colored Knights of Pythias had by the end of World War I become the state's largest black secret society and mutual aid organization. The same week that the Jacksonville clerks solidified their commitment to voter registration, the Pythians held their annual Grand Lodge meeting in Tampa.[14] Members were in a mood to celebrate. During World War I, KOP lodges had sponsored Liberty Loan drives and other activities for the task of supporting the Allied effort. A Pythian had boasted during the war, "More than a thousand of [our] members are either on the firing line or in camps awaiting the coming of the overseas transport, and thousands more are at home, with their satchels packed, awaiting the call, eager to join their brethren and offer up their sacrifices that democracy may reign and the world be made safe for all men and all men made citizens."[15] By 1919, the Pythians claimed fifteen thousand members in good standing in Florida. Nearly one out of every six adult black males of voting age in the state was a member of the lodge.[16]

The level of organization the Knights of Pythias had achieved gave the order the confidence to enter the realm of formal politics. The Tampa delegates called upon all members in the state to pay their poll taxes and register to vote. Those who did not register by January 1, 1920 would be suspended until they did so.[17] As black voter registration surged across Florida, a source informed W.E.B. Du Bois:

> This revival of the Negro's interest in becoming registered and paying his poll-tax began last May when the Grand Lodge Knights of Pythias passed a resolution prohibiting any member from entering the lodge in the state of Florida after January 1, 1920, until he had registered and paid his poll taxes. The Knights of Pythias has a membership of fifteen thousand men of voting age. It is a question in my mind whether this resolution could have been enforced had any member objected in the courts but no one objected, hence the other fraternities followed suit and as a result we have a heavy registration of Negro voters which has already had a telling effect on the attitude of white men toward the Negro.[18]

African American women were creating equally important social spaces where black Floridians could meet and discuss voter registration.[19] A. G.

Samuels, writing on behalf of the "Colored Voters of Cocoa-Brevard County," informed GOP presidential candidate Warren G. Harding that "since the Colored Women has begun to Register it has caused the Colored men voters to take on new life in Politics all over the state, as they has never before."[20] A leader of the Jacksonville movement was Eartha White, a community organizer who had been urging African Americans to register to vote for two decades.[21] After White and others led a number of voter registration workshops, African American women in Jacksonville marched to the polls in groups: "In the Seventh ward they began to arrive at 8 o'clock," an observer wrote in late September, "and many of them sat down on the curbing to rest, so many hours were they in line. . . . Some went with babies in their arms, and others took their lunches so that they would not have to fast while waiting to be registered at 7 o'clock last night when the books closed. "[22] Black women in Fort Pierce formed their own political club and embarked on voter education work.[23]

Democratic officials sounded a general alarm. A white man from Fort Pierce warned: "Surely no white man nor white woman wants to occupy a lower sphere in our political life than a negro washerwoman—refuse to register and vote, and you so place yourself, you cannot get away from that fact."[24] The Florida Ku Klux Klan reorganized during the summer of 1920 and began targeting black organizers and institutions involved in voter education work.[25] Alarmed by a vigorous African-American registration movement in Miami, local Klansmen papered the city with flyers reading: "Beware! The Ku Klux Klan is again alive! And every Negro who approaches a polling place next Tuesday will be a marked man. This is a white man's country, boys, save your own life next Tuesday."[26]

Between 1900 and 1930 Florida suffered the highest per capita lynching rate in America.[27] Black Floridians understood all too well the risks of engaging in political activity. On the eve of the 1888 election, the *Pensacola Daily Commercial* warned African Americans to stay away from the polls or suffer the consequences.[28] Two years later a white Floridian characterized race relations in his state by explaining that "Southern white men use it as a by word that no white man is hung for killing a negro."[29] African Americans were murdered for demanding higher wages, for falling into debt, and, in at least one case, for failing to kneel before a white man.[30] An African American worker was lynched because "He was a very impudent and fearless negro, and gave his employers, as well as the entire community a great deal of trouble and uneasiness."[31] A black building contractor's home in Palatka was bombed five times because he employed white labor.

His family was forced to flee the town.[32] As the promise of Reconstruction faded, black Floridians had to cope with what Rayford Logan aptly referred to as the "nadir" of American politics.[33]

African American defiance of white supremacy, however, belies the notion that this era was the nadir of black resistance. Existing accounts of black political activity in the Deep South have generally assumed that aspirations were channeled into safer venues, or, more recently, paths of "hidden resistance."[34] The evidence from Florida suggests otherwise.[35] On numerous occasions, black workers in Florida took up arms and organized self-defense committees to prevent a lynching from occurring.[36] Between 1901 and 1905, African Americans waged streetcar boycotts against segregation in Florida's major cities. The white press admitted that black Floridians did not accept segregation: "They get as good accommodation as the whites in the street cars, but they object to the tangible expression of the color line."[37] Given the risks of violent reprisals, many acts of assertion occurred more quietly. The members of Harmony Baptist Church in Lakeland staged a prayer service against Jim Crow in 1914—part of the national day of protest against railroad segregation called by Booker T. Washington.[38]

The Florida voter registration movement was rooted in this history of resistance to Jim Crow. Thousands of black Floridians registered to vote in 1919 and 1920 because they believed that the franchise offered them a way to break through a system that violated their ideas of justice. An A.M.E. Zion church official in Pensacola explained:

> We are urging our folks to register and vote for the same reason that other people are registering and voting. We want full protection of the law, representation where we are concerned, decent public accommodations; for equal pay, better schools and a living wage for our teachers, womanhood respected regardless of color, good roads, a fair share of public improvements and the free and unabridged right to vote like any other American citizens.[39]

The Florida voter registration movement was fueled not by a spontaneous awakening of black communities or by the emergence of the "New Negro," but by intergenerational aspirations to dignity. Institutions like the railway mail clerks' union in Jacksonville, the Knights of Pythias, and women's organizations were part of a rich tradition of mutual aid that black Floridians created to endure Jim Crow. Local movement activists were generally older men and women who played leadership roles in such organizations. Some, like Joseph E. Lee in Jacksonville, traced their political lineage back to Reconstruction.[40] The median age of black voter registrants in five Florida counties—Dade, Palm Beach, Marion, Columbia and Putnam—was nearly forty.[41]

In Florida, the New Negro had gray hair. T. S. Harris, a leader of the voter registration movement in Suwannee County, had been active in Republican Party politics since the late 1870s.[42] Harris had served in 1890 as a delegate of the "Colored Man's Political Protective League," an organization that vowed that "No Longer Will They Be Used by a Handful of White Republicans."[43] A Masonic lodge leader, Harris also served as a delegate to the 1916 state Republican Party convention.[44] After the Armistice, African Americans in Suwannee County set aside a day of "patriotic rejoicing" with a parade, barbecue, and rally at Florida Memorial College in honor of "every young man who served in the army and navy in the great war."[45] Harris gave the keynote address. A year later, white Democrats in Suwannee County confirmed Harris's success by complaining that African-American secret societies were spearheading a local voter registration movement.[46] Harris parlayed decades of organizing experience to conduct voter education seminars for black women and men. Terrorists firebombed Harris's house, but not before he had helped hundreds of African Americans to become registered voters.[47]

African Americans like T. S. Harris rooted their activism in beliefs about dignity and justice, ideas that black Floridians preserved through a wide array of remembrance day ceremonies that shaped historical memories of bondage, the Civil War, and freedom. "Decoration Day" was held in honor of African American Union Army veterans. "Fifteenth Amendment Day" was observed to commemorate passage of the Reconstruction amendments and to reinforce claims to equal citizenship.[48] Black Floridians transformed William Lloyd Garrison Day, Frederick Douglass (or "Lincoln-Douglass") Day, and other memorials into sacred moments of reminiscence, infusing these events with an egalitarian vision that clashed with the racist version of black history then current in Florida's schools and America's colleges.

Emancipation Day was the most important day of remembrance. In 1870, African Americans in Tampa observed the day by marching through the streets of the town to the court house, "where they were harangued for a couple of hours by speakers of their own color. They wound up their show by singing 'Old John Brown.'"[49] A minister who traveled to northern

Florida in the late nineteenth century remarked, "I was by the hospitable Pensacolians invited to participate in their Emancipation celebration. They celebrate the 20th of May because on that day, they were liberated from slavery by the order of the Union Generals . . . they truly celebrated on a grand scale."[50]

Black Floridians turned Emancipation Day into a mass event that bolstered African American pride and claims to equality.[51] In the months leading up to the fiftieth anniversary of freedom, African American communities formed Emancipation Day committees in cities, small towns, and rural areas in Florida. When the great day finally came in 1913, the survivors of slavery took center stage to share the stories of their struggles with younger people. In Sanford, "The afternoon was spent in listening to experiences of many of the ex-slaves."[52] In Bartow, "Hon. C. L. Livingston, an old veteran of slavery days, made the opening speech," to an audience of approximately one thousand people.[53] In Daytona, the survivors rode in a parade float of honor "which contained four old mothers who were eye witnesses to the liberating of the race. . . . The parade was one of the grandest ever witnessed here."[54] In Gainesville, African Americans held a torchlight parade and sang "The Battle Hymn of the Republic" and the "Star Spangled Banner," among other activities.[55] At Fort Pierce, A. J. Kershaw gave the primary oration, titled "Claim of the Negro to American Soil," while at St. Joseph's church in Jacksonville, the speaker of honor "reviewed with credit and pleasure to his anxious hearers, the United states History in that he showed that the Negro has a reasonable, merited and legitimate right to claim America as his country."[56]

African Americans kindled their faith in a democratic future by celebrating their past. Emancipation celebrations reaffirmed the dignity and self-respect that Jim Crow tried to erase from black citizens. By promoting historical memories of liberation, African Americans demonstrated an aversion to the white supremacist present. Black Floridians also accomplished this by naming their fraternal lodges, clubs, and secret societies for individuals they believed personified radical aspirations in the past. Lodge members named their organizations for individuals like: Antonio Maceo; J. C. Gibbs (the highest-ranking African American political leader in Reconstruction-era Florida); Frederick Douglass; John Brown; William Lloyd Garrison; Paul Laurence Dunbar (who had written a poem eulogizing the black Civil War dead at Olustee); Richard Allen; Wendell Phillips; Phyllis Wheatley; Crispus Attucks, and other freedom fighters.[57] When African Americans in Quincy named their Knights of Pythias lodge after Frederick

Douglass or when Mrs. L. J. Madison read a paper titled "Frederick and Freedom" to commemorate Douglass's ninety-seventh birthday in Jacksonville, black Floridians were asserting the righteousness of their struggle for equal citizenship in America.[58]

African Americans' practices of celebrating the past to bolster claims to equality in the present were reinvigorated by their participation in World War I. Before American troops embarked for France, one hundred African Americans met at Mt. Moriah Baptist church in Quincy to draft a series of resolutions on the Great War. They reminded authorities: "Our race constitutes a part of the citizenship of this great commonwealth and has always shown its patriotism and loyalty in all of its struggles from the Revolutionary War down to the recent trouble with Mexico."[59] While historians have stressed the important role returning black veterans played in the making of protests in the wake of the Armistice, they have not adequately examined the ways African Americans "back home" created the political context black soldiers returned to. At a religious conference in West Palm Beach, Rev. R. C. Ransome drew loud applause when he "admonished the people that there was a new era about to dawn. The boys from overseas would be coming home, and as they had been fighting for democracy abroad, they would expect to have the same brand of democracy at home —freedom of thought, equal opportunity and [an] open door for every man. If democracy means anything, it means just this."[60] Two months later, L. A. Alexander, a combat veteran from West Palm Beach, echoed Rev. Ransome's ideas on social change: "I voice the sentiment of every colored soldier in the United States when I say that we are hoping and expecting to reap the benefits of our toilsome struggles and that Democracy in its fullest meaning will be for the betterment of the Negro race as it will be for all other races."[61]

This gendered language of military service did not acknowledge the central place women played in sustaining a war effort that relied heavily on citizens' contributions.[62] Mary McCleod Bethune authored a series of plays, pageants, and other events that gave equal weight to the contributions of black soldiers, women, senior citizens, and young people alike to the Allied effort. Mrs. Bethune's students at Daytona Normal staged a performance titled "Echoes from France" in which the performers portrayed "the big soldier," "little sister," and "the brave mother," acting out the work that each character had to do in order for the country to win the war.[63] Bethune also celebrated "the birthdays of Washington, Lincoln and the Negro orator and abolitionist, Frederick Douglass."[64] Her students made a diorama depicting "the evolution of the Negro from a slave in chains to the Negro of today as teacher, Red Cross nurse, soldier and patriot. And over all waved the beloved flag of our common country." Bethune wanted her audiences to understood that all black Floridians, regardless of age or sex, deserved equal citizenship. She reinforced this message by inviting an ex-slave, R. A. Scott, to address the audience. Scott's talk was titled "Echoes of Emancipation."

"Echoes of emancipation" reverberated throughout Florida in 1919. A reception given at Laura Street Presbyterian Church in Jacksonville honored the congregation's heroes on their return from France. The church also reserved a place of honor for Matthew M. Lewey, a Civil War veteran of the Fifty-Fifth Massachusetts Infantry Regiment, who "was introduced and given a respectful hearing, while he spoke with much interest of the days of his youth fighting the battles of his country."[65] During Reconstruction, Lewey was an elected representative in Florida. In 1884, M. M. Lewey served as a delegate to a statewide gathering of African American leaders who demanded reparations for slavery that would be applied to Florida's public school system.[66] Now, Lewey shared his insights with young veterans and fellow church members who were as determined to claim their civil rights as he had been more than a half century earlier.

A few months later, M. M. Lewey became a featured speaker at the Jacksonville movement's voter education workshops.[67] When expanded suffrage came, his wife, Bessie K. Lewey, and their two daughters became registered voters.[68] The Leweys' intergenerational commitment to freedom characterizes the kind of movement black Floridians were creating. The earliest exhortations about paying the poll tax and registering to vote after the Armistice emerged from Florida's 1919 Emancipation Day celebrations.[69]

"To See that None Suffer"

It was no accident that secret societies became a primary organizing vehicle for the Florida voter registration movement. A spokesperson for a black women's secret society in Live Oak boasted: "Those who have joined it would not take anything for their membership. We care for our sick ones and bury the dead."[70] This ethos of organized mutual aid was the springboard for the Florida voter registration movement. Segregation placed black Floridians at the bottom of a dangerous, low-wage economy, and they created institutions that practiced reciprocity to sustain working families during crises and thereby lessened dependence on white employers.[71] A black correspondent in Palatka observed of his counterparts, "Next to his church duties come his society duties. He believes that every one should be connected with some secret society, if for no other purpose than to look after his remains when breath leaves the body. The consolation of knowing that he will be decently buried is sweet to his thoughts."[72] Secret societies, churches, and unions visited sick members, performed labor for each other in times of need, and, through their membership dues, gave one of the greatest gifts of all: a decent burial.[73] These organizations built a culture of dignity and self-respect within the shell of a social system that denied their humanity.[74]

The Florida Knights of Pythias, which called upon its members to pay their poll taxes and register to vote in the spring of 1919, exemplified the mutual aid tradition. The Knights grew to "cover Florida like water covered the sea," in the words of Quincy resident A. I. Dixie, because the fraternal order was a powerful engine for organized mutual aid in African American communities. Like other secret societies, the KOP adopted rigorous rules and procedures for ensuring that sick members and their families were not forgotten by the membership. In larger towns and cities where two or more Knights' lodges existed, members were required to organize a Relief Committee "to look after sick or distressed brothers, to pay them their benefits or make donations or loans."[75] Such visits were undertaken to bolster the morale as well as the material condition of the afflicted.

In a time of disenfranchisement, the local KOP lodge provided a model of self-government. The order's leader asked: "Will we as Pythians make use of our God-given opportunity and means, or will we fulfill the oft-repeated prophecy that we are incapable of self government?"[76] The Pythian *Manual* stated: "Every member, however humble he may be, has the same right with every other to submit his propositions to the Lodge, to explain and recommend them in discussion and to have them patiently examined and deliberately decided upon by the Lodge."[77]

The KOP's emphasis on sustaining African American dignity set it on a collision course with Jim Crow. In 1899, the order successfully fought a legislative effort to restrict the use of title "Knights of Pythias" to members "exclusively of the white race."[78] Later, a KOP member was attacked by a white mob and arrested in Santa Rosa County for insisting that he had the right to purchase a berth on a Pullman car.[79] In 1915, the Knights presented to Governor Park Trammell a strongly worded resolution protesting racial oppression in Florida.[80]

Segregation has been credited with enhancing black solidarity, but it also generated bitter class and gender tensions between African Americans. Such tensions often undercut organizing efforts against Jim Crow. T.V. Gibbs, a black leader, opposed waging an organized campaign against segregation because he believed that better hygiene, not protest, was the best strategy to challenge anti-black prejudice. Gibbs argued, "When our people as a mass learn to ride in railway cars without eating water melons, fat meat, and peanuts, throwing the rinds on the floor; when our women leave their snuff sticks, greasy bundles and uncouth manners at home, railroad discriminations will abate much of their injustice."[81] Sentiments like these angered working-class African American women who endured much of the abuse shelled out by white conductors on segregated street cars.[82] It is no accident that black women anchored the street car boycott movement in Florida.[83]

Zora Neale Hurston observed: "the Negro race was not one band of heavenly love. There was stress and strain inside as well as out. Being black was not enough. It took more than a community of skin color to make your love come down on you."[84] As if by way of illustration, African Americans in Pensacola initiated a boycott against black businessmen who had started a "blue blood" society that excluded darker-skinned members. "Negroes stated that if the applicants are too exclusive in their associations, they are also too good to receive their money."[85] Solidarity was not automatic in African American communities during segregation. The individuals who carried out the boycott against the "blue bloods" of Pensacola believed that the elitism expressed by the black businessmen was an insult to their self-respect.

"A General Strike by the Colored Laborers"

The African-American working class provided the catalyst for social and political change in Florida by engaging in four years of heightened labor struggle beginning in 1916. Black workers seized on labor shortages in the wartime economy and pioneered a Great Migration out of Florida. As World War I progressed, black workers organized unions, petitioned the federal government for redress of their grievances, and organized a wave of strikes against white employers. African American laborers collectively challenged the status quo while calling into question cautious strategies of racial uplift. In turn, black working-class activism encouraged Florida's African American "race leaders" to return to the tactics of mass struggle.

African Americans carried out an organized labor exodus out of Florida. A Daytona newspaper reported that "The platform at the railway passenger depot Sunday morning at the time of train No. 86, due north bound at 9:24, presented the appearance of a colored excursion, and was such for between 30 and 40 of the men who were leaving, in charge of a government recruiting agent, for government work at Brunswick, Ga."[86] Noting that "There is a moral reaction against ill treatment by the whites," Adam Clayton Powell stated that an Ocala, Florida minister, Reverend A. L. James, "discovered last week that his entire parish had moved to New York. He followed them and is preparing to organize them in a church in Harlem."[87]

Initially, many African American leaders advised workers to stay in the South and depend on their white employers.[88] Black workers were skeptical of such advice. A Department of Labor report found: "They will not allow their own leaders to advise them against going North."[89] S. W. Jefferson of Pensacola spoke for black Floridians who were finished with Jim Crow:

> Plenty of "sound advice" is given him [the black worker] about staying in the South among his friends and under the same old conditions . . . but not one word about better treatment is suggested to lighten the burden. . . . The world war is bringing many changes and a chance for the negro to enter broader fields. With the "tempting bait" of higher wages, shorter hours, better schools and better treatment, all the preachments of the so-called "race leaders" will fall on deaf ears.[90]

When black businessmen in Jacksonville urged an end to the Great Migration they were publicly chastised by African American trade unionists, who countered: "We are unalterably opposed to any person or persons acting as our agent or counselors, without our consent or authority . . . all labor troubles or controversies should be submitted to labor organizations."[91] This environment of popular insurgency swept many "race leaders" out of positions of influence, and enhanced the level of accountability remaining leaders would be subject to.

While thousands of black Floridians left the state, African Americans who remained seized the space offered by labor shortages and federal control of the railroads. Railroad laborers organized unions, some of which had ties to the Industrial Workers of the World (IWW).[92] Subsequently, railroad workers flooded Woodrow Wilson's administration with petitions demanding the eight-hour day and equal pay for equal work.[93] Firemen on the Florida East Coast Railway noted that they were faithful boosters of the Liberty Loan drives and argued: "We feel that there should be no discrimination in wages on account of color. We all do the same work."[94] In petitioning the Wilson administration, railroad workers rejuvenated the language of citizenship by making their economic grievances against Jim Crow a political problem that required federal intervention.

African American women also sought to take advantage of the relative shortage of labor in Florida. Domestic workers quit stingy bosses to seek better wages and resisted municipal "work or fight" ordinances that were passed to tie them to white employers.[95] A.M.E. Bishop John Hurst noted that "colored women in most cases demanded an increase in wages, this increase being necessary because of the increased cost of living, which applied in Florida as well as in other parts of the country. When these demands for an increase in wages were denied by their employers, they quit, and were arrested when their employers reported the cases to the police authorities."[96]

In the wake of the Armistice, African American laborers in Florida's packing houses, citrus fields, and service industries went out on strike for higher pay and to protest years of white business supremacy. In St. Petersburg, "The union idea, having been stirred up here lately, is spreading and now the negro women who do washing and ironing and general housework are to demand $3 a day, no matter what is their employment."[97] African-American longshoremen in Key West struck after a white railroad watchman severely beat a black employee and union member.[98] At the end of October, Crescent City "Negro orange pickers connected with the Sawyer & Godfrey packing house went on strike . . . demanding 10 cents per box for picking."[99] Black laborers in the potato fields of Putnam County began organizing for higher wages. A black newspaper enthusiastically noted that farm workers in the Hastings potato harvest were earning higher pay due to labor shortages.[100]

Labor activism without political power was a blunt-edged weapon. "The Hastings potato section is not going to sit idly by and witness agitators entering its confines to encourage laborers to strike," white employers warned. Black "agitators" were immediately arrested.[101] When five hundred African-American waiters in Palm Beach threatened to strike, a local sheriff vowed that the strikers "would be put to work, as peons, on the roads" and "stated that if any trouble arose he, the sheriff, would not get hurt, but [warned] the Colored waiters might."[102]

Caught in the vise of the one-party state, African-American workers began looking toward a political solution. As the presidential election of 1920 drew closer, Florida's race and labor struggles carried stronger overtones of political conflict. "There is much talk of a general strike by the colored laborers of all classes," wrote a black correspondent from St. Petersburg on July 2, 1920. "Pamphlets have been circulated among them urging that they demand equal rights with the white people, and it is claimed that the K. of P. society is behind the movement which resulted in so many colored men qualifying as voters by paying poll taxes."[103]

"If You Want Better Citizenship"

"Race leaders" took their cue from this popular upheaval and began charting a new solution to the crisis of Jim Crow. Drawing on their widespread support of the "War for Democracy" and borrowing from the rejuvenated language of equal citizenship invoked by African-American railroad workers and others, black Floridians began to coordinate their efforts. "The Negro Uplift Association," a new civil rights organization, called for a statewide political convention to take place in Ocala on April 23, 1919. The NUA sought an end to lynching, the promotion of "fairer economic and industrial conditions," and "the removal of individual political discrimination." The NUA wanted black Floridians to create a "workable program whereby we may secure to ourselves and to our children the enjoyment in larger measures the rights and privileges which are ours by right."[104] This was a sharp critique of Jim Crow.

Black Floridians in nineteen counties met to elect delegates. "The Negro Uplift Association movement is a live wire in this St. Lucie County," wrote a black correspondent. "Prof. H. R. Jenkins, chairman, has held several meetings, and every one of them drew out large crowds of interested people . . . there will be a mammoth mass-meeting held at Fort Pierce, the county seat of St. Lucie county at which time the delegates and other citizens will be present."[105] A local resident urged support for the cause: "If you have race pride, if you are loyal, if you want better opportunities, if you want better citizenship, you can be depended upon [to] be present."[106]

Negro Uplift Association delegates and officers had deep activist roots in their communities. Rev. S. H. Betts, a delegate from Jackson County, was an A.M.E. minister known throughout the Panhandle as an outspoken advocate for black education and civil rights. A colleague from Chaires wrote that Betts's "popularity with his race is almost unbounded. He speaks on their behalf fearlessly, which means danger of bodily harm in this section. In short no colored man has dared say such things in such places as has he."[107]

NUA delegates were leaders of older civil rights organizations, secret societies—especially the Knights of Pythias—and newly formed NAACP branches. J. S. Pottsdammer, an officer with the Tallahassee NAACP and a member of the KOP, was the NUA chair for Leon County. D. J. and B. J. Jones, brothers, insurance salesmen, Pythians, and organizers of the Lake City Republican party, were NUA delegates, as was Dr. W. S. Stevens, a Pythian officer and a leader of the Republican Party in Gadsden County. J. A. Gregg, president of the Jacksonville NAACP, was a delegate from Jacksonville, as was W. W. Andrews, Grand Chancellor of the Knights of Pythias. Rev. John Hurst, a national board member of the NAACP, was a delegate-at-large. The Ocala convention gave these community activists a space to meet and to discuss the crises facing African Americans in Jim Crow Florida.[108]

African-American women were absent from the upper echelons of NUA leadership.[109] Evidence from two local chapters, however, suggests that African-American women played a critical role in the development of the organization. In the St. Lucie county NUA, four of the seven elected officers were women.[110] In Tallahassee, women served on all of the branch's committees.[111] Still, black women remained underrepresented in the major positions of NUA leadership. As a way of addressing this structural weakness, Mary McCleod Bethune, president of the State Federation of Colored Women's Clubs, organized a "reconstruction conference" during the Federation's 1919 convention where NUA, NAACP, and "various women's organizations in the State" conferred.[112]

Delegates at the Ocala convention voted to deliver a civil rights memorial to Governor Catts and the Florida State Legislature. The NUA memorial "plead for better railroad conditions, protection against lynching, a longer school term, and a colored superintendent for the State Industrial School." The Uplift Association also called "attention to the part Negroes played in winning the war by serving their country both at home and abroad."[113]

An NUA delegation formally presented the memorial to the state legislature in May. In the midst of reading the NUA petition, however, the senate clerk was stopped by angry legislators who had discovered that the petitioners were African Americans.[114] The clerk immediately purged the memorial from the legislative record.[115]

The failure of the Negro Uplift Association's petition provided an important experience for black organizers. They had asked white authorities to acknowledge the dignity of black Floridians, and their rights to citizenship, and their claim had been denied. The Florida legislature had little incentive to consider any such petition from African Americans. African Americans had proposed to engage in politics without possessing any political power. They would not make this mistake again.

"We Are Urging Our Folks to Register"

Black Floridians interpreted the legislature's response to the NUA as a signal to step up the voter registration campaign. A week later, the Knights of Pythias passed their resolution on voter registration, and local activists redoubled their efforts. The methods African Americans used in this struggle illuminate the ways in which social movements can emerge in repressive societies. Black Floridians mobilized through the community institutions that played central roles in efforts to sustain black dignity while holding white supremacy at bay. Rev. W. N. Mitchell, a Madison County pastor, told Warren Harding: "I have organized a Club in my church named the Harding Club. We meet every Thursday evening to discuss plans for the coming Nov. election which we hope you will win."[116] In Polk County, angry Democrats searched in vain for "mysterious" white organizers who were said to be "coercing" black women and men to register, but they ultimately found no evidence of interracial collaboration.[117] Meanwhile, more than five hundred African Americans in Lakeland registered to vote.[118] After weeks of chasing ghosts, Democrats learned the truth: black citizens in Lakeland had used the local Knights of Pythias lodge as their primary organizing vehicle.[119]

African-American organizers made solid links between voting rights, economic justice, and segregation. Drawing on the hard lessons learned by black workers, activists integrated politics, economics, and dignity in their pleas for voter registration:

> Another law that works against the black man, is the one wherein a labor agent is compelled to pay a license of $2500, if he gives him transportation

to another place; if the man is out of work, and some one wants to send him to another place where he can make an honest living at good wages, he must sneak here and there like a hunted criminal to meet the agent who will furnish transportation. Can not the Negro see that this law, a relic of slavery is against him? Why not register and vote some one to the legislature who will work for the repeal of this old time slavery law?[120]

Black organizers tied the ballot to concrete needs. The "Civic League for Colored People of St. Petersburg" sponsored voter education workshops, pooled resources to help members pay their poll taxes, and agitated for educational reforms in Pinellas County. Black parents agreed with N. B. Young, president of Florida A & M College, who argued at the NUA's convention that segregated schooling, "with very few exceptions, is a failure."[121] Civic League members framed their activism around education and hoped to see "every man paying his poll tax, that our strength may be considered by the school board when lining up for the next term of school."[122]

By July 1919, the Civic League had raised enough funds to help pay poll taxes for nearly four hundred voters.[123] More than a year before the Nineteenth Amendment was ratified, Clara Blackman explained to U.S. Secretary of Labor William Wilson that the St. Petersburg Civic League was encouraging African American women to prepare to engage in electoral politics through political education workshops. Blackman also told Wilson that the Civic League was helping to spur the growth of an "Organized Women's Labor Union."[124] When expanded suffrage came to St. Petersburg in September 1920, African American women were ready. More than one hundred domestic workers registered to vote in a single day.[125]

Mary McLeod Bethune urged black women's clubs in Florida to mobilize their communities to spread the gospel of voting and civil rights.[126] She beseeched African Americans in Daytona: "Eat your bread without butter, but pay your poll tax!"[127] Black women took up Bethune's challenge. The Brooklyn Citizens and Improvement Club, an affiliate of the City Federation of Colored Women's Clubs in Jacksonville, met at the home of Mrs. Sadie Ash Bordner to hear "Rev. A. P. Postell deliver a very interesting address which was enjoyed by all. Many men have qualified themselves to vote through the activities of this club since its last meeting."[128] This club was affiliated with the City Federation of Colored Women's Clubs and had long emphasized citizenship, voting rights and the commemoration of Emancipation Day.[129] In 1916 the club women had canvassed black neighborhoods and urged men to register to vote in order to gain improved municipal services for African American neighborhoods.[130]

Secret societies, especially the Knights of Pythias, played critical roles in building the voter registration movement in rural Florida. The state Vice Chancellor of the KOP, Dr. W. S. Stevens, lived and worked in Gadsden County. After the death of his mother, Stevens had been adopted and raised by his uncle, Mr. Matthews, in Tallahassee. Matthews was assassinated by a mob of white men in his own home, in front of Stevens, his other children, and his wife.[131] No charges were filed. Under the dictates of Jim Crow, the white men had committed no crime.

Dr. W. S. Stevens arrived in Quincy in 1905 fresh from Meharry Medical College. Stevens had not planned to stay long in the rural county, but when he packed up to leave for a larger practice in Tallahassee, local African Americans, suffering from a severe lack of access to health care—one of the grimmest aspects of Jim Crow—begged the county's only black doctor to stay.[132] W. S. Stevens stayed in Quincy for the rest of his life, and he gained the trust and respect of local black residents.[133] He quickly assumed a leadership role in the local KOP lodge. In 1916 he was elected as a delegate to the state Republican party convention.[134] In 1919 he was elected as a delegate from Gadsden to attend the Negro Uplift Association convention in Ocala.[135]

As the voter registration movement gained momentum in urban Florida, Dr. Stevens began convening local Pythians as well as female members of their sister organization, the Courts of Calanthe, under the guise of lodge meetings in order to hold voter education meetings.[136] In this endeavor he was assisted by Rev. T. Phillyaw, a pastor and member of the local KOP.[137]

As the struggle gained momentum in Quincy, two allies emerged in rural Gadsden. T. L. Sweet, secretary of the Harding-Coolidge Club in nearby River Junction, began to facilitate voter registration meetings there, and the Greensboro NAACP branch, which consisted mainly of farmers and farm laborers, took up the same work in their locale.[138] In response, the Gadsden County sheriff warned that special deputies would be waiting at the polls on election day with handcuffs in order to arrest "ex convicts, who have registered as qualified voters."[139] J. T. Smith, a farmer and the branch president, explained: "The white peoples are very hot here on the account of the election. Some says they will be blood spilt here that day, and some say they will not let us vote they close out the Redistration Books A head of time as to keep some of our Peoples from redstring."[140] More ominously, Smith reported that Gadsden shopkeepers "ceased selling we Colored peoples any [ammunition] four weeks ago, although some of us are determined to go the pole that day regardless to the consequence."[141]

Mutuality, not militancy, explains the extraordinary tenacity of the Florida voter registration movement. African Americans in Gadsden pressed on in spite of the grave dangers that confronted them.[142] The relationships of trust that Pythian lodge members had forged over the years helps to explain the Gadsden movement. In truth, the oath that KOP members took to register to vote in 1919 was no ordinary resolution. It carried with it a momentum built up painstakingly through years of sick visits, shared labor, and common struggles. Faced with the specter of white violence, Rev. Phillyaw "told the boys, 'we took an oath to stand together,' and they did."[143]

African Americans approached white registrars *en masse* across Florida. Walter White, who passed for a white man so that he could conduct an undercover investigation of the election, was given a chilling account of how African-American male registrants in Orange County were received by the Democratic registrars: "A White lawyer told me laughingly of how a Negro would approach a registration booth in his county, Orange, and ask if he could register. The officials there . . . would reply, 'Oh, yes, you can register, but I want to tell you something. Some God damn black ____ ____ ____ is going to get killed about this voting business yet.'"[144]

"They Say They Will Kill Anybody"

Faced with a statewide democratic social movement, Florida's white supremacists began a systematic campaign of intimidation, fraud, and violence to choke off the black vote. The *Orlando Reporter-Star* warned: "The struggle for white supremacy in the South now confronts us."[145] Joe Earman, editor of the *Palm Beach Post,* told a leading Democratic official: "I am a white man, a southern democrat and for the supremacy of white man first last and all the time."[146] Palm Beach County election officials vowed to place "Democratic challengers" at the polls on election day to seize "illegal" black voters, and Sheriff R. C. Baker promised to "have several deputy sheriffs at the polls prepared to arrest black violators of the election laws as fast as they appear and ask for ballots."[147]

What ensued was one of the most violent election campaigns in American history.[148] Mass arrests of African Americans preceded election day.[149] Four Knights of Pythias lodges in Gadsden and Liberty counties were burned down.[150] Even though they were heavily outnumbered, KOP members near River Junction fought a desperate gun battle to defend their lodge from white paramilitary forces only to see it burned to the ground. Pythians who were captured after the shootout were beaten and executed.[151] Black activists across Florida were hunted down and assassinated.[152] In the week prior to the election, the KKK marched in full regalia in Jacksonville, Daytona, and Orlando.[153] In the weeks leading up to election day, the Ku Klux Klan controlled the U.S. Mail in Gadsden County in order to isolate local African American activists and to keep news of the mounting racial holocaust in Middle Florida from reaching the outside world.[154]

The events that transpired in Manatee County were replicated throughout Florida on election day. While African Americans in Manatee were determined to vote, local Democrats were equally determined to stop them. White gunmen broke into a Knights of Pythias meeting place in Palmetto shortly before the election and warned African-American women and men to stay away from the polls.[155] On election day, more than twenty carloads of white men armed with repeating rifles and pistols patrolled the approaches to the polling places in Manatee County. Miraculously, a group of black citizens found a way to reach the courthouse at Palmetto. They were led by a twenty-two-year-old farm worker, Dan Thomas, as well as by Rev. W. S. McGill, an A.M.E. minister.[156] As Thomas approached the door to the county courthouse a white man came from behind and shot him in the back.[157] Mr. Thomas fell, mortally wounded. A melee ensued, and a mob of white men descended on the black would-be voters. African-American women were kicked away from the polls and Rev. McGill was driven from the county. Dan Thomas died the next day, leaving behind a wife and two young children. "The Colored people can't talk for fear of their lives," wrote a group of African Americans in Palmetto who begged the NAACP to help them. "They say they will kill anybody that makes it known."[158] At nearly the same moment, hundreds of African Americans were physically driven from polling places in Miami by white paramilitaries.

An even worse fate befell African Americans in western Orange County. Facing a determined group of black voters in Ocoee, white supremacists pulled out all the stops and engaged in a spree of savage violence. After a physical altercation at the polls and a subsequent gun battle which they apparently lost, whites in Ocoee called for reinforcements. In short order, fifty carloads of heavily armed white men from Orlando and the surrounding area poured into Ocoee and drove five hundred African Americans out of the town, burning, looting, and lynching as they went.[159] The

Rev. R. B. Brooks, presiding A.M.E. elder in St. Augustine, stated that "the total number [of dead] will probably never be known because the bones of the murdered Negroes who were burned to death, were taken away as souvenirs by members of the mob."[160]

"I Pray the Day Will Come"

The Florida voter registration movement shows that people can create social movements by creating meaningful networks of trust and mutuality that overcome the fear and inertia of existing systems of political domination. Contrary to the assumptions of much of the literature on modern protest, it is not charismatic individuals who create movements; it is the relationships between individuals that convince ordinary people to take risks and engage in politics. Thousands of black Floridians risked their lives and registered to vote because the women and men who asked them to do so were deeply rooted in their neighborhoods and in the institutions that buffered their communities from white supremacy. Black Floridians temporarily defeated the forces of demobilization that have led to a declining voter turnout in American politics, especially among the nation's poor.[161] It is worthwhile to pause a moment to examine how African Americans in Florida achieved this renaissance of working-class political activity. When African American workers initiated the Great Migration, petitioned the federal government for redress of their grievances, and waged postwar strikes, they revived the broader struggle against white supremacy. In turn, voter registration activists took up the political issues that black workers cared most about—lynching, poverty wages, debt peonage, failing schools—and used these issues as rallying points. This tight fit between economic justice and political power was one of the great animating ideas of the movement. William Watson, a black labor leader speaking at a packed meeting held at Mt. Zion A.M.E. church in Jacksonville in 1919, ensured that his audience understood that labor and political struggles were synonymous: "admission into labor unions carries with it the prerequisite of the applicant being a registered voter with his poll tax paid up."[162]

The Florida voter registration movement affirms the continuity of African American resistance to Jim Crow. Black Floridians were able to capitalize on the economic and political changes ushered in by World War I to create a social movement only because they had preserved ideas of dignity and equal citizenship within mutual aid institutions that celebrated the experience of emancipation and freedom. This is not to downplay the degradation and violence that constituted the larger social fabric of segregation; it is only to point out that African Americans were able to create spaces white supremacists were unable to breach.

The freedom struggle that African Americans forged after World War I was rooted in a long history of striving for justice. An African-American woman from Butler County explained to James Weldon Johnson why she had risked her safety to vote:

> My Dear Father helped to fight three years to raise children as [R]epublicans and this year was the first year I voted and it was cast for Harding. . . . All that is needed is to let the southern white man know that the War of [18]63–4 and 5 has made us free, and the negroes are no longer their slaves, and have the right to be protected by our laws.[163]

This conflict between African Americans' search for justice and the tenacious power of white supremacy remains a defining theme in American politics. William Sutton witnessed the bands of armed white men who shut down the polls on election day in Liberty County. After this terrifying experience, Sutton hoped that one day things would be different:

> I am glad to read of so many who are in sympathy with the colored men and women who were not allowed to vote. I pray the day will come when all citizens regardless of color, will be able to cast their votes for whom they please, and think will lead our people to victory in political and civil rights in our country of America.[164]

NOTES

Author's Note: I am grateful to Vincent A. Brown, William Chafe, Derek Chang, Raymond Gavins, Glenda Gilmore, Lawrence Goodwyn, Adam Green, Nancy Hewitt, Ian Lekus, and Charles Payne for patiently reading various drafts of this project and offering insightful criticism. Sheila Payne offered a keen editorial eye and inspiration from start to finish.

1. *The Florida Times-Union* (Jacksonville), March 20, 1904. The *Times-Union* was Florida's premier daily newspaper.

2. "Postal Clerks Meet," NCP, *Florida Metropolis*, May 31, 1919. This announce-

ment appeared in the "News of the Colored People" (NCP) section of the *Metropolis*. Located in the rear section of the paper, this column was a single sheet of local and statewide African American news based on correspondence received from black informants across the state. Edited by W. I. Lewis, the page was read by black subscribers throughout Florida. Items cited from this page will be distinguished from other *Metropolis* items by the abbreviation NCP.

3. "National Convention of Railway Postal Clerks," NCP, *The Florida Metropolis*, July 8, 1919. The Railway Mail Association was an affiliate of the American Federation of Labor. For information on the National Alliance, see Abram Harris and Sterling D. Spero, *The Black Worker: The Negro and the Labor Movement* (New York: Atheneum, 1969), 123–24; Philip S. Foner, *History of the Labor Movement in the United States*, vol. 7, *Labor and World War I, 1914–1918* (New York: International Publishers, 1987), 242.

4. "Postal Clerks Meet," NCP, *Florida Metropolis*, May 31, 1919.

5. William Greider writes: "Politics begins in personal relationships. Indeed, without that foundation, politics usually dissolves into empty manipulation by a remote few. People talking to one another—arguing and agreeing and developing trust among themselves—is what leads most reliably to their own political empowerment." *Who Will Tell The People: The Betrayal of American Democracy* (New York: Simon & Schuster, 1992), 223–24.

6. Using city directories, census schedules, registration lists, and congressional testimony I have thus far identified the names, ages, and occupations of more than 1,500 African Americans who registered to vote in 1919 and 1920. These figures are taken from six counties: Duval, Marion, Columbia, Putnam, Palm Beach, and Dade. For an analysis of African American voter registration figures in 1919–1920, see: Paul Ortiz, "'Like Water Covered the Sea': The African American Freedom Struggle in Florida, 1877–1920" (Ph.D. dissertation, Duke University, 2000), 393–475.

7. For an excellent overview of black history from the colonial period to the present in Florida, see: David R. Colburn and Jane Landers, eds., *The African American Heritage of Florida*. (Gainesville: University Press of Florida, 1995). See also: Cantor Brown, *Florida's Black Public Officials, 1867–1924* (Tuscaloosa: The University of Alabama Press, 1998).

8. Works that stress intergenerational linkages in the making of civil rights struggles include: William H. Chafe, *Civilities and Civil Rights: Greensboro, North Carolina, and the Black Struggle for Freedom* (New York: Oxford University Press, 1980); John Dittmer, *Local People: The Struggle for Civil Rights in Mississippi* (Urbana: University of Illinois Press, 1994); Glenda Gilmore, *Gender & Jim Crow: Women and the Politics of White Supremacy in North Carolina, 1896–1920* (Chapel Hill: University of North Carolina Press, 1996); Charles M. Payne, *I've Got the Light of Freedom: The Organizing Tradition and the Mississippi Freedom Struggle* (Berkeley: University of California Press, 1995).

9. Colin A. Palmer has transformed the image of the "New Negro" into "The

Generation of 1917," by which he means "a new generation of blacks emerged who were more insistent in their demand for justice and that from then on, the style of protest in black America was more vigorous, sustained, and multifaceted." Palmer's analysis misses the intergenerational component that the present study argues is the key to understanding the emergence of the Florida voter registration movement. Palmer, *Passageways: An Interpretive History of Black America, Volume II: 1863–1965* (New York: Harcourt Brace College Publishers, 1998), 107.

10. "The 'Unseen Hand,'" *The St. Augustine Evening-Record*, November 1, 1920; "'Unseen Hand' Is Sending Negro Women Registrations Far Above That of Whites," *The Florida Metropolis*, September 21, 1920.

11. The *Afro-American* marveled: "Florida is getting to be something else besides a Land of Flowers, It is becoming a state of the far South where colored people are registering and preparing to vote in unprecedented numbers." See: "Mysterious Body in Florida," *The Afro-American* (Baltimore), April 2, 1920, in *The Tuskegee Institute News Clipping File*, ed. John W. Kitchens (Microfilm, 252 reels, Tuskegee Institute, 1978), Reel 11, Frame 933.

12. *The New York Age*, March 9, 1889.

13. Black Floridians viewed secret societies and lodges as a necessary tool of survival. See: William Artrell to Joseph Lee, May 3, 1881, Box 2, Joseph Lee Papers, Ike Williams III, Private Manuscript Collection, Jacksonville, Florida; "General Laws of the Independent Afro-American Relief Union of Gadsden County, Florida" (1932), Special Collections Library, Duke University; "Independent Brotherhood," *The Freeman* (Indianapolis), March 15, 1902.

14. "Pythian Grand Lodge," NCP, *The Florida Metropolis*, May 24, 1919; NCP, *The Florida Metropolis*, May 17, 1919.

15. NCP, *The Florida Metropolis*, October 11, 1918.

16. See *Fourteenth Census of the United States, Volume III, Population* (Washington, D.C.: Government Printing Office, 1923), 185–86; and *History and Manual of the Colored Knights of Pythias* (Nashville, Tenn.: National Baptist Publishing Board, 1917).

17. Florida's secret societies had a long record of promoting political activism. See Robert Gabriel to Joseph Lee, July 11, 1879, Joseph Lee Papers, Ike Williams III, Private Collection; NCP, *The Florida Metropolis*, December 9, 1905.

18. "Lo! The Poor Democrat!" *The Crisis*, June 1, 1920. The Jacksonville City Federation of Women's Clubs also congratulated the KOP on passing the voter registration resolution. See "Grand Chancellor Andrews' Official Visits," NCP, *Florida Metropolis*, April 1, 1920.

19. The term "social space" refers to places African Americans created for themselves in which to discuss politics and organizing. Within such spaces, black Floridians discussed what historian Charles Payne terms the "big" ideas: "citizenship, democracy, the powers of elected officials." Payne, *I've Got the Light of Freedom*, 74. Social movements rise or fall on their ability to generate such spaces, and

this is especially true in movements that arise in one-party states. See Linda Fuller, *Where Was the Working Class? Revolution in Eastern Germany* (Chicago: University of Illinois Press, 1999), 164.

20. A. G. Samuels to Warren Harding, October 1920, Roll 36, Frames 902–903, Warren G. Harding Papers, Ohio Historical Society (Microfilm Edition), Manuscript Division, Library of Congress. "White and Negro Voters in Brevard," *Star Advocate* (Brevard), October 29, 1920. After the passage of female suffrage, 639 African American women and men registered to vote in Brevard County. The Nineteenth Amendment was ratified on August 26. A week later, Clay Crawford, Florida Secretary of State, issued letters to the state's county supervisors of registration decreeing that women's suffrage was in effect. Generally, women in the state began registering to vote on Tuesday, September 7th. For ratification in the South see: Marjorie Spruill Wheeler, *New Women of the New South: The Leaders of the Woman Suffrage Movement in the Southern States* (New York: Oxford University Press, 1993).

21. Daniel L. Schafer, "Eartha M. M. White; The Early Years of a Jacksonville Humanitarian." Unpublished paper, May 1976, Eartha M. M. White Collection, Thomas G. Carpenter Library, University of North Florida.

22. "7,502 Women Registered in the City," *The Florida Times-Union* (Jacksonville), September 28, 1920.

23. Negro Womens' Harding and Coolidge Club of Fort Pierce to Warren Harding, September 22, 1920, Harding Papers, Roll 36, Frame 782.

24. Letter to the Editor, *Fort Pierce News-Tribune*, September 21, 1920. Democrats promoted white women's voter registration as a tool to nullify black women's suffrage. White middle-class women responded enthusiastically, organizing "Business and Professional Women's" political clubs in St. Augustine, Jacksonville, Franklin County, and other areas. See: "Why I Have Registered and Shall Vote in November," *St. Petersburg Daily Times*, September 30, 1920. For other examples, see: "Commissioner McRae Urges White Women to Register and Vote," *Orlando Morning Sentinel*, October 2, 1920; "White Women Must Register," *The Pensacola Journal*, September 29, 1920; "White Women Register," *St. Augustine Evening Record*, October 9, 1920.

25. "Ku Klux Klan Re-Organized in Florida," *Baltimore Herald*, August 1920, in *The Tuskegee Institute News Clipping File*, Reel 11, Frame 630; "To Organize," *The Jasper News*, August 6, 1920; "Ku-Klux-Klan Is Robbing Negro of Vote," *The New York Call*, November 1, 1920. A newspaper editor investigating Klan activity told a congressional committee that KKK organizations in Florida and Texas, states where African Americans were building political movements, were the most lethal. See: The U.S. House of Representatives' Committee on Rules, *The Ku-Klux Klan Hearings*, Sixty-Seventh Congress, First Session (Washington, D.C.: Government Printing Office, 1921), 12. For an excellent discussion of African American organizing in Texas during this era, see: Steven A. Reich, "Soldiers of Democracy: Black

Texans and the Fight for Citizenship, 1917–1921," *The Journal of American History* 92 (March 1996): 1478–1504.

26. "Ku Klux Warning," *The Afro American,* in *The Tuskegee Institute News Clipping File,* Reel 11, Frame 632.

27. See: Charles S. Johnson, *Southern Atlas of Southern Counties* (Chapel Hill: The University of North Carolina Press, 1941), 73. The *New York Times* cited a report showing that between 1908 and 1912 Florida's lynching rate was twice as high as Mississippi's. "Fewer Lynchings," *New York Times,* undated clipping, file "Clippings, 1912–1914," box C342, in Papers of the National Association for the Advancement of Colored People, Series I, Manuscript Division, Library of Congress. Also see: Stewart E. Tolnay and E. M. Beck, *A Festival of Violence: An Analysis of Southern Lynchings, 1882–1930* (Chicago: University of Illinois Press, 1995), 37–38.

28. "Race Battle," *The Pensacola Daily Commercial,* September 1, 1888. For a similar editorial, see: "The Negro's Status," *Florida Times-Union,* June 26, 1899.

29. John Porter to William Chandler, October 2, 1890, Volume 82, William E. Chandler Papers, Manuscript Division, Library of Congress.

30. "Instantly Killed in Pasco County: Negro Laborer Made Trouble and Was Shot," *The Florida Times-Union,* July 24, 1903; "A Double Killing," *The Florida Metropolis,* June 27, 1905; "Killed Aged Negro for a $5 Debt," *The Florida Metropolis,* January 23, 1913. "Duel at Sanderson Results in Two Deaths," *The Florida Metropolis,* July 31, 1905.

31. "A Negro Made Way with Near Bellville," *The Florida Times-Union,* April 7, 1904.

32. Anonymous interview by Paul Ortiz, July 1998, "Behind the Veil: Documenting African American Life in the Jim Crow South," Collection, Center for Documentary Studies, Special Collections Library, Duke University.

33. Rayford W. Logan, *The Betrayal of the Negro: From Rutherford B. Hayes to Woodrow Wilson,* with an introduction by Eric Foner (1965; reprint, New York: Da Capo Press, 1997).

34. The definitive work on "hidden resistance" in the context of African American history remains: Robin D. G. Kelley, "'We Are Not What We Seem': Rethinking Black Working-Class Opposition in the Jim Crow South," *Journal of American History* 80 (June 1993): 75–112.

35. Floridians clashed frequently over the "mores" of white supremacy in the state's cities, small towns, and rural areas. See: "White Man Had Difficulty with Darkey," *The Quincy Herald,* February 8, 1889; "Bob Williams," *The Quincy Herald,* October 4, 1890; "Whites and Blacks Have Trouble in Miccosukee Saturday Night," *The Florida Times-Union,* November 4, 1903; "Told Story of an Assault," *The Daily News* (Pensacola), March 31, 1903; "Negroes Threaten War vs. Whites at Palmetto in the Death of Watson," *Tampa Weekly Tribune,* July 19, 1900; "Negro Woman Creates Disturbance on Street Car," *Florida Metropolis,* June 5, 1907. For vivid testimonies of African American resistance in Florida before World War II, see: Mavis McClendon,

interviewed by Paul Ortiz, August 21, 1997; A. I. and Samuel Dixie, interviewed by Paul Ortiz, August 10, 1994; Bernal Montgomery, interviewed by Paul Ortiz, July 12, 1998, Behind the Veil Collection. See also: Ortiz, "Like Water Covered the Sea," 212–260.

36. For black armed self-defense in Florida, see: Ortiz, "Like Water Covered the Sea," 80–83; 111–38.

37. *The Pensacola Journal*, July 2, 1905.

38. "Lakeland News," NCP, *The Florida Metropolis*, June 11, 1914.

39. Letter to the Editor, *Pensacola Journal*, September 30, 1920.

40. See: "Republican Club House Warming and Installation," NCP, *Florida Metropolis*, June 10, 1919. For Lee's political career during Reconstruction, see: Joseph E. Lee Papers, Private Manuscript Collection of Ike Williams III, Jacksonville, Florida; and Brown, *Florida's Black Public Officials*, 103.

41. Tabulated voter registration figures in author's possession.

42. T. S. Harris to Joseph E. Lee, December 9, 1879; T. S. Harris to Joseph Lee, February 24, 1880. Joseph E. Lee Papers, Private Manuscript Collection of Ike Williams III. Charter members of NAACP branches in Palatka and Jacksonville also included survivors of Reconstruction. See: "Application for Charter, Palatka," July 1, 1919, Box G42, Folder "Palatka, Fla," NAACP Papers. George H. Mays, born in 1849, was the Jacksonville NAACP's treasurer. Mays served as a constable in Jacksonville in 1873 and later as a city marshal before embarking on a thirty-three-year career with the post office. Along the way, Mays helped organize the Grand United Order of Odd Fellows Lodge in Florida. See: "Application for NAACP Charter," February 20, 1917, Box G41, File "Jacksonville, Fla.," NAACP Papers; Brown, *Florida's Black Public Officials*, 109; NCP, *The Florida Metropolis*, December 26, 1918.

43. Brown, *Florida's Black Public Officials*, 65.

44. Florida Republican Party Delegates, 1916, Box 3, Folder "Republican Party Roll of Delegates to Republican State Convention, 1916, Palatka," Joseph E. Lee Papers, Florida State Archives, Department of State, Tallahassee, Florida.

45. "Live Oak to Honor her Soldiers," NCP, *The Florida Metropolis*, August 11, 1919.

46. *The Apalachicola Times*, September 25, 1920.

47. *The Bradford County Telegraph*, November 12, 1920; *New York Times*, October 7, 1920. At least 408 men and 256 women registered by the end of the registration period.

48. For an overview of black historical memory in Florida see: Ortiz, "Like Water Covered the Sea," 180–97.

49. "Negroes of Tampa Celebrate Emancipation," *The Florida Peninsular* (Tampa), January 5, 1870.

50. "An Uncalled for Attack on Ministers," *The Christian Recorder*, June 13, 1889.

51. Viola B. Muse, "Celebrations and Amusements among Negroes of Florida,"

January 19, 1937, Box 1, Folder "Celebrations, September, 1938," The Florida Negro Papers, University of South Florida, Tampa.

52. "Sanford Notes," NCP, *The Florida Metropolis,* January 14, 1913.

53. "Bartow News," NCP, *The Florida Metropolis,* January 15, 1913.

54. "Daytona Items," NCP, *The Florida Metropolis,* January 9, 1913.

55. "Gainesville Celebrates Emancipation Proclamation," NCP, *The Florida Metropolis,* January 6, 1913.

56. "Fort Pierce News," NCP, *The Florida Metropolis,* January 9, 1913; "Emancipation Day Celebration," NCP, *The Florida Metropolis,* January 3, 1913.

57. For a larger discussion of these naming practices, see Ortiz, "Like Water Covered the Sea," 180–97.

58. See: "Quincy News," *Florida Metropolis,* February 15, 1907; and: "Freedman's Day Successful," *Florida Metropolis,* February 18, 1907.

59. "Colored Citizens of Quincy Pledge Loyalty to America, *Gadsden County Times,* April 19, 1917.

60. "South Florida Methodist Conference," NCP, *The Florida Metropolis,* February 25, 1919.

61. "Soldier's Experience Overseas," NCP, *The Florida Metropolis,* April 4, 1919.

62. For women's initiatives to support the war effort in Florida, see: William J. Breen, "Black Women in the Great War: Mobilization and Reform in the South," *The Journal of Southern History* 46 (August 1978): 436–39.

63. "Daytona Normal and Industrial Institute," NCP, *The Florida Metropolis,* May 19, 1919.

64. "Unique Celebration of the February Birthdays," NCP, *The Florida Metropolis,* March 3, 1919.

65. "Presbyterian Honored their Soldiers," NCP, *The Florida Metropolis,* March 26, 1919. Information on Matthew M. Lewey obtained from Brown, *Florida's Black Public Officials,* 104.

66. "The Proceedings of the State Conference of the Colored Men of Florida" (Washington, D.C., 1884), Reel 10, Frame 34, *Frederick Douglass Papers* (Microfilm), Manuscript Division, Library of Congress.

67. "Citizens' Meeting at Grant's Memorial Church," NCP, *The Florida Metropolis,* October 25, 1919.

68. U.S. Congress, House Committee on the Census, *Hearings before the Committee on the Census,* Sixty-Sixth Congress, Third Session (Washington, D.C.: Government Printing Office, 1921), 67. The NAACP presented affidavits at this hearing from black Floridians who swore that they had been barred from voting on election day 1920.

69. NCP, *The Florida Metropolis,* January 11, 1919.

70. "Live Oak Notes," NCP, *The Florida Metropolis,* March 7, 1919.

71. "Negro Switch Tender Meets a Horrible Death," *Florida Times Union,* September 8, 1899; "Bad Accident to A Negro," *Daily News* (Pensacola), December 26,

1902; "Death of a Bayman While Unloading a Vessel," *The Florida Times-Union*, October 24, 1899; "Coast Line Engine Crushes Colored Man," *Lakeland Star*, October 14, 1920.

72. "Societies in the South," *The New York Age*, July 28, 1888.

73. The "Order of Emancipated Americans" flourished in rural north Florida. Lodge members helped each other in times of need. "If you was a farmer and your mule died," A. I. Dixie recalled, "the farmers in the community had to give you a day's work 'til you get another mule." A. I. Dixie interview with author, August 10, 1994, Behind the Veil Collection.

74. The historian Earl Lewis has explored the roles black fraternal organizations played in the Jim Crow era, noting that "membership in a spate of institutions enhanced one's ties to the community and, conceivably, one's willingness to work on behalf of broader community interests." Lewis, *In Their Own Interests: Race, Class, and Power in Twentieth-Century Norfolk, Virginia* (Berkeley: University of California Press, 1991), 72.

75. *History and Manual of the Colored Knights of Pythias* (Nashville, Tenn.: National Baptist Publishing Board, 1917), 492.

76. Ibid., 220.

77. Ibid., 482.

78. *Acts and Resolutions of the Legislature of Florida, Seventh Regular Session* (Tallahassee, Fla.: The Tallahasseean Book and Job Print, 1899), 261–62.

79. *History and Manual of the Colored Knights of Pythias*, 387.

80. "Florida Pythians Protest to Governor," *The New York Age*, June 10, 1915.

81. Letter to the Editor, *The New York Freeman*, July 23, 1887. When prominent national African American leaders like A.M.E. Bishop Daniel Payne or *Richmond Planet* editor John Mitchell Jr. were seized and thrown off of Florida trains for violating Jim Crow, Gibbs's argument was seriously undercut. "Bishop Daniel Payne's Reply," *The Christian Recorder*, August 10, 1882.

82. "Pulled from Street Car; Negress Got Awfully Mad," *Florida Times-Union*, November 14, 1911.

83. In a report on the first Jacksonville streetcar boycott, it was noted that "The backbone of the opposition originated with the women who threaten a boycott of the men of the race if they dared to ride in the separate cars." "Among the Exchanges," *Indianapolis Freeman*, March 22, 1902.

84. Zora Neale Hurston, *Dust Tracks on a Dirt Road* (1942; reprint, New York: HarperCollins, 1996), 190.

85. "Wanted 'Blue Blood' Charter," *Daily News*, January 19, 1903. Adolph Reed writes: "Black people are neither more or less capable of pettiness and class prejudice than anyone else. . . . Skin tone, family connections, and even more arbitrary considerations all created fissures in the phantom unity of the pre–civil rights community just as they do today." Reed, "Dangerous Dreams: Black Boomers Wax Nostalgic for the Days of Jim Crow," *Village Voice*, April 16, 1996, 27.

86. "Colored Labor Growing Scarce," *Gazette News* (Daytona), September 6, 1918, in *Tuskegee Institute News Clippings File*, Reel 8, Frame 25.

87. "Minister Asserts Brutality Drove Negroes North," *New York Tribune*, July 2, 1917, in *The Tuskegee Institute News Clippings File*, Reel 6, Frame 475.

88. "Labor Problem: Representative Negroes Urge Their Race to Remain Here," *Florida Times-Union*, August 6, 1916.

89. W.T.B. Williams, "The Negro Exodus from the South," republished in *Black Workers: A Documentary History from Colonial Times to the Present*, ed. Philip S. Foner and Ronald Lewis (Philadelphia: Temple University Press, 1989), 306.

90. "Negro View of the Exodus," *Montgomery Advertiser*, September 9, 1916, in *Tuskegee Institute News File*, Reel 5, Frame 473.

91. "Officers of Negro Labor Unions Would Solve the Labor Problems," *The Florida Times-Union*, August 14, 1916.

92. See "Convention of Railroad Men Opens in Chicago," *The Chicago Defender*, October 2, 1920. Philip S. Foner discusses the formation of independent black unions during the Great War in *History of the Labor Movement in the United States*, vol. 7, *Labor and World War I, 1914–1918* (New York: International Publishers, 1987), 242–43.

93. For example, see: Berry Tillman to W. S. Carter, November 11, 1919, in *Black Workers in the Era of the Great Migration*, ed. James Grossman, Reel 7, Frame 466.

94. Petition of Florida East Coast Railway Firemen to W. G. McAdoo, October 28, 1918, in *Black Workers in the Era of the Great Migration*, ed. James Grossman, Reel 7, Frame 462.

95. For similar struggles, see Tera W. Hunter, *To Joy my Freedom: Southern Black Women's Lives and Labors after the Civil War* (Cambridge: Harvard University Press, 1997), 219–38.

96. Walter White, "Florida, 1918 (?)" *Papers of the NAACP, Part 10: Peonage, Labor and the New Deal, 1913–1939* (Microfilm), Reel 23, Frame 283.

97. "Fight among Unions," *The Tampa Sunday Tribune*, September 11, 1919.

98. W. A. Armwood Diary Entries, January 23–29. Box 4, Folder "Literary Productions: Diaries-Transcripts, 1918–1919," Armwood Family Papers, Special Collections Library, University of South Florida, Tampa.

99. "Orange Pickers May Strike for More Pay," *Palatka Daily News*, November 15, 1919.

100. Quoted in the *New York Age*, May 29, 1920.

101. "Labor in the Potato Section," *Palatka Morning Post*, April 12, 1920; "Labor Agitators Arrested by Hastings Officers," *The Daily-Herald* (Palatka), April 16, 1920.

102. "Waiters' Strike Barely Averted," *Cleveland Advocate*, March 27, 1920.

103. "K. of P. Foment Strike," *The Afro-American* , July 4, 1919. The "K. of P." refers to the Knights of Pythias.

104. "To Colored Citizens of Florida," NCP, *The Florida Metropolis*, March 11, 1919.

105. "Fort Pierce News," NCP, *The Florida Metropolis*, March 18, 1919.

106. "Gifford News," NCP, *The Florida Metropolis*, April 4, 1919.

107. "Dr. Betts Strongly Encouraged," NCP, *The Florida Metropolis*, June 23, 1919.

108. For a broader discussion of the NUA delegates and their backgrounds, see: Ortiz, "Like Water Covered the Sea," 380–385.

109. Deborah Gray-White examines the obstacles African American women faced during this era in asserting political leadership within black communities. See: White, *Too Heavy a Load*, 116–20.

110. "Gifford News," NCP, *The Florida Metropolis*, March 13, 1919.

111. "Tallahassee News," NCP, *The Florida Metropolis*, April 21, 1919.

112. "Echoes from State Federation of Colored Women's Clubs," NCP, *The Florida Metropolis*, June 21, 1919.

113. "Colored Citizens' State Convention Closed," NCP, *The Florida Metropolis*, April 28, 1919.

114. "Florida Senate Refuses to Heed Race Complaints," *Cleveland Advocate*, May 24, 1919.

115. "Legislature Refuses to Hear Petition," *The Afro-American*, May 19, 1919.

116. W. N. Mitchell to Warren G. Harding, July 10, 1920, Roll 36, Frame 836, Warren G. Harding Papers.

117. "Negroes Out-Register White Women," *The Lakeland Star*, September 16, 1920.

118. "Interesting Program Arranged for Women," *The Lakeland Star*, September 21, 1920. Also see: "Tell Negroes to Register or Go to Jail," *The Lakeland Star*, October 8, 1920.

119. See: "Lodge Members Being Forced to Register," *The Lakeland Star*, October 14, 1920.

120. "Why the Negro Should Register 3,000 Votes," *The Colored Citizen*, April 30, 1920.

121. "Colored Citizens' State Convention Closed," NCP, *The Florida Metropolis*, April 28, 1919. Dr. N. B. Young was a staunch opponent of disenfranchisement in turn-of-the-century Florida. In 1905, he had scoffed at the idea (held by a youthful W.E.B. Du Bois as well as Booker T. Washington) that the so-called "educational qualifications" for suffrage would somehow improve the level of black citizenship, arguing that "Nothing common to American citizenship should be alien to him." "Sees Wrong to Race," *The Chicago Record-Herald*, May 5, 1905. At an early stage, Young became a strong supporter of the NAACP.

122. "St. Petersburg News," NCP, *The Florida Metropolis*, July 7, 1919.

123. NCP, *The Florida Metropolis*, July 22, 1919.

124. Clara Blackman to William Wilson, June 26, 1919, in *Black Workers in the Era of the Great Migration, 1916–1925* (Microfilm), ed. James Grossman, Reel 14, Frames 359–62.

125. "Republicans and Color," *St. Petersburg Daily Times*, October 10, 1920. See also: "Negroes Have Club," *St. Petersburg Daily Times*, September 24, 1920.

126. Taking part at the 1920 National Association of Colored Women's convention in a spirited discussion that attempted to define the term "reconstruction," Mrs. Bethune's focus group "stated that it involved the special interests of our people concerning the best consideration along all lines, such as jim-crow cars, lynchings, industrial affairs, etc." See: National Association of Colored Women, *Twelfth Biennial Session* (1920).

127. This account is taken from Mrs. Bethune's manuscript copy of *Mary McCleod Bethune: A Biography*, a work written by Rackham Holt that was eventually published in 1964. See: "Biography," in *The Bethune Foundation Collection, Part 1*, ed. Elaine M. Smith, Reel 1, Frame 412.

128. "Brooklyn Citizens' Club," NCP, *The Florida Metropolis*, August 6, 1919.

129. "Emancipation Day," NCP, *The Florida Metropolis*, January 3, 1920.

130. "City Federation of Colored Women's Clubs," Program, June 28–30, 1916, Folder "National Association of Colored Women," Eartha M. M. White Collection. Historian Glenda Gilmore discusses the ways African American women engaged in civic and political activism before attaining suffrage. See: Glenda Gilmore, *Gender & Jim Crow: Women and the Politics of White Supremacy in North Carolina, 1896–1920* (Chapel Hill: University of North Carolina Press, 1996).

131. Inez Stevens-Jones, interview with author, August 14, 1997, Behind the Veil Collection. Inez Stevens-Jones is Dr. Stevens's oldest living daughter. Stevens's medical skill is attested to in "Quincy Notes," NCP, *Florida Metropolis*, February 23, 1907. See also: "The Tallahassee Colored Column," *Daily Democrat*, August 15, 1916.

132. Indeed, when Dr. Stevens built a modest hospital to treat black patients, white citizens demolished it. An autonomous black hospital would have undermined the power white employers exercised over the health-care delivery system in Gadsden County. Inez Stevens-Jones interview. Also see: Spencie Love, *One Blood: The Death and Resurrection of Charles R. Drew* (Chapel Hill: The University of North Carolina Press, 1996.)

133. Samuel Dixie, interview with author, August 1997, Behind the Veil Collection.

134. Republican Party Convention Delegates List, 1916, Joseph E. Lee Papers, Florida State Archives.

135. "To Colored Citizens of Florida," NCP, *The Florida Metropolis*, March 11, 1919.

136. Inez Stevens-Jones interview; A. I. Dixie interview; "Statement of Walter F. White," December 17, 1920, Box C312, File, "KKK 1920," NAACP Papers, Library of Congress.

137. A. I. Dixie Interview.

138. T. L. Sweet to Walter White, December 6, 1920, in Box C285, NAACP Papers. This branch's members, who hailed from Greensboro, River Junction, and

Juniper, held their organizational meeting on September 20, 1919. See: Box G40, Folder "Greensboro, Fla. 1920–25," NAACP Papers.

139. "Quincy," *The Pensacola Journal*, October 10, 1920.

140. J. T. Smith to Walter White, October 23, 1920, Box G40, NAACP Papers.

141. Ibid.

142. After expanded suffrage came to Gadsden, a white correspondent snarled: "Something should be done quickly to arouse the white women of this and all other places and to help them see [and] realize the vast importance of registering to vote. . . . To date, of 112 who have registered here, only 36 are white; while the books show 76 newly qualified negro voters and only 8 white men." "White Women Must Register," *The Pensacola Journal*, September 29, 1920.

143. A. I. Dixie, interview with author.

144. Walter F. White, "Election Day in Florida," in "Disfranchisement of Colored Americans in the Presidential Election of 1920," Box C284, Folder "Voting Dec. 1920," NAACP Papers.

145. Quoted in *The Florida Times-Union*, September 21, 1920.

146. Joe Earman to James Hodges, November 1, 1920, Folder "Misc. Correspondence 1920: Nov.–December," James B. Hodges Papers, University of Florida.

147. "Officers Will Arrest Negroes Who Try to Vote Illegally November 2," *The Palm Beach Post*, October 30, 1920. The *Fort Pierce News-Tribune* announced a similar strategy in Fort Pierce: "it is well known that some of the negroes who have registered are not citizens; they were born in the Bahaman Islands and have never been naturalized. . . . And any one who presents himself at the polls who is not fully fitted for the ballot will find himself in the hands of the law! Let all take warning!" *News-Tribune*, October 29, 1920.

148. "Ku Klux Klan Demonstrates that White Supremacy Will Be Maintained in Volusia County," *The Daytona Daily News*, November 2, 1920; "Election Day Orgy of Murder in Florida," *The Atlanta Independent*, December 2, 1920; "Election Crookedness," *The National Republican*, January 1, 1921.

149. "Voting Heavy in Lakeland," *Lakeland Star*, November 2, 1920; "That Police Raid," *The Miami Herald*, October 20, 1920; "Officers Will Arrest Negroes Who Try to Vote Illegally November 2," *The Palm Beach Post*, October 30, 1920; Report of Walter White, Box C312, Folder "KKK 1920," NAACP Papers.

150. "Negro Lodges Are Burned to Ground," *The Daily Democrat* (Tallahassee), October 23, 1920; "That Election Day Orgy of Murder in Darkest Florida," *The National Republican*, November 27, 1920.

151. A. I. Dixie, interview with author.

152. "Body of Murdered Negro Found in the Ocklockonee River," *Gadsden County Times*, November 4, 1920, newspaper clipping in Box C312, Folder "KKK 1921–Jan," NAACP Papers; "Negro Assassinated," *St. Augustine Evening Record*, October 25, 1920; Anonymous to James Weldon Johnson, January 5, 1921, Box C312,

Folder "KKK 1921–Jan," NAACP Papers. "Try to Intimidate Negro Politician," *New York Times*, October 7, 1920; Inez Stevens-Jones interview; A. I. Dixie Interview, Behind the Veil Collection; "Woman Escaped from Florida Mob But Rest of Family Died," *New York Age*, December 18, 1920.

153. "Ku Klux Klan Parade in Streets of Jacksonville," *Times Plain Dealer*, November 6, 1920, in *The Tuskegee Institute News Clipping File*, Reel 11, Frame 628.

154. Dr. N. B. Young to Walter F. White, February 3, 1921, Box C312, file "KKK 1921–Feb," NAACP Papers.

155. Franklin Verun to James Weldon Johnson, January 8, 1920, Box C312, Folder "KKK 1921–Jan," NAACP Papers.

156. Information on Mr. Thomas appears in the unpublished 1920 U.S. Census schedules for Manatee County.

157. J. E. Timothy, J. Isaac, A. V. Billings, Tobi Fairbanks, N. Bigott, and J. C. Bigott to NAACP, December 31, 1920, Box C312, Folder "KKK 1921–Jan," NAACP Papers.

158. Ibid.; "Dan Thomas Shot," *The Manatee River Journal*, November 4, 1920.

159. "Ocoee Claims 2 White Victims," *Orlando Morning Sentinel*, November 3, 1920; Report of Walter White, Box C312, Folder "KKK 1920," NAACP Papers; "Notes Taken by Stetson Kennedy on Dialogue between Zora Neale Hurston and Dr. Carita Dogget Course," n.d., Box 1, Folder 13, Stetson Kennedy Papers, Federal Writers Project, 1936–1940, Southern Historical Collection, University of North Carolina, Chapel Hill; Zora Neale Hurston, "The Ocoee Riot," Box 2, Folder "Atrocities Perpetrated upon June 1938," The Florida Negro Papers, Special Collections Library, University of South Florida; Lester J. Dabbs, "A Report of the Circumstances and Events of the Race Riot on November 2, 1920 in Ocoee, Florida" (M.A. thesis, Stetson University, 1969).

160. Walter White Report, 2, NAACP Papers. I am indebted to the community historians of the Democracy Forum, a citizens' group in Orange County that seeks to bring to light the events of election day 1920 in order to bring a measure of justice to the victims and remaining survivors of the Ocoee Massacre. The Democracy Forum has sponsored public events in central Florida to insure that Americans never forget what happened in Orange County.

161. For a discussion of the forces of demobilization in modern American politics, see: Adolph Reed Jr., *Stirrings in the Jug: Black Politics in the Post-Segregation Era* (Minneapolis: University of Minnesota Press, 1999).

162. "Anniversary and Reconstruction Meeting," NCP, *The Florida Metropolis*, July 15, 1919.

163. Anonymous to Walter White, December 30, 1920, Box C312, Folder "KKK–Jan," Papers of the National Association for the Advancement of Colored People, Manuscript Division, Library of Congress.

164. "Wilma, Fla.," *The Atlanta Independent*, December 3, 1920.

Chapter 8

"With the Aid of God and the F.S.A."

The Louisiana Farmers' Union and the African American Freedom Struggle in the New Deal Era

Greta de Jong

Introduction

In August 1938, a member of the interracial Louisiana Farmers' Union (LFU) wrote in a letter to the union office, "My crop is coming along fine. With the aid of God and the F.S.A. I hope to establish a better home for myself and family and to help my fellow brothers."[1] This simple statement reflected some profound changes in the southern political economy that threatened to weaken plantation owners' control over their workers and encouraged greater militancy among black people in the 1930s. Widespread poverty caused by the Great Depression precipitated a decade of experimentation by the federal government in an attempt to find solutions to social problems. The limits of President Franklin Roosevelt's New Deal reforms were soon exposed in the South, where local elites' control over the administration of federal programs allowed for discrimination against African Americans and the displacement of thousands of sharecroppers and tenants from the land. In response to these developments, rural poor people joined together in organizations like the LFU to fight planter abuses of the New Deal and demand a fair share of federal aid.[2]

This article examines African Americans' participation in the LFU, showing how they used the union to attack inequalities and injustices that were the foundations of the white supremacist social order. Although studies of similar groups like the Southern Tenant Farmers' Union and the Alabama Share Croppers' Union exist, little attention has been given to the Louisiana Farmers' Union.[3] Viewed in isolation, or in comparison with the civil rights movement of the 1960s, the union's brief appearance and the activities of its members might not seem to be particularly important. Placing the events of the 1930s in a broader historical context helps to illuminate their significance. Prior to the emergence of the LFU, black people in rural Louisiana were actively engaged in attempts to gain economic, political, and social justice, although their efforts were usually confined to clandestine or unorganized forms. The New Deal and the arrival of union organizers in their communities provided a chance to take the freedom struggle to another level. African Americans embraced the union as an ally in their ongoing fight to gain fair compensation for their labor, adequate education for their children, a chance to participate politically, and protection from violence. Black Louisianians' involvement in the LFU showed an awareness of the power of collective action and an appreciation of the causes of their problems that resurfaced in the decades after World War II, when the disintegration of the plantation system enabled a more powerful protest movement to emerge. Examining African American activism in rural Louisiana over time reveals some continuity in the goals of rural black people, even though the methods of achieving them did not remain static.

The Post–Civil War Plantation System

The sugar and cotton plantation regions where the LFU focused its organizing efforts were among the most repressive areas in the nation. Situated along the Y-shape formed by the Mississippi and Red Rivers, parishes such as Pointe Coupee, Iberville, St. Landry, West Feliciana, Rapides, Natchitoches, and Concordia had reputations for the brutal treatment of African Americans dating back to the antebellum period.[4] The post–Civil War plantation system only slightly mitigated the harshness of slavery. Faced with a chronic shortage of capital and the necessity of borrowing heavily themselves, planters concluded that the only way to make the production of the state's staple crops profitable was to keep labor costs as low as possible. In the decades after Reconstruction, many Louisiana plantations came to resemble the rationalized, efficiency-driven enterprises associated with northern capitalism and industry. Corporate owners and absentee landlords gave little thought to the welfare of their workers, with whom they rarely had any direct contact. Agricultural laborers increasingly came to be viewed as statistics in plantation record books, important only to the extent that they counted as profits or losses.[5]

Most African Americans in the cotton parishes worked as sharecroppers or tenants, closely supervised by plantation owners or managers.[6] Payment for their labor was withheld until after the harvest, when they received a share of the income from the crops they had raised. Lacking cash for most of the year, plantation workers relied on their employers for housing, food, clothing, and other necessities. These were purchased on credit and the costs, plus interest, deducted from their wages at "settlement time." Planters often charged usurious interest rates on credit extended to their laborers, arguing that these were necessary because of the high risks involved. Landlords had sole responsibility for keeping accounts and selling the crops, so that employees had to take the plantation owner's word for how much they had earned and how much they owed. At the end of the year, it was common for sharecroppers and tenants to be told that they had come out in debt. Most had no choice but to stay and work for another year for the same planter even if they suspected they had been cheated. The system provided plantation owners with an effective way to maintain the stable supply of cheap labor that they depended on.[7]

In the sugar plantation regions further south, tenant farming was less common. African Americans in these parishes were mostly wage laborers who worked in gangs watched over by white supervisors.[8] Plowmen and their families provided the core labor supply, and were hired on year-long contracts. During the harvest season, planters employed extra workers from the surrounding areas, including many cotton farmers from northern Louisiana and Mississippi who came south to cut cane after their crops had been laid by.[9] Payment arrangements varied, but whatever the method, wages were universally low. On average, sugar workers received about 85¢ to $1.00 per day during the planting and cultivating seasons and slightly more during harvest times.[10] Though employers customarily provided houses, garden plots, firewood, and medical care, there was a growing tendency in the early twentieth century to eliminate these benefits. Plantation owners knew there was money to be made in furnishing employees with food and other necessities. Like their counterparts in the cotton parishes, some sugar workers never saw any cash. Employers either paid them in scrip redeemable only at plantation stores or simply kept a record of their purchases and labor.[11]

Low incomes, the centrality of credit, and the "furnish system" held many black families in perpetual poverty or indebtedness. Some employers deliberately cheated workers out of their earnings, either by overcharging them at commissaries or manipulating accounts. One sugar worker in

Pointe Coupee Parish whose daughter kept records of the family's purchases from a plantation store discovered when the time came to settle the
account that his employer had debited twice the correct amount.[12] Although it is difficult to quantify the extent of these practices, an article that
appeared in a Madison Parish newspaper in 1926 suggests that they were
common and that white people made no attempt to deny them. Under the
heading "Madison Parish; Its Customs—Yesterday and Today," an old-time
resident reminisced about the day one of the most prominent planters in
the area hired a woman to tutor his son, instructing her to "Teach him how
to figger. Teach him how to beat the nigger out of his half, take the other
half and leave him satisfied."[13] Many plantation owners used such methods
to hold their workers in peonage. At the beginning of one season, cotton
grower Henry Stewart of West Feliciana Parish commented on the difficulty of finding black tenants who were not too indebted to their previous
employers to move, saying, "I fear that the planters make as much money
selling negroes as they do selling cotton."[14]

Limiting black people's access to education was another way to ensure
that they remained relatively immobile. Educational policy in the rural
parishes reflected the belief shared by many landowners that "if you educate
a Negro, you lose a good field hand."[15] School terms accommodated planters' need for labor during the crop seasons, with most black children attending classes for only three or four months a year.[16] Teachers often lacked
proper qualifications and were poorly paid. Even those who were competent instructors faced difficulties such as overcrowding, lack of equipment,
and dilapidated buildings. In many parishes African Americans received
only an elementary education, as no high school existed.[17] Parish boards
spent only a fraction of the state funds they received for educating black
children on that purpose. In 1938, an analysis of the disparities in spending
on white and black schools in Louisiana forced even the state superintendent of education to admit that there was "no serious intention in most of
the parishes to provide school facilities for Negro children."[18]

Lack of education and inadequate incomes prevented most black Louisianians (and many poor white people) from meeting the requirements for
literacy and property ownership necessary for voting or holding office.
As a result, small cliques of wealthy white people dominated nearly all aspects of life in the rural parishes. Planters often owned not just most of the
land, but also the houses, stores, service stations, theaters, and other businesses in the towns that served their areas. Prominent names in local politics were likely to be the same as those that dominated the sugar and

cotton industries, or to be related to planters through business or family ties. Public policy reflected the interests of the rich white men who controlled police juries, school boards, and the courts. Law enforcement officers frequently acted as if they were the private employees of plantation owners rather than public servants who were supposed to protect the whole community.[19] Some parishes resembled personal fiefdoms, governed by a few individuals or families whose influence extended over everyone in the community, white or black. St. Landry Parish planter, merchant, and postmaster J. P. Savant, for instance, exercised almost absolute power in the town of Whiteville and its surrounding areas in the early twentieth century. Savant kept his workers in peonage, threatened them with death if they tried to leave, and beat them if they displeased him. "All the negros for several miles are afraid of him and do any thing he says," one resident reported. "The white as well as the negros are afraid to say a word for if they offend Mr Johnie they know that they will have to move or be carried out of the neighborhood."[20]

As this statement suggested, any attempts by black people to protest injustice risked a violent response. In 1908, when some African Americans who had been "worked without pay and . . . [been] horribly beaten" on a plantation in Madison Parish tried to escape, they were captured and whipped severely on the orders of their employer.[21] Moses Williams recalled that on the plantation where he grew up in Richland Parish, people were beaten if they were late for work or questioned an order given by the landlord. Once, when his mother became ill, Williams asked the man to call a doctor. The plantation owner denied that Williams's mother needed medical treatment, and became angry when Williams argued with him. "That man went back . . . and got a pistol," Williams said, "and I started to run. . . . He tried to kill me just because I told him my mother needed to go to a doctor."[22]

Within the boundaries of their own property and in the larger community, planters were the law. Their power was such that, if need be, they could monitor what African Americans did with their time outside of working hours in addition to supervising them during the day. Planters owned the houses black people lived in, the stores they shopped in, the land their churches and schools were built on. Landlords controlled the mail and telephones, enabling them to limit the amount of contact their employees had with the world outside the plantation. White people also bestowed money, gifts, and favors on African Americans who kept them informed of developments within the black community. The likelihood that planters would find out about any expression of dissatisfaction or any attempt to organize workers made challenging the plantation system extremely difficult. As former sharecropper Harrison Brown explained, "You couldn't be known resisting against the powers. . . . They always had a way to reach you and get you, you know. So . . . you'd have to take it slow."[23]

African American Strategies of Resistance in the Early Twentieth Century

The absence of organized protest did not mean that African Americans passively accepted their fate. Rural black people devised various strategies to resist plantation owners' efforts to deny them economic opportunity, education, legal protection, and political power. Although these activities did not directly confront white supremacy and affected the social order only slightly, they reflected participants' awareness of the sources of their oppression and provided the foundations of the twentieth-century freedom struggle.

In the rural South's low-wage economy, the central problem of most African Americans' lives was making a living. In search of better pay and working conditions, a high proportion of agricultural workers left their employers at the end of each year, often without paying their debts.[24] Although plantation owners attributed the constant movement of labor to black people's inherent "shiftlessness," such actions were not random or unpurposeful. The statement given by John Pickering to a notary public in Texas after he moved there from Louisiana in 1926 shows that his decision resulted from a carefully considered, accurate analysis of the plantation system and his chances of economic advancement if he had stayed with his previous employer. "I moved off of the place of the said William Wilson because he would not give me a fair settlement on what I had made and what I earned and would not account to me for my share of the cotton crop," Pickering said. "I being an ignorant negro he would not furnish me with a statement showing what the cotton sold for and what goods I had procured from him, but insisted that, notwithstanding his getting all the cotton, I still owed him three hundred dollars. When I found out he would not give me a fair settlement and was getting all of my earnings, I decided to move into the State of Texas because I knew that in the State of Louisiana the big planters buy and sell negroes and never let one get out of debt."[25]

In addition to seeking escape from economic exploitation, black Louisianians circumvented plantation owners' efforts to deny them education. By following their teachers as they moved from one regional classroom to the next, some students extended the length of time they attended school beyond the limits set by their parish school boards. Families living in communities that lacked high schools commonly sent older children to stay with friends or relatives in neighboring parishes to complete their secondary education.[26] When state and local governments refused to build schools for black communities, African Americans constructed their own or held classes in churches and fraternal society halls.[27] In a typical case, a study of schools in St. Helena Parish found that the school board owned only two of the buildings used for educating African Americans. The remaining twenty-eight, attended by over 80 percent of the black children, were "housed in churches and in buildings erected mainly at the expense and efforts of the Negroes themselves."[28]

Such practices reflected and reinforced strong community ties that African Americans developed in their families, schools, churches, benevolent societies, and fraternal orders. These institutions offered valuable support networks that black Louisianians relied on for survival. Sugar workers in Pointe Coupee Parish recalled that when people became ill and were unable to work, friends and relatives "took up orders" for them at plantation stores, charging food and other necessities to their own accounts so that families who had fallen on difficult times would not starve.[29] For a small fee, black Louisianians could join any number of organizations that offered similar safeguards.[30] As well as providing opportunities for socializing and enhancing members' economic security, black community institutions played other, more subversive roles. Churches and society halls provided some of the few spaces where rural black people were relatively free from white supervision, and within their walls African Americans engaged in decision-making and other political processes that were denied them in the world outside.[31]

Disfranchisement and lack of access to the law forced black people to find other ways to counter the violence and injustice that pervaded their lives. Given white Louisianians' frequent use of beatings, whippings, and lynchings, it should not be surprising that African Americans also resorted to aggressive tactics. In 1926, for instance, black sharecropper Joe Hardy raised what he thought was a good crop on the plantation of John S. Glover in Caddo Parish. Expecting to clear several hundred dollars, he was surprised when the time came to settle his account and Glover claimed that he owed sixty dollars instead. Hardy did not want to risk any trouble so he said nothing at the time. Later, he approached a neighboring planter who agreed to hire him for the next year and to pay his debt to Glover. When Hardy took his new employer's check to Glover, the planter attacked him and in the fight that followed, Hardy shot and killed his former landlord.[32]

African Americans who chose to defend themselves against harassment or violence took enormous risks, especially if a white person was killed or injured in the process. Joe Hardy narrowly escaped being lynched, but most were not so lucky. A black man in Tallulah and another from Caddo Parish both paid with their lives after shooting their white employers.[33] In a tragic incident that occurred near Alexandria in 1928, an angry mob retaliated against William Blackman's entire family after he shot a deputy in self-defense and was shot and killed himself. The mob lynched Blackman's two brothers, burned seven homes, and drove all his remaining relatives out of the parish.[34] Such stories suggest that African Americans were far from acquiescent in the first half of the twentieth century, but they also reveal the limits of protest in a setting where white people's political, economic, and fire power always overwhelmed any resources that black people had access to.

The New Deal and the Louisiana Farmers' Union

That setting began to be altered in the 1930s, when President Roosevelt's New Deal policies extended federal influence into the South on a scale not seen since Reconstruction. In the course of the decade, the Roosevelt administration enacted a string of measures aimed at alleviating poverty and restoring economic stability. The Federal Emergency Relief Administration (FERA) and later the Works Progress Administration (WPA) allocated approximately fourteen billion dollars to the states to be used either as direct payments to unemployed people or wages for work on public projects.[35] The National Recovery Administration (NRA) attempted to standardize business operations and improve conditions for workers by establishing industry-wide codes for maximum hours and minimum wages. To rescue the nation's farmers, the Agricultural Adjustment Administration (AAA) paid subsidies to those who voluntarily reduced their crop acreages in an effort to eliminate overproduction, increase prices, and raise rural people's living standards. The Resettlement Administration and its successor agency, the Farm Security Administration (FSA), provided low-interest loans and other assistance to marginal farmers to help them achieve self-sufficiency.[36]

The New Deal raised black people's expectations and encouraged them to believe they might finally be recognized as citizens. Federal policy prohibited racial discrimination by the newly established relief agencies, and First Lady Eleanor Roosevelt achieved notoriety among white southerners for speaking out against racism. Franklin Roosevelt's record in this respect was more ambiguous, but many black people nevertheless viewed his presidency as a positive development. For the first time since the Civil War and Reconstruction, African Americans believed the government was on their side.[37] A black sharecropper whose crops had been stolen by his landlord in Red River Parish reflected this new mood when he appealed to the Department of Justice for help. "I am told that President Roosevelt is a true friend to the negro people," he wrote. "I want you and him to aid me, please."[38]

The actual results of the New Deal were disappointing. Despite the administration's assurances that black people would receive the same treatment as white people from government agencies, it failed to enforce this policy at the local level. Discrimination was widespread, and white southerners were able to use their control over relief programs to reinforce existing power relationships. Throughout the region, administrators were selected by the same planters and business owners who dominated everything else. As had always been the case, the authority to decide who would or would not receive aid lay with the most powerful people in Louisiana's towns and parishes. Access to federal dollars in addition to their own wealth only increased their influence.[39]

One of the biggest disasters of the New Deal for rural black people was the displacement of thousands of sharecroppers and tenants as a result of the federal government's farm policies. With the reduction in crop acreages brought about by the AAA, plantation owners' need for labor decreased. Many growers invested their subsidy checks in tractors and other machinery that further reduced their need for workers. Employers were supposed to retain workers on their plantations and share AAA payments with them, but loopholes in the legislation allowed the less scrupulous among them to avoid these obligations.[40] Welfare officials in Louisiana noticed the prevalence of "old plantation negroes who are no longer able to work for a living," on their rolls, and concluded that many landlords were taking advantage of the New Deal to rid themselves of unproductive laborers.[41]

Workers who remained on the plantations were easily cheated out of their share of AAA payments. Officials within the Department of Agriculture decided that federal policy should not interfere with traditional labor contract arrangements in the South, allowing planters to continue manipulating accounts and limiting their employees' incomes. In its first two years of operation the AAA distributed subsidy checks to landlords and entrusted them with the task of disbursing the appropriate portions of these funds to sharecroppers and tenants. Many agricultural workers failed to receive their share, so in 1936 the administration began mailing plantation owners multiple checks made out in the names of individual employees. It remained an easy matter for landlords to coerce workers into signing the checks over to themselves. Illiterate sharecroppers were forced to mark these mysterious slips of paper with an "X" without fully understanding what that meant.[42] Another ploy was to make sure the money could only be spent at plantation stores. Harrison Brown remembered "when the government had ordered you'd get a check or something after you settled . . . they took that check. . . . And the way they took it you couldn't cash it in town nowhere, you had to go by your merchant and let him sign it to cash it in—that was so he could get his hands on it, but you'd have to go by them."[43]

Planter abuses of New Deal programs did not go unchallenged. The massive social upheavals caused by the Depression gave rise to radical workers' and farmers' movements that struggled to influence national policy and enhance equality, opportunity, and security for all Americans. In 1931, members of the Communist Party began working among rural black people in Alabama, encouraging them to form the Share Croppers' Union (SCU) in an effort to increase the bargaining power of agricultural workers and help them gain fair treatment from landlords. Socialists in Arkansas organized the interracial Southern Tenant Farmers' Union (STFU) in 1934 to fight the mass evictions of sharecroppers caused by the AAA. The STFU spread into Missouri, Oklahoma, Texas, and parts of Mississippi, attracting more than twenty thousand members. At the same time, liberals in the Farmers' Educational and Cooperative Union of America (more commonly called the National Farmers' Union or NFU) began to increase their influence over that union's leadership, advocating federal legislation more responsive to the needs of small farmers. The activities of these rural unions and the publicity generated by plantation owners' violent opposition were instrumental in drawing nationwide attention to the plight of southern sharecroppers. The modification of some AAA policies in the later half of the 1930s and the expansion of programs to help displaced and low-income farmers buy land of their own resulted in part from union agitation.[44]

The Louisiana Farmers' Union was formed in the mid-1930s, originating as an offshoot of the Share Croppers' Union. In Alabama, lynchings, beatings, and evictions had driven the SCU underground, forcing its members to meet secretly and placing limits on its effectiveness. After a strike by cotton pickers in Lowndes County was violently crushed in 1935, union leaders began searching for ways to strengthen the organization. Strong interest shown by black farmers in Louisiana encouraged the SCU to focus some of its attention on that state, and initially it seemed that the union would meet less resistance there than in Alabama.[45] In January 1936, SCU secretary Clyde Johnson reported from Louisiana, "We have locals of 20 to 175 members that meet in churches and school houses and when some little terror did start against one member one of our leaders went to see the Sheriff in the name of the Union and the Sheriff didn't say a word about him being a Union member."[46] Communist organizers worked with local people to make contact with black farmers and encourage them to attend meetings to discuss the union. Those who were interested in forming a local then elected officers, and recruited more members by approaching family, friends, and neighbors.[47] The social networks that existed within churches and other community institutions provided useful structures for disseminating information about the union.[48] By May 1936, the SCU had approximately one thousand members in Louisiana, and the union had moved its headquarters to New Orleans.[49]

The SCU's New Orleans office was staffed by a small group of activists that included (at various times) Clyde Johnson, Gordon McIntire, Peggy Dallet, Reuben Cole, and Clinton Clark. Most were white southerners in their early twenties who shared a commitment to progressive causes and viewed their work as part of the fight for social justice.[50] They acted as effective grassroots organizers, offering advice and aid to union members but encouraging local people to make key decisions about issues affecting them. The first issue of the union newspaper, the *Southern Farm Leader*, invited members to send in letters expressing their concerns and ideas for action, describing conditions in their communities, and reporting on the activities of their locals.[51] Clyde Johnson recalled that whenever a new policy or position needed to be formulated, "everyone available met to talk it over. If it involved a basic union position we discussed it all over the union and tried to have a state meeting approve a position. . . . We believed the

members had to understand and approve an action to have it be successful. Rubber stamps can't cooperate."[52]

Relationships between the communists and local union members were
characterized by mutual respect. At its first convention in 1936, the union
passed a resolution thanking Clyde Johnson for his tireless efforts on their
behalf, calling him "one of the outstanding champions of the Southern day
laborers, sharecroppers, tenants and small farmers."[53] Three years later,
Gordon McIntire noted the rapid growth of the union in Louisiana, saying, "Much of the credit must go to the Local leaders of the Union, whose
courageous desire to improve the economic conditions and protect the
democratic rights of brother farmers throughout the agricultural fields has
been repaid by the success of the Union."[54]

After establishing itself in Louisiana, the SCU attempted to further
strengthen its position by joining forces with other farmers' and laborers'
unions. In May 1936 Johnson wrote an editorial in the *Southern Farm
Leader* suggesting that all of the 60,000 southern sharecroppers, tenants,
and small farm owners who currently belonged to the SCU, the STFU,
or the NFU unite together in the largest of the three organizations, the
NFU.[55] Johnson had maintained friendly relations with STFU leader H. L.
Mitchell since 1934, and the two unions sometimes cooperated on issues affecting them both. However, Mitchell and others in the STFU were
wary of the SCU's communist affiliations, and they rejected the idea of
a merger.[56] The SCU's overtures toward the NFU were more successful.
Hard-pressed small farmers and tenants among the NFU's all-white membership were beginning to see the value of uniting with black farmers to
fight government agricultural policies that mostly benefited large corporate landowners. The more progressive elements within the union saw an
opportunity to strengthen their position by encouraging the transfer of
SCU members to their organization.[57] In return, NFU charters offered the
former SCU locals the protection they so badly needed.[58] Clyde Johnson
hoped the charters would enable union members to "meet openly without
interference," and that uniting with an established organization that had
more than one hundred thousand members in thirty-eight states would
"give the Black Belt farmers a much greater backing" in their struggles
against plantation owners.[59] In 1937 the SCU's locals in Alabama and Louisiana began transferring into the NFU, and the Louisiana Farmers' Union
was chartered as a state division of the national union.[60] At the annual
convention of the NFU in November, delegates from the southern states
played an important part in electing new executive officers and replacing

the union's traditional emphasis on banking and money reform with a program more in line with the needs of poor farmers. Resolutions called for legislation to help tenants achieve farm ownership, mortgage relief, crop loans, and price control, as well as cooperation between farmers' organizations and industrial workers' unions.[61]

Since the problems confronting agricultural day laborers were different from those of farm operators, SCU leaders urged that they be organized into a separate union affiliated with the American Federation of Labor (AFL).[62] In 1937 farm wage workers in Alabama gained an AFL charter to form a union, but shortly afterwards they joined the United Cannery, Agricultural, Packing and Allied Workers of America (UCAPAWA), a new organization of farm and food processing workers sponsored by the Congress of Industrial Organizations (CIO). Johnson then left the South to work with UCAPAWA lobbyists in Washington, leaving Gordon McIntire to head organizing efforts in Louisiana. McIntire encouraged wage laborers to join UCAPAWA and small farmers, tenants, and sharecroppers to join the LFU. The LFU maintained a stronger presence in the state than the CIO union, however, especially when financial difficulties forced UCAPAWA to abandon most of its rural labor organizing activities after 1938.[63] To complicate matters, many of the LFU's members worked as seasonal wage laborers at sugar cane cutting time in addition to raising cotton or other crops during the year. For these reasons the LFU did not limit its activities to issues affecting tenants and sharecroppers, and its locals were made up of all types of agricultural workers.[64]

The LFU welcomed white as well as black people, and strong local leadership was provided by members of both groups. The union's "family membership" structure also encouraged participation by women and young people. Dues were $1.50 per year for adult males; women and boys between the ages of 16 and 21 could join for free. Non-dues-paying members were called honorary members but they had the same rights and privileges in local, county, and state unions as dues-paying members.[65] Women took an active part in the union at both the local and state levels. Often more literate than men, they performed valuable services like writing letters, passing on information from printed sources, keeping records, and teaching other members how to read and write.[66] Women delegates at the union's 1936 convention confidently expressed their opinions and ideas for action. Among the resolutions passed were several calls for measures aimed at improving conditions for farm women. They included equal pay for equal work, higher wages for domestic workers, free medical attention for pregnant women, and a maternity insurance system.[67]

As with all interracial unions in the South, the LFU's mixed membership presented problems.[68] In keeping with the Communist Party's antiracism, organizers at first did not allow segregated locals, though they avoided challenging southern racial practices too openly.[69] According to Johnson, "To be for equal rights, for freedom and for self-defense was enough. It covered all our problems. We never advocated 'social equality' in those words because in the white mind it was synonymous with demanding that a black marry his daughter. The racist propaganda hung so heavy on this that it was futile to argue."[70] Later the policy on interracialism became more relaxed, particularly after opponents charged that the LFU was a "nigger union" in an attempt to discourage white people from joining. Gordon McIntire refuted the claim in the December 1937 issue of the *Southern Farm Leader*, explaining that the perception arose after a mass meeting in Opelousas where the black farmers appeared to overwhelm the white members in attendance. "They later realized that their enthusiasm had worked against them," he wrote. "Both white and colored generally prefer to have their own locals and meet separately."[71]

No precise statistics showing the ratio of white to black members are available, but the majority of LFU locals seem to have been made up of African Americans. The union did make some headway among poor white people in rural Louisiana. White farmer John Moore of Simmsport, for example, led efforts to organize a local in Avoyelles Parish before being attacked and driven from his home by a mob in July 1936.[72] Most of the other local leaders were black, including John B. Richard (who served as vice president of the state union), Abraham Phillips, and Willie and Irene Scott.[73] The black men and women who joined the union were cotton farmers and sugar workers who welcomed the legal assistance, skills, and resources that organizers brought to the freedom struggle. The grievances that LFU members expressed in letters to the union newspaper and in convention resolutions reflected many long-standing concerns of rural black people, including unfair crop settlements, inadequate schools, exclusion from decision-making on government policies that affected them, and lack of protection from violence.[74] Joining the LFU signaled their intention to intensify the fight against inequality and injustice.

The LFU's first real battle occurred in St. Landry Parish in 1936. The union had been active there for several months, becoming involved in a range of activities that included forming a farmer-labor cooperative with maritime workers in New Orleans and pressuring state and federal authorities to provide relief to farmers after the region was struck by drought.[75] In November, plantation owners in the parish made their first attempt to destroy the union, precipitating a fight that set LFU members against planters and their associates in local office. With the help of federal officials, the LFU gained a partial victory, but the incident showed that the union was far from welcome in Louisiana and that white landowners were determined to do everything in their power to prevent it from interfering with the plantation system.

The struggle began when twenty families on St. Landry Farm learned they were to be evicted because the bankers who owned the plantation wanted to sell the land to the federal government's Resettlement Administration. Local administrators responsible for choosing farmers to participate in the planned resettlement project decided that LFU members would not be among their number. Most of those who were told they would have to leave were African American sharecroppers and belonged to the union. According to former manager Albert de Jean, all were good farmers. The families were served eviction notices in late November and ordered to move off the place by the end of the following month. As a statement by the LFU pointed out, most rural workers made their arrangements for the following crop season in July and August. The only landowners likely to have farms available this late in the year were "'ornery' landlords" who abused their workers. The St. Landry Farm families did not want to move.[76]

Eight union locals joined together to protest the action, demanding that the sharecroppers either be allowed to stay and participate in the resettlement program or be placed on good farms elsewhere with loans to buy their own equipment and supplies. Planters and parish officials responded by intimidating organizers and members. A group of white men that included Sheriff D. J. Doucet harassed Gordon McIntire when he went to collect affidavits from plantation residents in December. At a meeting held in Opelousas, vigilantes threatened McIntire and other union leaders while local resettlement supervisor Louis Fontenot "stood among the hoodlums grinning."[77] In late December the Resettlement Administration sent Mercer G. Evans to investigate the LFU's charges of discrimination. After speaking to local officials, Evans said he found no evidence of policy violations, but suggested that the displaced sharecroppers might receive loans if they found new farms and applied for aid.[78] Under continued pressure from the union, federal administrators finally agreed to grant the evicted families loans of between four and five hundred dollars each to help them establish farms of their own.[79]

The LFU achieved similar success in a battle with landlords in Pointe Coupee Parish in 1939. Plantation owners had responded to stricter regulations forcing them to share AAA checks with workers by evicting sharecroppers and altering tenancy agreements so that they could keep a bigger proportion of the government subsidies for themselves.[80] Tenant families were told they must accept the new arrangements or leave. Union officials advised the farmers to stand firm while they lobbied the federal government to intervene. According to local leader Abraham Phillips, "One bad week followed another, for we never knew when the boss would stop bluffing and really put us out in the cold. But we kept building our membership during those anxious days, we appealed to the federal government, and finally won the support of the Farm Security Administration, so that we got better rent contracts for 1939 than we'd ever had before."[81] The FSA agreed to lease the plantations from the owners and arranged for tenants to pay cash rents of six dollars an acre. The settlement allowed the families to receive their full AAA payments, sell their own cotton, and follow a live-at-home program, offering a chance to save some money and get out of debt that most had not previously had.[82]

The LFU also became involved in efforts to improve conditions for sugar workers. Under the Sugar Act of 1937, growers who wished to take advantage of the AAA subsidy program had to adhere to certain regulations, including the payment of "fair and reasonable" wages. These were to be determined each year by the Department of Agriculture after hearings were held to give planters, processors, and laborers the opportunity to present testimony to government officials.[83] In October 1937, hearings to set wages for the coming harvest season were held at Louisiana State University, a segregated venue that prevented African Americans (who made up the majority of sugar workers) from attending. The morning session was taken up with growers who spoke of the poor prices they received for their product, implying that they could not afford to pay cane cutters any more than the current rates (on average, $1.10 per day or 65¢ per ton).[84] In the afternoon, Gordon McIntire spoke on behalf of approximately one thousand LFU members whose complaints included inadequate wages, inaccurate weighing of cane, being paid in scrip, the excessively high prices charged at company stores, and not being allowed to grow their own food.[85] Some of the planters responded by praising the "beautiful paternalism of the old plantation system," arguing that workers received free housing, medical care, and other benefits, therefore they did not need higher wages. Others claimed that black people were lazy and wasted all their money on gambling anyway so it was pointless to pay them more. However, since wage increases seemed inevitable, the growers indicated that they might accept rates of $1.25 per day or 75¢ per ton.[86] After the hearings the LFU urged members to write to Joshua Bernhardt, chief of the AAA's Sugar Section, telling him why they needed higher wages.[87] The final wage determination set minimum rates at $1.20 per day for women and $1.50 per day for men, or 75¢ per ton. The regulations prohibited growers from reducing wages "through any subterfuge or device whatsoever," and stated, "the producer shall provide laborers, free of charge, with the perquisites customarily furnished by him, e.g., a habitable house, a suitable garden plot with facilities for its cultivation, pasture for livestock, medical attention, and similar incidentals."[88]

The Department of Agriculture held additional hearings in February 1938 to establish wages and working conditions for the planting and cultivation seasons. Peggy Dallet presented a statement by the LFU describing the miserable poverty that year-round employees on the sugar plantations suffered and calling for minimum wages of $1.20 per day for women workers and $1.50 for men. She refuted planters' contentions that the provision of free housing and medical care compensated for low pay, saying that in most cases accommodations were not fit for human habitation and sick people paid their own doctors' bills. Dallet requested that all payments be in cash, and asked that workers be allowed to grow gardens and raise livestock for food.[89] The AAA announced its regulations for the coming season in July, requiring growers to pay women at least $1.00 and men $1.20 per day, and to provide the customary perquisites free of charge. Though the new wage determination was not as high as the LFU had hoped, it still represented a 20 percent increase over previous rates.[90]

These wage rates held steady for the next four years.[91] Once the rules were established, workers fought to ensure that planters abided by them. The LFU taught its members how to keep records of what they were owed for the labor they performed each day and encouraged them to file complaints against employers who violated the law.[92] Nearly four hundred wage claims were submitted to local and federal authorities in August and September 1939. At the request of the LFU, the Department of Agriculture withheld AAA subsidies from plantation owners until the claims were settled, and government agents investigated reports that workers in several parishes had been threatened and intimidated by their employers.[93]

The same year, union members in Pointe Coupee Parish refused to accept wages of $1.00 per day from a planter who had evicted some families the previous year for filing complaints. As a result, they reported, he was "forced to live up to the law."[94]

Support for the LFU grew steadily throughout the late 1930s. Between 1936 and 1938 the number of dues-paying members more than doubled, increasing from 400 to 891.[95] Although this represented only a tiny fraction (less than one percent) of the LFU's potential constituency of more than 200,000 white and black farm owners, tenants, and farm laborers, it was an encouraging start.[96] Organizers found the response from African Americans especially gratifying. In November 1939 more than three hundred delegates from locals in twenty-five parishes attended the third annual convention of black members held in Baton Rouge, where they presented reports of their activities and listened to guest speakers from the AAA and FSA informing them of their rights under the federal government's agricultural programs.[97] Gordon McIntire reported that it was "probably the largest meeting of sharecroppers and tenants ever held, but if not I will guarantee that it was the most unified meeting, and surely accomplished more than any that I have ever attended." The delegates voted to work toward establishing parish-wide organizations to coordinate the efforts of their union locals, and agreed to allow the collection of dues for 1940 after the current year's harvest, to make it easier for cash-deprived tenant farmers to join the union.[98]

Some white observers in Louisiana ridiculed black people's participation in the LFU, arguing that the communists wanted only to manipulate the state's poor, ignorant sharecroppers for their own purposes. One report on the union stated that it was "a trouble making organization in that it puts ideas in the minds of the negro tenant farmers in Louisiana which could not possibly have originated there."[99] But African Americans were not as easily misled as these analysts believed. Black Louisianians saw the union as a powerful ally in their fight against exploitation and discrimination. They did not need to read Karl Marx or be "duped" by communist propaganda to sense the logic in the LFU's initiatives. Union organizers could not have been so successful if their analysis had not accurately described many aspects of rural black people's lives. As the Urban League's monthly newspaper *Opportunity* pointed out, black tenant farmers in Alabama and Louisiana knew nothing about theories of economic determinism or Marxist philosophy, "But these things they do know. They know of grinding toil at miserably inadequate wages. They know of endless years of debt. They know of two and three months school. They know of forced labor and peonage."[100]

African Americans in rural Louisiana had been battling these evils in their own way before the arrival of union organizers. Membership in the LFU offered the chance to fight plantation owners on more even terms. Writing to the *Southern Farm Leader* "about the dirty landlords, and how they rob us poor tenants," one Pointe Coupee activist stated, "When I heard about this union and what it was for, I joined it and I am proud to be a member of the Farmers' Union and I am willing to help every good effort for our justice and rights."[101] Another member wrote, "When our Creator brought us into this world, He gave each and every man a right to inherit some of land that He created. I'm looking to the Union to open the door for me."[102] With the power of organization behind them and with the help of sympathetic federal officials, black Louisianians gained some limited concessions from plantation owners in the 1930s.

A key issue that had always concerned rural African Americans was gaining fair settlements at the end of the crop seasons. According to Clyde Johnson, one of the first things sharecroppers and tenants wanted was "a way of having a voice. They wanted their account with the landlord to be on paper."[103] The LFU taught its members how to keep records of purchases from plantation stores so that they would know if planters tried to cheat them. At the same time, the union lobbied to make the provision of written contracts with employers a standard practice under federal farm programs.[104] Although administrators had always encouraged the use of contracts, they were not compulsory. In 1938 the FSA announced that it would insist on having written leases drawn up between its clients and their landlords, attempting to pacify planters by saying that this was for the protection of both parties.[105] "We know from experience that both profit from having their agreement in written form," an FSA official stated.[106] Another supervisor explained, "The landlord must be protected against abuse of the land and improvements, abandonment of crops and the like, while the tenant must have assurance of occupancy, a fair division of crop proceeds and renumeration [*sic*] for improvements made."[107] These statements aside, most of the provisions on the FSA's standard lease form seemed designed to improve conditions for tenants, including minimum requirements for the quality of housing and a guarantee that renters be allowed to follow a live-at-home program.[108]

Complementing the campaign for written leases, black people used their union locals to continue the struggle for decent schools. Shortly after his arrival in Louisiana, Clyde Johnson reported that "The Negro people, contrary to the teaching of the landlords, are very hungry for education and culture. Union members are already writing to the state depart[ment] of education explaining that they get only 3 or 4 months schools with very poor facilities and insisting that they be given longer and better school terms."[109] In a resolution calling for resettlement loans for the evicted sharecroppers of St. Landry Farm, LFU Local 2 also demanded "better equipped school houses and free text books, longer school terms, higher salaries for Negro teachers, and free transportation for Negro children."[110] A few months later the *Southern Farm Leader* reported that a group of union women in the parish had successfully lobbied for improvements at their children's school. The women raised $15.50 for the purpose them-selves, then sent a delegation to request more aid from parish officials, who agreed to match the amount. The money was used to install new toilets, new steps, and a fence to enclose the school grounds.[111]

Union members in other communities carried out similar activities, often making education a top priority. The secretary of a newly established local reported in 1937 that "Our first demand is for a school bus, some of the children have as much as 5 miles to walk."[112] The following year, when the LFU endorsed the Harrison-Fletcher Bill providing for federal aid to education, one member told Gordon McIntire, "I saw in the Bulletin where you said you had been to Washington to get aid for rural schools. To my judgement that is one of the most important things you could have done for us especially in West Feliciana Parish. . . . I can see and under-stand that you are on the job and I pray that you and all others keep work-ing for improvement."[113]

The LFU also attempted to give members a voice in the administra-tion of federal farm policies. In 1937, Gordon McIntire represented the union at hearings held by the President's Committee on Farm Tenancy in Dallas, Texas. He joined three representatives of the STFU in urging the federal government to allocate more money to its rural rehabilitation pro-grams, so that assistance could be given to the thousands of farm families who needed it.[114] A common complaint among rural poor people was that agents of the federal government's Agricultural Extension Service often failed to address the needs of small farmers, tenants, and sharecroppers. "County agents are chosen by the landlords to be of service to the land-lords," an article in the *Southern Farm Leader* explained. "Its hard for a square dealing County Agent who wants to be of service to share cropers and tenants and small farmers, to keep his job. He is soon fired by the landlords." The newspaper encouraged readers to demand that county agents be elected by white and black farmers and farm workers so that they might be more responsive to the needs of the majority of rural people instead of serving the narrow interests of plantation owners.[115] Administrators of federal loan programs also came under attack for discriminating against African Americans and LFU members. Union leaders urged members to write to the heads of government agencies and their representatives in Congress to ask that administration of the programs be placed in the hands of committees elected by all the farmers in the areas they served.[116]

These efforts to democratize federal agricultural policy and increase black people's political influence were largely unsuccessful.[117] At the local level, however, union agitation gained access to New Deal programs for black farmers who otherwise would have been excluded. A measure of the LFU's achievement in this area is that in Pointe Coupee Parish, where the union had many strong locals, more than 80 percent of FSA clients in 1938 were black.[118] Union leaders disseminated information about federal loans that were available and helped members to complete the application process. Black farmers who encountered discrimination from local officials could call on the LFU to assist them in gaining fair treatment. Abraham Phillips, for instance, was repeatedly turned down for an FSA loan by his parish committee because of his "general reputation as a trouble maker and a busy body" (a reference to his union organizing activity). The LFU's persistent appeals on his behalf caused the committee members to relent in January 1942. They finally approved Phillips's application in an attempt to "harmonize the labor situation" in Pointe Coupee.[119]

African Americans were intensely interested in obtaining credit from sources other than white landowners and merchants. In letters and statements to government authorities, black farmers often expressed the belief that all they needed was a chance to prove their ability free from the constraints of exorbitant interest rates and the dubious accounting practices of landlords.[120] This theme permeated the affidavits collected by Gordon McIntire during the struggle to gain resettlement loans for the sharecroppers of St. Landry Farm. Almost all of those threatened with eviction wanted to buy the land they worked and believed they would be able to support themselves if they could borrow money at reasonable interest rates. Harry Jack Rose summarized the prevailing view when he stated, "If I can just have the chance I sure would like to buy this farm. . . . I know how to work and I have eight children and four good hands. I can work 40 acres or more. If I can get a little piece with the government I know I can defend myself."[121]

African Americans' faith in their own abilities was borne out by the experiences of many of those who did receive federal assistance. The first black farmer to pay back an FSA loan did so thirty-six years ahead of schedule.[122] Overall, in the six years following the creation of the first rural rehabilitation agencies, the number of farmers who defaulted on federal loans amounted to only 2.6 percent of borrowers.[123] As one study pointed out, a major achievement of the government's lending programs was the "liberation of the negro and white tenants from bondage to the 'furnish' system under which tenants paid an average of 20% to 50% for production credit and were consequently kept in perpetual debt—or perpetually in flight from unpaid obligations."[124]

Planter Reactions

The same developments that held such promise for rural poor people elicited negative and sometimes violent responses from their employers. Union organizers' initial hopes of operating free from harassment in Louisiana were not realized. After its early successes in the mid-1930s, the LFU encountered increasingly strong opposition from white landowners, politicians, and business people in the rural parishes. Opelousas newspapers accused the union of stirring up "class hatred" and turning "the negro against white man, the sharecropper against the land owner."[125] Planters tried to discourage farm workers from joining, claiming the LFU only wanted to exploit them. One member reported, "Ed B. went to his boss' office to get $2. that Mr. H. owed him. Mr. H. told Ed., 'Now don't take this money and give it to that Union because you are only making some fellow rich in New Orleans.'"[126] Another landlord called all his workers together one morning and told them not to join the union or there would be trouble: "You fellows going around writing to the government, it will be too bad. And anyone of you who joins that thing, you will have to move."[127] Gordon McIntire encountered intense hostility from planters, merchants, and local officials whenever he ventured into the rural parishes. One man told him, "We don't want a Union here. . . . We'll keep it out . . . with our lives if we have to."[128]

As always, plantation owners could rely on law enforcement officers and other public servants to protect their interests. Sheriff D. J. Doucet of St. Landry Parish visited the secretary of the LFU's Woodside local one night, threatened him, and gave him five days to leave the parish.[129] Union members in Natchitoches Parish reported in 1940 that "the landlords are telling the sheriff and deputies to visit all the meetings of the farmers and beat the people until they break up the unions." Police in the parish held and interrogated an elderly black sharecropper for two hours, telling him that it was illegal for people to pay any dues to the union.[130] Local administrators of federal programs also discouraged farmers from joining the LFU by withholding aid from members. Resettlement Administration officials in Pointe Coupee Parish relocated those who had joined the union to poorer land, took their equipment away so that the farmers had nothing to work with, and held up their AAA checks. The secretary of one local in the parish complained, "The landlords are bitterly against the union in this section," and added, "Resettlement and county agents are carrying on the same crooked work against us."[131] The danger that the frequent overlap of planter and public authority posed to organizing efforts was most clearly revealed in Rapides Parish during the struggle over sugar workers' wages in 1939. According to Gordon McIntire, immediately after wage claims were submitted to the local agricultural committee, "terror broke out in Rapides Parish, where one of the big landlords against whom we had entered several claims, was Chairman of the Parish Committee."[132]

Union members lived with constant threats of evictions, beatings, imprisonment, and death. One man who dared to ask his landlord if his AAA payment had arrived reported that his employer "seemed to get offended because I asked about my check, and he told me I had been with him too long for him to hurt me, so I had better move before he killed me. And he gave me 24 hours to be gone off the farm."[133] In June 1937, a group of white men broke into the home of Willie Scott in West Feliciana Parish, seeking to lynch him. Finding only his wife Irene at home, they beat her severely in an attempt to gain information. Irene Scott survived by pretending to be knocked unconscious and fleeing to some woods while the men waited outside the house for her husband to return. With the help of other union members, the Scotts escaped to New Orleans.[134] Frightening attacks like this were common. By the late 1930s most LFU members probably felt a lot like Joe Beraud, who feared he would soon be murdered by his landlord. "MR. WARREN is going all around telling both whites and blacks that he is going to kill me," he wrote in a letter to Gordon McIntire. "He is carrying his gun for me. . . . My life has come to be like a rabbit's."[135]

Black Louisianians who had joined the LFU in the hope of achieving better living and working conditions struggled determinedly against plantation owners' attempts to repress their efforts. African Americans in Woodside responded to the threats made against their union secretary by forming an armed guard to watch over his home and family.[136] Communist organizers supported the right of black people to protect themselves against violence and encouraged the use of armed self-defense. In a letter to LFU members during the St. Landry Farm fight, for instance, Gordon McIntire wrote, "If any members house is threatened by crazy hoodlums they have a right to protect their home with guns. We are not going to make trouble but must protect our rights."[137] In 1937, a report on the situation in West Feliciana Parish noted that "some of the negro union officers were quite capable of determined, courageous and effective leadership and quite competent to take care of themselves in a test of strength with the whites."[138] Despite planters' attempts to kill them, Willie and Irene Scott returned to the parish and continued their union activities. The LFU newsletter reported in February 1938 that members in West Feliciana had "bandaged up the victims and dug deep into their pockets for food and other aid," and that the parish locals remained strong even though they could not meet as openly as before. "Maybe poor folks just don't have good sense," the report stated, "but when other people are getting shot at, poor folks want to know why. And so more people join up and the Union rocks on, for Union men are hard to scare."[139]

The LFU's ability to call on federal assistance in the 1930s might have contributed to its members' tenacity. After Gordon McIntire had complained repeatedly to government officials, both the Department of Agriculture and the Federal Bureau of Investigation (FBI) finally sent investigators to the sugar parishes in 1939.[140] In its September newsletter, the LFU assured members that government officials were "determined to investigate every case of intimidation or any other violations of civil liberties."[141] Although this statement greatly exaggerated the Roosevelt administration's commitment to ensuring justice in the sugar parishes, the mere presence of the federal agents had a positive effect. The interest that events in rural Louisiana attracted from people outside the region threatened to undermine the tight control that planters had over their communities. Consequently, they sought to avoid actions that might provide material for sensational headlines in northern newspapers or draw national attention. Fear of federal intervention prevented officials in Natchitoches Parish from lynching black LFU organizer Clinton Clark after he was arrested and jailed there in 1940. According to one account, there was every likelihood Clark would be killed until the state attorney general made a telephone call to the parish district attorney. "No—no lynching!" he reportedly stated. "We've got to be careful. The State is on the spot. Can't afford that kind of thing with the federal government like it is."[142] Violence continued in Natchitoches and other parishes where the union was active, but the situation almost certainly would have been worse had it not been for the watchful eyes of officials in Washington.

Southern political and economic leaders deeply resented the encroachment of national authority into local affairs. Although they welcomed efforts to stabilize agricultural prices and benefited greatly from the AAA, planters viewed any attempt by the federal government to address more fundamental issues of poverty and inequality with suspicion. From the earliest days of the New Deal plantation owners had been wary of its implications. In the late 1930s it seemed that their worst fears were being realized. The increased federal presence in the South and the encouragement that liberal officials in Washington provided to organizations like the LFU threatened the existing social order. In the early 1940s, southern lobbyists joined forces with conservative northern business leaders to demand an end to the government's "socialistic" experiment.

Much of this opposition focused on the FSA. The agency was vilified in country newspapers and at mass meetings of plantation owners throughout the South. Critics charged that the FSA's efforts on behalf of poor farmers interfered with natural economic forces that dictated the failure of inefficient or incompetent enterprises, that its encouragement of cooperative farms was "communistic," and that efforts to combat the high incidence of disease among its poverty-stricken clients represented an attempt to introduce "socialized medicine" into the United States. In 1940, enemies of the agency in Congress succeeded in passing budget amendments that restricted appropriations for its tenant loan program. At its annual meeting in December of that year, the powerful American Farm Bureau Federation called for the abolition of the FSA and the transfer of federal loan programs to the Agricultural Extension Service, whose agents generally supported the interests of large producers. Although the FSA officially survived until its replacement by the Farmers Home Administration in 1946, its activities were sharply curtailed after 1942 by further budget cuts and the shifting of many of its responsibilities to the Extension Service. Assistance was denied the majority of poor farmers who applied for loans after the reorganization of the government's farm credit agencies. The displacement of plantation workers continued with little to cushion the effect, relegating many people to the status of seasonal wage laborers forced to work for low pay during the harvest seasons and dependent on public welfare services at other times of the year.[143]

The Demise of the LFU and the Emergence of the Civil Rights Movement

At around the same time, the fortunes of the LFU began to decline. After reaching a high point of about three thousand members in 1940, both membership and finances decreased dramatically over the next several years.[144] Organizing efforts had always been hindered by widespread poverty among the people the union aimed to recruit. Most rural families could barely afford to spare even the meager amount it cost to join the union, and the LFU had many members who paid their dues irregularly, if at all.[145] Union staff were therefore heavily dependent on donations from liberal sympathizers to finance their activities. Those funds became harder to obtain as the United States prepared to support the European democracies in World War II, a move that most liberals supported, while the Communist Party and union leaders advocated American neutrality and attempts to resolve European problems peacefully. In June 1941, one staff member wrote of the difficulties the LFU was experiencing in raising funds from former benefactors, saying, "the war has changed the attitudes of 'liberals' who once contributed liberally. . . . Try to appeal to the [deleted words] today! There's a red bogeyman hiding behind everything except a defense poster."[146]

The union also suffered from the loss of two of its most experienced organizers. Gordon McIntire contracted tuberculosis and was forced to give up work in January 1940. He left Louisiana six months later, and Peggy Dallet shortly followed. Two other staff members, Roald Peterson and Kenneth Adams, attempted to keep the New Orleans office functioning but insufficient funds and continued repression by plantation owners hindered their efforts. Failure to collect annual dues in the fall, the only time most rural workers had any cash, left the LFU with only one paid-up member on record in 1941. Peterson and Adams found themselves in an impossible predicament, lacking money because they were unable to visit union locals to collect it, and unable to visit locals because they had no money. The union's financial difficulties resulted in the suspension of its state charter by the NFU in December. Local officials in Concordia Parish took advantage of the situation to arrest Adams and Clinton Clark for "collecting money under false pretenses" when they ventured into the parish on a fundraising trip in January 1942.[147] The two organizers were not released until three months later.[148]

Meanwhile, the planter-dominated Louisiana Farm Bureau used its influence over the Agricultural Extension Service to encourage rural people to join the Bureau instead of the LFU. Extension agents printed and distributed notices of farmers' meetings, promoting the Farm Bureau as an organization that had close ties with the government and could do more for farmers than other agricultural unions. An additional "advantage" for poor sharecroppers and tenants was that their landlords were often willing to pay Farm Bureau dues for them.[149]

Developments during World War II also contributed to the demise of the LFU. New economic opportunities drew thousands of rural people to the cities, where they worked in factories for wages that were higher than they could ever hope to earn as farmers.[150] Wartime prosperity and the increasing demand for labor offered an easier solution to farm workers' problems than remaining on the land and fighting plantation owners. Many of the LFU's rural constituents drifted away, either migrating to urban areas or moving into non-agricultural employment.[151] In March 1942 Gordon McIntire wrote a circular letter to LFU members from a Denver sanatorium urging them to continue their union activities while organizers worked to collect enough dues to have the state charter restored, but his appeal failed to halt the disintegration of the union. Although a few locals continued to hold meetings and recruit members, the LFU was not rechartered and there is no trace of official union activity after the mid-1940s.[152]

Even more than the New Deal, the nation's participation in World War II drastically altered conditions in the South. Mechanization, new jobs in industry, better educational facilities, and improved communications networks eroded the tight control over rural black people that plantation owners had maintained in the first half of the twentieth century. The same economic transformations that hastened the death of the LFU simultaneously contributed to the emergence of another, more powerful movement for change: the civil rights movement.

When activists from the Congress of Racial Equality (CORE) arrived in rural Louisiana in the 1960s, black people were better placed than they had been in the 1930s to lend their support to organized challenges to white supremacy. Farm owners, business proprietors, factory workers, students, and unemployed people who had escaped agricultural labor and were no longer tied to the plantation economy provided the backbone of the civil rights movement in the region.[153] At least a few of these local activists were former members of the LFU, and those links might have been stronger were it not for the migration and other disruptions that accompanied World War II.[154] More significant than the overlap in membership, though, is that the issues that seemed important to local people showed some continuity with earlier struggles. Responding to what they soon discovered were the main concerns of rural black people, CORE workers eventually modified their narrow focus on voting rights and desegregation to embrace some familiar-sounding objectives: higher wages, access to good jobs and education, helping poor people to achieve economic independence, preventing white violence, and federal protection of African Americans' citizenship rights.[155]

In initiatives that were reminiscent of the LFU's efforts in the 1930s, CORE activists worked with local people to increase black participation in federal farm programs by disseminating information and encouraging African Americans to participate in elections for parish committees of the Agricultural Stabilization and Conservation Service (successor to the AAA).[156] With financial assistance from the Farmers' Home Administration and the Office of Economic Opportunity, black farmers in St. Landry Parish formed the Grand Marie Vegetable Producers' Cooperative (GMVPC) in an effort to bypass the discriminatory practices of corporate landowners who dominated the processing and marketing of sweet potatoes, which had superseded cotton as their primary crop. After purchasing storage facilities and processing equipment, the GMVPC assumed control over the preparation, packaging, and marketing of its members' potatoes, offering them prices that were double or triple those they had received before. In addition, the cooperative used some of its funds to launch an educational program that brought much-needed advice and assistance to rural poor people in St. Landry and three other parishes.[157]

Community organizing efforts like the St. Landry cooperative became the main focus of CORE activity in rural Louisiana in the later half of the 1960s. Civil rights workers from outside the region allowed local people to set the agenda, modifying their own programs to fit the needs of the African Americans they worked with. Plans for a "Louisiana Citizenship Program" drawn up by CORE staff after canvassing several parishes in September 1964 emphasized the need to combine voter registration with other activities like attacking discrimination in employment, establishing adult literacy programs, and building community centers where people could go for legal advice and other assistance.[158] The themes of the earlier freedom struggle reemerged in the era of the civil rights movement, as black people continued the fight for equal economic, educational, and political rights.

Conclusion

In the early twentieth century, the repressive plantation system severely limited black political activity in Louisiana's rural parishes. Yet within its confines, African Americans engaged in subtle forms of resistance to white supremacy that reflected their desire for equality. These efforts were translated into open protest when the New Deal and World War II extended federal influence into the South and transformed the region's economy. Changing conditions altered the methods that black Louisianians used to challenge their oppression, but their underlying objectives remained remarkably consistent throughout the century. Black people's participation in the rural unions of the 1930s and the civil rights movement of the 1960s should not be seen as separate and unrelated events. For African Americans, they were different parts of the same struggle.

NOTES

Author's note: Funding for the research and writing of this article was provided by the Department of History and the Research and Graduate Studies Office of the Pennsylvania State University, and by the Carter G. Woodson Institute for Afro-American and African Studies at the University of Virginia. The final version was vastly improved thanks to the many helpful comments and suggestions offered by the following people: Nan Elizabeth Woodruff, Thavolia Glymph, Daniel Letwin, Gary Cross, Clyde Woods, Charles Payne, Adam Green, Pete Daniel, Reginald Butler, Scott French, John Gennari, Natasha Gray, Phillip Troutman, Andrew Lewis, Vânia Penha-Lopes, Eve Agee, Daphne de Jong, and the anonymous readers who assessed the article before publication. I am very grateful to them all.

1. "Some Letters from the Field," *Louisiana Farmers' Union News*, 20 August 1938, 3.

2. The political and economic changes that swept the South in the 1930s are discussed in Pete Daniel, *Breaking the Land: The Transformation of Cotton, Tobacco, and Rice Cultures since 1880* (Urbana, 1985), 65–151 and Jack Temple Kirby, *Rural*

Worlds Lost: The American South, 1920–1960 (Baton Rouge, 1987), 51–79. Rural poor people's responses to the Depression and to federal agricultural policies are the subject of Donald Grubbs, *Cry from the Cotton: The Southern Tenant Farmers' Union and the New Deal* (Chapel Hill, 1971) and Robin D.G. Kelley, *Hammer and Hoe: Alabama Communists during the Great Depression* (Chapel Hill, 1990). Neil Foley also offers some very useful insights into this period in *The White Scourge: Mexicans, Blacks, and Poor Whites in Texas Cotton Culture* (Berkeley, 1997), 163–182, as does Jeannie M. Whayne in *A New Plantation South: Land, Labor, and Federal Favor in Twentieth-Century Arkansas* (Charlottesville, 1996), 157–218.

3. Adam Fairclough devotes a few pages to the LFU in his recent study of the black freedom struggle in Louisiana, concluding that its impact was limited. Fairclough states that rural Louisiana proved to be "a graveyard for black political organization" in the 1930s and 1940s, and that "attempts by some historians to link the work of the farmers' unions to the civil rights movement of the 1960s are unconvincing." Perhaps because the LFU organized around economic issues rather than segregation or disfranchisement, the connections have been obscured. Yet as historian Nan Elizabeth Woodruff has shown, rural black people's notions of citizenship encompassed economic as well as political and social rights. A closer look suggests that African Americans in rural Louisiana supported the civil rights movement for the same reasons they had joined the LFU—as a continuation of their struggles for citizenship, broadly defined. Adam Fairclough, *Race and Democracy: The Civil Rights Struggle in Louisiana, 1915–1972* (Athens, 1995), 51–54; Nan Elizabeth Woodruff, "African American Struggles for Citizenship in the Arkansas and Mississippi Deltas in the Age of Jim Crow," *Radical History Review* 55 (winter 1993): 33–51.

4. J. Carlyle Sitterson, *Sugar Country: The Cane Sugar Industry in the South, 1753–1950* (Lexington, 1953), 104–107; W.E.B. Du Bois, *Black Reconstruction: An Essay on the Part which Black Folk Played in the Attempt to Reconstruct Democracy in America, 1860–1880* (Cleveland, 1935), 453; Gwendolyn Midlo Hall, *African Americans in Colonial Louisiana: The Development of Afro-Creole Culture in the Eighteenth Century* (Baton Rouge, 1992), 150.

5. C. Vann Woodward, *Origins of the New South, 1877–1913* (Baton Rouge, 1951), 178–185; Jay R. Mandle, *The Roots of Black Poverty: The Southern Plantation Economy After the Civil War* (Durham, 1978); Robert L. Brandfon, *Cotton Kingdom of the New South: A History of the Yazoo Mississippi Delta from Reconstruction to the Twentieth Century* (Cambridge, 1967), 1–21; William Ivy Hair, *Bourbonism and Agrarian Protest: Louisiana Politics, 1877–1900* (Baton Rouge, 1969), 35–39; Sitterson, *Sugar Country*, 311–313; "Excerpt from Regional Director's Weekly Report, Region VI," 25 January 1937, 1, loose in box, box 4, Records Relating to the President's Special Committee on Farm Tenancy, 1936–37, Division of Land Economics, Divisional Records, Records of the Bureau of Agricultural Economics, Record Group 83, National Archives (hereafter cited as Farm Tenancy Committee Records, RG 83).

6. Tenancy arrangements throughout the South varied, offering farm workers different degrees of autonomy. Some tenants simply rented land from plantation owners and retained control over management decisions as well as the sale and division of their crops. Others more closely resembled wage workers who were paid with a share of the crops that they raised under the supervision of landowners or overseers. On large "business plantations" like those that emerged in the Mississippi and Red River delta regions of Louisiana, the more independent types of tenancy were rare, especially for African Americans. The only difference between sharecroppers and tenants on these plantations was that tenants provided their own farm animals and tools, whereas sharecroppers had only their labor to contribute to the making of the crop. When the crops were divided, tenants received a larger share (usually two-thirds) than sharecroppers, who received one half. In 1930, 63,213 (86 percent) of the state's 73,770 black farmers were tenants. Of those, only 6,692 (11 percent) were cash tenants (the most independent type). Fifty-one percent (32,214) were sharecroppers, and 38 percent (24,307) were listed as "other tenants." Two-thirds of the state's 107,551 tenant farmers were black. Harold D. Woodman, *New South—New Law: The Legal Foundations of Credit and Labor Relations in the Postbellum Agricultural South* (Baton Rouge, 1995), 105–106; Ralph J. Ramsey and Harold Hoffsommer, *Farm Tenancy in Louisiana* (Washington, 1941); Bureau of the Census, *Fifteenth Census of the United States: 1930, Agriculture, Volume 2, Part 2* (Washington, 1932), 1219.

7. Harrison Brown, interview by author, tape recording, 25 November 1996, T. Harry Williams Center for Oral History, Louisiana State University (hereafter cited as Brown interview); "The Problem," n.d., 3–4, file "LU-1 184-047, Farm Tenancy," box 1, Farm Tenancy Committee Records, RG 83; Hair, *Bourbonism and Agrarian Protest*, 51–52; Joe Gray Taylor, *Louisiana Reconstructed, 1863–1877* (Baton Rouge, 1974), 401–403; Paul E. Mertz, *New Deal Policy and Southern Rural Poverty* (Baton Rouge, 1978), 8–9.

8. Like cotton growers, sugar planters had experimented with tenants in the decades following the Civil War, but found these arrangements unsatisfactory. Sugar production required a highly disciplined, tightly supervised labor force, and the considerable financial investments that planters had in sugarhouses and other specialized equipment made them unwilling to rely on tenants for their maintenance. In addition, there was no way to accurately measure the amount of sugar that each tenant's cane produced, making a fair division of the proceeds difficult and discouraging more widespread use of tenancy in the sugar parishes. In the 1930s almost 80 percent of the Louisiana sugar crop was produced using wage labor, with African Americans making up 75 percent of the resident work force. Sitterson, *Sugar Country*, 240–241, 389–390.

9. Sitterson, *Sugar Country*, 114–133; Joseph P. Reidy, "Mules and Machines and Men: Field Labor on Louisiana Sugar Plantations, 1887–1915," *Agricultural History* 72 (spring 1998): 185–194.

10. To ensure that year-round employees fulfilled their contract obligations, some planters paid them half of their earnings every two weeks and withheld the other half until after the harvest. Others paid both permanent and temporary employees weekly or daily wages. Sugar wage rates fluctuated from year to year and during different times of the season, according to prices, market conditions, and the labor supply. Sitterson, *Sugar Country*, 318–322; Reidy, "Mules and Machines and Men," 184–185; Louis Ferleger, "The Problem of 'Labor' in the Post-Reconstruction Louisiana Sugar Industry," *Agricultural History* 72 (spring 1998): 149.

11. J. Bradford Laws, "The Negroes of Cinclare Central Factory and Calumet Plantation, Louisiana," Department of Labor Bulletin No. 38 (Washington, 1902), 107–112; Sitterson, *Sugar Country*, 391; Myer Lynsky, *Sugar Economics, Statistics, and Documents* (New York, 1938), 290; Gordon McIntire to Miss La Budde, 12 October 1937, 3–4, file 3, reel 13, Clyde L. Johnson Papers in *The Green Rising, 1910–1977: A Supplement to the Southern Tenant Farmers Union Papers* (Glen Rock, 1977), microfilm (hereafter cited as Johnson Papers).

12. "Abolish the Commissaries," *Louisiana Farmers' Union News*, 1 March 1938, 2.

13. "Madison Parish; Its Customs—Yesterday and Today," *Madison Journal*, 27 March 1926, 1.

14. H. M. A. [Henry M. Stewart] to Annie [L. Allain], 15 December 1905, 5, file 17, box 8, Turnbull-Allain Family Papers, Hill Memorial Library, Louisiana State University. See also Walter L. Jones to Department of Justice, 1 June 1903, frame 0045, reel 2, *Peonage Files of the U.S. Department of Justice, 1901–1945* (Frederick, 1989), microfilm (hereafter cited as Peonage Files); F. M. Tatum to Theodore Roosevelt, 9 September 1903, frames 0224–0025, reel 2, Peonage Files; "Negroes in Keen Demand," *New York Sun*, 30 June 1904, item 295, frame 30, *Hampton University Peabody Newspaper Clipping File* (Alexandria, 1988), microfiche; Fred R. Jones to Attorney General, 23 January 1909, frames 0542–0543, reel 13, Peonage Files; B. F. Wilmer to Attorney General, 24 October 1929, frames 0689–0691, reel 11, Peonage Files; and J. A. Persons to Richard Leche, 4 August 1938, file "Labor Miscellaneous," box 39, Richard W. Leche Papers, Hill Memorial Library, Louisiana State University.

15. R. F. Reden to R. G. Tugwell, 8 August 1933, 2 (encl. in Fred Hildebrandt to R. G. Tugwell, 9 August 1933), file "Negroes 1921," box 1, General Correspondence, Negroes, 1909–1923, Records of the Immediate Offices of the Commissioner and Secretary of Agriculture, Records of the Office of the Secretary of Agriculture, Record Group 16, National Archives.

16. Martin Williams, interview by author, tape recording, 24 November 1996, T. Harry Williams Center for Oral History, Louisiana State University (hereafter cited as Martin Williams interview); Johnnie Jones, Sr., interview by Mary Hebert, transcript, 1 September 1993, 6, 19, T. Harry Williams Center for Oral History, Louisiana State University (hereafter cited as Jones interview); Rovan W. Stanley, Sr., interview by Janie Wilkins, transcript, 19 March 1978, 1, Oral History Collection, Center for Regional Studies, Southeastern Louisiana University; "Official Proceed-

ings of the School Board," *St. Francisville Democrat*, 11 July 1936, 2; "Farmers' Union Asks Federal Aid for Rural Schools," *Louisiana Farmers' Union News*, 1 June 1938, 1.

17. Louisiana Education Association Department of Retired Teachers, *We Walked Tall* (n.p., 1979), 38–40; "Want Adequate Schools, Equal Salaries; State Parent-Teachers Association is Planning Action," *Louisiana Weekly*, 4 January 1941, 1.

18. T. H. Harris to Parish Superintendents and Parish School Board Members, Circular No. 1017, 2 April 1938, file "Cases Supported—Teachers Salary Cases—Louisiana 1938–1940," box 88, series D, part 1, Papers of the National Association for the Advancement of Colored People, Library of Congress (hereafter cited as NAACP-LC Papers).

19. Report of T. F. Wilson, Federal Bureau of Investigation, 1 August 1939, 16, file "144-32-2," box 17587, Classified Subject Files—Correspondence, Central Files and Related Records, 1904–1967, General Records of the Department of Justice, Record Group 60, National Archives (hereafter cited as Classified Subject Files, RG 60); Ernesto Garlarza, *The Louisiana Sugar Cane Plantation Workers vs. The Sugar Corporations, U.S. Department of Agriculture, et al.: An Account of Human Relations on Corporation-Owned Sugar Cane Plantations in Louisiana under the Operation of the U.S. Sugar Program, 1937–1953* (Washington, 1954), 27, filed at n.d. [Aug 1954], reel 39, *Southern Tenant Farmers' Union Papers* (Sanford, 1971), microfilm (hereafter cited as STFU Papers).

20. Fred R. Jones to Attorney General, 23 January 1909 and 6 July [1909], frames 0542–0544 and 0525–0527, reel 13, Peonage Files; "Planters Bank Ranks Among State's Big Financial Firms," *St. Landry Clarion-Progress*, 18 August 1923, 10.

21. "Elstner Reviews Joel Johnson Case," clipping from *Shreveport Journal*, n.d. [c. 1909], frames 0038–0039, reel 17, Peonage Files.

22. Moses Williams, interview by author, tape recording, 24 November 1996, T. Harry Williams Center for Oral History, Louisiana State University (hereafter cited as Moses Williams interview).

23. Report of T. F. Wilson, Federal Bureau of Investigation, 1 August 1939, 25, file "144-32-2," box 17587, Classified Subject Files, RG 60; Louisiana Education Association Department of Retired Teachers, *We Walked Tall*, 39; Jones interview, 34; Brown interview.

24. Researchers found that in the spring of 1935, between one-third to one half of all sharecroppers and tenants in the South had been on their present farms for less than one year. "Report of the President's Committee on Farm Tenancy: Findings and Recommendations," February 1937, 19, file "Tenancy (Jan 1–Feb 1)," box 2661, General Correspondence of the Office of the Secretary, 1929–1970, Records of the Immediate Offices of the Commissioner and Secretary of Agriculture, Records of the Office of the Secretary of Agriculture, Record Group 16, National Archives (hereafter cited as General Correspondence, RG 16).

25. Statement of John Pickering, 8 April 1926, frame 0633, reel 12, Peonage Files.

26. Leola Palmer, "The Evolution of Education for African Americans in Pointe

Coupee Parish (New Roads, Louisiana): 1889–1969," (Ph.D. diss., Ann Arbor, 1992), 230.

27. Palmer, "Evolution of Education," 35, 232, 412; Laurie A. Wilkie, *Ethnicity, Community and Power: An Archaeological Study of the African-American Experience at Oakley Plantation, Louisiana* (Columbia, 1994), 83; Jones interview, 10.

28. *Organizational Study, St. Helena Parish, Section II—Negro Schools*, State Department of Education of Louisiana, Bulletin No. 549, March 1945, 2.

29. Palmer, "Evolution of Education," 29.

30. Wilkie, *Ethnicity, Community and Power*, 83; Sepia Socialite, *The Negro in Louisiana: Seventy-Eight Years of Progress*, 5th Anniversary Edition (New Orleans, 1942), 89; "50 Year History of the Knights and Ladies of Peter Claver," *Claverite*, November/December 1959, 12, file 38, box 6, Alexander Pierre Tureaud Papers, Amistad Research Center; "Women's 4th Dist. Home Mission Baptist Association," 26 July 1938, 148, file 11-6, reel PP2.9, Robert Tallant Collection, microfilm, Amistad Research Center.

31. At monthly meetings of the Bethel Baptist Church in Natchitoches Parish, for instance, representatives of the church's various districts followed standard parliamentary procedures as they discussed and voted on issues such as the disbursement of funds to needy members, censure and fining of those who were guilty of misbehavior, and long-term policies and programs. Record Book, 1922–1924, Bethel Baptist Church Records, Hill Memorial Library, Louisiana State University. See also William A. Muraskin, *Middle-Class Blacks in a White Society: Prince Hall Freemasonry in America* (Berkeley, 1975), 123–132; Earl Lewis, *In Their Own Interests: Race, Class, and Power in Twentieth-Century Norfolk, Virginia* (Berkeley, 1991), 70–73; Evelyn Brooks Higginbotham, *Righteous Discontent: The Women's Movement in the Black Baptist Church, 1880–1920* (Cambridge, 1993), 5–11; and David T. Beito, "Black Fraternal Hospitals in the Mississippi Delta, 1942–1967," *Journal of Southern History* 65 (February 1999): 112–113.

32. Walter White to John Garibaldi Sargent, 26 January 1926, frames 0755–0756, reel 11, Peonage Files.

33. James A. Ray to President, 27 February 1912, file "158260, Section 1, #3," box 1276, Straight Numerical Files, 1904–37, Central Files and Related Records, 1904–67, General Records of the Department of Justice, Record Group 60, National Archives (hereafter cited as Straight Numerical Files, RG 60); John R. Shillady to R. G. Pleasant, 25 June 1918, frame 0319, reel 12, series A, part 7, *Papers of the NAACP* (Frederick, 1982), microfilm (hereafter cited as NAACP Papers).

34. "Kill Innocent Colored Men in Louisiana," clipping from *Philadelphia Tribune*, 16 June 1928, frame 1152, reel 11, series A, part 7, NAACP Papers; "Somebody Ought To Pay These Mob Bills," clipping from *Chicago Defender*, 26 May 1928, frame 0436, reel 12, series A, part 7, NAACP Papers.

35. James S. Olson, ed., *Historical Dictionary of the New Deal: From Inauguration to Preparation for War* (Westport, 1985), 177–178, 549.

36. William E. Leuchtenburg, *Franklin D. Roosevelt and the New Deal, 1932–1940* (New York, 1963), 118–142.

37. Harvard Sitkoff, *A New Deal for Blacks: The Emergence of Civil Rights as a National Issue, Volume I: The Depression Decade* (New York, 1978), 59–75; Nancy Weiss, *Farewell to the Party of Lincoln: Black Politics in the Age of FDR* (Princeton, 1983), 220–221; Patricia Sullivan, *Days of Hope: Race and Democracy in the New Deal Era* (Chapel Hill, 1996), 41–67; Hollinger F. Barnard, ed., *Outside the Magic Circle: The Autobiography of Virginia Foster Durr* (Tuscaloosa, 1985), 127.

38. Willie Dixon to Attorney General of the U.S., 24 April 1939, frame 0987, reel 9, Peonage Files.

39. For instance, a survey of the land holdings of AAA committee members in Louisiana found that the majority were large growers and corporation owners unsympathetic to the problems of small farmers, tenants, or sharecroppers. Control over crop acreage allotments enabled planters to ensure that they received the largest share, while the amount of land that other farmers could cultivate was drastically reduced. Gordon McIntire, Statement on Sugar Cane Wages, Federal Hearing, 16 June 1939, 7, 11–12, file 3, reel 13, Johnson Papers. See also Clyde Johnson, interview by Bob Dinwiddie, transcript, 4 April 1976, 46, file 1, reel 13, Johnson Papers (hereafter cited as Johnson interview); Daniel, *Breaking the Land*, 91–109; and Pete Daniel, "The Legal Basis of Agrarian Capitalism: The South since 1933" in *Race and Class in the American South since 1890*, ed. Melvyn Stokes and Rick Halpern (Oxford, 1994), 79–102.

40. David Eugene Conrad, *The Forgotten Farmers: The Story of Sharecroppers in the New Deal* (Urbana, 1965), 64–82; Grubbs, *Cry From the Cotton*, 23–25; Mertz, *New Deal Policy*, 23.

41. Tensas Parish Department of Public Welfare, "For the Welfare of Tensas Parish," 15 March 1937, 7, Tensas Parish Scrapbook, 1937–1975, Manuscript Volume 9, Gladys Means Loyd and Family Papers, Hill Memorial Library, Louisiana State University; Maude Barrett to Loula Dunn, 11 September 1935, frames 0015–0016, reel 1, *Selected Documents from the Louisiana Section of the Work Projects Administration General Correspondence File ("State Series") 1935–1943*, National Archives Microfilm Publication M1367, Historic New Orleans Collection (hereafter cited as WPA Papers).

42. Conrad, *Forgotten Farmers*, 105–119; Grubbs, *Cry From the Cotton*, 21–23; Johnson interview, 47.

43. Brown interview.

44. Kelley, *Hammer and Hoe*; Grubbs, *Cry from the Cotton*; Michael W. Flamm, "The National Farmers Union and the Evolution of Agrarian Liberalism, 1937–1946," *Agricultural History* 68 (summer 1994): 54–80; Kirby, *Rural Worlds Lost*, 51–52; Donald Holley, *Uncle Sam's Farmers: The New Deal Communities in the Lower Mississippi Valley* (Urbana, 1975), 82–104; Mertz, *New Deal Policy*, 20–44.

45. Johnson interview, 48; Kelley, *Hammer and Hoe*, 168–169.

46. Tom [Clyde Johnson] to H. L. Mitchell, 31 January [1936], reel 1, STFU Papers.

47. Dale Rosen, "The Alabama Share Croppers Union," March 1969, 89, file 2A, reel 13, Johnson Papers.

48. Johnson interview, 29.

49. C. L. Johnson, "The Sharecroppers Union," *Louisiana Weekly*, 16 May 1936, 6; Rosen, "Alabama Share Croppers Union," 138–139; Kelley, *Hammer and Hoe*, 63, 172.

50. Clyde Johnson was the only northerner in the group and Clinton Clark the only African American. Originally from Minnesota, Johnson had attended City College in New York and had worked as an organizer for the National Student League before joining the Communist Party and being assigned to Alabama in 1934. Though he eventually left the Party, he remained committed to workers' struggles for his entire life. In addition to his work with the SCU and LFU, he became involved in organizing beet workers in Colorado, pecan shellers and oil workers in Texas, and electrical workers in Pittsburgh before taking a job as a carpenter in California in the 1950s. According to Robin Kelley, after Johnson was elected business agent for Local 550 of the Carpenters' and Millmen's Union, he turned the local into "a powerful force for civil rights, trade union democracy, and antipoverty work in the Bay Area." Texan Gordon McIntire had attended Commonwealth College in Arkansas (a school that was closed down by the state in 1941 for "teaching anarchy") before arriving in Alabama to work with Johnson and the SCU in 1935. Clinton Clark was a native of Louisiana who helped establish union locals in St. Landry, Avoyelles, and Pointe Coupee Parishes in 1936. Peggy Dallet had been involved in organizing local chapters of various leftwing organizations in New Orleans, including the American League for Peace and Democracy, the League for Young Southerners, and the North American Committee to Aid Spanish Democracy. She became the LFU's office secretary in 1937, and later married Gordon McIntire. Reuben Cole came from a sharecropping family in Georgia. Like McIntire, he had attended Commonwealth College, and joined the staff of the LFU in May 1937. Rosen, "Alabama Share Croppers Union," 4, 89, 138–139; Kelley, *Hammer and Hoe*, 63, 169; Robin D. G. Kelley, "A Lifelong Radical: Clyde L. Johnson, 1908–1994," *Radical History Review* 62 (spring 1995): 254–258 (the quotation cited is on p. 257); Reuben Cole, "Southern Farm Students Praise College for Workers," *Southern Farm Leader*, February 1937, 2; Tex [Gordon McIntire] to Clyde and Anne [Johnson], 13 April 1956, file 3, reel 13, Johnson Papers; Clyde Johnson, "A Brief History, Share Croppers' Union, Alabama/Louisiana, 1931–1941," April 1979, 18, box 9, Clyde Johnson Papers, Southern Historical Collection, University of North Carolina; Federal Bureau of Investigation, "Louisiana Farmers' Union (Farmers' Educational and Cooperative Union of America, Louisiana Division)," 27 September 1941, 8, File 100-45768, Louisiana Farmers Union, Federal Bureau of Investigation Files, Amistad Research Center (hereafter cited as FBI Files).

51. "Southern Farm Leader," *Southern Farm Leader*, May 1936, 1.

52. Clyde Johnson quoted in Rosen, "Alabama Share Croppers Union," 89.

53. "Share Croppers Union Expresses its Thanks to Secretary Johnson," *Southern Farm Leader*, August 1936, 5.

54. "Your Paper—Our Bow," *Louisiana Union Farmer*, November 1939, 4.

55. "For Unity in the South," *Southern Farm Leader*, May 1936, 4.

56. Rosen, "Alabama Share Croppers Union," 99–106.

57. Kelley, *Hammer and Hoe*, 169–172; Rosen, "Alabama Share Croppers Union," 86–87, 99–107, 112–113.

58. A union newsletter explained, "The charter gives the local the legal right to hold closed meetings and it is unlawful for anyone who is not a member to break in a meeting." "Organization Information," *Union News*, 30 April 1937, 2, file 2, reel 13, Johnson Papers.

59. Clyde Johnson to J. M. Graves, 15 May 1937, 1, file 2, reel 13, Johnson Papers; "S.C.U. Locals Transferring to Farmers' Union," *Southern Farm Leader*, February 1937, 2.

60. Johnson interview, 48; [Clyde Johnson] to G. S. Gravlee, 23 September 1936, file 2, reel 13, Johnson Papers.

61. SCU leaders strongly supported working with organized labor, encouraging members to form local farmer-labor cooperatives and to support candidates of the Farmer-Labor Party when they ran for political office. In return, leaders of the American Federation of Labor (AFL) and the Congress of Industrial Organizations (CIO) promised support for the struggles of rural people in the South. At its annual convention in April 1937, the Louisiana State Federation of Labor endorsed the LFU's efforts. The editor of the state AFL's newspaper, William L. Donnells, provided office space for LFU organizers and helped produce the *Southern Farm Leader* for more than a year before the farm union's failure to pay its bills caused him to withdraw this support. "Farmers' Union National Convention," *Louisiana Farmers' Union News*, 1 December 1937, 1–2; Farmers' Educational and Cooperative Union of America, National Program, December 1937, file 3, reel 13, Johnson Papers; "Washington Hears Farm Workers' Plea for Recognition," *Southern Farm Leader*, May 1936, 1; "A New Party is Needed to Battle for Justice," *Southern Farm Leader*, August 1936, 5; "Louisiana Labor Pledges Support for Farm Union," *Southern Farm Leader*, April/May 1937, 1; "New Office for Louisiana Farmers' Union," *Louisiana Farmers' Union News*, 15 January 1938, 1; Gordon McIntire to Mack, Bob, and Clyde [Johnson], 23 June [1938], file 3, reel 13, Johnson Papers.

62. "For Unity in the South," *Southern Farm Leader*, May 1936, 4.

63. Although UCAPAWA represented agricultural workers at federal hearings and before government agencies concerned with labor, most of its organizing activity centered on the processing industries. [Clyde Johnson], "Activities in United Cannery, Agricultural, Packing and Allied Workers of America, 1938," 3 July 1976, file 4, reel 13, Johnson Papers; Kelley, *Hammer and Hoe*, 172; *UCAPAWA Yearbook*,

December 1938, 8, 14, file 5, reel 13, Johnson Papers; Rosen, "Alabama Share Croppers Union," 113–115.

64. Gordon McIntire to Miss La Budde, 12 October 1937, 3, file 3, reel 13, Johnson Papers.

65. "S.C.U. Locals Transferring to Farmers' Union," *Southern Farm Leader*, February 1937, 2; "Organization Information," *Union News*, 30 April 1937, 2, file 2, reel 13, Johnson Papers.

66. Rosen, "Alabama Share Croppers Union," 91; Whayne, *A New Plantation South*, 194. Women and girls typically spent less time working in the fields than men and boys, so they could attend school for a greater part of the year. Stephanie J. Shaw provides additional insight into rural black people's determination to educate their daughters, particularly, in *What a Woman Ought to Be and to Do: Black Professional Women Workers during the Jim Crow Era* (Chicago, 1996), 13–16.

67. "Women Delegates Discuss Schools, Adopt Program," *Southern Farm Leader*, August 1936, 1; "Women Are Entitled to Free Medical Aid," *Southern Farm Leader*, August 1936, 4.

68. The literature on this topic is extensive. White and black southerners were certainly capable of overcoming mutual suspicion and mistrust to form strong interracial alliances, but these organizations always remained vulnerable. If the racism of individual members did not weaken or destroy them, racist and sometimes violent attacks by members of the larger community often did. See for example Barbara S. Griffith, *The Crisis of American Labor: Operation Dixie and the Defeat of the CIO* (Philadelphia, 1988); Eric Arnesen, *Waterfront Workers of New Orleans: Race, Class and Politics, 1863–1923* (New York, 1991); Michael Honey, *Southern Labor and Black Civil Rights: Organizing Memphis Workers* (Urbana, 1993); Daniel L. Letwin, "Interracial Unionism, Gender, and 'Social Equality' in the Alabama Coalfields, 1878–1908," *Journal of Southern History* 61 (August 1995): 519–554; and Stephen H. Norwood, "Bogalusa Burning: The War Against Biracial Unionism in the Deep South, 1919," *Journal of Southern History* 63 (August 1997): 591–628.

69. Rosen, "Alabama Share Croppers Union," 90.

70. Clyde Johnson quoted in Rosen, "Alabama Share Croppers Union," 92.

71. In the same article, McIntire asserted that "The Farmers' Union is proud of its large colored membership. But just as America has more white farmers than colored so has the Union." It is (perhaps intentionally) unclear whether "Farmers' Union" meant the LFU or the NFU, but it seems likely that he was referring to the predominantly white national membership and not the state union. Gordon McIntire, "Between the Plow Handles," *Southern Farm Leader*, December 1936, 4.

72. "Simmesport Hoodlums Drive Organizer Moore Out of Town," *Southern Farm Leader*, August 1936, 2.

73. Rosen, "Alabama Share Croppers Union," 90, 139–140.

74. "Resolutions of Sharecroppers' Convention—A Call to Action," *Southern Farm Leader*, August 1936, 3–4.

75. "First Louisiana Union Label Farm Produce for Maritime Strikers," *Southern Farm Leader*, November 1936, 1; "St. Landry Farmers Need Corn Relief," *Southern Farm Leader*, November 1936, 2.

76. Gordon McIntire and Clyde Johnson, "Statement on the St. Landry Farm Case," n.d., 1–2, file 3, reel 13, Johnson Papers.

77. Gordon McIntire and Clyde Johnson, "Statement on the St. Landry Farm Case," n.d., 1, file 3, reel 13, Johnson Papers; "Editorial Notes," *Southern Farm Leader*, December 1936, 4.

78. Gordon McIntire and Clyde Johnson, "Statement on the St. Landry Farm Case," n.d., 3, file 3, reel 13, Johnson Papers; Mercer G. Evans to Clyde Johnson, 24 December 1936, file 3, reel 13, Johnson Papers.

79. Clyde Johnson to Louis Fontenot, 4 January 1937, file 3, reel 13, Johnson Papers; "St. Landry Farm Tenants Getting Teams and Tools," *Southern Farm Leader*, January 1937, 1.

80. "Seek AAA Relief Payments," *Southern Farm Leader*, September 1936, 4.

81. Louisiana Farmers' Union news release, 29 November 1939, 1, file "Southern Tenant Farmers' Union Jan 23–Dec 20," box 406, series A, part 1, NAACP-LC Papers.

82. "Cotton Tenants Win Rent Victory," *Louisiana Farmers' Union News*, March 1939, 1–2. To "live at home" meant that farm families grew as much of their own food as possible instead of purchasing it from landlords or merchants.

83. Sugar Act of 1937, in Lynsky, *Sugar Economics*, 215–216.

84. Although it is possible that some of the planters did have genuine financial difficulties, most were probably not as poverty-stricken as they claimed. Between 1930 and 1936, gross income from the Louisiana sugar crop more than doubled (increasing from $15,000,000 to $33,000,000), while wages remained relatively static. Godchaux Sugars, a company that owned a dozen plantations in seven parishes, reported a net income of $858,000 in 1936. At the 1937 hearings, when the owner of Burgaires Sugar stated, "It is not a question of how we are going to divide the profits but how we will share the losses," a small grower from his parish pointed out that the company had made $500,000 in profits the previous winter. In any case, plantation owners derived great benefits from the government's subsidy program, and it was not unreasonable to require them to share part of their increased earnings with their workers. Lynsky, *Sugar Economics*, 23, 93; Gordon McIntire to Miss La Budde, 12 October 1937, 1, file 3, reel 13, Johnson Papers.

85. Gordon McIntire to Miss La Budde, 12 October 1937, 3–4, file 3, reel 13, Johnson Papers.

86. Gordon McIntire to Miss La Budde, 12 October 1937, 5, 7, file 3, reel 13, Johnson Papers.

87. Godfrey G. Beck and Gordon McIntire to Sugar Cane Cutters and Friends of Field Labor in the Sugar Industry, n.d. [October 1937], file 3, reel 13, Johnson Papers.

88. This did not mean that all planters had to provide such benefits, only that those who had always done so could not withdraw these privileges in an effort to reduce wages. In a set-back for the LFU, the Sugar Section later determined that growers could deduct pay for board if this was agreed to in advance with their laborers. Gordon McIntire called the new ruling "simply a loophole" that allowed planters to pay less than the minimum wage. H. A. Wallace, "Determination of Fair and Reasonable Wage Rates for Harvesting the 1937 Sugar Crop of Louisiana Sugarcane, Pursuant to the Sugar Act of 1937," 12 November 1937, in Lynsky, *Sugar Economics*, 233; "The Check-up on Cane Cutting Wages," *Louisiana Farmers' Union News*, 1 March 1938, 5; Tex [Gordon McIntire] to Clyde Johnson, 14 September 1939, file 3, reel 13, Johnson Papers.

89. "Farmers' Union Asks Wage Increases for Sugar Workers," *Louisiana Farmers' Union News*, 1 March 1938, 1–3.

90. "Increased Wages for Sugar Cane Workers Specified in Rules," *Opelousas Clarion-News*, 28 July 1938, 3; Joshua Bernhardt, *The Sugar Industry and the Federal Government: A Thirty Year Record (1917–47)* (Washington, 1948), 208.

91. LFU organizers and members attended additional hearings in August 1938 (to establish rates for the 1938 harvest season) and June 1939 (to establish rates for the 1939 cultivation and planting seasons, and the 1940 harvest season), but the union was unable to gain further wage increases. With the start of World War II, however, wages rose to almost $3.00 per day and continued to increase after the war, reaching up to $3.70 per day or $1.74 per ton during the 1949 sugar harvest. "Cane Grower Denies Labor Intimidated," clipping from *New Orleans Item*, n.d. [6 August 1938], file 3, reel 13, Johnson Papers; Tex [Gordon McIntire] to Clyde [Johnson], 20 June 1939, file 3, reel 13, Johnson Papers; Bernhardt, *Sugar Industry*, 224–225, 242, 251–252, 266, 272, 275–276; Sitterson, *Sugar Country*, 393–394.

92. "The Check-up on Cane Cutting Wages," *Louisiana Farmers' Union News*, 1 March 1938, 5.

93. "Action on Cane Wages," *Louisiana Farmers' Union News*, August 1939, 3; "The Sugar Battle Still Rages," *Louisiana Farmers' Union News*, September 1939, 3; B. E. Sackett to Director, Federal Bureau of Investigation, 7 September 1939, file "144-32-2," box 17587, Classified Subject Files, RG 60.

94. "Sharecroppers and Tenants Hold Convention," LFU news release, 4 November 1939, 2, file 3, reel 13, Johnson Papers.

95. [Clyde Johnson] to G.S. Gravlee, 23 September 1936, file 2, reel 13, Johnson Papers; Federal Bureau of Investigation, "Louisiana Farmers' Union (Farmers' Educational and Cooperative Union of America, Louisiana Division)," 27 September 1941, 6, File 100-45768, Louisiana Farmers Union, FBI Files.

96. Bureau of the Census, *United States Census of Agriculture: 1945, Volume 1, Part 24* (Washington, 1946), State Tables 1 and 5. The census lists a total of 206,719 farm operators and laborers (excluding unpaid family labor) in Louisiana in 1940.

97. "Sharecroppers and Tenants Hold Convention," LFU news release, 4 No-

vember 1939, 1, file 3, reel 13, Johnson Papers; "Negro Conference in Baton Rouge," *Louisiana Union Farmer*, November 1939, 1.

98. Tex [Gordon McIntire] to Clyde [Johnson], 11 November 1939, 1, file 3, reel 13, Johnson Papers.

99. Federal Bureau of Investigation, "Louisiana Farmers' Union (Farmers' Educational and Cooperative Union of America, Louisiana Division)," 27 September 1941, 18, File 100-45768, Louisiana Farmers Union, FBI Files.

100. "Editorial Notes," *Opportunity*, August 1931, 234.

101. A New Member, "Slavery," *Southern Farm Leader*, October 1936, 3.

102. Quoted in "Sharecroppers and Tenants Hold Convention," LFU news release, 4 November 1939, 1, file 3, reel 13, Johnson Papers.

103. Johnson interview, 45.

104. Gordon McIntire and Clyde Johnson, "Statement on Farm-Tenancy," n.d. [c. January 1937], 3, file "Extra Copies Briefs from Hearings on Farm Tenancy, Dallas, Texas, Jan. 4, 1937," box 1, Farm Tenancy Committee Records, RG 83; "The Sharecrop Contract," *Southern Farm Leader*, April/May 1937, 3.

105. Mertz, *New Deal Policy*, 202.

106. "F.S.A. News," *Pointe Coupee Banner*, 8 June 1939, 1.

107. "FSA Insists on Written Farm Lease," *St. Francisville Democrat*, 1 October 1938, 2.

108. "FSA Farm News," *Pointe Coupee Banner*, 2 October 1941, 1.

109. C. L. Johnson, "The Sharecroppers' Union," *Louisiana Weekly*, 16 May 1936, 6.

110. "Local No. 2 Resolution," *Southern Farm Leader*, December 1936, 3.

111. "Mother's Club Gets Toilets for School," *Southern Farm Leader*, January 1937, 1.

112. "Want School Bus First," *Southern Farm Leader*, April/May 1937, 3.

113. "Farmers' Union Asks Federal Aid for Rural Schools," *Louisiana Farmers' Union News*, 1 June 1938, 1; "Some Letters from the Field," *Louisiana Farmers' Union News*, 20 August 1938, 3.

114. "Unions Ask Land for Landless at Texas Meeting," *Southern Farm Leader*, January 1937, 1.

115. "Your County Agent," *Southern Farm Leader*, June 1936, 4.

116. "Resettlement," *Southern Farm Leader*, May 1936, 4.

117. Pete Daniel has shown that government farm policies continued to privilege large, corporate landowners over small farmers while accommodation to southern traditions and prejudices allowed racism to become institutionalized within the Department of Agriculture. As late as 1992, only 417 African Americans served on county committees of the Farmers' Home Administration (successor to the FSA) out of a total of 6,611 members. Discrimination was so prevalent that black farmers filed a class-action lawsuit against the government, winning a settlement in January 1999 that promised hundreds of millions of dollars in back pay-

ments to African Americans who had wrongfully been denied credit, grants, and other benefits. Daniel, "The Legal Basis of Agrarian Capitalism," 100; Alan Jenkins, "See No Evil," *The Nation*, 28 June 1999, 16.

118. This was a much greater percentage than was typical for the South as a whole, where discrimination against black farmers kept the number of successful FSA applicants low. In 1939, for instance, only 722 loans were granted to African Americans in fourteen southern states, representing 23 percent of the loans that were available in those states. (Black people made up 35 percent of the tenant farmers in the same states.) African Americans constituted 70 percent of tenants in Pointe Coupee Parish in 1935. "Good Record for Pointe Coupee's FSA Farmers," *Pointe Coupee Banner*, 20 January 1938, 1, 4; *Report of the Administrator of the Farm Security Administration 1939* (Washington, 1939), 15, file "183-04 Annual Report 1937," box 27, General Correspondence, 1935–42, Records of the Resettlement Division, Records of the Central Office, Records of the Farmers Home Administration, Record Group 96, National Archives (hereafter cited as General Correspondence, Resettlement Division, RG 96); Bureau of the Census, *United States Census of Agriculture: 1935, Volume 1* (Washington, 1936), 703.

119. Douglas Robinson to Steve Barbre, 18 March 1941 and E. C. McInnis to A. M. Rogers, 31 January 1942, both in file "Pointe Coupee Parish, La. AD-510," box 193, General Correspondence Maintained in the Cincinnati Office, 1935–42, Records of the Office of the Administrator, Records of the Central Office, Records of the Farmers Home Administration, Record Group 96, National Archives (hereafter cited as General Correspondence, Cincinnati Office, RG 96).

120. See for example L. J. Billingsley to Secretary of Agriculture, n.d. [c. February 1934], file "Bero to Bill," box 3, Correspondence with the General Public to which Individual Replies were Made, 1933–35, Records of the Division of Subsistence Homesteads, Records of the Central Office, Records of the Farmers' Home Administration, Record Group 96, National Archives (hereafter cited as Subsistence Homestead Division Correspondence, RG 96); Willie Bates to Franklin Roosevelt, December 1934, folder "Bas to Beat," box 2, Subsistence Homestead Division Correspondence, RG 96.

121. Statement of Harry Jack Rose, 7 December 1936, file 3, reel 13, Johnson Papers.

122. "First Negro Farmer Pays Off FSA Farm Ownership Loan," *Louisiana Weekly*, 27 February 1943, 12.

123. Arthur Hatfield, "Farmers Able to Buy Farms Under Bankhead-Jones Farm Tenant Act," *Louisiana Weekly*, 9 August 1941, 7.

124. [Statistics on African American Gains under FSA Programs], n.d. [c. between 1937–1942], file "Investigation of Clients Preference (Veterans, Indians, etc.)," box 43, General Correspondence, 1937–42, Records of the Farm Ownership Division, Records of the Central Office, Records of the Farmers' Home Administration, Record Group 96, National Archives.

125. "Is Communism in Our Midst," *Opelousas Clarion-News*, 3 December 1936, 4; Statement by Gordon McIntire, 9 December 1936, 2, file 3, reel 13, Johnson Papers; "The Farmers' Union and the Negro," *Louisiana Farmers' Union News*, 15 February 1938, 1.

126. "Some Letters from the Field," *Louisiana Farmers' Union News*, 20 August 1938, 3. Some planters honestly believed that union organizers were taking advantage of their black laborers for mercenary reasons. Numerous references to the poverty of the New Orleans staff members in the papers of the LFU show that this was not the case. Organizers received no regular salaries and were dependent on donations from northern supporters in addition to some limited funds allocated by the NFU. When they traveled out to the rural parishes to visit union locals, they relied on members to feed and house them. "Racketeers Said to Be Robbing Poor as Alleged RA Workers," *Opelousas-Clarion News*, 2 January 1936, section 2, 4; George A. Dreyfous and M. Swearingen, "Report to the Executive Committee of the [Louisiana League for the Preservation of Constitutional Rights] on Investigations in West Feliciana Parish," n.d. [1937], 6, file 19, box 2, Harold N. Lee Papers, Howard Tilton Memorial Library, Tulane University (hereafter cited as Lee Papers); Tex [Gordon McIntire] to Clyde [Johnson], 17 February 1937, 16 April 1937, 22 May 1937, 22 June 1938, and 23 June 1938, all in file 3, reel 13, Johnson Papers.

127. Report of T. F. Wilson, Federal Bureau of Investigation, 1 August 1939, 25, file "144-32-2," box 17587, Classified Subject Files, RG 60.

128. Elma Godchaux to Louisiana League for the Preservation of Constitutional Rights, 17 October 1937, 2, file 7, box 1, Lee Papers.

129. Report of T. F. Wilson, Federal Bureau of Investigation, 1 August 1939, 28, file "144-32-2," box 17587, Classified Subject Files, RG 60.

130. "Natchitoches Farmers Rally to Defend Clark," *Louisiana Weekly*, 17 August 1940, 5.

131. "Trouble With Checks," *Southern Farm Leader*, January 1937, 3. Similar complaints were made by farmers in Alabama and Arkansas was well as other parishes in Louisiana. See "Resettlement," *Southern Farm Leader*, May 1936, 4.

132. Gordon McIntire to Gardner Jackson, 17 July 1939, 1, file 3, reel 13, Johnson Papers.

133. Report of J. O. Peyronnin, Federal Bureau of Investigation, 6 September 1939, 2, file "144-32-2," box 17587, Classified Subject Files, RG 60.

134. "Statement of Terror against Farmers' Union Leaders in West Feliciana Parish Louisiana," 2 July 1937, file 3, reel 13, Johnson Papers.

135. Report of J. O. Peyronnin, Federal Bureau of Investigation, 6 September 1939, 3, file "144-32-2," box 17587, Classified Subject Files, RG 60.

136. Report of T. F. Wilson, Federal Bureau of Investigation, 1 August 1939, 28, file "144-32-2," box 17587, Classified Subject Files, RG 60.

137. Gordon McIntire [to St. Landry Farm LFU Members], February 1937, 3, file

2, reel 13, Johnson Papers. See also Johnson, "A Brief History," 11–12 and Rosen, "Alabama Share Croppers Union," 92.

138. George A. Dreyfous and M. Swearingen, "Report of the Executive Committee of the [Louisiana League for the Preservation of Constitutional Rights] on Investigations in West Feliciana Parish," n.d. [1937], 3, file 19, box 2, Lee Papers.

139. "Union Men Don't Scare," *Louisiana Farmers' Union News*, 15 February 1938, 1–2.

140. Gordon McIntire to Gardner Jackson, 17 July 1939 and Gordon McIntire to Clyde Johnson, 19 July 1939, both in file 3, reel 13, Clyde Johnson Papers; Report of T. F. Wilson, Federal Bureau of Investigation, 1 August 1939 and Report of J. O. Peyronnin, Federal Bureau of Investigation, 6 September 1939, both in file "144-32-2," box 17587, Classified Subject Files, RG 60. The FBI's involvement was reluctant and its agents showed more empathy with plantation owners than with sugar workers. In his final report, the Bureau's Special Agent in Charge in New Orleans dismissed McIntire's complaints, saying, "The Bureau's attention is invited to the fact that McIntire is a labor union organizer who is trying to organize the negro workers in the cane fields and he, of course, is meeting with the usual opposition any such movement would have, especially in this part of the country, in connection with attempts to organize negro workers. His interests in the whole matter are purely mercenary, in attempts to secure members for his organization." B. E. Sackett to Director, Federal Bureau of Investigation, 7 September 1939, 2, file "144-32-2," box 17587, Classified Subject Files, RG 60.

141. "The Sugar Battle Still Rages," *Louisiana Farmers' Union News*, September 1939, 3.

142. Margery Dallet, "Case of Clinton Clark, Natchitoches, La.," 17 August 1940, file 15, box 3, Lee Papers.

143. H. L. Mitchell to Members of Executive Council of the STFU, memorandum, 7 March 1941, 1, reel 18, STFU Papers; "Farm Bureau Advocates Abolition of Tenant Program," *Tenant Farmer*, 15 July 1941, 1, file "Southern Tenant Farmers' Union 1940–1941," box 527, series A, part 3, NAACP-LC Papers; H. L. Mitchell, "The People at the Bottom of Our Agricultural Ladder," 7 October 1952, 1, reel 36, STFU Papers; Sidney Baldwin, *Poverty and Politics: The Rise and Decline of the Farm Security Administration* (Chapel Hill, 1968), 335–362; Holley, *Uncle Sam's Farmers*, 174–278; Mertz, *New Deal Policy*, 218–220; Daniel, *Breaking the Land*, 91–109; Kirby, *Rural Worlds Lost*, 51–79.

144. Federal Bureau of Investigation, "Louisiana Farmers' Union (Farmers' Educational and Cooperative Union of America, Louisiana Division)," 20 February 1943, 1, File 100-45768, Louisiana Farmers Union, FBI Files. This figure was an estimate given to an FBI agent by a former member of the LFU. It is unclear whether it refers to the union's total membership or only dues-paying members—if there were three thousand dues-paying members, then the union's total membership could have been several times that number.

145. Gordon McIntire, "Dear Friends," n.d. [1938], file 3, reel 13, Johnson Papers; Federal Bureau of Investigation, "Louisiana Farmers' Union (Farmers' Educational and Cooperative Union of America, Louisiana Division)," 20 February 1943, 1, File 100-45768, Louisiana Farmers Union, FBI Files.

146. Federal Bureau of Investigation, "Louisiana Farmers' Union (Farmers' Educational and Cooperative Union of America, Louisiana Division)," 27 September 1941, 22, File 100-45768, Louisiana Farmers Union, FBI Files.

147. Gordon McIntire to Members and Friends of the Farmers' Union in Louisiana, 10 March 1942, file 3, reel 13, Johnson Papers; Fred Kane, "Clinton Clark Threatened With Mob Violence," *Louisiana Weekly*, 31 January 1942, 1, 7.

148. "Farm Union Organizers Are Freed," *Louisiana Weekly*, 11 April 1942, 2.

149. Gordon McIntire to G. Warburton, 14 November 1939, file 3, reel 13, Johnson Papers; "Pointe Coupee Farmers Organize," *Pointe Coupee Banner*, 13 June 1940, 1; M. L. Wilson to H. C. Sanders, 9 June 1943, file "Dir. La. 1.43–6.43," box 886, General Correspondence of the Extension Service and its Predecessors, Correspondence, Records of the Federal Extension Service, Record Group 33, National Archives; Rosen, "Alabama Share Croppers Union," 79.

150. "Memorandum Concerning Economic and Employment Conditions in Louisiana, Notes on Individual WPA Districts," June 1941, frames 0753–0755, reel 6, WPA Papers; "Louisiana and National Defense, Second Report," 30 April 1941, 3, file 3, box 13, William Walter Jones Collection of the Papers of Sam Houston Jones, Howard Tilton Memorial Library, Tulane University.

151. Bureau of the Census, *Census of Agriculture: 1945, Volume 1, Part 24*, State Tables 1 and 5. Approximately 60,000 rural people left the land between 1940 and 1945. They represented more than one quarter of Louisiana's farm population.

152. Gordon McIntire to Members and Friends of the Farmers' Union in Louisiana, 10 March 1942, file 3, reel 13, Johnson Papers; Federal Bureau of Investigation, "Louisiana Farmers' Union (Farmers' Educational and Cooperative Union of America, Louisiana Division)," 6 August 1943, 1, File 100-45768, Louisiana Farmers Union, FBI Files.

153. Ronnie Moore to Vernon Jordan, memorandum, 16–18 December 1966, 4, file 4, box 23, Scholarship, Education, and Defense Fund for Racial Equality Papers, State Historical Society of Wisconsin (hereafter cited as SEDFRE Papers); John Zippert, interview by author, tape recording, 28 June 1998, T. Harry Williams Center for Oral History, Louisiana State University (hereafter cited as Zippert interview).

154. Local leader Abraham Phillips of Pointe Coupee Parish later became involved in the Deacons for Defense and Justice, an armed self-defense group that was formed to protect civil rights workers in Louisiana. A comparison of names that appear in the records of both the LFU and CORE suggests that several other residents of Pointe Coupee Parish who were active in the 1930s were also involved in the civil rights movement (Siegent Caulfield and Leon Lafayette, for example). Kelley, *Hammer and Hoe*, 169; Abraham Phillips et al. to Mr. Baldwin, 21 October

1941, file "Pointe Coupee Parish, La. AD-510," box 193, General Correspondence, Cincinnati Office, RG 96; Mimi Feingold, "Parish Scouting Report—Summer Project, Pointe Coupee Parish," 14 April 1964, 2, file 20, box 1, Congress of Racial Equality, Sixth Congressional District Papers, State Historical Society of Wisconsin (hereafter cited as CORE Sixth Congressional District Papers); "Report for Pointe Coupee Parish," n.d. [11 October 1963], 1, file 3, box 6, Congress of Racial Equality, Southern Regional Office Papers, State Historical Society of Wisconsin.

155. Oretha Haley, interview by Kim Lacy Rogers, tape recording, 27 November 1978 and Rudy Lombard, interview by Kim Lacy Rogers, tape recording, 9 May 1979, both at Amistad Research Center; August Meier and Elliott Rudwick, *CORE: A Study in the Civil Rights Movement* (Urbana, 1975), 338–339.

156. Henry Brown, et al., Field Report, West Feliciana Parish, 14–21 July [1965] and Henry Brown, et al., Field Report, West Feliciana Parish, 28 July–3 August [1965], both in file 15, box 1, CORE Sixth Congressional District Papers; Wilbert Guillory, interview by author, tape recording, 25 June 1998, T. Harry Williams Center for Oral History, Louisiana State University; Zippert interview; Meier and Rudwick, *CORE*, 351.

157. "History of Grand Marie Co-op," n.d., file 3, box 1, John Zippert Papers, State Historical Society of Wisconsin (hereafter cited as Zippert Papers); John Zippert to Marvin Rich, 2 August 1966, file 11, box 23, SEDFRE Papers; "Agricultural Stabilization and Conservation Service: A Report of the United States Commission on Civil Rights," 1965, file 5, box 1, CORE Sixth Congressional District Papers; National Sharecroppers' Fund, "Statement on Discriminatory Practices Affecting Programs of the U.S. Department of Agriculture," 29 August 1963, frames 01228–01231, reel 38, *The Papers of the Congress of Racial Equality, 1941–1967* (Sanford, 1980), microfilm (hereafter cited as CORE Papers); Sweet Potato Alert Proposal, Progress Report, 30 May–3 July 1966, 2, file 3, box 1, Zippert Papers; Zippert interview.

158. Ronnie Moore, "Louisiana Citizenship Program," September 1964, frame 00542, reel 20, CORE Papers.

Chapter 9

Beyond the "Talented Tenth"
Black Elites, Black Workers, and the Limits of Accommodation in Industrial Birmingham, 1900–1921

Brian Kelly

In the South industry is still in pioneer state. Its vast mineral wealth is to be uncovered, millions of feet of timber are to be cut, thousands of miles of railroad are to be constructed and kept in repair, great drainage projects are to be carried through, and the rough work of many growing industries is to be done promptly. Here is the opportunity for the masses of the negroes. . . . Today the South could not do without them for a week. If they should suddenly disappear, the South would be crippled for years to come.

—"The South & the Negro," in the
Manufacturer's Record, February 26, 1903

The dichotomy between protest and accommodation that has dominated study of turn-of-the-century black politics for almost two generations has largely obscured the lives—and historical significance—of black agricultural and industrial workers. Increasing numbers of Reconstruction scholars have noted the aspirations and the agency of freed men and women on the "bottom rail" of southern society, while richly textured and imaginative studies of civil rights activism after World War II have highlighted the key roles played by little-known local militants. Yet black workers remain neglected in treatments of the period in between, characterized famously by Rayford W. Logan as the "nadir" in African American history and, more recently, by Leon Litwack as "the most violent and repressive period in the history of race relations in the United States."[1] More than thirty years after calls for a new, more egalitarian "history from below," one must still search long and hard to trace the historical imprint of those who mined the coal and iron ore, felled the timber, and built the levees that propelled the South into the industrial age.[2]

Black workers' absence from the historical literature becomes more striking when one considers the prominent strategic role assigned black workers in elite designs to transform the region. Leading proponents of Southern industrialization routinely boasted that "cheap, docile black labor" would provide the means by which the region's unmatched natural resources could deliver prosperity[3] and allow it to "take the lead in the cheapest production on this continent."[4] If the overthrow of Reconstruction aimed, as W.E.B. Du Bois asserted, to "reduce black labor as nearly as possible to a condition of unlimited exploitation," then the central figures in that tale of suppression have curiously eluded historians.[5]

While the scant attention devoted to black working-class activism raises fundamental questions about the soundness of prevailing scholarship, the complex record of black elites during this period also invites revisionist thinking. All African Americans—elites as well as workers—operated within the narrow parameters established and maintained by the ever-vigilant wardens of white supremacy. Middle-class race leaders, many historians suggest, did the best they could in a difficult situation in which "most individuals, as well as most institutions, movements, and strategies . . . fell between the poles of collaboration and resistance, combining elements of both in complex, shifting ways." The three principal strategic responses to Jim Crow, John W. Cell writes—accommodation, militant confrontation, and separatism—"were all implicit in the situation."[6]

Cells's observations are borne out in much of the literature produced in recent years. Scholars of the period have moved away from any notion of a sharp dichotomy between protest and accommodation. Racism's potency in the years straddling the turn of the century forced black leaders to "shift between the tactics of accommodation and . . . protest" while negotiating "a safe path through the thicket of American race relations," one recent article concludes.[7] New studies, especially those concerned with black women's activism in the post-Redemption South,[8] reiterate the conclusion of earlier historians, including August Meier and Louis T. Harlan, that accommodation's passive deportment often masked patient and determined struggles against Jim Crow. Even the most "jelly-backed" race leaders, they insisted, surreptitiously practiced subversion in a system that offered meager rewards to proponents of gradualism and deference.[9]

That insight continues to serve as a central interpretive pillar in recent scholarship on African American resistance in the early twentieth-century South. The subversive potential of racial uplift is one of the common threads in much of the newer feminist scholarship, a theme that finds deep resonance in broader studies. Neil McMillen weaves the same premise into a sensitive treatment of Mississippi's small but influential black middle class, and in his elegant if harrowing montage of the Scottsboro frame-up James Goodman credits Booker T. Washington with "perfect[ing] and [taking to] its logical conclusion the cunning that had once assured the survival and sanity of slaves." "With danger all around them, [and] under the most unbearable pressure," he writes of Washington's Depression-era heirs in Birmingham's black middle class, "they displayed the most amazing grace."[10]

The attention to context in these recent studies is both necessary and potentially fruitful. The effectiveness of individual race leaders or indeed of various movements and race tendencies in confronting Jim Crow cannot be gauged arbitrarily; rather, it must be measured against the real possibilities and constraints imposed on them from without. In place of the more optimistic and collective élan exhibited by black southerners during their brief "day in the sun" under Reconstruction, the swaggering forward march of white supremacy naturally begat defensiveness, individualism, and racial insularity. It seems appropriate, therefore, to take seriously McMillen's admonition that "the study of black politics in the period before World War II" must begin with "an appreciation of feasible limits."[11]

It would be a mistake, however, to disregard the very real tensions that developed within southern black communities themselves. One corollary of the "accommodation as protest" approach has been the assumption that harsh circumstances forced all black southerners into the same mold, that there developed a unitary black experience of Jim Crow in the South during this period.[12] Such generalizations tend to perpetuate what Bayard Rustin once called the "sentimental notion of black solidarity,"[13] impeding a more dynamic understanding of the complex, varied response of African Americans to their predicament. Buried deep in the best analyses of racial uplift and black middle-class activism is a nagging acknowledgment that their stories are unrepresentative of the experience of a majority of black southerners.[14] Yet there has been no rush to unearth the parallel black working-class experience under Jim Crow. In one of the few departures from prevailing trends, Fon Louise Gordon insists in her Arkansas study that while "the systemic and hostile nature of caste operated to categorize the black community as an undifferentiated mass," the "black experience . . . at the turn of the century involved an internal struggle as well as an external [one]" for an African American population both "diverse and dynamic . . . not merely a monolith facing oppression."[15]

This study of black labor activism in early twentieth-century Birmingham suggests that the fundamental division within its African American community[16] during the period before World War I was not between elite advocates of protest and accommodation, but between black workers and middle-class "race leaders." The disparity in their respective attitudes to the New South social order manifested itself through a range of schisms: differing notions of domesticity and sexual morality; clashing perspectives on the regnant *petit bourgeois* mantra, which privileged individual over collective advance; and above all disagreement as to the level of collective deference owed to white society generally, and white elites in particular. Invariably, the axis around which these tensions revolved was the labor question.

The turbulent social history of industrializing Birmingham suggests a rancorous negotiation within the black community over how to respond to their predicament. Black workers who felt the burden of Jim Crow not only in their civic dealings but throughout their working lives attempted, where possible, to extend the "feasible limits" of protest to encompass a challenge to their employers. Indeed, their harsh treatment and meager compensation on plantations and in mines and mills of the New South seemed to black workers the very essence of what racial oppression was all about. Prominent Birmingham race leaders, however, steeped in the Washington tradition, frequently found themselves siding with Alabama's industrial employers against black workers. The resulting intraracial tensions reveal that accommodation reflected not only the harshness of life under Jim Crow, but also the distinct social position of a small minority of middle-class African Americans. And the response of black workers suggests that any notion of race progress that fell short of addressing the central problem of exploitation was deficient, if not irrelevant.

Birmingham provides an ideal setting in which to examine these tensions. By the turn of the century, northern Alabama's mineral district was the industrial showcase of the New South. Its prosperity rested upon a seemingly inexhaustible supply of cheap black and white labor. District mines and mills absorbed whites from outlying counties in northern Alabama, and efforts to import skilled labor brought some European immigrants, but from the mid-1880s onward employers satisfied their labor demand mainly through employment of blacks. By 1900, African Americans formed the largest group in the mines, and within ten years made up three-quarters of the iron and steel workforce. Birmingham became home to the largest concentration of black industrial workers in the nation.[17]

The first stirrings of labor unrest in the Birmingham district reinforced the employers' appreciation of their "cheap, docile negro labor" as a strategic counterweight to unionization efforts.[18] In iron foundries and steel mills, employers, abetted by a thin layer of white craftsmen, constructed a labor pyramid sharply defined along racial lines: at the bottom, a large mass of unskilled blacks confined to grueling and poorly paid jobs, and at the top a layer of skilled white craft workers whose "innate consciousness of race superiority" served as a "wholesome social leaven" in warding off labor unrest.[19] In the mines, however, a different situation developed. There, the harshness of mining camp life, the malleability of skill lines, and the residue of an egalitarian populist interracialism encouraged unified challenges to operators' authority. Birmingham miners mounted a series of powerful, interracial industrial actions from the late 1880s onward.[20]

Perceiving these strikes as a threat to the region's prosperity, coal operators groped for a remedy to their labor troubles, laying the foundations for a labor policy that would dominate the district well into the twentieth century. Borrowing from both the legacy of antebellum slavery and contemporary models of welfare capitalism imported from the North, leading operators embraced a strategy of racial paternalism that aimed to cultivate low-paid, defenseless black workers as a wedge against labor agitation. And in this project they enjoyed the cooperation of black conservatives, deferring to the new status quo.

Even before the turn of the century, Birmingham race leaders had played a prominent role in directing the Negro "welfare associations" created by employers to "fight the organization of Negro workers in the United Mine Workers" union. H. C. Smith, whose first foray into public life was the organizing of a convention of conservative black Democrats at Montgomery in 1892, declared in an interview some years later that "he made his living by doing 'welfare work' and that the 'industrial institutions' around Birmingham" contributed funds so that he did not "have to worry for support." The Hampton Institute's *Southern Workman* later noted that "Hampton and Tuskegee graduates are having a large part in such work," and at least one mining company offered an annual scholarship to Tuskegee.[21]

That industrial accommodation predated the rise of Booker T. Washington illustrates that the precarious position of black workers and not merely the lure of white clientage and sponsorship for the new black elite facilitated implementation of employers' plans. Nevertheless, the unmatched influence of Washington's accommodationist outlook among Birmingham's black middle class offered industrialists a crucial advantage. Washington was a frequent visitor to the district and wielded considerable influence; the local cadre of college-educated African Americans were graduates of either Washington's Tuskegee Institute (sixty miles to the southeast) or the State Normal School at Huntsville, overseen by another prominent race conservative, William H. Councill.[22] With the threat of black insurgency alleviated by accommodationist hegemony, white city officials expressed their relief that the "Birmingham negro," guided by such advisers, "has found his groove and moves quietly within it." NAACP officials sent south to organize branches in 1914 found Alabama "utterly Booker-T-Washingtonized": while the state as a whole was hard going for the Tuskegeean's adversaries, Birmingham proved their most difficult challenge. Over the next several years, NAACP organizers established branches in Selma and Montgomery, but none was present in Birmingham as late as 1918.[23]

Many of Birmingham's black businessmen were active in Washington's National Negro Business League, described by one historian as the national "organizational center of black conservatism." The most celebrated figure in the district's black business establishment and the president of the black-owned Alabama Penny Savings Bank, William R. Pettiford, was a close confidant of Washington's and a key figure in the early history of the NNBL. Washington enjoyed a close working relationship with the city's iron and steel kings, and for a time provided key financial backing for the black-owned Grate Coal Mining Company. His influence with the most powerful employer in the district, the Tennessee Coal, Iron, and Railroad Company (TCI), secured for Pettiford a position as an adviser on "negro welfare." Another Tuskegee operative, Melvin J. Chisum, was appointed "labor agent" by TCI and went on to a career securing black strikebreakers for northern industries during World War I.[24]

Birmingham's unique constellation of powerful industrial interests, an army of black industrial workers, and a cohesive black middle class made for the most systematic application of Washington's labor relations model anywhere in the United States. As well, the particular harshness of black life and lack of feasible alternatives there made employer paternalism robustly vital as a social paradigm. In a period when black Alabamians saw their formal political rights severely restricted, and when legislative restrictions were routinely backed up by extralegal violence, Birmingham employers promised a haven from discrimination and overt white hostility. In return Washington's local acolytes promised relief from the "strikes, labor wars, and lockouts" common in the North.[25]

The close collaboration between Birmingham industry and the black establishment derived in part from the compatibility of the black middle class's "missionary notions of uplift"[26] with white employers' understanding of the role of black workers. Following the defeat of Reconstruction, Kevin Gaines has argued, southern black leadership's sense of "collective ... struggles against the slave system and the planter class" was transformed into "a self- appointed personal duty to reform the character and manage the behavior of Blacks themselves."[27] At its most benign, this transformation manifested itself simply as an embrace of the regnant social Darwinism trumpeted by defenders of the new industrial order elsewhere throughout the United States.

On one level, there was nothing remarkable in the black middle class's sharing the faith of their white counterparts in the ameliorative powers of the market. But there *was* something disturbing about their separation of economic doctrine from the stark reality that engulfed the mass of black southerners during this period. The "rhetoric of uplift," Leon Litwack observes, "proliferated almost in direct proportion to its irrelevance to the working lives of most black Southerners."[28]

If individual black workers fell between the cracks of society, uplifters contended, the fault was to be located not in an unjust social order but in their own lack of industry and thrift. Indeed, the Jim Crow South was at times depicted as a color-blind meritocracy. "American civilization is a great highway," black *Birmingham Reporter* editor and William H. Councill protégé Oscar Adams explained in a speech before a group of black coal miners at Acton. "It isn't so much color, previous condition or race, it is who you are and what you are [which determine] whether you will ... be respected in the counsels of the best thought of American life." And in a context where few black southerners managed to advance far along the fast lane to prosperity, emphasis on individual responsibility often degenerated into denunciation of those who "drag [the race] down." "I wonder at times why we are so extravagant, why we spend so much for the showy, the fashion and care so little for the concrete," Adams harangued his readers. "Your making is in your hands, you can make it good or you can make it bad."[29]

Under Adams's direction the *Reporter* (Alabama's largest-circulation black weekly) became a "forum for conservative, middle-class morality and ethics," raising the alarm against the "'unworthy Negro,' the 'Negro swell,' the 'Negro gambler . . . of the crap-game gentry' and the 'dishonest Negro.'"[30] The paper's sycophantic tone elicited occasional protests from within the black community, but on the whole the *Reporter* was typical of Birmingham's black press during this period, which according to one observer made "little or no effort to incite Negroes to active resistance of any kind" and more often "seemed to avoid the race question altogether."[31]

How do we explain the public posture of Birmingham's black middle class during this period? What accounts for their silence on "the most pressing Negro problem[s]" deriving from the caste system? Did their public accommodation disguise "surreptitious" attempts to win advances for the race, as Meier suggested of Washington? Were they "sellouts" or "Uncle Toms," so concerned with ingratiating themselves among the "better class of whites" that they failed to provide needed leadership for "their" people? Were their lives so different from the lives of black workers that they themselves were shielded from, and oblivious to, the manifold effects of racism on ordinary blacks? The key to understanding the enigma of accommodationism during this period lies not in the shortcomings of individuals like Washington or Adams, but in their role as intermediaries between the "better class of whites" (in Birmingham, industrial employers) and the black working class.

The black middle class's gradualist approach cannot be explained as a function of their immunity from the indignities of Jim Crow. Although their relative privilege insulated them from the likelihood of being victimized by whites, race leaders felt keenly the humiliation of such incidents, perceiving them not only as an insult to the race but as an affront to their hard-won social status. In October 1917 the *Reporter* related the details of an incident involving P. M. Edwards, described as "no doubt the wealthiest colored man in Birmingham." Attempting to keep an appointment with a sheriff at the Jefferson County Courthouse, Edwards had been refused elevator service by an operator who insisted he walk up the back steps to the sheriff's office.[32] Though mild by comparison to the countless atrocities committed in defense of white supremacy, the incident illustrates that conditions were such that no African American went unaffected by the racial hostility pervading the South during this period.

With important exceptions,[33] accommodators did not indulge in sycophancy so much as put forward a restricted, class-specific brand of racial pride. Reconciled to the doctrine of separation of the races, and dependent for their livelihood upon maintenance of the color bar, the black middle class's understanding of racial solidarity revolved around two key elements. The first was the notion that black consumers owed a special allegiance to "their own" enterprises. Even Adams's most militant critics agreed on the importance of the "Buy Black" slogan. "Patronize your race institutions first, last and all the time," *Free Speech* editor F. P. McAlpine exhorted his readership.[34] Significantly, while racial pride of this brand was routinely invoked during industrial confrontations to dissuade black workers from joining the "white man's union," it never seemed to preclude deference toward white industrialists or the "better class of white men."

The other core tenet of the middle class's notion of race leadership was its fervent embrace of the charge to uplift the race, through patient moral reform of black workers themselves. The emergence of class distinctions in the black community represented, in their eyes, positive confirmation of race progress: those who had acquired the rudiments of culture and education and demonstrated thrift, industry, and sobriety had been rewarded with advance. The great work incumbent upon race leaders lay in bringing the light of middle-class morality to those still in the dark, and they undertook this work with great zeal—leavened, always, with a large dose of paternalism.[35]

While white patronage was not the only factor elevating individuals like Pettiford or Adams to race leadership, the compatibility of their outlook with that of employers ingratiated them to powerful whites, thus consolidating their public standing. Although material incentives cannot fully explain this arrangement, throughout this period many of Birmingham's most prominent "race men"—newspaper editors, ministers, leaders of the fraternal orders, welfare workers, and teachers—*were* financially dependent upon industrial patronage. Guy Johnson's characterization of Booker T. Washington as "in some respects a greater leader of white opinion than he was of Negro opinion" applies to many Birmingham blacks engaged in "uplift." Prominent race men like Adams and Republican Club chairman W. B. Driver spoke frequently at employer-sponsored welfare association meetings throughout the district, sharing the podium with management as they regaled black workers with lectures on "The Dignity of Labor" and "Race and Community Devotion." In return, Adams's newspaper benefited from the generous support of the district's most powerful employers.[36]

While it is possible to reconstruct the motivations of the spokesmen of middle-class "uplift," it is more difficult to gauge the attitudes of black laborers in Birmingham's mines and mills. One thing is clear, however: they were not the passive, docile mass depicted by local employers and race leaders. In the coal fields, in particular, black miners played a prominent role in every major confrontation with the operators. One of the leading pioneers of racial paternalism, coal operator Henry DeBardeleben, expressed his bewilderment that an "unexpected" feature of the 1894 strike had been the "stubbornness and unity" of black miners, who seemed to him "as determined in their purpose as the white." A white United Mine Workers (UMW) official complained during the same conflict that while "the colored [men] in and about Pratt City" were "true and noble," "mean scrubs of white men" were making themselves the "enemies" of the union by their strikebreaking. DeBardeleben was again stunned when, during the hard-fought 1908 strike, his "Negro Eden" at Blue Creek downed tools and voted to affiliate with the UMW. After union members ambushed a trainload of strikebreakers at Blocton, Major G. B. Seals of the Alabama Guard complained that black unionists were "armed to the teeth" and "seem to be . . . everywhere in predominance." When the strike went down to defeat, UMW President J. R. Kennamer lauded black miners for standing by their union. "There are no better strikers in the history of the UMW . . . than the colored men of Alabama," he said. "They struck, and struck hard. They fought manfully for their rights."[37]

Significantly, it was not until the threat of interracial unionism had been shattered, after the operators' rout of the UMW in 1908, that employers undertook the transformation of the district under the banner of welfare capitalism. Alabama industrialists overhauled their operations for complex reasons. They intended, quite obviously, to deter labor agitation and unionization, but in addition they hoped that substantial material improvements would stabilize their labor supply and raise productivity among native black and white labor. Though often presented as a model of racial philanthropy, the new departure not only failed to eliminate the color bar in industry, as some charmed observers imagined, but in fact elevated the importance of black labor as a check against rising labor costs. Not surprisingly, black elites were assigned a central role in reconciling black workers to the new arrangement. The system seemed to industrial accommodationists the very embodiment of the *quid pro quo* they sought to establish with Birmingham industry: theoretically, at least, black workers would reap the fruits of improved living and working conditions in return for a guarantee of labor peace. "Give the laboring field to the Negro, give him the contracts in the mines, the steel plants and many other fields," Adams beseeched employers in a tone reminiscent of Washington, "and strikes will cease."[38]

The new order was unilaterally imposed, of course. To the extent that the arrangement was at all a product of negotiation, its terms were negotiated by race leaders on behalf of black workers, and not by workers themselves. Observers therefore must be careful to distinguish black workers' acquiescence to the new order from the positive "enthusiasm" that employers and their accommodationist allies projected on their behalf. Its unilateral quality meant that welfare capitalism never retained the loyalty of industrial workers, black or white, and district employers therefore reserved physical coercion as a vital component of their labor policy. Despite their public promotion of new-style mining camps as model communities, coal operators went to extraordinary lengths to limit miners' mobility throughout the district. Armed company guards were a regular feature of camp life, not only in the more "backward" camps that had resisted the "newfangled" methods associated with welfare capitalism, but even in those "model" camps run by leading operators.

Thus, the new order proved fully compatible with techniques of harsh brutality and racial exploitation. Although TCI was forced to abandon its notorious convict lease system in 1911, it did so under protest, and the company's three hundred or so state convicts—nearly all black—were simply moved to mine properties run by competitors at Pratt Consolidated.[39] Black miners throughout the district complained of their treatment at the hands of company "shackrousters," who rode through camps "from sunrise until [sundown] with [their] billy [club] and . . . revolver hanging to [their] saddle, going from house to house beating up negro men and using [black] women to suit [their] fancy."[40]

Perhaps the most telling measure of the gap between the rhetoric of employer benevolence and the realities of mining camp life comes from the DeBardeleben Coal Company.[41] Significantly, the DeBardeleben operation won praise from Oscar Adams and others even as its high-handed authoritarianism elicited widespread condemnation from miners. The company's supervisor at Sipsey, Milton Fies, recalled in his memoirs a number of "unusual . . . Negro[es] of the old school" who served him with loyalty, diligence, and respect. He displayed less tolerance, however, for those who stepped out of line. When one of his night bosses killed an "impertinent" black miner for failing to show up for night work in October 1914, blacks at Sipsey became "considerably wrought up" over the incident, until Fies called in a deputy from nearby Jasper and discharged "some five or six negroes" who were "particularly impertinent and troublesome." On another occasion he discharged a black employee for allegedly insulting the wife of a company agent "in such a way . . . as to warrant our hanging the negro upon a limb and shooting him full of holes." Management at Sipsey "question[ed] all who desire[d] employment . . . very closely, to avoid hiring any men with union sympathies"; when Fies discovered one of his section foremen had been advocating union organization among miners at Sipsey, he immediately fired the individual and imported detectives to "make a thorough investigation as to just how much trouble" the man had "caused." Some years later, when employees at Payne's Bend stopped work to protest a missed payday, company officials instructed supervisors to "find out who is at the bottom of this movement and discharge him."[42]

Despite the best efforts of uplifters in the steel mills and coal camps, the disparity between rhetoric and reality was not lost upon black workers. While the absence of a collective alternative and the hostility they faced from white workers enhanced the appeal of racial solidarity, black workers' patience with the exhortations of uplifters inevitably wore thin. At times, the resulting tensions threatened to tear race organizations apart. When, during the 1908 strike, Grand Master Henry Claxton Binford of the Colored Masons warned UMW members in his ranks that he would deny death benefits to "any Mason killed while affiliating to these unions," his statement drew a sharp response from black unionists, one of whom objected that he could "not swallow every camel that Binford and the SCM tries to force down my throat. He is not the whole cheese so far as colored Masons are concerned." The "miners' union," this writer declared, "has done more for us than all the secret orders combined."[43]

With so much of their non-working lives increasingly coming under the supervision of company-appointed welfare workers, black workers valued the semi-autonomy offered by the fraternal orders and secret societies. During the low ebbs in union activism that inevitably followed UMW defeat, race institutions could play an important role in cementing the relationship between race leaders and the objects of their efforts. Though typically staffed at their upper echelons by representatives of the middle class, the orders won a wide following among both men and women in the coal camps. The orders provided a seemingly innocuous vehicle for race association in a society wracked with perpetual fears of black insurrection. Their extension of sickness and death benefits to members enhanced their appeal among laborers enjoying few other means of financial security. Above all, however, the popularity of the fraternal orders in the camps reflected the appeal of racial pride and autonomy: "Here only," a mining camp physician observed, "has the negro his best opportunity for self-government. There is no excuse for hiding the sins of a brother from fear of too harsh treatment at the hands of another race." Some measure of their élan can be gleaned from the fact that "some white men regard[ed] them with distrust, thinking they were for offensive rather than defensive purposes." No doubt substantial numbers of white Alabamians shared the fears expressed by Georgia officials in the postwar period that these organizations were "nothing more nor less than hotbeds of anarchy and Bolshevism . . . always plotting and scheming against the white race."[44]

While white hostility inspired cohesion within race organizations, the contrast between an overwhelmingly working-class membership and elites' identification with the employers inevitably generated intraracial conflict. During periods of tranquility and in the absence of labor strife, the orders could hold together, but cleavages invariably developed whenever events brought these contradictions to the surface. The same dynamic was apparent in church work. Elites were continually exhorting black workers to reject the emotional service and amateur gospel preached by itinerant ministers and unofficial sects in favor of the regular ministry subsidized by the employers. Black miners, on the other hand, complained that many of these preachers were "nothing more than stool-pigeons for the coal companies" who "instead of preaching the Gospel of the Son of God" were disseminating "the doctrine of union hatred."[45]

Class tensions proved no less capable of intruding upon relations between female uplifters and the objects of their reform work than they had among their male counterparts. Lynne Feldman found a "rather sharp delineation of fraternal membership among [black] women from different socioeconomic classes." The most prestigious of the female orders, the Court of Calanthe, "practiced an exclusionary membership which kept the order free from a lower class of women" and "removed themselves from more democratic organizations." The civic activism engaged in by elite black women, aimed largely at winning the franchise for themselves, offered little for black mining camp women. The experience of a black woman at TCI who was pistol-whipped by company guards in 1911 for complaining that the company was cheating her husband out of his wages, or of the scores of black women arrested and abused for their part in strikes in 1908 and 1920, was completely foreign to the experience of the wives and daughters of Birmingham's black establishment.[46]

In the absence of industrial conflict, the most troublesome feature of camp life from the perspective of black elites was the sexual permissiveness that seemed to them to pervade black working-class life. "Marital ties are regarded very lightly in many instances," one observer noted. "I have seen men living with as many as three different women in as many years. . . . Some marry each new wife without divorce, often under an assumed name, while others are never married to any of the women." A black miner, Bobby Clayton, recalled that the tendency of miners to move about in search of work rendered family life unstable: "some men had two wives and this one stayed . . . here and one stayed somewhere else and . . . the women would get along together. Men had double families and wasn't no conflict." No comparable testimony from black women survives to corroborate Clayton's positive rendering, but however they regarded their own stake in such arrangements, these women's lives were an affront to those attempting to implant middle-class morality in the camps. The broader national confrontation between elite women upholding chastity as "the litmus test of middle-class respectability" and black working-class women unconvinced of the merits of such propriety seems to have been played out with a particular intensity around Birmingham's mining camps.[47]

Birmingham employers' embrace of welfare capitalism rested on the belief that token amelioration of labor's grievances would stave off a more fundamental challenge to their low-wage regime. Race leaders signed up to the arrangement with different, but complementary, concerns. Racial paternalism never delivered on its promise to those seeking relief from the poverty and despotism of black-belt agriculture, however. There was work to be had in Birmingham's mines and mills, but only under conditions that kept black workers and their families living in poverty, and under a regime that replicated the brutality so familiar to black southerners. No system bearing such serious flaws could succeed in holding the permanent allegiance of black (or white) workers, and by early 1916 the disaffection of blacks from the paternalist arrangement was becoming obvious.

Its demise was accelerated by a number of developments unique to the Birmingham district. The failure of Pettiford's black-owned Alabama Penny Savings Bank and the "almost destruction of a number of [black] fraternal organizations" by financial scandals undermined the authority of established race leaders. The sense of crisis found its way into the *Reporter*, which attributed the decline of the Colored Odd Fellows to "right down meanness, ignorance, personal graft, and highway robbery." "What is the matter?" editors asked. "Leaders are dying, banks are falling, institutions of pride, church organizations, fraternal organizations are splitting . . . while the gambler, the alarmist and the unholy agitator go on with seeming prosperity."[48]

The local crisis coincided with national developments that would not only widen the gulf between black workers and race leaders, but seriously undermine the authority that area employers had enjoyed and dramatically transform the landscape of southern black politics. Increased demand brought on by the war presented black (and white) Alabamians with prospects of industrial employment beyond Birmingham, complicating employers' plans for maintaining prewar arrangements. "It has been necessary for us to offer inducements to our miners to prevent . . . them from migrating northward," Sipsey boss Milton Fies complained. Where wage increases failed to halt emigration, employers resorted to physical coercion aimed at retaining their black labor supply. "Shut the barn door before the horses get out!" urged a regional trade journal, and a number of employers followed the directive enthusiastically. In June 1917, the Birmingham *Labor Advocate* recounted an incident that occurred at a mine outside city limits where, after "many of the colored population had put on their best Sunday clothes and . . . gathered at the depot intending to come to Birmingham to a big baptizing . . . the superintendent and shack rouster appeared upon the scene and forced all the Negroes, without allowing them time to go home and put on their mining clothes, to go into the mines to work." Given such "intolerance," editors reasoned, it was no wonder that "the colored people . . . enter their protests in the way they have."[49]

True to form, race leaders denounced the "disgrace" of emigration as a product of black "ignorance" and warned that it would "put a stain, a suspicion on Negro labor that has never been on it before." "How can we expect the decent consideration of influential honest white citizens when we so deport ourselves?" asked the *Reporter*. By this time, however, the black middle class's project of racial solidarity was badly frayed, and their attempts to stem the "northern fever" only fueled the alienation of black workers. "Negro leaders and negro papers can no more keep Negroes here than they can fly to heaven backwards," one Birmingham minister conceded. That black workers discerned in the efforts of race leaders evidence of their subordination to area employers is evident in the bitter parting shot related by one of those heading north: "The Negro papers which you subsidize and the Negro leaders whom you pay, cannot hold [us]. Two [or] three years ago you promised us schools, you have not given them to us. The only thing you have offered us is an old Jail for our children."[50]

It is difficult to overestimate the scale of the transformation wrought by the complex crisis known as the Great Migration. But one consequence often overlooked is the way in which unprecedented opportunities for mobility and self-assertion undermined the authority of race conservatives and instilled new confidence among black workers. Booker T. Washington's death in 1915 coincided with a waning in the authority of the Tuskegee machine, but that decline was inevitable in the new circumstances, and in that sense Washington was perhaps fortunate to be spared a fresh (and very likely unwinnable) rivalry with the "New Negro." The effects of this transformation were felt nowhere more powerfully than in the Birmingham district, and can be seen in developments that unfolded at a molecular level.

The disintegration of employer-directed racial paternalism deprived Birmingham industrialists of a crucial asset in warding off working-class militancy and contributed directly to the reemergence of interracial unionism, a process aided by black self-assertion. In steel, organizing attempts had been continually hampered by the deeply rooted tradition of racial exclusion among white craft workers, but even that began to be called into question. Cognizant of the advantage that the lily-white policy had handed to their employers, white steelworkers resigned themselves to aiding the organization of black unskilled laborers in 1918 and supported a short-lived effort by the Mine, Mill and Smelter Workers' Union to organize district steel mills.

The campaign was less significant for the meager successes it registered than for the violent reaction it elicited from employers who had long posed as the guarantors of a fair deal for black workers. With Tuskegee operative Melvin J. Chisum employed under the direction of TCI to discourage black laborers against unionism, the steelmakers resorted to the first significant turn to vigilante violence since their rout of the UMW in 1908. An employer-directed paramilitary squad known as the Vigilantes scoured the district targeting Mine Mill meetings, assaulting black workers, and tar-and-feathering the black Mine Mill organizer assigned to the campaign. The vigilantes appear to have provided the core of the newly revived Birmingham Klan, which, according to Joseph McCartin, emerged in direct response to the organizing attempts in steel.[51]

In the coal fields, employers faced a much more difficult test. They had never succeeded in wiping out the UMW's exceptionally resilient interracial tradition, and it was here that the architects of the industrial order and their predominantly black workforce would clash dramatically in 1920. Coal operators responded to the UMW's wartime revival with an intensification of race-baiting and a renewed anti-union effort by Adams and others. Labor Department officials detected an attempt on the part of leading coal operators to "entirely . . . disrupt the [miners'] union by getting the negroes out," after which "negroes would rapidly and entirely displace white labor in the mines." The shift toward increased black mine labor coincided with an attempt to purge union militants, both white and black, and race leaders played an essential role in this effort. The "greatest bone of contention" among UMW officials, according to field agent H. P. Vaughn, was the fact that "all of the Negro preachers had been subsidized by the companies and were without exception preaching against the negroes joining the unions." Union officials complained that a "wagon load" of the rabidly anti-union *Workmen's Chronicle*, published out of TCI headquarters by black editor and former DeBardeleben employee P. Colfax Rameau, had been "dumped at one mine and that the paper is frequently distributed free throughout large sections of the mining district."[52]

In the end, however, the attempt to reinvigorate paternalism had little impact on black miners' loyalty to the UMW. By the time a strike was declared in September 1920, their sentiments were clear. Ms. G. H. Mathis, who had conducted a "patriotic" speaking tour of the mining district under the auspices of the Alabama Coal Operators' Association, claimed to have detected a "very considerable German influence at work" which "appear[ed] to be getting a hold on the negroes," who were "acting with a show of threat towards the white people." And when the strike finally broke out, every account noted the involvement of black strikers at the center of events. Of the 130 "most active and persistent of the strikers" at Marvel Mine, operator Ben Roden complained, eighty were black. Roden regretted that he was unable to enforce the color line in his camp during the strike "because in the negro camp, to a man, not a single negro has gone back to work. They just sat there in the negro quarters and held that camp." Jefferson County Sheriff J. C. Hartsfield wired an urgent request to Governor Thomas Kilby for mounted machine guns to be used in the event of "labor strikes, race riots, etc." He noted in particular that the "negroes are heavily armed and well equipped with pistols, guns and ammunition," raising the specter of having to confront "negro mobs of six hundred or eight hundred."[53]

Under the strain of events, the black middle class's behavior exhibited the earmarks of a desperate rearguard action. While Birmingham's press portrayed the strike as outside agitation against the settled order, and operators condemned the UMW's interracial policy as an affront to southern honor, the accommodators' actions demonstrate how disoriented their alliance with industrial elites had made them. Noting the "riotous spirit so prevalent in the mining fields," Oscar Adams complained that "organizers of the UMW . . . are insinuating that Negro miners and white miners are social and industrial brothers." "They are neither," he wrote. "Both are impossible, never have been possible, and never will be possible." P. Colfax Rameau went further, calling for a special session of the state legislature to pass a "'Law Prohibiting' [*sic*] Negroes from joining any white man's organization, fraternal or industrial," an act he claimed would "do more to help the Negro . . . than anything that has been done since the signing of the [Emancipation] proclamation." With black workers challenging the terms of their exploitation in the coal fields, the black middle class's strategy had come full circle, to a point where rather than hastening the demise of the paternalist arrangement, they instead encouraged the lynch-mob atmosphere being prepared by the operators and their allies in Birmingham's business community. The crisis of 1920 would pass: in the end, black and white miners could not prevail over the awesome power ranged against them. But the sharp division emerging between black workers and "race leaders" during the course of the strike was etched in the collective memory of Birmingham's black working class and would be brought to bear on the important struggles that lay ahead.[54]

Curiously, for a city that earned such notoriety as the citadel of segregation in the 1960s, scholars are only now beginning to explore the complex history of Birmingham's early black community. But any serious investigation will have to attend to the antagonism between a black elite that placed its influence at the disposal of the region's most powerful white employers and a black working class whose labor—under horrendous conditions—provided the source of that power.

What of the wider significance of the Birmingham story for the study of early twentieth-century black politics? No doubt Birmingham represents something of an anomaly in the early twentieth-century South. Its industrial character, its dependence on cheap labor, and the accommodationist hegemony all combined to magnify class tensions in Birmingham's black community. Doubtless these tensions assume other forms elsewhere in the New South. The story in Atlanta, with a more commercial orientation and an intellectually more diverse black middle class, might be different. The Carolinas, where black labor was excluded from important sections of industry rather than exploited within it, may have seen greater cooperation between black elites and black workers. Perhaps the closest comparison to the tensions present in industrial Alabama developed in the vast timber forests of Louisiana and East Texas, where the Southern Lumber Operators' Association pursued a paternalist strategy similar to the one embraced by Birmingham industrialists.[55] But generally, attention to the labor question illuminates intraracial tensions at work throughout the region. The key element in the New South's formula for advance, seldom acknowledged yet nonetheless central, was cheap black labor's role as cornerstone to the region's coming prosperity. At times willfully, more often unwittingly, black elites' alliance with white capital blinded them to the true lot of black workers ensnared within this arrangement. The New South was, in many ways, Birmingham writ large.

NOTES

1. Rayford W. Logan, *The Negro in American Life and Thought: The Nadir, 1877–1901* (New York: Dial Press, 1954); Leon F. Litwack, *Trouble in Mind: Black Southerners in the Age of Jim Crow* (New York: Alfred A. Knopf, 1998), xiv.

2. A number of groundbreaking studies of black industrial workers and their relation to the official labor movement have been published in recent years, but this scholarship has not been fully integrated into a broader reinterpretation of African American politics during this period. For examples of this scholarship, see Eric Arnesen, *Waterfront Workers of New Orleans: Race, Class, and Politics, 1863–1923* (New York: Oxford University Press, 1990); Joe William Trotter. *Coal, Class, and Color: Blacks in Southern West Virginia, 1915–1932* (Urbana: University of Illinois Press, 1990); Daniel L. Letwin, *The Challenge of Interracial Unionism: Alabama Coal Miners, 1878–1921* (Chapel Hill: University of North Carolina Press, 1998); Brian Kelly, *Race, Class, and Power in the Alabama Coalfields, 1908–1921* (Urbana: University of Illinois Press, 2001); Ernest Obadele-Starks, *Black Unionism in the Industrial South* (College Station: Texas A & M University Press, 2000). Useful surveys of recent southern labor historiography for this period include James B. Green and Paul B. Worthman, "Black Workers in the New South, 1865–1915," in *Key Issues in the Afro-American Experience*, ed. Nathan I. Huggins et al. (New York: Harcourt Brace, 1971), 47–69; Eric Arnesen, "Following the Color Line of Labor: Black Workers and the Labor Movement before 1930," *Radical History Review* 55 (1993): 53–87; Rick Halpern, "Organized Labor, Black Workers, and the Twentieth-Century South: The Emerging Revision," in *Race and Class in the American South*

since 1890, ed. Rick Halpern and Melvyn Stokes (Oxford, U.K.: Berg, 1994), 43–76; Glenn Feldman, "Research Needs and Opportunities: Race, Class, and New Direction in Southern Labor History," *Alabama Review* 51, no. 2 (April 1998): 96–106.

3. This was, of course, the central irony of the entire New South project: "prosperity" for the region—vaguely defined—would derive in large part from the thinly veiled exploitation of its agricultural and industrial laborers.

4. J. D. Kirkpatrick, "Testimony before the Kilby Commission," March 4, 1921, *Alabama Coal Operators' Association/Alabama Mining Institute Records* (hereafter *ACOA/AMI Records*), Department of Archives and Manuscripts, Birmingham Public Library (hereafter DAM/BPL); "Southern Bessemer Ores," *Manufacturers' Record*, October 25, 1890.

5. W. E. B. Du Bois, *Black Reconstruction* (New York: Simon & Schuster, 1995), 670.

6. John W. Cell, *The Highest Stage of White Supremacy: The Origins of Segregation in South Africa and the American South* (Cambridge: Cambridge University Press, 1982), 252, 257.

7. William Jordan, "'The Damnable Dilemma': African-American Accommodation and Protest during World War I," *Journal of American History* (March 1995): 1564. According to one recent article, no less a figure than Du Bois himself succumbed at times to "paralysis" in the face of racial hatred. Deeply shaken by the horror of the 1906 Atlanta Riots, the authors contend, Du Bois was forced to conclude that, "contrary to [the] boastings [of his] Niagara [Movement] . . . blacks had to 'pussy foot' and ignore their own rights or face annihilation." Dominic J. Capeci Jr. and Jack C. Knight, "Reckoning with Violence: W. E. B. Du Bois and the 1906 Atlanta Race Riot," *Journal of Southern History* 62, no. 4 (November 1996): 762. See also Edward Ayer, "An American Nightmare: Review of Leon Litwack's *Trouble in Mind*," *New York Review of Books*, May 3, 1988.

8. For studies focused specifically upon black women's activism see, in addition to Tucker and Hunter, Jacqueline Anne Rouse, *Lugenia Burns Hope: Black Southern Reformer* (Athens: University of Georgia Press, 1989); Cynthia Neverdon-Morton, *Afro-American Women of the South and the Advancement of the Race, 1895–1925* (Knoxville: University of Tennessee Press, 1989); Dolores Janiewski, *Sisterhood Denied: Race, Gender, and Class in a New South Community* (Philadelphia: Temple University Press, 1992); Evelyn Brooks Higginbotham, *Righteous Discontent: The Women's Movement in the Black Baptist Church, 1880–1920* (Cambridge: Harvard University Press, 1993); Glenda Elizabeth Gilmore, *Gender & Jim Crow: Women and the Politics of White Supremacy in North Carolina, 1896–1920* (Chapel Hill: University of North Carolina Press, 1996); Paula Giddings, *When and Where I Enter: The Impact of Black Women on Race and Sex in America* (New York: Harper Trade, 1996, reprint); Deborah Gray White, *Too Heavy a Load: Black Women in Defense of Themselves, 1894–1994* (New York: W. W. Norton, 1999); Lynne B. Feldman, *A Sense of Place: Birmingham's Black Middle-Class Community, 1890–1930* (Tuscaloosa:

University of Alabama Press, 1999); Darlene Clark Hine et al., eds., *Black Women in America: An Historical Encyclopedia* (Bloomington: Indiana University Press, 1994). For more general studies that examine the boundaries of black middle-class activism in the Jim Crow South, see Neil Mcmillen, *Dark Journey: Black Mississippians in the Age of Jim Crow* (Urbana: University of Illinois Press, 1982); Fon Louise Gordon, *Caste & Class: The Black Experience in Arkansas, 1880–1920* (Athens: University of Georgia Press, 1995); Janette Thomas Greenwood, *Bittersweet Legacy: The Black and White "Better Classes" in Charlotte, 1850–1910* (Chapel Hill: University of North Carolina Press, 1994); Kevin K. Gaines, *Uplifting the Race: Black Leadership, Politics, and Culture in the Twentieth Century* (Chapel Hill: University of North Carolina Press, 1996).

9. August Meier, "Negro Class Structure and Ideology in the Age of Booker T. Washington," *Phylon* 23 (fall 1962): 258–66, and *Negro Thought in America, 1880–1915: Racial Ideologies in the Age of Booker T. Washington* (Ann Arbor: University of Michigan Press, 1963); Louis T. Harlan, *Booker T. Washington: The Making of a Black Leader, 1856–1901* (New York: Oxford University Press, 1972), and *Booker T. Washington, The Wizard of Tuskegee, 1901–1915* (New York: Oxford University Press, 1983).

10. James E. Goodman, *Stories of Scottsboro* (New York: Vintage Books, 1995), 61, 60.

11. McMillen, *Dark Journey*, 287.

12. Here it is worth bearing in mind Judith Stein's caveat that "while Blacks shared a common victimization based upon color, that experience yielded a variety of responses." "The real consequences of racial oppression became clearer when considered in another context: was the experience of prejudice the same for worker and businessman, landowner and sharecropper, intellectual and illiterate?" See Stein, "Black and White Burdens," *Reviews in American History* (March 1976): 88–92. Gordon concurs, arguing that "teachers, domestics, and sharecroppers often seemed to have little in common other than race. Class, occupation, gender, and even color determined the precise way in which Jim Crow laws intersected with a person's life. The differences produced tension, particularly between urban and rural blacks and between elites and laboring classes." Gordon, *Caste and Class*, 63.

13. Rustin quoted in Willard B. Gatewood, "Aristocrats of Color, South and North: The Black Elite, 1880–1920," *Journal of Southern History* 54, no. 1 (February 1988): 3.

14. Although he deals with the problem only briefly, McMillen acknowledges that "black business and professional elites exercised influence out of proportion to their numbers and lived in a manner far removed from the black masses," and that on occasion the "inevitable tension between the two ends of the black spectrum" meant that "class antagonisms sometimes overrode caste solidarity" (*Dark Journey*, 194). In her important North Carolina study, Glenda Gilmore (*Gender & Jim Crow*, xviii, xix) criticizes the traditional focus "on a narrow stratum at the top of black society" and extends her own treatment to carefully reconstruct the ac-

tivist lives of predominantly middle-class black women, but she acknowledges that her own "focus on black leaders often slights the black working class point of view" and reminds readers that hers is "one story of African-American resistance; others remain to be told."

15. Gordon, *Caste & Class*, xii. Nell Irvin Painter suggested that the reluctance among historians to rigorously examine intraracial strife could be attributed in part to a "taboo" against close examination of "class differentiation" among African Americans and a "fear of opening a Pandora's box of racial disunity." See Painter, "Comment" on Armstead Robinson's "The Difference Freedom Made," in *The State of Afro-American History,* ed. Darlene Clark Hine (Baton Rouge: Louisiana State University Press, 1986). For other studies that acknowledge a distinct, if incipient, black working-class perspective on Jim Crow, see Greenwood, *Bittersweet Legacy*; Feldman, *Sense of Place*; White, *Too Heavy a Load*; Judith Stein, *The World of Marcus Garvey* (Baton Rouge: Louisiana State University Press, 1985); Kelly, *Race, Class, and Power in the Alabama Coalfields*.

16. One might indeed question whether it is useful to describe the socially and geographically segregated, economically stratified black population of Birmingham as a "community." Mindful of the limitations pointed out by a number of historians and attentive (as this essay will demonstrate) to intraracial tensions, I have used the term here in the most general sense, concluding that the legal and social enforcement of formal segregation, and to a lesser extent the racial self-identification that white hostility reinforced, renders the term appropriate.

17. Carl V. Harris, *Political Power in Birmingham, 1871–1921* (Knoxville: University of Tennessee Press, 1977), 108; Cell, *Highest Stage of White Supremacy*, 126–27; Bobby M. Wilson, "Structural Imperatives behind Racial Change in Birmingham, Alabama," *Antipode* 24, no. 3 (1982): 172–73.

18. J. D. Kirkpatrick, "Testimony before the Kilby Commission," March 4, 1921, *ACOA/AMI Records*. Their satisfaction that black labor was less prone to industrial militancy, immune from the disturbances associated with unionization, and less capable of resisting low wages and harsh treatment was almost universally expressed by industrial employers throughout the South during this period. For examples of the employers' faith in an innate docility and anti-unionism among African American workers see, in the *Manufacturer's Record*, "Labor in the South," May 15, 1886; "Cheap Southern Labor," August 16, 1890; "Foreign Immigration," August 15, 1891; "The Negro Problem," October 28, 1898; "For Labor in the South," December 22, 1904; "Difficulties of the Labor Problem in Southern Industries," July 20, 1905; "The South and Labor," August 10, 1905. On the perceived "general absence of the tendency among Negro workers to unite for collective bargaining," see also Lorenzo J. Greene and Carter G. Woodson, *The Negro Wage Earner* (New York: Russell and Russell, 1969), 132, 186.

19. Horace Mann Bond, *Negro Education in Alabama: A Study in Cotton and Steel* (Tuscaloosa: University of Alabama Press, 1994, reprint), 145.

20. On the formative period of coal-field unionism in the Birmingham district, see Letwin, *The Challenge of Interracial Unionism.*

21. Sterling D. Spero and Abram L. Harris, *The Black Worker: The Negro and the Labor Movement* (New York: Atheneum Press, 1931), 137, 364–66.

22. Harlan confers on Councill the dubious distinction of having "for years . . . sought to displace Washington in the hearts of white Alabamians by going farther than he in concessions to Southern white racial attitudes." Harlan, *Making of a Black Leader*, 299.

23. John R. Hornady, *The Book of Birmingham* (New York: Dodd, Mead, and Company, 1921), 69; "Address of Miss Kathryn M. Johnson to the Sixth Annual Conference of the NAACP," May 1914 (microfilm: 8:223), Annual Conference Proceedings, 1910–1950: *Papers of the NAACP* (hereafter *NAACP Papers*); "Branches Organized during the Year of 1918" (13:126), Annual Business Meetings, Proceedings and Correspondence, 1915–1950: *NAACP Papers.* Significantly, when an NAACP branch was finally established in Birmingham, its organization was the work of a newcomer to the city, Dr. Charles McPherson, a product of the Atlanta University system.

24. Gordon, *Caste & Class*, 78. Feldman reports (*Sense of Place*, 97) that "Pettiford rose to prominence in the NNBL and frequently spoke at their annual meetings. From there, his influence radiated across the country and reinforced his status in Birmingham." On NNBL support in Birmingham and Pettiford's role within it, see Feldman, *Sense of Place*, 52, 79–80, 93, 148. On Washington's relationship with TCI management and Chisum's appointment, see Marlene Hunt Rikard, "George Gordon Crawford: Man of the New South" (M.A. thesis, Samford University, 1971), 42, 151. On his relationship with southern industrial employers generally, see C. Vann Woodward, *Origins of the New South, 1877–1913* (Baton Rouge: Louisiana State University Press, 1971), 358–59. On Washington's involvement in the Grate Coal Mining Company along with Pettiford and black entrepreneur T. W. Walker, an endeavor that apparently had the approval of TCI, see "W. R. Pettiford to B. T. Washington," November 6, 1900, in *Booker T. Washington Papers*, ed. Louis R. Harlan. Among the duties Chisum performed at Washington's behest, according to Harlan, is his infiltration of William Monroe Trotter's Boston Suffrage League. See Harlan, *Wizard of Tuskegee*, 57; Chisum's strikebreaking activities are discussed on 93–94.

25. Booker T. Washington, "The Negro and His Relation to the Economic Progress of the South," in *Selected Speeches of Booker T. Washington*, ed. E. Davidson Washington (New York: Doubleday, Doran and Company, 1932), 81–82. Stein argues that Washington "offered Southern leaders a way to combat black insurgency" and that his "promises of industrial peace were welcomed by capitalists throughout the country [who] sought Tuskegee graduates to man schools and manage black labor within industrial corporations." These employers, she writes, "needed Tuskegee's trained men and women to confront the militancy of an in-

dustrial proletariat." Judith Stein, "'Of Mr. Booker T. Washington and Others': The Political Economy of Racism in the United States," *Science and Society* 38, no. 4 (winter 1974–75): 447–48.

26. Gaines, *Uplifting the Race*, 94.

27. Ibid., 20.

28. Litwack, *Trouble in Mind*, 148.

29. *Birmingham Reporter*, December 12, 1920. Elite denunciations of alleged black working-class extravagance were standard fare in the remarks of many of Adams's contemporaries throughout the South. Janette Greenwood finds similar concerns animating Charlotte's black elites: "The better class criticized the activities of poor blacks, especially those that reinforced white stereotypes . . . or undercut advancement. They expressly targeted camp meetings, public baptisms, and excursions—'three of the strongest agents in the demoralization and breaking down of our people.'" Greenwood, *Bittersweet Legacy*, 85. Washington loyalist Dr. R. H. Johnson of Georgia was credited by white elites with producing a pamphlet "on the condition of the race" that served as a "welcome alternative to the insane optimism which has characterized the treatment of the negro question in some quarters." In it he called for a campaign against "laziness, immorality, drunkenness, immoral ministers, teachers, physicians and reformers of all kinds . . . excursions, [and] hot suppers as now conducted." "Negroes Studying Themselves," *Manufacturer's Record*, October 22, 1897.

30. James L. Sledge III, "Black Conservatism in the Twentieth-Century South," *Proceedings of the Southern Conference on African-American History* 13 (February 1992): 14–15.

31. Martha C. Mitchell Bigelow, "Birmingham: Biography of a City of the New South" (Ph.D. dissertation, University of Chicago, 1946), 197.

32. *Birmingham Reporter*, October 20, 1917.

33. Feldman alternates between highlighting the elite disposition of race leaders like Pettiford and Adams, including their contempt for black workers, and crediting them (*Sense of Place*, 78) with pursuing a "cautious and deliberate" course that allowed them to "elicit change without incident," an argument I find unconvincing. The equivocation in her argument derives in large part, I would argue, from confusion on the labor question. See Feldman, *Sense of Place*, 19.

34. *Free Speech*, 1903, cited in Nancy Perrin Bailey, "In Their Own Voices: A Study of Birmingham's Weekly Press in the Progressive Era, 1900–17" (M.A. thesis, University of Alabama, Birmingham, 1983), 63.

35. Feldman writes that "many members of [Birmingham's] black middle class believed it was their duty to perform as role models for the downtrodden and that the crude behavior displayed by members of the lower classes was responsible for the race's problems, including Jim Crow legislation. . . . However, those outside the middle class often resented their interference, mocked their pretenses, and rejected their help." Feldman, *Sense of Place*, 189.

36. Guy B. Johnson, "Negro Racial Movements and Leadership in the United States," *American Journal of Sociology* 43 (1937–38): 63. In addition to touring industrial enterprises exhorting black workers to satisfy their employers, Adams apparently ran a clearinghouse providing black manual labor to industry, a field of endeavor in which Washington's NNBL involved itself nationally. On one occasion Adams expressed his disappointment when more than two-thirds of the "twenty-five or thirty" laborers referred by him to a plant employing black labor exclusively walked off the job. He attributed the stoppage to their failure to "see the need for so much money at the expense of their usual frolic." *Birmingham Reporter*, August 9, 1919.

37. Robert David Ward and William Warren Rogers, *Labor Revolt in Alabama: The Great Strike of 1894* (Tuscaloosa: University of Alabama Press, 1965), 73; *United Mine Workers' Journal*, June 7, 1894; Lewis, *Black Coal Miners in America: Race, Class, and Community Conflict, 1780–1980* (Lexington: University Press of Kentucky, 1987), 49, 50, 56. For a useful documentary record of black miners' involvement in the 1908 strike, see Philip Foner and Ronald L. Lewis, eds., *The Black Worker: A Documentary History*, vol. 5 (Philadelphia: Temple University Press, 1980), 156–98.

38. *Birmingham Reporter*, December 20, 1919.

39. For a documentary record of the conflict between TCI and the State of Alabama over the removal of convicts from TCI's mines, including the correspondence between TCI officials and the State, see "Testimony of President Oakley, Alabama State Board of Convicts," in United States Senate, *Hearings on United States Steel Corporation*, vol. 4, (Washington, D.C.: Government Printing Office, 1912), 3112.

40. *United Mine Workers' Journal*, June 1, 1916.

41. The records of the much larger TCI, which pioneered welfare capitalism in the district, remain closed to researchers. No doubt they contain a wealth of information that would add considerably to our knowledge of both the conditions district workers labored under and the methods by which they attempted to resist the employers' authority.

42. Fies, *The Man with the Light on His Cap* (Jasper, Ala.: n.p., 1983), 11–13; "Fies to DeBardeleben," 1914; "Fies to G. M. Bowers," January 26, 1915; "Fies to DeBardeleben," c. 1920; "Fies to DeBardeleben," February 23, 1914; "DeBardeleben to Fies," February 25, 1914; "Fies to R. H. Franklin," June 13, 1920; in *DeBardeleben Coal Company Records*, DAM/BPL.

43. *Hot Shots*, August 26, 1908; *Labor Advocate*, September 4, 1908.

44. Meier, *Negro Thought in America*, 15; Anonymous, "Alabama Mining Camp," *Independent* 63 (October 3, 1907): 791; *Birmingham Reporter*, May 17, 1919.

45. *United Mine Workers' Journal*, June 1, 1916; *Labor Advocate*, June 17, 1916.

46. Feldman, *Sense of Place*, 170–71. Details of the campaign for black women's suffrage in *Birmingham Reporter*, October 30, 1920. The pistol-whipping incident is related in "Xaridimos to Stefane," June 12, 1909, Alabama: Complaint of Peonage

upon Part of TCI, Peonage Files, *Records of the Department of Justice*, RG 60, National Archives, Washington, D.C. Repression against strikers and their supporters is detailed in *Van Amburg Bittner Papers*, West Virginia and Regional History Collection, West Virginia University, Morgantown.

47. Deborah Gray White, *Too Heavy a Load*, 70.

48. *Birmingham Reporter*, February 26, 1916; October 28, 1916; December 23, 1916; January 22, 1916.

49. *Labor Advocate*, October 7, 1916.

50. "Early Surveys: Migration Study—Birmingham Summary," n.d., 6–7, Series 6, Box 6, *Urban League Papers,* Manuscripts Division, Library of Congress, Washington, D.C.

51. The steel organizing campaign is detailed in Joseph McCartin, *Labor's Great War: The Struggle for Industrial Democracy and the Origins of Modern American Labor Relations* (Chapel Hill: University of North Carolina Press, 1997), and in Kelly, *Race, Class, and Power in the Alabama Coalfields*, chap. 5, "War, Migration, and the Revival of Coalfield Militancy."

52. Statement of Field Agent E. Newdick: Bitter and Dangerous Alignment—Employers Foster Race Prejudice, February 24, 1919; Chief Clerk's Files, "Special Problems—Birmingham," RG 174; *Records of the Department of Labor, 1907–42*; National Archives, Washington, DC.

53. *Birmingham Age-Herald*, September 3, 1917; Roden, "Testimony before the Kilby Commission," March 4, 1921, *ACOA/AMI Records*; "J. C. Hartsfield to Thomas Kilby," September 13, 1919, *Kilby Administrative Files*, Alabama Department of Archives and History (hereafter ADAH), Montgomery, Alabama.

54. *Birmingham Reporter*, September 11, 1920; October 2, 1920; October 30, 1920; Rameau to Kilby, September 6, 1920, Governor Thomas Kilby Administrative Files, ADAH.

55. On the SLOA and paternalism, see James E. Fickle, "Management Looks at the 'Labor Problem': The Southern Pine Industry during World War I and the Postwar Era," *Journal of Southern History* 40, no. 4 (February 1974): 61–76.

Chapter 10

The Power of Remembering

Black Factory Workers and Union Organizing in the Jim Crow Era

Michael Honey

The black freedom struggle is a long one. It is intergenerational, multilayered, and includes all classes of folk. More often than not, history tells us about educators, professionals, preachers, and others whom we perceive as leading the movement for change. To really understand the freedom struggle, however, we must know about the life histories of ordinary people, the disinherited, working-class and poor people who rarely appear in the history books. To locate their stories, historians have increasingly shifted their research to the local level and to the years and the generations prior to the 1954–1965 period, usually considered the high point of the civil rights struggle in the South. Attention to these earlier years has begun to redirect our vision toward connections between community, civil rights, and labor struggles, toward the crucial perspective and influence of women, and toward the role of ordinary people in creating the basis for change.[1]

This shift in freedom movement historiography intersects with recent directions in labor history. Marxists have long focused on links between African American workers and the larger labor movement. While mainstream labor scholars once focused mainly on the minority of workers, most of them male and white, who were organized, since the 1960s the whole field's attention has increasingly shifted to the unorganized majority and to people of color and women. "Proletarianization" of the black population—the process of becoming urban workers after slavery—has become a fundamental construct.[2] The role of black women domestic, factory, farm, and household workers in the working class and in the struggle for change has also become increasingly evident.[3] The black working class, rural and urban and in many occupations, is moving closer to center stage in labor history. It is doing so in African American history as well. After all, workers have always been the overwhelming majority of the black population; their fate should be fundamental to our understanding the larger picture. Such a perspective seems increasingly relevant in our own era, in which the decline of industrial jobs, unions, and all manner of reliable working-class employment in the inner cities is so heavily undercutting the achievements of past struggles.[4]

The power of memory as a means of recreating the twentieth-century experiences of black workers has become especially important. Their thoughts and experiences rarely appeared in the media or were recorded by anyone in a sympathetic manner. Recollections from "the survivors of the race," as Clarence Coe described himself and his age cohort who began factory work in the 1930s, thus help us to access a past that has been largely untold.[5] Oral history gets us behind the Jim Crow system to find what Robin Kelley has called the "hidden transcript" of sustained black oppositional culture and resistance to racism.[6] Behind the walls and masks of silence about black lives in the South, oral historians, including those at the Behind the Veil Project at Duke University and a variety of other places, are increasingly exposing how working-class and poor southern African Americans during the dark days of segregation became a force in history through church, family, work, play, unions, music, politics, and community organizations.[7]

This article focuses on the oldest surviving generation of black factory workers, part of a stream of migrants from the countryside to the cities during the early twentieth century who became part of community struggles by African Americans to improve their conditions in urban areas. These workers explained how whites constructed segregation in factories and how blacks challenged this construction by organizing unions, voting in workplace elections, and fighting for the right to hold union office and to act as negotiators with white bosses. In the 1950s they challenged white workers and employers alike by filing lawsuits, based on the *Brown V. Board of Education* ruling (and later, Title VII of the 1964 Civil Rights Act), to desegregate the factories and open up skilled jobs to African Americans. They also collected donations for the NAACP and joined civil rights struggles in the community. As black women during World War II and younger cohorts of black men and women in the 1960s moved into factory employment, black workers helped create an intergenerational base for labor and civil rights struggles. In their own lives and on their own terms, through labor organizing they also created the tangible economic benefits for themselves and their children that civil rights organizations were largely unable to deliver.

My contribution to this story comes from twenty years of return journeys to the Deep South city of Memphis, where I had initially spent six years as a community organizer, to talk with the pioneer black and white workers in the labor movement. The Mississippi Delta city of Memphis in many ways provides a fitting microcosm for such research. Memphis historically had been at the heart of slavery and the cotton trade and was the place where E. H. Crump and his cronies created one of the worst police states of the segregation era. From the early twentieth century to his death in 1954, Crump ran the most ruthless political machine in the United States, based largely on his manipulation of the poll tax. This tax on the right to vote, legislated into existence as part of the disfranchisement of the black population after Reconstruction, accumulated every year it was not paid, and most workers could not afford to pay it. Based on kickbacks from city employees and vice establishments, Crump's machine paid people's poll taxes and told the masses of workers and virtually the entire black community who to vote for. Crump thereby put his people in power, and he used a vicious police force to put down any protest. He directed the economic and political life of the city for some forty years, enforcing the plantation mentality of paternalism mixed with violent repression so common to his native state of Mississippi. Through the Crump regime, segregation's denial of rights to African Americans led to widespread denial of citizenship rights to working-class whites as well.[8]

Memphis also had a history of civil rights and labor struggles, dating back to Ida B. Wells's struggle against lynching in the 1890s, yet the Crump legacy of repression and elite control always remained very strong. As the crossroad for black and white musical interchange, the birthplace of blues and rock and roll, a certain amount of racial mixing inevitably went on. And in the early 1960s, a college-educated, youthful group led one of the more successful NAACP branches in the South in challenging segregation in public facilities. But the labor movement, strong in Memphis and some other southern cities in the 1940s, declined in the 1950s and 1960s. It took an independent thrust by black workers and the African American community as a whole to burst open the city's repressive history. Memphis became a storm center in the southern freedom movement during the 1968 sanitation strike in which Dr. Martin Luther King Jr. lost his life. Yet as I came into Memphis in the early 1970s after those climactic events, the town appeared quiescent, even stagnant. While civil rights organizations remained active, unions were weak, and it appeared that organized workers had done little to bring about social change prior to 1968. The reality, as I was to discover in my research for *Southern Labor and Black Civil Rights: Organizing Memphis Workers* (1993), was more complex. Although white supremacy had undermined both labor and civil rights organizing for many years, the pre-1960s generation had not been quiescent. On the contrary, various labor activists had resisted Crump's police state, struggled successfully to improve the living standards of black and white workers, and helped bring about fundamental shifts in the social order. One could only understand this, however, by viewing labor and civil rights struggles as part of a continuum, rather than as separate developments.

Oral histories heavily informed my work by revealing an unwritten history of grass-roots struggle and led me to a closer examination of what black workers can tell us about their long history of resistance to racism. Additional interviews with black factory workers over the years created a first-person narrative of working-class struggle and resistance to segregation, one that had begun long before and continued long beyond what most people think of as the modern civil rights movement. The hidden transcript revealed by black workers in Memphis suggested new ways to show that history is not so much the work of great men as it is the work of ordinary working-class men and women. This article accesses just a few of these oral histories, now published at length in book form as *Black Workers Remember: An Oral History of Segregation, Unionism, and the Freedom Struggle* (1999).[9] Perhaps this short review can offer some understanding of what black workers contributed to African-American, labor, and civil rights history in the South.

If You're Black, Get Back

Big Bill Broonzy aptly captured the nearly universal experience of black workers under Jim Crow in his 1946 song, "Black, Brown and White Blues." Virtually any black worker living in the Jim Crow South could recall the conditions he described. Serving as a replacement for slavery, segregation insured that few black workers could rise above minimal levels in wages, skills, or status. Whites confined them to plantation and day labor in the rural areas, and to domestic and personal service in both the cities and the countryside. In industry and the crafts, both white workers and employers barred them from higher-waged occupations. African Americans thus worked harder for less money, always subordinated to whites, regardless of their abilities and knowledge. As Broonzy sang, "if you're black, get back."

Lynchings and racial violence, control over the vote, segregation in the labor market and in public accommodations, the ever-visible "white" and "colored" signs, and constant racist propaganda in the news media affected all black southerners. But black workers in Memphis reminded me that the South's racial system was not just about race, but about wages, work, and profits. Like slavery before it, segregation drove down the price of black labor and undercut wages for unskilled whites, disunited the working class, and kept it from organizing and becoming politically powerful. Segregation incorporated both racial and economic forms of oppression.

White workers of course played a crucial role in creating and sustaining the racially segmented labor market. The stories of black workers confirm a growing number of historical studies that paint a depressing picture of how white male workers, not just capitalists, kept blacks at the bottom of the wage and job hierarchy, thereby denying them opportunities to feed their families and to accumulate household incomes. White workers' exclusionary practices reached a particularly ugly stage during the late nineteenth and the early twentieth centuries, when white craft unions and railroad brotherhoods virtually obliterated black workers from skilled labor markets. Not only craft unions in the American Federation of Labor (AFL), but the industrial unions of the Congress of Industrial Organizations (CIO) institutionalized discrimination through contracts negotiated and enforced by white male union members.[10]

Given the horrific record of many unions, one wonders why black workers would have supported them at all. The answer is that black workers, particularly in the low-waged and unskilled labor market they dominated in places like Memphis, saw far more clearly than whites that nothing would change for them except through unionization. Black workers often preferred all-black unions when they could get them, as in longshore employment. But they also remained consistently willing to join unions with whites, even if in segregated locals.[11] Even when blacks and whites sat on opposite sides of the room, and even when whites controlled most of the elected positions and kept blacks in the worst jobs, biracial CIO unions still offered black workers hope for a change in their relationship to employers and to white workers. Most African American workers in Memphis joined them and stuck by them whenever and wherever they could.

The relationship of black women workers to union organizing proved to be very different from that of black men, however. For reasons explained later, very few black women ever had the option of organizing or joining a union. This reality heavily weights the narratives of union organizing during the heyday of the labor movement from the 1930s to the 1960s toward black male workers. In the South, black men always worked in large numbers in many factories, warehouses, and sawmills, and on the docks, and it is their story that in large measure defines the CIO experience in places like Memphis up until the 1940s.[12] During World War II and again in the 1960s, black women increasingly came into the formal labor market and into union leadership. As the service economy displaced male industrial workers in the 1970s and 1980s, black women workers often took center stage in the southern labor movement. Their activism connected to earlier generations. Tera Hunter and others have demonstrated how important the work, associational activities, and family life of non-unionized and women workers always has been to working-class history. The non-union, minority, and female working class, Robin Kelley also suggests, needs to be seen and understood as an active force; workers cannot be understood merely in terms of their relationship, or lack of relationship, to the organized labor movement.[13]

Yet the genre of older labor studies that focus on unions and organizers still has a particular resonance when applied to the lives of the black men and women who were union pioneers in the CIO. Instead of white males, black men, and eventually black women as well, provided the animating force for a significant portion of the industrial labor movement, especially in the South. From the perspective of these black workers, the distance between labor organizing and civil rights struggles seems rather small. For proletarianized black men and women, issues of race and class intertwined, and the importance of unions in their story is not to be denied. What I found in Memphis, and what other researchers have found in other parts of the South and other parts of the United States as well, is that African Americans usually were the most willing to join union organizing, took the greatest risks to do it, and were the last to give up on it. Many of the great labor movements of the twentieth century would not have occurred without their active participation.[14]

Black workers in Memphis told me in chapter and verse how white factory owners divided workers and their jobs by race and gender. One of the oldest Memphis workers I spoke with, a man named Hillie Pride, explained to me that this could be changed only through organization: he felt that unionization, more than any other factor, determined his fate.

Mr. Pride and his wife, Laura, came from sharecropping in Arkansas, where conditions had been so bad that Mrs. Pride refused even to talk about them. Hillie began working at the Fisher Body factory when unions existed only among a few white skilled workers. If your skin was black, "you didn't have no union, no help, no nothing," Pride said. He remembered that African Americans making ten cents an hour lined up for their pay singing "the Lord will make a way somehow." Pride later moved to the Firestone Tire and Rubber factory, where wages were better but conditions were even worse. He never felt confused about the need for an organization that would unite all of the workers in the plant. "Nobody said nothing for you at all, until the union got there," he recalled. "You were just like mules and hogs."[15]

Matthew Davis also remembered being worked like a mule and treated like one as well. He and other African Americans at Firestone hauled, cut, and washed blocks of raw rubber weighing hundreds of pounds apiece, and worked in tire pigment called lamp black, a substance that washed out of their skins long after their work day and killed many of them with cancer during retirement. Unskilled white workers also suffered from bad job conditions, overwork, and lack of respect from supervisors, but blacks could never move out of their lower status, for the company assigned both jobs and wages on the basis of race. Blacks usually worked in departments separate from whites, but where they worked together the company classified them as "helpers" to the whites and paid them at lower rates. Whites got higher wages for the same work and had access to a promotional ladder denied to blacks. As Davis recalled, "all you had to do was come in there and your face be white, brother, and you'd move up."[16]

The CIO's promise of equal rights trade unionism sounded like the answer to these conditions. African Americans recognized that industrial unions could not succeed unless the CIO organized blacks and whites into the same union, something the white workers in the AFL craft unions refused to do. But most whites desperately resisted what the companies called the CIO's "nigger unionism." During an organizing drive at Firestone in 1940, white workers refused to unionize under the CIO and joined a segregated AFL local instead. They discovered only through hard experience how ineffective a racially and craft-divided union could be; they made no progress for several years under AFL representation. Reluctantly, whites at Firestone and elsewhere joined the CIO, tacitly recognizing the necessity of a single union that organized the whole workplace into one unit, black and white together. This recognition of a degree of common interest among blacks and whites would drive industrial unionism forward during the CIO's crucial period of expansion in World War II, and it created a number of strong unions by the end of the war.

Without the support of black workers, however, the CIO would never have survived in Memphis. Most CIO unions did not enlist blacks as full-time organizers, for under the extremely repressive conditions of the 1930s, employers would not bargain with them, white workers would not listen to them, and expulsion or even death would most likely be their fate.[17] Even so, black workers made up eighty percent of the unskilled labor force in Memphis factories, which could not be organized without their support. Black rank-and-file support provided the base for early CIO success, for African Americans proved the most eager to join, took the greatest risks to do it, and were the last to give up. George Holloway's story provides insight into why the CIO had such appeal for black factory workers.[18] In explaining to me the early history of southern unionism, he put it into a personal context leading us back to an earlier time:

> I was born in Memphis, Tennessee on June 8, 1915. My daddy's parents were slaves in Tennessee. Grandaddy died on a day farm in Somerville, Tennessee, when I was one or two years old. Daddy took me to the funeral. My Grandma died two or three years later. Daddy was a child of slaves; he wasn't a slave though. Daddy said that his parents were allowed to stay on the big farm, when they were free, as sharecroppers. Grandad handled a two-mule plow, and scraped cotton. Dad didn't want to work on a farm, so he went to Memphis and worked in the clothes pressing shops, maybe on Beale Street. Then, he went to the Pullman Company, as a way to travel.

Holloway, like many others of his generation, had direct links to slavery through his family, which had participated in the proletarianizing migration into the cities to escape the dreadful rigors of sharecropping and Jim Crow in the countryside. What he especially remembered, however, was how powerless he felt as he experienced the many indignities of urban segregation as a child. Secondhand schoolbooks and poor conditions in segregated schools, sitting in the Jim Crow balconies at theaters, abuse from white police on the streets, women being forced to try on clothes in the basement of the local department store—"we knew all of this was wrong as youngsters, and we didn't enjoy it, but there was nothing we could do about it," he said. There were no alternatives: the NAACP barely existed, driven underground by Memphis's repressive political machine and a brutal white police force. Boss Crump controlled jobs and city licenses and had ministers or anyone else who spoke against the Jim Crow system beaten up and run out of town. Murders of black people by police, and in a few cases by employers, demonstrated that they had no rights that whites felt bound to respect. For many black working-class people, unions provided the only light in the dark night of segregation. As an adult, Holloway told me, "I joined the union to help change these things."

Holloway knew about unions through his father, who taught him the good things they could do for workers and their families:

> My Daddy was a pullman porter and the second vice-president, and then president of the [Memphis] Pullman Porters' Union. They were part of the AF of L. He brought me my first union experiences. My daddy used to run [on the train] from Memphis to New York. I'll never forget, when I was nine years old, my daddy came home one night, singing. When people [passengers] would steal things off the train, such as towels, pillow cases, and water pitchers, my daddy would have to pay for it if he hadn't noticed. My sister, Amelia and I heard him singing one night for the first time in fifteen years since he had begun working there. Because they had formed the union, he would no longer have to deduct stolen and broken items from his pay check. That was my first notion and recollection of the unions. They had a band and would have parades and picnics. My daddy played in the band. Once the union came in, Porters made more than a letter carrier, and they were looked up to in the community. They made good money, enough to buy beautiful houses or cars. Back in the 20's, black people rarely owned cars, unless they were doctors or something like that.

Holloway early on understood why the authorities in Memphis were so dead set against unionization for blacks: it worked. The Pullman Porters union in the latter 1930s raised his father's wages to among the best wages in black Memphis. Holloway also learned about the Brotherhood of Sleeping Car Porters President A. Philip Randolph, who was run out of Memphis twice by the Crump machine. Randolph's continued struggle for equal treatment in society and within the labor movement provided a model he tried to emulate.

Holloway's father, however, also taught him the bad things about unions, which seriously hindered their ability to organize the multiracial working class in Memphis:

The only other AFL unions that had blacks at that time were the Carpenters' and Bricklayers' Unions. They [AFL] had a separate hall for blacks. Blacks and whites couldn't go to meetings together. They actually belonged to two different unions. The AFL trades building was right on Beale Street, and the black one was behind it. It was a big brick building for the white union, and a separate little wooden building in the back, at one time a servants' quarters, for the black union. The AFL machinists and electricians were all in the white union. The whites didn't want the blacks in the union, and they weren't going to have them. When Dad was forming the union, they couldn't meet at peoples' houses openly. They had to sneak people in different doors in secret, so no one would notice. Mr. Crump said there wouldn't be any black union.

AFL craft unions had largely excluded blacks from the best jobs and subordinated the few blacks who belonged to AFL unions by segregating them into separate, largely powerless units. Craft unionism organized workers based on their occupation or skill and used this organization to keep other workers out. This method had excluded not only blacks but other minorities, women, and the great mass of unskilled industrial workers. The CIO, which began in 1935 and 1936, emerged out of the AFL as a new spearhead for organizing the vast ranks of unrepresented workers, many of them racial and ethnic minorities. It sought to bring together all workers in an industry or workplace into one union, regardless of race, nationality, gender, or political creed. Communist and other leftist organizers fully committed to equal rights took on a special role in the CIO, leading many of the toughest organizing drives and fighting for the inclusion of black workers in union membership and leadership. In Memphis, CIO organizing began amongst a small group of activists on the waterfront, a number of them Communists. They organized and inspired river workers like Red Davis, a poor white sixteen-year-old who became extremely active in Communist and labor organizing for the next twenty years and who took a strong antiracist stand. Organization spread from there into other low-wage industries.

CIO unions grew episodically during the New Deal and then by leaps and bounds during World War II. But in places like Memphis it remained slow going. Police and company thugs in numerous instances beat organizers nearly to death for trying to organize the dreaded interracial CIO. When Holloway and the first generation of black union activists began their careers in the 1930s, organizing a union that included African Americans could easily cost one's life. When Holloway began work at the Firestone factory, a white organizer named George Bass came from Akron to convince workers to join the CIO's Rubber Workers union. Black workers had no difficulty supporting this, and Holloway became one of his lieutenants in the organizing drive. But white workers largely fell prey to the AFL and the company's line that they would be joining a "nigger union" if they enrolled in the CIO. Bass and another white organizer named Noel Bedgood were brutally beaten in front of the factory by company thugs; it took eighty-five stitches to close Bass's wounds. Holloway stood by horrified, with tears in his eyes. He was unable to intervene because he knew it would cause a race riot and undermine unionization even further. In a subsequent election, a segregated AFL union took control of the plant. Holloway left the industry before Firestone could fire him, but he remained a strong union man.

Holloway continued to view unionism as virtually synonymous with his struggle as a black man for equal rights, but like other black workers he recognized that industrial unions could not advance without reaching white workers. Breaking down white resistance to an inclusive union of whites and blacks together became the acid test for the CIO in many work places. Almost all white workers came from a culture steeped in white supremacy. They faced racial taunts and the fear of being physically attacked for joining a multiracial union. Nonetheless, a significant number of southern whites did join CIO unions. Self-interest dictated it. The segregated AFL union at the Firestone plant was like "a lost ball in high weeds," as rubber worker organizer Forrest Dickenson put it.[19] The AFL's racially bifurcated units could not develop an effective plant-wide strategy to handle industrial issues, and they made no progress for Firestone workers.

Whites therefore began to reconsider their attachment to the old unionism. Richard Routon came from a farm area where segregation was built into every aspect of life, and his father had been a member of a racially exclusionary white railroad union. Routon initially supported the AFL, but he became disgusted with AFL-company collusion and shifted his allegiance to the CIO. Interestingly, he became a CIO leader by advocating black and white unity during a confrontation between white and black workers in the factory parking lot. Like many other white workers in industries with large numbers of blacks, he came to realize that racial division meant poor wages, bad working conditions, and no power.[20]

In some cases white workers changed their attitudes significantly, and in other cases they hewed to white supremacy. Routon became a moderate supporter of integration based on his experiences with African Americans in the union. Red Davis went further; he became a race traitor and completely jumped the ship of white supremacy. He eventually married an African American woman and dedicated much of his life to fighting racism.[21] In other cases, white workers simply accepted interracial industrial unionism as necessary to improving conditions. Based on that logic, the CIO in Memphis blossomed to 32,000 members during World War II. However, the majority of white workers remained all too happy to support departmental and occupational segregation, separate seniority lines, and racially based wage differentials, and most sought to use their unions to control blacks and protect white privileges.

African Americans, on the other hand, became increasingly impatient. Once unionization was attained, and after many blacks fought in a "war for democracy" during World War II, they increasingly demanded an equal place in the factory and the union.

The postwar period and early 1950s thus became the decisive turning point for the CIO and for black workers and an era of vicious confrontations with white supremacists. In the late 1940s and early 1950s, increasing pressures for conformity resulted from cold war anti-communism and from the Ku Klux Klan, Dixiecrats, and later the White Citizens Councils and the John Birch Society. All of these pressures pushed union racial practices to the right. The Taft-Hartley act, passed by Republicans and southern Democrats in Congress in 1947, drastically modified the labor freedoms granted by the 1935 Wagner Act and undermined the ability of unions to organize, especially in the South. The split in CIO unions over support for the Progressive Party's integrationist Henry A. Wallace against the more racially conservative Democrat Harry Truman in the 1948 presidential campaign and conflict over Communist leadership in the CIO led to the purge of nearly all of the CIO's Left-led unions (with nearly a million members). As the CIO eliminated its most active antiracists, the segregationist and Christian fundamentalist upsurge decimated union and civil rights organizing. White racial conservatives took over the CIO in Memphis and many other places, and organizing stagnated.[22]

It was in this extremely difficult context that people like George Holloway and Clarence Coe took on struggles to open up skilled jobs in unionized factories to African Americans, and to eliminate separate bathrooms, time clocks, water fountains, and other facilities. Holloway, who had become a Pullman porter after leaving Firestone, in 1946 became one of the first people hired at the new International Harvester plant in Memphis, and the leading union activist in the plant. Some 3,000 white and black workers voted in the CIO practically unanimously, but whites still resisted demands for equality at the workplace or in the union hall. Holloway eventually became the first black United Auto Workers union regional representative in the South in the 1960s, but only after years of struggles both with and against white workers in Memphis.

While people like Holloway helped to lead organizing and to implement unionism on the shop floor, they fought a battle on two fronts: one with employers and the other with their fellow white workers. Employers continued to enforce customary segregated work arrangements and unequal wage rates. White workers also resisted any loss of their racial privileges. Many of them had undertaken strikes during the war to protect their higher-paid jobs from black competition, and they continued to uphold separate seniority lists, segregated departments, and discriminatory occupational wage differentials. They also refused to teach blacks how to operate machines so they could move into higher-paying jobs. The contractual relationship achieved by industrial unions more often than not codified discriminatory hiring and promotional practices, thereby consigning African Americans to the inferior positions established in the pre-union era.[23]

The efforts of their supposed white union allies to try to maintain segregated cafeterias, rest rooms, drinking fountains, and even time clocks and parking lots never ceased to amaze African Americans. Outraged, even decades later, at the indignities he suffered at the Firestone plant, Hillie Pride asked me: "What would you think, if it was a fountain here, and one over there, and the same water come up here as there, what would be the difference if you drank over there?" Yet even as whites struggled to maintain their control, blacks like Holloway were fully conscious that, in the era before the federal government stepped in with fair employment and civil rights laws, they also needed the support of those same white workers to attack the miserable conditions everyone suffered in the factories. Holloway and the more activist black unionists tried to build their unions for short-term gains, hoping to end segregation in the long run.

Civil Rights Unionism

Holloway and others like him walked a tightrope, on one hand trying to persuade whites to support mainstream unionism, which was concerned about wages and working conditions, and on the other trying to implement the CIO's equal rights philosophy by challenging workplace and union discrimination. Civil rights unionists such as Holloway wanted the opportunity not just to be in a union but to participate equally, to qualify for any available job, and to be paid equally for it. Many black workers were veterans of military service in World War II, and they expected more from unions than higher wages: they wanted to enlist the CIO unions in a more general campaign to end Jim Crow and to enact full civil and political equality. They paid dearly for their beliefs and their commitments to that struggle.

In 1948, Holloway joined the first union negotiating committee at International Harvester, an almost unprecedented situation at the time. One hotel refused conference rooms for union-company negotiations, proclaiming that "this hotel would not allow a black man disputing a white man's word." A second hotel rented its facilities but forced Holloway to enter through a service elevator in the back, where garbage and cleaning disinfectant splashed on him every morning. One company negotiator throughout the proceedings insisted on referring to Holloway as "the nigger," a slur none of his white union colleagues protested. Holloway told me:

> I want you to know that after we negotiated the contract in Memphis, for one year Mr. Bryson, the superintendent of International Harvester Memphis works, would use the word "nigger" at every grievance meeting. Such as "niggers are slow, they are not doing their work, we are going to get rid of them." I used to lay my head on the table and cry within, because the other six union committee men were white and wouldn't defend me. I was the secretary of the bargaining committee, therefore I kept the minutes and I didn't have time to speak up. Many times, I asked the bargaining committee to stop this, but they wouldn't.

Holloway suffered these indignities as perhaps the only college-educated man, undoubtedly a better secretary than most factory workers, on the bargaining committee. He had attended Tuskegee Institute for two years, but he had to go to work after the "Roosevelt recession" of 1937; the best work he could find, despite his above-average education, was factory work. But he put these skills to good use at Harvester, where blacks, who made up a third of the plant's population, elected him as committeeman and a trustee of the union. While constantly dogged by racism, he did his best to represent all the workers. As a committeeman in the plant, Holloway had jurisdiction over workers in the punch presses, foundries, warehouse, and among truck drivers, janitors, and others. He had perhaps a hundred different stewards, black and white, working under his jurisdiction. He was elected to more than ten union committees and was vice chair of the bargaining committee, working with stewards to decide which grievances to pursue. For more than a decade he remained at the center of negotiations, grievance procedures, and union affairs in the plant. He wrote many of the basic union policies, some of them adopted by International Harvester (now Norstar) around the country. He had extraordinary responsibilities, comparable to those of a political or administrative leader.

Yet for many years he still remained a "nigger" to many white workers, workers whose very futures in many ways depended upon his integrity and intelligence. White union leaders refused even to give him a ride, as he hitchhiked or walked miles to his job while white union members drove past him. He was the only black on the local's executive board, and none of the whites would ever second his motions, so none of his resolutions could even be discussed. In 1949, when Holloway became the first black at the Harvester plant to operate a machine, white workers tampered with it while he was on break. Had he not checked the machine before restarting it he could have been dismembered or killed. "I was the committeeman for the man in the department who tried to kill me," Holloway told me. "That's how relations were with whites at the time."

Throughout the 1950s, Holloway struggled with racist whites more often than he struggled against IH's relatively moderate white management. A clique of white supremacist "secessionists" illegally put union funds into a private account in their own names, planning to make the hall a "private club" in order to keep it segregated in violation of UAW equal rights policies. The national UAW put the local in receivership and closed the hall. Still, white unionists affiliated with the White Citizens Council carried guns to union meetings and intimidated white workers sympathetic to integration. Vigilantes broke all of the windows in Holloway's home, and for two years he and his wife Hattie regularly received threatening phone calls in the middle of the night. Several union meetings nearly turned into race riots, and during one entire summer a black worker from the Firestone plant named Lint Coe, brother of activist Clarence Coe, guarded the Holloway home at night with a shotgun. Carl Moore, the white regional director for the UAW, also lived under threat and carried a shotgun in his car. Despite these perils, eventually Holloway and his black (and a few white) allies integrated the union hall, the plant's facilities, and all the skilled occupations. White workers gradually swung toward support of the national

UAW against the secessionists. But Holloway's victories came at a very high cost to himself and his family. His wife told me that she still felt nervous about being around whites twenty years after these events, and she recalled days when Holloway left home for union affairs telling her he might not return.

The racial strife at International Harvester paralleled a similar fight taking place at Firestone in the postwar era. Clarence Coe was at the forefront of that fight. Like Holloway, his family background and his earlier experiences had instilled in him the determination that he would not bow down to Jim Crow.[24] He had came to Memphis from rural west Tennessee in the late 1930s. His civil rights awareness started, he said, "I guess, from my ancestors":

Back during slavery, right here at Madison, Tennessee, they called it the Magden Quarters, that's the neighborhood where my foreparents came from when they were in slavery. When they were freed, they allowed each slave to buy a tract of land, and my grandparents bought land there. Right up there in west Tennessee. My grandparents got this land. And their parents had been slaves, my grandparents and great-grandparents were slaves. I just grew up in that environment, and my parents taught me some things. They taught me. And then, when you grow up and you see this is the way it really is, you just kind of start fighting back.

Coe managed to get a high school education in nearby Jackson, Tennessee. Although his family had escaped sharecropping, they could not escape the other terrors of the countryside. The sight of a lynching and seeing white men kick black men in the seat of their pants for the fun of it set Coe's mind on leaving. "I wanted to get away from this environment," Coe said.

Coe followed the lead of a friend and joined the chain of migration from the countryside to the city, taking up the civil rights struggle as soon as he moved to Memphis. Here he worked on the campaign to stop the legal lynching of nine black youths in the Scottsboro case, wrote stories for the black press, collected NAACP memberships, and tried to organize a union in a small factory where he worked. For his union activity, a fellow black worker, aided by others, stabbed him with a knife and nearly killed him; many years later, the evidence of this encounter remained in the form of a large "X" across his abdomen. Coe concluded from this and other experiences that, despite a general black enthusiasm for the CIO, many black workers were frightened of the consequences of overt organizing, and some would even lash out against those who disturbed their relationship with employers. Many black workers secretly rooted for Coe during his life of struggle at the point of production, but he felt that most of them stood mute on the sidelines while he stuck his neck out for the betterment of the race.

In Boss Crump's town, Coe found "the same damned things" that had caused him to leave the countryside—namely, a pervasive atmosphere of white racism and paternalism. African Americans had to call whites "mister" or "sir"; whites used blacks' first names, called men "boys" or complete strangers "auntie" or "uncle," or, more simply, "nigger." Whites would never shake hands with blacks or sit with them in a mixed group, unless blacks sat behind or opposite them, and whenever African Americans held good jobs, ran businesses, owned homes, land, good tools, or a new car, some white person put them "in their place." For driving a new car onto his employer's parking lot, for example, Coe found his tires slashed by the company's security guard. Whites thought blacks should grin and bear such indignities with good cheer. But Coe, like Holloway and a number of others, would not be contained, and he sought out every opportunity for change, particularly where he spent most of his days: at work. Coe began work at the Firestone Tire and Rubber company in 1941, laboring seven days a week, twelve hours a day during the war, never seeing the sun rise or set. He continued there the rest of his working life.

For Coe, the struggle for equality became a life and death battle at work, day in and day out. During the war he sought merely to survive, but like Holloway, after the war he began to take on "the Jackie Robinson role," becoming an activist for equal rights on the shop floor. He became an informal leader among black workers, and later an elected committeeman. Throughout the 1950s and 1960s, he constantly fought with white workers and factory supervisors to end their use of the term "nigger," to end departmental seniority that discouraged blacks from bidding for better-paying jobs, to abolish segregated facilities in the plant, and to elect blacks to higher union offices. White workers twice tried to maim or kill Coe when he broke into previously white jobs, and by the 1960s he kept a gun in every room of his house and in his car. Desegregating the factory, gaining respect, and opening up better-paying and more prestigious jobs to African Americans was a grim struggle that lasted years: "You had to fight for every inch. . . . Nobody gave you anything," Coe recalled.

After the *Brown v. Board of Education* Supreme Court decision overturned school segregation, Lonnie Rowland, Coe, and other black workers secretly collected money at the plant and hired a private attorney who sued both the company and the union to overturn segregation at Firestone. As at International Harvester, some of the union meetings over desegregation nearly turned into bloodbaths, and black workers at Firestone did not completely attain integration until the early 1970s. Coe did not begrudge the struggle, but he felt disheartened about the cost of gaining even the simplest, everyday rights, such as using a convenient restroom or a fountain in the factory, bidding on a skilled job, or parking in the paved ("white") instead of the gravel ("black") parking lot. Looking back, he couldn't help exclaiming, "My God, man, when you'd given up thirty years of your life fighting for something that should have been yours to begin with, it's a little bit disheartening!"

In such battles, black workers sometimes had the rhetorical support of the unions and sometimes the backing of white union leaders. But they could not rely on them. When the CIO merged with the AFL in 1955–56, black activists had less clear support from their national unions than in a previous era of left-center unity. At the local level, and in the South particularly, they had to initiate heroic battles to end Jim Crow in the factories and union halls. Through their struggles, civil rights unionists sought something more than a union and something more than civil rights. They carried their hopes for change into a series of black-led struggles for factory and workplace desegregation, and they used their unions to register blacks to vote, to exert more power in the community, and as battering rams to break down many of the barriers that had been holding African Americans back economically for generations. Their actions even convinced some white workers that the barriers of white supremacy did not serve white interests either. After opening up all jobs to anyone and equalizing wage rates at Firestone, for example, older whites realized they might prefer to move out of fast-paced assembly line jobs into sweeping or other jobs previously reserved for blacks.[25]

Civil rights unionists also took their struggles into the streets. Encouraged by a Communist-led union that had long taken on larger civil rights issues, Leroy Boyd and seventeen other black members of Local 19 of the Food, Tobacco and Agricultural Workers (FTA) union in Memphis went further into the realm of outright protest activity than most dared during the repressive 1950s. Traveling to Mississippi to hold a vigil to stop the execution of Willie McGee, a black man falsely charged with the rape of a white woman, these seventeen men (along with Red Davis and a number of white protesters) were arrested and barely escaped lynching before they returned to Memphis. Shortly thereafter, Willie McGee was executed, with 500 whites celebrating outside. Back in Memphis, those who protested his execution came under heavy attack. But black Local 19 had something most black workers lacked: not only did some of its black members take the lead in the civil rights protest in the dark years of the 1950s, but they did so with strong white support, in a Left-led union that had always made the destruction of Jim Crow one of its goals. The FTA had been purged from the CIO, but it continued to struggle on (it was eventually subsumed by other international unions). Its Local 19 in Memphis, staffed in the postwar period by an extremely committed white organizer and leftist named Ed McCrea, offered strong support for civil rights initiatives.

Boyd's arrest in Mississippi, under the sponsorship of the Communist-led Civil Rights Congress, was only the most public step in a life-long struggle against white supremacy.[26] He came from a poor sharecropping family in Mississippi, and he remembered various acts of violence against blacks, especially when whites thought black men had been involved with a white woman. He always hated whites telling him who he could go out with, and the McGee case only reminded him of the racial terrorism justified by white men's fixation on interracial sex. In one incident he remembered, whites dragged a black man behind their car with chains. He knew that whites could be vicious, but his father always spoke up to them, and Boyd learned early how to protect himself with his fists or a knife.[27]

At age twenty-one, in 1946, he had become a part of the stream of thousands of rural people seeking to get out of Mississippi's mechanizing cotton fields by heading north to Memphis, St. Louis, and Chicago. He came to the city with no knowledge of unions, hoping to move on, but instead he spent the rest of his life in Memphis, battling for his rights as a worker in the low-wage cotton compress and seed oil industry. When he turned to a union for help, employers claimed he and his associates were "communists" or were being manipulated by communists. He rejected all such charges out of hand, saying anyone who took a stand for civil rights would automatically be labeled a communist. Said Boyd,

> if a white person took too much time with a Negro, they'd always call him a nigger-lover. That's what you'd be branded, a nigger-lover. So they [whites] wouldn't associate with us too much. And that's a mistake with the whites, not to associate with the Negro. The union representatives were branded with another name, they were called nigger-lovers, and also communists.

Boyd knew that "communist" was a scare word, and he also knew that a small number of radical whites had long promoted explicitly integrationist activities within the local CIO. Both black and white Communist organizers built his and other unions from the ground up, and in his opinion there was nothing wrong with being a Communist.

However, most white radicals were run out of the labor movement after Senator James Eastland of Mississippi held hearings in Memphis attacking Local 19 and other unions with a Left tinge as communistic in 1952. Boyd commented on how the anticommunist hysteria eliminated most of the active integrationist whites from the unions. But it did not end agitation for civil rights or unionization among black workers. Boyd, Earl Fisher, and other black workers continued over a period of years with work slowdowns and unacknowledged strikes to establish rights at work and to open up jobs previously reserved for whites only. These workers made the same demands as civil rights protestors in the streets. "We told them [employers and whites] we wanted to be treated like other decent Americans," Boyd remembered.

Boyd had always worked with Communists, and never said whether he had ever joined the Communist Party. Ideologically, what appealed to him about the CP was its philosophy of struggle. His own struggle for dignity through unionization not only improved his working life, but also provided him with a means to involve members of his union and his family in various struggles throughout the 1960s. He didn't pay any attention when people called him a Communist, and he didn't study on it too much either. His philosophy was straightforward, and it guided him throughout his working life: "The union is the people. You got to have your people with you. If everybody fighting for one cause, you got a strong union."

A Way Out of No Way: Black Women Factory Workers

The labor struggle was by no means confined to black men, although they dominated industrial employment until the 1960s. In the early years of industrialization, white employers virtually excluded black women from all but the very worst industrial jobs. At the beginning of the Great Depression more than eighty percent of black women in Memphis worked in domestic and personal service, and they usually made so little that even many working-class white families could afford to hire them. The vast bulk of black women working for wages until the 1960s did so in white people's homes or did laundering, waiting, and cleaning jobs with no upward mobility. Those few black women who did get factory jobs worked not as machine operatives but as floor sweepers or cleaners and in other laboring positions, and they experienced even worse wage and occupational discrimination than black men. Most white employers thought of black women as servants, not as workers, and at best treated them paternalistically.[28]

Black women finally came into industry in a major way during World War II, although employers dispensed with most of them at war's end. Those black women who did make it into the factories and into the unions did so under the worst of conditions. Most manufacturers hired white women to replace white men who went off to war, often choosing them over black men when they could. When they got more desperate for labor, employers hired black men; only after that would they hire black women, who often did the hottest, hardest, dirtiest work that black men normally did, at even lower wages. Wood, furniture, and food processing came to rely on black women for unskilled labor, often supervised by white women. At Firestone during the war, the work force of 7,000 became majority women, and a number of black women found unionized jobs there. But they got little aid from federal agencies supposed to enforce equal access to jobs and job training in defense industries.

Irene Branch and Evelyn Bates both falsified their body weights to get jobs at Firestone, and they clung to miserable jobs hauling tires in the fields and doing cleaning and other dirty work.[29] These jobs still provided far higher pay than household, servant, and field labor. Under segregated conditions, few bathrooms existed for black women in the plant, and these were little better than outhouses. Other indignities crowded their days in the factory, as these women struggled with fellow white workers as much as they did with management. White women supervisors could act just as viciously as the men, and they did everything they could to keep black women from learning skills that would allow them to apply for higher-wage jobs. In their world of constricted opportunities, black women nonetheless had no choice but to "take it"—to keep working despite abuse. Although the United Rubber Workers union existed in the plant, it remained weak. According to Ms. Branch:

> Those supervisors would curse you, call you names, do you any kind of way. They'd call you "nigger" and everything else, and spit on you. Do *any-*

thing to you. Blacks was really treated bad. And they'd fire you in a minute. I know a lot of men—women too—quit out there. But I didn't quit. I had a hard time, but I stuck on in there.

Because of black women's precarious position in the labor market, Branch told me, "you couldn't do nothing else but take it or get going on." Knowing how to "take it" meant staying at the job, whatever the company and white workers dished out, without protest. One could count the number of unionized plants that would hire black women in Memphis on one hand. "There was no use, if they didn't have a union." Black workers "just didn't have the privilege" of whites, and without a union they couldn't do much to change conditions.

Both Branch and Bates became their family's main providers after husbands died or left, and, as with the generation of black men who came into industry earlier, unionization provided the key to doing this. As Branch put it, "If it wasn't for that union I wouldn't have stayed in there." Indeed, when it looked like all the black women would be drummed out of the industry after the war, black men pressured the union to make an agreement with the company that saved the jobs of the most senior women, white as well as black. Like black men that I talked to, Ms. Branch saw unionization as critical to her work life. "Nothing didn't go right, we didn't see freedom until we got that union." Without it, she recalled, she never would have been able to stay in the industry, or to double and triple her real wages, send children to college, or have a pension that allowed her to retire.

However, while both Branch and Bates supported the union as much as anyone did, their experience of it was different from that of black men. Wage work was central to their lives, but it combined with traditional core values that placed raising children before anything else; hence, they had little time for union affairs. Ms. Branch, whose husband died early, had begun work life as a domestic worker, and under the financial pressure of being the family breadwinner she continued to take care of white folks' children and her own in the day, working at Firestone at night. She kept up an exhausting routine of constant labor that included only three or four hours of sleep a night for twenty-eight years. Branch survived this regime of incessant work, but like many black women raising families, she had no time to go to union meetings. But as with black men, her incessant labor and determination rested on strong family models of hard work and persistence. Said Ms. Branch,

I was raised in Athens, Georgia. My dad got his eye knocked out in that railroad strike, somebody beat him up, around 1924. He had a brother here, and my parents moved to Memphis in '24. I was a little girl then, and I went to school here. But I left when I was eighteen, because I had a mean stepmother. Then I married at nineteen, been workin' ever since. I didn't go around these honky tonks, just went to church and worked all the time. They called me a work horse.

So when I got grown and I married, then my husband died. I worked practically all my life from eighteen years old, nursing white children and cooking for white people, 'til I got the Firestone job. I had to do the cooking, and I had to go to the back door. You nursed those children and everything, and then you'd eat after they got through eating.

This stoic and heroic routine allowed Ms. Branch to raise her first husband's two children and send one to college, and her position as a unionized factory worker ultimately made her an independent woman. When a second husband tried to make her quit her factory job, "I told him he had to get going." She remained single and independent, working two jobs, for the rest of her life.

Evelyn Bates had similar difficulties in finding any time beyond work and child care. She likewise suffered from supervisor abuse and bad working conditions as she too raised a family largely alone. She identified not just unionization, but the civil rights movement and resultant court decisions, as opening a new day for her and other black women workers:

The integration of jobs happened after the Supreme Court Decision in '54 [*Brown v. Board of Education*]. Before that, only thing a black woman could do in Firestone was sweep, work on the line doing heavy work like I was talking about, work up on the belt sweeping, where all that lamp black [a carcinogen] was, or clean the restrooms as a maid. They had a few black womens up in the cafeteria, on the black side. The white worked on the white side. That's all a black woman could do before they integrated the jobs. But the idea was, the white women didn't want to sweep, she didn't want to clean up no restroom, so that was a black woman's job. It was just like you had black and white men's jobs. That's the way it was with the womens, too.

Bates eventually broke into one of the higher-paying jobs that had been the exclusive preserve of white women, despite the fact that no one would teach her how to do the work. Ultimately, she recalled, she became good friends with some of the white women who had been most vehement in opposition to her. Like Irene Branch, she felt the union had been at the core of her success, the measure of which remained the success of her children.

Accommodation and Resistance

Later generations of black women broke many of the barriers that had held them back in the unions. Alzada Clark in the 1960s organized the furniture and related industries in some of the worst places in Mississippi, going to jail and fighting virtually for her life against some of the most violent anti-union employers in the United States. Ida Leachman organized some of the lowest-wage workers in the country in the 1980s and 1990s. Black women in the Deep South increasingly became union leaders and organizers as the economy shifted from industrial to service employment, and their militancy exhibited the sea change that had taken place in black attitudes since the years of "taking it." Indeed, the generation of African Americans who obtained jobs during the civil rights era would not "take it" as she and other members of the earlier generation had, Ms. Branch and other workers told me.

Edward Lindsey provided an example of the new generation.[30] He had participated in the Nashville sit-in movement in 1960 before taking a job at Firestone, and he had intended to become a doctor, not a factory worker. His response to workplace segregation was straightforward: he sat in the "white" cafeteria, drank out of the "white" fountain, and violated segregation every chance he got. Older black workers like Hillie Pride did not object to such confrontational tactics; in fact, they admired them. But even Clarence Coe and Matthew Davis, themselves involved in civil rights actions most of their lives, felt that many young blacks in the 1960s became too materialistic. They simply would not work the long hours, and they took the higher wages and decent working conditions the union had achieved by then as a given. Some of them had Cadillacs, and once you had such a car, "you got to ride," said Coe. Almost uniformly the older generation felt the younger group had lost the work ethic, and that the next generation in the 1980s and 1990s, a period of union-busting and factory closings, had lost its way entirely.

Evelyn Bates reflected on the timing of a worker's entrance into the Firestone plant and how it influenced their understanding of struggle over time:

The younger people thought that things had always been better for us like they were when they started. They thought we were making big money all the time, and that we always had a easy job. It wasn't like that. The younger people came in and really didn't understand the struggle that the older people had gone through. No they did not. We went through with something! The mens were the ones that were hired in '37 and '38. To hear some of them tell you what they went through! They really went through with something. We thought we went through something, but we didn't near go through what they went through. When I first started, they had a jack, and the men was pulling all this heavy rubber. When the younger generation come in, all the new equipment was there for them, so they thought we had an easy time all of the time. But, we went through hell! Sure did. When the younger folks came in, they could get a job anywhere. I always figure they thought, "Easy go, easy come."

On the other hand, those who came into industry in the 1960s often thought the generation whose lineage had gone from sharecropping and segregation to factory work were too humble, too willing to "take it" in order to survive. Some of them felt that Hillie Pride and many in his generation had accepted too much of the white man's ways, even while they acknowledged that many in his generation had also displayed great dignity and courage. Indeed, attitudes of the pre–civil rights generation, as Clarence Coe tells us, varied enormously, and of course changed with circumstances.

The testimony of black workers reminds us of the fine line they walked between accommodation and resistance during the segregation era. They had a limited range of options, all of which demanded some degree of accommodation to the racial system. The price people paid in the struggle for change always remained high. Most African Americans in the South, at least until the 1950s, worked as sharecroppers or as agricultural wage laborers. Many others, like the vast majority of black women, did domestic work or, like Memphis black men working in sanitation, some kind of service work, all at rock-bottom wages. Those who could get work in the factories often did better, and those few who unionized did far better. But most older people with families, wherever they worked, feared to risk their jobs by joining mass marches and struggling for rights in civil society. Labor and civil rights pioneers like George Holloway, Clarence Coe, Matthew Davis, Leroy Boyd, Edward Lindsey, and other activists proved exceptional in their willingness to assault Jim Crow at all levels.

A growing historiography demonstrates how the black militancy of the

1960s, whether in the mode of nonviolent direct action or that of armed self-defense, turned the Jim Crow South around. But what of the earlier generation? The role of ordinary working-class African Americans in the freedom struggle is complex and difficult to document. On one level, their accomplishment was survival: being able to keep working, put food on the table, and raise the next generation, hoping for an opportunity to right the many wrongs of segregation. The right to work, they believed, was the right to live. Many people, Hillie Pride among them, focused on that level of struggle. Unlike Coe and Holloway and others, most black workers did not overtly rebel. Yet in discussing his past, Pride displayed anger and incredulity when describing the segregation system; he spoke of his pride in the work he did and how he taught others to work hard and well; and he castigated the cruelties of 1980s-style capitalism in the United States, telling me that African Americans as a group were being "ripped up by the moral structure of this country." He had strong opinions and understood the sacrifices he and his generation had made in order to endure.

Pride and others in the early generation of factory workers knew that "taking it" was to some degree necessary for the "survival of the race." They worked harder than most people could imagine today, applying the regimen of hard labor they had learned on the farms to the brutal labor required in the factory. They took pride in their ability to withstand these tests, but they had not acquiesced to the system of racial segregation. The accomplishments of this generation also included, by the mere fact of unionization, significant achievements in breaking down barriers between whites and blacks; and union wages strengthened black communities at their core, providing economic support for families, churches, and community organizations. In varying degrees, most black workers fought the racial system at some level, some of them tooth and nail and others covertly. They did not accept white supremacy, they did not devalue their own labor, and most of them applauded, if they did not take part in, the civil rights struggle.

While many black workers resisted by enduring, some, like Holloway, Coe, and others, played the "Jackie Robinson role" of standing up and taking threats and abuse in order to challenge segregation openly. All of those who came of working age during the 1930s, however, bore a special relationship to the history of racism and black resistance to it. Most of them knew grandparents who had once experienced slavery. All of them had parents who had lived under the worst years of the Jim Crow system. They understood the necessity of accommodating to whites in order not to get killed, and to some degree they conformed to the racial etiquette of their times, but they also had parents and other family members who had modeled some form of resistance to the system. Both humility and resistance were ingrained in their characters.

One can understand the accomplishment of these union pioneers in part by looking to their later years. People such as Holloway and Coe through their unions became politicians in their plants and ambassadors in the community. Holloway chaired many of the International Harvester plant's committees and led much of its negotiating for whites as well as blacks, while Coe at Firestone became a walking union textbook, able to spell out the provisions of a complicated union contract relevant to virtually any situation. Both participated heavily in the civil rights movement. Matthew Davis supported the NAACP and marched with the sanitation workers, and he used his union at Firestone as a means to play a key role in many of the civic, church, and fraternal organizations of the north side of Memphis. His union sent him to conventions, to represent the workers at city hall, and to attend hearings and public events concerning workers and the black community. He joined the Firestone union's singing group and became a deacon in his church, frequently preaching the sermons. When he retired in 1982, 300 people, including the mayor and other city leaders, honored him, and he received an honorary sheriff's badge. Davis felt the union had provided him with a vehicle to participate in the affairs of the larger society, a degree of power nonexistent for most blacks in civil society, as well as a means to send his children to college.

Civil rights unionists, male and female alike, did not fight only for justice on the plant floor. They led the NAACP's mass membership drives among black factory workers. They supported many of the civil rights efforts, from the Scottsboro case in the 1930s to the student sit-ins in the 1960s, and became leaders in their churches and communities as well as in their unions. Many of the children of these black workers went to college as a result of the rising incomes and status unionization brought their parents. In some cases it was the children of unionized workers who broke the barriers of segregation at Memphis State University, the public library, and other important institutions. Black workers and their children, with Ph.D.'s, medical degrees, or "no d's," became leading citizens in Memphis and other parts of the United States.[31] Leroy Boyd and his children played humble roles as foot soldiers in the civil rights demonstrations in Memphis and northern Mississippi. He and many of the black labor activists

I spoke with played a critical role in supporting the black sanitation workers whose strike shook Memphis to its core in 1968. The United Rubber Workers union hall became the center for daily mass meetings and was bombed as a result. Unionized black factory workers joined sanitation workers, black ministers, teachers, and the larger black community in finally breaking open the politics of paternalism and racial subordination through this momentous strike. In the aftermath of Martin Luther King's death, labor and civil rights struggles practically merged for a time. Organizing and strikes at the city's public hospital and later and the Memphis Furniture factory continued to raise the issues of black labor in the city. Furniture Worker leader Leroy Clark also led the NAACP in street demonstrations and school boycotts, while Matthew Davis, Alzada Clark, and other black unionists led voter registration drives and community mobilization, leading to the election in 1974 of Harold Ford, the first black Congressman in the Deep South since Reconstruction, and to the election of black Mayor Willie Herrenton in 1991. As civil rights unionist Edward Lindsey put it, these people saw the civil rights and labor struggles as parallel, not separate.[32]

The Power of Remembering Depends on What We Remember

Ultimately, de-industrialization and assaults on the Right to organize undermined unions and shattered the economic base for much of the black community. A new phase of struggle began, led increasingly by women and the working poor. Retirees of the United Rubber Workers union remained an important force in trying to save their neighborhood from the plagues of de-industrialization and crack cocaine, while black union retirees continued to work in their churches and communities in a variety of ways. But the things they struggled to achieve in the workplace were disrupted or destroyed.

The stories and perspectives of this generation of workers who suffered the worst of American apartheid need to be recognized and made visible. Black workers challenged many of the economic aspects of apartheid and helped to lay the groundwork for more systematic attacks on Jim Crow. They not only changed their own lives, but created the basis for advances by their children, who became part of the new generation of college students who so significantly influenced the course of the black freedom struggle. Black workers also changed the character of the labor movement, challenging white control over jobs, unions, and public spaces and creating a black leadership cadre within it.

They were a transitional generation, moving from farm to factory and from Jim Crow to Freedom Now. This generation, which created many of the cracks in the wall of segregation, is swiftly passing from the scene. Any efforts we can make to fill in the silence created by segregation with the active voices of such workers will help us to understand a little better the dynamics that led to the destruction of America's apartheid. Recovering lost voices, oral historian Steven Caunce tells us, "allow[s] us to examine life at a level of detail that would be quite impossible to achieve for whole populations." Even talking to one such person can change our perspective dramatically; interviewing many can "have a cumulative effect when linked together."[33] These workers, George Holloway says, are "witnesses," and their testimonies suggest some of the complexity and the often subterranean character of black struggles for equality and justice.

We need to link the black working class more explicitly to the origins and development of the civil rights movement and to highlight economic justice as one of the unresolved issues raised by the movement. The persistent demand for economic justice by poor and working-class people, addressed so clearly by Martin Luther King in the Poor People's campaign and the Memphis sanitation strike, remains to be achieved. What generations of factory unionists and other black workers learned through organizing should be researched, understood, and incorporated into freedom movement history, carrying it beyond the framework of civil rights to the concerns for economic justice and labor rights that are both long-standing and increasingly urgent in our own era.

Despite the limitations placed upon their lives, black working-class activists felt they had gained something by organizing and fighting back. For them, unions meant more than better wages, shorter hours, and decent working conditions. As Robert Beasley, a sanitation worker who participated in the 1968 sanitation strike, commented to filmmakers, "'I Am A Man,' that really meant something, didn't it."[34] This slogan adopted by the workers signified a demand for complete citizenship and full human rights, and resonated throughout the Memphis black community. The stories of such black workers, rural and urban, women and men, can help us to locate the origins and judge the results of a freedom struggle that had many dimensions, took many forms, and outlasted the oppressor's rope.

NOTES

1. For an excellent review and critique of the literature, see the bibliographic essay in Charles Payne, *I've Got the Light of Freedom: The Organizing Tradition and the Mississippi Freedom Struggle* (Berkeley: University of California Press, 1995), 413–42. This book clearly places the freedom movement in the context of an inter-generational organizing tradition that largely evolved from the bottom up, even while being influenced by national and international developments. In a similar vein but with a focus on the NAACP, Adam Fairclough shows the diverse and community-based origins of the freedom movement, in *Race and Democracy, The Civil Rights Struggle in Louisiana, 1915–1972* (Athens: University of Georgia Press, 1995). John Dittmer makes a deep exploration into local origins in *Local People, The Struggle for Civil Rights in Mississippi* (Urbana: University of Illinois Press, 1994). Patricia Sullivan suggests the many ways the 1950s and 1960s are tied to the 1930s and 1940s, in *Days of Hope: Race and Democracy in the New Deal Era* (Chapel Hill: University of North Carolina Press, 1996). Certainly this focus on the previous generations and local organizing is not entirely new, however. Clayborn Carson, *In Struggle: SNCC and the Black Awakening of the 1960s* (Cambridge: Harvard University Press, 1981), sensitively details the relationship between cadres and local people, and a variety of books on the earlier generations of white and black organizers exist, including Linda Reed's *Simple Decency and Common Sense: The Southern Conference Movement, 1938–1963* (Bloomington: Indiana University Press, 1991). Recent autobiographies by Black Panther Party members David Hilliard and Elaine Brown, and studies of Black Power and northern urban struggles, such as James R. Ralph Jr., *Northern Protest: Martin Luther King, Jr., Chicago, and the Civil Rights Movement* (Cambridge: Harvard University Press, 1993), have creatively moved freedom movement studies into non-southern terrain; Robin D. G. Kelley, *Hammer and Hoe: Alabama Communists during the Great Depression* (Chapel Hill: University of North Carolina Press, 1990). Michael K. Honey's *Southern Labor and Black Civil Rights: Organizing Memphis Workers* (Urbana: University of Illinois Press, 1993), and Robert Rodgers Korstad, *Civil Rights Unionism: Tobacco Workers and the Struggle for Cemocracy in the Mid-Twentieth-Century South* (Chapel Hill: University of North Carolina Press, 2003) link freedom movements to African-American labor and radical organizing in the 1930s and 1940s South.

2. This literature is synthesized by Joe Trotter, "African-American Workers: New Direction in U.S. Labor Historiography," *Labor History* 35, no. 4 (fall 1994): 495–523, and by Trotter's and Eric Arneson's papers presented at the Southern Historical Association, November 7, 1997, in Atlanta. For another summation of this scholarship, see Bruce Nelson, "Class, Race and Democracy in the CIO: The 'New' Labor History Meets the 'Wages of Whiteness,'" *International Review of Social History* 41 (1996): 351–74; and "Working Class Agency and Racial Inequality," *International Review of*

Social History 41 (1996): 407–20. The growing intersection of race and labor studies became apparent at the conference on "Racializing Class, Classifying Race," at St. Antony's College, University of Oxford, July 11–13, 1997. But it should be noted that a focus on African American workers, men and women, has existed in Marxist literature for a long time. Philip S. Foner in particular explored black labor history in depth long before the new wave of scholarship. See Foner, *Organized Labor and the Black Workers, 1619–1981* (New York: Praeger, 1973, revised and reprinted by International Publishers, 1981), and his multivolume history of the American labor movement. Foner and Ronald L. Lewis published an eight-volume history of the black worker, summarized in *Black Workers, A Documentary History from Colonial Times to the Present* (Philadelphia: Temple University Press, 1989).

3. See Jacqueline Jones, *Labor of Love, Labor of Sorrow: Black Women, Work and the Family, from Slavery to the Present* (New York: Random House, 1985). On multiethnic women's labor scholarship and questions of race, gender, and class, see Dana Frank, "White Working-Class Women and the Race Question," *International Labor and Working-Class History* 54 (1998): 80–102. Literature is also cited in Bruce Nelson, "Class, Race and Democracy in the CIO," 372 n. 36, cited above. A model study is Tera Hunter, *"To Joy My Freedom": Southern Black Women's Lives and Labors after the Civil War* (Cambridge: Harvard University Press, 1997). See also Dolores E. Janiewski, *Sisterhood Denied: Race, Gender, and Class in a New South Community* (Philadelphia: Temple University Press, 1985); and Elizabeth Clark-Lewis, *Living In, Living Out: African American Domestics in Washington, D.C., 1910–1940* (Washington, D.C.: Smithsonian Institution Press, 1994).

4. See William Julius Wilson, *When Work Disappears, The World of the New Urban Poor* (New York: Alfred A. Knopf, 1997).

5. Personal interview with Clarence Coe, Memphis, Tennessee, May 27 and 28, 1989.

6. Kelley and others in African-American labor studies are steadily finding new ways to reveal the truth of Richard Wright's admonition that "we are not what we seem." See Robin D. G. Kelley, *Race Rebels: Culture, Politics, and the Black Working Class* (New York: The Free Press, 1994).

7. Recent and compelling oral histories linking black workers to civil rights struggles include Rick Halpern and Roger Horowitz, *Meatpackers: An Oral History of Black Packinghouse Workers and Their Struggle for Racial and Economic Equality* (New York: Twayne Publishers, 1996), and Michael Keith Honey, *Black Workers Remember: An Oral History of Segregation, Unionism, and the Freedom Struggle* (Berkeley: University of California Press, 1999). On the historiography, see Rick Halpern, "Oral History and Labor History: A Historiographic Assessment after Twenty-five Years," *Journal of American History* 85, no. 2 (September 1998): 596–610. The Behind the Veil project at Duke University has scoured the South collecting precious testimonies from hundreds of black southerners. The transcripts are held at the Center for Documentary Studies, Duke University. See William H.

Chafe, "'The Gods Bring Threads to Webs Begun,'" *Journal of American History* 86, no. 4 (March 2000): 1531–52; and William H. Chafe, Raymond Gavins, and Robert Korstad, *Remembering Jim Crow: African Americans Tell about Life in the Segregated South* (New York: The New Press, 2001).

8. For chapter and verse of this story, see Honey, *Southern Labor and Black Civil Rights.*

9. Honey, *Black Workers Remember.* Laurie Beth Green documents the crucial role of black women in working-class and freedom struggles, in "Battling the Plantation Mentality: Consciousness, Culture and the Politics of Race, Class and Gender in Memphis, 1940–1968" (Ph.D. dissertation, University of Chicago, 1999).

10. Not to exhaust the list of contributors to the recent literature on racism and labor organizing, see works by David Roediger, Alexander Saxton, Herbert Hill, Jeffrey Norrell, Bruce Nelson, Eric Arneson, Roger Horowitz, Dolores Janiewski, Rick Halpern, Earl Lewis, Joe Trotter, myself, and others. Much of this work focuses on white working-class racial identity and racism, but it also explores transracial labor solidarity. It is peculiar (or maybe not) that white males so heavily dominate this phase of historiography. On multi-ethnic women's labor scholarship and questions of race, gender, and class, see Frank, "White Working-Class Women and the Race Question." See also the work by Tera Hunter, Jacqueline Jones, and other women cited in this article. Bruce Nelson, in *Divided We Stand: American Workers and the Struggle for Black Equality* (Princeton, N.J.: Princeton University Press, 2001), provides an important overview. And see Eric Arnesen, *Brotherhoods of Color: Black Railroad Workers and the Struggle for Equality* (Cambridge: Harvard University Press, 2001).

11. See accounts by Earl Lewis, *In Their Own Interests: Race, Class, and Power in Twentieth-Century Norfolk, Virginia* (Berkeley: University of California Press, 1991); and Eric Arneson, *Waterfront Workers of New Orleans: Race, Class, and Politics, 1863–1923* (Urbana: University of Illinois Press, 1991).

12. For confirmation of the pattern of black female exclusion from industry before the 1940s on a national basis, see Jacqueline Jones, *Labor of Love, Labor of Sorrow: Black Women, Work and the Family, from Slavery to the Present* (New York: Random House, 1985).

13. Tera W. Hunter, *To 'Joy My Freedom: Southern Black Women's Lives and Labors after the Civil War* (Cambridge: Harvard University Press, 1997), and Kelley, *Race Rebels.*

14. See the recent treatments by Roger Horowitz, *"Negro and White, Unite and Fight!": A Social History of Industrial Unionism in Meatpacking, 1930–90* (Urbana: University of Illinois Press, 1997), and Rick Halpern, *Down on the Killing Floor: Black and White Workers in Chicago's Packinghouses, 1904–54* (Urbana: University of Illinois Press, 1997). For a sampling of recent labor scholarship on the South, see Gary M. Fink and Merl E. Reed, eds., *Race, Class, and Community in Southern Labor History* (Tuscaloosa: University of Alabama Press, 1994); Robert H. Zieger,

Organized Labor in the Twentieth-Century South (Knoxville: University of Tennessee Press, 1991), and *Southern Labor in Transition, 1945–1995* (Knoxville: University of Tennessee Press, 1997). See Rick Halpern's essay "Organized Labor, Black Workers, and the Twentieth Century South: The Emerging Revision," in *Race and Class in the American South Since 1890,* ed. Rick Halpern and Melvyn Stokes (Oxford: Berg Publishers, 1994), 43–76.

15. Personal interview with Hillie Pride, May 26, 1983, Memphis.

16. Personal interview with Matthew Davis, October 30, 1984, and April 1996, Memphis.

17. Examples of such repression against black workers in the cases of William Glover and Thomas Watkins are given in detail in *Black Workers Remember.*

18. Personal interview with George Holloway, March 23, 1990, Baltimore, Maryland.

19. Personal interview with Forrest Dickenson, February 20, 1983, Memphis.

20. Personal interview with Richard Routon, February 18, 1983, Memphis.

21. Personal interview with W. E. Davis, January 28, 1983, St. Louis, Missouri.

22. See Sullivan, *Days of Hope,* and Honey, *Southern Labor and Black Civil Rights,* on the postwar schisms. And see accounts by Karl Korstad, Ellen W. Schrecker, and others in Steven Rosswurm, ed., *The CIO's Left-Led Unions* (New Brunswick, N.J.: Rutgers University Press, 1992). Michael Honey gives more detail in "Labor, the Left, and Civil Rights in the South: Memphis during the CIO Era, 1937–1955," in *Anti-Communism: The Politics of Manipulation,* ed. Judith Joel and Gerald M. Erickson (Minneapolis: MEP Press, 1987).

23. These patterns of white worker behavior were widespread. Robert J. Norrell, "Caste in Steel: Jim Crow Careers in Birmingham, Alabama," *Journal of American History* 73 (1986): 669–94, identifies this pattern and concludes that industrial unions, by enforcing departmental seniority and occupational segregation, played a crucial role in undermining black economic progress. In this sense, even industrial unions can be seen as an obstacle rather than a support for black advancement. For a compelling account of white worker resistance to desegregation in the South, see Alan Draper, *Conflict of Interests: Organized Labor and the Civil Rights Movement in the South, 1954–1968* (Ithaca, N.Y.: ILR Press, 1994).

24. Personal interview with Clarence Coe, op. cit.

25. Personal interview with George Clark, October 30, 1984, Memphis.

26. Personal interview with Leroy Boyd, February 6, 1983, Memphis.

27. My interview with Leroy Boyd is supplemented by an interview with him conducted by Paul Ortiz, June 19 and 22, 1995, Memphis, used by permission of the Behind the Veil: Documenting African American Life in the Jim Crow South Oral History Project at Duke University.

28. In 1930, 17,349 black women (and 5,511 black men) worked in domestic and personal service in Memphis—more than the 10,588 black men who worked in factories. Some 5,000 black women also labored in the hottest and most miserable

of conditions in steam laundries. Honey, *Southern Labor and Black Civil Rights*, 36–38.

29. Personal interviews with Irene Branch, May 25, 1989 and May 27, 1989, and with Evelyn Bates, May 25, 1989, Memphis.

30. Personal interview with Edward Lindsey, May 27, 1989, Memphis.

31. As one example, George Isabell, who worked at the Buckeye Factory and belonged to Local 19, had a daughter who got arrested "integrating" the public library and later became a medical doctor. Personal interview with George Isabell, February 7, 1983, Memphis.

32. Personal interviews with Alzada Clark, May 24, 1989, Leroy Clark, March 27, 1983, and Leroy Boyd and Edward Lindsey, op. cit.

33. Steven Caunce, *Oral History and the Local Historian* (London and New York: Longman Publishers, 1994), 116–17 on deceiving appearances, and quote on 28.

34. Beasley quoted in *At the River I Stand,* a film by Steve Ross, David Appleby, and Allison Graham, available from California Newsreel.

Chapter 11

Being Red and Black in Jim Crow America

On the Ideology and Travails of Afro-America's Socialist Pioneers, 1877–1930

Winston James

> Men make their own history, but not of their own free will; not under circumstances they themselves have chosen but under the given and inherited circumstances with which they are directly confronted.
>
> —Karl Marx

> And some there be, which have no memorial; who are perished as though they had never been; and are become as though they had never been born. . . . But these were merciful men, whose righteousness hath not been forgotten. . . . The people will tell of their wisdom, and the congregation will shew forth their praise.
>
> —Ecclesiasticus 44:9–15

Although there is a welcome and growing body of literature on black socialists[1] in the United States, it is largely concentrated on the Depression years when the Communist Party and its influence among Afro-Americans, and indeed others, was at its height.[2] Despite the valiant efforts of the late Philip Foner and a few others, the black socialist presence in America before the 1930s is understudied and largely unknown.[3] Yet the prominence of black people within the Communist Party from the 1930s to the 1960s cannot be separated from the earlier existence and efforts of black socialists. There is in fact a strong and organic connection between the developments during the half century before 1930 and the later influence of black socialists in American political life.

Though numerically small, perhaps never exceeding more than a few thousands up to 1930, black socialists constituted a significant presence within the wider Afro-American community. The political and ideological influence they exerted, especially between 1910 and 1930, extended well beyond their numerical weight. Concentrated in New York, Philadelphia and Chicago, they demanded equality and struggled for a wider emancipation based on socialist principles. They joined the Socialist Party and the Industrial Workers of the World. Others formed the African Blood Brotherhood, the leadership of which became the nucleus of black membership within the newly formed American Communist Party by the middle of the 1920s. Chief among them were Hubert Harrison and Ben Fletcher, pioneering black members of the Socialist Party and the Industrial Workers of the World; A. Philip Randolph and Chandler Owen, who edited the black socialist magazine, the *Messenger*; Cyril Briggs, founder of the African Blood Brotherhood and editor of its organ, the *Crusader*, and an early member of the Communist Party; Otto Huiswoud, the only black charter member of the Communist Party; Grace Campbell, a Socialist-turned-Communist; Claude McKay, Wilfred A. Domingo, Lovett Fort-Whiteman, Richard B. Moore, Otto Hall and his brother Harry Haywood. Huiswoud, Campbell, McKay, Domingo and Moore had joined Briggs in founding and leading the African Blood Brotherhood.[4] A disproportionately large number of these radicals, as I have documented and explained elsewhere, were of Caribbean origin.[5]

What attracted these black men and women to the ideology of revolutionary socialism and the building of socialist organizations on the sandy ground of America? As black people in a racist society, how did their condition inflect their class politics and ideology? What was the extent of their influence? And what were the forces that hindered their political practice and inhibited their impact and organizational growth within the black community?

In this paper I shall argue that the answer to these questions are not as self-evident as they may at first seem; that the socialist ideology developed by these Afro-Americans was even more profoundly influenced by considerations of race than it was by those of class, though class and race largely overlapped; that the black socialists were not as quixotic as some commentators made them out to have been; that they provided pertinent analyses —especially of the relation between race and class—about the condition of

Afro-America under capitalism that still merit respectful attention; and that the challenges that these black socialists faced in developing their project came not just from American capitalism, and not just from racism within the socialist and trade union movements, but also from important structural, institutional and ideological obstacles located within the black community itself.

If American socialism has lacked the capacity to retain Afro-American adherents, it has never failed to attract them to its banners. Peter Humphries Clark (1829–1925) was the first Afro-American to answer the call of modern American socialism. Within a year of the founding of the Workingmen's Party of the United States (WPUS), the first socialist party of the Americas, in 1876, Clark had joined its ranks. Like so many other Afro-Americans after him, his conversion to the socialist cause was full-hearted, his work for the movement, zealous. Insofar as Afro-Americans were the most oppressed and exploited layer of the working class, then socialism would redeem the race as it liberated the class. That was the idea that attracted Clark to Marxism. A child of the working class himself, a cogent, agile and bold thinker, Clark appreciated and succumbed to the socialist ideal. But after joining the movement, he quickly recognized that the struggle for socialism was hindered by its supposed agents in the United States, the white working class. Like thousands of black comrades after him, Clark discovered that the practice in America did not live up to the European theory. Racism within the movement or, at best, the inattention to the specificity of what would later become known as the Negro Question, disappointed and nullified the promise.

Clark has no biography and the profiles of him generally ignore his engagement in the socialist movement. Yet Clark's encounter with American socialism is remarkably instructive and deserving of our attention. And from his experience, a pattern emerged—enthusiastic conversion to the cause, committed work, frustrated hopes, disillusionment, defection, and a drift toward black nationalism—that would be repeated many times over by future generations of Afro-American radicals.

Born in Cincinnati in 1829, Clark, was the eldest child of Michael Clark and his wife. Michael Clark's own father was a Kentucky slave owner, who in 1817 sent Michael's mother, a slave woman, and her children across the Ohio River to Cincinnati and set them free. He apparently made provision for the children until they were grown.[6] Michael Clark became a barber and did his best to provide an education for Peter. But there was little available for black Cincinnatians. Up to the early 1840s, Peter had only a few months of schooling each year during the winter. But in 1844, the Rev. Hiram Gilmore, an English clergyman and philanthropist, established the Cincinnati High School (generally referred to as Gilmore High School), the first secondary school for black children in the city.

Gilmore High provided Clark with an exceptionally rounded liberal education. Praised by black and white educationalists alike, Gilmore and his supporters spared no expense to make the school a success, though money was always short. "Good teachers were employed, and besides the common branches of an English course, Latin, Greek, music, and drawing were taught," noted one commentator.[7] Unlike most nineteenth-century philanthropic ventures to educate "the Negro," Hiram Gilmore's was not the limiting one of industrial education. Carter G. Woodson reported that the school was patronized and appreciated by black Cincinnati "as the first and only institution offering them the opportunity for thorough training." The school, he said, became popular throughout the country, attracting Afro-Americans from as far South as New Orleans. Gilmore's black pupils were prepared for college and a significant proportion went on to Oberlin "and such colleges which drew no color line on matriculation." Among Gilmore's distinguished nineteenth-century alumni were P.B.S. Pinchback, John Mercer Langston, James Monroe Trotter, and John I. Gaines.[8] Clark, a quick study, excelled at Gilmore and within two years of entering, was made a pupil teacher. He graduated in 1848 and sought work in the city.

His father managed to partially shield him from the harshness of Cincinnati's racially segmented labor market. Michael Clark managed to place Peter with a white stereotyper, Thomas Varney, as an apprentice. As the *Cleveland Gazette* suggested in its 1886 profile of Peter Clark, for a colored boy to be given a chance to learn a trade "was then and is still a remarkable thing in Cincinnati."[9] But the anomaly is largely explained by the fact that the Varneys were relatively liberal-minded—Mrs. Varney was a correspondent for the radical *New York Tribune*, a paper for which Marx and Engels wrote. But the clincher was, more than likely, the two hundred dollars Michael Clark paid Varney to train his son. This was a major sacrifice for the Clark family to make.

Peter's apprenticeship ended abruptly and sadly. Varney caught the California fever, closed his business and left for the West coast, apparently with the Clarks' hard-earned two hundred dollars in his pocket. The man who took over Varney's business had "no use for colored apprentices." And according to the *Gazette*, "Mr. Clark stepped out of the shop and has not found a minute's work at his trade from that day to this."[10]

In the meantime, Michael Clark had become ill and Peter, who learned the trade from him, took over and ran the barbershop. His father died within months of Peter's joining him in the business. Peter was a reluctant barber. Unlike many of the black barbers in the city, Clark ran a "civil rights" barbershop—he insisted on not serving white customers only, but black ones too. He resented the white customers' racism and arrogance, but apparently needed their patronage to stay in business. Matters came to a head when one day he quarreled with a white customer. The white man wanted Clark to introduce him to "colored ladies" at a fair. Clark refused. The white man declared that he would no longer patronize Clark's business. The excuse was that Clark's barbershop also served "niggers." According to Clark's friend, William Simmons, Clark became so angry that he threw the shaving cup on the floor in rage and disgust and declared "he would never shave another white man, and, if he did, he would cut his throat."[11] He closed the business.

In 1849, while still a barber, Clark was examined and appointed a teacher. In that year, the Ohio legislature under the influence of Free-Soilers had allowed black people to organize and run their own schools with public finance for the first time. Clark led in organizing the first black-run public school in Cincinnati and became its first black teacher. But the Cincinnati city council refused to appropriate money to pay Clark's salary on the grounds that black people, not being citizens, could not be school trustees and handle public monies.[12] The matter was pursued in the courts, right up to the Ohio Supreme Court, which ruled in the school's favor. But this was fully two years after the dispute began. Clark was once again unemployed.

It was the coincidence of this personal experience of racism and the wider calamity of the passage of the Fugitive Slave Law—an act that imperiled even further the limited liberty of the so-called "free" colored population in the United States—which led Clark to decide to leave the country for good.[13] Liberia, as it had been for thousands of other Afro-Americans, was his intended destination. In his letter to the American Colonization Society, written within days of the passage of this infamous law, he informed them that he, and two friends who were students at Oberlin College, had "resolved to emigrate to the Republic of Liberia." His inquiry addressed to the Society revealed the seriousness of his intent:

We would like to know at what time [and] at what place we would be able to embark[.] I at present know of no chance this year excepting the vessel which Governor McDonogh will dispatch from N[ew] Orleans[,] of this we are not certain whether we can obtain a passage. We think of taking a course in Book-keeping and penmanship before we go, would there be any chance for us to obtain situations as book-keepers, if so what salary. The chance for a school teacher, what amount of clothing it would be advisable to carry out with us, the price of boarding, clothing, what prices flour, pork, and other articles of western produce will command in the Liberia market.[14]

It is not clear if his student companions—L. W. Minor and William R. Carey—went with him in the end, but Clark reached the port of New Orleans in January 1851 ready to leave for Africa. But the ship provided being "a dirty little lumber schooner," he was advised to wait for a more suitable vessel. He spent over a year in New Orleans during which time he got a job as a clerk. But he was called back to Cincinnati to help organize the public schools, which had won their court battle for public funding. He returned home.[15]

Back in Cincinnati, he threw himself once again into the struggle, especially around the question of public education for the black population of the city. He finally received the three months' salary that the Cincinnati council owed and had refused to pay him back in 1849 when he began the school. Clark gave all of it, $105, to help defray the legal cost of the action against the city council.[16] He collaborated with Frederick Douglass in the Negro Convention movement and acted as an editor and correspondent of the *North Star* and *Frederick Douglass' Paper*, and with Douglass became an anti-emigrationist.[17]

Like Douglass, Clark was a Republican in the 1850s. Though frustrated and angered by the treachery of the Republicans, Douglass maintained, right to the end, that, as far as black people were concerned, there was no alternative to Lincoln's party. The Republican Party was the ship and all else was the sea, he famously declared in 1871. In subsequent years, he became increasingly seasick on the Republican ship, he criticized conditions on the vessel, he often disagreed with its turns, he was impatient with its speed, and frequently quarreled with its various captains. But Douglass never abandoned ship.[18] Clark did, and did so relatively early and noisily. He would reluctantly return to it. But before he did, he at one stage thought he had found an alternative, more congenial vessel heading in the right direction. Clark had joined forces with the socialists of Cincinnati.

He helped to form the Colored Teacher's Co-operative Association and served as its delegate to the 1870 convention of the National Labor Union. It was there that Clark first met William Haller, a former militant abolitionist and fellow Cincinnatian who edited *The Emancipator*, the leading English-language socialist paper in the Midwest. The men became lifelong friends and Clark soon became convinced that the socialism propounded by Haller and his comrades offered the best answer to the problems faced by Afro-Americans. As his faith in the Republican Party declined, so grew his attraction to socialism. And on March 26, 1877, Clark publicly renounced his allegiance to the GOP at a large meeting of socialists in Cincinnati and expressed his support for the WPUS. Clark was appalled at the growing inequalities that accompanied the rise of American capital during and after the Civil War, and was especially outraged at the oppression of his fellow Afro-Americans in the South. "Go to the South," said Clark, "and see how the capitalists banded together over the poor whites."

> They carefully calculate how much, and no more, it will require to feed the black laborer and keep him alive from one year to another. That much they will give him for his hard labor, on which the aristocracy live, and not a cent more will they give him. Not a foot of land will they sell to the oppressed race who are trying to crowd out the degradation into which capital has plunged them.[19]

Clark viewed with scorn and alarm the growth in the number of millionaires as the misery of the poor became more unbearable and widespread. He recalled in his speech the suicidal despair that gripped him when, as a young man, he could not find work for several months to feed his hungry wife and baby. "Capital," said Clark, "must not rule, but be ruled and regulated. Capital must be taught that man, and not money, is supreme, and that legislation must be had for man." Government, he told his audience, "is good; it is not an evil." And it was the government's responsibility and duty "to so organize society that honest labor should not feel such oppression to drive it to desperation."[20]

Clark's turn to socialism possessed him like a religious conversion. Although he apparently remained a Unitarian, his enthusiasm for his new faith was unbounded. He spoke at street-corner meetings and at trade union gatherings on behalf of the WPUS and wrote for the party press. But it was not until the great railroad strikes of 1877 that Clark came to wider public attention.

1877 was one of the most turbulent years in the nation's history and one of the most momentous for the labor movement. Reeling under the blows of a severe depression that began in 1873, workingmen who managed to hold on to their jobs experienced a downward spiral in their standard of living. While the cost of food, which devoured three-fifths of their income, fell by 5 percent between 1873 and 1876, their wages plummeted by an estimated 25 to 60 percent over the same period. Unemployment was rife. Some estimated that as many as 60 percent of the non-farm workers were unemployed; others about 25 percent. The estimates varied, but the misery of the poor, especially in the growing urban centers of the nation was plain for all to see.[21] For the first time, the tramp became a familiar figure of the American landscape. But the large corporations, which were still fat from the bonanza of the Civil War and its aftermath, conspired to push the workers into an even deeper state of degradation in the name of profit. The railroad workers became one of their primary targets for wage cuts. And after an attempt to cut their wages by 10 percent for the second time within a year, the workers of the Baltimore and Ohio Railroad at Martinsburg, West Virginia struck. It began on July 17, 1877 and quickly spread to a dozen railroad centers across the North and the West. Nationwide, local militias and federal troops were mobilized to suppress the strike, which had spread to America's major cities and had expanded beyond the railroad workers. Scores of workers were killed, hundreds injured, property worth millions was destroyed during the struggle. Cincinnati was one of the centers of discontent. And it was there on July 22, 1877 that Peter Clark addressed a huge crowd of striking railroad workers and their supporters.

Coolly, but passionately cogent Clark expressed his sympathy for the strikers, condemned the callousness of the railroad companies and the federal government for siding with the corporations. But his discourse went beyond the immediacy of the strike, extending to a critique of capitalism and a recommendation of socialism to cure its ills.

"The poor man's lot is at best a hard one," Clark said.

His hand-to-hand struggle with the wolf of poverty leaves him no leisure for any of the amenities of life, his utmost rewards are a scanty supply for food, scanty clothing, scanty shelter, and if perchance he escapes a pauper's grave [he] is fortunate. Such a man deserves the aid and sympathy of all good people, especially when, in the struggle for life, he is pitted against a powerful organization such as the Baltimore and Ohio Railroad or the Pennsylvania Central.[22]

He pointed out that the Baltimore and Ohio was taken over by the government during the Civil War and that on top of the substantial investment made in tunnels, bridges, rails, etc.—expenditure that effectively amounted to the rebuilding of the corporation's infrastructure—the company also received millions of dollars of government money for its use during the war. At war's end, the Baltimore and Ohio, with improved infrastructure was handed over by the government to its previous operators. Little wonder that the company could pay dividends of 10 percent to its shareholders. "Yet," he declared, "this road, so built, so subsidized, so prosperous . . . declares itself compelled to put the wages of its employees down to starvation rates."

The government's support of the companies during the strike "cannot be too severely condemned," said Clark. "Has it come to this, that the President of a private corporation can, by the click of a telegraphic instrument, bring state and national troops into the field to shoot down American citizens guilty of no act of violence?" He supported the wronged men meeting force with force. And even if he was in the end defeated, Clark expressed gratitude, that the American citizen, as represented by these men, "was not slave enough to surrender without resistance the right to appeal for redress of grievances." Clark optimistically predicted that within twenty years the railroad companies would be under government control—"all will be owned by the government and worked in the interests of the people." The factories and the land will in time, undergo a similar transformation. "[C]ooperation instead of competition will be the law of society." The "miserable condition" into which American society had fallen, Clark declared, had "but one remedy, and that is to be found in Socialism."

He brought to the attention of his audience the violent ups and downs in the capitalist economic cycle, the increased distress caused by each succeeding downturn, and the decrease in the number of capitalists and how those who survive "grow more wealthy and powerful." He graphically depicted the chaotic nature of these fluctuations and their human cost: prosperity, overproduction, glutted markets, reduced prices, goods sold at cost and below cost, bosses fail, shops are closed, men are idle, "and the miserable workmen stand forth, underbidding each other in the labor market." If the competition is too sharp, said Clark, "they resort to strikes as in the present instance. Then comes violence, lawlessness, bloodshed and death." This is the cruel dynamic of the capitalist cycle that the apologists of the system are unwilling to acknowledge. "People who talk of the anarchy of socialism," said Clark echoing Marx, "surely cannot have considered these facts. If they had, they would have discovered not a little of anarchy on their side of the question." Clark reiterated that from his reading of the various theories of political economy, there is "but one efficacious remedy" proposed for the maladies of capitalism, "and that is found in Socialism."

> The present industrial organization of society has been faithfully tried and proven a failure. We get rid of the king, we get rid of the aristocracy, but the capitalist comes in their place, and in the industrial organization and guidance of society his little finger is heavier than their loins. Whatever Socialism may bring about, it can present nothing more anarchical than is found in Grafton, Baltimore and Pittsburgh today.

Cooperatives may help to ameliorate the condition of some workers— "poultice the ulcer in the body politic"—but they are also subject to the periodic crisis of the wider capitalist system. This deduction led Clark to the inexorable conclusion:

> The government must control capital with a strong hand. It is merely the accumulated results of industry, and there would be no justice should a few scores bees in the hive take possession of the store of honey and dole it out to the workers in return for services which added to their superabundant store. Yet such is the custom of society. . . .
>
> Machinery too, which ought to be a blessing but is proving to be a curse to the people should be taken in hand by the government and its advantages distributed to all. . . .
>
> Machinery controlled in the interests of labor would afford that leisure of thought, for self-culture, for giving and receiving refining influences, which are so essential to the full development of character. "The ministry of wealth" would not be confined to a few, but would be a benefit to all.

He saw similar benefits being derived from the nationalization of the railroad companies. For those who object to his collectivist vision, Clark pointed out that

> Society has already made strides in the direction of Socialism. Every drop of water we draw from hydrants, the gas that illumines our streets at night, the paved streets upon which we walk, our parks, our schools, our

libraries, are all outgrowths of the Socialistic principle. In that direction lies safety.

Choose ye this day which course ye shall pursue.

Given the indictment of capitalism laid out in his speech, Clark had a strangely sanguine view of the American political system. In his coda, he seemed to have overlooked the interconnection between the political and the economic—which he himself alluded to—and expressed misplaced faith in the judicial system and the power of the ballot. "Let us, finally," he concluded,

> not forget that we are American citizens, that the right of free speech and of a free press is enjoyed by us. We are exercising today the right to assemble and complain our grievances. The courts of the land are open to us, and we hold in our hands the all-compelling ballot.
>
> There is no need for violent counsels or violent deeds. If we are patient and wise, the future is ours.

The speech, reported the *Emancipator*, was "characterized by the deep pathos of feeling that is to be expected of one who can look back at the time when the wrong and injustice of capital abused his race, which by its labors and sorrows helped to build the greatness of this nation."[23] It was indeed a *tour de force* and much appreciated by his audience.

Clark rose in the WPUS, running on the party ticket in the fall of 1877 for the state superintendent of schools. Haller praised his candidacy, seeing it as "most thoroughly represent[ing] the contest between laborers and capitalists, of the proscribed race, whose sorrows made the name of the United States the synonym of robbery and murder throughout the world." Clark's nomination was "above all others the finest vindication of the claim that the Workingmen's Party is a purely cosmopolitan organization."[24] Clark fared best of all the WPUS's candidates in Ohio, but they all failed in their electoral bids. In 1878 he was elected to the National Executive of the newly formed Socialist Labor Party, the left wing of the WPUS, which split at the end of 1877. But Haller's antiracist influence in the party declined after 1877, and factionalism absorbed much of the Socialists' energies. Clark was disillusioned with the party's racism and its ignoring of the plight of Afro-Americans as well as the enervating effects of the factional fights. On July 29, 1879, Clark resigned from the SLP. Fiercely independent in political outlook, somewhat of a maverick in temperament, he objected to what he regarded as the party's doctrinaire tendency "to hold members down to a rigid pattern of ideas." He did not, however, renounce his socialist ideology. Indeed, he announced that he was still a socialist, but would wait for a movement to arise that speaks to the interests and needs of Afro-America. "The welfare of the Negro is my controlling political motive," he told his erstwhile comrades as he bade farewell to the SLP.[25]

Clark returned to the Republican fold in 1879, but three years later he had once again bolted, sick once again of the party's policy on the Negro Question. He counseled black political independence, that black people should dispose of their votes to the highest bidder, not to the Republican Party out of blind loyalty—any party that extended and protected their interests, regardless of label, should be the one given support. Clark declared that "as soon as we have a few thousand colored men in each of the evenly balanced States . . . who will vote for the friends of the race, without regard to the party label they bear, the fight will be won . . . for neither party can afford to despise such a political body actuated by such motives."[26]

In accordance with this calculus he joined the Democratic Party in Ohio in 1882 and in so doing earned the opprobrium of black Republicans across the nation. Harry C. Smith, staunch Republican and founder-editor of the *Cleveland Gazette*, one of the most influential black newspapers of the time, mounted an unrelenting attack upon Clark.[27] It was an understandable and predictable one. For, at the time, as Wendell Dabney put it, black people regarded white Democrats as "the Devil's chosen children, and a Negro Democrat was a creature of such depravity that hell was far too good for him."[28] But Clark's political logic, at least for the local setting, was reasonable.[29] The Civil Rights Act of 1875 had been struck down in 1883 by the U.S. Supreme Court, all of whose members were appointed by Republican presidents. In the absence of federal law, black Ohio had no protection of their civil rights. Remnants of the discriminatory "Black Laws," which dated back to 1804, were still on the state's statute books.[30] Black Republican state legislators in 1880 and 1883 had urged their white Republican colleagues, who controlled the Ohio legislature, to repeal them, but without success. The white Republicans refused to allow the matter to even come to the floor. It was Clark's rebellion against the Republicans that led to action.

Ohio Democrats nominated George Hoadly for the governorship in 1883. Hoadly, a distinguished lawyer and former judge, had been an abolitionist and Radical Republican before the Civil War. He joined the Ohio Democrats in the 1870s but remained an antiracist and a close friend of

Clark's. Clark's campaign in support of Hoadly was made easier by the fact that the Republicans had nominated a well-known racist, Joseph Foraker, as their candidate. Hoadly won by a narrow margin and explicitly attributed his success to the crossover votes of three to seven thousand black Ohioans. He moved fast and repealed the Black Laws that the Republicans had conspicuously left alone. Belatedly, the Republicans in the legislature, in their attempt to curry favor with the black electorate, joined the Democrats in changing the law.

Clark had won a tangible and important victory, but at a high personal cost. When the Republicans returned to power in 1886, he was ingloriously removed from his job by the Cincinnati Board of Education.[31] He was effectively sent into exile, first to Alabama, where in 1887 he became principal of the State Normal and Industrial School in Huntsville. Hating the Deep South's Jim Crow ambience, he left within a year and took on the principalship of Sumner Negro High School in St. Louis. There he worked until his retirement in 1908, somewhat disengaged from political action and became more and more disillusioned with the prospect of black America as he grew older.

As late as the 1880s, he still held to his socialist dreams, however insecurely.[32] But his political career through the decades of the 1870s into the new century is marked by a parabola of despair relieved by hope, conquered once again by an even deeper trough of disillusionment. The dark vortex which he inhabited in the early 1870s is forcefully revealed in a remarkable Emancipation Day address he gave in Dayton, Ohio, in 1873:

> I do not forget the prejudice of the American people; I could not if I would. I am sore from sole to crown with its blows. It stood by the bedside of my mother when she bore me. It darkens with its shadow the grave of my father and mother. It has hindered every step I have taken in life. It poisons the food I eat, the water I drink and the air I breathe. It dims the sunshine of my days, and deepens the darkness of my nights. It hampers me in every relation of life, in business, in politics, in religion, as a father or as a husband. It haunts me walking or riding, waking or sleeping. It came to the altar with my bride and now that my children are attaining their majority, and are looking eagerly with their youthful eyes for a career, it stands by them and casts its infernal curse upon them. Hercules could have as easily forgotten the poisoned shirt which scorched his flesh, as I can forget the prejudices of the American people.[33]

Four years later, when he joined the Workingmen's Party, he must have felt more optimistic. And he was cheered by the reforms that Governor Hoadly brought in to ease the plight of black Ohioans.[34] But although he campaigned for the Democrats up to 1888, the rising tide of Jim Crow in the South with the attendant epidemic of lynchings and disenfranchisement of Afro-Americans brought home to him that what might have worked in Ohio did not now work in Alabama and never did.[35] And so the darkness returned.

Criticized by black preachers a few years earlier for not being sufficiently religious, Clark surprised everyone when in the spring of 1892 he organized a national day of prayer and fasting to summon God's intervention against Southern lynching. A greater power than government and parties was needed for the job because, he thought, they were impotent.[36] His prayer unanswered, in 1901 Clark regretted not having gone to Africa after all. The old man implicitly chided himself for having opposed the emigrationists in the 1850s. He now recalled that the "most memorable" of the Negro Conventions was that held in Ohio in 1852. John Mercer Langston, whom he vigorously opposed at the time, "delivered," he now reports, "the best speech of his life, defending the thesis, 'there is a mutual repellency between the white and black races of the world.'" Amidst what Paul Laurence Dunbar aptly called the "evil days" that had befallen Afro-America, Clark declared: "Time has vindicated the position taken by Mr. Langston in that memorable address."[37]

On June 25, 1925, and in his ninety-seventh year, Peter Humphries Clark quietly passed away at his home in St. Louis. Little is known about the last twenty years of his life. He clearly deserves a biography. Despite the fact that he was "somewhat below the middle size" and "thin,"[38] Clark was clearly no mean fighter. He had more than his fair share of detractors, but, especially in the later years, he had ardent admirers too, especially among the younger and bolder generation of black men and women in the North. Even some of his former critics sought to bring his body home to a final resting place in Cincinnati. "Dead, he was no longer dangerous and therefore more desirable," noted Wendell Dabney, another Cincinnati black rebel and Clark eulogist. In his tender portrait of black Cincinnati, Dabney described Clark as "Cincinnati's greatest colored product from the standpoint of intellectuality, courage and racial loyalty." He declared that in Clark's veins "coursed no bootlicking blood."[39]

*

One of the younger men inspired and influenced by Clark's example was Timothy Thomas Fortune. Born a slave in Marianna, Florida, in 1856, Fortune had a most curious career. While still in his twenties, he launched and edited two of the nation's most influential black newspapers, the *New York Globe* and the *New York Freeman*. Because of his excellent prose and forthright and politically courageous journalism, he quickly acquired a reputation as a radical civil rights advocate in the 1880s. Some even viewed him as Frederick Douglass's legitimate political heir. He then surprised and disappointed his most loyal admirers in the 1890s by joining forces with the arch accommodationist, Booker T. Washington. Fortune not only became Washington's ghost writer, but one of his most effective propagandists and Northern attack dogs, snapping at the heels of "kickers" such as Du Bois and William Monroe Trotter like a black rotweiler. Breaking with Washington in 1907, he tried to retrieve his radical credentials, but he had harmed and alienated too many of his former allies to effectively repair the breach; he was viewed, a little unkindly, as an opportunist. Fortune entered a seven-year bout with depression and alcoholism, emerging into the light only in 1914 when he recommenced his journalistic career. In 1923 he joined the staff of Garvey's *Negro World*, serving as editor up to his death in 1928.[40]

Fortune, like Clark and several notable Afro-American spokespersons, had become disgusted with the Republican Party after the Compromise of 1877 and counseled political independence. It was during this radical phase that Fortune wrote his remarkable book, *Black and White: Land, Labor and Politics in the South*.[41] Fortune's, however, is a strange and contradictory book that has been more frequently praised than carefully analyzed. It deserves our attention here because of the apparent centrality of class and the class struggle in its analysis. Fortune attempted to show that black and white workers have

a *common cause*, a *common humanity* and a *common enemy*; and that, therefore, if they would triumph over wrong and place the laurel wreath upon triumphant justice, without distinction of race or of previous condition *they must unite!* And unite they will, for "a fellow feeling makes us wond'rous kind." When the issue is properly joined, the rich, be they black or be they white, will be found upon the same side; and the poor, be they black or be they white, will be found on the same side.

Necessity knows no law and discriminates in favor of no man or race.[42]

Not only is it implausibly suggested here that this unity of black and white labor will be brought about inevitably, elsewhere, Fortune stated explicitly that he had "no faith in parties." In republics, he wrote, parties are always manipulated by "demagogues, tricksters, and corruptionists."[43] Little wonder, then, that he never joined any party of the Left.

Even more problematic is the fact that the white workers of the South with whom he suggested black workers should join are described by him in another passage as a "class of vermin," monsters of cruelty, a "servile, cruel, heartless set of men," a "careless, ignorant, lazy, but withal, arrogant set, who add nothing to the productive wealth of the community because they are too lazy to work, and who take nothing from that wealth because they are too poor to purchase."[44] Elsewhere he drew a sharp contrast between black and white workers of the South:

> When I think of the absolutely destitute condition of the colored people of the South at the close of the Rebellion; when I remember the moral and intellectual enervation which slavery had produced in them; when I remember that not only were they thus bankrupt, but that they were absolutely and unconditionally cut off from the soil, with absolutely no right or title in it, I am surprised,—not that they have already got a respectable slice of landed interests; not that they have taken hold eagerly of the advantages of moral and intellectual opportunities of development placed in their reach by charitable philanthropy of good men and women; not that they have bought homes and supplied them with articles of convenience and comfort, often luxury,—but I am surprised that the race did not turn robbers and highwaymen, and, in turn, terrorize and rob society as society had for so long terrorized and robbed them. The thing is strange, marvelous, phenomenal in the extreme.

Set against this loving portrait of the black South are, in his italics,

> *the white men of the South, the capitalists, the land-sharks, the poor white trash, and the nondescripts, with a thousand years of Christian civilization and culture behind them, with "the boast of chivalry, the pomp of power," these white scamps, who had imposed upon the world the idea that they were paragons of virtue and the heaven-sent viceregents of civil power, organized themselves into a band of outlaws, whose concatenative chain of auxiliaries ran through the entire South, and deliberately proceeded to murder innocent*

men and women for POLITICAL REASONS *and to systematically rob them of their honest labor because they were too accursedly lazy to labor themselves.*[45]

Black and White, then, is torn apart by the struggle of the would-be anti-capitalist on the one hand, and the rage of the former slave as a race man, on the other.

True, there are lovely passages of anticapitalist rhetoric in character with that of critics of Gilded Age America: "Capital has placed its tyrant grip upon the throat of the Goddess of Liberty. The power of railroad and telegraph corporations, and associated capital invested in monopolies which oppress the many, while ministering to the wealth, the comfort and luxury of the few, has become omnipotent in halls of legislation, courts of justice, and even in the Executive Chambers of great States, so the poor, the oppressed and the defrauded appeal in vain for justice." There is even a gesture to Marx's labor theory of value: "capital is the offspring of labor, not labor the offspring of capital. Capital can produce nothing. Left to itself, it is as valueless as the countless millions of gold, silver, copper, lead and iron that lie buried in the unexplored womb of Nature." But in the end, with its emphasis on land monopoly, not only does the book owe more to Henry George than Karl Marx, it is more antiracist than it is anticapitalist. For Fortune was more of a social Darwinian than an egalitarian. As he put it, "men of natural parts, of superior culture and ambitious spirit usually, in all societies, manage to rise to the top as the natural rulers of the people. You cannot keep them down; you cannot repress them. They rise to the top as naturally as sparks fly upward to the heavens." He even went so far as to claim that in America "if a man *has it in him* the way is open for him to mount to the topmost round of the social ladder." He suggested that the "intelligent, the ambitious and the wealthy men in *both races* will eventually rule over their less fortunate fellow-citizens without invidious regard to race or previous condition."[46]

Fortune desired not the overthrow of American capitalism as such, but the removal of the wall of "color-prejudice" that blocked the progress of Afro-Americans within the existing order. He attacked millionaires: "What are millionaires, any way, but the most dangerous enemies of society, always eating away the entrails, like the vultures that preyed upon the chained Prometheus? Take our own breed of these parasites; note how they grind down the stipend they are compelled to bestow upon the human tools they must use still further to swell their ungodly gains!" But he then blunted his own attack by declaring that he objected to millionaires not because they have property, but because, as a rule, "they have acquired it by unjust processes and use it tyrannically."[47] For the implication here is that some millionaires acquired their property justly and do not use it tyrannically. But if one adheres to the basic socialist principle that property is theft, how would it be possible for one to acquire millions, especially in those days, without committing an injustice or being implicated by an injustice (through inherited wealth, for instance) along the way? Whatever happened to the idea of expropriating the expropriators?

Fortune painted a sunny picture of the emergence, despite the difficult environment, of the black bourgeoisie in the North as well as the South.[48] He was confident that black people, especially those in the South, have the capacity to succeed. All they lacked was "intelligence," by which he means general training. When the black man has this desideratum of intelligence, "he will no longer labor to enrich men more designing and unscrupulous than he is; he will labor to enrich himself and his children." Indeed, with his "powerful muscle and enduring physical constitution, directed by intelligence," the black man of the South will "ultimately turn the tables upon the unscrupulous harpies who have robbed him for more than two hundred years; and from having been the slave of these men, he, in turn, will enslave them." From having labored to enrich others, "he will force others to enrich him." The laws of nature are "inexorable, and this is one of them," Fortune declared. "The white men of the South may turn pale with rage at this aspect of the case, but it is written on the wall." Fortune protested, perhaps a little disingenuously, that he was of no disposition to "infuriate any white man of the South, by placing a red flag before him." He was simply presenting to these men a glimpse of the future, one which their grandchildren will view with "complacent indifference." The world moves forward, he wrote, and the white man of the South is forced to move with it. "Like the black man, he must work, or perish; like the black man, he must submit to the sharpest competition, and rise or fall, as the case may be. And so it should be."[49]

In the end, then, the argument of *Black and White*, snaps from the tug-of-war of its own contradictions. But the race man wins over the class man in the book. Given such problems, it is odd that the book has been so often and so lavishly praised as an anticapitalist work, even by those on the Left. Philip Foner, for instance, declared that the publication of *Black and White* marked "the first time that a black spokesman had stated with such clarity and vigor the thesis of class conflict and the identity of interests of black and white workers." The book is certainly vigorous, even audacious, but lacks clarity. Foner's further proposition that not even Peter Clark had analyzed "the class forces in American society and the inevitability of the struggle as cogently as T. Thomas Fortune," is difficult to support. True, Clark did not write on the subject at the same length as Fortune did, but his argument was far more clearly and convincingly put forward, as his 1877 speech to the Cincinnati railroad workers makes evident. And as Foner himself admits, Clark followed the logic of his analysis and joined forces with the socialists.[50]

Fortune did support the Knights of Labor, its biracial unionism, and its struggle against the "odious and unjust tyranny of capital." Preempting sentiments that would be echoed by black socialists more than a generation later, Fortune declared:

> since we are largely of the laboring population it is very natural that we should take sides with the labor forces in their fight for a juster distribution of the results of labor. We cannot afford to stand off from or to antagonize the army under whose banner we labor in the common lot of toil. . . . All we can do is to fall into line on the right or left, and which side it will be depend entirely upon whether we are a capitalist or a laborer.[51]

Fortune's support for the Knights was by no means uncritical. He was equally forthright in his criticism when they veered from their non-racist principles in the face of white supremacist opposition.[52] He criticized black leaders who advocated strike-breaking. He was not afraid, as he said in 1886 to "lay it down dogmatically" that the interests of black and white workers are "identical in every particular." Thus: "The black man who arrays himself on the side of capitalism as against labor would be like a black man before the war taking sides with the pro-slavery as against the anti-slavery advocates."[53]

A couple years after *Black and White*, Fortune wrote a much more coherent and forceful pamphlet, *The Negro in Politics*, an elaboration of one of the chapters in the earlier book.[54] Equally passionate, but far more focused and considered than the first book, it makes the most sustained statement of all the late nineteenth-century Afro-American documents for the political independence of the Negro. Fortune sought an end to the "political vassalage of the race" and "sentimental politics."[55] His was a savage indictment of the Republicans. Boldly exposing Lincoln's feet of clay, Fortune wrote that the "great Emancipator" was "more of a politician than an Abolitionist." Lincoln, he said, "freed the slave by proclamation more as a war measure than from the motives of love for the slave . . . he did not believe that the slave could be made a citizen but should rather be colonized." In an even more heretical mode, Fortune went on: "I firmly believe that, had he not been martyrized by a skulking assassin, the treatment of questions affecting us would have been vastly less favorable to us than they have been."[56] From the smashing of one icon, he moved to another, the venerable Frederick Douglass. He, more respectfully, accused Douglass of "Utopian" folly for his continued belief in and support of the GOP.[57] Although he in places wrote of Reconstruction in an overly negative tone, a tone surprisingly similar to that which became known as the Dunning School of Reconstruction historiography, Fortune's is a fine work.[58] It is also, in the end, a melancholy document, a black *cri de coeur*, for it shows through the force of its own logic the limited political choices available to Afro-Americans within the national context. Fortune rejected emigration as a choice. He was not a Socialist. Thus in the end, the pamphlet was in fact a plea for black people in the North to vote the Democratic ticket, if only to punish the Republicans for building up a mountain of political insults and betrayals and taking the black vote for granted. Like Clark and other prominent black spokesmen who supported the Democrats, Fortune suggested that black people should vote Democratic with their eyes wide open. He had no illusions about the Northern Democrats and nothing but contempt for the "Bourbon Democracy" of the South, which he called a "curse" to the nation. "No colored man can ever claim truthfully to be a Bourbon Democrat. . . . But he can be an independent, a progressive Democrat." He urged the strategic and intelligent use of the black ballot. "You do not need to be a Democrat or a Republican to force from politicians your honest rights," he declared. "*You simply need to be men*, conscious of your power."[59] And as in the case of Peter Clark in Ohio, black Northern Democrats did win significant concessions from the party in various states above the Mason-Dixon Line. But by the beginning of the 1890s the systematic disenfranchisement, Jim Crowing and lynching of Afro-Americans in the South led, or carried out at the behest and complicity of Southern Democrats, it became even more difficult for black people in the North to support, what was after all, the sister party of the one in the South.[60] It was not until Franklin Roosevelt ran for his second term that there was a marked shift in northern black vote in favor of the Democrats.[61]

It was during the 1880s that Fortune emerged as the most uncompromising advocate of black retaliatory violence. "[R]esist an injury promptly," he insisted. And he had a solution to the lynching epidemic in the South:

"the only way to stop it is for colored men to retaliate by the use of the torch and dagger. The white man who stabs or lynches a colored man should be stabbed or lynched in return." He pointed out that he did not seek violence; it was a defensive, last resort: "We propose to accomplish our purposes by the peaceful methods of agitation, through the ballot and the courts, but if others use weapons of violence to combat our peaceful arguments it is not for us to run away from violence. A man's a man, and what is worth having is worth fighting for."[62]

Fortune, alas, underwent a drastic change in the 1890s. In 1890, he condemned the Colored Farmers' Alliance as "offensively Socialistic in most of its demands" and "warn[ed] Afro-Americans everywhere to be cautious of committing themselves to the support of the Farmers' Alliance and its revolutionary purposes and aims."[63] He inveighed against the People's Party (the Populists), long before its racist degeneration, denouncing it as "a menace to the nation."[64] Unions in general, racist or non-racist ones, had, to Fortune, become a menace. By 1907 he was writing of the "determination of trade unionism to arbitrarily dominate capitalism," which he claimed amounted to the "robbery of consumers and employers." He called for "even-handed justice to all—to invested capital, to producing capital and to the vast army of consumers."[65] Conspicuously absent is a call for justice to the vast army of laborers; a remarkable omission for a man who had previously recognized capital as the offspring of labor. After Booker T. Washington's Atlanta Exposition address in 1895, Fortune's blood did not boil, as it would have done less than a decade earlier. Instead, in his column in the New York *Sun*, he praised Washington and dubbed him, the "Negro Moses."[66] Fortune the lion had metamorphosed into a lamb.

It is thus, for his eloquent plea for black political independence and his audacious call for black self defense and retaliation, that the radical Fortune should be most accurately remembered. For despite his anticapitalist rhetoric in *Black and White*, closer inspection reveals that he was not a socialist, but one, who, at a relatively tender age, had the courage to declare: "Race first; then party!"[67] And like the New Negro radicals a generation later, he did not believe in turning the other cheek. Unlike Mohandas Gandhi and Martin Luther King who preached that an eye for an eye would in the end leave everybody blind, Fortune thought that an eye for an eye, would, in the end, stop the racist "scamps" from gouging out black people's eyes.

*

George Washington Woodbey, not Fortune, was the next major figure to emerge following Clark's socialist footsteps. Twenty-one years after Clark's resignation from the Socialist movement, Woodbey, a Baptist minister, would become one of Afro-America's most distinguished socialist thinkers and activists. George W. Slater, another Baptist pastor, heard Woodbey speak in Chicago in 1908 and soon thereafter joined the Socialist Party. Relatively little by the way of biographical detail is known about these men. Woodbey was born a slave in Tennessee in 1854, had two terms of schooling after emancipation, lived in Kansas and Nebraska but did most of his political work in California, mainly Los Angeles and San Diego. He served on the executive board of the California Socialist Party and became the party's first black national organizer. A most remarkable man, Woodbey educated himself, becoming an outstanding pamphleteer and orator. He had a fine, analytical mind that he put to excellent work in the cause of socialism. Evident from his surviving body of writings, is an exceptional ability to make complex ideas clear in his attempt to reach a wide, and in particular, a black audience.[68] His turn to socialism was like a religious conversion. And when he joined the Socialist Party in 1900 he resigned from his church in Omaha and vowed that his life henceforth would be "consecrated to the Socialist Movement."[69] But he never abandoned his Christian faith, for he saw no contradiction between his religious beliefs and his socialist politics. Indeed, he saw Marx as a descendant of the Hebrew prophets and was "convinced that Socialism is but the carrying out of the economic teachings of the Bible."[70] As he put it in one of his pamphlets, "Why the Negro Should Vote Socialist":

> For my part as a preacher, I know that we would all be far better off if we had Socialism. The Bible says: "Your Heavenly Father knoweth that you have need for all these things." Meaning by that, food, clothing and houses. But God has put the things that you need here on the earth and the capitalist class has gobbled them up and you must by your votes change the condition.[71]

Woodbey moved to San Diego in 1902 where his ill mother was living and was made minister of Mount Zion Baptist Church. He became deeply involved in Socialist politics in California and nationwide. His black congregation liked him and, despite his dissident views, was patient with him, but in the end they were not convinced, despite his great powers of persuasion, that socialism and Christianity were as compatible as he made out. They eventually got rid of him, and one of his flock reported that his dismissal was "a direct result of [his] mixing too much Socialism with his Bible, and this the members of his church resented."[72] He was apparently very adept at "[loosening] up his flock with the Bible, then finished his sermon with an oration on Socialism,"[73] but in the end it failed him. That George Woodbey, of all people, had been unsuccessful in persuading his congregation of the compatibility of Christianity and socialism is a stern lesson that the black socialists who came after him would have done well to ponder. For Woodbey, perhaps more than any other black socialist to operate in the United States, was keenly aware of the deep resistance that many black Christians had toward socialism. Moreover, he consciously devised strategies to reach those who were religious and explicitly chided his comrades who believed that it was "necessary to make atheists, infidels or agnostics of the professed Christian before you can make a Socialist out of him." In "Why the Socialists Must Reach the Churches with Their Message," he complained that

> I have not only been told by this class of comrades, but have read from the pens of others that man cannot be a Christian and a Socialist. Because our party circulates these opinions and declares them from the soap box, occasionally, I find myself compelled to keep on explaining when I speak to church people.[74]

He argued that the only way to reach church people is to show them that the "economic teaching of the Bible and of Socialism are the same" and that for them "to stand consistently by the teaching of [their] own religion" they must accept socialism. He suggested that when the socialist is speaking to the Christian on socialism from the Biblical standpoint, he or she should confine himself or herself "strictly to its economic teachings." He went on to say:

> It is my experience, that when you show the church member how the Bible, in every line of it, is with the poor as against their oppressors, and that it is only because we have not been following out its teaching, that professed Christians have been found among the worst oppressors of the poor and that no man is entitled to be called a Christian who does not measure up to the teaching of the Bible, you have made the first step toward converting him to the idea that it cannot be done in its entirety without the collective ownership and operation of industries.[75]

Woodbey pointed out that through its ineptitude or arrogance the Socialist Party was making it difficult for him to win converts among church members. "It will not do," he declared, "to send those who do not understand the Christian people, to carry this message, for the reason that they are sure to say something that will spoil the whole thing." He argued that he was not particularly concerned with the merits of religious belief and disbelief, but simply drawing attention to "the difficulties" he found in reaching church people and how to deal with them. He was confident that "When once we have succeeded in showing the church people and the pastors of small churches, that if they are to follow the teachings of the Bible, they must be with us in advocating the overthrow of the capitalist system, we will have made the greatest step yet made in the cause of socialism."[76]

There are a number of unanswered questions about Woodbey's departure from Mount Zion Baptist. Were his congregation so deeply committed against his socialism to the extent that they would throw him out on that account only? Were there other considerations at work in his ousting? Was there any pressure from higher authorities to have him removed? Important though these questions are, as of now, we have no clear answers to them. And Philip Foner, who has done the most digging—wonderful digging for which we are deeply in his debt—to resurrect Woodbey, is mute on these questions.

It is a pity that Randolph, Owen and the *Messenger* magazine did not heed Woodbey's wise counsel. They perhaps were not aware of it. Hubert Harrison, however, knew him and heard him speak. Woodbey was, said Harrison, "very effective."[77] But Harrison ignored Woodbey's advice and indeed advocated a militant rationalism and atheism that Afro-America had not seen before among its ranks. And the political consequences were predictable.

Nothing is known about Woodbey after 1915, when his last article appeared in the Socialist press. The Reverend George W. Slater, however, attributed his political awakening to the work of Woodbey. We know even less about Slater's life. We do not know when or where he was born or when he died. We know he lived in Chicago between 1907 and 1912, where he served as the minister of Zion Tabernacle church. Between 1912 and 1919 he lived in Clinton, Iowa, where he was pastor of the Bethel African Church. Like Woodbey, he was a distinguished orator, pamphleteer and contributor to the socialist press. And like him, Slater saw no distinction between socialism and Christianity. "Scientific Socialism," wrote Slater in a 1915 article, "is the only systematic expression of the social message of Jesus."[78]

Slater had served as Secretary to the Colored Race for the Christian Socialist Fellowship, and as a Socialist Party lecturer. In 1909, Eugene Debs
publicly praised Slater for his "excellent work in educating the black men
and women of the country and showing them that their proper place is in
the Socialist movement." Debs described Slater as "a fine example of the
educated, wide-awake teacher, of his race, whose whole heart is in the
work and who ought to be encouraged in every possible way to spread the
light among the masses."[79] And during the 1911 municipal elections in New
York, Harrison reported that he used, with some success, a pamphlet by
Slater, "The Colored Man's Case as Socialism Sees It," in an effort to win
Afro-Americans to the Socialist cause.[80]

Clark, Woodbey and Slater were better known than all the other black socialists in the late nineteenth century and the first decade of the twentieth
century. But they were not the only ones of renown. Frank J. Ferrell, a New
York machinist, was not only an important member of the Socialist Labor
Party in the 1880s, he was also the most famous Afro-American in the
Knights of Labor. Ferrell served as secretary-treasurer of the Knights' powerful District Assembly 49 of New York. Although his speeches have not
survived, he was celebrated as an orator and was praised by the black press
for his role in building interracial solidarity in District 49. Ferrell stood up
for non-racist and egalitarian principles in the order.

Despite the fact that the national leadership of the Knights under Vin-
cent Powderly excluded Asians from membership, Ferrell and Timothy
Quinn, the leader ("district master workman" in Knights' parlance) of District 49 helped to successfully organize two groups of Chinese workers in
New York. Ferrell and Quinn sought and fought hard to secure charters for
them as regular local assemblies. But the General Executive Board of the
Knights, in part due to the pressure of the virulently anti-Chinese West
Coast members of the order, rejected the request. Ferrell and three others
on the GEB spoke in support of granting the charters and issued a minority report dissenting from the majority decision. The dissenters, two of
whom were white comrades of Ferrell's in District 49, noted that "the first
basic principle of the organization was the obliteration of lines of distinction in creed, color or nationality." They also noted that Chinese workers
had conducted a militant strike in California in 1884 and concluded that
Asian workers could make a valuable contribution to the labor movement
once they were organized. Although the charters were refused, Chinese

workers, contrary to the leadership's edict, were welcomed as members in mixed locals in District 49.[81]

Ferrell was brought to the public's attention during the 1886 national convention of the Knights held in Richmond, Virginia. A few months before the convention Quinn had sent a group from District 49 to secure hotel accommodation for the sixty-member New York delegation. On the basis of the group's report, arrangements were made for the delegates to stay at the hotel of one Colonel Murphy, a Confederate veteran. When Murphy discovered that a member of the delegation, Ferrell, was black he cancelled the booking, saying that "customs here must be respected." He offered to provide separate accommodation for Ferrell in a black hotel.

District 49 unanimously passed a resolution, introduced by master workman Quinn, stating that none of their delegates will be allowed to stay in a hotel that discriminates on the basis of "color, creed or nationality." The delegates from District 49, many of them socialists, turned up in Richmond with tents, indicating their determination not to forsake their principles and brother workman Ferrell. The good black citizens of Richmond saw to it that the tents were not used. They opened their homes to District 49 delegates. Some of the more religious-minded delegates worshipped at Richmond's only black Catholic Church, transgressing Richmond's convention of segregation. The delegates of District 49, in a body, attended Richmond's Mozart Academy of Music to see a performance of *Hamlet*. Ferrell was comfortably seated between two white socialist comrades in the orchestra. According to Philip Foner, this made Ferrell "the first Negro in Richmond's history to occupy an orchestra seat in a theater."

Before the beginning of the convention, master workman Quinn, the leader of New York's delegation, explained to Powderly what had happened with the Murphy hotel booking and suggested that it would be a wonderful expression of the Knights' creed to have Ferrell introduce the Governor of Virginia to the assembly. Powderly thought this was going too far. "[I]t would not be pleasant for either the Governor or the convention to attempt to set at defiance a long established usage," he told Quinn. Powderly did agree, however, to have Ferrell introduce him after the governor had spoken. Workman Ferrell took his moment in the limelight to tell the 800 assembled delegates and the governor, who was sitting on the platform, that one of the goals of the Knights of Labor was "the abolition of those distinctions which are maintained by creed or color." Powderly, anxious not to antagonize the white South, was not only somewhat embarrassed by Ferrell's defiant words, but also a resolution introduced by Quinn. Master workman Quinn's resolution declared that the Knights of Labor recognized "the civil and political equality of all men and women in the broad field of labor, and recognizes no distinction on account of color." Powderly managed to successfully water down Quinn's noble resolution with a big "but." Genuflecting to white delegates from the South, Powderly added to Quinn's words: "but it [the Knights of Labor] has no purpose to interfere with or disrupt the social relations which may exist between different races in any portion of the country." The amended resolution was adopted by the convention over District 49's objection.[82]

Predictably, the white racist press did not like the goings-on at Richmond. It accused the Knights of an attempt to force "social equality" upon the South. The Knights, it said, was a "Socialist conspiracy to overthrow existing social relations in our communities," and advised white members to leave the organization and form their own white-only order. Powderly was alarmed by the attacks of the white Southern press and sent a letter to the Richmond *Dispatch* to appease his racist critics. Published while the convention was still in session, Powderly explained that he had no wish to "interfere with the social relations which exist between the races in the South." He assured them that "There need be no further cause for alarm. The colored representatives to this convention will not intrude where they are not wanted, and the time-honored laws of social equality will be allowed to slumber undisturbed."[83] This was not the first nor the last time that socialist egalitarianism would be trumped by what Hubert Harrison would later call "Southernism."

The black press criticized Powderly for not having a strong enough backbone to stand up to the white supremacists, but praised the order as a whole. Fortune, in the New York *Freeman*, had special praise for District 49. "District 49 of New York," he suggested, "should be placed at the head of the class for a squared-toed manifestation of true manhood and most unusual courage." Harry Smith's Cleveland *Gazette*, noted: "Taking all things into consideration, time, place, surroundings, it is the most remarkable thing since emancipation. The race's cause has secured a needed ally in the Knights of Labor organization."[84]

At the end of the convention, the black community in Richmond held a banquet in honor of District 49. A hundred delegates and their friends were seated "without reference to color" on two tables which stretched the length of the hall. Victor Drury, socialist, close friend of Ferrell's and one of the leaders of District 49, was so moved by the occasion that, according to a reporter present, he entered "a flight of oratory unusual even in him." He spoke on the brotherhood of man, invoking the example of John Brown, among others, who were willing to die for the ideal.[85] Sadly, the Knights of Labor, viciously persecuted by the ruling class, quickly degenerated into a white supremacist organization. By 1894, with the support of its white locals, it called for the deportation of Afro-Americans to the Congo Basin, Liberia, "or some other parts of Africa." By 1895, it was effectively dead as a union.

The names of William Costley, John H. Adams and Edward D. McKay ought also to be listed on the roster of Afro-American socialist pioneers. The three were delegates to the founding conference of the Socialist Party of America held in Indianapolis in July 1901. They are particularly noteworthy, especially Costley and Adams, because of their role in getting the conference to adopt a relatively radical resolution on the Negro Question.

The resolution was introduced by Costley, one of the delegates from San Francisco. The resolution condemned the capitalist class for fostering racism among black and white workers. It similarly condemned both the Democrats and Republicans, educational and religious institutions for betraying the Negro "in his present helpless struggle against disfranchisement and violence." The resolution went on: "we declare to the negro worker the identity of his interests and struggles with the interests and struggles of the workers of all lands, without regard to race or color or sectional lines." It closed with an invitation to Afro-Americans to membership and fellowship with the Socialist Party "in the world movement for economic emancipation by which equal liberty and opportunity shall be secured to every man, and fraternity become the order of the world." Adams and McKay, two coal miners from different parts of Indiana, initially objected to the resolution, arguing that the Negro should not be singled out from other workers in this way. As Adams put it, the Negro "must stand up with every other man, without special favor." But after Costley explained that the history of the Negro worker, who had only recently escaped the shackles of slavery, was different from that of white workers, Adams agreed to go along with the resolution. An important clause condemning "the innocent persecution of innocent members of the race, their severe punishment for trivial offenses, their lynching, burning and disfranchisement," was objected to by a white delegate, Algie Simons. Simons, a socialist editor and historian, admitted openly that he sought the removal of the clause because it would "make a great deal of trouble in the South."

This was enough to put Adams and McKay firmly behind Costley; they recognized capitulation to white chauvinism when they saw it. They had several distinguished white allies among the delegates, but the offending clause was removed from the resolution when it was finally passed.[86]

The Socialist Party leadership, including Morris Hillquit, who spoke against the resolution's passage at the convention, in subsequent years treated it as an embarrassment, as if the resolution had nothing to do with the party. The resolution was never re-affirmed for more than a decade after its passage, and, up to 1912, the Negro Question was never discussed by a national convention of the party. As F. Laurence Moore put it, the party was "militantly cautious about mentioning black Americans in their official party statements."[87] Indeed, this American *samizdat* was generally pulled out of the archives by the party primarily to disabuse racist critics of the idea that the Socialists advocated "social equality" for the Negro.[88] Eugene Debs expressed the hope in 1903 that the next convention will repeal the resolutions on the Negro Question. "The negro does not need them and they serve to increase rather than diminish the necessity for explanation," Debs wrote. "We have nothing special to offer the negro, and we cannot make special appeals to all the races. The Socialist party is the party of the working class, regardless of color—the whole working class of the whole world."[89]

William Costley evidently recognized far more clearly than Debs, a good man, that formulated in this manner, Debs's "negro" and "working class" were politically debilitating abstractions. For boldly putting the Negro Question and in such clear terms to a reluctant Socialist Party, Costly, Adams and McKay made an important contribution to the black socialist tradition. The problems they encountered would be repeated many times over in the subsequent years.

The Afro-American socialists active during the inter-war years were, therefore, not by any means ancestorless. With the exception of Hubert Harrison, it does appear, however, that the black radicals' knowledge of their illustrious predecessors was poor. The names Peter Humphries Clark, George Woodbey, George Slater, Frank Ferrell and William Costley never appeared in the *Messenger*, the *Crusader*, nor the *Challenge*. The example of these black socialist fighters was never evoked, their struggles and sacrifices, unremembered and unlearned from.

Although it is impossible to tell with any precision how many black socialists there were between 1900 and 1930, we do know that their number was relatively small; certainly minuscule when set beside the large army, numbering perhaps as many as two million in the United States alone, recruited by Marcus Garvey and the Universal Negro Improvement Association. Though concentrated in the Northern states, black socialists were widely distributed across the United States. And the efforts of Clark, Woodbey and Slater bore fruit.

In 1913 the Socialist Party conducted a survey to ascertain the status of black members in its locals across the country. All the secretaries of the Northern states who replied reported the presence of black members, but could not specify numbers because, they said, records were not kept on the basis of race. Of the nine secretaries who replied from Southern states and the District of Columbia, eight—Florida, Georgia, Kentucky, Louisiana, Maryland, Mississippi, Tennessee and the District of Columbia—indicated that they had black members. In addition to these, the party in Texas in 1915 also reportedly had some black members. Through its courageous fight against the disenfranchisement of black citizens, the Socialist Party in Oklahoma, apparently won a significant, though undetermined, number of Afro-Americans to its flag.[90] Wherever it operated and there were black workers, the Industrial Workers of the World—which was originally aligned to and founded by the more radical members of the Socialist Party —recruited black members.[91]

By 1919 however, the center of gravity of black membership in the Socialist Party had shifted dramatically to the North. The locals in the South had either ceased functioning or were in terminal decline, the IWW had been smashed ferociously in the South and the West and barely survived in the North after 1919.[92] New York's Harlem became the unrivalled center of black radicalism, nationalist as well as socialist, by 1919. It was there that the *Messenger*, the *Crusader*, the *Emancipator*, and the *Negro World*, among others, were published; it was there that the headquarters of the Liberty League of Afro-Americans, the African Blood Brotherhood, and the UNIA were located.

While the *Negro World* was black nationalist in outlook, the *Messenger*, the *Crusader* and the short-lived *Emancipator* were, albeit with different admixture of black nationalism, explicitly revolutionary socialist publications. By 1922 the black socialists were in sharp opposition to Garvey. But the *Messenger*, the *Crusader* and the *Emancipator* were run by men and women who not only wrote, analyzed and propagandized, but also engaged in sustained political activity in a variety of other ways. The *Messenger* was the publication around which black members of the Socialist Party organized in New York and nationally. The *Crusader*, likewise was the propaganda arm of the African Blood Brotherhood, while the *Emancipator* was edited by W. A. Domingo and Richard B. Moore, two staunchly anti-Garveyite members of the black Left.

Hubert Harrison (1883–1927), whom A. Philip Randolph dubbed the "father of Harlem radicalism," started the ball rolling. A brilliant and erudite orator and writer, Harrison had been one of the pioneering black members of the Socialist Party in New York. He joined the party in 1909, but tiring of the racism of its leading comrades, he left it in 1914 and concentrated his effort on mobilizing black people in the struggle against racism. He advocated a defensive policy of "race first," but never abandoned or renounced his deeply ingrained Marxism. He was greatly admired by all of Harlem's black radicals and intellectuals. Even those who later disagreed with him acknowledged their debt to Harrison and his pioneering effort.[93]

Harrison must be credited with undertaking the first sustained analysis of the class position of black people in the United States and the coincidence of black people's interest with anticapitalist projects.[94] Thus he provided unstinting support to William "Big Bill" Haywood and the IWW, which he greatly admired. When Haywood was recalled from the National Executive Committee and expelled from the Socialist Party in 1912, Harrison, himself a supporter of direct action, publicly protested and was one of the signatories to the resolution of protest put together by leading left-wing members of the party.[95] He was an active participant in the Paterson, New Jersey, silk strike and spoke at the strikers' rallies. Harrison defended Africa against both European and Euro-American racism on the one hand, and the patronizing civilizationism advocated by New World Africans for their continental brothers and sisters, on the other. Connected to this effort was his unassailable critique of scientific racism in America. Brought up in the church in his native St. Croix, he broke from it in America and became one of the nation's first black freethinkers.[96] He invested great faith in rationalism and advocated a scientific outlook on life, including the Negro Question. In language similar to that of Fortune, Harrison told black Harlemites that their loyalty to the Republican Party was misplaced; that they owed neither Lincoln nor the Republicans anything. On the contrary, the Republicans, he argued, had used and betrayed black Americans and were deeply indebted to them. Harrison was merciless in his attacks upon Booker T. Washington, his allies and heirs who sought accommodation with American racism. His attacks on Washington would cost him his nice, little civil service job at the Post Office. He vigorously advocated black self-defense against racist violence in the South as well as the North, and denounced black leaders who counseled otherwise.

Harrison made three especially noteworthy contributions to the Afro-American socialist tradition he inherited. First, to him must be attributed the development of not only a secular, but anti-clerical, black socialist political culture in the United States. He effected a sharp break with the Christian Socialist tradition begun by Peter Clark and so ably developed by Woodbey and Slater. (Creditable though it may be intellectually, as I shall argue, this aggressive atheism was, at best, a dubious political distinction.) Harrison was forthright in his condemnation of Christianity and religion in general. He was perplexed and disappointed by the absence of a free-thought tradition among Afro-Americans, especially the intelligentsia. In a 1914 article first published in the *Truth Seeker*, a freethought and agnostic newspaper, he acknowledged that there were "a few" black agnostics in New York and Boston, but these were generally from the Caribbean. He particularly noted the prominence of Puerto Rican and Cuban cigar-makers—"notorious Infidels," he affectionately called them—among their number. Here and there, he said, "one finds a Negro-American who is reputed to have Agnostic tendencies; but these are seldom, if ever, avowed." Harrison expressed sympathy for their predicament. "I can hardly find it in my heart," he wrote, "to blame them, for I know the tremendous weight of the social proscription which it is possible to bring to bear upon those who dare defy the idols of our tribe. For those who live by the people must needs be careful of the people's gods."[97] This recognition of the problem did not stop him, however, from attacking religion in the most ferocious terms. He invoked Nietzsche's contention that "the ethics of Christianity are the slave's ethics." "Show me a population that is deeply religious," Harrison declared, "and I will show you a servile population, content with whips and chains, contumely and the gibbet, content to eat the bread of sorrow and drink the waters of affliction. The present condition of the Negroes of America is a touching bit of testimony to the truth of this assertion."[98]

Second, unlike Clark, Woodbey and Slater who were all somewhat pacifist, repeatedly counseled against the use of violence, and had an elevated view of the efficacy of the vote, Harrison advocated the use of violence on the part of black people, if only in self-defense. Like Fortune before him and Malcolm X two generations later, he did not believe in turning the other cheek. Harrison made his views known in no uncertain terms in the aftermath of the East St. Louis Massacre. On July 2, 1917, scores, if not hundreds, of black people—men, women, children (including little babies)— were wantonly murdered, largely by white workers and members of the police force in an extraordinarily savage orgy of violence.[99] Harrison was so enraged by the "Horror of East St. Louis," as the event was commonly dubbed by Afro-America, and so vociferous in his advocacy of armed self-defense on the part of black people that the Department of Justice sought his deportation. In the very first issue of his magazine, the *Voice*, published on July 4, 1917, a mere two days after the events, Harrison declared: "If white men are to kill unoffending Negroes, Negroes must kill white men in defense of their lives and property. This is the lesson of the East St. Louis massacre."[100] The editor of the *New York Age*, the city's oldest black newspaper, told an interviewer that "The representative Negro does not approve of radical socialistic outbursts, such as calling upon the Negroes to defend themselves against the whites." He condemned Harrison, though not by name, in an *Age* editorial. Harrison responded, noting that such "cringing," "lickspittle," "conspicuous and contemptible cowardice" will avail Afro-Americans nothing but more attacks. He pointed out that where the mob in East St. Louis found black people "organized and armed, *they turned back.*"[101] "When murder is cheap," Harrison observed, "murder is indulged in recklessly; when it is likely to be costly it is not so readily indulged in." He went on:

> Will *The Age* venture to deny this? No? Then we say, let Negroes help make murder costly, for by so doing they will aid the officers of the city, state and nation in instilling respect for law and order into the minds of the worst and lowest elements of our American cities. And we go further: We say that it is not alone the brutality of the whites—it is also the cowardice of Negroes and the lickspittle leadership of the last two decades which, like *The Age*, told us to "take it lying down"—it is this which has been the main reason for our "bein' so aisily lynched," as Mr. Dooley puts it. . . . We are aiming at the white man's respect—not at his sympathy.[102]

Harrison made a third and very significant contribution to the black socialist tradition. It is this: he was the first black member of an American Socialist organization (the Socialist Party in his case) to publicly criticize its racism while he was still a member. Others, from Clark to Du Bois voiced their criticisms publicly only after they had left. Despite its bold and militant stance you will look in vain in the pages of the *Messenger* for any criticism of the Socialist Party. Indeed, Harrison felt that Randolph and Owen—"lackeys," he called them—were guilty of misleading their black readers in not criticizing the racism of the Socialist Party.[103] Well before he finally gave up on the Socialist Party, Harrison was at war with "Southernism" that corrupted the politics of the party's leadership. While Woodbey, Slater, Randolph and Owen confined their work to winning black adherents to the Socialist Party, Harrison concentrated his effort on making the party a suitable, worthy and welcoming political home for black people. While Woodbey, Slater and Randolph and Owen wrote frequently on "Why the Negro Should Vote the Socialist Ticket," Harrison was the only one to pen articles about "The Duty of the Socialist Party," to Afro-Americans.[104] From the 1920s on, Briggs, Moore, Harry Haywood and Otto Huiswoud would raise similarly pointed questions about the internal health of the Communist Party in relation to Afro-Americans.

Harrison, then, was the great pioneer and others followed in his footsteps. At the height of their radicalism, nothing appeared in the *Messenger* and the *Crusader* that had not been prefigured and articulated by Harrison. The antithetical relationship between the interest of black people and that of capital; Christianity as a backward and imprisoning superstition; the power of scientific analysis; the need for a non-parochial and internationalist outlook; the need for black people to meet force with force; the necessity to abandon the old leadership and replace it with that of the New Negro—all these positions articulated by Harrison became the stock-in-trade of the black Left. Harrison died unexpectedly and young in 1927, but his organizational, if not his intellectual and political influence, had diminished years before with the rise of Garvey.

Why were these black men and women attracted to Marxism? They were—from Peter Clark in the 1870s to William Patterson in the 1970s—attracted to it because they saw the ideology as, first and foremost, a means of solving the race problem. As black people were, as Slater put it, "almost to a man . . . of the working class,"[105] it made sense for them to support the ideology and the party that fought for and defended the interest of the working class. The race stood to benefit from the general emancipation of the class. Randolph and Owen perhaps put it best:

> Socialism is the political party of the working people. Now 99 percent of the Negroes are working people, so they should join the working people's party. The Republican party is the party of monopoly, big business and wealth. It represents plutocracy. Negro plutocrats should belong to the

Republican party, but Negro working people should join and support the workingmen's party. That is the Socialist party in all countries.[106]

After 1917, many were drawn to revolutionary socialism through the res-onant anti-colonialism and anti-imperialism of the Bolsheviks and the Communist International. The Bolsheviks handling of the "national ques-tion," and especially the "Jewish question," at least up to the rise of Stalin, also attracted Afro-American adherents. Bolshevik anti-colonialism was the major force that brought Cyril Briggs over to Marxism; and he was not the only one to make the journey to Marxism via Moscow and the Comintern.[107]

The membership of black Left organizations, such as the ABB, and the presence of black people in predominantly white left-wing organizations during these years was small, but the influence of black socialists was con-siderable. Through the written and spoken word, black socialists reached and influenced large numbers of Afro-Americans.

It is difficult to gauge with any precision the circulation of the radical magazines put out by the black Left. Randolph claimed that the *Messenger* reached a peak circulation of 33,000 per issue. But the correct figure is per-haps nearer 26,000.[108] Cyril Briggs, more likely than not, exaggerated too when he claimed that the *Crusader* had reached a peak of 36,000; a New York State Senate inquiry estimated a circulation of 4,000 for April 1920.[109] The true figure is perhaps nearer 20,000 at the peak of its popularity. The *Emancipator* is estimated to have had a circulation of 10,000 at one time, and William Bridges's *Challenge*, 6,000.[110] Frederick Detweiler, in his 1922 study, *The Negro Press in the United States*, conservatively estimated that each copy of these publications was read by at least five people.[111] These magazines, especially the *Messenger* and the *Crusader*, were widely distrib-uted, but circulated more readily in the North and West than they did in the South. In 1922, Owen gave a detailed breakdown of the stores in vari-ous cities that ordered the *Messenger* and the numbers they took. Briggs told a historian that the *Crusader* "reached many Negro communities throughout the country," and that in fact the ABB recruited most of its members through the magazine.[112] These publications were also available in many college and university libraries. Thus it is reasonable to assume that hundreds of thousands of black readers were exposed to the ideas of the black Left through their organs.

But the radicals did not only write, they also spoke, and spoke elo-quently. Harlem was the central site of radical oratory and the gospel of socialism addressed to Afro-America. Professor Kelly Miller, a follower of Booker T. Washington, complained that during the First World War "Harlem was filled with street preachers and flamboyant orators haranguing the people from morning till night upon Negro rights and wrongs." The Justice Department intelligence reports bear eloquent testimony to this and to the large crowds that gathered to listen.[113] Among these were the black socialists—Harrison, Randolph, Owen, Moore, Domingo, Bridges, Otto Huiswoud, Grace Campbell, Anna Brown, Elizabeth Hendrickson, Tom Potter, Frank Crosswaith and a host of others. But the preaching was not confined to Harlem. The radicals traveled widely across the country and addressed black people and white sympathizers in various states; Huiswoud and Moore on behalf of the African Blood Brotherhood and later the Communist Party; Randolph, Owen and Crosswaith on behalf of the Socialist Party.[114] Their socialist message reached tens, perhaps hundreds, of thousands of Afro-Americans during these decades through the spoken word alone.

Who were the black readers of the black socialist publications? Speaking of the *Messenger*, the most widely circulated of the black socialist magazines, Charles Johnson claimed that "it cannot be said that the socialistic principles made any considerable headway, or that it reached as many Negro workers as it did merely restless Negroes of all stations." In a similar vein, Jervis Anderson suggested that the black readership was "mainly among the lower-middle-class intelligentsia, since the bulk of the masses were by then reading Marcus Garvey's *Negro World*." Spero and Harris went so far as to suggest that the *Messenger*, as early as 1918, directed its appeal at "enlisting the support of the middle-class Negro."[115] There is some truth in all of these statements. But the evidence also suggests that they all underestimated the extent to which the *Messenger* and similar journals reached ordinary black workers. In 1921 alone, the Marine Transport Workers Industrial Union of Philadelphia, aligned to the IWW, with over 60 percent black membership at the time, contributed $1,200 to the magazine and purchased 3,600 copies for its members.[116] And in 1917, largely through the work of the *Messenger*, Randolph, Owen and other black members of the Socialist Party, Morris Hillquit, the party's mayoral candidate, won an estimated 25 percent of the Harlem vote. This was not solely or even largely attributable to black middle class support. (The Afro-American middle class at the time was still closely attached to the party of Lincoln.) When Randolph himself ran for New York state comptroller in 1920, he won 202,381 votes, only 1,000 votes less than that received in the state by Eugene Debs in his Presidential bid that year.[117] Most significantly, the formation of the Brotherhood of Sleeping Car Porters and the choice of Randolph to lead its fight came from the influence of the magazine upon a group of radical Pullman porters. Ashley Totten, the man who first approached Randolph in June 1925 seeking his help to form and lead a union of his fellow porters, had for many years been a keen reader of the *Messenger*, had listened to Randolph's soapbox speeches on the need for unionism among Afro-Americans, and was a great admirer of both magazine and man.[118] Totten was by no means the only *Messenger*-reading porter, and through the influence of the magazine and the porters' admiration for Randolph came the first large-scale unionization of Afro-Americans since the glory days of the IWW.[119]

Similarly, the African Blood Brotherhood, whose leaders by 1924 had joined the Workers' (Communist) Party of America, formed the organizing body around which the American Negro Labor Congress was formed in 1925. It took time to develop, but by the 1930s it had borne fruit, representing through its allied unions, thousands of black workers across the country.[120]

The influence of socialist magazines such as the *Messenger* on black youth and the rapidly expanding black population of students in general during this period is still in need of exploration and documentation.[121] But there is sufficient evidence already available to indicate that its influence was considerable. The 1920s was a period of great turbulence on black college campuses. The presidents of these schools were overwhelmingly white as was the faculty. Run with an admixture of paternalism and despotism, a new generation of black students refused to go along with the old ways. They protested against the curriculum, incompetent white teachers, their treatment as if they were children—when to get up, when lights are out. Claude McKay who arrived from Jamaica at Tuskegee in the late summer of 1912, left before courses began in the fall. He could not stand what he called the "semi-military, machinelike existence" there, so he left for Kansas State College. Ben Davis recalled the intellectually stultifying environment at Morehouse and resented the fact that "the methods of a kindergarten were being imposed upon grown men, some as old as faculty members." It was even worse at Hampton Institute, Virginia, where "All hell broke loose," on October 8, 1927, when the faculty insisted on keeping the lights on during a film show. They did not trust the young men with the young women in the darkened auditorium. Who knows what they could get up to?[122] At Howard University, a distinguished black professor,

Kelly Miller, was said to have been called "a black dog" by the college's white president, James Durkee. The *Messenger* and other journals, including the *Crisis*, intervened and fanned the flames of revolt.[123]

Writing in 1923, Abram Harris, an Afro-American student of Marxist political economy, reported that despite the hostility of the government and some middle class Afro-Americans towards the *Messenger*, Randolph and Owen had a following which comprised "some of the best trained minds in the race." Some of these, said Harris, "are to be found in the Northern and Southern Universities."[124] Harris, who in 1930 became the first Afro-American to receive a Ph.D. in economics from Columbia, was himself very much influenced by the radicalism of the early *Messenger* and was a great admirer of the magazine before it entered its reformist phase around 1923. The young E. Franklin Frazier, who would become America's most influential black sociologist, also fell under the magazine's spell, and went so far as to focus his 1920 master's thesis, "New Currents of Thought Among the Colored Population of America," around the arguments developed by Randolph and Owen in its pages. Like his friend Harris, he, too, was disappointed by the "petty bourgeois" turn of the magazine in the mid-twenties. In a 1928 article, Frazier noted that the *Messenger*, once the shining star of black radicalism, "is now no longer the spokesman of economic radicalism but has become an organ chiefly devoted to advertising negro enterprises and boosting black capitalists. Such," he lamented, "is the irony of fate."[125]

What many of the commentators did not realize at the time was that Chandler Owen's brother, Toussaint, a master tailor from Columbia, South Carolina had been encouraged by Chandler to come to New York after his business had failed. With strong connections to the socialist unions in New York's needle trades, Chandler was confident that his brother could find a job commensurate with his undoubted skills. Toussaint failed to find work in the needle trades. George Schuyler was only slightly off the mark when he remarked that the unions in the needle trades were "Jewish and Italian unions rather than labor unions." Toussaint died in March 1923, but the circumstances of his death remain unclear. Disillusioned, Owen left New York in 1923 on a speaking tour and never returned to the city. He left the Socialist Party, settled in Chicago and ran unsuccessfully for the Republican nomination for Congress in 1926. He subsequently worked in public relations for both the Democrats and Republicans in Chicago.[126] In 1925, Randolph also left the Socialist Party. "The Socialist Party," he said, explaining his withdrawal, "had no effective policy toward Negroes, and didn't spend enough time organizing them."[127] Randolph thereafter focused his energies in organizing the Brotherhood of Sleeping Car Porters. He remained a socialist for the rest of his life. The *Messenger* ceased publication in June 1928.[128]

The most vivid recollection of the profound impact that the *Messenger* had upon him as a black student, came from a young man who ran across the magazine at the height of its radicalism when he was a struggling, working-class and disillusioned youth studying law at the University of California, Berkeley. He wrote in his memoir, published more than five decades after the event:

> I read the *Messenger*, a magazine published in New York by two young Black radicals—A. Philip Randolph and Chandler Owen. I was stirred by its analyses of the source of Black oppression and the attempt to identify it with the international revolution against working-class oppression and colonialism. This was an enriching and exhilarating experience. For the first time I was being made aware that the study of society and the movement to change it constituted a science that had to be grasped if Black America was ever to attain equal rights.[129]

William L. Patterson spent the rest of his life in an unrelenting, costly and selfless fight on behalf of Afro-America and the working class. He became a distinguished lawyer and member of the Communist Party who drafted the historic petition to the United Nations, delivered by his comrade and friend, Paul Robeson, in 1951. The petition, outlining the dark deeds committed by the United States government against its African-descended citizens, was aptly titled *We Charge Genocide*.[130]

Given the historical record, then, David Levering Lewis's declaration that the *Messenger* "had an extremely modest impact in the Afro-American community," should not be taken seriously. He provides no evidence to support his claim, and informed contemporaries gave a contrary verdict. Abram Harris in his 1923 assessment regarded the impact as significant; five years later, E. Franklin Frazier, speaking of the black socialists around the *Messenger*, reported that their influence among Negroes was "strong"; James Weldon Johnson, one of the early black residents of Harlem and one of its keenest observers, writing in 1930 noted with particular reference to the *Messenger* and the *Challenge* that "These journals shook up the Negroes of New York and the country and effected some changes that have not been lost"; and Roi Ottley, Harlemite and Afro-American journalist, reported in his 1943 book that the *Messenger* was "influential."[131]

Of the black socialists who were politically formed during the two decades between 1910 and 1930, those of the African Blood Brotherhood wielded the greatest influence on left currents in America and upon unions aligned to the Communist Party during the 1930s and later. Otto Huiswoud, Cyril Briggs, Richard B. Moore, Lovett Fort-Whiteman, Otto Hall, Harry Haywood, Grace Campbell, were all to rise to prominence in the Party during the late 1920s and 1930s.[132] And they were instrumental in recruiting other black people into the CP, including members of the intelligentsia with whom they had some success especially during the 1930s. Thus William Patterson, who was radicalized by the Sacco and Vanzetti case, quickly moved to joining the Party under the influence of Richard B. Moore, Grace Campbell—"a magnificent Black woman," he called her— and Cyril Briggs. It was Briggs who sold him a copy of *The Communist Manifesto* at the offices of Patterson's Harlem law firm, Dyett, Hall and Patterson. "I want to suggest that you read this," Briggs told him. "It won't take anything from your law practice—it could add something to it." Patterson reported that after reading the volume, "A door opened for me." He was later handed a copy of Lenin's *State and Revolution* which proved to the lawyer that "the state was the organ of class rule."[133] Not long after, he joined the Party, and quickly rose to a leadership position. Thus the growth in influence of the Communist Party among Afro-Americans in the 1930s substantially issued out of the formation of the early black cadres, such as Briggs and Moore, and their efforts in the previous decades.

Black socialists, however, even in the 1930s, did not enjoy the level of influence in the Afro-American community that they had anticipated and striven for. They never came close to creating a following the size of that generated by Garvey and the UNIA in the 1920s. Black nationalism was a far more powerful magnet than the socialism advocated by the black radicals. Why was this so?

Black radicals turned to socialism not through any blind or facile idea of class loyalty per se, but through the double recognition of the racial and skewed class position of Afro-Americans. Socialism, in theory, draws no color line. Of course, in racist America, the practice was very different from the theory—and there was the rub. Unions blocked the entry of black workers into their ranks; socialist leaders, more often than not, espoused and practiced racism in their parties; the Socialist Party of America generally turned a blind eye to the racism of its members, especially those in the Southland.[134] Proletarian solidarity is fine in theory, but impossible when there is virulent racism.

The conventional riposte to black people advocating socialism in the United States is that the white working class is irremediably racist. It is a powerful one, but not entirely adequate. It is in fact ahistorical and undialectical. It is a response that issues from horrendous events such as the East St. Louis Massacre. But just as there was East St. Louis, so there were the radical wing of the Knights of Labor, the IWW, and the brave and principled white socialists in Oklahoma who stood shoulder to shoulder with Afro-Americans. The challenge for the historian is to the divine the laws of the conjunctures of solidarity and alliance, and conjunctures of dissolution and conflict. How may we systematically analyze what one historian has called the "crazy-quilt patterns of biracialism and hate"?[135] In other words, under what circumstances do cross-racial alliances develop and thrive? And under what circumstances do these alliances breakdown and antagonisms develop? These are difficult but important questions to address, but some historians have begun to address them, if only implicitly.[136]

In short, the lazy shorthand—the white working class is incurably racist —that passes itself off as analysis will not do. It cannot account for Timothy Quinn and District Assembly 49, Big Bill Haywood, Joe Hill and the Wobblies; it cannot account for the principled antiracism of Oscar Ameringer, who did splendid antiracist work among the Oklahoma Socialists; nor can it account for Elizabeth Gurley Flynn and Robert Minor in the Communist Party or for the later phase of Eugene Debs's life. One may respond by saying that these are aberrations in American history that need not detain us. But not only is such a response too easy, and too cheap, the fact is that there are *too many* aberrations of this kind, even in these racist United States, for them to be so lightly dismissed. We need, therefore, to explain them.

The early black radicals were not fools when they advocated socialism and sought cross-racial alliance among the proletariat. Nor were they naive, quixotic dreamers. They had fine minds, and certainly minds by no means inferior to those who accused them of foolishness. (From Peter Humphries Clark on, socialism has always attracted some of the brightest of the race.) They carefully read their conjuncture during and after the First World War. It was an historical moment filled with revolutionary promise—the impact of the war itself, revolution in Russia, Germany and Hungary, the Seattle and record mass strikes of 1919, the black energies released through the Great Migration, the revolutionary courage and actions of the Wobblies, Indian and Irish nationalisms—and this gave every sign of a world being turned upside down. They threw in their lot with the working class struggle because black people had undergone a forced and mass proletarianization (agrarian and urban) at the end of slavery. The mistake that they made—Harrison was the major exception here—was to not recognize early enough that the conjuncture had changed decisively by 1922 and that new tactics and strategies were called for; that Afro-Americans needed to aggregate as a people, to rely more heavily upon their own political resources, upon what they could do on their own, as the revolutionary tide turned, domestically and globally. After all, in 1921 Big Bill Haywood—the most principled and honorable leader the U.S. labor movement had ever produced—jumped bail and had fled the United States for Russia. For Haywood, especially given the ferocious repression of the Wobblies, the Statue of Liberty was a mockery. As his ship passed her, he cursed "the old hag": "Good-by[e], you've had your back turned on me too long. I am now going to the land of freedom."[137]

In short, after the high tide of 1919, the *annus mirabilis*, black nationalist projects were far more attractive to Afro-Americans and, I would say, far more viable than socialist ones. Because Garvey squandered the opportunity and resources of the UNIA on the Black Star Line, does not mean that options such as black co-operatives in the urban North could not have been pursued to ameliorate the condition and improve the economic and political prospects of Afro-Americans. Indeed, contrary to the commonly held view, the UNIA's economic activity was not confined to the Black Star Line endeavor. Under the Negro Factories Corporation, the primary economic arm of the movement, the UNIA in Harlem alone had by 1922: three grocery stores, two restaurants, a printing plant, a steam and electric laundry, a bakery and a millinery store. Located at 62 West 142nd Street, the Universal Mart of Industry, apart from the laundry, housed a number of other enterprises, including a Men's Manufacturing Department, which made UNIA uniforms, insignia, and the like; and a Women's Manufacturing Department and Bazaar, which made Black Cross Nurses' uniforms, shirts, ties and Panama hats.

Ulysses Poston, the UNIA's Minister of Labor and Industry, had overall responsibility for the Negro Factories Corporation, but it was J. Raymond Jones, his assistant, who carried out most of the everyday management of these enterprises. And it is Jones who provides the most authoritative and vivid portrait of these operations in his memoirs. Black Southern farmers sold their sweet yams and other farm produce directly to the UNIA, bypassing white middlemen and their greed; courageous defiance of Southern conventions, which Jones and Poston recognized could have cost these Southern members "economic reprisals at best and physical horror at worst." With similar audacity, some in Florida sold oranges and grapefruits to the organization. And from the Caribbean still others sold limes to the Negro Factories Corporation. On one occasion, two members in Georgia contacted UNIA headquarters and sought the Corporation's help in selling two rail tanks of molasses. Jones, who was by this time an avid reader of the *Journal of Commerce*, knew what to do and successfully disposed of the cargo for a good price to the American Molasses Company on Wall Street. Expenses were deducted and the money was sent to his happy UNIA brethren in Georgia. From Africa, farmers in Ghana sent word that they would like to sell their cocoa to the UNIA, thus bypassing the commodities sharks in London. The UNIA could not help, they had not the resources to do so.

Jones points out that with the exception of the Black Star Line and what he called "Mrs Garvey's clothing factory," all the enterprises were profitable—despite some difficulties, including Garvey's unwarranted and harmful interference. But with the imprisonment of Garvey in 1925, the infighting within the organization, the defection of members involved in the enterprises, the fall in confidence of suppliers, the Negro Factories Corporation declined and died.[138]

Jones leaves no doubt that the UNIA enterprises were viable, could have developed and continued to thrive had it not been for the crisis of 1925 within the organization. He conceded that there was a shortage of trained personnel, but despite that, the Corporation was viable and managed to make a profit up to at least 1925. In other words, contrary to the pessimism of scholars such as E. Franklin Frazier and Abram Harris about black enterprises at the time, Jones persuasively argued that they did and could succeed, especially given the collective, ideological underpinnings of an organization such as the UNIA.[139]

The ABB certainly believed that co-operatives could succeed and, no doubt inspired by the UNIA effort, seriously attempted to establish co-operatives in Harlem and elsewhere. But Briggs and his comrades in the ABB, unlike the Garveyites, lacked the necessary resources. In 1923, the ABB appealed to the Workers' Party for support to get the project off the ground, but the party refused and the idea was stillborn.[140] Strangely, the ABB never appealed directly to its members or the wider black population more generally for financial support to begin the black co-operative grocery store in Harlem that Briggs dreamed of.

There were other areas in which the black socialists made mistakes. As more and more racist blockages occurred in the Socialist and the Communist parties and trade unions, as the economic recession hit in the early twenties, political energies should have been more systematically diverted to projects of greater self-reliance and the establishment of black unions such as the Brotherhood of Sleeping Car Porters that Randolph helped to build in the late 1920s.

The black Left, especially that around the *Messenger*, severely wounded itself and diminished its effectiveness in reaching the mass of Afro-Americans through its unrelenting and generally indiscriminate attack upon religion in general and Christianity in particular. The *Messenger* denounced "pigmy-minded [*sic*] preachers who infect many of the Negro churches." A couple years earlier, in 1919, they wrote: "In the Negro Church, the ministers are largely ignorant, venal or controlled," adding in parentheses, "There are certain marked exceptions, of course."[141] But few took notice of the rider. They did not think highly of the spirituals, especially coming from Fisk, Hampton and Tuskegee, which they said, "served to instill the spirit of servility into Negro youths."[142] Even though they praised radical black ministers such as George Frazier Miller and Francis Grimké, and radical white ones such John Haynes Holmes and Charles Williams, the editors frankly declared, "we don't think very much of ministers." It was the mildest rebuke they uttered.[143]

In March 1919, the Rev. George Frazier Miller joined the *Messenger* as a contributing editor, but that did not attenuate the anti-religious language of the magazine. True, W. A. Domingo, who was still at the time editor of Garvey's *Negro World*, wrote a forceful article entitled "Socialism[:] The Negroes' Hope" in which he echoed the earlier sentiments of Woodbey and Slater on the relation between Christianity and socialism:

> Socialism as an economic doctrine is merely the pure Christianity preached by Jesus, and practiced by the early Christians adapted to the more complex conditions of modern life. It makes no distinction as to race, nationality or creed, but like Jesus it says "Come unto me all ye who are weary and heavy laden and I will give you rest." It is to procure that rest that millions of oppressed peoples are flocking to the scarlet banner of International Socialism.[144]

But this could hardly cancel out the impression left in the minds of the religious of Randolph's programmatic statement, "A New Crowd—A New Negro," in the previous issue. "In the church," Randolph wrote,

> the old crowd still preaches that "the meek will inherit the earth," "if the enemy strikes you on one side of the face, turn the other," and "you may take all this world but give me Jesus." "Dry Bones," "The Three Hebrew Children in the Fiery Furnace" and "Jonah in the Belly of the Whale," constitute the subjects of the Old Crowd, for black men and women who are over-worked and under-paid, lynched, jim-crowed and disfranchised —a people who are yet languishing in the dungeons of ignorance and superstition.[145]

In a 1919 editorial on Thanksgiving, the *Messenger* boldly declared: "We do not thank God for anything nor do our thanks include gratitude for which most persons usually give thanks at this period. With us we are thankful for different things and to a different Deity. Our Deity is the toiling masses of the world and the things for which we thank are their achievement."[146] Black Chicagoan Fenton Johnson, a radical himself, rightly dubbed those like Owen and Randolph as "extreme rationalists."[147]

But the editors of the *Messenger* were not alone. In a debate at the Harlem Community Church, Richard B. Moore expounded on the topic, "How I lost Jesus," in opposition to Rev. Ethelred Brown's "How I Found Jesus."[148] Claude McKay, one of the most militantly atheistic of his generation, declared in 1922 that "Karl Marx's economic theories are hard to digest, and the Negroes, like many other lazy-minded workers, may find it easier to put their faith in that other Jew, Jesus."[149] A year later another New Negro radical, Ulysses Poston who was associated with the UNIA and then the *Messenger*, lamented the "superior-religious consciousness" of the Negro. This consciousness has led to the belief that "the solution of his most minute problems is [to be] entrusted to God." According to Poston, this "false conception of God and religion has held back the negro in his attempts at material and political advancement. Such songs as 'You Can Take All the World, But Give Me Jesus' have had an unhealthy effect on the material progress of the negro." He accused black ministers of "commercializing this superior-religious consciousness." Poston in fact went on to denounce the sorrow songs and spirituals in general as "weird, unintelligent" and "detestable" music.[150]

Harrison, Randolph, Owen, McKay and others made the mistake—a mistake that Woodbey had vigorously warned against—of believing that because one is an atheist others had to be, too, in order to establish a movement for struggle. True, there were some backward and reactionary black church men and women who ought to have been criticized when they did harm. A quite legitimate target, and one attacked by the *Messenger*, was the black minister who before a large convention in Georgia in 1919, declared:

> Bolshevism was begotten in Germany, or that it is of German parentage, or that it was born in Russia, it took its name from a man named Bolsheviki, an insurrectionist or rioter, who raised an army to overthrow the recognized government of Russia. At that time the Government was tottering under the great blows of the German army. Bolsheviki thought that the time was ripe to establish new ideas and a new government that was somewhat after the idea of the Socialist. The definition or meaning of Bolshevism, as may be determined by research, is analogous to anarchy, the state of society where there is no law or supreme power, a state of lawlessness and general disorder. A condition where human life and property, human rights and justice, all that is noble and great [is] trampled under the feet of human beasts.[151]

But to make a bonfire of all black Christians with the incendiary language of Chandler Owen, a master of invective, was a major error that cost them dearly—and not only among the black working class, but large segments of the black intelligentsia, too.[152] Fenton Johnson was not the only contemporary to draw attention to the counterproductive, anti-religious dimension of the *Messenger*. Sterling Spero and Abram Harris thought that the black socialists' atheism was "most potent among the factors responsible for their failure." For, as they noted in 1931, "few Negroes were then or are today tolerant of atheism. . . . [A]ny Negro movement which rests upon a social theory strongly tinged with atheism is not likely to receive large support from Negroes."[153] Strictly speaking, however, it was not the atheism of the radicals that repelled black people; it was the fact that it was arrogantly and gratuitously flaunted in the faces of the religious. The Communist Party, even during its Popular Front phase, encountered difficulty in recruiting and, especially, retaining black members because of its secular worldview.[154]

Garvey made no such error, partly because he was himself a believer. He appropriated the symbols of Christianity and turned them black. Garvey did not banish Jesus; he canonized him as the Black Man of Sorrows. He did not reject God, but worshipped the God of Ethiopia: he called upon his followers to worship God, as he put it, "through the spectacles of Ethiopia."[155] It resonated with, rather than alienated his Afro-American supporters and won new followers to the UNIA.

The black socialists had formidable structural obstacles to overcome in their attempts to win over black workers. One was the fact that the overwhelming majority of the black population still lived in the South and it became increasingly difficult and dangerous to carry out political work there. Socialists, black and white, encountered the double tyranny of racist white workers and white capitalists, along with the vehement objection of many of the small and besieged Afro-American middle class, who understandably, sought a quiet life.

On top of this, many Afro-Americans were confined to atomized and isolating service jobs such as domestic work, which made it difficult to develop a trade union consciousness and even more difficult to put such ideas into practice. How does one, for instance, strike effectively as a domestic servant?[156] Randolph managed, after a titanic struggle, to succeed in organizing the Pullman porters, not only because discontent among them was widespread in the mid 1920s, but because they were all employed by one and the same company. And this structural condition helped the porters, albeit after protracted struggle, to prevail during the New Deal period.

Although Hubert Harrison and the *Messenger* were fervent supporters of women's suffrage, the black socialists had relatively few women among them prior to the Great Depression. It is not entirely clear why this should have been so, but the fact that both the *Messenger* and the *Crusader* failed to address the specific plight of black women probably contributed to the dearth of female members. The black socialist men seemed to have held a position on the woman question similar to that held by the white socialists on the Negro Question: they had nothing special to offer black women; socialism would solve the problem of black women as it would that of black men. Nevertheless, there was one prominent black woman among the black socialists, Grace Campbell, one of the leaders of the African Blood Brotherhood and one of the early black members of the Communist Party. She ran on the Socialist Party ticket for the New York state assembly in 1919 and 1920, but by 1922 she had joined the Workers' (Communist) Party.[157] She tried to win black women over to socialism in the 1920s, but with limited success. In 1921, according to a Justice Department intelligence report, Campbell was "conducting an active campaign among the colored women, but so far is unsuccessful as these women are not at all interested in Socialism and don't care to learn."[158] There were, however, other distinguished black women in the socialist movement in the 1920s, most notably Elizabeth Hendrickson, a distinguished Harlem orator, and Lucille Randolph, A. Philip Randolph's wife.[159] The major breakthrough in the recruitment of black women to the socialist cause occurred in the 1930s with the defection of former Garveyite Audley Moore (later known as Queen Mother Moore) to the Communist Party and the emergence of the younger generation of black women, including Claudia Jones and Louise Thompson Patterson.[160]

Once again, the Garveyites were more successful than the socialists. Not only in absolute terms, but proportionately, the UNIA attracted more women, had more in leadership positions and retained them longer. And when Amy Jacques Garvey had her women's page in the *Negro World* between 1924 and 1927, the specific problems of women were given much greater attention and more effectively addressed than they ever were in any of the black socialist publications of the time.[161] In fact, apart from its vigorous campaign for women's suffrage, there is virtually nothing on women in the pages of the *Messenger* and even less in the *Crusader*.

Probably the greatest structural obstacle to the work of the black socialists was the pervasive racism within the labor movement. It was difficult to persuade black workers that white workers were their natural class allies given the chauvinism of the white working class, which too often manifested itself in bloody pogroms such as that of East St. Louis. Like their white counterparts, the black socialists typically conceptualized the working class as an abstraction: a class opposed to capital, that would transcend its artificial divisions, that would be conscious of its long-term interests, and would pursue them without regard to race. The real working class was quite different. It was overwhelmingly white, short-sighted, and the majority of its members with whom Afro-Americans came into contact were Southerners. Moreover, it was typically racist and mean-spirited—bent on keeping the crumbs from the table of capital to its white self. In short, the white working class of whom Randolph and Owen spoke and wrote were, alas, not the ones that Afro-Americans encountered in their everyday life in Chicago, Detroit, Birmingham, Atlanta or Boston. True, there were pockets of those who approximated to the *Messenger* model—most notably the Wobblies, whom Randolph and Owen praised and encouraged— but they were relatively small in number and diminished during the 1920s due to the ferocious repression by the bosses and the state. The problem of cross-racial alliance was compounded further by the fact that, on the rare occasions when white workers extended the hand of friendship they were frequently distrusted by black workers. Moreover, black workers realized that engagement in radical movements could be costly, and was indeed dangerous. Thus, the young Harry Haywood was rebuffed when he sought to recruit his progressive black friend, a postal worker in Chicago, to the Young Communist League. "I'm sorry, [Haywood]," said his friend, "but I find being Black trouble enough, but to be Black and red at the same time, well that's just double trouble, and when you mix in the whites, why that's triple trouble." In the course of the exchange, Haywood accused his friend of being a "racialist who saw everything in terms of Black and white." "Why not," he replied. "Being a Negro, how else should I see things?" What made matters even more perplexing for Haywood, was the fact that his friend was a socialist, who nevertheless "would not put it beyond the whites . . . to distort socialism in a manner in which they could remain top dogs." Black people, Haywood's friend felt, had to remain vigilant and operate under their own leadership and organization. The whites simply could not be trusted.[162]

Within such a context, then, the work of black socialists was virtually impossible, and this was especially so when even leading members of the ostensibly socialist movement were themselves racists or did little or nothing to counter the chauvinism of their followers.

Little wonder, then, that Garvey and the UNIA did so much better in their recruitment than the black socialists. Garvey's worldview corresponded with the commonsensical experience of the black working class. Garvey did not see a white working class as such; he saw white men who were determined to keep all the good things of this world to themselves. The disillusioned Harrison who had left the socialist movement in 1914 and later supported the UNIA, put the black nationalist position best: "We say Race First, because you [the white socialists] have all along insisted on Race First and class after."

> Any man today who aspires to lead the Negro race must set squarely before his face the idea of "Race First." Just as the white men of these and other lands are white men before they are Christians, Anglo-Saxons or Republicans; so the Negroes of this and other lands are intent upon being Negroes before they are Christians, Englishmen, or Republicans.
>
> Sauce for the goose is sauce for the gander. Charity begins at home, and our first duty is to ourselves. It is not what we wish but what we must, that we are concerned with. The world, as it ought to be, is still for us, as for

others, the world that does not exist. The world as it is, is the real world, and it is to that real world that we address ourselves.[163]

Harrison did not live to see it, but the Depression of the 1930s rearranged the political landscape—this time even more profoundly than the Great War had done—which improved the conditions for cross-racial class alliances. The pressure of the Communist International, especially the resolution of its 6th Congress in 1928, placed the American CP in a position where it had to give greater attention and priority to the Negro Question. This gave black comrades such as Briggs, Huiswoud, Haywood and Moore (who had been fighting white chauvinism in the party for years) and their white allies within the party greater power to effect changes in key areas. The attention paid by the CP to the Scottsboro case and black Southern workers came from a combination of favorable domestic conditions and pressure from Moscow.[164]

The cold war, McCarthyism and structural changes within the American economy in the postwar years would significantly diminish, truncate and, indeed, reverse many of the gains made by black socialists in the 1930s.

To conclude: Peter Humphries Clark and the black socialists of the first three decades of the twentieth century struggled against formidable odds. They dealt with difficult and still unresolved problems and questions. Most significantly, they wrestled with the question of the relation between race and class in a racist society in which the proportion of the population made up of black people was (and is) relatively small. How can a small, economically weak, racialized and maligned group—turned into a "minority" through the gerrymandered aggregation of Euro-Americans, and overwhelmingly proletarianized—how can such a group organize to defend its interests? Can it pursue its demands and defend itself without making alliances? Can alliances be made if one is rebuffed by those with whom one seeks to align? In Ghana the Asante say that one can't clap with one hand. Do Afro-Americans have to learn how to clap with one hand? Is it possible to do so? Is it desirable? Are the prospects for alliance better today than they were in the time of the *Messenger*? Is it possible or desirable to make alliances when Afro-America itself is not politically organized as a group? What are the internal obstacles to Afro-America's advancement, how may they be overcome?

Randolph, Owen, Moore, Campbell, Domingo, Huiswoud, Harry Haywood and other black socialists struggled with such questions. They answered the questions in one way, and a few of them answered the questions differently over time. Garvey and the black nationalists answered such questions in a radically different manner—and asked different ones too. The UNIA gained mass support; the black socialists did not.

But as we have seen, despite the difficulty of their political project, the black socialists won support, and perhaps to an extent greater than one should have expected. In fact, their influence was considerable, especially among sectors of the black intelligentsia, but not only there. The black socialists made some gains, but suffered many defeats, some self-inflicted. They nevertheless, richly deserve our respect and appreciation for they struggled not just for themselves and their oppressed contemporaries, but also to make the world a more decent place for us and all the oppressed and exploited. Despite their courage and great personal sacrifice, they have been largely ignored, unremembered and uncelebrated. But even when we do not recognize it, the line of continuity between their struggles and those of the later period is strong and discernible. Interviewed in 1969, the high noon of the Black Power movement, the eighty-year-old Randolph said "I *love* the young black militants." But he also complained that he was "greatly concerned about the lack of historical knowledge on the part of some of [them]." The old man displayed a remarkably Olympian overview of the links between the different periods and phases of the black struggle:

> We are creatures of history . . . for every historical epoch has its roots in a preceding epoch. The black militants of today are standing upon the shoulders of the "[N]ew Negro radicals" of my day—the '20s, '30s and '40s. We stood upon the shoulders of the civil rights fighters of the Reconstruction era and they stood upon the shoulders of the black abolitionists. These are the interconnections of history and they play their role in the course of development.[165]

NOTES

1. By socialists I mean anti-capitalists, whether in the Socialist Party, the Communist Party or the Industrial Workers of the World (IWW). The IWW membership comprised socialists as well as anarcho-syndicalists. For present purposes I will ignore the finer distinctions between socialists and anarcho-syndicalists because both groups were committed anti-capitalists. In what follows, when *Socialist* is written with a capital "S", it refers as a noun to a member of the Socialist Party, and as an adjective it pertains to the Socialist Party. Uncapitalized, *socialist* refers generically to anti-capitalists and their activities.

2. See, in particular, Mark Naison, *Communists in Harlem During the Depression* (Urbana: University of Illinois Press, 1983); Mark I. Solomon, *Red and Black: Communism and Afro-Americans, 1925–1935* (New York: Garland Publishing, Inc., 1988) idem., *The Cry Was Unity: Communists and African Americans, 1917–1936* (Jackson: University of Mississippi, 1998); and Robin Kelley, *Hammer and Hoe: Alabama Communists During the Great Depression* (Chapel Hill: University of North Carolina Press, 1990).

3. Philip Foner, *American Socialism and Black Americans: From the Age of Jackson to World War II* (Westport: Greenwood Press, 1977); idem., ed., *Black Socialist Preacher: The Teachings of Reverend George Washington Woodbey and his Disciple, Reverend G. W. Slater, Jr.* (San Francisco: Synthesis Publications, 1983), hereafter referred to as *Black Socialist Preacher*; Jervis Anderson, *A. Philip Randolph: A Biographical Portrait* (1972; Berkeley: University of California Press, 1986); Theodore Kornweibel, *No Crystal Stair: Black Life and the* Messenger, *1917–1928* (Westport: Greenwood Press, 1975), and Winston James, *Holding Aloft the Banner of Ethiopia: Caribbean Radicalism in Early Twentieth-Century America* (New York: Verso, 1998). See also Henry Williams's interesting but rather tendentious monograph, *Black Response to the American Left: 1917–1929* (Princeton: History Department, 1973).

4. See James, *Holding Aloft the Banner of Ethiopia*, esp. pp. 155–82.

5. James, *Holding Aloft the Banner of Ethiopia*.

6. "Peter Humphries Clark," *Cleveland Gazette*, March 6, 1886. In a brief 1942 biographical sketch of Clark, Dovie King Clark asserts that William Clark, partner of Meriwether Lewis on what became know as the Lewis and Clark Expedition of 1804, was Peter Clark's grandfather. This has been repeated ever since in biographical profiles of Clark. But the connection is questionable: Clark himself never made this claim, nor did any of the many statements about him prior to that of Dovie King Clark's. Furthermore, the *Cleveland Gazette*'s profile of 1886, the first major one of the nineteenth century, which claimed that the family moved to Ohio in 1817 was never contradicted by Clark himself, which goes against King Clark's assertion that William Clark moved Clark's grandmother and her children across the Ohio River in 1804 before embarking on his expedition. Dovie King Clark, "Peter Humphries Clark," *Negro History Bulletin*, May 1942, p. 176. Lawrence Grossman who has written the most detailed profile of Clark also questions the William Clark connection. David Gerber, subscribes to the King Clark thesis but like King Clark, does not provide any supporting evidence for the new genealogy. Philip Foner and Paul McStallworth also endorse the William Clark ancestry. See Lawrence Grossman, "In His Veins Coursed No Bootlicking Blood: The Career of Peter H. Clark," *Ohio History*, vol. 86, no. 2, Spring 1977, pp. 79–95; David Gerber, "Peter Humphries Clark: The Dialogue of Hope and Despair," in Leon Litwack and August Meier, eds., *Black Leaders of the Nineteenth Century* (Urbana: University of Illinois Press, 1988), pp. 173–90; Foner, *American Socialism and Black Americans*, p. 45, and Paul McStallworth, "Peter Humphries Clark," in Rayford Logan and

Michael Winston, *Dictionary of American Negro Biography* (New York: W. W. Norton, 1982), p. 114. Also see, William Wells Brown, *The Rising Son; or, The Antecedents and Advancement of the Colored Race* (Boston: A. G. Brown & Co., 1874), pp. 522–24; William J. Simmons, *Men of Mark: Eminent, Progressive and Rising* (Cleveland: Geo. M. Rowell & Co., 1887), p. 244–49; I. Garland Penn, *The Afro-American Press, and its Editors* (Springfield: Willey & Co., 1891), pp. 76–78; Wendell P. Dabney, *Cincinnati's Colored Citizens: Historical, Sociological and Biographical* (Cincinnati: Dabney Publishing Company, 1926), pp. 103–08, and 114.

7. Quoted in Dabney, *Cincinnati's Colored Citizens*, p. 103.

8. Dabney, *Cincinnati's Colored Citizens*, pp. 103–05; Grossman, "In His Veins Coursed No Bootlicking Blood," p. 80; Carter G. Woodson, "The Negroes of Cincinnati Prior to the Civil War," *Journal of Negro History*, vol. 1, no. 1, January 1916, pp. 19–20; Foner, *American Socialism and Black Americans*, p. 46; Foner also reported that Hiram Gilmore was a utopian socialist and that his ideology may have influenced Gilmore's students (p. 375).

9. "Peter Humphries Clark," *Cleveland Gazette*, March 6, 1886. For more on the proscriptions against black men entering the skilled trades in the city, see Woodson, "Negroes of Cincinnati," pp. 5–6; David Gerber, *Black Ohio and the Color Line, 1860–1915* (Urbana: University of Illinois Press, 1976), pp. 5–7; idem., "Peter Humphries Clark," pp. 176–77; and Joe William Trotter, *River Jordan: African American Urban Life in the Ohio Valley* (Lexington: University of Kentucky Press, 1998), pp. 27 and 29.

10. "Peter Humphries Clark," *Cleveland Gazette*, March 6, 1886; Simmons, *Men of Mark*, p. 244; Grossman, "In His Veins Coursed no Bootlicking Blood," p. 81.

11. Simmons, *Men of Mark*, p. 245.

12. Dabney, *Cincinnati's Colored Citizens*, pp. 105–106; Grossman, "In His Veins Coursed No Bootlicking Blood," p. 81.

13. The best analysis of the Compromise of 1850 of which the Fugitive Slave Law was an important and most controversial component is Holman Hamilton, *Prologue to Conflict: The Crisis and Compromise of 1850* ([Lexington]: University of Kentucky Press, 1964).

14. Peter H. Clark to the American Colonization Society, September 17, 1850, reprinted in "Letters to the American Colonization Society (Part 5)," *Journal of Negro History*, vol. 10, no. 2, April 1925, pp. 285–286.

15. *Cleveland Gazette*, March 6, 1886; Gerber, "Peter Humphries Clark," p. 178.

16. Dabney, *Cincinnati's Colored Citizens*, p. 106.

17. *Cleveland Gazette*, March 6, 1886; Simmons, *Men of Mark*, pp. 245–246; Wells Brown, *Rising Son*, p. 523; Floyd Miller, *The Search for a Black Nationality: Black Emigration and Colonization, 1787–1863* (Urbana: University of Illinois Press, 1975), p. 158; Howard Bell, ed., *Minutes of the Proceedings of the National Negro Conventions, 1830–1864* (New York: Arno Press, 1969).

18. Waldo Martin's *The Mind of Frederick Douglass* (Chapel Hill: University of

North Carolina Press, 1984), esp. chap. 3, remains the best analysis of Douglass's politics.

19. Foner, *American Socialism*, pp. 48–9. The details of Clark's political biography are drawn from Simmons, *Men of Mark*, pp. 244–49; Herbert Gutman, "Peter H. Clark: Pioneer Negro Socialist, 1877," *Journal of Negro Education*, vol. 34, no. 4, Fall 1965; Foner, *American Socialism*, pp. 43–60; McStallworth, "Peter Humphries Clark"; Grossman, "In His Veins Coursed no Bootlicking Blood"; Gerber, "Peter Humphries Clark" among others. Foner, however, provides the most detailed account of Clark's socialist politics.

20. Foner, *American Socialism*, p. 49; Gutman, "Peter H. Clark," p. 414.

21. Robert Bruce, *1877: Year of Violence* (1959; Chicago: Quadrangle, 1970), esp. p. 19.

22. Clark's speech was printed in its entirety in the *Cincinnati Commercial*, July 23, 1877, under the heading: "Socialism: The Remedy for the Evils of Society." It has been partially reprinted in Gutman, "Peter H. Clark," pp. 415–18; and in its entirety in Philip Foner and Robert James Branham, eds., *Lift Every Voice: African American Oratory, 1787–1900* (Tuscaloosa: University of Alabama Press, 1998), pp. 581–86.

23. *Emancipator*, July 28, 1877, quoted in Foner, *American Socialism and Black Americans*, p. 51.

24. Quoted in Foner, *American Socialism*, p. 56.

25. Gerber, *Black Ohio and the Color Line*, p. 233; Foner, *American Socialism*, p. 59.

26. Quoted in Grossman, "In His Veins Coursed no Bootlicking Blood," p. 90.

27. See, *Cleveland Gazette*, especially, March 29, and September 13, 1884; June 26, and July 3, 1886. Smith would himself become impatient with the Republican Party, but his defection occurred many years later in the 1920s. Kenneth Kusmer, *A Ghetto Takes Shape: Black Cleveland, 1870–1930* (Urbana: University of Illinois Press, 1976), pp. 240–43.

28. Dabney, *Cincinnati's Colored Citizens*, p. 114.

29. Similar defections to the Democrats were taking place elsewhere in the North. See August Meier, *Negro Thought in America, 1880–1915: Racial Ideologies in the Age of Booker T. Washington* (Ann Arbor: University of Michigan Press, 1963), chap. 2; Lawrence Grossman, *The Democratic Party and the Negro: Northern and National Politics, 1868–92* (Urbana: University of Illinois Press, 1976).

30. Woodson, "Negroes of Cincinnati Prior to the Civil War," esp. pp. 2–6; Richard Wade, "The Negro in Cincinnati, 1800–1830," *Journal of Negro History*, vol. 39, no. 1, January 1954; Gerber, *Black Ohio and the Color Line*, pp. 3–5.

31. Grossman, "In His Veins Coursed No Bootlicking Blood," pp. 91–93; Gerber, *Black Ohio and the Color Line*, chap. 8; idem., "Peter Humphries Clark," pp. 187–190.

32. Foner, *American Socialism and Black Americans*, pp. 59–60.

33. *Dayton Herald*, September 26, 1873, quoted in Grossman, "In His Veins

Coursed No Bootlicking Blood," pp. 94–96; also see Gerber, "Peter Humphries Clark," p. 173.

34. See Clark's letter to the *New York Freeman*, March 29, 1887, where he celebrated the victory of the black militants, the "kickers," in Ohio in bringing about reform.

35. For post-Reconstruction developments in the South see especially, C. Vann Woodward, *Origins of the New South, 1877–1913* (Baton Rouge: Louisiana State University Press, 1951); Rayford Logan, *The Negro in American Life and Thought: The Nadir, 1877–1901* (New York: Dial Press, 1954); Walter White, *Rope and Faggot: A Biography of Judge Lynch* (New York: Alfred Knopf, 1929); William Cohen, *At Freedom's Edge: Black Mobility and the Southern White Quest for Racial Control, 1861–1915* (Baton Rouge: Louisiana State University Press, 1991), esp. chaps. 8 and 9.

36. Grossman, "In His Veins Coursed No Bootlicking Blood," p. 94.

37. Clark to John W. Cromwell, December 21, 1901, reprinted in John W. Cromwell, *The Negro in American History: Men and Women Eminent in the Evolution of the American of African Descent* (Washington, D.C.: American Negro Academy, 1914), pp. 36–38; Paul Laurence Dunbar, "Douglass," in idem., *The Complete Poems of Paul Laurence Dunbar* (New York: Dodd, Mead & Co., 1922), p. 208. Dunbar, like Clark, was a native of Ohio.

38. Wells Brown, *The Rising Son*, p. 523; see also *Cleveland Gazette*, March 6, 1886, which sought to use Clark's small stature against him.

39. Dabney, *Cincinnati's Colored Citizens*, p. 114. For similar appraisals of Clark by black contemporaries, see also Wells Brown, *Rising Son*, pp. 522–524; Simmons, *Men of Mark*, pp. 246–247; Garland Penn, *Afro-American Press and Its Editors*, pp. 76–78.

40. Emma Lou Thornbrough, *T. Thomas Fortune: Militant Journalist* (Chicago: Chicago University Press, 1972); August Meier, *Negro Thought in America, 1880–1915: Racial Ideologies in the Age of Booker T. Washington* (Ann Arbor: University of Michigan Press, 1963). William Seraile, "The Political Views of Timothy Thomas Fortune: Father of Black Political Independence," *Afro-Americans in New York Life and History*, vol. 2, no. 2, July 1978; Jean Allman and David Roediger, "The Early Editorial Career of Timothy Thomas Fortune: Class, Nationalism and Consciousness of Africa," *Afro-Americans in New York Life and History*, vol. 6, no. 2, July 1982. There are also revealing sidelights on Fortune in Louis Harlan, *Booker T. Washington*, 2 vols. (New York: Oxford University Press, 1972 and 1982); Stephen Fox, *The Guardian of Boston: William Monroe Trotter* (New York: Atheneum, 1971); Tony Martin, *Race First: The Ideological and Organizational Struggles of Marcus Garvey and the Universal Negro Improvement Association* (Westport: Greenwood Press, 1976); and David Levering Lewis, *W. E. B. Du Bois: Biography of a Race, 1868–1919* (New York: Henry Holt, 1993).

41. Timothy Thomas Fortune, *Black and White: Land, Labor and Politics in the South* (1884; New York: Arno Press, 1968).

42. Fortune, *Black and White*, pp. 241–42; see also p. 174; emphasis in the original, as are all the others in Fortune's texts quoted below.

43. Fortune, *Black and White*, p. 131.

44. Fortune, *Black and White*, pp. 198–99.

45. Fortune, *Black and White*, pp. 239–40.

46. Fortune, *Black and White*, pp. 173–74; 147; 176; 157; 178.

47. Fortune, *Black and White*, pp. 151–52.

48. Fortune *Black and White*, chap. 13.

49. Fortune, *Black and White*, pp. 194–95.

50. Foner, *American Socialism and Black Americans*, p. 90. Meier and Rudwick make a similar mistake in their assessment of the book: August Meier, *Negro Thought in America*, p. 47; August Meier and Elliott Rudwick, "Attitudes of Negro Leaders Toward the American Labor Movement from the Civil War to World War I," in Julius Jacobson, *The Negro and the American Labor Movement* (New York: Anchor Books, 1968), p. 37. Likewise, in a thoughtful essay, Allman and Roediger, while acknowledging Fortune's "eclecticism" and describing the book as "complex and contradictory," still persist in arguing that the "most striking" feature of the book's "economic radicalism" is Fortune's "insistence that class and not race was the ultimate cause of oppression in America." Allman and Roediger, "The Early Editorial Career of Timothy Thomas Fortune," pp. 40–43. Seraile is nearer the mark when he noted that Fortune wrote *Black and White* and the *Negro in Politics* "to acquaint blacks with the need for independent political thinking." Seraile, "The Political Views of Timothy Thomas Fortune," p. 17.

51. New York *Freeman*, March 20, 1886. Fortune's friend, D. Augustus Straker, a distinguished black lawyer and an immigrant from Barbados, also voiced strong support for the Knights of Labor, and its anti-racist stance. See Straker, *The New South Investigated* (Detroit: Ferguson Printing Company, 1888), pp. 196–97.

52. Philip Foner, *Organized Labor and the Black Worker, 1619–1981* (New York: International Publishers, 1982), pp. 51–56. There were limits to the Knights of Labor egalitarian creed. Founded in 1869, women were not allowed to join until 1881 and they persisted in excluding Chinese workers, despite the efforts of the more radical members, including Frank J. Ferrell, a black Socialist from New York and one of the Knights' leading members. Ibid., p. 47.

53. Quoted in Thornbrough, *T. Thomas Fortune*, p. 81.

54. Fortune, *Black and White*, chap. 9; T. Thomas Fortune, *The Negro in Politics: Some Pertinent Reflections on the Past and Present Political Status of the Afro-American, Together with a Cursory Investigation into the Motives which Actuate Partisan Organizations* (New York: Ogilvie & Rowntree, Publishers, 1885). The copyright notice suggests that it was actually published in 1886.

55. Fortune, *The Negro in Politics*, pp. 8 and 12.

56. Fortune, *The Negro in Politics*, pp. 15–16.

57. Fortune, *Negro in Politics*, pp. 27–29.

58. Named after William Dunning, a former professor of History at Columbia, the Dunning School viewed Reconstruction as an error, a "tragedy," at best, in American history. See W. E. B. Du Bois, *Black Reconstruction in America: An Essay Toward a History of the Part which Black Folk Played in the Attempt to Reconstruct Democracy in America, 1860–1880* (1935; New York: Atheneum, 1969), chap. 17; and Eric Foner, "Reconstruction Revisited," *Reviews in American History*, vol. 10, no. 4, December 1982.

59. Fortune, *Black and White*, pp. 126–27; idem., *The Negro in Politics*, p. 58.

60. See Lawrence Grossman's excellent study of the subject, *The Democratic Party and the Negro*.

61. Nancy Weiss, *Farewell to the Party of Lincoln: Black Politics in the Age of FDR* (Princeton: Princeton University Press, 1983).

62. Allman and Roediger, "The Early Editorial career of Timothy Thomas Fortune," pp. 46–47; Thornbrough, *T. Thomas Fortune*, p. 107.

63. Foner, *American Socialism and Black Americans*, p. 91.

64. New York *Sun*, December 16, 1894.

65. New York *Age*, August 8, 1907.

66. New York *Sun*, October 13, 1895.

67. Fortune, *The Negro in Politics*, p. 38.

68. His most important writings, and those of Slater may be found in *Black Socialist Preacher*.

69. *Black Socialist Preacher*, p. 6.

70. Ibid., p. 201.

71. Ibid., p. 255.

72. Ibid., p. 35.

73. Ibid., pp. 27–28.

74. *Black Socialist Preacher*, p. 260.

75. Ibid., p. 261.

76. Ibid., p. 262.

77. Hubert Harrison, "How To Do It—And How Not," *New York Call*, December 16, 1911.

78. *Black Socialist Preacher*, p. 352.

79. *Black Socialist Preacher*, pp. 336 and 346.

80. *New York Call*, December 16, 1911.

81. Foner, *American Socialism and Black Americans*, pp. 64–65.

82. Foner, *American Socialism and Black Americans*, pp. 65–67.

83. Quoted in Foner, *Organized Labor and the Black Worker*, pp. 54–55.

84. New York *Freeman*, October 2, 1886; Cleveland *Gazette*, October 23, 1886.

85. Foner, *Organized Labor and the Black Worker*, pp. 53–56; idem., *American Socialism and Black Americans*, pp. 67–68.

86. Ira Kipnis, *The American Socialist Movement* (1952; New York: Greenwood Press, 1968), p. 130; R. Laurence Moore, "Flawed Fraternity—American Socialist

Response to the Negro, 1901–1912," *The Historian*, vol. 32, no. 1, November 1969, pp. 1–3 (where the text of the resolution and the omitted clause are reprinted); Foner, *American Socialism and Black Americans*, pp. 94–98.

87. Kipnis, *The American Socialist Movement*, p. 130; Moore, "Flawed Fraternity," p. 3.

88. See, for example, Eugene Debs, "The Negro and His Nemesis," *International Socialist Review*, vol. 4, no. 7, January 1904, which opened with an anonymous letter from a racist "Socialist," accusing Debs of advocating "social equality." "You get social and political equality for the Negro, then let him come and ask the hand of your daughter in marriage . . . and we will see whether you will still have a hankering for social and political equality for the Negro," wrote the correspondent (p. 391).

89. Eugene Debs, "The Negro in the Class Struggle," *International Socialist Review*, vol. 4, no. 5, November 1903, p. 260.

90. James Weinstein, *The Decline of Socialism in America, 1912–1925* (1967; Rutgers University Press, 1984), pp. 67–69; H. L. Meredith, "Agrarian Socialism and the Negro in Oklahoma, 1900–1918," *Labor History*, vol. 11, no. 3, Summer 1970; James R. Green, *Grass-Roots Socialism: Radical Movements in the Southwest, 1895–1943* (Baton Rouge: Louisiana State University Press, 1978), pp. 94–110; Foner, *American Socialism*, chap. 10. See also Charles Leinenweber, "The Class and Ethnic Bases of New York City Socialism, 1904–1915," *Labor History*, vol. 22, no. 1, Winter 1981, p. 47.

91. See in particular, Philip Foner, "The IWW and the Black Workers," *Journal of Negro History*, vol. lv, no. 1, January 1970; William Seraile, "Ben Fletcher, I. W. W. Organizer," *Pennsylvania History*, vol. xlvi, no. 3, July 1979; Lisa McGirr, "Black and White Longshoremen in the IWW: A History of the Philadelphia Marine Transport Workers Industria Union Local 8," *Labor History*, vol. 37, no. 3, Summer 1995; Peter Cole, "Shaping Up and Shipping Out: The Philadelphia Waterfront During and After the IWW Years, 1913–1940," Ph.D. diss., Georgetown University, 1997; Howard Kimeldorf, "Radical Possibilities? The Rise and Fall of Wobbly Unionism on the Philadelphia Docks," in Calvin Winslow, ed., *Waterfront Workers: New Perspectives on Race and Class* (Urbana: University of Illinois Press, 1998). The best general history of the IWW is Melvyn Dubofsky, *We Shall Be All: A History of the Industrial Workers of the World*, 2nd. ed. (Urbana: University of Illinois Press, 1988).

92. Weinstein, *The Decline of Socialism in America*, pp. 73–74; Dubofsky, *We Shall Be All*.

93. Harrison's career is discussed in James, *Holding Aloft*, esp. pp. 123–34, from which some of the details here are drawn, and Jeffrey Perry, "An Introduction to Hubert Harrison: 'The Father of Harlem Radicalism,'" *Souls*, vol. 2, no. 1, Winter 2000. Also see Perry's forthcoming study, *Hubert Henry Harrison: "The Father of Harlem Radicalism"* (Baton Rouge: Louisiana State University Press).

94. Some of Harrison's essays were published in two volumes: *The Negro and the Nation* (New York: Cosmo-Advocate Publishing Company, 1917), and *When*

Africa Awakes: The "Inside Story" of the Stirrings and Strivings of the New Negro in the Western World (New York: The Porro Press, 1920). Jeffrey Perry has recently edited a splendid collection of Harrison's writings: *A Hubert Harrison Reader* (Middletown, Conn.: Wesleyan University Press, 2001).

95. See "What Haywood says on Political Action," *International Socialist Review*, February 1913, pp. 622–23.

96. I can think of no native born Afro-American who espoused atheism or even agnosticism before Randolph and Owen in the *Messenger* magazine, founded in 1917. David Walker, Martin Delany, Frederick Douglass, T. Thomas Fortune, James Weldon Johnson—all professed a religious faith. Even the iconoclastic Du Bois began his 1920 volume, *Darkwater: Voices from Within the Veil* (New York: Schocken Books, 1969) with the first item of his Credo being: "I believe in God, who made of one blood all nations that on earth do dwell" (p. 3). Despite the many shifts in his ideology up to his death in 1963, there is no evidence to suggest that he lost his religious faith.

97. Harrison, *The Negro and the Nation*, pp. 45–46.

98. Ibid., p. 44.

99. Despite its problematic character, Elliott Rudwick's 1964 study still stands as the only full-scale analysis of the East St. Louis riot: *Race Riot at East St. Louis, July 2, 1917* (1964; Urbana: University of Illinois Press, 1982).

100. Harrison, *When Africa Awakes*, p. 15.

101. Ibid., p. 18; emphasis in original.

102. Ibid., pp. 18–19.

103. Harrison, *When Africa Awakes*, p. 81.

104. *New York Call*, December 13, 1911.

105. *Black Socialist Preacher*, p. 346.

106. *Messenger*, May-June 1919, p. 9.

107. See James, *Holding Aloft the Banner of Ethiopia*, esp. chap. 5.

108. *Messenger*, August 1919, p. 19; *Messenger*, April 1922, p. 390; Frederick Detweiler, *The Negro Press in the United States* (Chicago: University of Chicago Press, 1922), p. 171; Kornweibel, *No Crystal Stair*, p. 54.

109. Cyril Briggs to Theodore Draper, March 17, 1958, Theodore Draper Papers, Special Collections, Robert W. Woodruff Library, Emory University, Atlanta; *Revolutionary Radicalism: Its History, Purpose and Tactics With an Exposition and Discussion of the Steps Being Taken and Required to Curb it, Being the Report of the Joint Legislative Committee Investigating Seditious Activities. Filed April 24, 1920, in the Senate of the State of New York; Part I, Revolutionary and Subversive Movements Abroad and at Home, Vol. II*, (Albany: J. B. Lyon Co., Printers, 1920), Table 1, p. 2004.

110. *Revolutionary Radicalism*, p. 2004.

111. Detweiler, *Negro Press*, p. 11.

112. *Messenger*, April 1922, p. 390; Briggs to Draper, March 17, 1958, Draper Papers.

113. Kelly Miller, "After Marcus Garvey—What of the Negro?" *Contemporary Review*, vol. 131, April 1927, p. 494; James, *Holding Aloft the Banner*, passim.

114. Owen went on an extensive "coast to coast" tour in 1922 during which he wrote vivid dispatches of his experience for the *Messenger*. See *Messenger*, April 1922, pp. 389–91; May 1922, pp. 407–410; June 1922, pp. 424–26; July 1922, pp. 447–48.

115. Charles Johnson, "The Rise of the Negro Magazine," *Journal of Negro History*, vol. 13, no. 1, January 1928, p. 17; Anderson, *A. Philip Randolph*, p. 119; Sterling D. Spero and Abram L. Harris, *The Black Worker: The Negro and the Labor Movement* (1931; New York: Atheneum, 1968), p. 390.

116. *Messenger*, April 1922, p. 391; for more on this remarkable union, see Foner, "The IWW and the Black Workers"; Seraile, "Ben Fletcher"; McGirr, "Black and White Longshoremen in the IWW"; Cole, "Shaping Up and Shipping Out"; Kimeldorf, "Radical Possibilities?"

117. *Manual for the use of the Legislature of the State of New York, 1921* (Albany 1921), p. 786; Weinstein, *Decline of Socialism in America*, pp. 73, 114–15.

118. Anderson, *A. Philip Randolph*, pp. 153–55.

119. For more on the birth and struggles of the Brotherhood of Sleeping Car Porters, see Spero and Harris, *Black Worker*, chap. xx; Anderson, *A. Philip Randolph*, pp. 151–225; and William Harris, *Keeping the Faith: A. Philip Randolph, Milton P. Webster, and the Brotherhood of Sleeping Car Porters, 1925–37* (1977; Urbana: University of Illinois Press, 1991).

120. Solomon, *The Cry Was Unity*, esp. chap. 4.

121. Students enrolled in black colleges increased sixfold between 1917 and 1927, from 2,132 to 13,580; by 1927 there were another 1,500 in predominantly white colleges outside the South. In 1920, 396 black students received bachelor's degrees; in 1929, 1,903 had done so. Raymond Wolters, *The New Negro on Campus: Black College Rebellions of the 1920s* (Princeton: Princeton University Press, 1975), pp. 17 and 313; Herbert Aptheker, "The Black College Student in the 1920s—Years of Preparation and Protest," in his, *Afro-American History: The Modern Era* (New York: Citadel Press, 1992), p. 175; also see *Crisis*, July 1923, pp. 108–116.

122. Claude McKay, "A Negro Poet and His Poems," *Pearson's Magazine*, vol. 39, no. 5, September 1918, p. 276; Benjamin J. Davis, *Communist Councilman From Harlem: Autobiographical Notes Written in a Federal Penitentiary* (1969; New York: International Publishers, 1991), pp. 31–39, quotation from p. 38; Edward Graham, "The Hampton Institute Strike of 1927: A Case Study in Student Protest," *The American Scholar*, vol. 38, no. 4, Autumn 1969, pp. 668–682; Wolters, *The New Negro on Campus*, chap. iv.

123. The *Messenger*, carried a large number of articles pertaining to these subjects, especially during the period 1923 to 1926. Of special note is the fine essay by Zora Neale Hurston on the Howard crisis: "The Hue and Cry about Howard University," *Messenger*, September 1925, pp. 315–19, 338.

124. Abram Harris, "The Negro Problem As Viewed by Negro Leaders," in his,

Race, Radicalism, and Reform: Selected Papers, William Darity, ed. (New Brunswick: Transaction Publishers, 1989), p. 48; the essay was first published in *Current History*, vol. 18, no. 3, June 1923.

125. Anthony M. Platt, *E. Franklin Frazier Reconsidered* (New Brunswick: Rutgers University Press, 1991), esp. chap. 4; E. Franklin Frazier, "The American Negro's New Leaders," *Current History*, April 1928, p. 58. Langston Hughes and Claude McKay, early admirers and contributors to the magazine, registered similar disappointment with the later *Messenger*. Hughes in his autobiography referred to the "curious career" of the *Messenger*. "It began by being very radical, racial, and socialistic, just after the [First World War]," he recalled. "Then it later became a kind of Negro society magazine and a plugger for Negro business, with photographs of prominent colored ladies and their nice homes in it." Langston Hughes, *The Big Sea: An Autobiography* (1940; London: Pluto Press, 1986), p. 233. In a 1928 letter, McKay similarly remembered the *Messenger* as "a splendid magazine during and right after the War. It had the *Crisis* licked miles and miles, it was so well-edited and strong in opinion. . . . But afterwards the tone of the *Messenger* went down a great deal in my opinion. I don't know why and how, one cannot always tell how decay begins." McKay to James Ivy, May 20, 1928, in Wayne Cooper, ed. *The Passion of Claude McKay: Selected Prose and Poetry, 1912–1948* (New York: Schocken Books, 1973), p. 146.

126. *Messenger*, March 1923, pp. 632–33, and April 1923, p. 657; *Chicago Defender*, May 5, 1923; George Schuyler, *Black and Conservative: The Autobiography of George S. Schuyler* (New Rochelle: Arlington House, Publishers, 1966), pp. 137–38; Anderson, *A. Philip Randolph*, pp. 142–44.

127. Quoted in Anderson, *A. Philip Randolph*, p. 149.

128. Kornweibel, *No Crystal Stair*, esp. pp. 270–75, provides a persuasive explanation of the *Messenger*'s "decline."

129. William L. Patterson, *The Man Who Cried Genocide: An Autobiography* (New York: International Publishers, 1971), pp. 30–31.

130. William L. Patterson, ed., *We Charge Genocide* (1951; New York: International Publishers, 1970).

131. David Levering Lewis, *When Harlem Was in Vogue* (New York: Oxford University Press, 1989), p. 9; Harris, "The Negro Problem As Viewed by Negro Leaders," p. 48; Frazier, "The American Negro's New Leaders," p. 58; James Weldon Johnson, *Black Manhattan* (New York: Knopf, 1930), p. 251; Roi Ottley, *New World A-Coming: Inside Black America* (1943; New York: Arno Press, 1968), p. 272.

132. For more on the ABB and the politics of the group that came out of it, see James, *Holding Aloft the Banner of Ethiopia*, esp. chap. 5, and Postscript.

133. Patterson, *The Man Who Cried Genocide*, pp. 81, 92–93. In a similar vein, James E. Jackson, Jr., a black Virginian who joined the Party in the 1930s, told me that hearing Richard B. Moore speak at Howard University was a turning point in

his life, which led to his joining the CP. (Telephone conversation with Jackson, 1996).

134. The literature on the subject is vast and growing, but see in particular, Moore, "Flawed Fraternity"; Sally M. Miller, "The Socialist Party and the Negro, 1901–1920," *Journal of Negro History*, vol. lvi, no. 3, July 1971; Foner, *American Socialism*; idem., *Organized Labor and the Black Worker*.

135. David Roediger, *Towards the Abolition of Whiteness* (London and New York: Verso, 1994), p. 135.

136. See, in particular, Eric Arnesen, *Waterfront Workers of New Orleans: Race, Class, and Politics, 1863–1923* (Urbana: University of Illinois Press 1994), and Winslow, ed., *Waterfront Workers*, a fine collection of studies.

137. William D. Haywood, *Big Bill Haywood's Book: The Autobiography of Big Bill Haywood* (1929; New York: International Publishers, 1983), p. 361.

138. John C. Walter, *The Harlem Fox: J. Raymond Jones and Tammany, 1920–1970* (Albany: State University of New York Press, 1989), pp. 37–43. (Despite its formal title and nominal author, the book is written in the form of an autobiography.) See also Tony Martin, *Race First*, pp. 33–35; Robert Hill, ed., *The Marcus Garvey and Universal Negro Improvement Association Papers*, vol. vii (Berkeley: University of California Press, 1990), pp. 982–85.

139. Frazier's and Harris's views on black businesses which began to emerge in the 1920s are summarized in E. Franklin Frazier, *The Negro in the United States* (New York: Macmillan Co., 1949), chap. xvi; and Abram Harris, *The Negro As Capitalist* (Philadelphia: American Academy of Political and Social Sciences, 1936).

140. James, *Holding Aloft the Banner of Ethiopia*, pp. 171–73.

141. *Messenger*, March 1921, p. 197; September 1919, p. 19.

142. *Messenger*, September 1919, p. 19.

143. *Messenger*, July 1921, p. 213, and December 1919, p. 21; see also *Messenger*, November 1917, p. 27; May-June 1919, p. 27; February 1923, pp. 614–15; April 1923, pp. 668–69.

144. *Messenger*, July 1919, p. 22.

145. *Messenger*, May-June 1919, p. 27.

146. *Messenger*, December 1919, p. 4.

147. [Fenton Johnson], "Religion is not Retarding the Race," *Favorite Magazine*, December 1919, p. 209.

148. Joyce Moore Turner, "Richard B. Moore and His Works," in *Richard B. Moore, Caribbean Militant in Harlem: Collected Writings, 1920–1972*, W. Burghardt Turner and Joyce Moore Turner, eds. (Bloomington: Indiana University Press, 1988), p. 40.

149. Baltimore *Afro-American*, August 11, 1922.

150. Ulysses S. Poston, "The Negro Awakening," *Current History*, December 1923, p. 474.

151. Quoted in *Messenger*, May-June, 1919, p. 20.

152. Owen was not, of course, the only one who attacked religion in the pages of the *Messenger*, but he had a particularly ferocious polemical style. Randolph himself remarked years later that "Chandler was gifted in writing in what you might call . . . the spirit of attack, especially with respect to individuals." "Reminiscences of A. Philip Randolph," p. 181, Oral History Research Office, Butler Library, Columbia University. See also Schuyler's portrait of Owen: Schuyler, *Black and Conservative*, pp. 137–38. Ben Davis provides a particularly vivid depiction of the intolerant and repressive religious atmosphere that existed in some of the black colleges. In the case of Morehouse College, intolerance of freethought and atheism was as strong among the faculty as the student body. Davis, *Communist Councilman From Harlem*, esp. pp. 35–36.

153. Spero and Harris, *Black Worker*, pp. 399–400. See also George E. Haynes, *The Trend of the Races* (New York: Council of Women for Home Missions and Missionary Education Movement of the United States and Canada, 1922), p. 14.

154. Naison, *Communists in Harlem*, pp. 281–82. In Alabama, the local CP tended to be more tolerant of the religiosity of its black members. Kelley, *Hammer and Hoe*, pp. 107–108. Manning Johnson, an Afro-American trade unionist who joined the Party in 1930 and served on the national committee of the CP between 1936 and 1938, left in 1940 and became an anti-Communist Quisling. He, nevertheless, plausibly claimed that the Party's attitude toward religion was a key factor in his leaving. "When I came into the Communist movement I was profoundly religious," he said. "After I was in the Communist movement a while I was told I had to abandon my religious convictions, and that to be a good Communist I had to be an atheist. Finally they agreed to accept me, and they assured me that in the course of my experience in the party I would lose my religious convictions." *Hearings Regarding Communist Infiltration of Minority Groups—Part 2 (Testimony of Manning Johnson), Hearing Before the Committee on Un-American Activities, House of Representatives*, 81st Congress, 1st session, July 14, 1949 (Washington, D.C.: Government Printing Office, 1949), p. 506.

155. Cited in Randall K. Burkett, *Black Redemption: Churchmen Speak for the Garvey Movement* (Philadelphia: Temple University Press, 1978), p. 7. Burkett has provided the most detailed discussion of the religious side of Garveyism: *Garveyism as a Religious Movement* (Metuchen: Scarecrow Press, 1978).

156. Despite her triumphalist tone in discussing the black washerwomen strikes in Jackson (1866), Galveston (1877) and Atlanta (1881), Tera Hunter provides no evidence that any of these strikes yielded the results demanded by the women. The fact that successful organized action eluded the washerwomen, the most independent of the domestic workers, showed the major obstacles that such workers had to face. Tera W. Hunter, *To 'Joy My Freedom: Southern Black Women's Lives and Labor After the Civil War* (Cambridge: Harvard University Press, 1997), esp. chap. 4.

157. Campbell's political career is discussed at length in James, *Holding Aloft the Banner of Ethiopia*, esp. chap. 5.

158. Quoted in James, *Holding Aloft the Banner of Ethiopia*, p. 175.

159. Turner and Moore Turner, eds., *Richard B. Moore*, pp. 55, 165–66, 217; Anderson, *A. Philip Randolph*, esp. pp. 69–73; Melinda Chateauvert, *Marching Together: Women of the Brotherhood of Sleeping Car Porters* (Urbana: University of Illinois Press, 1998).

160. Barbara Bair, "Audley Moore," and Robin Kelley, "Louise Thompson Patterson," both in Darlene Clark Hine, Elsa Barkley Brown, and Rosalyn Terborg-Penn, eds., *Black Women in America: An Historical Encyclopedia*, vol. 2 (Bloomington: Indiana University Press, 1994); Buzz Johnson, *"I Think of My Mother": Notes on the Life of Claudia Jones* (London: Karia Press, 1985); Marika Sherwood, *Claudia Jones: A Life in Exile* (London: Lawrence & Wishart, 1999); Naison, *Communists in Harlem During the Depression*; Solomon, *The Cry Was Unity*.

161. James, *Holding Aloft the Banner of Ethiopia*, pp. 137–55.

162. Harry Haywood, *Black Bolshevik: Autobiography of An Afro-American Communist* (Chicago: Liberator Press, 1978), pp. 135–36. Similarly, in a 1923 Harlem debate with Otto Huiswoud, George Schuyler told him that "the Negro had difficulties enough being black without becoming Red." Schuyler, *Black and Conservative*, p. 146.

163. Harrison, *When Africa Awakes*, pp. 81 and 40.

164. James, *Holding Aloft the Banner*; Naison, *Communists in Harlem*; Solomon, *The Cry Was Unity*.

165. Phyl Garland, "A. Philip Randolph: Labor's Grand Old Man," *Ebony*, May 1969, pp. 31 and 36.

Part III

World War II

A Certain Hope Died

The idea that the years during and after World War II constituted a turning point in the tenor of Black politics has become more evident—and better developed—in recent scholarship. Sweeping changes—trade unionization, especially the growth of the CIO; war mobilization of millions, in particular in the South with its disproportionate number of boot camps; expansion of the public sector to a degree unprecedented since the Civil War; and the concentrated condition of a society on the verge of becoming majority urban—all fundamentally agitated Black life, exciting institutional and organic leaders alike to extend their conception of struggle. Certainly landmark initiatives of this time, such as the March on Washington movement or the NAACP's class action campaign against segregated education, provided a clear precursor to some of the most celebrated instances of later antiracist reform. What becomes clear among the more contemporary essays, however, is the status of the World War II cohort of organizers, agitators, and leaders as what Michael Honey calls a "transitional generation," a bridging group that challenged conditions on shop floors and in civic associations, in polling places and city buses, pointing the ways to the modes of confrontation and direct action that would characterize the decades to come.

Naturally, the processes of change worked differently in different parts of the South. Tracy K'Meyer, in one of the most instructive analyses we have of the movement in a border state, takes seriously Winston James's call for historians to try to divine the laws of cross-racial "solidarity and alliance . . . dissolution and conflict." The once promising interracialism of the populist movement was overwhelmed by the white supremacist tides sweeping the South at the end of the nineteenth century. If biracialism in the union movement was sporadic, we can still point to cases like the communist and socialist organizers working with the agricultural workers in the 1930s, who were inspiring for their sheer audacity, even if their work did not lead to lasting interracial organizations, even if their work was sometimes tainted by racial paternalism. K'Meyer finds that in Louisville changes in schooling, hiring practices, and the delivery of health care all resulted from a high degree of interracial fellowship within the city, fashioned through spiritual, workplace, and electoral ties. "Fellowship" is the right word for what she describes, something that goes beyond merely functional cooperation. In Kentucky, Blacks never completely lost the right to vote and were never subject to the degree of racial terrorism common in the Deep South, which may explain why interracialism had a better chance to root itself there. Together with the piece by Scott Sandage on "memory activism" and its impact on civic culture throughout the past century, K'Meyer's piece reinforces the motivating power of what Gunnar Myrdal famously termed the "American creed" of democratic participation and rule of fair play within the development of traditions of struggle among Black Americans.

Scott Sandage's discussion of the African American appropriation of the public meaning of the Lincoln Memorial reminds us again of the centrality of "memory work" as a form of struggle, this time more explicitly at a national rather than local level. Blacks challenged official representations of the Memorial as a shrine to sectional reconciliation through elaborate public rituals spanning the middle of the twentieth century, from the storied 1939 Easter Concert of Marian Anderson to the 1963 March on Washington. By doing so, they suggested—and in the end consecrated—the image of Lincoln as Emancipator, and therefore of African Americans as irreversibly American. Sandage's provocative claim that the civil rights struggle "came of age" not in 1963, but in 1939, might give pause to those who have worked to uncouple the development of Black civil critique from the NAACP. Nevertheless, the "memory-work" of the activists described authorized African Americans as citizens in principle, if not immediately in practice. At an even more basic level, the changing meaning of the Lincoln Memorial illustrates again the capacity of Blacks to reinvent the idea of "America" to fit their needs.

In the Deep South, the story of the war years is one of increasingly aggressive mobilization of African American communities, much of it in an attempt to secure "the all-compelling ballot," as Peter Humphries Clark called it. The essays by Caroline Emmons and Wim Roefs recover significant episodes in the postwar drama. There are many ways to frame the stories of Florida's Harry T. Moore and South Carolina's John McCray, but certainly they should be seen in part as a commentary on the political potential of the postwar Black middle class in the South. Along with Amzie Moore, Medgar Evers, Modjeska Simpkins, Vernon Dahmer, T.R.M. Howard, E. J. Stringer, Fred Gray, Aaron Henry, Osceola McKaine, Ella Baker, and Septima Clark, they represent a tradition of middle-class activism, some of it operating under the most dangerous conditions to be found in the postwar South. They were druggists and doctors, small business owners, dentists, attorneys, farm owners, social workers, and crusading journalists; a few—a very few—were teachers. Some were ministers, of course, but at least in the rural South, ministers of activist bent were still far outnumbered by their more accommodationist brethren.

Many middle-class Black activists in the South were still ducking bullets when E. Franklin Frazier published his scathing *Black Bourgeoisie* (1957), premised on the idea that slavery "annihilated the Negro as a person" (p. 10) and characterizing the Black middle class as riddled with inferiority complexes, compensating with conspicuous consumption and other forms of make-believe, refusing to identify with the Black masses and their struggle.[1] "The black bourgeoisie suffers from 'nothingness' because when Negroes attain middle-class status their lives generally lose both content and significance" (Frazier, 195). Perhaps it is the most aggressive rendition we have of the theme of "disremembrance." Frazier's analysis fits well with Kelly's description of Birmingham and with the emerging trends Barkley Brown identified in Richmond, but it hardly fits the situation Ortiz found in early-twentieth-century Florida and it would be a very misleading guide to the movement in the postwar South, where part of the Black middle class was temporizing while another part was crusading—and some were doing both by turns. Frazier trafficked in caricature, but his arguments are profoundly resonant both with some identifiable historical trends and with recurrent themes in Black popular thinking. Much popular discourse in the African American community, even on contemporary college campuses, differs little from Frazier. To be authentically Black, one must be from the working class, from the street corner, the ghetto—Malcolm's field Negro, not his house Negro.

Until recently, mainstream academic analysis of the civil rights movement created very nearly the opposite caricature, a benign portrait in which middle-class Blacks get virtually all credit for leading the civil rights movement. (For example, William J. Wilson saying "These . . . civil rights acts were mainly due to the efforts of the black professional groups [ministers, lawyers, teachers, students].")[2] This, of course, is just a variation on traditional top-down analysis in which only elites count.

Race and class are ideas that Americans have trouble thinking about separately, so there is no reason to be surprised if the combination of the two leads to particularly reductionist thinking. One need not look very far into the historical record to see that virtually any social status position is subject to both "progressive" and "reactionary" pressures, varying in form and intensity over time and across situations. The analytical task is to understand how these potentials play themselves out in particular cases. The middle-class activists of the postwar era may not represent their class, but they do represent its possibilities. In the case of John McCray, for example, it seems important that his early education gave him a very positive sense of the historical contributions of Black people and models of racial self-confidence among his teachers. The more detailed our portraits of the lives of people who played important roles in making change, the less vulnerable we are to ahistorical stereotyping of whatever variety.

McCray and Moore also invite us again to consider the utility of the term "activism." Moore, writing his earnest letters to government officials as if they cared, and McCray, insisting that positive alliances with white southerners were possible, seem more the epitome of critical citizens, determined, like the Lincoln Memorial protesters, to recreate this country in their own images. Taken literally, of course, they are activists, but that term fails to do justice to their passionate attachment to the American possibility.

It is hard, though, to take the term literally, given its powerful connotations. In an age of mass media, activism gets reduced to its theatrical, dramatic components, devaluing the kind of unexciting persistence that marked the life of Harry T. Moore and hundreds like him. In terms of real-world consequences, the heroic conception of activism may be as disempowering as the Great Man theories of history. Activism becomes a morally attractive social category, but for most people, an unattainable one.

At its worst, "activism" for the Left serves the same functions that "patriotism" serves for the Right, both labels so encased in positive moral overtones as to preclude critical discussion. Replacing a dialogue about the bad character of welfare cheats with one about the sterling character of social activists continues the tradition of a national discourse that tries to understand social inequality in terms of individual character rather than in terms of social structure and process. If Dr. King plagiarized his dissertation and violated his marriage vows, if Marion Barry, once a leader of the sit-in movement, became a drug user, it is an embarrassment because such behaviors are inconsistent with the high level of morality we want to ascribe to "activists." It might be more realistic to think of it the other way and rejoice over the fact that people who had the normal human frailties were able, for a moment in their lives, to make extraordinary contributions to democracy.

Perhaps we need a more cautious assessment of the value of the recent bottom-up scholarship on the movement. In its romanticized forms, the idea of the "movement" becomes an intellectual ghetto of the Left, separating analysis of the lives of those Blacks whom we most admire from the lives of those other kinds of Black folks who are just—other. Perhaps the emphasis on bottom-up movement scholarship in the academy, perhaps all the nostalgia about movement days outside of the academy functions to divert analyses from the places where most Black people live most of their lives, which is not at the barricades. That we need to understand the importance of the John McCrays and Harry Moores is a major theme of this volume, but this volume also suggests that we need to understand what was happening to, say, Black social clubs and block clubs at the same time. Understanding how "ordinary people" participated in making history is important, but it is also important to deepen our understanding of the factors shaping their participation in everyday life. Deepening our understanding of the "movement" at the cost of losing our grasp on Black civic life may prove a poor trade.

A decade after his death, few young Black Floridians, the people for whom he died, would have recognized the name of Harry T. Moore. In Mississippi, there has been a campaign in recent years to revive the name of Medgar Evers, but prior to that his memory too had faded in the state where he lived and died. Despite much good work in the last decade and a half, postwar African American leadership in the South had slipped out of our collective understanding of the movement even before all of them were dead. It is easy enough to explain that in terms of the dominance of top-down perspectives, but that can't be a complete explanation. Emmons points out that emancipation celebrations similar to those Ortiz and Glymph describe in earlier generations were still happening in post–World War II Florida. As suggested earlier, under the conditions of modernity, their impact was unlikely to be what it had been and few functional equivalents seem to have been found (although NAACP Youth Councils, which grew rapidly during the 1950s, seem to have performed some of the same functions for a much more delimited audience).

At the same time, we should probably think in terms of a will to forget, a will to disremember as always coexisting and contending with the will to remember, with now one and now the other more powerful. Peter Wood noted that some aspects of African American history are so painful that African Americans prefer not to think about them, like the young Black people of the 1920s who refused to sing spirituals because they were reminiscent of the "shame" of slavery. James Baldwin speaks of

> This past, the Negro's past, of rope, fire, torture, castration, infanticide, rape; death and humiliation; fear by day and night, fear as deep as the marrow of the bone; doubt that he was worthy of life, since everyone around him denied it; sorrow for his women, for his kinfolk, for his children, who needed his protection and whom he could not protect. . . .[3]

This, of course, like E. Franklin Frazier's discussion of the annihilation of the Negro personality, is a Black way of saying that Black people have done nothing but sing spirituals and strum banjoes. If that is how one sees the past, there is nothing to identify with. More, in the postwar South, parts of the Black population may have had a vested interest in the homogenizing of more recent history. Only a fraction of the Black population was participating in the movement in anything like a sustained way. One can see how the people John McCray was blasting for being "spineless and unworthy," the people Harry Moore admonished for their lethargy ("Mere talk will not suffice"), the ones who didn't speak up for Moore until he was gone, the ones who crossed the street when they saw Medgar Evers coming, might not be interested in preserving the whole history. Teachers and preachers, who as groups tended to have ambivalent reactions to activism from roughly the turn of the century until the mid-1960s, were also probably among the groups who were coming to have the most influence in shaping the communal sense of the past. For them, top-down, normative analysis was face-saving.

Charise Cheney reminds us that the motives of activists are normally mixed, that people who are noble and selfless in their efforts to undermine one kind of inequality may be simultaneously undergirding another. Her analysis of the masculinist underpinnings of much of what styles itself Black nationalism takes us back in particular to issues raised by Elsa Barkley Brown, to the dangers inherent in unconsciously equating the welfare of Black people with the welfare of Black men. Aptly termed by Cheney a "politics of substitution," masculinist nationalism discourages full appreciation of the breadth of group ambition, leaving only the fantasy of one day exerting power equivalent to that of the oppressor. Here one can see clearly how a certain view of history, the view of history described by Baldwin, in which the central theme of the Black experience becomes the denial of Black manhood, feeds a hunger for respect that then becomes the grounds for justifying gender subordination.

The war years and immediate postwar years accelerated ferment and change but they also accelerated the forces encouraging cynicism and dis-remembering, sometimes in the form of masculinist nationalism or in the form of the glorification of street culture. James Baldwin remarked that "The treatment accorded the Negro during the Second World War marks for me, a turning point in the Negro's relation to America. To put it briefly, and somewhat too simply, a certain hope died, a certain respect for white Americans faded."[4] Explicitly racist formulations of Black inferiority were less acceptable after the war but they were too often supplanted by conceptions of Black men, women, and children alike as manifestations of pathology. For many, the promise of increased industrial wages and union assurances of occupational mobility were summarily repudiated by seismic waves of economic restructuring—first automation, then de-industrialization, and finally the mocking recovery of a service-intensive economy, where dignity of labor and the option of collective action alike have become ever more rare. Even the concentrating effects of urbanization, presumed by scholars since the Chicago School to constitute the doorway to social integration, became instead for Blacks the trapdoor to a race-based separation more comprehensive than that of Jim Crow, and arguably more demeaning. Given these conditions, perhaps it is not so surprising that the younger generations of Memphis—like those in so many cities and communities across the country—came to forget the figures of the transitional generation, instead believing that African Americans' normal response to oppression was one of cowardly acquiescence.

The young people Honey describes in Memphis at least had a foot on the economic ladder. Those who were less lucky may have been even more powerfully drawn to oppositional forms that provided for individual self-respect but in ways that could be collectively problematic. In his brilliant discussion of the zoot suit as cultural warfare, Robin Kelley describes an oppositional subculture of young hipsters in World War II Harlem, men who equated wage labor with exploitation, who were more interested in having a good time than in working, who saw the war as a white man's war in which they had no stake. It seems a safe guess that for many of them, cynicism about the American promise must have been verified by the continued tenacity of postwar racism and by their continued inability to break out of menial jobs. Aggressively disassociating themselves—in their speech, their dress, their entire self-presentation—from anything that smacked of being "country"—which, in part, means from being the exploited—creating their own symbolic world of respect, they were also disassociating themselves from the communal traditions and memories that had sustained generations of their forebears, leaving themselves no sense of collective history but that offered by mass culture, no standards by which to judge themselves except by an inversion of the standards of a world that looked on them with amused contempt and pity, to use Du Bois's immortal phrase. They were buying self-respect, in short, by sacrificing their ancestors. Internalized racism is reinscribed as hipness, as toughness, as all the things their ancestors, were, presumably, not.

As a heuristic device, it may be very important to see the most feared contemporary Black icon, that of the urban tough, and the most valorized, that of the civil rights worker of the 1960s, as ultimately responding to the same problems and, as different as their responses are, still having to negotiate some of the same terrain. As Cheney makes clear, we have to understand some of the swaggering masculinity of the contemporary ghetto as a dialogue with the past, men and boys trying to do, in the context of their lives, what Black Civil War soldiers were trying to do in the context of theirs. Compensatory masculinities, of course, can make communal life all but impossible. Similarly, where activism is informed by what Gutmann called "a truncated and shrunken historical consciousness" we may be most likely to get activism in its theatrical, heroic forms, which repeatedly turns out to be unable to recreate the social conditions prerequisite to its own continuance.

Methodologically, this means that it is not enough to pay more attention to the ways everyday life informs social change. We need analytical schemes that go further, that allow us to pose questions about urban gangsters that may shed light on activists and vice versa, schemes that do not fall into the trap of glorifying activists while vilifying urban youth by contrast. If we just ask how they understand their history as Black people and how those understandings inform their social behavior, their sense of their own possibilities, we at least begin a dialogue that puts both in the same discussion. Like Cheney, we believe that one of the most fruitful points of entry is the presence of masculinist posturings across contexts.

To put the point differently, an engaged view of Black activism at the present moment should take into account the numbing effects of disremembering in all parts of the Black community but might also encourage all parties, movement veterans as well as alienated youth, to consider what it means to discern activity and intervention within the political context of Black life today. What do labor dignity and collective action look like in a service economy, particularly one in which the workers' pool is increasingly young, Black, and female? Are champions of Black misogyny and masculinity the accommodationists of the twenty-first century, advocating a world view that presumes the exercise of autonomy but in reality justifies a profoundly restricted view of Blacks' true collective capacity? What contemporary trends—punishment and incarceration, urban land use and conservation, fiduciary redlining, immigration from within as well as beyond the African diaspora—presently catalyze society and excite African American group outlook as world wars and internal migrations did in the twentieth century, and contraband camps and constitutional conventions did during and after the Civil War? What capacities exist among Black people for civic action—plain, undramatic civic action—and how have those capacities been changing over time? Though "activism" is often taken as a timeless aspect of Black life, the pieces assembled here speak loudly on behalf of social and historical specificity. Perhaps we presume ourselves to live in a deactivated age because we do not work hard enough to see society as it in fact is. Perhaps we must take care not to overlook current possibilities for social challenge because our imaginations are still dominated by Birmingham in 1963.

Time longer than rope. Oppression doesn't last forever. The phrase, which has been used in reference to the long struggle in South Africa,[5] appears to come from the West Indies. It suggests something of the tenacity of the struggle, a theme that resonates throughout this volume. It suggests something of the optimism (albeit guarded) that allowed African Americans to believe against all proofs in their ability to reshape America. Still, it is neither alarmist nor defeatist to wonder if that optimism is still appropriate. Time is longer than rope, but that may be most true where a rich, complex historical consciousness has been sustained. If African Americans are becoming less able, for whatever reasons, to convey a usable past across generational lines, less able to maintain the social patterns, often rooted in mundane, day-to-day activities, that sustained activism in the past, less able to reinvent the idea of activism to speak to changing realities, then the anti-triumphalist tendencies current in some parts of African American popular thought may not be so far-fetched. What was bought so dearly easily slips away.

NOTES

1. E. Franklin Frazier, *Black Bourgeoisie* (New York: Collier Books, 1962).

2. William Wilson, *The Declining Significance of Race* (Chicago: University of Chicago Press, 1978), 135.

3. James Baldwin, *The Fire Next Time* (New York: Vintage, 1992), 98.

4. Ibid., 54.

5. Edward Roux, *Time Longer Than Rope; a History of the Black Man's Struggle for Freedom in South Africa* (London: Gollancz, 1948).

Chapter 12

Building Interracial Democracy
The Civil Rights Movement in Louisville, Kentucky, 1945–1956

Tracy E. K'Meyer

In 1956, as Louisville, Kentucky celebrated its nationally renowned peaceful integration of public schools, local activist Anne Braden gave credit for the accomplishment to "a long history of struggle on the part of Negroes and white liberals which has steadily chipped away at the structure of segregation through the years."[1] By this time Louisville had seen more than a decade of progress fighting segregation and discrimination in public libraries, city auditoriums and offices, hospitals, recreational facilities, and higher education. These gains were accomplished by a coalition of black and interracial organizations working concurrently and in cooperation through persuasion, petition, legislation, and legal challenges toward the goal of equal citizenship. A combination of factors contributed to this distinctive "organizing tradition," including the local impact of the national postwar interest in civil rights, a sense of responsibility regarding leadership on race, and the presence of constituencies increasingly concerned about relations between whites and blacks. Most important, however, and most characteristic of the Louisville context, was black community pressure backed by political participation.[2]

While historians have paid increasing attention to civil rights activism in the postwar period across the South, very little has been written on border areas in this era.[3] The story of Louisville's efforts reveals the extent of what was possible in the racial and political setting of the border region. In addition, the story contributes to our understanding of the number and complexity of grassroots organizations committed to improving conditions, relations, and access to equal opportunity in the pre-*Brown* period.

A close examination of the story, however, also reveals how the nature of the movement—its interracial makeup, the decision to target public discrimination, and widespread concern for the city's progressive reputation —determined what could, and could not, be accomplished. In short, the history of the early movement in Louisville enables us to view both the strengths and the weaknesses of an interracial political movement against discrimination and segregation in the border South.

Many factors shaped postwar civil rights activism in Louisville, beginning with the city's geographic setting on the border between North and South. Louisville was most obviously southern in its pattern of segregation. Blacks were limited to separate and unequal parks, schools, and hospitals. They were restricted in downtown restaurants, theaters, and stores. The city had a rigid pattern of housing segregation, with blacks confined to the oldest and most crowded sections. Economic discrimination prevented large numbers of African Americans from rising above unskilled or service jobs. Beyond these specific manifestations of Jim Crow, Louisville was politically and emotionally oriented toward the South. Even though Kentuckians had been emotionally divided during the Civil War, after Reconstruction white residents, including those in its leading city, identified more with their southern neighbors. Elite white sentiment memorialized the Confederacy and honored it with monuments. Finally, the Democratic Party dominated just as it did elsewhere in the solid South.[4]

Other characteristics gave Louisville a more northern or midwestern atmosphere. The city was home to a broad ethnic and religious mix, including relatively large Catholic and Jewish populations, who provided leaders and rank-and-file participants in the civil rights movement. The presence of a diverse industrial base and unions also informed the local climate. During the Second World War the city ranked eighteenth nationally in number of defense factories, and in peacetime it attracted even more. Of the thirty-five largest plants in the urban area, all but nine were owned and managed by absentee leadership, providing links between the city and national corporations. The unions in the largest plants were also directed by decisions made in national headquarters. Negotiations between national unions and corporate leaders had direct results in racial policy in some Louisville businesses. For example, in its contract with the Farm Equipment Workers (FE), International Harvester agreed to institute a nondiscrimination rule in hiring and promoting that applied to the Louisville plant. This strengthened the hand of the FE, the most interracial and aggressive union in the city on civil rights issues. Although the numbers of African Americans employed in these plants, especially in skilled jobs, were always low, the firms added to the cosmopolitan outlook of some of the city's business leaders and heightened union sensitivity to racial issues.[5]

The most important northern characteristic of Louisville for the civil rights movement was black political power. Unlike cities further south, in Louisville African Americans had enjoyed uninterrupted access to the vote since 1870 and had a history of improving racial conditions through political pressure. Louisville's black leaders always regarded the vote and political processes as their most important weapons in the fight against discrimination. In contrast to the rest of the South, which actively subverted the fifteenth amendment's protection of black suffrage, in Louisville at least there was no organized effort against the black vote. Before World War I blacks supported Republicans and hoped for patronage positions and concessions in return. After the war, when the Republican Party's political fortunes rose in Kentucky, blacks became more aggressive and insisted that their loyalty be repaid. In 1921 a group of young leaders bolted the GOP and formed the Lincoln Independent Party (LIP). Although the LIP was soundly defeated, the Republican administration responded to the challenge by appointing blacks to white-collar city jobs and hiring black police and firemen. Throughout the 1920s African-American leaders used their political influence to pressure party leaders to fight racial violence and support black education. In the 1930s intensifying party competition gave African Americans leverage to elect their candidates to local and state offices. Most notably, in 1936 Charles W. Anderson won a seat in the Kentucky General Assembly, the first black elected to a southern legislature since Reconstruction.[6]

During and after World War II, a number of factors increased the impact of African Americans' political power. Although they made up just under 20 percent of the voting population, residential segregation concentrated African Americans into a small number of wards and increased their influence. Thus, because candidates for alderman were nominated by wards it was increasingly common for African Americans to win a few aldermanic seats. Likewise, because state representatives were elected by districts blacks had a good chance of securing seats in heavily African-American sections. Another factor, much noted in the black press, was the mobility of black voters between political parties. Historically the vast majority of blacks were Republican, but with the New Deal Democrats actively recruited voters. Louisville's blacks voted for Roosevelt and the

Democratic Party in national elections while continuing to support Republicans at the city level. It should be noted that although the Progressive Party attracted support from militant blacks and whites, as a group African Americans refused to invest their vote in what many considered a losing campaign. The result of shifting party allegiances and Democrats' improved treatment of blacks was that by 1956 47.7 percent of registered blacks were Republican and 47.1 percent were Democrats. This made African Americans the swing constituency, forcing each party to work to keep their loyalists and to recruit from the other side.[7]

This political power resulted in direct and indirect black influence in public affairs. African Americans held appointed positions in important decision-making offices including the housing commission, the Mayor's Legislative Committee, and the Commonwealth Attorney's Office. Elected officials such as Representative Felix Anderson and Alderman William W. Beckett used their positions to keep equal rights on the legislative agenda. Indirectly, the black vote prompted white politicians to make campaign promises and public statements on racial equality. For example, Andrew Broaddus, the 1953 Democratic candidate for mayor, declared that in his administration "there will be equal protection under the law for all our citizens, regardless of race, creed, or any other circumstances." Shortly after that fall's election the new director of public safety bluntly promised, "I do not believe in racial segregation of any sort."[8] In short, the result of black political participation was at the minimum white lip service to equality and at times a black voice in the process of governing. Because of their influence as the swing vote between parties, African Americans, along with their white allies, could approach local and state elected officials through persuasion and petition and could reasonably expect favorable legislation. This potential for political action created the environment in which progress on civil rights issues was possible.

The roots of Louisville's postwar interracial movement lay in the preceding decades' record of gradual progress in race relations. Since the turn of the century black leaders, backed by the community, had cooperated with white politicians and liberal leaders to bring about some amelioration of racial conditions and relations. Blacks successfully prevented the segregation of streetcars, for example, and in 1917 convinced the Supreme Court in *Warley v. Buchanan* to overturn housing segregation ordinances. Black leaders united with white politicians to combat racial violence by lobbying for passage of the first state anti-lynching law in 1920, barring Ku Klux

Klan organizers from the city, and convincing the mayor to order protection for black families who were bombed after moving into white neighborhoods. Throughout the period Louisville had relatively low levels of racial violence and elites and officials expressed opposition to it. There were no post–World War I or II riots or disturbances, for example, and the white press spoke out against extreme instances of police brutality.⁹ Finally, African-American leaders collaborated with the Commission on Interracial Cooperation (CIC) to pressure the government to set aside money for black education, specifically for a black campus of the University of Louisville, leading in 1931 to the creation of Louisville Municipal College. These gains, limited though they seem in retrospect, earned the city a reputation as fair-minded and progressive on race issues, a reputation that became important to local leaders and to the evolution of postwar activism.¹⁰

The relationship between black and white leaders during these early years gave the movement a particular character and influenced the extent and nature of the changes accomplished. At the turn of the century some white civic leaders believed Louisville was different from other southern cities, especially in its lack of racial problems, and they wanted to keep it that way. Black leaders determined that the best way to prevent a deterioration of conditions was to ally with these whites. To do so they played down calls for social equality and emphasized self-help, education, and better living conditions. In return they were rewarded with prestigious positions in the community. After World War I, some more militant leaders, including newspaper editors I. Willis Cole and William Warley, criticized white city officials and called for independent black action against segregation. At the same time, however, black moderates, including churchman George Clement and CIC leader Reverend James Bond, continued to seek alliances with whites in order to gain concessions for the black community. They allied with prominent businessman and philanthropists such as Robert W. Bingham and Theodore Ahrens who wanted to keep the lines of communication open and to ensure Louisville's continued reputation for good race relations. In his comprehensive examination of Louisville's black community prior to 1930, George Wright argues that moderate blacks got more attention because they were willing to work for change on terms set by whites and to help keep up the façade of good relations. Moreover, they received much of the credit when progress was made. In short, while there were militants, most often the alliance of moderate leaders and their white counterparts determined the content and extent of change. In the prewar years that meant an acceptance of segregation with efforts to improve conditions within it.[11]

In the post–World War II era the interracial movement in Louisville expanded and more aggressively fought segregation and discrimination. This change was the result of several factors, including the national trend toward liberalism on race issues. During the war the rejection of fascism raised consciousness about racism at home and its incompatibility with the freedom for which the country was ostensibly fighting. Many people concluded, as did Gunnar Myrdal in *An American Dilemma*, that racism was the fundamental moral flaw in American society. Because of wartime mobility blacks gained political influence in northern communities, and at the same time returning veterans energized the NAACP in the South. In Louisville, the black press publicized this swelling assertiveness, while local leaders organized rallies to garner support for the civil rights campaigns sprouting up around the country. Black agitation convinced whites to address racial problems. As a 1944 meeting in Louisville concluded, "The war and war effort have created problems and misunderstanding in interracial relations in Louisville" that needed to be solved. Sentiments such as these gave rise to urban interracial committees across the South and Midwest. Finally, the cold war fostered a new attention to race relations because discrimination came to be seen as a liability in foreign relations.[12]

Prompted by wartime and cold war propaganda that contrasted Nazi and Soviet totalitarianism with American pluralism and democracy, civil rights advocates challenged the country to live up to its ideals by fighting racism. The connection between pro-democracy and antiracism was one of the main ideological underpinnings of the early movement in Louisville. Activists both black and white attacked racial discrimination, arguing that "Anyone who accepts the Declaration of Independence should oppose segregation" and that "segregation [was] the greatest blot on the Constitution in the United States in its history." Moreover, local black leaders used wartime symbols to urge the community to uphold democratic principles. As one prominent black journalist noted, "The boys who died on beachheads, who were instilled with the four freedoms, are beginning to ask questions now that they are home." The link between saving democracy and fighting racism gained importance in the early cold war years, when local and national leaders warned that communists and fascists might exploit the weaknesses of prejudice, segregation, and the denial of equal rights.[13] Local activists used democratic rhetoric to argue for equal rights, declaring that democratic governments should not discriminate or segregate. The idea that in a democracy African Americans should have equal access to the benefits of citizenship came to serve as one of the principal arguments of the postwar Louisville movement.

A second ideal informing the Louisville movement was the city's self-image as progressive and its desire to maintain its reputation as a leader in race relations. Louisvillians, black and white, often commented on the positive atmosphere in the city. The city's leading black newspaper, the *Defender*, promoted this image by publishing an annual honor roll of individuals and institutions—black and white—who contributed to the concerted movement to "make Louisville one of the most progressive cities in the entire nation." Meanwhile the *Courier Journal* commented on the good relations and calm acceptance of change. For example, in reaction to the proposal to integrate the public libraries in 1942 the editors remarked, "The relations between the races in Louisville have been good. By comparison with other communities they have been almost utopian." Certainly, racial peace could not be upset merely by allowing blacks into the libraries. This self-image was reinforced by national journalists and civil rights leaders who recognized Louisville as "exceptional among southern cities in its community efforts to solve racial problems." Along with the praise came expectations from local and national observers that Louisville, and Kentucky generally, would lead the way in the elimination of segregation.[14]

In the postwar era activists regularly wielded this progressive reputation as a measuring stick of the city's racial progress. Black leaders acknowledged that Louisville had race relations "finer than any southern city" and "a good name among people all over the United States for its fair dealings toward Negroes," especially in the realm of political equality. But that was not enough. As long as there continued to be segregation, according to Frank Stanley, owner and publisher of the *Defender*, "We are not in the position to boast." Louisville's blacks and sympathetic whites needed to fight harder to wipe out prejudice and segregation in the parks, public facilities, and schools. Using the reputation to their advantage, activists argued that "Louisville, the self-styled 'Gateway' to the South is morally obligated to make even greater progress to justify its leadership claims." Citing neighboring states' civil rights laws as inspiration, and comparing the city to others like Indianapolis, Cincinnati, and Baltimore, Louisville activists called on the city to live up to its reputation.[15]

*

National and regional attention to civil rights, democratic rhetoric, and many Louisvillians' desire to be on the cutting edge of racial progress combined to create an environment conducive to an expanded interracial movement working for better race relations and equal citizenship. Before World War II elite white and black leaders had dominated interracial cooperation; now more than twenty black, white, and biracial religious, labor, and secular groups formed a coalition to bring about progress. The first component of this coalition was black civil rights organizations. As it did elsewhere, the Louisville NAACP stepped up its activity and enlarged its membership base after the war. The local group was in close contact with its national officers and followed their lead fighting against the poll tax and in favor of a permanent Fair Employment Practices Committee (FEPC). The Louisville branch also conducted fundraisers and sponsored rallies to support the national organization's legal defense work. Locally the NAACP attacked segregation in parks, professional associations, employment, and education. While it was primarily a black organization, the NAACP cooperated in interracial projects, usually providing legal advice.[16]

Louisville was also home to smaller indigenous and in many ways more militant black organizations. Black attorney C. Eubank Tucker founded the Kentucky Bureau of Negro Affairs (KBNA) in order to protect the "Negro in his social, economic, educational, political, and Constitutional life." The KBNA was almost a one-man show, with Tucker urging blacks to assert their legal rights, promising to defend them, and constantly egging on other organizations to be more militant. Likewise, the Jefferson County Sunday School Association (JCSSA), which started as a church group, quickly became a militant leader. In the early 1950s the JCSSA was a prime mover in coalition-building in campaigns against discrimination in jobs and health care.[17]

A second constituency in the postwar coalition was white and interracial religious groups. During this period a brotherhood movement was making inroads into the southern churches, influencing a minority subculture of southern white Christians, and in some cities Jews, to adopt a more liberal perspective on race relations.[18] The founding statement of the Militant Church Movement in 1951 expressed a basic principle of faith-based civil rights activism: "No church or person is Christian that does not believe in the principles laid down by Jesus Christ, the founder of the church, namely the Fatherhood of God, the Brotherhood of man, and the Golden Rule." From this premise the Louisville Council of Churches, representing diverse denominations, drew the conclusion that the churches had a special responsibility "to show that the solution of the race problem is the gospel of Christ." With that in mind, prominent clergymen and seminary professors lent their names to public appeals and integrated ecumenical organizations such as the Louisville Council of Churches and the National Council for Christians and Jews sponsored meetings and participated in public pressure campaigns.[19]

While it is always difficult to measure the involvement of rank-and-file members in any church activity, there is evidence that lay people got involved, especially women and youth groups. For example, black and white high school students from the YMCA, YWCA, Young Men's Hebrew Association, and Catholic organizations formed Youth in Action to promote better racial and religious understanding. Methodist women in Louisville matched the regional pattern of dedicating their organizations to better race relations.[20] The primary work of these religious groups was to change attitudes within their congregations and in the city at large through public forums, fellowship hours, and exchanges on Brotherhood Sunday. But in addition they cooperated in coalitions to petition local and state government on specific issues.

Working alongside these groups were some of the major unions and labor organizations of the city. The Farm Equipment Workers and Teamsters worked to change attitudes within their own organizations and also provided rank-and-file support for direct action and political pressure. A local branch of a new organization, the Negro Labor Council, ran public relations campaigns encouraging interracial solidarity among workers while also coordinating pressure for a permanent FEPC and jobs in large local firms. Closely allied with these labor groups was the Louisville Progressive Party. To some extent these local groups were influenced by national trends. The FE, as a CIO union, was led by their national practice of insisting on integrated unions and nondiscrimination policies in hiring. More generally, the labor movement was influenced by its alliance with the national Democratic Party and to a lesser extent the Progressive Party. Locally activists argued that equality of black and white workers on the job would raise living standards for both, and in the process would contribute to the prosperity and well-being of the whole community. In this period at least, some labor groups were stalwart partners in petition drives and boycotts, turning people out for meetings and testifying for legislation.[21]

The final major constituency was the secular interracial organizations. Louisville had branches of the CIC and Urban League in the 1920s. The CIC was subsumed under the new statewide Kentucky Commission on

Interracial Cooperation (KCIC) during the war and then changed its name and incorporated as the Kentucky branch of the Southern Regional Council (KSRC), following the lead of the regional organization. During the war the group emphasized the need to forestall postwar racial tension by working for the FEPC and for educational opportunity and by cosponsoring public forums on race relations. The Urban League concentrated on opening employment opportunity through negotiations with local businesses. In 1944 Mayor Wilson Wyatt followed a national trend and established the Louisville Interracial Committee, composed of twenty people and charged with mediating racial conflict. All of these groups drew their members from "leading citizens"—businessmen, ministers, professors, and other professionals.[22] Locally the secular interracial groups were relatively quiet between 1948 and 1954, but they set a precedent of city government and elite white support for racial improvement. And they reawakened in the mid-1950s to help guide the process of school integration.

Though not identifiable as a group or organization, a number of prominent white liberals contributed to the interracial movement. The prewar interracial coalition had been dominated by men and women like them and their elite black allies. Although the postwar movement included a wider variety of grassroots organizations, elite whites still played a role. For example, outspoken faculty at the Southern Baptist Theological Seminary, Bellarmine College, and the University of Louisville influenced the intellectual centers of the city. Successful businessmen including Dan Byck, Arthur Kling, and Harry Schachter worked behind the scenes negotiating incremental desegregation. Perhaps most important, however, were Barry Bingham and Mark Ethridge, owner and publisher respectively of the *Courier Journal* and *Louisville Times*. Bingham was a well-respected leader whose main concern was protecting the city's positive reputation. Ethridge was known for his fight against the Klan in Georgia and his work on the FEPC during the war. Under their guidance, the daily papers molded "public opinion in favor of better race relations."[23] Although they did not always agree with black activists about the pace or extent of desegregation, these white liberal leaders often came down on the side of ending particular cases of discrimination and thus smoothed the way for community acceptance of change.

In the postwar years these constituencies conjoined to assail segregation in Louisville through a mixture of persuasion, petition, legislation, and court challenges. Some small changes came when black community pressure convinced white civic leaders and politicians to end discrimination at government-owned facilities and jobs. For example, a citizens committee representing the NAACP, Urban League, Pan-Hellenic Council, Citizens of Parkland Committee, and the Peter Salem Post of the American Legion held a sit-in, wrote letters to the editor, and testified at a library board meeting, convincing the library board to integrate the public library system gradually between 1948 and 1952.[24] The NAACP sponsored rallies, sent resolutions to the mayor's office, and convinced the Board of Aldermen to recommend lifting all racial discrimination in the city civil service, arguing that "It is criminal for government subdivisions to practice . . . [segregation] while America preaches democracy to the world." In 1952 the city began hiring black clerks at city hall and in February 1954 Mayor Andrew Broaddus, citing the right to equal opportunity and pledges he had made in his campaign, ordered an end to all discrimination in the civil service.[25] Perhaps the quickest result came when C. Eubank Tucker, as head of the KBNA, wrote letters asking that all Jim Crow signs be removed from the county government buildings. Within one month the signs of segregation were gone.[26] These gains nudged the Louisville city government slowly toward desegregation and demonstrated the efficacy of black community and political pressure on white officials.

The first extensive example of interracial coalition-building and effective rank-and-file lobbying for legislation was the campaign to eradicate segregation from hospital care. The movement arose in 1950 after three African Americans injured in a car wreck spent hours on the floor of a hospital emergency room in Breckinridge County. They were denied treatment until an ambulance took them to the black hospital seventy miles away in Louisville. The Progressive Party of Kentucky and the Farm Equipment Workers launched a protest and started a petition drive to ask the governor to open all hospitals. The drive quickly garnered enough support that leaders decided to establish the Interracial Hospital Movement (IHM), a coalition of ministerial, student, labor, and traditional civil rights groups. The Episcopal Diocese of Kentucky, the Louisville Council of Churches, the Baptist Ministers and Deacons Meeting, and other religious groups endorsed the drive. Thirty organizations, including student groups from Southern Baptist Theological Seminary, the University of Louisville, and Louisville Municipal College, and several local unions including the FE, Public Workers, and Teamsters, circulated petitions. In order to show the support of local residents, the IHM also put petitions in corner drug and grocery stores. The goal was to demonstrate the breadth of support

from across the spectrum of the white and black community by giving the
governor 10,000 names on petitions.[27]

The movement drew on the ideas and strengths of different constituencies and pursued a variety of strategies. In order to advertise the ongoing
petition drive, the IHM organized a Brotherhood Rally in November 1951,
attended by a racially mixed audience of more than 200 people. Speakers
included union representatives (to demonstrate "that the unions are in the
forefront of this struggle"), student body leaders from the University of
Louisville and Southern Seminary, and a long roster of clergymen. At the
rally the Reverend J. C. Olden appealed to the conscience of the faith-
based constituency. Quoting Jesus, he said, "'In as much as ye have done
unto one of the least of my brethren, ye have done it unto me,' Jesus died
on the floor of a hospital in Breckinridge County." At the end of the rally,
supporters signed a pledge promising "to deal with all human beings without prejudice."[28]

Next, in January 1951, 150 members of the IHM visited Governor Lawrence Wetherby. Spokesmen Allen L. Coones of the FE and Reverend
J. Albert Dalton of St. Stephen Episcopal Church argued that desegregated hospitals were a matter of constitutional principle. The state had
no right to support financially institutions that served only a part of the
population. Specifically, the delegation asked the governor to require tax-
supported and tax-exempt hospitals to accept black patients. Almost immediately Wetherby opened the state tuberculosis facility, Hazelwood
Sanatorium, to blacks, and a few months later he ordered all forty-four
state-operated hospitals to admit African Americans.[29]

Rather than resting on these laurels the IHM utilized its resources to
pressure all hospitals to open, including the state's 100 private hospitals.
Carl Braden and the Urban League investigated those that did not serve
blacks, in the process reminding officials that if they received federal dollars they could not discriminate. Meanwhile Anne Braden consulted with
lawyers on the legal basis for a suit against private hospitals. The lobbying
efforts of the IHM paid off. In 1952 the Kentucky Senate stipulated that no
hospital licensed by the state could discriminate in the provision of emergency treatment. The IHM continued to press for all treatment, calling for
federal laws to be enforced, applying "moral pressure" on hospital officials,
mobilizing public opinion, and asking the NAACP to take over the job of
protecting black patients' legal rights under the new law.[30]

The success Louisville became most known for—the peaceful integration of its schools—also best illustrates the character of the postwar move-

ment and what it could accomplish. The campaign followed the lead of national efforts by starting with graduate and professional schools. In 1944 Charles Anderson introduced a bill to amend the state's Day Law, which since 1904 had mandated segregation in the classroom, to allow integration of postgraduate education. The Anderson bill passed the General Assembly, making it the "first favorable effort in any legislature of the South to abolish segregation and discrimination in education by legislative action." The bill failed in the Senate, however.[31] A few years later the NAACP tried again through court action. In 1949 they succeeded when a court decision forced the University of Kentucky to admit Lyman Johnson of Louisville to graduate school, making him "the first Negro to enroll in a 'white' University east of the Mississippi and south of the Mason-Dixon line."[32] Meanwhile, the KSRC, the Urban League, and the *Defender* lobbied for another amendment to the Day Law, to allow exceptions for nursing training. In 1953, after passage of the amendment, they convinced Mayor Broaddus to guarantee unrestricted participation of black women in the nursing program at the city General Hospital.[33]

In late 1949 a campaign began to open the undergraduate institutions of Louisville. After the court decision against the University of Kentucky the NAACP began pressing the University of Louisville to admit blacks to its medical school. They prepared a test case, but it was dropped on a technicality. Meanwhile the Board of Trustees debated the issue. The pro-integration minority on the board, including former mayor Wilson Wyatt, quietly began laying the groundwork for voluntary desegregation by surveying the university's constituencies, determining the legal applicability of the Day Law, and convincing Jesse H. Lawrence, black state representative from Louisville, to introduce a bill amending the law again to allow integration of undergraduate institutions. The amendment passed on March 2, 1950, and almost immediately the two local seminaries and Bellarmine College, a private Catholic school, opened their doors to blacks. With the legislative barrier removed the University of Louisville pledged to open the graduate and professional schools in fall 1950 and the rest of the school the next year. As part of the plan, Louisville Municipal College closed in June 1951 and its students were allowed to transfer schools. Many Municipal College students could not afford the higher tuition at University of Louisville, however, and only one of the college's black faculty, Charles Parrish Jr., was hired by the university. Still, Parrish noted a year later that for those who did attend the transition to integrated college classrooms was successful. The smooth acceptance of integration at the university, and the fact that barriers had been lifted without a court order, further enhanced the city's self-image as progressive.[34]

With higher education desegregated, attention shifted to the lower grades. In the years leading up to *Brown* local groups began lobbying for legislation and garnering public support for complete integration. In 1951 the Committee on Education for Kentucky Youth, led by Monsignor Felix N. Pitt of Louisville, asked for an amendment to the Day Law to allow local boards of education to integrate. The Mayor's Legislative Committee approved the proposal, which would allow private or parochial schools to admit blacks, but it failed at the state level. A year later, the Militant Church Movement started a petition drive, hoping to achieve desegregation through a grassroots campaign rather than by court decisions. Finally, in January 1953 a new interracial group, the Citizens Committee for Democratic Schools in Kentucky (CCDSKy), formed and made Louisville its headquarters. This new committee was composed of representatives from churches, unions, and civil organizations—a constituency very similar to that of the IHM—and based its critique of school segregation on the taint it put on American democracy and the damage it did to children's psyches.[35]

The new Committee for Democratic Schools quickly became the spearhead of a coalition effort to end or amend the Day Law. In January 1954 Senator C.W.A. McCann (D-Louisville) introduced Senate Bill 6, which would overturn the law and the part of the state constitution mandating segregation and would require that all but religious schools accept students without discrimination. At the same time Felix Anderson introduced another bill to leave segregation up to local school boards, but civil rights groups supported the more encompassing McCann measure. The Citizens Committee on Desegregation, a primarily black organization, circulated pamphlets and rounded up endorsements for the measure. The climax of the campaign was a public hearing at the legislature. Representatives from the Kentucky State Federation of Labor, the Americans for Democratic Action (ADA), the Baptist Ministers and Deacons Meeting, the United Electrical workers, the Women's International League for Peace and Freedom, student groups, and others spoke, giving, according to one witness, "a very graphic demonstration of the support that exists in the state for non-segregated schools."[36] Legislators hesitated, however, preferring to wait for the Supreme Court's decision in *Brown*, and both bills died in committee. Though legislative efforts were unsuccessful, the campaign demonstrated support for integration across a broad range of constituencies in the city.

The CCDSKy pledged to continue to pave the way for the acceptance of the expected court decisions.[37]

The *Brown* decision was not a surprise to local leaders or officials. Indeed, various groups had been discussing the impending ruling and how to respond to it. The Louisville chapter of the ADA sponsored a forum in late February 1954 at which Catholic School Board leader Monsignor Felix Pitt, Alexander Erlen of the Confederation of Jewish Organizations, and Whitney Young of Lincoln Institute discussed the need to prepare parents for the transition to integration, especially to the idea of their children being taught by black teachers. The Kentucky Education Association also set up a committee to study the legal implications of the decision.[38] When the *Brown* decision was announced, state and city officials responded positively. On May 18, Governor Wetherby immediately declared, "Kentucky will do whatever is necessary to comply with the law." Local officials meanwhile remarked that they had expected the decision and could now openly start planning for integration. From all quarters came the prediction that Louisville would not have a problem and would lead the South in a smooth adjustment to the ruling. Nevertheless, state school officials decided that local boards should take a year to prepare and hear what the Supreme Court had to say about implementation.[39]

In the meantime the city school system began the process of planning for integration. In fall 1954 Superintendent Omer Carmichael polled the faculty, asking them to submit their ideas about what problems might arise and how to solve them. White teachers began to prepare their classes by introducing black history and talking to their students about the upcoming change. The principals' meetings were already integrated and soon the PTAs followed suit, eventually merging black and white units. During the year Carmichael made numerous speeches and participated in forums to answer parents' questions. As Evelyn Jackson, a black principal in the system, recalled, "He went into the communities, met with city fathers, political groups, Lions and Rotary Clubs, at the library." Other employees of the system did the same. The goal, particularly after *Brown II*, was to prepare the community and to make a "prompt and reasonable start" toward integration of the schools in 1956.[40]

While Carmichael and others worked through the school system, the civil rights coalition worked to build a consensus in the community. One advocate asserted: "The important thing is that people with an interest in smoothing the way for desegregation get together to talk about it and by doing so hopefully pave the way for others to get interested too." With that in mind, a group of parents in the east end formed the Eastern Council on Moral and Spiritual Education and published a pamphlet of pro-integration speeches. Youth Speaks, an interracial group of high school students, encouraged other young people to support integration. Many groups, including the local affiliates of the National Council of Jewish Women and the National Council of Christians and Jews, organized informational forums. Meanwhile, "ministers discussed it with their congregations to get everybody to lose this fear of what's going to happen." The court decision also reinvigorated the local Southern Regional Council affiliate, which incorporated as the Kentucky Council on Human Relations and began a campaign to provide information and guidance to communities undergoing integration.[41]

Over time, some local activists grew impatient and pushed harder. On the statewide level the Citizens Committee on Desegregation proposed three steps to insure not only a rapid transition, but one that would not hurt black teachers in the process. Then in summer 1955 the NAACP became more aggressive. The state branches voted to push local boards to integrate that fall. The Louisville branch wanted the Board of Education to make its plans public in order to insure that it was not just stalling. They backed up their request with a petition to the local board in the name of twenty black parents asking for immediate desegregation in fall 1955. The board headed off this criticism by announcing its plan and its September 1956 goal.[42]

Louisville city public schools integrated according to the board's schedule, with a redistricting and pupil transfer option plan. The board redistricted schools without regard to race and placed students according to residence and the capacity of buildings. Parents had the option of requesting a transfer for their children to a school that was a majority of their own race. Carmichael justified the transfer option by saying that the court had ordered the end of compulsory segregation but not the enforcement of compulsory integration.[43] Summer classes were the first to be integrated, but the big day for the city was September 4, 1956, when students enrolled at their new schools. Attendance was a little lower than expected, due, officials thought, to parents keeping their children home to see how things went. By the end of the first month, however, officials reported that integration was a success, with statistics showing that 73.6 percent of pupils went to schools with mixed student bodies.[44]

Not everyone was satisfied with Louisville's desegregation of the schools, however. Some civil rights leaders questioned the transfer plan and complained that integration was "uneven, sometimes limited to High School" and dependent on black students' willingness to attend a white school, where they were the minority. In short, they warned that results would be merely token.[45] Another major concern was for the fate of black teachers. Ever since the *Brown* decision white officials had been questioning whether white parents would accept their children being taught by black teachers, while civil rights leaders urged that provisions be made to protect the faculty. Carmichael caused a furor when in an interview in *U.S. News and World Report* in late 1956 he argued that black teachers were never as good as white teachers regardless of education or experience. When pressured by the NAACP in 1957 to integrate the teaching staff, he put off the decision and any action for at least another year. Thus despite the declarations of success, the pupil transfer option and the failure to integrate the faculties kept the number of white students low in schools with large numbers of black students or teachers.[46]

Louisville school desegregation drew some opposition from segregationists, but the effort was small and relatively unorganized. Millard Grubbs, a former Klan member, started a White Citizens' Council unit and published a newsletter to argue against integration. The Citizens' Council tried to organize a boycott of the schools and had five members picketing the board of education on the first day of class. The only hint of violence was the burning of crosses at three schools and a scuffle involving a small group of students during registration. Some parents did keep their children out of school, and one couple was prosecuted for contributing to the delinquency of minors as a result. The system also faced a prolonged battle with a teenage boy from Michigan who moved to Louisville and formed an alliance with Grubbs in order to organize student opposition. He was kicked out of school, however, on the grounds that he was not a legal resident. The white press dismissed the significance of the organized opposition, and in retrospect white participants in the integration process characterized the objectors as "kooky, far right, militant." "They were almost like an embarrassment to the white people." More important, "there were no important citizens of the community" in the ranks of the opposition. Although in many ways integration was no more or less token than in other southern communities, in Louisville whites did not respond with anger or violence and opposition groups were not able to awaken much reaction.[47]

Peaceful school desegregation in Louisville earned praise at the time and in retrospect for the community and its leaders, both locally and nationally. Carmichael acknowledged the community, especially the religious leaders who created a favorable climate and the teamwork of parents, teachers, and others. The *Courier Journal* saw success as a product of state politics and the absence of demagogues using the issue for selfish gain, and cited the record of slow desegregation over the last few years in libraries, universities, parks, and transportation facilities. In retrospective interviews people give credit to strong leadership from city and school officials, the careful preparation done by teachers and the community, and the safety valve of the transfer option, which gave diehard parents a way to opt out of integration. The national media featured the Louisville story, contrasting the city's actions to those elsewhere in the state and region. These reports echoed the *Courier Journal*'s theme, noting that school integration was part of a larger pattern of progress and a result of Carmichael's actions. The superintendent received honorary degrees, was invited to speak at numerous forums, and visited the White House.[48] These events reinforced Louisville's national reputation as a leading southern city in racial progress and were pointed to with pride by both white and black citizens.

Despite the accolades and self-congratulation for the progress of desegregation in government-owned facilities, hospitals, and schools, some black leaders were critical of the priorities and pace of the postwar movement. One of the most insistent was Frank Stanley. In 1947 he challenged the biracial Committee for Kentucky to support open accommodations. When chairman Harry Schachter refused, claiming it was better to move slowly and not risk losing opportunities for progress, Stanley quit the committee. Shortly thereafter, in 1948, an Urban League study found many blacks believed that too many civil rights groups emphasized racial uplift and accommodation. When asked why Louisville did not go further in the 1940s, Lyman Johnson recalled that white leaders often used the city's good reputation to slow down change, suggesting "'Look how good we are to you. Now don't bug us too much.'" He further explained, "Whites said blacks 'should be satisfied because they were better off in Louisville than in Atlanta or Birmingham.'" On the eve of school integration, militant black leaders reminded the community that it had not progressed as far as it liked to think. While whites and moderate blacks argued for going slowly, radicals argued that Louisville's blacks should not rest until there was full integration of public spaces. As Stanley reminded his readers, "There are still problems."[49]

Moreover, not all the campaigns orchestrated by the interracial coalition succeeded. The battle to open the city park system was one of the longest. After the war interracial groups tried to persuade the city to integrate the parks, arguing that discrimination was morally wrong and that taxpaying citizens should have equal access to city-owned property. Youth in Action, the Civil Rights Committee of the Progressive Party, and the FE each tried to hold integrated picnics in the parks but were dissuaded by threats of violence or by officials who feared trouble.[50] The campaign to achieve park integration was hindered because it was unclear who had the authority to make the decision—the mayor, the aldermen, or (as it was eventually decided) the city park director. As an appointed position, the director was relatively less susceptible to political influence than other officials. With the failure of political pressure, the NAACP sponsored a number of lawsuits based on the inequality of facilities. In 1952 a judge ordered the city to equalize or integrate its golf courses, and in 1954 after continuing threats of legal action the Iroquois Park Amphitheater opened to blacks.[51]

However, at each step in the battle the city government steadfastly resisted, arguing that opening the parks would lead to racial mixing and conflict. Moreover, there is some evidence that white citizens did not want the parks opened. Soon after the 1952 decision, for example, white golfers petitioned the city to resegregate the courses. In addition, Frank Stanley reported in 1954 that blacks were routinely accosted, harassed, and arrested just for driving through a park.[52] Technically the campaign to desegregate the parks was a success. The parks were opened completely in 1955 after court decisions elsewhere indicated that segregated parks, like schools, were unconstitutional.[53] Yet the resistance to the process and the fact that action came only under intense court pressure revealed the difficulty the Louisville movement had making progress in an area that involved primarily social contact of a private nature, even if in a public space.

During the same period various groups in Louisville worked for equality of economic opportunity for African Americans. These campaigns resemble the integration efforts in their strategies of cooperative effort, persuasion, petition, and attempts at legislation, but they were much less successful. For several years the main focus was securing a permanent FEPC. The local unions, NAACP, Progressive Party, and branch of the Negro Labor Council joined a national campaign to collect petitions and lobby legislators for passage of the law. These groups, joined by political clubs and the Militant Church Movement, testified before the Board of Aldermen for local legislation. Rhetoric during this effort revealed that local activists saw the FEPC as a way to guarantee equal opportunity through the democratic process. Unfortunately, neither local, state, nor national legislation passed.[54] With legislative channels closed off, local activists initiated a number of public pressure campaigns, using negotiations, petitions, and boycotts to convince individual businesses to hire more blacks. While there were some successes in government jobs, progress was slow; and in private employment it was even slower.[55] While these campaigns reinforced alliances between labor and civil rights organizations, they could not bring about integration in an area that was considered to be primarily in private, as opposed to government, hands.

Ironically, at the time the national press was praising Louisville for its peaceful acceptance of school integration, a case involving the dynamiting of an African-American home in 1954 was winding its way through the local courts. Andrew Wade, an African-American electrician and former member of the Progressive Party, had asked his friends Anne and Carl Braden to help him acquire a house in Shively, a white subdivision just south of Louisville. The Bradens bought the house and transferred the deed to Wade. After the Wades moved in both families were harassed, and on June 26 the Wade house was bombed. Later that summer the Bradens and several others—but not Wade—were arrested and accused of conducting a communist plot to blow up the house and foment racial trouble.[56]

Segregated housing was not a target of the postwar interracial coalition, although the issue had been percolating. The increasingly tight housing market and crowded conditions in black neighborhoods led to pressure for expansion into nearby white blocks. The late 1940s and 1950s saw court decisions holding that courts and state agencies could not enforce discriminatory real estate agreements, but that private individuals and financial institutions could voluntarily practice segregation. As black migration into white neighborhoods continued, white hostility grew. Neighborhood associations bought houses preemptively to keep them out of the hands of blacks. On one occasion in summer 1953 the Klan burned a cross at the home of the only black family on a white block.[57] Intermittently white liberals had voiced support for African Americans' right to live wherever they wanted, in keeping with laws against government-sponsored segregation. But there was no local campaign to confront the issue. When the Wades were attacked the community reacted against the violence. But the *Courier Journal* criticized the tactics by which Wade got the house, and once the Bradens were labeled as communist white liberal and black moderate support faded. Only a few militant whites and some black organizations—but not the NAACP or the Urban League—remained vocal supporters of the two families. Quite telling is Anne Braden's critique of the labor movement. As she later recalled, labor leaders told her "We can talk about equality on the job and things like that. But in housing it's different. . . . This gets to social equality and they don't believe in that."[58]

The timing of the two events raises interesting questions and implications. The harassment of Wade and destruction of the house occurred within months of the *Brown* decision. As Anne Braden pointed out in her report on Louisville's school integration, "Housing integration of course remains a strong brake on actual [school] integration."[59] While public officials in Louisville were promising a smooth transition to public school integration, private gangs were reacting violently to the housing integration that would produce real change. The successful integration of public schools also occurred at the same time that anticommunist furor and attacks by the Commonwealth Attorney's office were railroading Carl Braden to prison. The juxtaposition of the two events highlights a basic contradiction in Louisville's postwar movement: an interracial coalition of white and black church, labor, political, and community groups worked to open public schools in the name of equal educational opportunity, equal access to the benefits of public institutions, and better race relations. At the same time interracial cooperation failed to integrate housing, protect the Wades, or support the Bradens. Housing, like jobs and recreational facilities, was an expression of private association and could not be secured by the methods used in Louisville's postwar tradition.

In retrospect it is possible to discern particular patterns in what was fought for and what was accomplished by Louisville's postwar interracial movement. The city's movement was distinctive because of the power of the black vote. In addition, it enjoyed a tradition of interracial cooperation, which although dominated in the 1920s and 1930s by elite whites and blacks, was expanded after the war to include more grassroots activism. The influence of black political power and the ideology of various white constituencies combined to ensure that the local movement took seriously both postwar democratic rhetoric and the city's responsibility to be a leader in southern race relations. This movement made gains in fighting government-sponsored segregation in city facilities, hospitals, and schools. However, there was less headway made against discrimination in jobs and housing, areas contemporaries considered a realm of private decision making. Although the case of the parks is more ambiguous, it reflects similar limitations. Despite being publicly owned, parks were primarily a forum for private activity.

The nature of the movement produced both its strengths and its weaknesses. The influence of black political power, rhetoric of racial democracy, and white liberal participation led to campaigns for progress in areas that could be defined as citizenship rights and were susceptible to political pressure. But the acceptance of gradualism in order to maintain Louisville's relatively good race relations, and the focus on government-sponsored segregation, kept the movement from making a serious challenge to private discrimination and social inequality. The postwar movement in Louisville thus demonstrates what black voters with white allies could accomplish. But it also demonstrated that an expanded notion of the rights of citizens was required before more extensive change could occur.

NOTES

1. Anne Braden, "Draft Report on School Desegregation in Kentucky," 1956, Box 53 File 12, Carl and Anne Braden Papers, State Historical Society of Wisconsin, Madison (hereafter cited as Braden Papers, followed by box number: file number).

2. My ideas about "organizing traditions" are informed by Charles Payne, *I've Got the Light of Freedom: The Organizing Tradition and the Mississippi Freedom Struggle* (Berkeley: University of California Press, 1995).

3. On the postwar movement see Aldon Morris, *The Origins of the Civil Rights Movement: Black Communities Organizing for Change* (New York: Free Press/Macmillan, 1984); John Egerton, *Speak Now against the Day: The Generation before the Civil Rights Movement in the South* (Chapel Hill: University of North Carolina Press, 1994); Patricia Sullivan, *Days of Hope: Race and Democracy in the New Deal Era* (Chapel Hill: University of North Carolina Press, 1996); Linda Reed, *Simple Decency and Common Sense: The Southern Conference Movement, 1938–63* (Bloomington: Indiana University Press, 1991); Anthony Dunbar, *Against the Grain: Southern Radicals and Prophets, 1929–59* (Charlottesville: University Press of Virginia, 1984); also see larger works that study this period including Adam Fairclough, *Race and Democracy: The Civil Rights Struggle in Louisiana, 1915–1972* (Athens: University of Georgia Press, 1995); John Dittmer, *Local People: The Struggle for Civil Rights in Mississippi* (Urbana: University of Illinois Press, 1994); and Payne, *I've Got the Light of Freedom*. For works on the border region see Sandy Shoemaker, "'We Shall Overcome Some Day': The Equal Rights Movement in Baltimore, 1935–1942," *Maryland Historical Magazine* 89 (1994): 261–74; Andor Skotnes, "The Black Freedom Movement and the Workers' Movement in Baltimore, 1930–1939" (Ph.D. dis-

sertation, Rutgers University, 1991); Henry Louis Taylor Jr., ed., *Race and the City: Work, Community, and Protest in Cincinnati, 1820–1970* (Urbana: University of Illinois Press, 1993); and Patricia L. Adams, "Fighting for Democracy in St. Louis: Civil Rights During World War II," *Missouri Historical Review* 80 (1985): 58–75.

4. On segregation in Louisville in this period see George C. Wright, *Life Behind a Veil: Blacks in Louisville, Kentucky, 1865–1930* (Baton Rouge: Louisiana State University Press, 1985). On Louisville's southern orientation see Omer Carmichael and Weldon James, *The Louisville Story* (New York: Simon and Schuster, 1957), 12–14.

5. Wilson Wyatt, interview by John Egerton, 12 July 1990, Southern Oral History Collection, Wilson Library, University of North Carolina, Chapel Hill (hereafter cited as SOHC); "Louisville: A Blend of Almost Everywhere," *Business Week,* 7 May 1955, 84–85; on the history of the Farm Equipment Workers see Toni Gilpin, "'Left by Themselves': A History of the Farm Equipment and Metalworkers Union, 1938–1955" (Ph.D. dissertation, Yale University, 1992).

6. On black politics in Louisville before World War II see Ernest Collins, "The Political Behavior of the Negroes in Cincinnati, Ohio and Louisville, Kentucky" (Ph.D. dissertation, University of Kentucky, 1950), 6–41; and Wright, *Life Behind a Veil,* 176–96, 246–61.

7. On black voting behavior in the 1940s see Collins, "Political Behavior," 70–133, 182–210; and Louis C. Kesselman, "Negro Voting in a Border Community: Louisville, Kentucky," *Journal of Negro Education* 27 (1957): 273–80.

8. "Negroes Active in Louisville Municipal Government," *American City,* April 1945, 86; Goldie Winstead Beckett, interview by Kenneth Chumbley, 12 September 1978, Oral History Collection, University Archives, University of Louisville (hereafter cited as OHC); "Political Parties Start Fall Campaigns," *Defender,* 8 October 1953, 1; "New Director of Safety Says He's Not Biased," *Defender,* 17 December 1953, 1.

9. The number of lynchings in the state steadily dropped decade by decade, with eight between 1919 and 1939. The last lynching involving a victim from Louisville was in 1913. Both the *Kentucky Irish American* and the *Courier Journal* carried criticisms of police violence against black suspects. See Wright, *Life Behind a Veil,* 237, 239–41,255–56; and *Kentucky's Black Heritage* (Frankfort: Kentucky Commission on Human Relations, 1971), 50–52, 80–81.

10. For an overview of black and interracial activism in Louisville in the pre–World War II era see Wright, *Life Behind a Veil*; and Wright, *A History of Blacks in Kentucky, Volume 2: In Pursuit of Equality, 1890–1980* (Frankfort: Kentucky Historical Society, 1992).

11. Wright, *Life Behind a Veil,* 199–212.

12. "Civic Leaders Will Confer on Racial Ills," *Courier Journal,* 10 May 1944, sec. 2, 1; on motivations leading to city and state interracial committees see Robert A. Burnham, "The Mayor's Friendly Relations Committee: Cultural Pluralism and the Struggle for Black Advancement," in *Race and the City,* ed. Henry Louis Taylor

Jr., 258–79; for a documentation of the government's association of civil rights with anticommunism in the pre-*Brown* era see Mary L. Dudziak, "Desegregation as a Cold War Imperative," *Stanford Law Review* 41 (1988): 61–120.

13. Amelda B. Ray, Letter to Editor, *Courier Journal*, 26 July 1946, sec. 1, 6; Reverend Carl J. Stanley to NAACP, 5 March 1956, Group 3 File C50, NAACP Papers, Library of Congress (hereafter cited as NAACP Papers, followed by group number: file number); "White and Negro Students Discuss Problem," *Louisville Leader*, 23 February 1946, 1; "Granger Says Peace Demands Racial Amity," *Courier Journal*, 23 January 1947, sec. 1, 11; "Nation Must Be Strong through Faith in Our Beliefs, Urban League Is Told," *Courier Journal*, 9 February 1951, sec. 1, 13; "League Told U.S. Fights Reds Negatively," *Courier Journal*, 27 February 1953, sec. 1, 14.

14. L. E. Woodard, "Progress Noted in City's Race Relations during '52," *Defender*, 31 December 1952, 1; see for example "Defender Honor Roll," *Defender*, 12 January 1952, 1; "Let Us in Louisville Keep Our Perspective," *Courier Journal*, clipping, [January 1942], Box 2 File 12, John and Murray Walls Papers, University Archives, University of Louisville (hereafter cited as Walls Papers, followed by box number: file number); "Urban League Told Life not so Bright for Negroes," *Courier Journal*, 13 April 1948, sec. 2, 1; "Granger Says Peace Demands Racial Amity," *Courier Journal*, 23 January 1947, sec. 1, 11; "Authority Warns against Haste in Steps to End Racial Segregation," *Courier Journal*, 13 December 1944, sec. 1, 2; William Patterson, interview by Darlene Eakin [n.d.], OHC.

15. Frank L. Stanley, "People, Places and Problems," *Defender*, 25 March 1954, 6; "Judge Shelbourne's Decision," *Defender*, 22 September 1951, 6; Frank L. Stanley, "People, Places and Problems," *Defender*, 18 March 1954, 7; J. Harvey Kerns, "A Survey of the Economic and Cultural Conditions of the Negro Population of Louisville, Kentucky," January-February 1948, Box 2, Arthur Kling Papers, University Archives, University of Louisville (hereafter cited as Kling 2).

16. See, for example, "$200 Reward Offered Here for Lynchers," *Courier Journal*, 5 August 1946, sec. 1, 4; Gloster B. Current to James Crumlin, 27 January 1948, NAACP Papers 2:C66; for examples of coverage of national events see *Louisville Leader*, 1946–50.

17. "Organization Formed to Protect Negroes," *Courier Journal*, 24 November 1940, sec. 2, 1; "KBNA Launches Fight on Jim Crow Waiting Rooms," *Defender*, 18 March 1953, 1; "Tucker's Charge of 'Partisan' NAACP is Just a Publicity Stunt, Crumlin Says," *Defender*, 28 January 1953, 3; Radio Script, 14 February 1954, Braden Papers 54:4.

18. For faith-based concern about race relations in this period see Tracy E. K'Meyer, *Interracialism and Christian Community in the Postwar South: The Story of Koinonia Farm* (Charlottesville: University Press of Virginia, 1997); William H. Crook and Ross Coggins, *Seven Who Fought* (Waco, Tex.: Word Books, 1971); Alice G. Knott, "'Bound by the Spirit, Found on the Journey': The Methodist Women's Campaign for Southern Civil Rights, 1940–1968" (Ph.D. dissertation, Iliff School of

Theology, 1989); and Robert Martin, *Howard Kester and the Struggle for Social Justice in the South, 1904–1977* (Charlottesville: University Press of Virginia, 1991).

19. Militant Church Movement, "Statement," 12 June 1951, Braden Papers 55:12; Good Will Conference Flyer [1945], Box 2 File labeled WECC, 1961–68, Harvey C. Webster Papers, University Archives, University of Louisville (hereafter cited as HCW Papers, followed by box number:file title); Edward A. McDowell, Letter to Editor, *Courier Journal*, 11 February 1944, sec. 1, 6.

20. "Youth of Various Faiths Plan Forum," *Courier Journal*, 16 December 1945, sec. 1, 17; "Youth in Action to Become Permanent," *Courier Journal*, 10 February 1946, sec. 1, 10; Henlee Barnett, interview by Linda White, 28 March 1984, OHC; Statement by Mrs. E. H. Menart et al., 17 February 1950, Reel 59, File 1, Southern Regional Council Papers, Clark Atlanta University Center, Robert W. Woodruff Library, Atlanta (microfilm); Charles Steele, "Urban League Reminders," *Defender*, 1 July 1954, 9.

21. Untitled article, *CUB* [newsletter of the FE-CIO Local 236], 17 September 1946, 1; see also scripts for radio broadcasts by the Negro Labor Council over local station WLOU, winter 1953–54, Braden Papers 54:4. For more on the relationship between labor and civil rights see Robert Korstad and Nelson Lichtenstein, "Opportunities Lost and Found: Labor, Radicals, and the Early Civil Rights Movement," *Journal of American History* 75 (1988): 786–811; Michael K. Honey, *Southern Labor and Black Civil Rights: Organizing Memphis Workers* (Urbana: University of Illinois Press, 1993); and special issue of *International Labor and Working Class History* 44 (1993).

22. For a history of the local Commission on Interracial Cooperation and Urban League see Wright, *Life Behind a Veil*, 262–82. For a regional history of interracial groups see Julia Ann McDonough, "Men and Women of Good Will: A History of the Commission on Interracial Cooperation and the Southern Regional Council, 1919–1954" (Ph.D. dissertation, University of Virginia, 1993); Thomas A. Krueger, *And Promises to Keep: The Southern Conference for Human Welfare, 1938–1948* (Nashville, Tenn.: Vanderbilt University Press, 1967).

23. Anne Braden, *The Wall Between*, 2d ed. (Knoxville: University of Tennessee Press, 1999), 43; David Gittleman, interview by Tracy E. K'Meyer, 1 December 1999, in possession of author; Kerns, "Survey," Kling 2. For a more mixed review of Bingham and Ethridge see Lyman Johnson, interview by John Egerton, 12 July 1990, SOHC.

24. "Negroes Ask Unrestricted Library Use," clipping [1942], Walls Papers 2:12; "Segregation at Library Banned," *Louisville Leader*, 22 May 1948, 1.

25. "NAACP Considers Board Decision 'Challenging,'" *Defender*, 26 May 1951, 1; "Aldermen Advise Civil Service Board to Stop Race Discrimination," *Defender*, 5 May 1951, 1; "Members of NAACP Protest City's Decision," *Defender*, 23 June 1951, 1; "Colored Clerk Employed in City Hall for First Time," *Defender*, 16 July 1952, 1; "Department Heads Are not Surprised, *Defender*, 4 February 1954, 2.

26. "County Asked to End Restroom Segregation," *Courier Journal*, 4 February 1953, sec. 1, 22; "Bias Signs Removed from Courthouse," *Defender*, 4 March 1953, 1.

27. Press Release, 10 September 1950, Anne Braden to Caesar Bell, 24 October 1950, Anne Braden to Pat Ansboury, 22 November 1950, Braden Papers 50:9; Rev. J. C. Olden, "Lest We Forget," *Defender*, 1 March 1952, 6; "Campaign for Louisville Interracial Hospital Moves Ahead," Federated Press release, 8 November 1950, Folder 26, Social Action Files, State Historical Society of Wisconsin.

28. Anne Braden to Pat Ansboury, 22 November 1950, Anne Braden to James Smith, 22 November 1950, series of letters 23 November 1950 to black ministers, Program for Brotherhood Rally, 26 November 1950, Press Release, 27 November 1950, Braden Papers 50:9; Rev. J. C. Olden, "Lest We Forget," *Defender*, 1 March 1952, 6.

29. Press Release from IHM, 27 November 1950, untitled statement [1951], Carl Braden to Charles Steele, 13 June 1951, Braden Papers 50:9; "Hospital Protest Committee Plans Confab with Governor Wetherby," *Defender*, 20 January 1951, 3; Fletcher Martin, "Aid Denied Because of Patient's Color Immoral, Governor Told," *Defender*, 27 January 1951, 1; "Hazelwood Sanatorium Opens Doors to All People after Group Protest," *Defender*, 17 February 1951, 1.

30. Carl Braden to Charles Steele, 13 June 1951, Anne Braden to Rev. J. W. Adams, [1951], Rev. J. Albert Dalton to James Crumlin, 8 May 1952, Braden Papers 50:9; "State Hospital Licensing Act Would Ban Race Discrimination," *Defender*, 16 February 1952, 1.

31. "Kentucky Votes 41-40 to Admit Negroes to White Universities," Press Release, National Bar Association, 26 February 1944, Section 3B Reel 12, NAACP Papers, Library of Congress (microfilm, University of Kentucky) (hereafter cited as NAACP MF, followed by section number: reel number); "Kentucky Senate Defeats Bill to Admit Negro Students to White College," Press Release in letter, Charles Anderson to Thurgood Marshall, 16 March 1944, NAACP MF 3B:12.

32. "NAACP to Fight for Admission of Negroes to Kentucky Schools," *Courier Journal*, 15 January 1949, sec. 1, 9; "Subsiding of Prejudice Is a Slow process," *Courier Journal*, 7 April 1949, sec. 1, 8.

33. Charles Steele, "Urban League Reminders," *Defender*, 17 December 1953, sec. 2, 11; *Kentucky's Black Heritage*, 99.

34. Wilson Wyatt, interview by John Egerton, 12 July 1990, SOHC; "Student Relations at U. of L. Cited," *Defender*, 8 March 1952, 1. For a complete history of Louisville Municipal College and the desegregation of the University of Louisville see James Blaine Hudson, "The History of Louisville Municipal College: Events Leading to the Desegregation of the University of Louisville" (Ph.D. dissertation, University of Kentucky, 1981).

35. "Committee Favors Ending of Segregation in Schools," *Courier Journal*, 19 September 1951, sec. 1, 1; "Pitt Proposal Seems Doomed," *Defender*, 9 February 1952, 1; Militant Church Movement Letter to Editor, *Defender*, 13 August 1953, 6; "New

Group Here Asks School Ban on Segregation," *Courier Journal*, 13 February 1954, sec. 1, 2; "Proposed Constitution—Committee For Democratic Schools in Kentucky" [n.d.], Statement of M. M. Perdue [1953], Braden Papers 48:11.

36. "Bill Would Kill Law Segregating Schools," *Courier Journal*, 7 January 1954, sec. 1, 5; "Leaving Segregation Up to Local Boards Urged," *Courier Journal*, 15 January 1954, sec. 2, 1; Series of letters in March 1954 planning hearings, [?] to Olof Anderson [n.d.], Anne Braden to Jim [Dombrowski], 27 February 1954, Braden Papers 48:11; John Briney, "Segregated Schools Are Deplored by All Speakers at Public Hearing," *Courier Journal*, 25 February 1954, sec. 1, 8.

37. Governor Lawrence W. Wetherby to Anne Braden, 9 March 1954, Daniel Hughlett and Lillian Elder to members of CCDSKy, 16 April 1954, Braden Papers 48:11; "Railroad Plan, Segregation Bill Die in Senate," *Courier Journal*, 20 March 1954, sec. 2, 1.

38. Charles Steele, "Urban League Reminders," *Defender*, 4 March 1954, sec. 1, 5; "KEA Group to Study Segregation-Ruling Effect," *Courier Journal*, 22 April 1954, sec. 1, 1.

39. Hugh Morris, "Decision Voids State's Day Law," *Courier Journal*, 18 May 1954, sec. 1, 1; "City, County Are Planning Integration," *Courier Journal*, 18 May 1954, sec. 1, 1; "What Louisvillians Think of the Supreme Court Decision," *Defender*, 20 May 1954, sec. 1, 2; Frank L. Stanley, "Being Frank about People, Places, and Problems," *Defender*, 17 June 1954, sec. 2, 9; Allan M. Trout, "Desegregation Delayed in State," *Courier Journal*, 18 June 1954, sec. 2, 1; "Kentucky State Board of Education Says Wait on Final Court Decree," *Defender*, 24 June 1954, sec. 1, 2.

40. "Desegregation Study Asked by Carmichael," *Courier Journal*, 2 November 1954, sec. 1, 1; Evelyn Jackson, interview by Darlene Eakin [n.d.], Duard J. Pate, interview by Darlene Eakin [n.d.], Milburn Maupin, interview by Darlene Eakin [n.d.], in OHC; Jean Howeton, "September '56 Is Still Integration Target Here," *Courier Journal*, 1 June 1955, sec. 1, 1; "Board to Begin Planning Now for Desegregation," *Courier Journal*, 7 June 1955, sec. 2, 1. For a first-person account of the process of school integration see Carmichael and James, *The Louisville Story*.

41. Marion Porter, "'Climate of Approval' Is Called Key to School Desegregation," *Courier Journal*, 30 January 1955, sec. 3, 5; "County Group Publishes Data on Integration," *Courier Journal*, 3 April 1955, sec. 1, 22; Margaret Yeager, interview by Darlene Eakin, 1 July 1973, Milburn Maupin, interview by Darlene Eakin [n.d.], OHC; Galen Martin, interview by Tracy E. K'Meyer, 11 November 1999, in possession of author; "Council Set Up to Aid Integration," *Courier Journal*, 9 April 1955, sec. 1, 12.

42. "Preliminary Integration Steps Urged," *Courier Journal*, 17 December 1954, sec. 2, 1; M.M.D. Perdue Letter to Editor, *Courier Journal*, clipping [1954], Braden Papers 48:11; Press Release, NAACP, 16 July 1955, Donald Jones to Gloster B. Current, 24 July 1955, "20 Demand Integration Here Now," clipping [n.d.], NAACP 2:A227; William Patterson, interview by Darlene Eakin [n.d.], OHC.

43. "Desegregation Plan for City Provides for Redistricting 'Without Regard to Race,'" *Courier Journal*, 22 November 1955, sec. 1, 1; "Pupil Transfer Plan Criticized, Defended," *Courier Journal*, 23 November 1955, sec. 1, 1.

44. "Things Go Smoothly as First Negroes Enroll in Manual Summer School," *Courier Journal*, 12 June 1956, sec. 2, 1; "Estimates Seem Awry on Integrated Classes," *Courier Journal*, 6 September 1956, sec. 1, 1; "76 Percent of City Pupils Integrated," *Courier Journal*, 23 October 1956, sec. 1, 1.

45. "Pupil Transfer Plan Criticized, Defended," *Courier Journal*, 23 November 1955, sec. 1, 1; Braden, "Draft Report," Braden Papers 53:12.

46. "Butler Says Kentucky White People Will Balk at Use of Negro Teachers," *Defender*, 8 July 1954, 2; "Kentucky's Negro Teachers Warned to Prepare Themselves for Desegregation," *Courier Journal*, 6 November 1954, sec. 2, 1; Omer Carmichael, "Is 'Voluntary' Integration the Answer? Interview with Louisville's School Superintendent, Dr. Omer Carmichael," interview by editors, *U.S. News and World Reports*, 5 October 1956, 142; "Integrate Teachers Here, NAACP Urges Board," *Courier Journal*, 11 July 1957, sec. 2, 1.

47. David Gittleman, interview by Tracy E. K'Meyer, 1 December 1999, in possession of author; William Patterson, interview by Darlene Eakin [n.d.], Milburn Maupin, interview by Darlene Eakin [n.d.], OHC.

48. Carmichael and James, *The Louisville Story*, 101–3; "The Story Behind the Story of Successful Integration Here," *Courier Journal*, 13 September 1956, sec. 1, 6; Galen Martin, interview by Darlene Eakin [n.d.], Ruth Higgins and Margaret Yeager, interview by Darlene Eakin [n.d.], Milburn Maupin, interviewed by Darlene Eakin, 2 October 1978, William Patterson, interviewed by Darlene Eakin [n.d.], OHC; "How to Integrate," *Time*, 24 September 1956, 53; "The Quiet Zone," *Newsweek*, 24 September 1956, 37; Robert Riggs, "Ike Lauds City's Desegregation," *Courier Journal*, 12 September 1956, sec. 1, 1.

49. Untitled article, *Defender*, clipping, 5 July 1947, Box 6 File 55, National Urban League Papers, Library of Congress; Kerns, "Survey," Kling 2; J. C. Olden, "Militant Church," *Defender*, 19 November 1953, 6; Frank L. Stanley, "People, Places and Problems," *Defender*, 18 March 1954, 7 and 25 March 1954, 6; Lyman Johnson, interviewed by John Egerton, 12 July 1990, SOHC.

50. I. Willis Cole, Letter to Editor, *Courier Journal*, 29 July 1946, sec. 1, 6; Youth in Action, Letter to Editor, *Courier Journal*, 29 July 1946, sec. 1, 6; "Negro-White Picnic Set to Test Park Segregation," *Courier Journal*, 10 September 1948, sec. 2, 1; "Civil Rights Group Votes to Postpone Interracial Picnic," *Courier Journal*, 30 September 1948, sec. 1, 1; Gilpin, "'Left by Themselves,'" 521–26.

51. "Aldermen Refuse to Act on Park Segregation," *Courier Journal*, 25 July 1946, sec. 1, 1; "Judge to Try Two Phases of Antisegregation Suit," *Courier Journal*, 11 March 1950, sec. 1, 1; "Park Suit Is Firm Test of Rights Guaranteed under Law, Lawyer Says," *Defender*, 28 April 1951, 1; "City Integrates Golf Course; Other Inequali-

ties Studied," *Defender*, 26 January 1952, 1; "Supreme Court Asked to Hear Amphitheater Suit," *Defender*, 26 March 1953, 1; "Amphitheater Racial Bars Are Lifted," *Courier Journal*, 11 March 1954, sec. 1, 1

52. "Aldermen Asked to Rule on Segregation in Parks," *Courier Journal*, 23 July 1947, sec. 1, 1; "Judge Quite Technical in Park Suit," *Louisville Leader*, 2 August 1947, 1; "Golfers Circulate Petitions for Segregated Courses," *Courier Journal*, 13 April 1952, sec. 1, 16; "Broaddus Again Refuses to Desegregate Parks," *Defender*, 3 June 1954, 1; Frank L. Stanley, "Being Frank about People, Places, and Problems," *Defender*, 19 August 1954, 7.

53. "Ruling May End Park, Pool Segregation Here," *Courier Journal*, 8 November 1955, sec. 1, 1; "Ban on Mixing Races at Parks in State Upset," *Courier Journal*, 17 December 1955, sec. 1, 1.

54. "Board to Continue Local Campaign for FEPC Bill," *Courier Journal*, 24 February 1946, sec. 1, 15; "20,000 Signatures Sought Here for FEPC Proposal," *Defender*, 15 March 1952, 1; "3,000 Signatures for FEPC, Goal is 20,000," *Defender*, 9 April 1952, 1; "Why Signing the FEPC Petition Is an Important Factor," *CUB*, 6 June 1952; "Aldermen Will Hear Petition for City FEP Ordinance," *Defender*, 2 July 1952, 1; "For a Healthy and Prosperous Community—Pass FEPC Now," Testimony of Louisville Area NLC before Louisville Board of Aldermen, 8 July 1952, Braden Papers 54:4; "Aldermen Will Introduce City Fair Employment Practice Law," *Defender*, 29 October 1952, 20; Radio Script for Broadcast by Louisville Area NLC over WLOU, 18 October 1953, Braden Papers 54:5; Radio Script for Broadcast by Louisville Area NLC over WLOU, 24 February 1954, Braden 54:4; "House Gets Bill for State FEPC," *Courier Journal*, 3 March 1948, sec. 1, 1. The death of the bill was confirmed by author's phone conversation with a research specialist at the Kentucky Legislative Research Commission, November 1999.

55. "Once a Letter Carrier Always a Letter Carrier," *Defender*, 20 January 1951, 1; "Ministers Urge Transit Co. to Change Employment Policy," *Defender*, 21 January 1953, 1; "Groups Urging Negroes to Tighten Beer Boycott," *Defender*, 7 May 1952, 3; "GE Hiring Policy Discussed with Plant Official," *Defender*, 14 May 1952, 1; "Better Group Relations Seen for GE Plant," *Defender*, 27 August 1953, 2.

56. For the story of the Wade house incident see Braden, *The Wall Between*.

57. "Court Bans Real-Estate Color Bars," *Courier Journal*, 4 May 1948, sec. 1, 1; Grady Clay, "Neighbors Buy House to Keep It from Negroes," *Courier Journal*, 14 May 1950, sec. 5, 9; "Klan Cross Burned at Upper Grand Ave. Home," *Defender*, 23 July 1953, 1; "House Offer to Negroes Causes Stir," *Courier Journal*, 8 February 1954, sec. 2, 1.

58. "Woman Told Negroes May Live Anywhere," *Courier Journal*, 23 November 1948, sec. 2, 1; "Contrast in Approaches to Goal of Race Justice," *Courier Journal*, 16 January 1949, sec. 3, 2; Braden, *The Wall Between*, 76–82, 116–27.

59. Braden, "Draft Report," Braden Papers 53:12.

Chapter 13

"A Bland, Scholarly, Teetotalling Sort of Man"

Harry T. Moore and the Struggle for Black Equality in Florida

Caroline Emmons

Florida has long debated its identity as a Southern state, at times releasing a "faintly tropical rebel yell," while at other times, its leaders and citizens have insisted that their state is not really Southern at all.[1] This confusion has extended to race relations as well. While Florida's leaders have claimed their state to be "moderate" in its racial policies and history, the historical record provides plenty of evidence that Florida was far from immune from racial violence and hatred. Some of the region's most vicious lynchings occurred within the state and by the 1930s, one historian has described Florida as the "most lynch-prone state in the South."[2] Another long-standing belief about Florida is that if there is a typically Southern section of the state, it is confined to the Panhandle; while there may be some truth to this, the record, once again, contains evidence that racial violence and discrimination against African Americans could be found throughout the state. Miami, for example, was known throughout the first half of the century as perhaps the most racist city in Florida.[3]

African Americans in Florida have never found the state to be racially moderate. From Reconstruction to the present, they have resisted discrimination and violence through a variety of organizations and with an effective, although largely unrecognized, cadre of leaders. Perhaps foremost among these organizations in the twentieth-century has been the NAACP, which chartered its first branch in Florida in Key West in 1915. Over the next twenty years, the NAACP in Florida participated in voting rights cases, teachers' pay equalization suits, and a variety of criminal defense cases. By the late 1930s, mirroring a trend evident throughout the South, the NAACP stood poised to achieve its greatest membership gain and entered its most active period of civil rights litigation, with a particular focus on voting rights.

By the 1930s, black Floridians also had an organizer who relished the opportunity to get African-Americans on the voting rolls. Harry T. Moore, the first President of the Florida State Conference of NAACP branches, emerged as a leader in the struggle for civil rights at a time when opportunities for black political involvement were expanding rapidly. Moore believed that blacks could not improve their situation in any substantial sense without being able to effectively utilize the ballot. Working with the national office, Moore agitated tirelessly, both among white politicians and the black population in Florida, to secure the right of blacks to vote and to mobilize them to go to the polls and capitalize on that right.

Like other black intellectuals of the period, Moore believed that securing the ballot for blacks was essential in overcoming other abuses blacks faced. He had come to this belief partly through his struggle during the 1930s to win equal pay for black teachers and it was a view he would continue to hold as his work in the late 1940s moved to resisting racially-motivated violence. With voting rights the main focus of his energies during the 1940s, Moore also became deeply involved with the Progressive Voters' League, Inc., one of several black voting rights organizations in Florida whose policies Moore would significantly influence.

Harry Moore was born in Houston, Florida, a small town in the Florida Panhandle on November 18, 1905. His father, Johnny Moore, died when he was ten, but his mother, Rosa, would outlive her only child. The region of North Florida in which Moore was born is typical of the Florida Panhandle: heavily agricultural with a scattered population of only 26,780 in 1990.[4] When writing to the national NAACP office in reference to a 1944 lynching in the county, Moore noted that he knew from his own experiences growing up there that the Klan was active and brutality toward blacks not uncommon.[5] Moore attended several schools around the state, including the high school in Houston, Stanton High School in Jacksonville, and Florida Memorial in Live Oak, from which he graduated in 1925. An excellent student, he acquired the nickname "Doc" because of his talent for math and science problems. While in Jacksonville, he lived with several of his aunts, who were schoolteachers and whom his daughter later described as having the most significant influence on him.[6] Trained as a teacher, a profession he pursued in Houston, Titusville, Cocoa, and Mims, Florida, Moore received his bachelor's degree in 1951, the summer before he died, from Bethune-Cookman College, by taking summer classes. He is remembered as a shy, quiet man, slow to anger or to laugh, but intensely dedicated to the struggle for black equality. *Time* magazine described Moore in his obituary as a "bland, scholarly, teetotalling sort of man."[7] In 1925, Moore moved to Mims, Florida, to pursue his teaching career. A friend of Moore's, Crandall Warren, recollects giving literature he had received on the NAACP to Moore.[8] By 1934, Moore had organized the Brevard County Branch of the NAACP and become its first president.

Early activities of the Brevard County branch were typical of the organization's emphasis on education and "consciousness-raising." The "Branch News" column in *The Crisis* contained occasional pieces of information about the Brevard County chapter's activities; it is the only Florida branch to appear in that column with any regularity during the 1930s. The first mention of the new group came in January 1935 in an item which noted that the chapter had "aided its neighboring branches in such cases as need whole-hearted cooperation. In Volusia County, a colored boy said to have killed a white woman was taken from his county cell to the death cell at Ralford [*sic*], Florida, and, with aid from the local branches, ours included, the sentence was commuted, for further investigation."[9]

The January 1936 issue contained a short piece on the 2nd Annual Meeting of the chapter, held at Mims Junior High School. Among the officers elected was Harry T. Moore for another term as President and J. E. Gilbert as assistant secretary. Gilbert would be the plaintiff in the first suit filed in Florida for equalization of teachers' pay. Also in January 1936 the group sponsored a "county-wide emancipation celebration" at St. Paul Missionary Baptist Church in Cocoa. There was a parade, a mass meeting, and a "big, free dinner." Basketball games finished up the day. The Brevard County chapter planned another celebration for Negro History Week.[10] Moore continued to organize educational activities that might serve to galvanize community support. During the winter of 1936/37, these activities included: youth council meetings to discuss "educational inequalities" and observances of Emancipation Day and Negro History Week. At the latter celebration, Moore and T. W. Everett of Titusville "discussed the Negro in literature and his political activities from emancipation to the present."[11] While these activities are not unlike those carried out by most NAACP branches, Moore was conscientious in sending word of them to *The Crisis* for publication. This served to increase interest in and awareness of the branch throughout the community, which in turn spurred membership. Branches valued mention of their programs, officers, and accomplishments in *The Crisis* and complained when their news was left out.

Moore's name became familiar to black Floridians outside Brevard County primarily through his work on the teachers' pay suits which began in earnest in Florida in the late 1930s. He wrote to the national office in August 1937 noting "For several years, we have investigated protests against these (pay) inequalities in the form of petitions to the School Board . . ." He forwarded in this letter details of the unfair pay schedules used by the Brevard County School Board and said African American attorney S. D. McGill of Jacksonville had been retained to investigate the possibility of initiating a suit. Moore hoped the national office would help, but clearly was prepared to take the initiative.[12] Moore also served as president of District 4 of the Florida State Teachers' Association, the largest black teachers' organization in Florida; the FSTA would play a major role in supporting pay equity suits throughout the state. While John Gilbert was chosen for the first, ultimately unsuccessful, suit over teachers' pay in Florida, Moore took the lead in writing to the national office, soliciting legal help from Charles Houston, Thurgood Marshall, and others on the legal staff. His name was becoming known to the national NAACP staff as well as to black Floridians across the state.

Beginning in the spring of 1940, the national NAACP office began exploring the possibility of hiring a full-time organizer for Florida.[13] Moore had already petitioned the national office for the establishment of a state conference of branches. The NAACP operated in a technically decentralized fashion, with local branches retaining a good deal of independence from the national office. Local branches were responsible for raising their own funds and setting their own agenda. In reality, the national office did exert significant pressure, particularly in terms of political positions taken by local branches, because of the national office's cautious approach to charges of Communism and radicalism. As a result, the national office did interfere in local branches' decision-making when it felt the situation warranted it. Moore's name was acceptable to both NAACP officials in New York and black leaders in Florida and in 1941, Moore became the first President of the Florida State Conference of NAACP branches. The position was unsalaried, despite Thurgood Marshall's recommendation that the person hired in that position should be compensated.[14] Regardless of pay,

Moore now had a state-wide audience for his plans to secure equal rights for African-Americans and he chose to focus on the empowering realm of voting rights.

The Southern Democratic white primary, although only one of a variety of methods used to deny African-Americans the vote, proved to be the most difficult to eliminate.[15] Because of the ambiguous position political parties have always had in American politics, the state and Federal courts reached confusing and occasionally contradictory decisions in cases addressing the right of political parties to exclude certain individuals from membership. And because the Democratic primary was the only meaningful election in a region overwhelmingly Democratic until the 1960s, the exclusion of blacks from participation in those primaries effectively meant the exclusion of blacks from the political process.

Florida followed the pattern of other Southern states in erecting barriers to black political participation. In 1897, the Florida Legislature passed the first primary law and by 1902, the Democratic party had limited participation to whites only.[16] At this time, virtually all blacks who were registered in Florida were Republicans anyway, a holdover from the Reconstruction period. But blacks throughout the South knew that Republican candidates almost never won and they also knew that until they could register as Democrats and vote in the Democratic primary, they would not have a political voice. This is why the NAACP chose the Democratic white primary for one of its first legal campaigns.[17]

In 1927, they won their first major victory in *Nixon v. Herndon*, in which the Supreme Court ruled that a Texas law prohibiting blacks from participating in the Democratic primary was an unconstitutional state action. In Florida as early as 1928, the NAACP assisted local efforts to fight the primary law, in light of the *Nixon* decision. African-Americans in Pensacola, led by Nathan Jones, President of the Pensacola NAACP, and A.M. Johnson, President of the Escambia County Voters' League, began a voter registration drive in 1928 that enrolled 1500 black Democrats by the April 10 primary. However, when H. D. Goode and several other newly-registered black Pensacolans went to vote on April 10, the election officials refused to accept their ballots. The local NAACP chapter hired Attorney Fred Marsh and contacted the national NAACP office for assistance. In June, 1928, the national office contributed $100 and Louis Marshall, an NAACP attorney, offered his services as consultant. Although Circuit Court Judge Thomas West ruled that the Democratic Party in Florida could legally exclude black participation, an appeal to the Florida Supreme Court ended in victory for

Goode on the basis of the Nixon ruling.[18] The NAACP suffered a major setback in 1935 in *Grovey v. Townsend*, when the Supreme Court upheld a Texas Democratic party resolution that excluded African-Americans. The justices concluded that as long as the state of Texas itself did not specifically legislate against black political participation, the party could set its own qualifications.[19] The Florida Legislature, heartened by the *Grovey* decision, voted in 1937 to repeal the state poll tax, believing it was unnecessary in light of *Grovey* and out of fear that the tax discouraged poor whites from voting.[20] Unwilling to accept this decision as final, the NAACP continued to search for another test case.

They found it in 1944 with *Smith v. Allwright*, in which the Supreme Court declared the Democratic white primary to be the most significant election in the South and thus the exclusion of blacks from participation a clear violation of the Fifteenth Amendment.[21] With this decision, African-Americans eagerly anticipated wielding their hard-won right to the ballot. Although the NAACP victories in the courts were crucial in allowing blacks into the political process, grassroots organization would be essential in getting African-Americans to register and utilize their new power. Decades of economic and physical intimidation by the white power structure against blacks made this type of organization that much more dangerous.[22]

While little information is available on Moore's activities as president of the State Conference of the NAACP from 1941 until he assumed the paid position of executive secretary in 1946, it is apparent that he grew increasingly impatient with the pace of civil rights reform including the reluctance among blacks themselves to challenge their situation.[23] Moore wrote, during World War II, that blacks in America

> complain bitterly about the injustices that we suffer in this country. We bemoan the inequalities in educational opportunity, the segregation, police brutality, lynching, and other evils that are heaped upon Negro citizens; but so few of us are willing to take positive action for the alleviation of these conditions. Mere talk will not suffice. If we are to receive the proper respect from those who govern us, we must exercise some voice in their election.[24]

Moore recommended that African-Americans consider registering as Republicans or Independents, if they wished, to prevent Democrats from assuming they would win or that they had the black vote secured. He later disavowed this recommendation, as the power of the Democratic primary

became more apparent to him. Moore attacked politicians advocating segregation and said the causes of violence and discrimination against blacks
"should arouse black citizens" to vote. "We firmly believe in the doctrine
of that writer who said: He who would be free must himself strike the
first blow."[25]

As World War II came to a close and black veterans returned home,
demands for greater political and social equality began to accelerate. The
Smith decision in 1944 made it clear that blacks were gaining support in
their campaign for voting rights. In 1944, there were approximately 20,000
registered black Republicans in Florida, representing 5.5% of Florida's
black population, and no black Democrats.[26] In March 1945, Tom Watson,
Florida's Attorney General, remarked that black participation in Democratic primaries was "inevitable" and that "the Negro and the white man in
American idealism are entitled to the same political rights."[27] However,
Watson made clear his continuing commitment to the practice of racial
segregation.

In February 1945 blacks had freely voted in the Miami and Daytona
Beach Democratic primaries. But other parts of Florida were less inclined
to permit blacks to vote. With this in mind and emboldened by *Smith*, several NAACP leaders in Florida, including Moore, decided to form a new
organization that would focus on issues related to obtaining and using the
ballot. This group, the Progressive Voters' League, Inc. (PVL), outlined a
plan for registering blacks to vote in Florida and identified contact people
across the state to help organize the effort.[28] Moore served as the first Treasurer of the Progressive Voters' League.

In June 1945 the League released a manifesto listing its goals, among
them being to promote "goodwill at all times between the two races in this
state" and the belief that in the fight for the vote, "we should approach our
white friends as potential friends rather than as adversaries and enemies."
The group also assured whites that the League "recognize[d] a distinction
between the two races."[29] Even as the organization committed itself to vigorous pursuit of voting rights for blacks, it acknowledged that true social
and political equality between the races remained highly controversial to
most whites.

In November 1945 Moore distributed open letters about the PVL's activities, and was identified on the letterhead as Executive Secretary. By this
time, Moore had repudiated his earlier suggestion that blacks register to
vote under whatever affiliation they preferred. He asked potential black
registrants to consider the following issues:

Are Negro citizens of Florida suffering more from the discriminatory practices of local officials or of national officials? Who are more directly responsible for the inequalities in educational opportunities, the lynchings, the police brutality and other injustices suffered by Negroes, our state and county officials or the Administration in Washington? . . . Who controls the election of these state and county officials, the Republicans or the Democrats? Regardless to [*sic*] our party beliefs, we must now face facts. And the fact is that practically every city, county, and state official in Florida is selected in the Democratic Primaries. In order to help select these officials, Negroes must vote in the Democratic Primaries. In order to vote in the Democratic Primaries, Negroes must register as Democrats.[30]

In making this argument, Moore was directly contradicting the policy of the national NAACP office, which prohibited its officers or branches from making partisan recommendations.

In February 1946 the Florida Supreme Court ruled that blacks could vote in the Democratic primary. This meant that "for the first time in modern history, Negro citizens of Florida [could] cast their votes in the Democratic primary in the coming month of May."[31] Moore wasted no time capitalizing on the victory, anxious to encourage blacks to exercise their new rights. He was equally anxious to personally enjoy his right to the ballot.

Moore met with difficulty registering as a Democrat because he had been previously registered as a Republican.[32] In May 1946 Moore wrote to E. L. McIlrath, a Jacksonville attorney who had agreed to take on voting rights cases, to describe how an attempt by a group of blacks to vote and his own efforts to register had been unsuccessful. Moore had escorted a group of black voters, who had registered previously as Democrats, to the polling place and waited while they went in to attempt to vote. When they returned, they said the clerks had refused to let them vote. Moore went in himself to see why they had been turned back and was told that no Republican ballots had been received yet. Moore informed the clerks that several of those attempting to vote were registered Democrats. At this point, those blacks registered as Democrats were allowed to vote, but Moore and others originally registered as Republicans still met resistance in trying to change their affiliation.[33] Although Moore wished to pursue this case, an Assistant Attorney General in the Department of Justice informed him there did not appear to be a Florida law permitting an oral change of party affiliation, which Moore claimed to have done, and that, therefore, the case could not be pursued.[34] Other African-Americans in Florida were more successful. By 1946, Florida had 32,280 black Democrats and 15,877 black Republicans, together representing 13.1% of the black population.[35]

Moore attempted to register as a Democrat in Brevard County again in January 1947. He wrote to Thurgood Marshall's assistant, Marian Perry, in reply to a request from her for more information about his efforts to register. He said he had not received a reply from W. J. Bailey, the Brevard County Superintendent of Elections, to his request for instructions for registering. He sent the letter registered mail and felt sure Bailey had received it. He had also gone to Bailey's office "three or four times," but was unable to speak with him.[36] Moore reported that another group from Mims had tried to register as Democrats with the precinct clerk, "Mr. Duff," who told them he could only register them as Republicans. Mr. Duff later told Moore that Bailey had instructed him to refuse to register these individuals as Democrats. Although it is not clear when, or if, Moore was ever able to register as a Democrat and vote in Democratic primaries, he clearly was the most significant individual behind motivating and organizing other blacks in Brevard County to register and demand their right to vote. By 1950, over 50% of the adult black population in Brevard County had registered to vote, a testament in large part to Moore's efforts.[37]

Despite Moore's difficulties, the *Pittsburgh Courier* noted that "more than 32,000 civic-minded Negro citizens" from Florida "helped make political history," by voting in the Democratic primary in 1946. "A cordial relationship prevailed. . . marked by harmony and a noticeable lack of friction."[38] In Moore's annual address as President at the NAACP 1946 State Conference meeting, he observed that, "Undoubtedly, the most momentous development in Florida this year was the participation of Negro voters in Democratic primaries. In winning this right we have struck at the very core of our evils." Moore commended "Negro organizations" in Pensacola, Jacksonville, and West Palm Beach for "spearheading this important drive." He noted that "Negroes voted unhampered" in several counties but "lack of interest" and interference from voting officials kept the black vote down in others. "The Brevard County Branch of the NAACP is bringing legal action against officials who refused to register Negroes as Democrats in that county."[39] As noted earlier, the Department of Justice dropped the Brevard County case, on the grounds that some blacks had tried to change their affiliation orally and because of a lack of witnesses. Caught between Supreme Court decisions increasingly favorable to black voting rights and intransigent white Southern politicians, reluctance by the Department of Justice to prosecute voting rights violations during this period was not unusual.

Not only did Moore urge blacks to register and to vote, he also investigated which candidates most deserved black voters' support. In response to Moore's requests for candidates' positions on various issues of significance to black voters, Joe Hendricks, a Congressman from Florida, wrote that, "The negro of the state of Florida will vote in the primaries for the first time this election. His advancement is strictly within his own hands. If he votes independently and thinks before he votes, he will advance himself. If he is herded by Communists or those kin to them into voting in groups for measures which are opposed to the best interests of this nation, then he will retrogress."[40] Hendricks's response indicates the enormous difference in priorities that separated white politicians and the newly-enfranchised black electorate. For example, in this instance, Moore quizzed white politicians on their support for anti-lynching legislation. Hendricks responded that, "I deeply abhor lynching and will never take part in one regardless of the circumstances." Yet he refused to vote for the anti-lynching legislation then being considered because he believed it to be unconstitutional, especially in terms of its "infringement of states' rights." Despite the unsatisfactory nature of Hendricks's reply, Moore noted that Hendricks was the only Congressman to reply at all to his request for support for the bill. For most black voters in Florida, violence perpetrated by whites was a far more pressing concern than the Communist menace.

Having moved from Treasurer to Executive Secretary for the Progressive Voters' League, Moore wrote an open letter to candidates regarding the May 1946 primaries. He outlined the position of black voters as follows: "We seek merely the fundamental rights of American citizenship, equality of opportunities, equal protection of the law, justice in the courts, and free participation in the affairs of our government." He especially urged support for anti-lynching legislation, action against police officers who "permit lynchings or mistreat prisoners," equal job and educational opportunities, equal travel accommodations, and support for the Fair Employment Practices Committee.[41]

As Moore continued to meet resistance to his efforts to register and to evaluate political candidates, he turned his attention to a piece of legislation before the Florida Legislature that represented an attempt by some white politicians to resist the progress made by black voters. The Mathews Primary Bill, as it was known, attempted to separate primary elections from state control and "thus make the Democratic Party in Florida a private club."[42] It would also have facilitated the exclusion of African-American voters from the primary. The Florida State Conference of the NAACP and the Progressive Voters' League strongly opposed the bill, in an open letter penned by Moore to Florida legislators. Moore now served as executive secretary of both organizations and, in fact, signed letters identifying him as such. This practice would add to Moore's later difficulties with the national office of the NAACP.[43]

Moore outlined the two most significant problems he saw with the measure. "In the first place, it seeks to disfranchise a third of the voting population of Florida. In the second place, it would remove the primaries from state control and thus leave our electoral machinery open to the worst form of fraud and corruption . . . Senator Mathews has frankly admitted that his Bill is designed to keep Negroes from voting in Democratic primaries." Moore added another twist to his argument against the bill, playing on the political fears of the times, by predicting that the "Passage of the Mathews Bill will help to promote Fascism and Communism in our state."[44] Such a bill, Moore contended, eroded the intent of the Constitution regarding the rights of citizens to vote.

The Senate rejected the Mathews Bill, but did pass and send on to the House a proposed constitutional amendment that would have had a similarly negative impact on black voting. This amendment required those wishing to register to vote to be able to read any portion of the State or Federal Constitution, a device effectively used in many Southern states to prevent blacks from voting. Moore again strongly urged the members of the Florida House to defeat the bill. The bill did not pass.

Moore continued to issue statements as executive secretary of both the NAACP in Florida and the Progressive Voters' League. Although the programs of the two organizations were quite similar and Moore may have found it expedient to write one letter on these issues to save money and time, the national office of the NAACP expressed dissatisfaction with this arrangement. In July 1947 Gloster Current, Director of Branches, wrote Moore, commending him on the "excellent" letters on lynching and mob violence that he had forwarded to the national office. However, he added, "May I suggest that in the future, you not sign your name as representing both the NAACP and the Progressive Voters' League of Florida, Inc. on the same communication. A separate communication might better be sent from each organization. Otherwise, the impression may get out that the two organizations are interlocking."[45] Moore, however, continued, on occasion, to sign on the same letter as a representative of both groups, perhaps feeling that the similarity of the groups' goals was more important than the NAACP's reluctance to be associated with other civil rights groups.

Nineteen forty-eight was an important election year for black voters in Florida. African-Americans understood that this would be a closely fought Presidential race and viewed it as an opportunity to demonstrate that black voters could play a pivotal role in the election. This was the first Presidential race in the twentieth century in which Southern blacks would be able to vote and Harry Moore stepped up his activities in anticipation of the opportunity.

The abuse of power by white elected officials toward prospective black voters was widespread throughout the South. Part of Moore's responsibilities as head of the NAACP in Florida and as head of the Progressive Voters' League were to investigate and report on instances of interference in attempts by blacks to vote. Although the Federal government would eventually accept responsibility for insuring the safety of those attempting to vote, during the 1940s and 50s, the Justice Department responded slowly to complaints. State governments in the South were even less likely to investigate complaints, but Moore continued to petition the state to correct such problems, at the same time he alerted the national office of the NAACP to these situations.

In April 1948 Moore wrote Governor Millard Caldwell to urge him to take action in North Florida, where many blacks were afraid to even go to the polls for the primary on May 4. He explained to the Governor that many blacks had been intimidated from voting during the 1946 primaries, and they were reluctant to try again. Moore appealed to the "Chief Executive of our state" to take whatever action was necessary to prevent a recurrence of such interference in the upcoming elections. In response, Moore received a letter three lines long, in which the governor said, "I hope there will be no violations in the coming election."[46] He circulated copies of the governor's response and indicated his dissatisfaction with the noncommittal nature of this reply. Moore advised black voters to go to the polls in groups of at least three, so that if there was interference "we shall have evidence that can be presented to the Department of Justice for possible action."[47]

In addition to circulating among his "co-workers" the governor's reply, Moore again wrote the governor to urge more decisive action. "You did not give us any assurance that you would take definite action to forestall any attempt to keep Negroes from voting. We feel that it will not be safe just to sit back and 'hope.'"[48] He noted that since receiving the governor's letter, he had gotten word that in Calhoun County, whites had forbidden blacks to vote. "It seems to us that this situation must be faced squarely." Moore wanted Caldwell to instruct the sheriffs of North Florida counties, in particular, to protect black voters and to send any additional law enforcement officials that might be needed to make sure the law was observed. Moore's willingness to aggressively confront state government about its own racist policies insured that his name became increasingly familiar to many state officials, who almost certainly resented the presence of such an agitator in their midst.

Despite Moore's attempts to secure protection for black voters in the primaries, several incidents of voter intimidation occurred. In the small town of Greensboro, located in Gadsden County, J. T. Smith, the president of the local NAACP chapter, voted in the May 4 primary, along with several other blacks. As a result, whites detonated a bomb at the home of Smith's brother, one of the men who voted. Taking the advice of a white friend to leave town, Smith went to New Jersey, where he contacted the NAACP in New York. Marian Wynn Perry, Assistant Special Counsel to Thurgood Marshall, wrote Moore informing him of the incident and telling him that they hoped to get an affidavit from Smith. In the meantime, Perry asked Moore to initiate a state or local investigation and referred him to a woman in Quincy for more details.[49]

In Quincy, Mrs. D. H. Spencer, an NAACP member, reported to Moore that six blacks had voted in Gretna, "although they were 'advised' not to come to town that day. She also reported that the teacher in their school [was] now being moved to another school just because she voted." In another letter, Mrs. Spencer reported that "several white men had just visited her home and warned her to 'be darned sure you don't come to Gretna all day Tuesday.'"[50]

Clearly dissatisfied with the response to such problems by state officials, Moore wrote to the chairman of the National Democratic Platform Committee, Francis J. Myers, to impress upon the committee the need for strong civil rights language in the platform, despite white Southerners' call for protection of states' rights. Moore described to Myers the continuing threat of "lynching, mob violence, police brutality, disfranchisement, and racial discrimination" in Southern blacks' lives and disputed the claim of many white Southerners that lynching "has been reduced to a minimum." He cited the case of Leroy Bradwell, a black veteran who had disappeared in Gadsden County in 1945 while in the custody of "Sheriff Edwards and

Deputy Maple." Moore complained that, although none of Bradwell's family ever saw or heard from him after that, Governor Caldwell "readily accepted the officer's alibi" that they had dropped him off at the county line.

He also mentioned the case of J. T. Smith which both the state conference and the national office of the NAACP were pursuing.[51] Moore was interested in "making an example of someone," by involving the Department of Justice in the investigation to try and discourage future interference with black voters.[52] However, Moore and the NAACP legal staff were disappointed by the response from a Department of Justice Assistant Attorney General, Alexander M. Campbell. He wrote Franklin Williams, an NAACP lawyer in the national office, that "an investigation of this complaint has failed to disclose any evidence of the identity of the persons who caused the destruction of part of the home of James Smith, or any connection between this explosion and the attempted intimidation of the Negroes who voted." Campbell said in light of this, no further action would be taken.[53] By September, Moore had contacted the Department of Justice himself about voter intimidation in Florida. With the national elections only two months away, he was anxious to protect those black voters he was so vehemently urging to go to the polls. Moore mentioned the Smith case in his letter to the Department as well as cases in Taylor, Suwanee, Madison, and Calhoun counties, where "we know Negroes have been kept from voting." He complained of Governor Caldwell's unwillingness to intercede in such cases and requested that the Justice Department do whatever it could to protect black voters and punish those who interfered with them.[54]

Despite his concern over the ability of blacks to gain entry to the polls, and the safety of those who were able to vote, Moore continued to write circular letters as head of the Progressive Voters' League, endorsing candidates for national and state office. The P.V.L. endorsed Harry Truman for President because of the stand he had taken on the issue of civil rights. Moore wrote several eloquent appeals on Truman's behalf and especially saluted Truman's willingness to stand up to the pressures placed upon him by the Dixiecrats.[55] In one, he noted

> In 1948, as in 1860, we find our nation again divided on the race question. In 1860, it was called the slavery question. In 1948, it is called the question of civil rights. But the fundamental issue is the same in both cases. The basic question is this: shall America continue to treat Negroes as slaves, inferior beings, and second-class citizens, or shall Negroes be treated as free human beings with all of the rights and privileges of full citizenship?

When this question was raised at the Democratic Convention in Philadelphia this year, the reaction was about the same as it was at the Democratic Convention in Charleston and Baltimore in 1860. The reactionary "States Rights" Southerners walked out in 1860 . . . the reactionary Dixiecrats walked out again in 1948. . . . In advocating the civil rights program, Mr. Truman has stuck his neck out further for the Negro race than any president, perhaps even further than did Abraham Lincoln. . . . Fellow citizens, the Negro vote may prove to be the balance of power in the presidential race in Florida this year. We are the ones who need civil rights. Therefore, let us get prepared to throw a strong vote for the liberal forces that are trying to secure the complete emancipation of our race.[56]

Moore's activism as a representative of the NAACP and the Progressive Voters' League had continued to trouble the national office. Although Moore appears to have curtailed his practice of signing for both organizations on various communications, he continued to do so on occasion. In June 1948 Executive Secretary Walter White wrote a memo to Gloster Current, expressing his concern over the issue by saying "Is there any danger of the Association becoming involved in this inasmuch as Moore is Executive Secretary of the Florida State Conference as well as the Progressive Voters' League of Florida."[57] Current responded that he had advised Moore against using both titles in his letters, but admitted that Moore "apparently is continuing to do this. . . . There is nothing wrong as I see it with serving the two organizations but communications should always be on separate stationery and ought not to be sent at the same time and on the same subject."[58]

Despite the apparent similarities between the objectives of the PVL and the NAACP, the national NAACP office concluded that Moore's level of visibility in both groups was unacceptable. In November 1951, Moore's position as Executive Secretary for the Florida State Conference of the NAACP was abolished. The termination of this position appears to have been partly fueled by concerns over Moore's fundraising and membership recruitment abilities, although national membership numbers were also in decline during this period.[59] Moore himself attributed the decline in memberships to the fact that the national office decided to double membership dues from $1 to $2 in 1949.[60] Another problem may have been Moore's focus on rural areas at the expense of wooing more powerful African Americans in Florida's metropolitan areas (many of whom were Republicans).

Less than a month after his position was terminated, white reactionaries would find a way to silence him permanently. Most investigators and

NAACP activists concurred that Moore was targeted at least in part because of his work on the Groveland rape case. Sometimes referred to as "Little Scottsboro," the Groveland case involved allegations made against four young black men that they had kidnapped and raped a young white woman in 1949. Groveland is located in Lake County, the Central Florida home of one of the most notably racist sheriffs in Florida's history, Sheriff Willis T. McCall. McCall had led a posse after one of the young men who was shot and killed near Perry, one hundred miles from Lake City, as he attempted to flee. The other three were held for questioning and beaten severely during their incarceration. After quick convictions, two were sentenced to death and one, who was 16, to life in prison. The national NAACP legal team, including Thurgood Marshall, came to Florida to organize their appeal. While being transported back to Lake County for a new trial in November 1951, McCall claimed the two suspects tried to escape; he shot them both, killing one and seriously injuring the other.[61] Moore had vigorously protested the treatment of the young men, the behavior of McCall, and the failure of the State of Florida to protect the rights, and even lives, of the accused. The Moores' murder came a month after the two defendants were shot by McCall.

On Christmas night, 1951, after a traditional meal of ham and turkey, the Moores went to bed at about 10:15. Presents were left to be opened the next day when daughter Evangeline arrived. Almost as soon as the lights were turned off, a bomb containing three pounds of dynamite exploded directly under the Moores' bedroom. The explosion blew the mattress of the Moores' bed up to the ceiling and then flung it out into the yard, with Moore still on it. The blast "completely demolished the northeast corner of the house."[62] The Moores' injuries were severe; Moore's brother-in-law and neighbor George Sims said later, "He didn't feel like there was an unbroken bone in his body."[63] Sims rushed the Moores to a Sanford hospital, approximately thirty miles away, but Harry died on the way and Harriett was admitted with a 50/50 chance of recovery.

Moore's death quickly "stirred a storm of protest heard all the way to the United Nations."[64] Walter White flew to Central Florida to demand quick action on Moore's murder and, upon arrival, he and Governor Fuller Warren began exchanging heated charges. A flood of telegrams and letters poured into the Governor's office, the NAACP offices in New York, and a variety of newspapers and magazines expressing outrage over the murder. A number of letter-writers vowed to boycott Florida as a tourist destination until Moore's killer or killers were found. Harry Moore was buried on

New Year's Day, following a service held at St. James Missionary Baptist Church, located about a mile from his home. Estimates of attendance at the funeral range from 500 to more than 1000, although one newspaper reported that the funeral took place "without too much fanfare." "At least seven" FBI agents attended, along with J. J. Elliot, the Governor's special investigator. The police reputedly searched "every nook" of the church before the service.[65] Walter White did not attend the service, with one report claiming he had planned to attend but was unable to get plane reservations.[66]

Two days after her husband was buried, Harriett Moore died of injuries sustained in the bombing. She had been "improving steadily until the day of her husband's funeral, (when) she left the hospital, against her doctor's wishes, to view the body."[67] On January 8, she was buried, after a service attended by 250 people, including Roy Wilkins.[68]

As responses to the Moores' death poured into Florida from around the country, the investigation to find their killer continued. On January 10, the Governor announced that an "Army explosives expert" had arrived to conduct an investigation. Although their results were not conclusive, the amount of planning and effort they put into their work suggest the investigation was undertaken with a degree of seriousness that was previously not common in Federal investigations of racially motivated crimes.[69]

A grand jury convened in March 1952 to consider the "wave of terrorism" which had swept Florida during the preceding couple of years. Nineteen acts of violence were examined by the grand jury, including the bombing of the Moores' home; one hundred witnesses were interviewed and more than 3200 pages of testimony recorded.[70] Although no indictments were returned, the grand jury agreed to remain in session and finally in June, indicted six men for perjury. They had lied to the grand jury about being members of the Klan "or that they had taken part in a series of violent acts in Middle Florida from 1949 to 1952." Their report said the incidents in Florida represented "a catalog of terror that seems incredible."[71]

The mystery over who killed the Moores has continued to the present, with the investigation reopened in 1991, although it was closed in 1992 without any new arrests. It seems certain that whites targeted Moore for death because of the work he did. One magazine observed that the "shy, graying" Moore "seemed to personify a new and subtle change in the mores of the South: the indisputable fact that the white Southerner is slowly accepting the Negro's right to the vote and fuller freedom under the law."[72] It also seems certain that the white reactionaries who killed Moore were determined that the racial inequalities that existed at that time, and for so many years before, would remain in place. But as Moore "always told" his mother, Rosa, "If I die, I was only trying to help my people. If I go that way, I'll go as a hero. Somebody has got to do that work."[73] Moore did go as a hero and his example led others to carry on that work. But it was not only his death that made him a hero, it was, more significantly, the work he had carried on during his life.

The first NAACP official killed in the line of duty, Moore represents a bridge between the method typically employed by the NAACP at the time of relying on court action to achieve change and the more activist methods that would first be popularized in the Montgomery bus boycott four years after his death. Between 1948 and 1950, more African-Americans registered to vote than at any other time in Florida's history, with the percentage rising from 16.9 to 31.7%.[74] Although a variety of other factors were significant in this growth, Moore's efforts to register blacks played a critical role. Moore's death also renewed interest in the work of the NAACP within Florida. Only a couple of months after he was killed, the Branches Committee of the national NAACP office resolved to hire a new staff person in Florida because of this increased interest. On the other hand, Gloster Current noted that some NAACP workers in Florida were understandably more fearful in the wake of the bombing and he hoped the presence of a paid staff member might alleviate some of their concerns.[75] And in Brevard County, voter registration figures dipped from 51%, one of the highest percentages in the state among African Americans eligible to vote, to only 33%. Some in the area attributed this to "a real fear of participation," although it may have also been because the area had lost its most vigorous and committed leader.[76] Ella Baker said that after his death, "you could go into that area of Florida , and you could talk about the virtue of the NAACP, because they knew Harry T. Moore. They hadn't discussed a whole lot of theory. But there was a *man* who served *their* interests and who *identified* with them."[77]

The murder of the Moores, and the wave of violence that spread across Florida during the late 1940s and early 1950s, also challenges the image of Florida as a state that escaped the racial violence which plagued other parts of the South. Moore's story proves that the sort of activism he undertook during this period required enormous courage and was extraordinarily risky, no matter where in the South such organizing took place.

The indisputable contributions of Moore to the struggle for equal rights make it difficult to understand why his role has been so neglected.

Moore's name is not included on the Civil Rights Monument in Montgomery, Alabama, and it is difficult to find reference to him in secondary works on the period. He did not achieve the same type of national attention that later civil rights leaders received, but his work was essential to laying the foundations upon which later leaders built. Moore wanted to move quickly during a period in which other leaders, black and white, advocated patience. His activism offers a glimpse into organizing methods which would become familiar a decade later but in many respects were innovative at the time he advocated them: an emphasis on rural areas, a willingness to cooperate with other organizations, and a decision to focus on pressuring the Democratic Party as the only real political party in the South. Each of these decisions alienated him from the national NAACP, which by the time of his death was moving increasingly towards an emphasis on the needs of middle-class urban African Americans. The life and career of Harry T. Moore serves as yet another important example of how we must reevaluate the traditional periodization of the civil rights movement which "began" in 1955. Not only does doing so deepen our understanding of the origins of that movement, but it also allows us to recognize the heroic contributions of forgotten civil rights warriors like Harry and Harriett Moore.

NOTES

1. V. O. Key with Alexander Heard. *Southern Politics in State and Nation.* (Knoxville: 1949), p. 83.

2. Walter Howard. *Lynching: Extralegal Violence in Florida During the 1930s.* (Selinsgrove: 1995), p. 15. See also Arthur Raper. *The Tragedy of Lynching.* (Chapel Hill: 1933), p. 483.

3. Frank McCallister to NAACP national office, 27 July 1937. NAACP Papers.

4. *Florida Statistical Abstract, 1993.* (Gainesville: 1993), p. 19.

5. H. T. Moore to R. Weaver, 25 March 1944. NAACP Papers. Manuscript Division, Library of Congress. Washington, D.C. Hereafter referred to as NAACP Papers.

6. Interview with Evangeline Moore, by Ben Green. 29–30 May 1993. For more on Moore's childhood, see Ben Green. *Before His Time: The Untold Story of Harry T. Moore, America's First Civil Rights Martyr.* New York: Free Press, 1998.

7. *Time,* 7 January 1952, p. 14.

8. Interview with Crandall Warren, by author. 28 May 1992.

9. *The Crisis,* February 1935, p. 28.

10. *The Crisis,* March 1936, p. 90.

11. *The Crisis*, April 1937, p. 119.

12. H. T. Moore to W. White, 2 August 1937, Pt. 3, Series A, Reel 9. *Papers of the NAACP.* Schipper, Martin Paul, ed. (Frederick, MD: 1986). Hereafter referred to as NAACP Papers-Edited.

13. N. Griffin to T. Marshall, 23 March 1940. NAACP Papers.

14. T. Marshall to W. White, 8 April 1940. NAACP Papers.

15. Steven F. Lawson. *Running for Freedom: Civil Rights and Black Politics in America Since 1941.* (New York: 1991), p. 15–16.

16. Hugh Price. *Negro and Southern Politics.* (Westport, CT: 1957), p. 18.

17. Richard Kluger. *Simple Justice: The History of Brown v. the Board of Education and Black America's Struggle for Equality.* (New York: 1975), p. 167–168.

18. Darlene Clark Hine. *The NAACP and the Destruction of the White Primary, 1924–44.* (Ph.D. Dissertation: Kent State University, 1975), p. 47.

19. Kluger, p. 167.

20. Price, p. 2.

21. John Hope Franklin. *From Slavery to Freedom.* (New York: 1988), p. 319.

22. Aldon Morris. *The Origins of the Civil Rights Movement: Black Communities Organizing for Change.* (New York: 1984), p. 15.

23. *The Crisis*, February 1952, p. 75.

24. Open Letter from H. T. Moore, n.d. William Gray Papers. Florida Agricultural and Mechanical College. Black Archives. Tallahassee, FL.

25. Ibid.

26. Price, p. 33.

27. *Pittsburgh Courier*, 3 March 1945, p. 1.

28. This memo also contained the constitution and by-laws of the new group. Press Release by the Progressive Voters' League, 11 October 1944. Part 4, Reel 6. NAACP Papers-Edited.

29. Press Release from PVL, 20 June 1945. Pt. 4, Reel 7. NAACP Papers-Edited.

30. Letter to 'Co-Workers' from H. T. Moore, 15 November 1945. Pt. 4, Reel 7. NAACP Papers-Edited.

31. *Pittsburgh Courier*, 2 February 1946, p. 1.

32. T. Watson to H. T. Moore, 19 February 1946. Pt. 4, Reel 6. NAACP Papers-Edited.

33. H. T. Moore to E. L. McIlrath, 23 May 1946. Pt. 4, Reel 6. NAACP Papers-Edited.

34. Theron Caudle to M. W. Perry, 5 December 1946. Pt. 4, Reel 6. NAACP Papers-Edited.

35. Price, p. 33.

36. H. T. Moore to M. W. Perry, 21 January 1947. Pt. 4, Reel 6. NAACP Papers-Edited.

37. Price, p. 45.

38. *Pittsburgh Courier*, 18 May 1946, p. 1.

39. Annual Address to 1946 State Conference, 6 June 1946. NAACP Papers.

40. Joe Hendricks to H. T. Moore, 27 March 1946. William Gray Papers. Florida Agricultural and Mechanical University. Black Archives. Tallahassee, Florida.

41. H. T. Moore to "Candidates", 12 April 1946. William Gray Papers. Florida Agricultural and Mechanical University. Black Archives. Tallahassee, Florida.

42. *The Crisis*, June 1947, p. 185.

43. G. Current to E. Montgomery, 19 April 1951. NAACP Papers.

44. H. T. Moore to Florida Legislature, 4 April 1947. NAACP Papers.

45. G. Current to H. T. Moore, 3 July 1947. NAACP Papers.

46. M. Caldwell to H. T. Moore, 23 April 1948, and note added by H. T. Moore, 2 May 1948. NAACP Papers.

47. M. Caldwell to H. T. Moore, 23 April 1948, and note added by H. T. Moore, 2 May 1948. NAACP Papers.

48. H. T. Moore to M. Caldwell, 2 May 1948. Pt. 4, Reel 6. NAACP Papers-Edited.

49. M. W. Perry to H. T. Moore, 26 May 1948. Pt. 4, Reel 6. NAACP Papers-Edited.

50. Reported in a letter from H. T. Moore to J. T. Smith, 26 May 1948. Pt. 4, Reel 6. NAACP Papers-Edited.

51. H. T. Moore to Francis J. Myers, 8 July 1948. Part 4, Reel 6. NAACP Papers-Edited.

52. H. T. Moore to Thurgood Marshall, 12 July 1948. Pt. 4, Reel 6. NAACP Papers-Edited.

53. A. M. Campbell to Franklin Williams, 30 November 1948. Pt. 4, Reel 6. NAACP Papers-Edited.

54. H. T. Moore to Civil Rights Division of the Justice Department, 1 September 1948. Pt. 4, Reel 6. NAACP Papers-Edited.

55. "Why the Progressive Voters' League Is Supporting Harry S. Truman" by H. T. Moore, 27 October 1948. NAACP Papers.

56. Circular letter from H.T. Moore, 3 September 1948, Pt. 4, Reel 6. NAACP Papers-Edited.

57. W. White to G. Current, 4 June 1948. NAACP Papers.

58. G. Current to W. White, 22 June 1948. NAACP Papers.

59. *Pittsburgh Courier*, 28 October 1950, p. 1.

60. H. T. Moore to G. Current, 8 October 1949. NAACP Papers.

61. For more information on the Groveland case, see Steven Lawson, David Colburn, and Darryl Paulson. "Groveland: Florida's Little Scottsboro," *Florida Historical Quarterly* 65, July 1986, 1–26.

62. FBI Report, 16 December, 1952. Records of Federal Bureau of Investigation. Manuscript Division, Library of Congress. Washington, D.C.

63. *Newsweek*, 7 January 1952, p. 15.

64. *Miami Times*, 29 December 1951, p. 1.

65. *Pittsburgh Courier*, 12 January 1952, p. 1.

66. *New York Times*, 2 January 1952, p. 13.

67. *New York Times*, 4 January 1952, p. 14.

68. *New York Times*, 9 January 1952, p. 60.

69. FBI Report. Memorandum to the Director. 11 January 1952.

70. *New York Times*, 26 March 1952, p. 35.

71. *New York Times*, 4 June 1953, p. 26.

72. *Time*, 7 January 1952, p. 14.

73. *Pittsburgh Courier*, 5 January 1952, p. 1.

74. Price, pp. 32 and 33.

75. Memo from Branches Committee, 28 March 1952. NAACP Papers.

76. James Button. *Blacks and Social Change: Impact of the Civil Rights Movement in Southern Communities.* (Princeton: 1989), p. 70.

77. Charles Payne. *I've Got the Light of Freedom: The Organizing Tradition and the Mississippi Freedom Struggle.* (Berkeley: 1995), p. 238.

Chapter 14

Leading the Civil Rights Vanguard in South Carolina

John McCray and the Lighthouse and Informer, *1939–1954*

Wim Roefs

By 1954, South Carolina blacks had made considerable political progress. In the 1940s, through the courts, they had ended their exclusion from the primary of the one party that mattered in the state, the Democratic Party. They founded the South Carolina Progressive Democratic Party, the PDP, and forced national Democrats to address their position within the Democratic Party. The PDP also organized successful voter registration drives throughout the 1940s. In 1950, it was instrumental in Strom Thurmond losing a race for the U.S. Senate.[1]

Furthermore, during the 1940s, again through the courts, black South Carolinians won equal pay for black and white teachers. Perhaps most importantly, they were the first to challenge the constitutionality of segregated education, with NAACP lawyer Thurgood Marshall leading the effort in court. In 1954, their case, *Briggs v. Elliott,* was part of *Brown v. the Board of Education of Topeka, Kansas.*[2] In charge of most of the action was the South Carolina NAACP, a vibrant organization whose membership grew by the thousands in the 1940s.

John Henry McCray and his newspaper, the *Lighthouse and Informer,* played an important role in these achievements. McCray was part of an aggressive 1940s South Carolina civil rights leadership that also included James Hinton, Modjeska Simkins, and Osceola McKaine. McCray was a core organizer for the state NAACP, of which Simkins and Hinton, an insurance salesman and Baptist preacher, were the top officials. He was the co-founder, president, and, with McKaine, main organizer of the PDP, which effectively became the political and voter-registration arm of the state NAACP. The *Lighthouse* was the unofficial organ of the teachers' salary campaign, the NAACP, and the PDP, and McKaine became its associate editor. The wealthy Simkins, a member of Columbia's black upper class, was the *Lighthouse* society editor.[3]

Together, McCray, Hinton, Simkins, McKaine, and their close associates initiated and directed substantial and sustained civil rights agitation, which had been absent in South Carolina during the 1930s. Through political action and the courts, they pushed South Carolina's white Democratic leadership into a corner. And they were among the most militant elements within the state's African-American leadership. They put conservative blacks on the spot for obstructing progress and relegated black Republicans as a group to second-tier leadership. The *Lighthouse* also replaced the meek *Palmetto Leader* as the state's largest and most influential black newspaper.

McCray, McKaine, Hinton, and Simkins were radical in that they demanded what the state's white leadership was most unwilling to give up. They didn't compromise on goals, they were only to a degree willing to accept compromises for strategic purposes, and they put their activist fervor and organizational skills where their mouths were. "Thank God," the *Pittsburgh Courier*'s executive editor, P. L. Prattis, wrote in 1952, "that the gradualists are not in the saddle in South Carolina. Thank God that the stalwarts like McCray . . . are giving people the courageous, uncompromising leadership they need."[4]

McCray's "personal history as a newspaper publisher, NAACP organizer, voting-rights activist, and co-founder of the Progressive Democratic Party," Patricia Sullivan writes, "embodies the political struggles of many of his contemporaries and invites further study."[5] A look at McCray the newspaperman is a look at a brand of 1940s black journalism that defied the judgment of contemporary commentators, as well as some later ones, who thought of the black press, especially in the South, as scared and conservative, particularly with respect to local issues.[6]

While McCray was probably more strident than most of his southern peers, there were other black newspapers that didn't unequivocally qualify as conservative. McCray thought of himself as part of an exclusive fraternity of crusading editors that included Roscoe Dunjee of the *Black Dispatch* in Oklahoma, Louis Austin of North Carolina's *Carolina Times*, and Emory O. Jackson of the *Birmingham World*. Historians also have called the *Atlanta World*, the *Shreveport Sun* and *Louisiana Weekly*, several Texas papers, and the *Arkansas State Press* anything but conservative. They called them militant and crusaders and foes of Jim Crow.

McCray was a fighting editor, according to the *Carolina Times*. In South Carolina, the prominent journalist William Workman, a noted segregationist, wrote that McCray belittled and belabored "South Carolina political figures whose views run counter to his own on race issues." And a Columbia police court recorder declared that in his city, the *Lighthouse* had "done more than any 1,000 other things I can think of to agitate conditions." McCray took it as a compliment.[7]

A look at McCray and other South Carolina leaders as activists is a look at black leadership that, in Barbara Woods's words, "was in many ways in the vanguard of the civil rights movement in the South." John Egerton and Patricia Sullivan agree in their 1990s books on pre-*Brown* activism in the South. "After the white primary fell in Texas in 1944," Sullivan argues, "South Carolina became the primary battleground over the enforcement of that decision. By the mid-1940s black South Carolinians were in the vanguard of the movement for voting rights and for full participation in the Democratic Party." When the PDP in 1944 challenged the all-white South Carolina Democratic Party delegation's seating at the National Democratic Convention, it "threatened to explode the uneasy accommodation that the national Democratic Party had maintained between its northern black constituency and its white supremacist southern wing." The PDP, Egerton writes, became "a vehicle to force open the political process in [the] state and in the nation."[8]

South Carolina's activism was noticed outside of the state at the time. In North Carolina in the early 1940s, grassroots NAACP organizer Ella Baker held up the South Carolina NAACP as a model. The Southern Conference of Human Welfare offered both McCray and McKaine jobs as field organizers because of their success in organizing black voters in South Carolina. In 1952, the headline of Prattis's commentary in the *Pittsburgh Courier* proclaimed: "The North Would Do Well to Take Note: South Carolina's Leaders Are Men of Inspiring Courage." In the fight to "complete citizenship TODAY, not tomorrow," Prattis wrote, "perhaps the most encouraging and inspiring reports come from the state of South Carolina. Throughout the last decade, South Carolina Negroes in leadership positions, have been making known their determination to regain their political power and to use it for their own and the state's advantage. . . . One of these brave Negroes, the kind the race must have if it is ever to win full citizenship in this country, is John H. McCray, the Negro editor."[9]

McCray's Road to Activism

Growing up, McCray did not lack examples of black folks taking matters into their own hands. Lincolnville, South Carolina, where he grew up, was a rare all-black town governed by blacks. McCray was born in Youngstown, Florida, in 1910, but around 1916 his parents moved the family to Lincolnville, just outside his mother's hometown of Charleston. McCray was the oldest of five brothers and three sisters.

McCray's father, Donnie, became Lincolnville's marshal and assistant pastor at Ebenezer AME Church. Rachel McCray, his mother, was on the city council, active in civic organizations, and involved in voter registration and the NAACP. Both parents stressed education, including reading and learning beyond the classroom setting.[10]

"Growing up and attending school at Lincolnville and Avery Institute in Charleston," McCray recalled in 1981, "I got the idea that Negroes were very special people—virtually saints—who did all good things for history, [and seldom] anything bad enough to notice. Even when something was bad, you could always understand [why] it happened because of the treatment our exploited people had to undergo from whites." As a child, McCray also thought blacks were in charge everywhere, as they were in Lincolnville. That, he later thought, may have given him an attitude as a child that made him relatively fearless as an adult.[11]

After graduating first in his class at Lincolnville Grade School, McCray went to Charleston's Avery Normal Institute, a college prep school for black students. There he became editor of the *Avery Tiger* and president of the Debating Society. He met one of the great influences in his life, the strident instructor J. Andrew "Pearly" Simmons. "He taught other things—a great many of them not 'out of the book,'" McCray recalled. Simmons was "what they called then a dyed-in-the-wool 'race man.' In my own book, he was the first person to really impress and indoctrinate young people—his students—with ideas of their being just as good, and the equal of all others created by God."[12]

Avery's lack of reading materials written by blacks meant reading books McCray didn't care for. One, he recalled, included "the author's alluding to Negroes as having kinky hair, flat noses and a horrible odor." At Avery, segregation suddenly became real for young McCray when "For Whites Only" signs went up on the benches at Colonial Lake in a fashionable white section of Charleston. McCray and some of his Avery friends used to enjoy Easter Sundays there, sitting on a bench, looking at teenage girls. "The fact that we couldn't sit while watching ended what had been a pleasant experience for youngsters growing up in that part of Charleston."[13]

McCray graduated valedictorian of the class of 1931 and went to Talladega College in Alabama, where his political awareness developed further. McCray revived the college's debating club and wrote opinion essays for a campus publication, *The Mule's Ear*, a monthly journal.[14] He criticized the lack of contact at Talladega between students and faculty, and the faculty's unwillingness to engage students in frank discussions. McCray assessed "the general progressiveness of local student reflection" and found it wanting. In the Scottsboro case, "this world-wide disgrace to white American citizens," Talladega students showed little interest, McCray charged. "We may not possess the financial or political influence necessary to save the lives of the boys but we can offer our resentment to the manner in which many of the local and neighboring whites regard them." McCray, a *Mule's Ear* columnist wrote in jest, is "inclined to be a great leader but he lacks the followers."[15]

What Pearly Simmons had done for McCray at Avery, Professor Clarence Harvey Mills did at Talladega when he involved McCray and four of his college mates in a sit-in. Mills invited the five students to join him for soda fountain treats at the Owl Drugstore in downtown Talladega. The students automatically headed for the store's counter, but Mills sat down at the round, stone-topped tables, then ordered his young guests over. The students were stunned and hesitant but did as told.

"We don't serve colored at the tables," the white waiter told Mills. The professor showed a roll of bank notes "big enough to choke a horse," McCray recalled, and threw it on the table, saying, "serve this, dammit." The waiter disappeared, and an older white man appeared. What did Mills want? Soda fountain service, the professor replied. The man and the waiter talked. With nobody else around to witness the event, the man told the waiter to serve the college crowd. The students, McCray wrote, "gulped down the sodas and milkshakes in nothing flat, all the while just half-sitting on their chairs ready to run out. . . . Dr. Mills was in no hurry. He said nothing just then but later, back on campus, he told us it was wrong when we couldn't spend our money for whatever could be afforded because of the color of our skins."[16]

McCray's Early Activism

In 1935, after graduating with a chemistry degree, McCray settled in Charleston. In 1936 he married Satis Victoria Ballou, a fellow student from

Talladega, with whom he had three sons and a daughter. McCray became debit manager and sales instructor for the Charleston District of the North Carolina Mutual Life Insurance Co., a job he would hold for three years. At the same time, he became the city editor of *The Charleston Messenger*, a local black weekly.[17]

At the request of the president of the dormant local NAACP, McCray took over as the new president. He quickly encountered blacks who were less inclined to take action than he was. In the summer of 1936 he took up the case of two black men accused of killing a police officer. McCray established a defense fund for the accused, which did not sit well with many black Charlestonians. McCray recalled that they accused him of "stirring up race trouble" and "backing a criminal."[18]

In 1937, McCray again caused controversy among fellow blacks when he spoke out on federal anti-lynching legislation, for which the NAACP nationally and in South Carolina was campaigning. McCray wrote a remarkable letter to Charleston's *News and Courier*, a newspaper known for its extreme segregationism. He opposed the anti-lynching campaign by "our Northern brothers and sympathizers." Such campaigns only offered "forced and temporary benefits" while provoking southern whites. Fighting for voting rights, on the other hand, would mean that "soon or late, no one will care to lynch. And so we are content to wait."[19]

The letter foreshadowed McCray's 1940s emphasis on voting rights but did not sound like the man who would soon become one of the state's most militant civil rights leaders.[20] The local NAACP chapter demanded and received McCray's resignation. NAACP national secretary Walter White wrote to the *News and Courier*, saying that McCray did not speak for the Association, nor for intelligent and courageous blacks and whites in the South. McCray, White said, had misused his position and was no longer allowed to speak for the organization. Eventually, McCray and White would make up.[21]

McCray's appearance on the civil-rights scene came in a decade of limited political activity among South Carolina blacks. Still, there was some, and new young leaders emerged.[22] New Deal programs undermined the traditional power structure in South Carolina as local white elites were no longer the sole source for employment, financing, and credit. Tenant farmers and sharecroppers were a little less dependent on their old bosses.[23]

Already in 1931, unemployed Greenville blacks had protested with unemployed whites, triggering intense intimidation by the Greenville police and the Ku Klux Klan. After the establishment of the Works Progress Administration in 1935, black leaders in Greenville talked city officials into a WPA project that provided black neighborhoods with their first sewer lines. In Columbia, Modjeska Simkins was among those protesting the WPA's systematic exclusion of blacks from white-collar relief jobs. In 1936, voter registration jumped among South Carolina blacks, who registered as Democrats in support of FDR and the New Deal.[24]

By the late 1930s, the NAACP in South Carolina began to rise to the occasion. Greenville blacks, including the NAACP, began a voter registration campaign, triggered in part by the city's refusal to accept federal aid to build low-cost housing in black neighborhoods. There was more Klan intimidation, and several black leaders were arrested on trumped-up charges.[25]

The persecution in Greenville may have been a catalyst for the unification of the state NAACP. The Cheraw chapter, led by plumber Levi Byrd, organized a defense fund for the arrested Greenville members. Byrd then initiated the meeting at which the state's eight NAACP chapters established the S.C. State Conference of Branches. The statewide infrastructure and nonstop statewide organizing by the likes of McCray, Simkins, Hinton, and McKaine would turn the few isolated and weak local branches into a force to reckon with in the 1940s and one of the country's strongest state NAACPs. In 1939, South Carolina had eight NAACP branches and less than a thousand members. By 1945, there were forty branches and more than 10,000 members. By 1950, there were close to a hundred branches, as well as twenty-two youth councils and two college chapters.[26]

Enter the Lighthouse and Informer

In addition to James Hinton and Modjeska Simkins becoming the State Conference president and secretary, the South Carolina NAACP received much of its organizational strength at the top from John McCray, Osceola McKaine, and the *Lighthouse* moving to Columbia, the capital, located in the center of the state.[27] McCray moved the newspaper at the end of 1941, almost three years after he started it as the *Charleston Lighthouse* early in 1939. He had started it because no other paper dealt with discrimination against blacks.[28]

Because he wanted to expand its coverage, McCray soon changed the paper's name to the *Carolina Lighthouse*. He suspected that his widely acclaimed stand on a student strike at Columbia's Allen University put the *Lighthouse* on the statewide map. It is unclear what the conflict was about, but it involved officials of the American Methodist Episcopal church, with which Allen was affiliated. "Hell is going to be so full of AME preachers and presiding elders," McCray editorialized, that "the rest of us need not worry about where we're going when we die." He recommended a new president, who, to his surprise, was appointed.[29]

In 1940, the *Lighthouse* merged with the Sumter, South Carolina, *People's Informer*, creating the *Lighthouse and Informer*. It was the beginning of the partnership between McCray and Sumterite Osceola McKaine. When the paper moved to Columbia, McKaine became associate editor. Black Columbia activists Seymore Carroll and Modjeska Simkins had urged the move. They wanted a "fighting news organ" in the capital, and Simkins provided the building that became the *Lighthouse*'s home. McCray also moved because he expected that a more central location would increase circulation. Furthermore, he was tired of the harassment by the city of Charleston. In 1939, Charleston police had first arrested McCray and then forced him to pay a fine after he printed a story about a white mob ambushing a black medical doctor in nearby McClellanville. Then, in 1940, the city increased the business license fee for weeklies.[30]

When McCray in 1942 absorbed the *Aiken Journal*, he ran one of only two major black newspapers in the state. The other one, the *Palmetto Leader* in Columbia, was conservative and avoided politics. Like many black newspapers nationwide, the *Lighthouse* achieved its widest circulation after World War II, with 14,000 issues sold per week. By 1952, when nationally many black newspapers had peaked, circulation had decreased to 6,400.[31]

"There is something about working on a newspaper that haunts you forever," McCray wrote. "It's more than the smell of printer's ink, the sight of it on your hands and clothing. It's more than writing a story, an editorial piece and helping them get into print. Whatever it is, say oldtimers in the profession, it gets into your blood." But it was a constant ordeal. "If you happen to be non-white and get into this business," McCray wrote, "you are definitely on a shoe string in resources, plagued by meeting payrolls, the rent, utilities and the various and sundry other expenses connected with the business. . . . Invariably, you are committed to fighting for an ethnic group that doesn't patronize you enough to pay even the rent. You have to find some way of trading enough with white concerns that will work with you, while you consistently blast away at some other whites. Sort of crazy business."[32]

McCray seldom had enough money to run his operation. "The poor boy is working hard and is having to pull hills in low gear many times," Simkins commented in 1942. In Charleston, McCray couldn't meet fees and fines by himself. At the end, in Columbia, he was operating his own printing press because of lack of personnel. In between, he never stopped pleading with tardy advertisers, agents, and subscribers to send him his money.[33] The *Lighthouse* never received consistent financial support from a political party, church, or other organization, as many black South Carolina newspapers had since Reconstruction.[34]

McCray and the *Lighthouse* gave readers a version of the world that no other newspaper in South Carolina presented. In its varied mix of news and features, the *Lighthouse* told black Americans about black America, including its attempts to become part of the America that whites reserved for themselves. South Carolina's dailies virtually ignored blacks altogether, and the *Palmetto Leader* ignored national news and in-state civil rights activities.[35]

As an integral part of the South Carolina movement, the *Lighthouse* would announce and report on meetings of the NAACP, PDP, and interracial and citizens' committees. It announced and covered speaking engagements of McCray, McKaine, Hinton, Simkins, and others.[36] McCray wrote and editorialized about big civil rights issues such as the teachers' salary and white primary fights, voter registration, and the establishment of the PDP.[37] The paper wrote about Ku Klux Klan rallies, which McCray attended, and black interests in the 1950 race for the U.S. Senate between incumbent Olin D. Johnston and Governor Strom Thurmond.[38] The paper took up the fight for due process for black defendants and against the use of black inmates as cheap labor on private, white-owned farms.[39] It collected statistics about the presence or absence of black policemen in thirty-one southern cities.[40] There were special issues about black education and black South Carolinians in World War II.[41]

In his editorials, McCray took on both blacks and whites he disagreed with. In the first editions, he urged the Charleston NAACP to get moving. In 1940, he chastised a leading black Georgetown minister for refusing to set up a defense fund for a black man accused of raping a white woman. Part of his 1944 editorial policy was "firm denunciation of those race members 'hostile' to progressive programs." At the same time, he would promote membership in organizations he thought acceptable.[42]

McCray called for "knocking over wrong to make room for the right" as the only way of "getting first class status and ending the race issue."[43] He argued that blacks should file lawsuits in any area in which they did not enjoy "full equality of opportunity and services." Take your pick, McCray invited his readers.[44]

When South Carolina's college expansion plans stiffed South Carolina State College, the state-funded college for blacks, McCray targeted the powerful chairman of the South Carolina Senate Finance Committee, Edgar A. Brown.[45] McCray also ridiculed the $10,000 South Carolina reserved for the total operation of a new law school at S.C. State. "We are dramatically told and are supposed to believe, that the ten thousand dollar school is 'equal but separate.'"[46]

When the state of New York was reluctant to approve the extradition of a black South Carolina chain-gang escapee, McCray expressed his pleasure. Blacks were often beaten and killed on the state's penal gangs, he argued. "It is better to die and go to hell than to live and get in jail in South Carolina."[47] When an all-white jury acquitted twenty-six white men who had confessed to involvement in the lynching of Willie Earle, a black man in Greenville, McCray wrote that blacks weren't a bit surprised.[48] Both races should be represented on juries in cases involving both races, argued McCray, now less indifferent to the issue than earlier in Charleston. "Lynchers would be less inclined to lynch were they assured beforehand that their penalty would be partially fixed by the people they wronged."[49]

Teachers' Salary Equalization

In 1941, McCray told black teachers they should sue for salaries equal to those of white teachers. "There is no valid reason why Negro teachers in the employ of the state, should DONATE their services for the benefit of their race or humanity, while the white teachers are getting real taxpayer's dollars for their services."[50]

The salary issue, which caused perhaps the 1940s' greatest clash between conservative and militant black leaders in South Carolina, initially was Osceola McKaine's project. In 1940, McKaine had returned to his native Sumter after a sixteen-year stay in Europe. He owned a club in the Belgian city of Ghent. After World War II broke out and Germany occupied Belgium, he trusted friends with the club and went back to the United States. In 1941, a group of younger black teachers, including one of McKaine's cousins, approached him about helping them prepare for a salary equity suit.[51]

For some time, McKaine considered the salary issue of more immediate importance than voting rights. He went to work. The NAACP's Thurgood Marshall, who had just won a similar case in Virginia, had told South Carolina teachers they needed solid data about salary differences. They also needed a defense fund to pay for legal expenses and reimburse teachers fired because of their involvement in a lawsuit. McKaine traveled the state to collect data. With the help of the Sumter NAACP and a group of black Sumter businessmen, he started the defense fund.[52]

McKaine turned to the Sumter folks after it became clear that the Palmetto State Teachers' Association for black teachers was not behind the effort. Many in the PSTA leadership were senior educators and principals with a relatively good livelihood and prestigious positions within their communities. The PSTA leadership, Modjeska Simkins recalled later, simply wouldn't go against the white power structure. Simkins, deeply involved with the salary campaign, attacked the PSTA, calling its "moronic" leaders "cringing, groveling" creatures and "whimpering slaves." McKaine criticized them for their nearsighted views of potential civil rights progress in the state.[53]

McKaine's attack was part of a running feud he and McCray had with the PSTA over the salary campaign. In 1943, they ran an editorial entitled "The 13 Devils," referring to the PSTA executive committee. For 1944, McCray planned a campaign to get rid of the old order in the PSTA; if that didn't work, he thought the organization should be destroyed and replaced. The *Lighthouse* went after the PSTA president, John P. Burgess, when in a public speech he ridiculed black teachers for thinking they could get equal pay. Burgess indicated, McCray recalled, that he didn't want to risk his job as the highest-paid black teacher in the state. "We virtually 'roasted' him up to his dying day. And roasted him a little more afterwards. However, though not so intended, Mr. Burgess gave the equal pay campaign the big impetus to steam ahead."[54]

The salary campaign went ahead with full force in 1943 after the state NAACP put its organizational and fund-raising abilities behind it. At first, state NAACP president Hinton had reservations about the campaign. Hinton thought black teachers should finance their own lawsuits since they were among the state's best-paid blacks. He also preferred action for equal educational facilities for blacks and whites. He eventually agreed to campaign for both facilities and salaries. Since the salary campaign was already on track, it would be phase one of the NAACP education campaign. The equalization of facilities was to be phase two. Few were thinking of challenging segregated education itself.[55]

Finding a plaintiff was an ordeal. The first one, in Charleston, bailed out a few months after her case was filed. The next plaintiff, Viola L. Duvall, also of Charleston, stayed the course, albeit not without difficulty.

"She called us in Columbia some three weeks before the trial," McCray recalled, "saying she was getting depressed and feeling the pressure of being cut-off by her fellow teachers." Without the support of her family, the NAACP, and the *Lighthouse*, Duvall wrote to McCray, she would not have been able to withstand the pressure.[56]

Following the results in similar Virginia and Maryland cases, the suit was won in February 1944. Another was filed in Columbia. It was won, too, which led other school districts to formally equalize salaries to avoid further litigation. Columbia teachers, like their Charleston counterparts, failed to support the case, despite the success in Charleston. "More and more (though it is a sinister feeling)," McCray wrote in the *Lighthouse*, "I am reaching the conclusion that Negro teachers, as spineless and unworthy as those of Columbia have proven themselves, should be left to slave and starve and receive the wages of the serf."[57]

The Progressive Democratic Party

In 1944, McCray led the formation of the South Carolina Progressive Democratic Party. The party came about somewhat coincidentally after South Carolina NAACP leaders considered the formation of "Fourth Term for Roosevelt Clubs." South Carolina blacks wanted to vote again for the president, but it was uncertain whether the state Democratic Party, suspicious of the Roosevelt administration's attitudes on race issues, would support the president. South Carolina law allowed for separate electoral clubs entering slates of presidential electors. In the *Lighthouse*, McCray and McKaine supported the "Fourth Term Clubs."

McCray soon became the main spokesman for the fast-growing grassroots movement for FDR, and the *Lighthouse* office became the organizational center. In a March 18, 1944, editorial, McCray further explained the idea. "In South Carolina," he wrote, "despite overwhelming appreciation for President and Mrs. Roosevelt, because of their race, Negroes cannot vote in the Democratic Party, the party of the President and the commander-in-chief." For a self-addressed, stamped envelope, the *Lighthouse* offered copies of the plan for "Fourth Term Clubs." McCray suggested that the name for the clubs' statewide organization be "Colored Democratic Party."

The *Columbia Record*, one of Columbia's two dailies, picked up McCray's editorial, announcing that blacks were organizing their own party. That, McCray wrote much later, "wasn't exactly what *The Lighthouse* had in mind." The *Record* stretched the point. In fact, two years earlier, McCray had rejected the notion of a new party. Still, after the Associated Press distributed the Record's story, the *Lighthouse*'s office was inundated with requests for information about the new party. "Public reaction," McCray recalled, "led to the organizing for the first Deep South Negro Democratic Party."[58]

The choice of the adjective "colored" was no more deliberate than the idea for the party itself. Four days after McCray's March editorial, one Mrs. Howe, "an elderly white lady" of a prominent Columbia family, as McCray remembered her, came to the *Lighthouse* office. The Lord had answered her prayers with the new party, she told McCray and McKaine. But, she added, the party "must not be a reactionary party like that we have. It must be progressive. That's it. Let's name it Progressive Democrats." On her way out, she had another thought. "O yes, we will need money for our party," she said. She didn't have much on her, she said, but went into her handbag, finding a $4.50 pension check and two quarters. "We hadn't thought about raising money," McCray remembered, "just as [we hadn't] thought of leading a political party."[59]

Mrs. Howe was not the only white person suggesting that, to attract whites, the party not be called "Colored" or "Negro". The teachers' salary campaign had invited liberal whites to join its platform, and in the PDP, too, white folks were welcome. "I think we can count on the moral support of the better class of whites," McCray told the PDP's first convention in May. "But the real answer is up to us." Without support from "liberal Christian white people," McKaine said, most blacks "would have to become bloody revolutionaries." When McKaine in the fall of 1944 ran for the U.S. Senate against Governor Olin D. Johnston, both the candidate and his campaign manager, McCray, stressed the party's inclusion of whites. Poor whites and blacks equally suffered from segregation, McKaine argued during his campaign.[60]

Even before the May 1944 convention, the PDP had, according to McCray, more than 70 branches and 14,000 members. At the convention, in Columbia, were 172 local delegates and observers from eight southern states. McCray was elected party chairman and McKaine secretary. The regular state Democratic Party had refused to offer the PDP eight of its eighteen delegates to the Democratic National Convention in Chicago in July, and so the PDP decided to send its own delegation to challenge the regular party's seating. McCray and McKaine were elected co-chairs of the Chicago delegation. By the end of July, the PDP claimed 45,000 members.[61]

What had begun as an attempt to vote for an FDR electoral slate became a means to break open the Democratic Party in South Carolina and elsewhere in the South. Already in the early 1940s, McCray had in the *Lighthouse* led a statewide movement to open up the electoral process. Earlier attempts by others in the 1930s had been to no avail. In 1942, hundreds of blacks in Columbia enrolled again for the Democratic primary, but the state Democratic convention voted down a motion to allow blacks to vote. The South Carolina NAACP began to prepare for a legal challenge to the all-white Democratic primary. It set up a parallel organization, the South Carolina Citizens Committee, to raise funds for court cases. This allowed for contributions from teachers and government employees, who risked retribution if they contributed to the NAACP. McCray, Hinton, Simkins, and Pearly Simmons were among the usual NAACP suspects running the Citizens Committee.[62]

The U.S. Supreme Court's April 1944 decision in *Smith v. Allwright,* that the all-white Democratic primary in Texas was unconstitutional, did not obviate the need for action in South Carolina. On the contrary, leading southern defiance of the decision, South Carolina's legislature immediately repealed all state primary laws. This, Governor Johnston and others argued, turned primaries into private affairs of private organizations, to which federal law did not apply. South Carolina became the battleground for regional implementation of the Texas decision. In addition to the courts, South Carolina's black leaders took their fight to the national Democratic Party.

The PDP's challenge in Chicago was to be the first to a regular party delegation by an all-black delegation. As he began to campaign for the PDP's seating, McCray was well aware that the plan could upset the party's attempt to appease both southern whites and northern blacks. A Chicago challenge would put "the matter of discrimination firmly in the laps of the greater Democratic Party," he had told the PDP rank and file before the party's May convention. Seating the PDP was not just about South Carolina; it would "emancipate the approximately eight millions of Negroes living in the South." He asked President Roosevelt in a letter whether the national party approved of the exclusion of blacks down South. He reminded Eleanor Roosevelt of the importance of the black vote. The Democratic party had "merely winked at a problem it probably does not approve" of, he told Harlem's Adam Clayton Powell, who was campaigning for Congress. McCray asked for his help and that of black Illinois U.S. Representative William Dawson.[63]

Dawson arranged a meeting in Washington between McCray and the national committee leadership. A second meeting in Washington with a PDP delegation led by McCray followed five days later. The NDC asked the PDP not to challenge. It would cause a southern walkout and hurt Roosevelt's election prospects. "Gentlemen," McCray responded, "we are going to Chicago. Now if you care to, you can start talking from that point."

Chicago was the first of three PDP convention challenges. The Progressive Democrats didn't make it to the credentials committee; a special subcommittee denied the delegation seating on technicalities. Some PDP delegates wanted to stage a floor fight, but McCray and McKaine argued that the PDP show its loyalty to Roosevelt by accepting the ruling. There were indications that the NDC promised to help South Carolina blacks in their primary fight and to provide money for the PDP's organization effort.[64]

But by 1946 McCray had become disgruntled with the national Democrats' lack of effort. If the Democratic Party were interested in the fight of southern blacks, he argued, "we wouldn't have the curse of a Democratic white primary." A 1948 PDP delegation to the Democratic convention again failed to be seated. In 1956, the PDP delegation received a pledge that the national party would revise the rules to prevent future all-white delegations from states that practiced any form of discrimination against blacks trying to become delegates. It was that pledge, McCray would argue repeatedly, that opened the door for the 1964 convention challenge of the Mississippi Democratic Freedom Party. After 1956, the Progressive Democrats were slowly absorbed into the regular party. McCray, for instance, became vice-chairman of Columbia's Ward 18, a ward with a white majority.[65]

In the fall of 1944, the PDP ran McKaine against Johnston for the U.S. Senate. It was the first time in the twentieth-century South that an African American ran as a Democrat for a major federal office. McKaine and the PDP knew they couldn't win, but they felt the race would be a good recruiting tool and would show that African Americans could conduct a campaign. They also were happy to target the then-despised Johnston, who after the *Allwright* decision had threatened that South Carolina would "use the necessary methods to retain white supremacy in our primaries." McKaine thought it was "an open invitation to the Klan to get busy." Officially, McKaine received just over 3,200 votes, but McCray thought he had received more than 6,000 votes and perhaps even as many as 10,000.[66]

The formation of the PDP also provided South Carolina blacks with an alternative to the Republican Party. Black South Carolinians voted for Roosevelt, but as late as the early 1940s, black South Carolina leaders participating in electoral politics belonged to the GOP. In Charleston, McCray and the *Lighthouse* were associated with the Republicans. But South Carolina's Republicans were a small, impotent bunch, deeply split into one lily-white and two racially mixed factions, in which blacks often played only limited roles. The PDP, McCray said, would be an escape for blacks from the ineffective GOP.

But several black Republicans stayed with the GOP. A separate party was a setback for blacks, they thought, and, in any case, a move toward the dreaded Democrats. White Republicans resented the formation of the PDP, too, but they also perceived it as an opportunity. All three factions proposed political alliances with the PDP, but it was clear to McCray that they hoped black progress within the Democratic Party would drive white Democrats to the GOP. McCray and the PDP leadership rejected financial help from the Republicans; they didn't want to encourage charges that the PDP was a GOP front.[67]

Within the PDP context, some of the more obvious conflicts within the 1940s South Carolina movement took place. McCray was usually involved. For one, McCray's sometimes abrasive and overbearing approach antagonized others within the party. His control over the party led to accusations that he was a dictator, once even by McKaine. There was some disagreement within the party about the forcefulness of the 1944 PDP challenge, and there were accusations that McCray had sold out in Chicago, literally. Some claimed McCray had used party money for a personal trip to New Orleans. Most of the rumors involving money apparently originated from PDP members whom McCray opposed during a power struggle in a local PDP branch.[68]

More crucial differences existed, especially between McCray and McKaine, about PDP cooperation with other groups. In 1945, a black Columbia Republican, I. S. Leevy, had a chance to win a special election for the South Carolina House of Representatives because the field of white Democratic candidates was crowded. McKaine thought the PDP should help Leevy become the state's first twentieth-century black legislator. Others in the PDP, including McCray, opposed the idea. Leevy had publicly belittled the PDP, and Progressive Democrats considered his recent revival of an all-black adjunct organization to the GOP an open challenge. Leevy lost badly, and McKaine complained that the PDP had squandered a chance to show its potential electoral power.[69]

McCray and McKaine had a more intense conflict about associating with out-of-state leftist organizations. The militancy of McCray, McKaine,

Hinton, and Simkins was not defined by left-wing politics directed against the country's political and economic system. McCray did not even look much at politics in class terms, unlike McKaine, who developed class themes, promoted cooperation between working-class blacks and whites, and helped union organization in South Carolina. Both McKaine and Simkins worked with leftist organization from out of state, but while McCray happily formed coalitions with white South Carolina liberals, he was suspicious of non-southern, radical whites trying to organize southern blacks.[70]

McCray's concern was that such organizations would infiltrate and take over the PDP. He was suspicious of the Southern Conference of Human Welfare (SCHW), the Congress of Industrial Organizations' Political Action Committee (CIO-PAC), and especially the American Communist Party. The SCHW opened an office in Columbia, and both the CIO-PAC and the Communist Party made overtures to Progressive Democrats. In the *Lighthouse*, McCray spoke out against those trying "to capture the hearts of members of the PDP and bring the whole party into the Communist ranks."[71]

Within this context, a speech by McKaine at a 1945 meeting of the Southern Negro Youth Conference in Birmingham, Alabama, didn't sit well with McCray. Advocating interracial class politics and praising democracy and racial tolerance in the Soviet Union, McKaine stressed that African Americans could not hope to gain justice in the South without the help of progressive whites. McCray was even less enthralled when McKaine took a job as field representative of the SCHW, the organization's first black one. McCray himself declined an SCHW job offer, considering it an attempt to buy him out and control the PDP. He was annoyed that McKaine served two masters and publicly suggested that McKaine supported an SCHW attempt to take over the PDP. "Those who go around calling for alliances don't mean native white people," McCray said during a public speech, referring to McKaine. "They mean white Communists and PAC people who . . . a thousand miles away would dictate to us." Simkins, too, was deeply involved with the SCHW. She was not a PDP official, but she was close to the party's leadership; because of his distrust of the SCHW, McCray probably didn't like Simkins's involvement, either.[72]

McKaine denied McCray's charge and suggested that McCray was getting bad information from "unproved friends." The conflict led McKaine to stop writing his *Lighthouse* column for several months. As McKaine had health problems and traveled a great deal for the SCHW, he then made what may have been an inevitable step. In May 1946, he resigned as executive secretary of the PDP, although in July he resumed his *Lighthouse* column. In November, McKaine resigned as the *Lighthouse*'s associate editor to return to Belgium to take care of his club in Ghent. From there, he kept in contact with McCray and occasionally wrote for the *Lighthouse*.[73]

Voting in the Democratic Primaries

"Successful enforcement of the *Smith v. Allwright* decision," U.S. Attorney General Francis Biddle said in 1944, "will . . . depend on public opinion." The South Carolina movement wasn't willing to wait for that. What it didn't achieve through the national Democratic Party, it would achieve through the courts. In August 1948, 35,000 blacks, 7 or 8 percent of the electorate, voted in a South Carolina Democratic primary.

Within five months of the failed attempts to vote in 1942, the state NAACP through the Citizen Committee raised more than $6,000 for a legal challenge, $500 of which went to Texas to help with the primary case there. After South Carolina's government tried to turn political primaries into a private affair, a court case became inevitable.[74]

When primary enrollment came again in 1946, George Elmore, a Richland County PDP official, stumbled into history. Hinton and a group of hand-picked "guinea pigs" made the rounds to get on the books. McCray-the-reporter followed, note pad in hand. Wherever they went, white drug store or liquor store clerks put the enrollment books away. "The books aren't here," a clerk would say with a smile, and white folks who had just enrolled would smile along. The final stop, near closing time, was at a small store on Millwood Avenue, but the woman in charge said there was no book.

"We stood across the street," McCray recalled, "knowing there was still no guinea pig and prospects were not likely [to come up] for another two years." Hinton turned to McCray. "Chief, you can tell them that we tried as hard as we could, but we'll be back." Then Elmore arrived. "Almost instinctively, everybody turned his back to George," McCray remembered. "George talked a lot and nobody was especially in the mood for him at that time."

After Hinton had explained the situation, Elmore, a light-skinned man who could easily pass for white, popped the question. Could he try? Sure, the others replied. Elmore went in and asked for a coke. "Them niggers out there tried to get their names in our books," the woman behind the counter said; she was glad the books would close soon. Had he enrolled yet? Elmore hadn't, he replied. It was very important, she explained, that every white person enroll and vote.

"Yes m'am," Elmore said, and the women reached for the book, still fussing about "them damn smart alecky niggers." The woman asked his name, turned to the "E" section and told Elmore to write down his address, too.

She looked. "907 Tree Street. That's . . . 907 Tree Street. Then you're a damn nigger, too."

"Yes m'am," Elmore replied.

Back outside, Elmore had a message for Hinton and the rest. "She says you other niggers might as well come on in and enroll too."[75]

After Elmore was turned back at the primary polls in August, the NAACP filed suit in February 1947. That same month, the Georgia legislature, having asked advice from South Carolina Democrats, repealed its primary laws. Following the 1944 Texas decision, the Georgia NAACP had taken the state's all-white primary to court and won, twice, but the legislature's action neutralized the effects of the rulings. Through the South Carolina case, the NAACP prepared to demolish the last line of defense for the all-white primary.[76]

As Marshall and other lawyers prepared for the case, McCray went around the state, as usual, explaining the importance of the vote. Because blacks can't vote, he told African-American women in Charleston in January, the state spent much more per white child than per black child on education. Because blacks couldn't vote, they saw every day "little colored boys and girls trekking several miles to and from schools . . . while little white boys and girls whizzed by on modern, up-to-date buses." The ballot, he told students at Orangeburg's all-black Claflin College, "holds the answer to 99 percent of our present worries."[77]

On July 12, 1947, presiding Judge J. Waties Waring told South Carolina that it was time to "rejoin the union." It was time "to fall in step with the other states and to adopt the American way of conducting elections." But the state of South Carolina wasn't quite ready yet. After the ruling, the Democratic Party decided that blacks would have to take an oath in support of racial segregation before they could vote in the primary, but Judge Waring nixed that scheme in July 1948. One month later, South Carolina blacks took to the polls.[78]

As the state of South Carolina prepared an appeal of Waring's latest ruling, McCray advised in the *Lighthouse* that it should just begin preparing "for the day that is already here." The state lost the appeal and had to decide whether to appeal again and, in McCray's words, "continue to get a little common sense beaten into them until the issue is finally settled." South Carolina, he added, "prefers to go down swinging for white supremacy. Indicators are that it will go down but the manner is not clear yet." When the party leaders ultimately decided against further appeals, McCray promised no "gloating or haughtiness" but referred to them as "losers" after all.[79]

In 1950, South Carolina blacks went back to the polls, this time to defeat Governor Strom Thurmond, the Dixiecrats' presidential candidate two years before. Thurmond ran for the U.S. Senate against the PDP's old foe, incumbent Olin Johnston. Johnston was lucky, Modjeska Simkins recalled twenty years later, that Thurmond was perceived by black leaders as even worse.[80] McCray, in the *Lighthouse*, urged blacks to vote for Johnston over Thurmond, "whose every point and line was built about the Negro and who made it clear—if it wasn't clear before—that his doctrine of states' rights is nothing but the same old kicking Negroes around."[81]

Johnston got the black vote because he went after it, McCray wrote thirty years later. He was a racist and segregationist and blacks didn't like him then, McCray wrote, but PDP leaders decided to back him anyway. "Johnston's only requirement was not to engage in any anti-Negro shenanigans during the campaign. He kept the commitment, deviating just once, but with our knowledge and permission." That permission came when Thurmond went after Johnston for chasing the black vote. "Johnston wanted just one time to answer him," McCray wrote. "We didn't like the answer at all but Johnston kept his seat with the Negro vote."[82]

Blacks had won the race for Johnston, McCray claimed. There were 60,000 black votes, he wrote after the election, while Johnston won by fewer than 30,000. The Charleston *News and Courier* agreed. In the predominantly black ward where McCray and Hinton voted, the paper's William Workman reported, Johnston had received 1,249 votes against 72 for Thurmond. "I contend," Workman argued, "that the attitude of the two men as regards negroes would never have resulted in so lopsided a vote had not the word been passed by negro bigwigs to support Johnston."[83]

The End of the Lighthouse

By the time Waring made his second decision in the primary case, the next important court case was on its way. In Clarendon County, black parents had had enough of seeing "little colored boys and girls trekking several miles to and from schools." In 1947, some of them petitioned for school buses for their children. Two years later, this became a suit for equal school facilities in general, and then a challenge to school segregation itself.[84]

The impetus for the challenge came from James Hinton, who in June 1947 in Columbia addressed a gathering of rural preachers. Hinton gave one of the "give 'em hell" speeches he was known for, this time about equal schools. "No teacher or preacher in South Carolina," Hinton proclaimed, "has the courage to find a plaintiff to test the legality of the discriminatory bus-transportation practices in this state." In the audience, Rev. J. A. DeLaine of Summerton in Clarendon County was especially struck.

DeLaine spoke to Hinton afterward, and Hinton rushed to the *Lighthouse*. "Chief, it just may be we have a guinea pig," a flushed Hinton told McCray. Hinton grinned, as, McCray remembered, he always did after reading some audience the riot act. "What Jim Hinton didn't like to say to his audience," McCray recalled, "was [that] all of us involved had been frustrated for months in a search for a guinea pig for Phase II of our 1942 agreement." Hinton had told DeLaine that the state NAACP would only help if Summerton had an NAACP branch. A few weeks later DeLaine contacted Hinton. With McCray, Hinton drove down to Summerton on a Sunday morning to form NAACP and PDP chapters; that afternoon, the two did the same in nearby Kingstree.[85]

The school desegregation case was probably a factor in McCray's ending up on a chain gang for two months, the premier harassment he endured at the *Lighthouse*. First, there were the Charleston officials. In 1943, McCray faced a grand jury investigation after he wrote about a white judge being rude to a black woman, but a case never materialized. McCray also received hate mail from white folks and was well aware that his activism and that of others could be dangerous. "McKaine and I," McCray wrote, "often spent entire nights in the office drilling and schooling each other. That was a precaution should the unexpected happen to either of us."[86]

In January 1950, McCray was indicted after he reported the testimony of a black man accused of raping a white woman that the woman had consented to the sex. The charge was "criminal libel," a crime "unheard of today," McCray's NAACP lawyer, Jack Greenberg, wrote in 1994. An Associated Press reporter charged with the same crime was never called up for trial. McCray was, but his case never came to trial because McCray pleaded guilty to avoid jail. "The atmosphere was so hostile," Greenberg wrote, "that a white lawyer in Columbia, who covertly helped us, asked us to enter his house at night through the back door. He would have been ruined if his involvement became known."[87]

McCray was sentenced to three years' probation. He was not allowed to leave the state, but his parole officer explained that he could take short out-of-state business trips. In October 1950 in Chicago, McCray gave the keynote address at a function for Congressman Dawson. In November 1950, McCray delivered the Negro Achievement Week address for the Omega Psi Phi fraternity in Durham, North Carolina. Nothing happened until McCray was arrested nine months later, in August 1951. At first, the matter seemed to have been settled, the *Pittsburgh Courier* wrote in December 1952, "but when [McCray] continued to belabor state officials who favor continuation of segregation in public schools, and supported solidly the pending case from Clarendon county . . . the case against him was brought out again last spring." Greenberg agreed this was the real reason for "the court's anger with" McCray.[88]

McCray was convinced that James Byrnes, South Carolina's governor, had ordered his arrest. McCray had opposed Byrnes in his 1950 gubernatorial campaign. He campaigned for Adlai Stevenson, while Byrnes supported Eisenhower. "It is apparent that Editor McCray is a marked man," the *Courier* wrote, "because of his crusading tactics." Off to the chain gang it was.[89]

Financial struggles had always made the *Lighthouse* vulnerable, and this became more apparent when by the early 1950s the South Carolina movement had lost some of its vibrancy, and *Lighthouse* circulation went down.[90] McCray also never again had the kind of help at the *Lighthouse* that McKaine provided through 1946. And his relationship with Simkins had deteriorated, by 1954 beyond repair. The exact reason for the conflict is not clear. There were probably political differences, perhaps about Simkins's involvement with out-of-state leftist groups. There were probably personal and business conflicts, too. Simkins had provided financial aid to the *Lighthouse* and to McCray's family when he went to prison. McCray lost control of the *Lighthouse* to Simkins; sometime in 1953, Simkins became the paper's manager and publisher. In March 1954, McCray suddenly left the *Lighthouse*, leaving the paper with Simkins. In June, she criticized McCray in the *Lighthouse* for campaigning for a white politician with a dubious reputation on civil rights and against his opponent, H. D. Monteith, Simkins's brother. The *Lighthouse* folded a few months later.[91]

The *Lighthouse*, McCray said in 1955, had met its main objectives: stimulating black South Carolinians' participation in politics and improving their education. "We weren't making any money," he added a decade later. "So, with the accomplishments of our goals in sight, why should the paper struggle any longer? And why should we go on starving ourselves so that it would be printed? We had earned the right to turn away from the newspaper and give some of our energy to our own personal problems."[92]

Epilogue

After the *Lighthouse*, McCray became the Carolina reporter for the Baltimore *Afro-American*. He also would work for the *Pittsburgh Courier*, the *Atlanta World*, and the *Chicago Defender*. He stayed involved in the movement but not on the same level as before, and certainly not with the same influence. In 1964 McCray went to work for Talladega College; he retired in 1981, six years before his death.[93]

The civil rights movement of the 1960s mostly passed McCray by. He didn't care for the 1960 sit-ins in Columbia. He thought they were improper and that negotiations with Columbia's white leadership would be sufficient.[94] His main link with the 1960s movement was, therefore, his earlier contribution to building a strong statewide NAACP. McCray helped organize one of the most vibrant NAACP organizations in the country. Its strengths were evident in its prominent position on the national level. It was also evident in the way the organization dominated its home turf, to the extent that other civil rights groups never established much of a presence in South Carolina. Certainly on an organizational level, this was still true in the 1960s.[95]

The 1940s South Carolina NAACP was no example of the kind of bureaucratic, strictly legalistic group dominated by the national organization that frustrated an organizer like Ella Baker in the 1940s. Instead, South Carolina's NAACP combined vigorous grassroots organization, including voter registration, with vigorous legal action. While South Carolina leaders necessarily and happily coordinated legal action with the NAACP Legal Defense Fund and acted within its national strategy, they usually worked at their own pace. In the teachers' salary case, the initiative came from the local level, in Sumter, albeit after an assist from the national NAACP. In the white-primary case, grassroots action preceded legal action in South Carolina. The school desegregation case started as a fight for equal facilities, which started independently of the national NAACP through the interaction between the state NAACP and local blacks in Clarendon County.

The pace for legal action in South Carolina was largely set by progress at the grassroots level; without funds, plaintiffs, and general political support among South Carolina blacks, there would be, after all, no legal action, either. McCray, Hinton, Simkins, and McKaine were constantly on the road, activating the grassroots and initiating or facilitating the establishment of new NAACP and PDP chapters. The South Carolina NAACP of the 1940s fit the characterization that Raymond Gavins and Adam Fairclough have applied to the North Carolina and Louisiana NAACPs: "less bureaucratic and more people-oriented". Its history also confirms what historians increasingly acknowledge—that studying the civil rights struggle on the local, state, or national level should include an analysis of the interaction across these levels.[96]

NOTES

1. Hanes Walton Jr., *Black Political Parties: A Historical and Political Analysis* (New York: The Free Press, 1972), 69–77.

2. Richard Kluger, *Simple Justice* (New York: Vintage Books, 1975), *passim*; Miles Richards, "Osceola E. McKaine and the Struggle for Black Civil Rights: 1917–1946" (Ph.D. dissertation, University of South Carolina, 1994), chapters 6 and 7.

3. See also: Patricia Sullivan, *Days of Hope: Race and Democracy in the New Deal Era* (Chapel Hill: University of North Carolina Press, 1996), xii.

4. Prattis, "The North Would Do Well to Take Note: South Carolina's Leaders Are Men of Inspiring Courage," *Pittsburgh Courier*, June 21, 1952.

5. Sullivan, *Days of Hope*, xii.

6. E. Franklin Frazier, *Black Bourgeoisie: The Rise of A New Middle Class in the United States* (1957; London: Collier Books, 1969), 146, 150–61. Gunnar Myrdal, *An American Dilemma: The Negro Problem and Modern Democracy* (New York: Harper & Row, 1944, 1962), chapter 42; Armistead Scott Pride, "Negro Newspapers: Yesterday, Today and Tomorrow," *Journalism Quarterly* 28, no. 2 (spring 1951): 179–88; Armistead S. Pride and Clint C. Wilson II, *A History of the Black Press* (Washington, D.C.: Howard University Press, 1997), 214; John Egerton, *Speak Now Against the Day: The Generation before the Civil Rights Movement in the South* (New York: Alfred A. Knopf, 1994), 354.

7. See the chapters by Allen Woodrow Jones, Calvin Smith, Thomas J. Davies, and James Smallwood in: Henry Lewis Suggs, ed., *The Black Press in the South 1865–1979* (Westport, Conn.: Greenwood Press, 1983); Armistead S. Pride, "The Arkansas State Press: Squeezed to Death," *Grassroots Editor*, January 1962, 6; William S. Sullins and Paul Parsons, "Roscoe Dunjee: Crusading Editor of Oklahoma's Black *Dispatch*, 1915–1955," *Journalism Quarterly* 69, no. 1 (spring 1992): 204–13; W.D. Workman Jr., "Tax Sale Will Mark the End of *Lighthouse and Informer*," Charleston *News and*

Courier, February 5, 1955; Letter from the *Lighthouse and Informer* "To Whom It May Concern," August 23, 1943, McCray Papers at the South Caroliniana Library, University of South Carolina, Box 1, Folder 2 (hereafter "McCray Papers"); Margaret Vale, "Negroes Organize Democratic Party to Contest White Supremacy in Deep South," manuscript, McCray Papers, Box 2, Folder 21; *Carolina Times* (Durham, N.C.), August 18, 1951, McCray Papers, Oversize, Scrapbooks, 1942, 1952; "Report to the University of South Caroliniana Society Fifty-Fourth Annual Meeting, 1990"; McCray, "The Way It Was," date unknown and March 3, 1984 (manuscript).

8. Barbara Woods Aba-Mecha, "Black Woman Activist in Twentieth-Century South Carolina: Modjeska Monteith Simkins" (Ph.D. dissertation, Emory University, 1978), 1; Sullivan, *Days of Hope*, 143, 170; Egerton, *Speak Now*, 227. For a recent study of the civil rights struggle in South Carolina, see: Peter F. Lau, "Freedom Road Territory: The Politics of Civil Rights Struggle in South Carolina during the Jim Crow Era" (Ph.D. dissertation, Rutgers University, 2002).

9. Sullivan, *Days of Hope*, 196–97; Raymond Gavins, "The NAACP in North Carolina during the Age of Segregation," in *New Directions in Civil Rights Studies,* ed. Armstead L. Pride and Patricia Sullivan (Charlottesville: University Press of Virginia, 1991), 108–9; Prattis, "The North Would Do Well to Take Note.".

10. The McCrays: Forebears and Siblings, Personal Papers, Carrie Allen McCray, John McCray's third wife; written communication from Carrie Allen McCray, n.d. (1996).

11. John McCray, "South Carolina—The Way It Was," *Charleston Chronicle*, February 7, 1981, November 27, 1982. "The Way It Was" is a column that McCray, from 1980 to 1986, wrote for another black weekly newspaper, the *Charleston Chronicle*; Personal communication, Carrie Allen McCray.

12. McCray, "The Way It Was," December 26, 1981.

13. McCray, "The Way It Was," April 10, October 4, and November 20, 1982; John Henry McCray: Vita Sheet, Personal Papers, Carrie Allen McCray. See also: Edmund L. Drago, *Initiative, Paternalism, & Race Relations: Charleston's Avery Normal Institute* (Athens: University of Georgia Press, 1990), 239–40.

14. McCray Papers, South Caroliniana Library (SCL), Box 1, Folder 1; Coles, Jewel, "Prominent Editor Sees Bright Future for Negro Journalists," n.d. (1945, February), in McCray Papers, Box 1, Folder 4; "Report to the University of South Caroliniana Society Fifty-Fourth Annual Meeting," 1990.

15. John H. McCray, "In Defense of Student Education," *The Mule's Ear* 10, no. 1 (October 1933): 2–3, and "The Arraignment of Student Inertia," *The Mule's Ea* 11, no. 3 (February 1935): 1, 4–5; "Sappie Susie," "Who's Who in the Senior Class," *The Mule's Ear* 11, no. 5 (May 1935): 12.

16. McCray, "The Way It Was," July 25, 1981.

17. McCray, "The Way It Was," April 18 and June 6, 1981; "Report to the University of South Caroliniana Society Fifty-Fourth Annual Meeting, 1990."

18. McCray, "The Way It Was" (manuscript), February 16, 1985, McCray Papers,

Box 2, Folder 16. McCray writes that the two defendants eventually were executed by electric chair.

19. Charleston *News and Courier*, April 13, 1937; Edwin D. Hoffman, "The Genesis of the Modern Movement for Equal Rights in South Carolina, 1930–1939," *Journal of Negro History* 44, no. 1 (1959): 363–64; Theodore Hemmingway, "Beneath the Yoke of Bondage: A History of Black Folks in South Carolina" (Ph.D. dissertation, University of South Carolina, 1976), 384–86; Howard H. Quint, *Profile in Black and White: A Frank Portrait of South Carolina* (Washington, D.C.: Public Affairs Press, 1958), vi.

20. Hoffman, "Genesis," 364; Drago, *Avery Normal Institute*, 237–38.

21. *News and Courier*, April 24, 1937; McCray, "The Way It Was" (manuscript), February 16, 1985, McCray Papers, Box 2, Folder 16.

22. Hoffman, "Genesis," 253, 368–69; I.A. Newby, *Black Carolinians: A History of Blacks in South Carolina from 1895–1968* (Columbia: University of South Carolina Press, 1973), 203.

23. Walter Edgar, *South Carolina: A History* (Columbia: University of South Carolina Press, 1998), chapter 21; Newby, *Black Carolinians*, chapter 5; Hoffman, "Genesis," 361.

24. Hoffman, "Genesis," 353, 357–65; Edgar, *South Carolina*, chapter 21.

25. *The Crisis,* October 1939, 312–13, and January 1940, 20; Hoffman, "Genesis," 365–66; Sullivan, *Days of Hope*, 144–45; Hemmingway, "Yoke of Bondage," 387–88.

26. Hoffman, "Genesis," 367–68; Sullivan, *Days of Hope*, 141–42; Hemmingway, "Yoke of Bondage," 388–90; Woods, "Modjeska Simkins," 211–12.

27. Woods, "Modjeska Simkins," 172, 210–11.

28. Coles, "Prominent Editor"; Workman, "Tax Sale"; McCray, "South Carolina —The Way It Was: Legends from a Negro Editor" (1982). As part of his regular column in the *Charleston Chronicle* from 1980 to 1986, McCray in 1982 wrote a seven-part series called "Legends from a Negro Editor," specifically about his experiences as the editor of the *Lighthouse.*

29. McCray, "The Way It Was," February 27, 1982 and June 26, 1982.

30. During the arrest episode in 1939, the city had initially but in conflict with its own ordinance raised McCray's license fee from $25 to $100. He paid but eventually received a refund. In 1940, however, Charleston raised the fee for weeklies from $25 to $50. McCray, "Negro Editor," February 20 and 27 and March 12; McCray, "The Way It Was," June 6, 1980 and August 22, 1981; McCray, "The Way It Was" (manuscript), December 10, 1983, McCray Papers, Box 2, Folder 16; Richards, "Osceola E. McKaine," 106–7; Woods, "Modjeska Simkins," 173–74.

31. Hemmingway, "South Carolina," 290, 293; Charles F. Behling, "South Carolina Negro Newspapers: Their History, Content, and Reception" (M.A. Thesis, University of South Carolina, 1964), 14–15; Frazier, *Black Bourgeoisie*, 148; Roland E. Wolseley, *The Black Press, U.S.A*, 2d edition (Ames: Iowa State University Press, 1991), 81; Pride and Wilson, *Black Press*, 183.

32. McCray, "Negro Editor," February 20, 1982.

33. McCray, "The Way It Was," April 2, 1983; Letter of John H. McCray to Henry D. Pearson, July 5 and 16 and September 28, 1945, McCray Papers, Box 1, Folder 4; Letter of John H. McCray to James R. Bonds, January 14, 1946, McCray Papers, Box 1, Folder 5; Statement, *Atlanta Daily Word* for *Lighthouse and Informer*, February 9, 1946, McCray Papers, Box 1, Folder 5; Richards, "Osceola McKaine," 115.

34. Hemmingway, "South Carolina," 292–95; Woods, "Modjeska Simkins," 258.

35. Wim Roefs, "Expanding the Media Landscape for African Americans: South Carolina's *The Lighthouse and Informer* in the 1940s," paper presented at the American Journalism Historians Association Annual Convention, Pittsburgh, Pa., October 2000.

36. See, for instance, the *Lighthouse and Informer*, January 10, 1943, February 6, 1944, and October 29, 1949; "Lighthouse Headings," February 5, 1946, February 19, 1946, February 26, 1946, March 25, 1946, March 26, 1946, McCray Papers, Box 1, Folder 5.

37. See for instance: letters by Viola Louise Duval to John H. McCray, November 14 and 21, 1943, McCray Papers, Box 1, Folder 2; "Explanation of the Plan for 'Beating the Primary,'" presumably by John H. McCray, scheduled for publication in the *Lighthouse and Informer*, April 2, 1944, McCray Papers, Box 1, Folder 3; "The *Lighthouse and Informer*. 1944 Policies and Programs," McCray Papers, Box 1, Folder 3; McCray, "The Way It Was" (manuscript), November 26, 1983, McCray Papers, Box 2, Folder 16; Walton, *Black Political Parties: A Historical and Political Analysis* (New York: The Free Press, 1972), 70–72; "Lighthouse Headings," February 4, 1946, February 5, 1946, February 26, 1946, March 5, 1946, March 19, 1946, March 25, 1946, March 26, 1946, McCray Papers, Box 1, Folder 5.

38. The *Lighthouse and Informer*, October 29, 1949; Nadine Cohodas, *Strom Thurmond & the Politics of Southern Change* (Macon, Ga.: Mercer University Press, 1993), 213–15.

39. See, for instance: McCray, "The Way It Was," February 6, 1982; Letter of J. B. Drake to John H. McCray, May 7, 1943, McCray Papers, Box 1, Folder 2; Letter of Nat J. Humphries to John H. McCray, May 27, 1943, McCray Papers, Box 1, Folder 2; Letter of B. F. Kirkley to John H. McCray, November 13, 1943, McCray Papers, Box 1, Folder 2.

40. Letter of Ira De. A. Reid of the Southern Regional Council to John H. McCray, June 6, 1945, McCray Papers, Box 1, Folder 4.

41. Various letters to John H. McCray, April 1942, McCray Papers, Box 1, folder 1; letters by Olin D. Johnson and Fred D. Marshall to John H. McCray, March 20, 1943, McCray Papers, Box 1, Folder 2.

42. "The *Lighthouse and Informer*. 1944 Policies and Programs," McCray Papers, Box 1, Folder 3; McCray, "Negro Editor," February 27 and March 6, 1982.

43. *Lighthouse and Informer*, March 5, 1949.

44. *Lighthouse and Informer*, February 16, 1947.

45. *Lighthouse and Informer*, May 11, 1947 and May 18, 1947.

46. *Lighthouse and Informer*, June 1, 1947.

47. *Lighthouse and Informer*, June 4, 1949, and July 9, 1949.

48. *Lighthouse and Informer*, June 1, 1947.

49. *Lighthouse and Informer*, June 1, 1947. See also June 8, 1947 and June 15, 1947.

50. *Lighthouse and Informer*, October 19, 1941.

51. Richards, "Osceola McKaine," chapter 5 and 102–4; Woods, "Modjeska Simkins," 176–78.

52. Woods, "Modjeska Simkins," 177; Richards, "Osceola McKaine," 101–6, 120–21.

53. Richards, "Osceola McKaine," 109–12; Woods, "Modjeska Simkins," 176–77, 183–87.

54. McCray, "The Way It Was," September 6, 1980; "The *Lighthouse and Informer*. 1944 Policies and Programs," McCray Papers; McCray, "1940–70: 30 Glorious S.C. Years for Civil/Human Rights," speech delivered at the University of South Carolina, June 18, 1979; Richards, "Osceola McKaine," 129.

55. McCray, "The Way It Was," September 6, 1980; Richards, "Osceola McKaine," 115–16, 131–32, 148; Woods, "Modjeska Simkins," 178–79.

56. Letters by Viola Louise Duval to John H. McCray, November 14 and 21, 1943, McCray Papers, Box 1, Folder 2; McCray, "30 Glorious S.C. Years"; Richards, "Osceola E. McKaine," 103–24, 129–51; Woods, "Modjeska Simkins," 173–91.

57. McCray, "30 Glorious S.C. Years," 4–5; Richards, "Osceola McKaine," 143–46; Woods, "Modjeska Simkins," 188–92.

58. John McCray, "An Impact: S.C. Negroes and Political Action," speech delivered at the Avery Institute in Charleston, S.C., 1982; McCray, "Re: 'Black and Tan S.C. Delegations,'" paper, "To: Miss Rutha Green," n.d.; McCray, "30 Glorious S.C. Years"; "Explanation of the Plan for 'Beating the Primary,'" presumably by John H. McCray, slated for publication in *The Lighthouse and Informer*, April 2, 1944. McCray Papers, Box 1, Folder 3; Letter of A. J. Clement to John H. McCray, April 15, 1944, McCray Papers, Box 1, Folder 3; Richards, "Osceola E. McKaine," 162–64; Walton, *Black Political Parties*, 70–72; Newby, *Black Carolinians*, 281.

59. McCray, "30 Glorious S.C. Years."

60. "Negroes Organize Democratic Party to Contest White Supremacy in Deep South, by Margaret Vale," McCray Papers, 2–21; Richards, "Osceola McKaine," 167–73, 194–98.

61. Richards, "Osceola E. McKaine," 163–76; Walton, *Black Political Parties*, 73–74; Sullivan, *Days of Hope*, 170.

62. Sullivan, *Days of Hope*, 146–48; Woods, "Modjeska Simkins," 194–205.

63. John McCray, letters to "Fellow Citizen," May 17, 1944; to H. L. Bruce, June 22, 1944; to A. Clayton Powell, June 8, 1944; to Mrs. Franklin D. Roosevelt, June 9, 1944; to Wm. L. Dawson, June 22, 1944, McCray Papers, 2–21; McCray, letter to The President (Franklin D. Roosevelt), n.d., McCray Papers. McCray wrote several

letters to Powell. Also: Sullivan, *Days of Hope*, 170–71; Walter Edgar, *South Carolina*, chapter 22; Walton, *Black Political Parties*, 69–77; Richards, "Osceola McKaine," 163–67.

64. John McCray, letters to Wm. L. Dawson, June 22, 1944, and to A. Clayton Powell Jr., June 21, 1944, McCray Papers, 2–21; McCray, "30 Glorious S.C. Years"; Sullivan, *Days of Hope*, 170–71; Walton, *Black Political Parties*, 74–75; Richards, "Osceola E. McKaine," 177–88.

65. Cohodas, *Strom Thurmond*, 159–63; Walton, *Black Political Parties*, 75–76; John McCray, speech to the Seventh Youth Legislature, Southern Negro Youth Congress, October 18, 1946, Papers of the SNYC at Howard University, Box 7 (provided by Peter Lau); McCray, "30 Glorious S.C. Years"; McCray, "Black and Tan," n.d.

66. Walton, *Black Political Parties*, 73–74; Richards, "Osceola E. McKaine," 164–65, 192–206; McCray, SNYC speech, 1946.

67. Richards, "Osceola McKaine," 157–58, 169–70, 193–95; Woods, "Modjeska Simkins," 320–32; John McCray, "An Impact"; McCray, "Black and Tan"; McCray, "Negro Editor," March 13, 1982; "Explanation of the Plan for 'Beating the Primary,'" presumably by John H. McCray, McCray Papers, Box 1, Folder 3; letters of J. Bates Gerald to John H. McCray, April 25 and 30, 1944, McCray Papers, Box 1, Folder 3.

68. Richard, "Osceola McKaine," 184, 187–88, and chapter IX.

69. Ibid., 219–20.

70. Ibid., chapter 9; Woods, "Modjeska Simkins," 173–74, chapter 5; Linda Reed, *Simple Decency & Common Sense: The Southern Conference Movement, 1938–1963* (Bloomington: Indiana University Press, 1994), 95.

71. Richards, "Osceola McKaine," 232.

72. Ibid., 238–39; Woods, "Modjeska Simkins," chapter 5.

73. McKaine would not return to America alive; he died in Ghent in November 1955, one month shy of his sixty-third birthday. At his funeral in Sumter, McCray delivered the main eulogy. He would fondly remember McKaine in his later writings. Richards, "Osceola McKaine," chapters 9 and 10; McCray, "The Way It Was," March 5, 1985.

74. Sullivan, *Days of Hope*, 147–48; Newby, *Black Carolinians*, 281–86; Steven F. Lawson, *Black Ballots: Voting Rights in the South, 1944–1969* (New York: Columbia University Press, 1976), 48.

75. McCray retold what Elmore told him. McCray, "The Way It Was," December 6, 1980; McCray, "30 Glorious S.C. Years."

76. Lawson, *Black Ballots*, 47–55; Cohodas, *Strom Thurmond*, 114–115.

77. Cohodas, *Strom Thurmond*, 101–4.

78. Lawson, *Black Ballots*, 51–54; Newby, *Black Carolinians*, 274–89; Cohodas, *Strom Thurmond*, 101–4, 114–19.

79. *Lighthouse and Informer*, April 9 and June 11 and 18, 1949.

80. John G. Sproat, "The Limits of Moderations in South Carolina," paper presented at the annual meeting of the Organization for American Historians, 1987.

81. Cohodas, *Strom Thurmond*, 206–16.

82. McCray, "The Way It Was," November 29, 1980.

83. Cohodas, *Strom Thurmond*, 213–15.

84. Kluger, *Simple Justice, passim*; Edgar, *South Carolina*, chapter 22; Newby, *Black Carolinians*, 274–89; Nadine Cohodas, *Strom Thurmond*, 101–4, 114–19; Woods, "Modjeska Simkins," 228–33.

85. Kluger, *Simple Justice*, 13–14; McCray, "The Way It Was," September 20, 1980; Woods, "Modjeska Simkins," 227–31.

86. Letter of C. A. Scott to John H. McCray, September 2, 1943. McCray Papers, Box 1, Folder 2; Letter of R. B. Herbert to J. M. Hinton, September 4, 1943, McCray Papers, Box 1, Folder 2; Letter J. Clarence Colclough to John H. McCray, n.d. (probably late August, early September, no later than November), 1943, McCray Papers, Box 1, Folder 2; Postcard of "A Southern Lady" to John H. McCray, March 7, 1946, McCray Papers, Box 1, Folder 5; McCray, "The Way It Was," March 5, 1985; Richards, "Osceola McKaine," 128–29; Woods, "Modjeska Simkins," 257–58.

87. Jack Greenberg, *Crusaders in the Courts: How a Dedicated Band of Lawyers Fought for the Civil Rights Revolution* (New York: Basic Books, 1994), 54–55; *Carolina Times*, August 18, 1951; *Pittsburgh Courier*, December 13, 1952; McCray, "The Way It Was," February 26, 1983.

88. Greenberg, *Crusaders*, 55; *Pittsburgh Courier*, December 13, 1952.

89. *Pittsburgh Courier*, December 13, 1952; Greenberg, *Crusaders*, 55.

90. Wim Roefs, "John Henry McCray: Journalism, Influence, and Political Leadership in South Carolina's Early Civil Rights Movement, 1939–1954," paper presented to the 65th Annual Meeting of the Southern Historical Association, November 1999, Fort Worth, Texas.

91. Hill's Columbia City Directory 1953, 1954 (Hill Directory Co., Inc., Publishers); *Lighthouse and Informer*, June 12, 1954; Woods, "Modjeska Simkins," 247–60.

92. Workman, "Tax Sale" (1955); Behling, "South Carolina Negro Newspapers" (1964), 80–81.

93. McCray, Vita Sheet; McCray, "The Way It Was," August 22, 1981, December 5, 1981, July 17, 1982.

94. Newby, *Black Carolinians*, 328–29.

95. August Meier and Elliott Rudwick, *CORE: A Study in the Civil Rights Movement 1942–1968* (New York: Oxford University Press, 1973), 87–90, 116–19, 216–17; August Meier, "Epilogue: Toward a Synthesis of Civil Rights Activism," in Robinson and Sullivan, *New Directions*, 221; Adam Fairclough, *Race & Democracy: The Civil Rights Struggle in Louisiana, 1915–1972* (Athens: University of Georgia Press, 1995), xiv-xv.

96. Gavins, "North Carolina NAACP," 105–6; Fairclough, *Race & Democracy*, xv; Meier, "Epilogue," *passim*; Steven F. Lawson and Charles Payne, *Debating the Civil Rights Movement, 1945–1968* (Lanham, Md.: Rowman & Littlefield, 1998), *passim* and for Ella Baker, 103–5.

Chapter 15

A Marble House Divided

The Lincoln Memorial, the Civil Rights Movement, and the Politics of Memory, 1939–1963

Scott A. Sandage

Around 1910 the graduating eighth graders in Omega, Virginia, a conservative town on the Old Dominion's southern border, held a taffy pull to raise money for a class gift to their school. They earned five dollars and elected a boy named Oscar to spend it. At an emporium in a nearby town, he chose a dandy picture "in a fine-looking frame." The storekeeper asked, "Are you sure you want that one?" Oscar was sure; he went back and hung it in the school. "The next morning . . . the teacher came, and she was horrified," Oscar's widow recalled. "The pupils went home at lunchtime and told their parents. By afternoon there was great commotion about it," and the school board expelled Oscar the next day. The ornate frame held a portrait of Abe Lincoln. Oscar was quickly reinstated after his guardian offered ignorance as the boy's defense: McGuffey's reader had taught him nothing of Lincoln's crimes against the Old South, still a living memory in Omega. But Oscar graduated having learned "a stern lesson in intolerance." Thirty years later, as Franklin D. Roosevelt's assistant secretary of the interior, Oscar L. Chapman did not hesitate when a civil rights leader asked permission to use the Lincoln Memorial for an open-air concert by contralto Marian Anderson, whom the Daughters of the American Revolution (DAR) had refused to book into Constitution Hall because she was black.[1]

On Easter Sunday 1939, Anderson sang to an integrated crowd of seventy-five thousand at the Lincoln Memorial: "My country 'tis of thee, Sweet land of liberty, To thee we sing." Not "Of thee I sing," as the lyric usually goes, but "*To* thee *we* sing." The change made the national hymn subtly political, painting "land of liberty" as more aspiration than description and catching both the communalism and conflict of that famous day. White editors and Washington power brokers praised the concert as a stirring but welcome end to an embarrassing controversy. But black leaders saw it as an exciting beginning: an epiphany that brought forth a format for mass politics. "We are on the right track," wrote activist and black New Dealer Mary McLeod Bethune the next day. "Through the Marian Anderson protest concert we made our triumphant entry into the democratic spirit of American life."[2]

Tactically, the modern civil rights movement came of age on Easter Sunday 1939. The concert was not the first African American political use of Lincoln's memory, nor even the first civil rights gathering at his memorial. But it was, significantly, the first black mass action to evoke laudatory national publicity and earn a positive place in American public memory (our sometimes collective, always political sense of our past). Without fiery speeches or banners, without even mentioning the DAR, black organizers transformed a recital of sacred music at a national shrine into a political rally. In an era obsessed with defining Americanism, activists successfully portrayed their adversary as un-American. It was a formula civil rights activists and other protesters would repeat at the Lincoln Memorial in more than one hundred big and small rallies in subsequent decades—most notably in the 1963 March on Washington for Jobs and Freedom, when Martin Luther King, Jr., proclaimed his Dream from the steps where Marian Anderson had sung.

This essay argues that African Americans' struggles to hold a series of rallies at the Lincoln Memorial between 1939 and 1963 constituted a tactical learning experience that contributed to the civil rights movement's strategies of nonviolent action. Black protesters refined a politics of memory at the Lincoln Memorial. Within the sacred, national space of the monument, activists perfected a complex ritual of mass politics, one that exploited the ambiguities of cherished American values to circumvent opposition, unify coalitions, and legitimate black voices in national politics. Memory and ritual have been central concepts in the writing of cultural history but remain mostly unexplored in studies of black activism after 1940; this essay looks toward a cultural history of the civil rights movement. It is necessarily a dual inquiry into not only political tactics but also political imagery—in particular, the ambivalent relationship between African Americans and the icon called Abraham Lincoln. Blacks strategically appropriated Lincoln's memory and monument as political weapons, in the process layering and changing the public meanings of the hero and his shrine. But this political style was double-edged. The amalgam of a ritual-ized format, a sacred and public site, and nationalistic imagery constrained activists even as it empowered them. The power of these protests always lay in their inherent tensions between celebration and confrontation, between commemoration and politics, between sacred and profane, between race and nation.[3]

The Lincoln Memorial may be the best American example of what Pierre Nora has called a "memory site": a place where we struggle over ten-sions between our experience of the past (memory) and our organization of it (history). Ritual is a powerful weapon in these contests because it can be used conservatively or radically, to confirm or to transform social ar-rangements by affixing useful meanings onto sites and symbols. Civic leaders, for example, often try to forge a usable past by erecting monu-ments. But as Oscar Chapman's school expulsion attests, symbols such as Abraham Lincoln are always contested. Thus, memory sites are loci of struggle between the official groups that often create them and the vernac-ular groups that inevitably interpret and reinterpret them in competing ways. This essay employs John Bodnar's terms "official" and "vernacular" because they convey both the political essence of memory formation and the reality of unequal power relationships among competitors.[4]

However, prevailing concepts of public memory cannot fully absorb the interactions among the diverse political actors at the Lincoln Memorial. Architects, bureaucrats, editors, Hollywood filmmakers, patriotic societies, presidents, and protesters struggled against one another—ironically, by often cooperating with one another—to define often irreconcilable mem-ories of Abraham Lincoln. Such paradoxical alliances defy our analytical categories. Further, the Lincoln Memorial case forces us to grapple with the ideology of race in the making of American public memory. When black protesters worked with the Department of the Interior to arrange Anderson's Lincoln Memorial concert, what kind of memory was being made? Official or vernacular? White or black? Even within distinct cate-gories of actors, such as bureaucrats or black protesters, internal differ-ences of motive, style, and historical interpretation make it difficult to speak of collective memory with any precision. Yet our past is composed of broadly resonant cultural moments like the 1939 Anderson concert and the marches on Washington.

A cultural history of civil rights struggles must wrestle with these di-lemmas, and it must analyze blacks' symbolic tactics in terms of the cul-tural mood that made Americans receptive to their appeals for the first time since Reconstruction. This essay views the 1939 concert and 1963 march as brackets around what Warren I. Susman described as "a new era of nationalism," a time when depression and war kindled a search for common values and an "American Way of Life." But Susman imagined cultural nationalism as merely underpinning a Cold War consensus that curbed dissent until the militant 1960s. Likewise, some critics of the civil rights movement argue that coalitions with white liberals led inevitably to accommodation, manipulation, and fragmentation.[5]

Such views overlook exactly what studies of ritual and memory can show: that it was often activists who did the manipulating. Protesters mobilized mainstream symbols to further alternative ends, to constitute (not just reflect) shared beliefs, and to open spaces for social change. It was precisely the unrelenting nationalism that reigned from the 1930s to the 1960s that finally offered black activists a cultural language to speak to white America and to elicit support. The black church and Gandhian nonviolence were not the movement's only wellsprings of unity and strength; the stories and values of American history were equally vital resources. The famous picket sign, "I AM A MAN" may have been morally compelling, but winning political and legal rights for African Americans required a more focused message: I AM AN AMERICAN. Nowhere was this idea dramatized more vividly than in the Lincoln Memorial protests held from 1939 to 1963.

Among the most conspicuous gaps in the large historical literature on Abraham Lincoln, man and symbol, is the lack of any sustained analysis of the dynamic and complex relationship between African Americans and Lincoln's memory in the 138 years since his death.[6] The Lincoln Memorial and the foremost civil rights organization of the twentieth century both originated in impulses to honor Lincoln on the hundredth anniversary of his birth, February 12, 1909. During the week of Lincoln's centennial, while Congress debated proposals to erect a national monument, civil rights pioneers issued their famous "Lincoln Birthday Call" for a meeting to organize what became the National Association for the Advancement of Colored People (NAACP). The monument and movement were in this sense twinned, but their incompatible interpretations of Abraham Lincoln contributed directly to the rise of a racial politics of memory. Like the nation he had described in his celebrated 1858 speech, Lincoln's own marble memorial would quickly become a house divided.[7]

African Americans had tried to construct a usable public memory of Lincoln as early as 1876, when Frederick Douglass dedicated a Washington,

D.C., statue, which was paid for by freedmen and portrayed Lincoln emancipating a slave. Douglass criticized the statue for showing "the Negro on his knees," but he also saw strategic potential in publicly honoring Lincoln as the Great Emancipator. Blacks were thereby "fastening ourselves to a name and fame imperishable and immortal," Douglass said, and fulfilling a political duty to show public gratitude for emancipation. Historian David W. Blight has shown that Douglass was trying to "make Lincoln mythic" and to create a mood for racial justice by promulgating a public memory of the Civil War as an emancipatory struggle. Likewise, the NAACP founders in 1909 wrote that Lincoln's centennial should be a day for "taking stock of the nation's progress" toward racial justice. They noted ironically that on January 1, 1909 (Emancipation Day and only a month before Lincoln's hundredth birthday), Georgia had become the last Southern state to enact black disfranchisement laws. If Lincoln were alive, they ventured, he would be "disheartened and discouraged."[8]

Such views did not prevail in 1911 when Congress created a commission to memorialize Lincoln, chaired by President William Howard Taft. Turn of the century statesmen celebrated the economic and political reunion of North and South. Lincoln's ties to black freedom waned as politicians and scholars sculpted him into a "pro-Southern conservative" venerated on both sides of the Mason-Dixon Line: the patron saint of what Richard Nelson Current has called "reunion with reaction . . . nationalism revitalized at the expense of racial justice." As Lincoln assumed the role of Christ in American civil religion, signifying national redemption, it seemed he could not be both the Great Emancipator and the Savior of the Union. *Emancipator* became a casual synonym for *Lincoln,* not necessarily meant to evoke black freedom. When British dramatist John Drinkwater, in his popular 1920 book *Lincoln: The World Emancipator,* hailed "a profound unity of being in our two races," he meant not blacks and whites but Americans and Britons.[9]

Whitewashed views of Lincoln guided the design of the memorial, constructed between 1912 and 1921. Even its Potomac River site opposite Robert E. Lee's former Virginia home bespoke sectional reunion by design.[10] The Taft Commission's forty-one-page report to Congress made clear *which* Lincoln they honored, alluding twenty times to "the man who saved the Union" but to "emancipator" just once, in a rejected design. Architect Henry Bacon's final plan promised an exterior that expressed a single message, with columns and festoons embodying the states as "a symbol of the union." Inside, Daniel Chester French's stony Lincoln presides beneath an inscrip-

Fig. 2. Dedication of the Lincoln Memorial, May 30, 1922. Photo by Herbert L. French. Taken well after Robert Russa Moton's speech, this photograph of Moton standing at his seat (with program, at left) proves that he was not forced to sit in the "colored" section, as has often been alleged. Other photographs show black Civil War veterans seated among the dignitaries. (Photo no. 18882, vol. 5, p. 53, Lot 12294, Prints and Photographs Division, Library of Congress.) Courtesy Library of Congress.

tion: "In This Temple as in the Hearts of the People for Whom He Saved the Union the Memory of Abraham Lincoln Is Enshrined Forever." Art critic Royal Cortissoz wrote these lines and explained their subtlety to Bacon: "The memorial must make a common ground for the meeting of the north and the south. By emphasizing his saving the union you appeal to both sections. By saying nothing about slavery you avoid the rubbing of old sores." Lincoln himself supplies the only allusions to American slavery in the temple; his Gettysburg Address and Second Inaugural Address are carved into the walls. But as Dixon Wecter observed in 1940, these orations have been "worn so smooth by a million tongues that we are not apt to feel the edge of Lincoln's words." The Lincoln Memorial was conceived as a symbol of national consensus, linking North and South on holy, national ground.[11]

The shrine's 1922 dedication threw the racial schism over Lincoln's memory into stark, if fleeting, relief (figure 2). Taft, now chief justice of the Supreme Court, mentioned slavery not once in a long address. President Warren G. Harding reassured the South that Lincoln "would have been the last man in the republic to resort to arms to effect . . . abolition. Emancipation was a means to the great end—maintained union and nationality." One speaker breached the consensus. Robert Russa Moton, successor to Booker T. Washington at Tuskegee Institute, granted that "Lincoln died to save the union" but countered that the martyr's greatness stemmed from the fact that he "put his trust in God and spoke the word that gave freedom to a race, and vindicated the honor of a nation conceived in liberty and dedicated to the proposition that all men are created equal." But even as Moton spoke, prominent black Washingtonians were being confined by military ushers to a "colored" seating area at the rear of the crowd. The black press denounced the biased speeches and segregated seating as a mockery of Lincoln's ideals. Mainstream newspapers simply ignored the furor and headlined Moton's remark that African Americans were obliged to justify their emancipation by being loyal citizens. This round in the contest over Lincoln's memory went to the politicians.[12]

But a renewed battle between official and vernacular memories of Lincoln now existed, particularly at the national temple honoring him. "Proving that Lincoln will be remembered less as emancipator than as the man who kept the states together would tax a world of genius," balked a columnist for the black weekly *Chicago Defender*. In fact, there was a contrived, vulnerable quality to the bowdlerized Lincoln consecrated by politicians in the 1910s and 1920s. Surely the townsfolk in Omega, Virginia, who expelled young Oscar Chapman were not fooled by revisionist memories of Lincoln as nonsectional hero—nor were the United Confederate Veterans, who caused a furor only weeks after the temple's dedication by publicly blaming Lincoln for the Civil War. The consensus Lincoln seemed to need regular maintenance; starting in 1923, politicians and patriotic societies annually reaffirmed the primacy of Savior over Emancipator in Lincoln's Birthday ceremonies at the shrine. Black leaders continued to contest such interpretations; their first organized gathering at the memorial was a mass religious service in August 1926. The main speaker, a bishop of the African Methodist Episcopal Zion church, predictably told an audience of two thousand that "the immortality of the great emancipator lay not in his preservation of the Union, but in his giving freedom to the negroes of America."[13]

Conceived and dedicated as holy ground, the Lincoln Memorial became, as early as 1922, racially contested ground. By chance or design, the shrine straddled boundaries: between North and South, between black and white, and between official and vernacular memory. As both temple and tourist attraction, it sat on the cusp between sacred and secular. The memorial is a liminal space in Victor Turner's sense of being "betwixt and between" customary social categories. Liminal space is a realm of ambiguity—and therefore of possibility—where public rituals and appeals to sacred symbols possess an unusual potency to effect both social change and group unity, or *communitas*. African Americans were what Turner called liminal personae. Despite emancipation, they remained betwixt and between: no longer slaves, not yet full citizens. By invoking and reinterpreting a national icon, black protesters explored the ambiguities and possibilities of American society in the mid-twentieth century. Their protests at the Lincoln Memorial were repeated, standardized rituals that evolved from experience and that ultimately constituted a formidable politics of memory. The strategy was born, as Mary McLeod Bethune wrote, in the epiphany of Anderson's concert on Easter Sunday 1939.[14]

Maestro Arturo Toscanini said in 1935 that a voice like Anderson's was "heard once in a hundred years." Her fame by 1939 caused Howard University to seek a larger, off-campus auditorium for her annual Washington recital. On January 9, the Daughters of the American Revolution barred Anderson from their tax-exempt Constitution Hall, stating flatly and in writing that it was open "to white artists" only. The hall was the largest and most prestigious venue in the nation's capital; the shortage of options for the renowned international contralto was soon underscored when the District of Columbia Board of Education likewise refused Anderson the use of a high school auditorium. Anderson was neither the first nor last black performer banned by the DAR, but in 1939 First Lady Eleanor Roosevelt's public resignation from the DAR and black activists' skill at press relations elicited a flurry of pious editorials about national values. Eleanor Roosevelt had not only rejected the ubiquitous racism that burdened even celebrities like Marian Anderson; the First Lady had also publicly refused to countenance the DAR's petty and narrow definition of the American Way.[15]

An outraged coalition of black civic leaders and NAACP officers (as well as Anderson's shrewd manager, Sol Hurok) soon realized that bringing Abraham Lincoln into this fray, by what seemed an unprecedented use of his memorial, "would double the news value" of the event. On March 13, the NAACP board of directors decided that, rather than finding another

Fig. 3. Marian Anderson, Lincoln Memorial, April 9, 1939. *Life* Magazine photograph by Thomas McAvoy, © 1939, Time Warner.

concert hall, "it would be far better . . . for Miss Anderson to sing out-of-doors, for example, at the Lincoln Memorial, erected to commemorate the Memory of Abraham Lincoln, the Great Emancipator, or not to sing in Washington at all until democracy can surmount the color line in the nation's capital." Permission was quickly secured from Secretary of the Interior Harold L. Ickes—through his deputy, Oscar Chapman. Ickes cleared the idea with President Roosevelt, who reportedly quipped, "She can sing from the top of the Washington Monument if she wants to!" To be sure, the president and the secretary would later regret this precedent, but their making the memorial available in 1939 was a faint but significant harbinger of government support for civil rights; opening the national space of the memorial was a telling rebuke to the prejudice that ruled the commercial spaces of lunch counters and concert halls.[16]

The symbolic and logistical mastermind of Anderson's outdoor recital was NAACP secretary Walter White, a gifted publicist who had once called Herbert Hoover "the man in the lily-White House." White took care that plans for the concert would avoid any "impression that propaganda for the Negro was the objective instead of the emphasizing of a principle." He rejected as undignified an early proposal that Anderson sing in a park opposite Constitution Hall, "because that would be like a naughty boy thumbing his nose at the back of a larger boy who had socked him." Activists had more to gain by taking the high road. Even so, behind the scenes, White took every opportunity to tweak and embarrass the DAR, belittling them in correspondence with journalists and politicians as the "funny old ladies of the DAR" and attempting to get Grant Wood's satirical painting, *Daughters of Revolution,* printed on the cover of *Time* magazine.[17]

Having secured sacred ground for the concert site, White intensified his attention to symbolism. Anderson would begin by singing "America" because of the "ironic implications." Members of the cabinet, Congress, and the Supreme Court were recruited as public sponsors and invited to sit on the landing where Anderson would sing. "Boy Scouts, white and colored," were enlisted to hand out the concert's printed program—with the Gettysburg Address quoted on its cover. A script provided to radio commentators (and incorporated nearly verbatim into Harold Ickes's introduction) read, "It is both fitting and symbolic that [Anderson] should be singing on Easter Sunday on the steps of the Memorial to the Great Emancipator who struck the shackles of slavery from her people seventy-six years ago."[18]

On the afternoon of April 9, these elements came together brilliantly. After the brief introduction by Secretary Ickes, the singer descended the steps in front of the statue and, in White's words, "Poured out in her superb voice 'sweet land of liberty' almost as though it was a prayer." Those who attended remember the concert, which was captured by newsreel cameras and broadcast live by national radio networks, as "like a religious service" and "a great spiritual experience of common sympathy and understanding." Civil rights attorney Joseph L. Rauh, Jr., recalled, "It was quite a beautiful awakening of blacks in the city there. Everyone was there in their best clothes. . . . You got this feeling, there she was in front of Lincoln, and what a great step forward this was." The next day activists discussed making the concert an annual event to hold public attention on racial issues. In the ensuing two decades, planners repeatedly hearkened back to the Anderson concert as a formative moment (and the singer herself renewed public memories of the event in 1952 when she sang again on the steps of the shrine at a memorial service for Ickes). The Easter recital seemed a tactical epiphany to black activists because it suggested a site and format for injecting the civil rights cause into the mainstream of debates about national values and the American Way.[19]

Hagiographers have made the Anderson affair into a story about Eleanor Roosevelt, who neither planned nor attended the concert. Notwithstanding her exemplary courage, emphasis on the First Lady obscures the event's larger importance: With the concert, the civil rights movement began to develop a strategy of mass, symbolic protest that used ritual and appeals to memory to make racism a national issue. In 1939, Robert Sherwood's play, *Abe Lincoln in Illinois*, won the Pulitzer Prize and shared the Broadway footlights with *The American Way* by George S. Kaufman and Moss Hart. Abraham Lincoln increasingly became a coveted cultural and political symbol of the American Way of Life, a symbol wielded by everyone from Franklin D. Roosevelt to Carl Sandburg, from Hollywood moguls to the American Communist party. American veterans of the Spanish Civil War's Abraham Lincoln Brigade had marched to the memorial in 1938. Amid so many claims on Lincoln, his connection to racial justice remained controversial. Two months before Anderson's concert, Lincoln scholar Paul Angle had declared unequivocally that the president's fame as an emancipator was "unhistorical," unsupported by fact. In one bold stroke, the Easter concert swept away the shrine's official dedication to the "savior of the union" and made it a stronghold of racial justice. One concertgoer, the black baritone Todd Duncan, recalled that the performance seemed to transform the memorial into "a wonderful citadel, a cathedral," a place both to affirm the nation and to struggle to make it just.[20]

Fig. 4. Untitled cartoon, by [Jack] Sparling. Copyright 1939, *The Washington Post*. Reprinted with permission.

White America recognized one half of the metamorphosis—affirmation—and a catharsis of nationalism followed. A Massachusetts editor predicted that DAR members would not attend the concert. "We expect they would feel uncomfortable on that ground, and a little out of place," he wrote, sensing that the memorial had become a powerfully charged site. Likewise, a *Philadelphia Inquirer* editorial proclaimed a "New Message of the Lincoln Shrine." The influential columnist Franklin P. Adams compared the DAR to the Nazi German-American Bund, and vocal members of the public agreed. Those "Daughters of the American Reactionaries" were "stuffed petticoats" who had been unmasked as "un-American." "That's the stuff," one citizen wrote Ickes, "Give the colored girl a show. The D.A.R. don't own this country which is still free, thank the Lord. And it's most fitting that the spirit of Lincoln will be at this concert." Another wrote, "It's a strange world when you find the DAR in the same pew with the Ku-Kluxers." A Sunday concert had become a national referendum, polled at barbershops and breakfast tables across the land.[21]

Of course, not all the editorials and citizens' letters were supportive. And in the segregated capital, Marian Anderson had to sleep in a private home because no reputable hotel would accommodate a black guest. Some African Americans were appalled that Anderson had to sing out of doors, regardless of the noble setting. White newspapers referred to the forty-two-year-old contralto as "the Negro Girl from Philadelphia" and "this colored girl out of the slums" or paternalistically, by her first name only. The symbolic triumph left much unchanged. Even Eleanor Roosevelt was not always a reliable ally. Ironically, only a year after the concert she crossed a picket line for perhaps the only time in her life, bypassing black protesters to attend the 1940 premiere of the Raymond Massey film *Abe Lincoln in Illinois* at a segregated Washington theater.[22]

These contradictions in what has become a towering moment in American folklore, the Marian Anderson concert of 1939, reveal the inherent ambiguity of symbolic black protest at the Lincoln Memorial. Memory, theorists tell us, is a deeply visual medium. The concert and the ritualistic rallies that ensued in the 1940s and 1950s presented a compelling mnemonic image—the juxtaposition of the Great Emancipator with descendants of freed slaves. Like the "invented traditions" described by Eric Hobsbawm, that image used "history as a legitimator of action and cement of group cohesion." The political resonance of such an appeal hinges on what scholars call the social dimensions of memory, the extent to which an image tells an instantly recognizable "mythic story." Viewers connect such images idiosyncratically to their private understandings of the collective past. Black protesters at the memorial evoked the American cultural masterplot that "Lincoln freed the slaves." This catechism proved remarkably resilient despite official efforts to suppress it.[23]

But even as activists used the masterplot to argue for justice, they could not avoid replicating a stereotypical image of black subordination: that of the "grateful Negro at Lincoln's feet." Among the most familiar tableaux of American race relations, this duo appears in the 1876 monument dedicated (and criticized) by Frederick Douglass, in myriad popular prints, and even on a United States postage stamp that appeared in 1940, less than a year after Anderson's concert. David Brion Davis located the image within a genre he called the "Emancipation Moment," arguing that its subtext of racial hierarchy imposes on real-life African Americans a posture of indebtedness and moral obligation. We have already observed this at the memorial's 1922 dedication, when the white press focused on Robert Moton's remarks about "Negro loyalty."[24]

Themes of self-congratulatory nationalism and implicit racial hierarchy pervaded responses to Anderson's concert. A *Washington Post* columnist wrote that concertgoers felt "a little nobler" gazing at "the slender colored girl on the front steps . . . with the massive figure of Lincoln looking down benevolently." Compare this to *Life* magazine's photograph of the majestically poised singer in the mink coat she wore during the chilly recital. Then consider an admiring 1939 editorial cartoon in which the diva becomes a pickaninny, clad in the limp cotton dress of a field hand, sleeves rolled to the shoulder and arms thrown up rapturously to the towering emancipator. An artist of the Popular Front lampooned the DAR, but his drawing likewise subordinated a tiny, featureless singer to the colossal Lincoln (figures 3–5). The ubiquitous emancipation moment also appeared in Frank Capra's 1939 film *Mr. Smith Goes to Washington*. Filming for this paean to the American Way of Life began in the capital a mere eleven days after Anderson's recital. In James Stewart's famous scene at the memorial, as a white boy and his grandfather read aloud "new birth of freedom" from the Gettysburg Address, Capra crosscut to an elderly black man, eyes glistening as he doffs his hat and looks up at the statue. In 1947 a photo showing National Park Service janitors crouched on Lincoln's statue and captioned to evoke the stock figure of the black shoeshine boy appeared in *National Geographic* the same month that the NAACP held a large rally at the memorial. Two years later, the New York City Housing Authority graced a low-rent project in Harlem with George Keck's bronze, "Lincoln and Boy,"

Fig. 5: "It's All Lincoln's Fault," by [Fred] Ellis. Courtesy *Indianapolis Recorder.*

showing the kindly president with his arm around a reverent, black youth. In all these venues, the emancipation moment validated the status quo; Lincoln's noble work is done, it seemed to say, and the Negro must now remember his place. Just as Eleanor Roosevelt eclipsed Marian Anderson, in a broader sense Lincoln, as a symbol of the nation and of white magnanimity, became more important than emancipation or civil rights.[25]

From the time of Frederick Douglass, black leaders had known that whites might construe their use of Lincoln's memory in this way. NAACP secretary James Weldon Johnson ritually re-enacted the emancipation moment on Lincoln's Birthday, 1925; wrapping himself in a chain of flowers, he stood near Lincoln's statue in New York City's Union Square and symbolically broke the chain. Such performances imply a political choice, not a natural affinity of African Americans for "Father Abraham." Historians have obscured this point by assimilating the perspective of the emancipation moment; many assume uncritically that blacks felt "almost universal admiration for Lincoln" until the Black Power backlash of the 1960s. This simplistic view ignores earlier ambivalence among both leaders and ordinary members of the community. In 1927 a black teenager wrote W.E.B. Du Bois that youths in her Illinois town opposed celebrating Lincoln's Birthday. What, she asked, had Lincoln ever done for blacks? A famous rejection of the gratitude forced upon black citizens by the emancipation moment followed in 1932, when the African American editor of the Pittsburgh *Courier* advised his readers to defect from the Republican to the Democratic party. "My friends, go turn Lincoln's picture to the wall," wrote Robert Vann. "That debt has been paid in full." The *Washington Afro-American* likewise questioned Lincoln's relevance in 1946. Many who staged rallies at the memorial shared these doubts. Whitney M. Young, Jr., of the National Urban League, confessed "mixed feelings about Lincoln." Martin Luther King, Jr., called Lincoln "vacillating" but also saw him as the only president who had ever earned the confidence of African Americans. James Farmer, founder of the Congress on Racial Equality (CORE), recently emphasized the conscious strategy of black protest at the memorial. "It doesn't say anything about what we thought about Lincoln," Farmer explained. "It says something about how great the image of Lincoln was, and it was something we could use to achieve our noteworthy objectives, that's all." Black leaders regarded public appeals to Lincoln and national memory as the only symbolic language available to them to communicate with white America. The potential gains seemed worth the compromises.[26]

The emancipation moment and black ambivalence about Lincoln are directly relevant to the advent of a racial politics of memory at the memorial because they expose the gap between black and white perceptions of the protests and underscore the terms of struggle after 1939. Anderson's concert came to symbolize the promise of protest—at least to African Americans. But at a public ceremony in 1943, Ickes promulgated a very different official memory of Easter Sunday 1939, in the light of rising wartime domestic unrest among African Americans. "Marian Anderson's voice and personality," Ickes declared, "have come to be a symbol—a symbol of American unity at a time when a lack of it might well prove fatal to us as a people." Here, as in the white response to Robert Moton in 1922, was the grateful Negro at Lincoln's feet. Ickes's emphasis on national unity echoed earlier official attempts to use Lincoln's memory to obscure national differences (such as the subtle inscription Royal Cortissoz composed for the memorial). Despite Anderson's symbolic triumph, the inertia of white attitudes remained an obstacle. Using Lincoln to affirm national values was one thing; using him to struggle for change, quite another.[27]

Government cooperation was not forthcoming in the decades after 1939, when African Americans began to seek the memorial for more overt protests, rather than Sunday concerts. Activists gradually learned that the skillful use of ritual and memory could circumvent such opposition. A standardized civil rights protest ritual evolved from the elements in Marian Anderson's concert, such as using mass rallies instead of pickets, performing patriotic and spiritual music, choosing a religious format, inviting prominent platform guests, self-policing the crowds to project an orderly image, alluding to Lincoln in publicity and oratory, and insisting on using the memorial rather than another site. The civil rights ritual absorbed the profane into the sacred, coating politics with civil religion. It confronted racism powerfully but indirectly, shrewdly emphasizing national values over direct political criticism. Protesters refined this approach during the 1940s and 1950s as they engaged bureaucrats in sporadic tugs-of-war over using the memorial.

In 1941 black labor leader A. Philip Randolph coerced Roosevelt into issuing Executive Order 8806 (which created the Fair Employment Practices Committee) by threatening "an 'all-out' thundering march on Washington, ending in a monster and huge demonstration at Lincoln's Monument" to "shake up white America." Roosevelt's capitulation averted the rally, but Randolph's bid for a permit for a similar event the next year was denied. FDR and Ickes worried that the memorial was becoming a soapbox. Ickes confided to his diary, "If we allow one controversial subject to be discussed" at the memorial, "it would be difficult for us to deny its use on other similar occasions." Ickes wrote Randolph and explained that a protest would "dim the glory" of Anderson's historic concert, adding, "I do not believe that even such a meeting as you propose would be in the true spirit of the Lincoln Memorial." Grateful negroes were welcome; protesting ones were not.[28]

Randolph persevered. His next proposal revealed how activists were learning that access to this powerful symbol might depend on projecting peaceful, ritualistic images approximating the emancipation moment. In 1943 Randolph organized a small, interracial, interfaith prayer pilgrimage to the memorial on Lincoln's Birthday. The Howard University Glee Club sang "The Battle Hymn of the Republic" and "Go Down, Moses," juxtaposing their refrains of "His truth is marching on" with "Let my people go." Eleanor Roosevelt was invited to this exercise in civil religion but chose instead to attend an official wreath-laying ceremony there with her husband earlier in the day. Undaunted, Randolph planned for the future. "Next year," he wrote, "I hope that we shall have not one such ceremony, but hundreds, all over America, *wherever there is a statue of Lincoln,* and wherever groups of enlightened citizens of both races, both churchmen and laymen, can be brought together to re-affirm Lincoln's high faith and to advance the cause he served."[29]

Randolph prescribed ritual appeals to Lincoln's memory not just to legitimate political action but to unify a coalition, to evoke *communitas*. Rallies at the memorial could help rejuvenate frontline activists and unify leadership factions. For example, NAACP secretary Roy Wilkins reacted skeptically to the direct actions led in the 1950s by Martin Luther King, Jr. In 1957 the third anniversary of the Supreme Court's *Brown v. Board of Education* ruling neared without Southern compliance, however, and the two leaders agreed that an uplifting event was needed, in Wilkins's words, to "allow our people to participate in something and express themselves in some way."[30]

Again the Department of the Interior balked, claiming that holding the envisioned Prayer Pilgrimage for Freedom at the shrine would "inconvenience" tourists and deprive them of "undisturbed contemplation of this inspiring Memorial." Instead, officials offered an amphitheater near the Washington Monument. In appeal the NAACP's Clarence Mitchell stressed the memorial's power as a place for unity and regeneration, explaining "that the symbolic value of the Lincoln Memorial for this meeting was of tremendous importance in overcoming the despair, disillusionment and anger which have been generated by recent acts of racial violence and intimidation in the South." Incredibly, still determined to protect the memorial, the bureaucrats in turn suggested that the demonstrators gather on the plaza in front of the Supreme Court! When Mitchell rejected this and other counterproposals, the officials finally capitulated. The NAACP issued a special press release: "Secure Lincoln Memorial for Prayer Pilgrimage."[31]

The format exalted principle over direct confrontation. "There will be no picket lines, resolutions or attempts to call on the President," assured the NAACP, only prayers "for deliverance from the cancer of racism." On May 17, 1957, thirty thousand people prayed "in the presence of the memory of Abraham Lincoln and of the God and father of our people." Lest a zealous crowd unmask the day as a political rally, the printed program (above even the title of the event) warned that applause was improper at a religious service. Wilkins raised the flag of nationalism: "We are

Americans. . . . We believe in our Constitution and its Bill of Rights." King affirmed his place as the movement's preeminent spokesman with his oration, "Give us the ballot—We will transform the South." Mahalia Jackson led the crowd in the hymn that Marian Anderson had politicized, "My Country 'Tis of Thee."[32]

The 1957 event concluded with an addition to the politics of memory, the mass recitation of an "Affirmation and Pledge." Entreating "all Americans to join us in prayer and in work to eradicate racial and religious prejudices," the pledge not only served the ritual function of building *communitas,* it fostered a subtle transition from the realm of memory to that of politics. Protesters were asking Americans not merely to remember, but to act. Adding a pledge to the civil rights ritual also completed the underlying pattern of nonviolent action that had been evolving at the Lincoln Memorial. A few days before the pilgrimage, the activist Bayard Rustin explained that pattern to King. In the context of helping King focus a draft of the speech he would deliver at the memorial, Rustin wrote that "the form in creative action is always Yes-No-Yes. That is to say a positive action such as the idea of brotherhood, followed by a rejection—a No. Rejection of segregation, discrimination; injustice." The activist concluded, "this must be followed by a positive action . . . a common action.[33]

The pattern resonates strongly with the American jeremiad, a rhetorical convention favored not only by many black speakers but also by Abraham Lincoln. Rustin's explanation in 1957 underscores how ritual aims to bring people together and energize them for a common purpose. But the larger point is this: Years before activists like Rustin and King began to espouse a Gandhian philosophy of nonviolence in the South, the basic pattern had already taken shape in the rituals performed at the Lincoln Memorial. The essence (masking power and politics beneath a peaceful, communal gathering) was there in 1939, and it became more focused in later decades.[34]

By 1957 that essence was attracting notice; the Lincoln Memorial protests were starting to transcend the emancipation moment. To a point, responses to the 1957 pilgrimage echoed 1939: African Americans were again seen as taking the high road, painting their adversaries as un-American, and charging the sacred space of the memorial with a special force. How, asked Edward P. Morgan in his radio commentary for ABC News, could the Ku Klux Klan or white citizens' councils match the power of "a respectable and respectful gathering of American citizens in clean shirts and chic dresses" whose only weapons were the law and human dignity? "A burning cross, a bomb, floggings, a lynching party," Morgan continued, "these are blunt, cumbersome weapons against a force of this kind. Of course, the racists might refine their approach. They might henceforth picket the Lincoln Memorial as contaminated by such a host of Negroes." The monument continued to be seen as a contested space, but one that was becoming ever more identified with the civil rights movement and its politics of memory and ritual. Moreover, the ritual was reaching maturity in its dual functions of unifying protesters and legitimating black voices in national politics. Morgan urged his nationwide audience in 1957 to look again at the "respectable and respectful" assemblage at the memorial: "Here, if you looked at it closely, was a demonstration of power."[35]

Randolph never abandoned his idea of a big march on Washington. Even before the 1957 pilgrimage, his associate Rustin was jotting down ideas for a larger event, later realized as the 1963 March on Washington for Jobs and Freedom. "Efforts should be made as early as possible to get a permit to march in Washington and to hold a mass meeting before the Lincoln Memorial," Rustin wrote, fully aware of the publicity value of tussling with officials for a permit. "There may be trouble, but this could make the situation all the more lively if handled carefully." In late 1962, as local activism swelled in the South and the movement sought a federal civil rights bill, Randolph proposed "a mass Protest rally" at the memorial to proclaim a concrete "Emancipation Program" in the centenary year of Lincoln's proclamation. These early plans rebut the frequent assertion that the memorial was a compromise site for the March on Washington, chosen when more confrontational locales were abandoned. Organizers did discuss sit-ins at the Capitol and a White House demonstration, but a rally at the Lincoln Memorial was always at the core of their plans.[36]

As initial thoughts about the March evolved into a concrete plan, organizers eschewed militant activities. This story has been well told elsewhere; moderating influences included the tension between the movement's old and new guards, the addition of church and labor groups to the march coalition, and the choice to negotiate for the cooperation of the Kennedy administration (which concurrently introduced the bill that would become the Civil Rights Act of 1964). On the day of the march, even signs and banners had to be approved by planners, and last-minute changes were demanded of Student Nonviolent Coordinating Committee (SNCC) leader John Lewis's hard-hitting speech. Despite such moderations in the 1963 march, no event since Marian Anderson's concert left a more indelible public memory of the civil rights movement or, indeed, of the Lincoln Memorial.[37]

The march culminated the politics of memory begun in 1939. On August 28, 1963, four hundred thousand people massed at the shrine. In this "living petition," as Lerone Bennett, Jr., wrote in *Ebony*, marchers "said with their bodies that the Negro . . . was still not free." Marian Anderson was there; slated to open the program with the national anthem, she was delayed by dense crowds and later sang a spiritual. Marchers prayed and orated, and Randolph led the throng in a pledge: "Standing before the Lincoln Memorial . . . in the centennial year of emancipation, I affirm my complete personal commitment for the struggle for jobs and freedom for all Americans." Here again was the final "Yes" in Rustin's formula for an effective protest: the common action that nurtured both *communitas* and political commitment. "What mattered most at the Lincoln Memorial," Rustin later wrote, was not the eloquent speeches, but rather "the pledge of a quarter million Americans, black and white, to carry the civil rights revolution into the streets."[38]

In American memory the most eloquent speech of the day was King's. The final speaker, he wanted his remarks to be "sort of a Gettysburg Address." He began with the emancipation moment: "Five score years ago, a great American, in whose symbolic shadow we stand today, signed the Emancipation Proclamation." King alternated between confrontation (musing that Negroes had been given "a bad check") and the visionary nationalism of a dream "deeply rooted in the American dream." Near the end of his oration, he recited the hymn that Marian Anderson had sung from the same spot twenty-four years earlier, "My Country, 'Tis of Thee." Once more, black leaders offered America an inspiring and reverent national moment that subtly portrayed the movement's adversaries as un-American. As historian Richard Lentz has observed, "the power of King's oration ultimately derived from the confluence of two antithetical symbols—the Birmingham of Bull Connor with its snarling police dogs and lashing fire hoses, and the March with its assemblage of Americans sharing King's dream of America made whole." As the crowd and nationwide broadcast audience heard King's call and response, "Let Freedom Ring!", Lincoln brooded over his shoulder—the statue bathed in special lights to enhance its visibility on television and in news photographs.[39]

Journalists filed dozens of mood pieces to convey the ambience of the day: how dressed up the marchers were, the overwhelming aura of celebration "and utter determination," and a sense that the rally had somehow changed the memorial. "The shrine that was the assembly point was so entirely appropriate," Richard S. Bird wrote in the *New York Herald Tribune*, "that you looked at it in a new way." The ritual imbued participants with

> a feeling that is often hard for people to get in their every-day life.
>
> A feeling for country. Tens of thousands of these petitioning Negroes had never been to Washington before, and probably would never come again. Now here they were. And this was their Washington . . . and that great marble memorial was their own memorial to the man who had emancipated them.[40]

Marchers absorbed the mix of memory and *communitas*. One woman told a reporter, "I think Lincoln is moved by this: he must know what is happening." But she also knew the day was not really about Lincoln at all, exclaiming, "I am so proud of my people!" Lerone Bennett, Jr., pinpointed the day's legacy: "If the March changed no votes in Congress or no hearts in America, it did, at least change the marchers themselves. Those who thought, in the beginning, that it was too respectable, and those who thought it was too radical . . . for a moment in time they were one."[41] Pundits before and after the march predicted that it would change no votes on the civil rights bill. This cry originated among moderate and right-wing opponents, who warned that the event would be counterproductive. Later it figured in left critiques by activists and scholars, who felt the march had devolved from a protest into a "church picnic."[42]

Such critics missed the point of the march and the strategy it fulfilled. In the summer of 1963, called the "Summer of Discontent," 1,122 civil rights demonstrations occurred nationwide; an unprecedented 20,000 protesters were arrested in the South. The tactical brilliance of the march, as of earlier rallies at the memorial, was to raise subtly the threat of similar militancy in Washington—and to do it in a way that attracted public support and evaded government suppression. The Kennedy administration did press for moderation; but protesters had long before learned how to outmaneuver bureaucrats and arrive at the Lincoln Memorial. They were there again in spring 1964; while the civil rights bill languished in filibuster, seminarians of many races and faiths held a twenty-four hour vigil at the shrine for months. They were certain, one of them recalled, that "Lincoln was on our side." Just before the bill passed on June 10, Hubert H. Humphrey confided to activists, "The secret of passing the bill is the prayer groups." Who could ban a church picnic?[43]

Looking broadly from 1939 to the mid-1960s, then, the civil rights rituals at the Lincoln Memorial had repeatedly served two functions: uniting and invigorating activists, and legitimating political action by African Americans. Black leaders assembled at the shrine a compelling universe of national symbols—Marian Anderson and Eleanor Roosevelt, the American flag and the national anthem, preachers and church choirs, senators and presidents, boy scouts and Abraham Lincoln—all of which linked the African American political agenda to the regnant cultural nationalism of the era. In turn such icons were held up in opposition to a growing rogue's gallery of un-Americans that included the DAR, the lynch mob, the Ku Klux Klan, Mississippi senator Theodore G. Bilbo, Arkansas governor Orval Faubus, the white citizens councils, and Theophilus Eugene ("Bull") Connor.[44]

Randolph's press release for the 1958 Youth March for Integrated Schools made such pairings explicit; a rally at the Lincoln Memorial would "highlight the American Way of Life" and "alert public opinion to the grave danger of the poison of Little Rock Faubusism infecting the bloodstream of American life." Organizers understood exactly what they were doing at this national shrine, and they knew that public memory hinged on compelling visual images. To compete for public attention against modern distractions such as baseball's World Series and the sputniks, Randolph wrote, "any human cause, though great and imperative, must be given sharp picturization." The elder statesman of civil rights added, "The propaganda of the deed is more powerful than the propaganda of the word."[45]

A politics of memory might have worked just as well if protesters had gone to the White House or the Capitol. But a ritual strategy at the Lincoln Memorial had special advantages, both in getting a message to the public and in broadening participation. The distinction between protests at the Lincoln Memorial and those at other sites, Joseph L. Rauh, Jr., asserted, was in "how you're aiming." Smaller events were "directed right at the president," but mass meetings at this shrine were aimed at public opinion. Protesters transformed a monument into a kind of Supreme Court of Public Opinion; they chose to affirm cherished principles, not to criticize the policy makers who ultimately had to decide whether to change the system. Paul Robeson, leader of a 1946 anti-lynching rally at the memorial, observed this distinction. His blunt demands in a White House meeting with President Harry S. Truman created a minor furor; but at the Lincoln Memorial later the same day, Robeson merely sang and read a new emancipation proclamation.[46]

Activists also used the memorial to bring more people into the movement. Norman Hill, a leading organizer of the 1963 march, explained that protests there had a "diffused" impact and recalled that in 1963,

> as the march unfolded and developed, there was a growing sense that in fact the mood . . . of the country was shifting toward the movement. Therefore, if one wanted . . . to pass [the civil rights bill] and also to generate real numbers in the march itself—tactically it became more important to do that than to do the direct confrontational things like sitting-in in various halls of government.[47]

Even with the ritualistic format used at the Lincoln Memorial, assembling before government buildings would have been more directly confrontational, more accusatory, more likely to be counterproductive. Moreover, many nonactivists, both black and white, might have feared to join a chanting (possibly violent) throng outside the president's house or the Capitol. A "church picnic" at the Lincoln Memorial seemed less forbidding. Repeatedly, observers of the rallies remarked how they brought new people into the movement. "An awful lot of black people who'd never been at a *protest* were there," Rauh recalled of the 1939 concert. Paula Sandburg, the poet's widow, caught the ambience of the shrine when she chose it for her husband's memorial service: "It would be especially appropriate, as people from all walks of life would feel welcome there."[48]

Efforts at inclusion and indirect confrontation intensified the symbolism of protests at the Lincoln Memorial. The shrine was distant from government buildings, but it was by no means neutral ground or a compromise site that diluted the power of black protest. Conceived in a quest for white consensus, Lincoln's national monument had been subsequently redefined through interracial conflict. African Americans transformed the temple into a moral high ground from which to exhort the nation to finish what Lincoln called "the great task remaining before us." In this way the memorial became a powerfully confrontational site. Protesters presented themselves as orderly, patriotic citizens. They made the past a resource and made Lincoln a signifier of the dissonance between America's professed and achieved values. Rachelle Horowitz, transportation director of the 1963 march, remembered that marchers wanted to communicate a simple message: "We represent the core of what this country believes in." Rallying again and again at the memorial (hammering their message home and

drawing strength to keep fighting) was like returning to home base, Horowitz said. She and other protesters

> had to keep going back. . . . It's a sense of whether you have just a protest
> rally or whether you're having something with historical dimensions. And
> I think that Lincoln does add that. You're standing there in the face of
> history. In the face of history that has to be completed. . . . In terms of
> both symbolism and the need to go forward, the memorial is the per-
> fect place.[49]

Symbolic needs, of course, change over time. After 1963 many African
Americans deserted both the rituals and symbols that had been so forcefully merged at the Lincoln Memorial. The politics of memory had involved
choices between militant confrontation and longer-term public education,
between separatism and coalition building. The ritual that evolved from
those choices, the sacred status of the memorial itself, and the fact that using
the site required government permission narrowed protesters' tactical options. Wisconsin fair housing activists did hold an eight-day vigil there
in 1967, and the antiwar March on the Pentagon stepped off from the
memorial the same year. But as the general climate of protest turned more
militant in the late 1960s, black leaders, including King, explored new tactics. The disastrous Poor People's Campaign of 1968—the last action King
helped plan—built a shantytown within sight of the Lincoln Memorial, finally bringing to Washington the kind of long-term direct confrontation
pursued in Birmingham and Selma, Alabama.[50]

Likewise, African American activists abandoned Lincoln after 1963, as
the success of their movement transformed protesters' sense of identity.
In 1964 the black novelist John Oliver Killens attempted to explain the
widening gap between blacks and sympathetic white liberals. "You give us
moody Abraham Lincoln, but many of us prefer John Brown, whom most
of you hold in contempt and regard as a fanatic," he wrote. Malcolm X declared that Lincoln "probably did more to trick Negroes than any other
man in history." It surely did not help that (just as newsman Edward Morgan had predicted in 1957) the shrine's growing identification with African
American freedom was increasingly rebutted by racists—from the anonymous graffitist who scrawled "NIGGER LOVER" on an outside wall of the
shrine after a 1962 commemoration of the centennial of the Emancipation
Proclamation (figure 6), to a 1972 wreath-laying ceremony there by the National Socialist White People's Party (the American Nazis).[51]

Fig. 6: Graffiti at the Lincoln Memorial after the centennial celebration of the Emancipation Proclamation, September 22, 1962. Courtesy National Park Service, U.S. Department of the Interior.

By 1968 journalist Mary McGrory could write with certainty that "the Negroes are repudiating [Lincoln] as their champion and friend. . . . They have decided that he has been imposed upon them as 'a folk symbol.'" That repudiation applied equally to the Lincoln Memorial. "How many times," asked Julius Lester that same year, explicitly rejecting the emancipation moment,

has the photograph been reprinted of the small Negro boy staring up at the huge statue of Lincoln at the Lincoln Memorial? The photograph would mean nothing if the boy doing the staring were white. What is the catechism the black child learns from Grade One on? "Class, what did Abraham Lincoln do?" "Lincoln freed the slaves," and the point is driven home that you'd still be down on Mr. Charlie's plantation working from can to can't if Mr. Lincoln hadn't done your great-great-grandmama a favor.[52]

Earlier, Lincoln had been the only symbol honored by both whites and blacks on whom protesters could lay claim; the martyrdom of King, Malcolm X, and others, the rise of Black Power, and the advent of black history programs gave protesters a constellation of contemporary African American heroes. An interracial politics of memory, placing blacks at the center of the American story by juxtaposing them with its noblest hero, was no longer tactically useful if freedom remained a gift rather than the product of struggle—and if whites, influenced by the emancipation moment, continued to see the Lincoln symbol as bigger than the movement that was using it. Memory thereby threatened to become an end in itself, rather than an incentive to further action.[53]

Ironically, the African American rejection of Lincoln in the late 1960s was in part a denial of an icon they themselves had profoundly remade. The extent of the African American appropriation of national memory was attested by the counter-efforts of government officials and others after 1960 to recapture Lincoln and his memorial. The Civil War Centennial Commission, organizing the 1962 Lincoln Memorial ceremony for the hundredth anniversary of the Emancipation Proclamation, was so eager to control the message imparted there that it neglected to invite any African American speakers. (Thurgood Marshall was added to the program after activists threatened a boycott.) During their presidential crises Lyndon B. Johnson and Richard M. Nixon both gave formal speeches at the shrine to defend their policies and compare themselves to Lincoln. In 1970, soon after Nixon's embarrassing, predawn visit to the antiwar demonstrators encamped at the memorial, the president's aides prevailed upon entertainer Bob Hope and evangelist Billy Graham to organize a jingoistic rally called Honor America Day. On July 4 a crowd of thirty thousand at the Lincoln Memorial heard Graham deliver a sermon that was a remarkable response to the protest tradition that began when Marian Anderson politicized a national hymn. Graham declared, with unintended irony, "Let the world know that the vast majority of us still proudly sing: 'My Country 'tis of thee, sweet land of liberty.'" In a time when dissenters were turning to violent resistance Graham urged his hearers to "never give in! Never give in! Never! Never! Never! Never!"[54]

One of the enduring tragedies of the 1960s may be that African American protesters abandoned their rituals of alternative patriotism just when they had become most effective. In the late sixties, the commingling of the civil rights and anti-Vietnam War movements yielded new symbolic strategies. Peace historian Charles Chatfield argues that burning flags and draft cards did not represent anti-Americanism, but rather anti-"Americanism." Instead of using and subverting the patriotic icons and nationalism that Warren Susman argued had dominated American culture since the 1930s, anti-war strategists rejected them outright. The cultural journey from the 1930s to the 1960s was marked by the stark difference between Easter 1939, when Marian Anderson sang "My Country 'Tis of Thee," and Christmas 1971, when eighty-seven members of Vietnam Veterans Against the War were arrested for attempting to seize and seal off the Lincoln Memorial. Cultural nationalism was no longer a resource; protesters now saw it as part of the problem. And where some determined to go next, their broad coalitions would not follow. As balladeer Phil Ochs sang mockingly in 1966,

> I go to the civil rights rallies,
> And I put down the old D.A.R. . . .
> But don't talk about revolution;
> That's going a little bit too far.
> So love me, love me, love me; I'm a liberal.[55]

Civil rights rallies at the Lincoln Memorial were more than just protests in a dramatic setting; they were transformative rituals that reveal the complexity of American nationalism and the context of the civil rights movement's symbolic strategies. The format that evolved after Marian Anderson's 1939 concert foreshadowed blacks' later philosophy of nonviolent action. It unified and rejuvenated activists, broadened support and participation among white (and even black) citizens, and evaded bureaucratic roadblocks. Striving to make racial justice an essential component of the American Way of Life during decades ruled by a complacent cultural nationalism, African Americans redefined the American Way by counterexample—praying in their "Sunday best" on a national stage and creating events that could be neither ignored nor suppressed. Protesters used a national shrine as a kind of Trojan horse, evoking the specter of militancy in the capital through peaceful gatherings that celebrated national values even as they strove to change them.

This was the essence of the politics of memory: Activists brought politics into the temple, but in a way that preserved the temple's holiness and allowed them to partake of its power as a national site. Remarkably, after the Jim Crow incidents at the memorial's 1922 dedication ceremonies, a black newspaper editorialist had prescribed exactly this course. The shrine had been opened to the public, he wrote, "but not dedicated." Asking readers not to visit the memorial until black Americans could affirm its rightful message of emancipation, he described with uncanny foresight the rites of national memory that would become so important to the African American freedom movement. "With song, prayer, bold and truthful speech, with faith in God and country," he wrote, "later on let us dedicate the temple thus far only opened." Marian Anderson believed that her 1939 recital had accomplished exactly this goal. "That Easter Sunday concert was more than a concert for me," she remarked in 1943. "It was a dedication. . . . [E]veryone present was a living witness to the ideals of freedom for which President Lincoln died. When I sang that day, I was singing to the entire Nation." By transforming the memorial from a symbol of consensus into what Joseph L. Rauh later called "the protest palace," black activists claimed it as their own, powerful, memory site. Langston Hughes had prophesied as much in a 1927 poem, "Lincoln Monument." Brooding in stone sat Old Abe, "Quiet—And yet a voice forever." African Americans conferred on cold marble an enduring voice of protest.[56]

The Lincoln Memorial protests were celebratory moments when national collective memory seemed to be at its most inclusive, when there seemed to be the widest agreement about Abraham Lincoln's legacy—yet precisely then was the Lincoln symbol most hotly contested. The point here is not merely that there was room for oppositional expression during decades of Cold War consensus but that nationalism and public memory, often viewed as servants of the status quo, were themselves used to subvert or change the consensus; they were even used to demonstrate, as in the 1960s, that there really was no consensus. White Americans' persistent tendency to see national unity rather than protest in symbols like the Lincoln Memorial suggests that conflicts over public memory were integral to protesters' tactical shift in the late 1960s from a universalist, coalition-based approach to more militant and particularist strategies. It was not so much that their early tactics had transformed black activists into accommodationists, but rather that their sophisticated attempts to manipulate dominant symbols could never fully overcome irreducible differences between black and white ways of remembering the American past.

Given the fragmented oppositional politics of our own time, activists might revive the strategy of a politics of memory, with its remarkable ability both to unify protesters and to legitimate protest. Although mass demonstrations did resume at the memorial after the hiatus coinciding with King's assassination and the Vietnam War, these efforts have more often reflected a particularist politics of identity than a broad-based strategy. In the past twenty years activists there have demanded Native American rights, abortion rights, fetal rights, lesbian and gay rights, rights for people with disabilities, and the right to smoke marijuana. Other groups demonstrating there have implored the American people to end the arms race, intervention in El Salvador, housing discrimination, world hunger, the Persian Gulf War, and even the presidency of Richard M. Nixon. Rallies at the memorial have spotlighted the plight of soldiers missing in Vietnam, embassy hostages in Iran, victims of drunk drivers, persons living with Acquired Immune Deficiency Syndrome (AIDS), and American children living in poverty. Demonstrators have sought freedom for the people of Cuba, Taiwan, Czechoslovakia, Thailand, Pakistan, South Africa, and China. The 1963 March on Washington was itself commemorated with large rallies on its anniversaries in 1983, 1988, and 1993. Since 1982 Lincoln's shrine has been adjoined by a newer site of contested memory, the Vietnam Veterans Memorial.[57]

Not surprisingly, many of these recent protests invoke King's memory more than Lincoln's. The heavy hand of official memory is now sculpting King into the kind of consensus hero made of Lincoln in the 1910s. When King's birthday became a national holiday in 1986, conservative Georgia congressman Newt Gingrich observed, "No one can claim Dr. King. He transcends all of us." Gingrich completed the thought a decade later, again invoking King as he assured cheering delegates to the 1996 Republican party convention, "We, too, have a dream." How much these expropriations echo the apotheosis of Lincoln: the icon who belongs to all can be the weapon of no faction in particular. Manning Marable speaks for many contemporary activists when he deplores "the gradual ossification of Martin Luther King, Jr., his ideological and political development frozen on the steps of the Lincoln Memorial. . . . Half forgotten and deliberately obscured are the final radical years of King's public life" (figure 7).[58] King's induction into the pantheon of official memory threatens to construct a new national savior whose work is, of course, finished. King on those steps, reciting his Dream: Is this the new emancipation moment, at once liberating and limiting?

Struggles over public memory continue. Each year on King's birthday, a wreath-laying ceremony is held for him on that hallowed spot at the Lincoln Memorial; the National Park Service will honor King and his immortal speech by erecting a plaque on the steps of the memorial and by building a major King monument nearby. One wonders how the embittered residents

Fig. 7: "Martin Luther King," drawing by David Levine. The superimposition of King's head onto the familiar body of Daniel Chester French's monumental seated Lincoln underscores both how much the Lincoln Memorial has come to symbolize African American protest and how completely King himself has been rendered a marble saint. Reprinted with permission from the *New York Review of Books.* Copyright © 1994 Nyrev, Inc.

of long-ago Omega, Virginia, the town that expelled Oscar Chapman from grammar school, might react to this. Or to the African American schoolgirl who visited the memorial one day in the 1980s and stood staring up at the huge statue. "Do you know who that is?" an adult asked the child. "That's Lincoln," she replied. "Do you know who freed the slaves?" She completed the catechism by rote: "Martin Luther King."[59]

NOTES

Author's note: This essay originally appeared (with additional photographs) in the *Journal of American History* 80 (June 1993): 135–67, and it is reprinted by permission of the Organization of American Historians. Materials from the NAACP papers at the Library of Congress are quoted with the permission of that organization. Along with all those whom I thanked at the first publication of this essay, I am newly grateful to several who offered suggestions in the interim, including Gregory Cherpes, Blanche Wiesen Cook, T. K. Hunter, Allan Keiler, William E. Leuchtenburg, Reynolds J. Scott-Childress, Todd Shepard, John David Smith, and Joanna Schneider Zangrando.

1. Ann Chapman interview by Scott A. Sandage, November 6, 1989, transcript, pp. 3–4 (in Scott A. Sandage's possession). Oscar Chapman recounted his expulsion at the time of Marian Anderson's concert. See *Washington Daily News,* April 6, 1939, p. 29.

2. The subtle change in lyrics has not been noted by other scholars but is clearly discernible on the radio broadcast recording. See "Marian Anderson Concert at the Lincoln Memorial," April 9, 1939, tape RWA-2850, NBC radio collection (Division of Recorded Sound, Library of Congress, Washington, D.C.). *Washington Post*, April 10, 1939, p. 8; Mary McLeod Bethune to Charles H. Houston, April 10, 1939, folder 4, box 1-1, Marian Anderson/DAR Controversy Collection (Moorland-Spingarn Research Center, Howard University Library, Washington, D.C.). Although the collection is labeled "Marian Anderson/DAR Controversy Collection," it actually consists of the papers of the Marian Anderson Citizens' Committee.

3. The logistical benefits of the memorial may be an additional factor in protesters' choosing it; the shrine's steps are an ideal speaker's platform, and the adjacent open spaces accommodate large crowds, albeit with broken sight lines. However, crowds of more than ten thousand were a rarity before 1963, and if this essay's thesis holds, by then protesters' choice of site was already a matter of tradition and symbolic strategy, not logistics.

4. Pierre Nora, "Between Memory and History: *Les Lieux de Mémoire,*" *Representations* 26 (spring 1989): 7–25. See also David Thelen, ed., *Memory and American History* (Bloomington: Indiana University Press, 1990); Barry Schwartz, "The

Social Context of Commemoration: A Study in Collective Memory," *Social Forces* 61 (December 1982): 374–402; and John Bodnar, *Remaking America: Public Memory, Commemoration, and Patriotism in the Twentieth Century* (Princeton: Princeton University Press, 1992), esp. 13–20.

5. A useful overview of recent work is Steven F. Lawson, "Freedom Then, Freedom Now: The Historiography of the Civil Rights Movement," *American Historical Review* 96 (April 1991): 456–71. For an emerging new interpretation that interprets federal civil rights policy within the international context of the Cold War, see Mary Dudziak, "Desegregation as a Cold War Imperative," *Stanford Law Review* 41 (November 1988): 61–120. Warren I. Susman, *Culture as History: The Transformation of American Society in the Twentieth Century* (New York: Pantheon Books, 1984), 150–83; Warren I. Susman with Edward Griffin, "Did Success Spoil the United States? Dual Representations in Postwar America," in *Recasting America: Culture and Politics in the Age of Cold War*, ed. Lary May (Chicago: University of Chicago Press, 1989), 19–37; Manning Marable, *Black American Politics: From the Washington Marches to Jesse Jackson* (London: Verso, 1985), 87–97. For insights into the challenges that oppositional politics present to critical theory, see Gerald Graff, "Co-optation," in *The New Historicism*, ed. H. Aram Veeser (New York: Routledge, 1989), 168–81.

6. Since the original publication of this essay, several new works have continued to underplay the complex bonds between Lincoln and African Americans. Merrill D. Peterson's long-awaited *Lincoln in American Memory* (New York: Oxford University Press, 1994) subsumes a surprisingly brief analysis of civil rights protests within a section on civil religion (pp. 167–75, 348–58). Lincoln's aura continues to lure the most careful scholars into hagiography. Even Garry Wills, whose rhetorical exegesis of Lincoln's most famous speech merited a Pulitzer prize, could not resist the silly argument of his subtitle, *Lincoln at Gettysburg: The Words that Remade America* (New York: Simon & Schuster, 1992). Wills's exuberant claim that "because of [Lincoln's speech], we live in a different America" (p. 147) is rendered preposterous by the century of black struggle required to realize even minimal civil rights. Likewise, in *The Next American Nation: The New Nationalism and the Fourth American Revolution* (New York: The Free Press, 1995), the neoconservative pundit Michael Lind permits himself (p. 92) the astonishing aside that "Black Americans, indeed, played almost no role in the mid-century Lincoln cult."

Peterson's otherwise comprehensive book will remain the standard work at least until the appearance of a forthcoming study by the sociologist Barry Schwartz; see his "Memory as a Cultural System: Abraham Lincoln in World War II," *American Sociological Review* 61 (October 1996): 908–27, and his other works cited therein. More broadly, a helpful introduction to the sprawling literature of Lincoln studies is Gabor S. Boritt, ed., *The Historian's Lincoln: Pseudohistory, Psychohistory, and History* (Urbana: University of Illinois Press, 1988); see also the essays in James M. McPherson, ed., *"We Cannot Escape History": Lincoln and the Last Best Hope of Earth*

(Urbana: University of Illinois Press, 1995); and Frank J. Williams and William D. Peterson, eds., *Abraham Lincoln, Contemporary: An American Legacy* (Campbell, Calif.: Savas Woodbury, 1995). For brief references to blacks' feelings about Lincoln, see Benjamin Quarles, *Lincoln and the Negro* (New York: Oxford University Press, 1962), 208–10; Lawrence W. Levine, *Black Culture and Black Consciousness: Afro-American Folk Thought from Slavery to Freedom* (New York: Oxford University Press, 1977), 88, 137; Nancy J. Weiss, *Farewell to the Party of Lincoln: Black Politics in the Age of FDR* (Princeton: Princeton University Press, 1983), 28–29, 91–93, 196, and 224–25 n. 55; William H. Wiggins, Jr., *O Freedom! Afro-American Emancipation Celebrations* (Knoxville: University of Tennessee Press, 1987); John E. Washington's memoir, *They Knew Lincoln* (New York: E. P. Dutton & Co., 1942); Yvette Fulcher's survey of black attitudes toward Lincoln, summarized in Mark E. Neely, Jr., "Emancipation: 113 Years Later," *Lincoln Lore* 1653 (November 1975): 1–3; and John David Smith, "Black Images of Lincoln in the Age of Jim Crow," *Lincoln Lore* 1681 (March 1978): 1–4.

7. For debates over House Joint Resolution 247 and House Joint Resolution 254, see *Congressional Record*, 60 Cong., 2 sess., January 26, 1909, pp. 1418–19; ibid., February 10, 1909, pp. 2147–48, 2175; and ibid., February 11, 1909, pp. 2201–2. "Lincoln Birthday Call 1909," reprinted in NAACP fiftieth anniversary meeting invitation, February 12, 1959, box A255, group III, National Association for the Advancement of Colored People Papers (Manuscript Division, Library of Congress). Abraham Lincoln, "A House Divided," in *The Collected Works of Abraham Lincoln,* ed. Roy P. Basler, 9 vols. (New Brunswick, N.J.: Rutgers University Press, 1959), vol. 2, 461–69.

8. Frederick Douglass, "Oration in Memory of Abraham Lincoln," in *The Voice of Black America: Major Speeches by Negroes in the United States, 1797–1971,* ed. Philip S. Foner (New York: Simon & Schuster, 1972), 434–43, esp. 443; Freeman Murray, *Emancipation and the Freed in American Sculpture* (1916; Freeport, N.Y.: Books for Libraries Press, 1972), 199; Basler, *Lincoln Legend,* 286; David W. Blight, "'For Something Beyond the Battlefield': Frederick Douglass and the Struggle for the Memory of the Civil War," in *Memory and American History,* ed. Thelen, 27–49, esp. 36; "Lincoln Birthday Call 1909" (see n. 7 above).

9. Public Law 61-346 (passed February 9, 1911) established the Lincoln Memorial Commission. See reprint in Lincoln Memorial Commission, *Report of the Commission* (Washington, D.C., 1913), 62 Cong., 3 sess., Sen. doc. 965, pp. 7–8. Richard Nelson Current, *Speaking of Abraham Lincoln: The Man and His Meaning for Our Times* (Urbana: University of Illinois Press, 1983), 166; Michael Davis, *The Image of Lincoln in the South* (Knoxville: University of Tennessee Press, 1971); John Drinkwater, *Lincoln: The World Emancipator* (Boston: Houghton Mifflin, 1920), 6; Roy Basler, *The Lincoln Legend: A Study in Changing Conceptions* (Boston: Houghton Mifflin, 1935), 202; Eyal J. Naveh, *Crown of Thorns: Political Martyrdom in America from Abraham Lincoln to Martin Luther King, Jr.* (New York: New York University Press, 1990), 58–59, 202 n. 45; Robert N. Bellah, "Civil Religion in America,"

Daedalus 96 (winter 1967): 1–21, esp. 10–11, 14, 18. See also Eyal Naveh, "'He Belongs to the Ages': Lincoln's Image and the American Historical Consciousness," *Journal of American Culture* 16 (winter 1993): 49–57.

10. On the Lincoln Memorial as a symbol of white consensus and sectional reunion, see Kirk Savage, *Standing Soldiers, Kneeling Slaves: Race, War, and Monument in Nineteenth-Century America* (Princeton, N.J.: Princeton University Press, 1997); Kirk Savage, "The Politics of Memory: Black Emancipation and the Civil War Monument," in *Commemorations: The Politics of National Identity,* ed. John R. Gillis (Princeton: Princeton University Press, 1993), 127–49; and Christopher A. Thomas, *The Lincoln Memorial and American Life* (Princeton, N.J.: Princeton University Press, 2002).

11. Lincoln Memorial Commission, *Report,* 12–14, 25–27, 31, 33, 34, 36, 39, 40; John Russell Pope, "Appendix C: Report of the Architect on Designs for the Meridian Hill and the Soldiers' Home Sites," ibid., 29–31; Henry Bacon, "Appendix D: Report of the Architect on Alternative Designs for the Potomac Park Site," ibid., 33–34; Royal Cortissoz to Henry Bacon, April 6, 1919, quoted in *Washington Evening Star,* March 2, 1977, sec. C, pp. 1, 3; Dixon Wecter, *The Hero in America: A Chronicle of Hero Worship* (1941; Ann Arbor: University of Michigan Press, 1966), 254. Jules Guerin's murals in the memorial depict slavery allegorically, but Guerin, like Henry Bacon, saw the Union motif as primary. See Jules Guerin, "The Great Lincoln Memorial," *Ladies' Home Journal* (October 1921): 14–15, 160–61.

12. Rexford L. Holmes, Inc., ed., "Dedicatory Exercises Incident to the Formal Dedication of the Lincoln Memorial," May 30, 1922, not paginated, in entry 372, Records of the Lincoln Memorial Commission, RG 42 (National Archives, Washington, D.C.). The Robert Russa Moton legend is repeated in, among many examples, Constance McL. Green, *The Secret City: A History of Race Relations in the Nation's Capital* (Princeton: Princeton University Press, 1967), 199–201. Black press reports make no mention of Moton having sat in the "colored section." See *Washington Tribune,* June 3, 1922, pp. 1, 8, and June 10, 1922, p. 1; *Chicago Defender,* June 10, 1922, p. 1; and "Lincoln, Harding, James Crow, and Taft," *Crisis* 24 (July 1922): 122. For reception of Moton's speech, see *Washington Post,* May 31, 1922, p. 2; and *New York Times,* May 31, 1922, pp. 1, 3.

13. *Chicago Defender,* June 10, 1922, part II, p. 1. For the Confederate controversy, see *Washington Post,* June 22, 1922, p. 3; ibid., June 24, 1922, p. 3; and *Washington Evening Star,* July 7, 1922, p. 6. For Northern and Southern homage to Lincoln, see *Washington Post,* February 14, 1928, p. 5; *New York Times,* February 13, 1925, p. 4; and *Washington Post,* February 13, 1928, pp. 1–2. Bishop E.D.W. Jones, speaker at the 1926 gathering, is paraphrased in the *Washington Post,* August 6, 1926, p. 8.

14. In Victor Turner's view, liminal rituals are performed in "privileged spaces and times," after which one returns "changed in some way, to mundane life." Some public rituals invite rededication to shared values and the teachings of a society's "establishers of morality." Others can criticize public policies and "ritually trans-

form" the sites themselves. See Victor Turner, *The Anthropology of Performance* (New York: PAJ Publications, 1988), 25–26, 102; and idem., *The Ritual Process: Structure and Anti-Structure* (Chicago: Aldine Publishing Co., 1969). See also Kathleen Ashley, ed., *Victor Turner and the Construction of Cultural Criticism: Between Literature and Anthropology* (Bloomington: Indiana University Press, 1990); and David I. Kertzer, *Ritual, Politics, and Power* (New Haven: Yale University Press, 1988), 11.

15. For Arturo Toscanini's comments, see S. Hurok, with Ruth Goode, *Impresario: A Memoir* (New York: Random House, 1946), 240. Sarah Robert, Daughters of the American Revolution president general, to Harold Ickes, Feb. 3, 1939, box 2967, entry 1-280, Marian Anderson Subfile, Central Classified Files 1937–1953, Records of the Secretary of the Interior, RG 48 (National Archives); *New York Times,* February 28, 1939, pp. 1, 5. Many editorials are reprinted in Anson Phelps Stokes, *Art and the Color Line* (Washington, D.C.: n.p., 1939), 12–20. The singer's recollections are in Marian Anderson, *My Lord, What a Morning: An Autobiography* (New York: Viking Press, 1956); and see Barbara Klaw, "'A Voice One Hears Once in a Hundred Years': An Interview with Marian Anderson," *American Heritage* 28 (February 1977): 51–57.

Two useful scholarly accounts (which, however, do not analyze the concert planners' attention to symbolism) are Weiss, *Farewell to the Party of Lincoln,* 257–66; and Allida M. Black, "Championing a Champion: Eleanor Roosevelt and the Marian Anderson 'Freedom Concert,'" *Presidential Studies Quarterly* 20 (fall 1990): 719–36. See also idem., *Casting her Own Shadow: Eleanor Roosevelt and the Shaping of Postwar Liberalism* (New York: Columbia University Press, 1996), 41–44.

In recent years, the DAR has repeatedly attempted to rewrite the history of the Anderson incident and to deny that racism led to her exclusion from Constitution Hall. Fortunately, the documentary record makes the organization's revisionist position untenable. Among the other performers whom the DAR barred from Constitution Hall were Paul Robeson, the Hampton Institute Singers, and Harry Belafonte. See *Washington Star,* September 9, 1979, sec. G, p. 2; *Washington Herald-Tribune,* February 23, 1939, p. 16; and *Washington Tribune,* March 22, 1941, clipping in "Black Segregation and Discrimination/Marian Anderson Concert" folder, Washingtoniana Collection (Martin Luther King, Jr., Public Library, Washington, D.C.). For the DAR's most recent denial (following Marian Anderson's death) and my published rebuttal, see *New York Times,* April 23, 1993, p. A23, May 18, 1993, pp. C1, C14, and June 7, 1993, p. A16. See also Patrick Hayes, "White Artists Only: Fifty Years Ago Marian Anderson Sang at the Lincoln Memorial, and All Eyes Were on Washington," *Washingtonian* (April 1989): 95–103. Hope for a definitive account rests on Allan Keiler, *Marian Anderson: A Singer's Journey* (New York: Scribner's, 2000).

16. "News Value," in Walter White to Charles H. Houston, March 21, 1939, box C59, group I, NAACP Papers. Oscar Chapman claimed to have thought of using the memorial, but black leaders were discussing the idea at least two weeks before

their first recorded meeting with him. Chapman's self-serving version is in Joseph P. Lash, *Eleanor and Franklin: The Story of Their Relationship, Based on Eleanor Roosevelt's Private Papers* (New York: W. W. Norton & Co., 1971), 527; and see also T. H. Watkins, *Righteous Pilgrim: The Life and Times of Harold L. Ickes, 1874–1952* (New York: Henry Holt, 1990), 649–53. These influential but inaccurate accounts (on which Peterson, *Lincoln in American Memory*, 352, and many other uncritical retellings rely) are easily disproved by White to Houston, March 6, 1939, box Ll, group II, NAACP Papers; and [White], "Minutes of the Meeting of the Board of Directors," March 13, 1939, p. 4, box L2, ibid. Roosevelt quoted in Ann Chapman interview, p. 1.

17.   Walter White, *A Man Called White: The Autobiography of Walter White* (New York: Viking Press, 1948), 104, 182; "Marian Anderson Will Sing in the 'Open Air' as Rebuke to D.A.R.," press release, February 24, 1939, box L2, group II, NAACP Papers; White to Gertrude [Stone], March 14, 1939, box Ll, ibid.; White to Harry E. Davis, February 24, 1939, box L2, ibid.; White to Fiorello LaGuardia, April 21, 1939, ibid.; White to Lester B. Granger, June 13, 1939, ibid.; White to Edward G. Robinson, March 1, 1939, ibid.

18.   White to Charles H. Houston and V. D. Johnston, March 31, 1939, box Ll, group II, NAACP Papers. [Charles H. Houston], radio script, April 8, 1939, folder 35, box 2-2, Marian Anderson/DAR Controversy Collection. "Remarks of the Secretary of the Interior Harold L. Ickes in Introducing Marian Anderson at the Lincoln Memorial Concert to be Held at 5:00 p.m. (EST), Sunday April 9, 1939," box L2, group II, NAACP Papers. Although many sources (such as Peterson, *Lincoln in American Memory*, 353) allege that Anderson sang the national anthem and "America, the Beautiful," in fact she sang only "America," sometimes known as "My Country, 'Tis of Thee," followed by arias and spirituals. For the tumultuous history of "America," see Robert H. Branham, "'Of Thee I Sing': Contesting 'America,'" *American Quarterly* 48 (December 1996): 623–52.

19.   White, *Man Called White*, 184; Chapman interview, 1; Charles H. Houston, remarks on the presentation of a Marian Anderson concert mural, untitled typescript, January 6, 1943, p. 2, folder 49, box 2-2, Marian Anderson/DAR Controversy Collection. In 1941, Joseph L. Rauh, Jr., drafted Franklin D. Roosevelt's antidiscrimination rule, Executive Order 8802, and he attended or helped organize nearly all the demonstrations discussed in this article; see Joseph L. Rauh, Jr., interview by Sandage, November 11, 1989, transcript, p. 1 (in Sandage's possession). Houston to Oscar L. Chapman, April 11, 1939, folder 4, box 1-1, Marian Anderson/DAR Controversy Collection. For strategists' later references to Anderson, see White to Chapman, April 11, 1947, box A34, group II, NAACP Papers; and Roy Wilkins to Sol Hurok, telegram, April 12, 1957, box A245, group III, ibid. On Anderson's performance at the Ickes service, see *Washington Post*, April 21, 1952, sec. B, p. 1.

20.   Nancy J. Weiss, Allida M. Black, and many other scholars inflate Eleanor Roosevelt's role in planning the concert, for which Weiss admits there is little writ-

ten evidence. See Weiss, *Farewell to the Party of Lincoln*, 260. George S. Kaufman and Moss Hart, *The American Way* (New York: Random House, 1939). Robert Emmet Sherwood, *Abe Lincoln in Illinois: A Play in Twelve Scenes* (New York: Charles Scribner's Sons, 1939). For other contemporary evidence of the debate over "The American Way," see the winning essays of a contest to define the phrase, in *Harper's Monthly* 174 (April 1937): 556, and 176 (1938): 225–38, 395–404, 487–95, 633–44. On the Abraham Lincoln Brigade, see *Washington Post*, February 13, 1938, p. 10. Paul Angle quoted in Wecter, *Hero in America*, 251. On Lincoln in the 1930s, see Alfred Haworth Jones, *Roosevelt's Image Brokers: Poets, Playwrights, and the Use of the Lincoln Symbol* (Port Washington, N.Y.: Kennikat Press, 1974); and Michael Kammen, *Mystic Chords of Memory: The Transformation of Tradition in American Culture* (New York: Alfred A. Knopf, 1991), 509. Todd Duncan interviewed in the documentary, "Marian Anderson," prod. Dante J. James, Bernard Seabrooks, and Tamara E. Robinson (WETA, May 8, 1991).

21. *Worcester Gazette*, April 1939, clipping in scrapbook 494, Harold L. Ickes Papers (Manuscript Division, Library of Congress); *Philadelphia Inquirer*, April 1, 1939, p. 8; "Bund and D.A.R. Are Stable Mates, Says NY Columnist," press release, February 24, 1939, box L2, group II, NAACP Papers; anonymous letter to DAR from "an obscure, middle aged, red-blooded, old-fashioned, native-born American housewife out here in Canton, Ohio," n.d., ibid.; Beatrice Gurry to Rand School of Social Science, n.d., ibid.; Charles S. Cuney to the editor, unidentified newspaper, ibid.; Henry Lee to Ickes, April 3, 1939, Herbert Friedenwald to Ickes, March 30, 1939, Records of the Secretary of the Interior.

22. The singer stayed at the home of Mr. and Mrs. Gifford Pinchot. See Chapman interview, 2. *Washington Evening Star*, March 31, 1939, p. A20; *Washington Times-Herald*, March 29, 1939, p. 10; *Washington Post*, April 12, 1939, p. 9. Raymond Massey, who played Lincoln on Broadway and in the film *Abe Lincoln in Illinois*, wrote that the First Lady told him she decided to ignore the protest because "the picketing organization was not approved by the NAACP." See Raymond Massey, *A Hundred Different Lives: An Autobiography* (Boston: Little, Brown, and Co., 1979), 257; and the critical editorial, "Lincoln Memorial," *New Republic* (February 5, 1940): 166. Eleanor Roosevelt later spoke at an NAACP rally at the memorial, along with President Harry Truman and Senator Wayne Morse, on June 29, 1947. Walter White arranged the event with the cooperation of Oscar Chapman, by then Truman's secretary of the interior. "Largest Mass Meeting in Nation's History Planned by NAACP," press release, June 6, 1947, box A33, Group II, NAACP Papers.

23. Patrick H. Hutton, "The Art of Memory Reconceived: From Rhetoric to Psychoanalysis," *Journal of the History of Ideas* 48 (1987): 371–92. Eric Hobsbawm, "Introduction: Inventing Traditions," in *The Invention of Tradition*, ed. Eric Hobsbawm and Terence Ranger (Cambridge: Cambridge University Press, 1983), 1–14, esp. 12. David Thelen, "Introduction: Memory and American History," in *Memory and American History*, ed. Thelen, vii–xix. I am indebted to Rhys Isaac for discussing

with me his concept of "mythic recognition" as a component of successful public messages about the past.

24. Postage stamp in Wiggins, *O Freedom!* For analyses of various nineteenth- and twentieth-century images of the grateful Negro at Lincoln's feet, see Savage, "Politics of Memory," esp. 140; Michael Hatt, "'Making a Man of Him': Masculinity and the Black Body in Mid-Nineteenth-Century American Sculpture," *Oxford Art Journal* 15, no. 1 (1992): 21–35; Harold Holzer, Gabor S. Boritt, and Mark E. Neely, Jr., *Changing the Lincoln Image* (Fort Wayne, Ind.: Louis A. Warren Lincoln Library and Museum, 1985), 44–52, 123. See also examples in *Washington Evening Star*, February 12, 1947, p. A2; Weldon Petz, *In the Presence of Abraham Lincoln* (Harrogate, Tenn.: Lincoln Memorial University, 1973), 92; Kammen, *Mystic Chords*, 123, 125; and Peterson, *Lincoln in American Memory*, 159, 172, 349. Two striking unpublished images are "Negro Boys Admiring the Lincoln Memorial," Marjory Collins's series of three photos for the U.S. Office of War Information, spring 1942, reel 14, lot 216, Prints and Photographs Division, Library of Congress; and a photograph sent to the NAACP by a freelance photographer, Lawrence Needleman to Henry Lee Moon, January 16, 1957, box A255, Group III, NAACP Papers. David Brion Davis, "The Emancipation Moment," in *Lincoln, the War President: The Gettysburg Lectures*, ed. Gabor S. Boritt (New York: Oxford University Press, 1992), 63–88.

25. *Washington Post*, April 12, 1939, p. 9; untitled cartoon, by [Jack] Sparling, *Washington Times-Herald*, March 31, 1939, p. 18; "It's All Lincoln's Fault," cartoon by [Fred] Ellis, *Indianapolis Recorder*, May 6, 1939, p. 13. (This citation is from an African American newspaper, but Ellis drew for and seems to have been distributed by the *Daily Worker*.) *Washington Post*, April 20, 1939, p. 8; *Mr. Smith Goes to Washington*, dir. Frank Capra (Columbia Pictures, 1939). An updated variant appears in Oliver Stone's heavily didactic film, *JFK*; as Kevin Costner muses at John F. Kennedy's grave, a reverent black father and son stand to the side (*JFK*, dir. Oliver Stone [Camelot Productions, 1991]). *Seated in His Memorial, Abraham Lincoln Gets White Marble Shoes Shined*, photograph by B. Anthony Stewart, in *National Geographic Magazine* 91 (June 1947): 703. (See also a photograph of a black White House butler polishing silver under a portrait of Lincoln, ibid., 709). George Keck's 1949 "Lincoln and Boy" is in F. Lauriston Bullard, *Lincoln in Marble and Bronze* (New Brunswick, N.J.: Rutgers University Press, 1952), 191, 300.

It is worth noting that new photographs of Lincoln's statue in the memorial being cleaned by government janitors, almost always African Americans, are printed annually in major newspapers; many of these are apparently intended as comic poses, showing staff cleaning the Lincoln statue's ears and mouth with enormous cotton swabs and brushes. See, among dozens of examples, *Washington Post*, August 5, 1987, p. B1; *Washington Post Magazine*, February 18, 1990, p. 11; *New York Times*, August 3, 1994, p. A17; *Washington Post*, April 13, 1995, p. B3;. For criticisms, see Darrow Montgomery's ironic photograph, *Lincoln Memorial, November 30*, [Washington, D.C.] *City Paper*, December 8, 1989, p. 3; and Christopher Hitchens's account of the work-related death of a much photographed African American janitor at the Lincoln Memorial, "Minority Report," *The Nation* (August 9/16, 1993): 164. On the implied status quo in the emancipation moment, see Hatt, "'Making a Man of Him,'" 26.

26. *New York Herald Tribune*, February 13, 1925, p. 5; Davis, *Image of Lincoln in the South*, 153. The letter to W.E.B. Du Bois hints at black intergenerational conflict over Lincoln as well as white authorities' success in purging emancipation from Lincoln's memory; "my attending white school," the girl wrote Du Bois, "may be the cause of me not knowing what [Lincoln] has done for the Negro Race." Gertrude M. Banks to W.E.B. Du Bois, February 9, 1927, reel 21, W.E.B. Du Bois Papers (Manuscript Division, Library of Congress). Du Bois to Banks, March 9, 1927, ibid. Robert Vann quoted in William E. Leuchtenburg, *Franklin D. Roosevelt and the New Deal, 1932–1940* (New York: Harper Torchbooks, 1963), 187. For a slightly later analysis of the same issues, see "Lincoln and the Negro Youth," *New Masses* (February 16, 1937): 22. *Washington Afro-American*, February 16, 1946, p. 4; Whitney M. Young, Jr., quoted in Robert Penn Warren, *Who Speaks for the Negro?* (New York: Random House, 1965), 168; James M. Washington, ed., *A Testament of Hope: The Essential Writings of Martin Luther King, Jr.* (San Francisco: Harper & Row, 1986), 279–86, esp. 279; Martin Luther King, Jr., *Why We Can't Wait* (New York: Harper & Row, 1963), 162; James Farmer interview by Sandage, November 29, 1989, transcript, p. 8 (in Sandage's possession).

27. Harold L. Ickes, remarks on the presentation of a Marian Anderson concert mural, untitled typescript, January 6, 1943, pp. 3–4, folder 49, box 2-2, Marian Anderson/DAR Controversy Collection.

28. [A. Philip Randolph], "Call to Negro America: 'To March on Washington for Jobs and Equal Participation in National Defense,'" in A. Philip Randolph to Eleanor Roosevelt, June 5, 1941, in *Papers of Eleanor Roosevelt, 1933–1945*, ed. Susan Ware and William H. Chafe (microfilm, 20 reels, Frederick, Md.: University Publications of America, 1986), reel 15; Herbert Garfinkel, *When Negroes March: The March on Washington Movement in the Organizational Politics for FEPC* (New York: Atheneum, 1969), 38–42, 82–83; Ickes to Randolph, April 13, 1942, box 213, Ickes Papers; Harold L. Ickes Diary, April 11, 1942, p. 6530, ibid. For a re-evaluation of Randolph's important tactical role in the movement, see Paula F. Pfeffer, *A. Philip Randolph, Pioneer of the Civil Rights Movement* (Baton Rouge: Louisiana State University Press, 1990); Lucy G. Barber, *Marching on Washington: The Forging of an American Political Tradition* (Berkeley: University of California Press, 2002).

29. Randolph and B. F. McLaurin, "Special Release," February 14, 1943, box 26, A. Philip Randolph Papers (Manuscript Division, Library of Congress), emphasis added; Malvina C. Thompson to Winifred Raushenbush, February 15, 1943, box 24, Brotherhood of Sleeping Car Porters Papers, ibid. In 1943, four hundred Orthodox rabbis held a similar event, praying at the "symbol of liberation" for the United States to admit Jewish refugees. See *Washington Post*, October 7, 1943, p. 1.

30. On the tactical conflict between Roy Wilkins and Martin Luther King, Jr., see David J. Garrow, *Bearing the Cross: Martin Luther King, Jr., and the Southern Christian Leadership Conference* (New York: William Morrow & Co., 1986), 91. Wilkins quoted in NAACP Board of Directors minutes, March 11, 1957, p. 2, box A14, group I, NAACP Papers.

31. E. T. Scoyen to Clarence Mitchell, April 16, 1957, box A245, group III, NAACP Papers; Mitchell to Roy Wilkins, April 22, 1957, ibid.; "Secure Lincoln Memorial for Prayer Pilgrimage," press release, April 25, 1957, ibid.

32. For comments about picket lines, see "'Prayer Pilgrimage' to Nation's Capital Launched; Rev. L. Sylvester Odom to Chair Northwest Effort," press release, April 29, 1957, box A245, group III, NAACP Papers. For the prayer, see Mordecai Johnson, remarks at the Prayer Pilgrimage for Freedom, May 17, 1957, ibid. Roy Wilkins, remarks at the Prayer Pilgrimage for Freedom, May 17, 1957, ibid.; "Prayer Pilgrimage for Freedom, Lincoln Memorial, Washington, D.C., May 17, 1957, 12 Noon, Program," box 157, NAACP Washington Bureau Papers (Manuscript Division, Library of Congress); Washington, ed., *Testament of Hope*, 197–200.

33. Pledge quoted in "Prayer Pilgrimage for Freedom"; Bayard Rustin to Martin Luther King, Jr., May 10, 1957, typescript copy, Bayard Rustin Papers (Manuscript Division, Library of Congress). On Rustin, see Jervis Anderson, *Bayard Rustin: Troubles I've Seen* (New York: HarperCollins, 1996).

34. David Howard-Pitney, "The Enduring Black Jeremiad: The American Jeremiad and Black Protest Rhetoric, from Frederick Douglass to W.E.B. Du Bois, 1841–1919," *American Quarterly* 38 (1986): 481–92. On pledges, see Harriet Hyman Alonso, *The Women's Peace Union and the Outlawry of War, 1921–1942* (Knoxville: University of Tennessee Press, 1989), 19.

35. "Edward P. Morgan and the News," radio typescript, May 17, 1957, box A245, group III, NAACP Papers.

36. [Bayard Rustin], "Some plans and suggestions for a March to Washington for Civil Rights, October 1956," Rustin Papers. This memo, which calls for a full-time staff and a broad sponsorship, clearly envisions a march on the scale of 1963, not the smaller 1957 event. The memorial is also specified in early 1963 memos, meeting agendas, and correspondence. See BR, TK & NH [Rustin, Tom Kahn, and Norman Hill], untitled memo, January 1963, ibid.; "Proposals for Emancipation March on Washington" [March 22–23, 1963]; and Randolph to Hon. Stewart L. Udall, May 24, 1963, ibid.

37. Among many works that inaccurately suggest that the memorial was a compromise site, see Harvard Sitkoff, *The Struggle for Black Equality, 1954–1980* (New York: Hill & Wang, 1981), 160. For a discussion of Capitol sit-ins, see BR, TK & NH [Rustin, Kahn, and Hill], untitled memo, January 1963. For a discussion of a White House demonstration, see "Proposed Plans for March," July 2, 1963, box 26, Randolph Papers. Marable, *Black American Politics*, 91–97; Garrow, *Bearing the Cross*, 281–83. For slogan restrictions, see *Organizing Manual no. 2: Final Plans for*

the March on Washington for Jobs and Freedom, 10, Rustin Papers; and [Randolph], "Slogans," n.d., box A229, Group III, NAACP Papers. Several approved slogans refer to Lincoln and emancipation.

38. Although most sources number the 1963 marchers at 250,000, Thomas Gentile analyzed crowd-counting procedures and made a case for 400,000. See Thomas Gentile, *March on Washington: August 28, 1963* (Washington, D.C.: New Day Publications, 1983), 230. See also Farmer interview, 6–7. Lerone Bennett, Jr., "Masses Were March Heroes," *Ebony* 19 (November 1963): 35–40, 42, 44, 46, 119–20, 122, 124, esp. 35, 36; *Washington Post*, August 29, 1963, sec. E, p. 1; "March on Washington for Jobs and Freedom, August 28, 1963: Lincoln Memorial Program," leaflet, Rustin Papers; *New York Times*, August 29, 1963, p. 16; Bayard Rustin, typescript excerpt of article in *Liberation* 3 (October [1963]), Rustin Papers.

39. Nicolaus Mills, "Heard and Unheard Speeches: What Really Happened at the March on Washington?" *Dissent* 35 (summer 1988): 285–91, esp. 285; Washington, ed., *Testament of Hope*, 217–20; Richard Lentz, *Symbols, the News Magazines, and Martin Luther King* (Baton Rouge: Louisiana State University Press, 1990), 76–78, 109.

40. *New York Herald Tribune*, August 29, 1963, pp. 1, 8.

41. *Washington Post*, August 29, 1963, sec. A, p. 1; Lerone Bennett, Jr., "The March," in *The Day They Marched*, ed. Doris E. Saunders (Chicago, 1963), 3–14, esp. 14.

42. The classic statement here is Malcolm X (with Alex Haley), *The Autobiography of Malcolm X* (1965; New York: Ballantine Books, 1973), 278–81. The phrase "church picnic" originated among journalists as an approbation, not a condemnation, of the march. See *New York Herald Tribune*, August 29, 1963, pp. 1, 8; *New York Times*, August 29, 1963, pp. 1, 17; and Kay Boyle, "No Other Place to Be," *Liberation* 3 (September 1963): 9.

43. James W. Vander Zanden, "A Sociologist's Appraisal," *Midwest Quarterly* 5 (January 1964): 99–108; Marable, *Black American Politics*, 89–90; *Washington Evening Star*, April 28, 1964, sec. A, pp. 1, 4; *Washington Post*, May 11, 1964, sec. A, p. 6; John C. Raines interview by Sandage, October 25, 1989, transcript, p. 2 (in Sandage's possession). Hubert Humphrey quoted in Charles Whalen and Barbara Whalen, *The Longest Debate: A Legislative History of the 1964 Civil Rights Act* (Cabin John, Md.: Seven Locks Press, 1984), 164.

44. Sen. Theodore G. Bilbo was the villain of two 1946 anti-lynching rallies at the memorial. See note 46, below.

45. Randolph, "Why the Interracial Youth March for Integrated Schools?" [1958], Rustin Papers. For other evidence that black leaders invoked Lincoln's memory as part of a broad public relations strategy, see the NAACP's annual national radio broadcasts on Lincoln's Birthday throughout the 1950s and early 1960s. On the 1956 broadcast Roy Wilkins asked the South African humanitarian Alan Paton, "Can the peoples of South Africa invoke the memory of Lincoln in the

struggle against apartheid?" See "Suggested opening remarks and questions for NBC radio program to be recorded on Feb. 7," box A255, group III, NAACP Papers.

46. Rauh interview, p. 6; Paul Robeson's anti-lynching rally competed with a similar NAACP-Sponsored event, also held at the memorial. See *Washington Post,* September 29, 1946, sec. B, p. 5; *Washington Evening Star,* August 6, 1946, sec. A, p. 2; and *Washington Afro-American,* September 28, 1946, p. 1.

47. Norman Hill interview by Sandage, December 7, 1989, transcript, p. 2 (in Sandage's possession).

48. Rauh interview, p. 1; *Washington Evening Star,* September 20, 1967, clipping in "Lincoln Memorial 1960–1970" folder, Washingtoniana Collection.

49. Rachelle Horowitz interview by Sandage, December 20, 1989, transcript, p. 4 (in Sandage's possession); Abraham Lincoln, Gettysburg Address, in *Collected Works of Abraham Lincoln,* ed. Basler, vol. 7, 17–23.

50. *Washington Post,* October 8, 1967, sec. A, p. 32; *Washington Evening Star,* October 21, 1967, sec. A, pp. 1, 2; Washington, ed., *Testament of Hope,* 64–72; *Washington Post,* June 20, 1968, sec. A, pp. 1, 8–9; ibid., June 21, 1968, sec. A, pp. 1, 23.

51. John Oliver Killens, "Explanation of the 'Black Psyche,'" *New York Times Magazine,* June 7, 1964, pp. 37–38, 42, 47–48, esp. 47. Malcolm X quoted in Warren, *Who Speaks for the Negro?* 262. Lerone Bennett, Jr., "Was Abe Lincoln a White Supremacist?" *Ebony* 23 (February 1968): 35–40, 43; *Washington Evening Star,* September 27, 1962, sec. B, p. 1; *Washington Post,* February 12, 1972, sec. A, p. 2. For a Citizens Councils of America advertisement quoting allegedly racist comments by Lincoln, see *New York Times,* February 12, 1968, p. 36. The media often quoted Lincoln's speeches to discredit protesters in the late 1960s. See David Levering Lewis, *Martin Luther King: A Critical Biography* (New York: Praeger, 1970), 316; and "Riots and Mob Spirit: America's Greatest Danger," *U.S. News and World Report* (August 28, 1967): 92, 91.

52. *Washington Evening Star,* February 13, 1968, sec. A, p. 3; Julius Lester, *Look Out, Whitey! Black Power's Gon' Get Your Mama!* (New York: Grove Press, 1968), 57–58.

53. On the historical roots of this problem, see Vincent Harding, *There Is a River: The Black Struggle for Freedom in America* (New York: Harcourt Brace Jovanovich, 1981), 236–37.

54. On the emancipation centennial, see *Washington Afro-American,* September 22, 1962, p. 4; *Washington Evening Star,* September 19, 1962, p. 1; and *Washington Post,* September 19, 1962, sec. B, p. 1. Bodnar, *Remaking America,* 210–11. On Lyndon B. Johnson, see *New York Times,* February 14, 1968, p. 46; on Richard M. Nixon, see *Washington Post,* February 13, 1974, sec. A, pp. 1–2. For an account of Nixon's visit to the antiwar students, see William Safire, *Before the Fall: An Inside View of the Pre-Watergate White House* (Garden City, N.Y.: Doubleday, 1975). On Honor America Day, see *Washington Post,* July 5, 1970, sec. A, pp. 1, 22. Billy Graham quoted ibid., sec. A, p. 1.

55. Charles DeBenedetti with Charles Chatfield, *An American Ordeal: The Antiwar Movement of the Vietnam Era* (Syracuse, N.Y.: Syracuse University Press, 1990), 395–96. On the links between the Lincoln Memorial and the symbolism of the antiwar movement, see Kertzer, *Ritual, Politics, and Power,* 121–23. *Washington Post,* December 29, 1971, sec. A, p. 1, sec. D, p. 1. Phil Ochs, "Love Me, I'm a Liberal," on Phil Ochs, *There But for Fortune,* compact disc, Electra, 9-60832-2, 1989 (originally released on *Phil Ochs in Concert,* 1966).

56. *Chicago Defender,* June 10, 1922, p. 1. Marian Anderson, remarks on the presentation of a Marian Anderson concert mural, untitled typescript, January 6, 1943, p. 5, folder 49, box 2-2, Marian Anderson/DAR Controversy Collection. Rauh interview, p. 1. Langston Hughes, "Lincoln Monument," *Opportunity* 4 (1927): 85; quoted in Peterson, *Lincoln in American Memory,* 217.

57. National Park Service Ranger Logbooks, Lincoln Memorial, December 17, 1955–November 9, 1989, 21 vols. (Office of Mall Operations, National Park Service, Washington, D.C.). Clever landscaping prevents large rallies from being staged at the Vietnam Veterans Memorial, and the Park Service restricts permits for political actions there because of the "sacred and personal nature of the site." John Williams interview by Sandage, September 26, 1989, notes, p. 2 (in Sandage's possession). Williams is supervisory park ranger of mall operations, National Park Service. On the symbiosis of the memorials to Lincoln and to Vietnam veterans, see Bodnar, *Remaking America,* 4; and Charles L. Griswold, "The Vietnam Veterans Memorial and the Washington Mall: Philosophical Thoughts on Political Iconography," *Critical Inquiry* 16 (summer 1986): 688–719.

58. Newt Gingrich quoted in Naveh, *Crown of Thorns,* 189. "Speeches to G.O.P. Delegates by Representatives Gingrich and Molinari," *New York Times,* August 14, 1996, p. A14. For Manning Marable's comments, see [New York] *Guardian,* February 21, 1990, pp. 10–11. See also "A Round Table: Martin Luther King, Jr.," *Journal of American History* 74 (September 1987): 436–81.

59. *New York Times,* January 21, 1992, sec. A, p. 18; *Washington Post,* January 16, 1990, sec. B, p. 3; *Washington Post,* September 6, 2002, sec. B, p. 3; schoolgirl quoted in Frederick T. D. Hunt interview by Sandage, December 21, 1989, transcript, p. 4–5 (in Sandage's possession). Hunt attended the memorial's 1922 dedication and from 1955 to 1981 organized the annual Lincoln's Birthday ceremony held at the memorial by the Military Order of the Loyal Legion of Honor of the United States.

Chapter 16

"We Men Ain't We?"
Mas(k)ulinity and the Gendered Politics of Black Nationalism

Charise Cheney

The 1989 film *Glory* dramatizes the story of the Massachusetts 54th, one of the first all-Black Union regiments of the American Civil War. It is a tale of the human spirit, of triumph and heroism—of glory—against enormous odds. Yet despite its billing as a war epic, *Glory* unwittingly reveals a lot about American political culture and Black cultural politics. In particular, terrific moments of clarity enable the student of gendered realities to explore not only how war is figured as a rite of manhood, but how manhood is figured by the act of war. The most fascinating revelation of this compelling story (and the most relevant for this essay) is its conspicuous display of the race and gender politics of the Civil War era. In a war that is emblazoned in the American memory as one that pitted (white) brother against (white) brother, it was Black men that stood to lose the most. For in this contest of masculine wills theirs was a battle for freedom—and as *Glory*'s histrionics illustrated, this freedom was defined in terms of both the right to self-determination and in the right to exercise masculine privilege. These ex-slaves, freedmen, and free men risked their lives to claim their humanity and to demonstrate their manhood.

The cinematic moment that brings this point home most dramatically is the scene that leads into the film's culminating event: the Massachusetts 54th's courageous but fatal assault on the Confederacy's Fort Wagner in South Carolina in 1863. The evening before the men of the 54th commence their heroic death march, they gather around a campfire for a moment of inspiration and reflection before battle. In a style assumed to be familiar to the slave quarters of the antebellum South, these soldiers break out into an improvised melody (as Black folks in movies are so prone to do) and begin to conjure God through song and sermon. While harmonizing "Oh my Lord, Lord, Lord, Lord" to the syncopated rhythm of hand-clapping, tamborine-shaking, and washboard-scraping, they ask Him for the strength and courage to face the battle ahead—a battle they sense they are destined to lose.

There are three testimonials in this scene, the first by Jupiter Sharts, the Sambo/Coon who is a good-hearted but dim-witted runaway from South Carolina. The second is a sermon given by Rawlins, a character molded in the tradition of Harriet Beecher Stowe's Uncle Tom: his masculine exterior balanced by a feminine interior. And the final, most emotionally raw testimonial in this spontaneous secular/sacred pre-battle worship is delivered by Trip, the bad-ass nigger/runaway slave. Trip, played by Denzel Washington, is *Glory*'s counterpart to John Blassingame's "Nat"—a "not-Sambo" recognizable by his defiant will and righteous anger. He stands outside of what social scientists consider the traditional institutions of the Black community: he has no religion ("I ain't much about no prayin' now") and no family ("kill'd off my momma"), and it is because of this independence from familial and community attachments that he is able to openly challenge authority—both white and Black. Despite his history of loss, Trip maintains the one thing that white folks cannot take away from him: his manhood.[1] Prompted to testify by Rawlins ("You better get your butt on in there boy!"), Trip stands before the campfire in this riveting scene as a man before men; his gendered script is short, but to the point. And he concludes with a pointed statement that provides the audience with valuable insight into the minds of the men, both Black and white, who risked their lives in America's wars.

"It ain't much a matter what happen tomorrow, 'cause we men ain't we?" he declares with pause: "We men ain't we?"[2]

What Trip's speech lacked in eloquence, it made up for in poignancy. On that fateful evening, when he came face to face with his mortality, his only comfort was his belief that the heroic sacrifice of the 54th would confer upon them manly recognition. It is a sentiment indicative of a compulsion that seduced 180,000 African-American men to enlist in the ranks of the Union Army at the onset of the Civil War. By participating in the ultimate display of masculine contestation and aggression, the Black soldiers of the Massachusetts 54th, and of other Black Union regiments, hoped to acquire the privileges of male power and patriarchal authority enjoyed by (many) white men during the antebellum era. For them, the spoils of war ranged from citizenship (or male representation in the public sphere) to manly respect (and male repositioning in the private sphere). As Gail Bederman notes in *Manliness & Civilization: A Cultural History of Gender and Race in the United States, 1880–1917* (1995), these Black men enlisted in the Union Army, despite "unequal and offensive treatment," because they understood what was at stake, "that enlisting was their most potent tool to claim that they were men and should have the same rights and privileges as all American men."[3] But most importantly, she stresses, they did so because they recognized the gendered realities of nineteenth-century America. "These African Americans understood that the only way to obtain civic power was through gender—by proving that they, too, were men."[4]

By breathing life into the stereotyped supporting roles around Matthew Broderick's Colonel Shaw, the Black actors of *Glory* bore witness to the burdens and privileges of Black manhood during the antebellum and Civil War period.[5] In fact, this narrative is so meaningful because the Civil War provided the first major backdrop for the public staging of strong Black masculinity; it marked the beginning of an enduring claim by Black American men to hegemonic masculinity that was summed up in one compelling line: "We men ain't we?" In the form of a query, these four words unmask the uncertainty and instability in the status of Black manhood in the United States and give the historian of the American Black experience some insight into an issue that is not only omnipresent, but is accorded primacy, in Black culture and politics. Often expressed in the singular and in the affirmative, "We men ain't we?" becomes the declarative statement "I'm a Man," recognizable in multiple expressions of African-American popular and political culture. For instance, in Spike Lee's 1992 film interpretation of the life of Malcolm X, Malcolm's father, a Garveyite and Baptist preacher, bellows "I'm a Man!" while unloading his gun in the air and forcing night riders to retreat from their attack on his home. On the music scene, James Brown, also known as "The Godfather of Soul," wails "I'm a Man! I'm a Man!" as he threatens to exact revenge on the brother trying to steal his money and his "honey" in the 1973 hit "The Big Payback"; and 1980s R&B crooner Alexander O'Neal softly assures his lady that he is a sensitive and attentive lover while countering "I'm A Man! I'm A Man!" in the background of the 1991 hit "All True Man." Meanwhile in the political arena, this pronouncement can be found, among other places, in the publications of Black nationalism's premier theorists, David Walker ("we are MEN") and Martin Delany ("I am a Man") and could be understood as the overarching theme of the 1995 Million Man March.[6] Yet this masculinist politicking is not the sole province of Black nationalists. The power of the photographic record of the 1968 Memphis Sanitation Strike lies in the workers' struggle for manly dignity, signified by their protest signs that read simply: "I Am A Man."

This essay explores the masculinization of Black nationalist ideology and politics by its predominantly, but not exclusively, male ideologues and activists.[7] As political discourse Black nationalism is an ideology that has historically proven itself to be inspired by a crisis of masculinity and translated in a manner akin to what psychologist Alfred Adler deemed "masculine protest."[8] Its claims to the social, political, and economic power of patriarchy highlight the rhetorical dependence on the subordination of the feminine in the oral and literary works of Black nationalists. Most feminist scholars concentrate on the sexism of Black nationalist discourse, specifically the subordination of women, and attempt to amend androcentric historical accounts by spotlighting the political activism of women and women's organizations; this essay, however, attempts to explain the masculine ideals that both influence and emanate from Black nationalist theory and praxis. Rather than demonstrate how Black nationalist discourse works to exclude women and/or to relegate them to the margins of Black nationalist movements, organizations, and (consequently) histories, I scrutinize the masculinist ways in which Black nationalist ideologues consistently and systematically shape the Black political agenda. My particular interest is in how Black power in the United States is defined in terms of what Anne McClintock deems a "politics of substitution,"[9] or the tendency among African (male) nationalists to covet, or displace, the political, social, and economic position of European (male) colonials, as well as in how the process of Black empowerment is defined in terms of violent resistance.

Black nationalism has, historically, proven itself to be a politics obsessed with (and therefore limited by) the reclamation of Black manhood; this chapter is an attempt to reveal how, like the Black men in the soldier's story *Glory*, Black male nationalists are in an undying struggle over the question: "We Men ain't We?"

Rediscovering the Phallic Nation: Black Nationalism as a Politics of Masculine Protest

Until recently, scholars of U.S. Black nationalism have mistakenly assumed that its significance as a political theory is based simply in its positioning as a racial politics. Yet if, as R. W. Connell suggests in his 1995 book *Masculinities*, the definition of gender politics can be reduced to an "embodied-social politics," Black nationalism must be recognized as a race and gender politics. For as Paul Gilroy wrote in 1993: "gender is the modality in which race is lived."[10] It has become quite clear among feminist scholars, male and female, that people do not experience life in the disjunctive and/or hierarchical categorizations that have become the great analytical triumvirate of race, class, and gender; instead they move through their lives as Black and female and middle-class, for example. In the United States, our life chances are shaped, in part, by our class and our corporealities, for, among Americans, power and privilege are largely determined by the ways in which race and gender are inscribed on the body. And because power relations have a tremendous effect on material and cultural realities, it is only logical to assume they will also affect political activism, particularly how people organize and why.

With virtually exclusive access to the political arena, Black men have, historically, enabled themselves with the power and authority to determine the Black political agenda. And many among the ranks of Black nationalists have consistently abused that power and defined the boundaries of the imagined Black nation in terms of a sexual politics that institutionalized male domination and the subordination of the "feminine." For instance, Black women's sexuality was the subject of scrutiny by classical Black nationalists like Alexander Crummell who intimated that one of Black women's primary (political) duties was to protect their virtue and maintain sexual purity, while modern Black nationalist Stokely Carmichael conversely asserted that the only position for women in his movement was prone. This phallocentric politics necessitated the subordination of not only women, but "effeminate" men as well. In a desperate attempt to prove their manhood (We men ain't we?), Black heterosexual male nationalists strictly patrolled the borders of their masculine domain, a truth that is manifest in the idealized heterosexism displayed by nineteenth-century theorists like Henry Highland Garnet who demanded both freedom and franchise in terms of the patriarchal privilege and is confirmed by the explicit homophobia exhibited in the mid-twentieth century by Black Power advocates who deemed homosexuality "counterrevolutionary." This sexual politics continues to be manifest in the late twentieth century by rap nationalists like Ice Cube, who pronounced "true niggas ain't gay."[11]

Whether the hypermasculine positioning of Black nationalists is mildly disagreeable or violently offensive, it is meaningful because it stands as evidence of a self-perceived crisis among Black men present in Black political culture. Paul Gilroy characterizes this phenomenon as a movement to counteract manly dis-possession: "An amplified and exaggerated masculinity has become the boastful centerpiece of a culture of compensation that self-consciously salves the misery of the disempowered and subordinated."[12] The preoccupation with masculine status described by Gilroy betrays a semiotic approach to a race and gender politics dominated by men who have been historically denied access to the signs and symbols of "manhood."[13] And because this symbolic castration transcends time and space in African-America, Black nationalists from the nineteenth century to the present have projected "manhood" as a signifier for their liberation politics. Among many Black nationalists, the definition of what constitutes "manhood" has remained, in effect, static. Masculinity was/is defined as not-femininity; thus Black nationalism has evolved as a politics that, more often than not, sanctions the subordination of the feminine, symbolized by women, gay men, and all that is emotional/nonrational.[14] It is an embodied-social politics—and an identity politics—that many times reveals a thinly veiled crisis of manhood among Black men. And it is a crisis that is resolved through what psychologist Alfred Adler labeled "masculine protest."[15]

Take, for example, the sexual politics of two Black nationalist periods, the classical and the modern, which on the surface appear to be contradictory. With few exceptions, Black nationalists have been, and continue to be, conscientiously conservative—almost Puritanical—about issues of gender and sexuality, in part as a response to white supremacist stereotypes that rationalized sexual terrorism against Black men and women. This was especially the case among the Black elite, nationalist and integrationist, male and female, during the post-Reconstruction era. After slavery, men and women in the Black elite enthusiastically embraced conventional gender standards in an effort re-present African-America to white America as a form of resistance to anti-Black propaganda that was popularized, for example, by minstrelsy. As Gail Bederman explains in *Manliness & Civilization*, for men during this period "manliness," characterized by rational self-restraint, was the ideal representation of manhood. It is therefore easier to understand why classical Black nationalists like Alexander Crummell, who were trying to defy racial characterizations of Black Americans as savage, intellectually backward, and sexually depraved, comported themselves with cosmopolitan refinement.[16] For women, the gender standard was modeled after a bourgeois Victorian ideal that was discussed in terms of sexuality and defined by words like "morality," "social purity," and "chastity."

During the late nineteenth century some members of the Black elite set out on a political project to regenerate Black womanhood, in part by redeeming Black women's sexuality. And many, like Crummell, who was an Episcopalian minister, sought to impose Victorian sexual ethics on what he considered the nation's most neglected population: "The Black Woman of the South." Victims of "rude, coarse labor of men" and "ruthlessly violated" by white men, Crummell argued that southern Black women were subject to a "gross barbarism which tended to blunt the tender sensibilities, to obliterate feminine delicacy and womanly shame."[17] Thus, he declared the need for a "domestic revolution." Crummell urged upstanding Christian women of the North to travel south, for he argued that only women with "intelligence and piety," with "delicate sensibility and refinement," could restore the "instinct of chastity" in their degraded sisters. Without this rehabilitation Crummell believed there could be no racial uplift; in this he presaged the Nation of Islam's adage that a nation can rise no higher than its women: "If you want the civilization of a people to reach the very best elements of their being . . . you must imbue the *womanhood* of that people with all its elements and qualities."[18]

For Alexander Crummell, like the bourgeois feminists in the Black women's club movement, racial uplift was defined by the fulfillment of conventional gender roles. Because, in his words, according to some white men "black men have no *rights* which white men should regard, and black *women* no virtue which white men should respect!"[19] Interesting, but fitting, that Crummell chose to appropriate the language of the 1857 Dred Scott Supreme Court decision in this context, during his discussion of the sexual exploitation of Black women. For so determines the defining struggles of the race: Black men aspire to "manhood rights," a form of empowerment that necessitates Black women's subordination in the public and private spheres. A critical part of this coveted patriarchal role, as described by Crummell, is the right to protect the "virtue" of Black women, that is, the right to sovereignty over the sexual (re)production of Black women.

While classical Black nationalists like Alexander Crummell responded to stereotypes by systematically contradicting them, modern Black nationalists like rhetoricians in the Black Panther Party defied these representations, ironically, by engaging them. The Victorian manliness Crummell exhibited during the late nineteenth century was no longer the masculine ideal during the mid-twentieth century. According to Gail Bederman, as economic conditions shifted during the mid- to late nineteenth century, so did atti- tudes toward manliness. Some middle-class white men, deeming the Victo- rian ideal "effeminate," felt a need to "re-virilize" society. So at the turn of the century, "masculinity" became an alternative to "manliness" as a male identity that idealized aggression and virility—ideals that are more congru- ent with contemporary conceptions of manhood. In the mid-1960s most young Black nationalists, like Huey Newton and Bobby Seale, responded to the Civil Rights Movement by embracing this masculine model of man- hood, choosing militancy over nonviolent resistance, a political method they judged effeminate.[20] And at this time shedding a feminized male gen- der identity was critical, for it was not the characters popularized by min- strelsy that haunted Black activists and intellectuals. Instead, modern Black nationalists were compelled to address another, no less damaging represen- tation of African-America: the matriarchal Black family. Therefore in the midst of social science theories about the emasculation of the Black man, the rehabilitation of Black manhood became a primary issue on the politi- cal agenda. Case-in-point: The Black Panther Party.

During the early stages of the Black Panther Party's development, its leaders, from co-founders Huey Newton and Bobby Seale to Minister of Information Eldridge Cleaver, were profoundly influenced by the Moyni- han controversy. From the Party's beginnings in 1966, the men of the Central Committee set forth to reclaim their manhood through macho rhetoric and virile display—a phenomenon bell hooks called the "'it's-a- dick-thing' version of masculinity."[21] The creation of phallic/ies was cen- tral to Panther ideology: witness Newton's theory that the gun was an "extension of the body"[22] or the praxis of the community-patrol program. In fact, Panther leaders were so successful at this ideation that the Party was never able to overcome its early imaging as a macho gang of pistol- packing, "pig"-hunting, hypersexual Black men. Yet as impressive as their masculine performance in the public arena was, it was matched by their demonstrative gender politics.

Eldridge Cleaver's work is a good example of the tone that characterized race/gender theorizing during the Black Power movement. And like the writings of Alexander Crummell, Cleaver's work implicates Black woman- hood and Black women's sexuality. While he embodied the Black male rapist in *Soul on Ice*, Cleaver propagandized the Black female Jezebel in an essay entitled "Pronunciamento." In this address delivered at the Berke- ley Community Center in 1968, Cleaver describes the rationale behind "Pussy Power," a recruitment strategy with which Panther women were to (re)produce members.[23] To illustrate his point, Cleaver analogizes the biblical narrative of Adam and Eve, concluding that Eve could have altered the course of humanity if she had only utilized her powers of seduction.

> So Eve was a jive bitch. Because if she had been hip to Pussy Power, all she had to do was just sit down and say well you just go on and jack off because I'm gonna stay right here and fuck the devil. If Eve had done these things I'm sure that Adam wouldn't have held his ground.[24]

The profane nature of the above excerpt shows how far Black Power theorists strayed from the gender politicking of their predecessors as Cleaver encouraged Black women to flaunt their sexuality—not repress it.[25] Nevertheless it reflects a radical departure in rhetorical style, not substance; for while it may evidence a shifting sexual ethic, it also reveals the conservation of patriarchal authority, confirming the dynamic reproduction of cultural traditions Paul Gilroy named the "changing same." The conceptualization of "Pussy Power" was deceptively dis-empowering—it was not, as bell hooks imagined thirty years later, "power to the pussy."[26] However, it represented a continuing, contemporary manifestation of an effort to control Black women's sexuality: female bodies were subject to male desire and were the object of male consumption.

The sexual politics of classical and modern Black nationalists Alexander Crummell and Eldridge Cleaver described here exemplify a phenomenon R. W. Connell names "protest masculinities." Protest masculinities, according to Connell, can be a response to a perceived sense of powerlessness—particularly among men in marginalized communities (communities of color, impoverished communities) whose limited access to resources jeopardizes their claim to a gendered position of power.[27] For many Black men, this "crisis" of masculinity is inspired by a material reality, specifically a history of political disfranchisement, economic exploitation, and social discrimination, that has denied them the patriarchal "right" to provide for and to protect their families and communities. The proscriptions of racism have contributed to a sense of gendered deprivation that is consistently reflected in the oral and literary work of premodern, modern, and postmodern Black nationalists. A 1967 article written by Huey Newton, cofounder and Minister of Defense of the Black Panther Party, exemplifies this point. In this article, descriptively called "Fear and Doubt," Newton laments the self-perceived state of emasculation in modern African-America: "As a man he finds himself void of those things that bring respect and a feeling of worthiness," he explains.[28] This lack of manly respect, according to Newton, was due to the depressed economic conditions of Black communities.

> In a society where a man is valued according to occupation and material possessions, he is without possessions. He is unskilled and more often than not, marginally or unemployed. . . . He is, therefore viewed as quite worthless by his wife and children. His is ineffectual both in and out of the home. He cannot provide for or protect his family. He is invisible, a nonentity. Society will not acknowledge him as a man.[29]

As this quote demonstrates, for many Black nationalists, hegemonic masculinity—a political economy of male domination that ranges from influence to exploitation—becomes an ideal that is embraced and/or exaggerated. Eldridge Cleaver's rationalization of rape as an "insurrectionary act" and his diagnosis of male homosexuality as a "sickness" not unlike "baby-rape"[30] is an example of the lengths to which Black nationalists have gone in an effort to prove their manhood. Yet as extreme as Cleaver's work is (and it is clear that *Soul on Ice* is evidence of a crisis), it illustrates an integral element of masculine protest: performance. For what is masculinity if not camp? Witness Alexander Crummell, who was recognized for his display of genteel and civilized manliness during the mid-nineteenth century, or Huey Newton and Bobby Seale, who were infamous for their spectacle of virile and dangerous masculinity during the mid-twentieth century.

The difference in male representation portrayed by Alexander Crummell and the co-founders of the Black Panther Party is an illustration of the historical dynamics of gender identity. If, as Gail Bederman suggests, gender is the process that links identity to anatomy,[31] Black nationalists like Crummell, Newton, and Seale show that in a politics based in race and gender rationales this process is often projected into the public domain as a performative, or demonstrative, politics. Gender provides the guise—the mask—through which the male theorist/activist translates his social role into a political one.[32] This explanation is not intended to minimize the stimuli for and consequences of gender performance, for the script, the actors, and the audience are very real. And as Anne McClintock warns: "All nationalisms are gendered; all are invented; and all are dangerous."[33]

While Black nationalism is a politics that creates a sense of collective identity, it is deceptively hierarchical; for as a form of masculine protest, Black nationalist ideology has been shaped in part by a hegemonic masculinity that undermines a communal ideal. As an embodied-social politics that demarcates not only race, but gender and sexuality, Black nationalism is a politics that recreates a system of domination and exploitation. For although the work of women and gay men has proven essential to the progression of the Black nationalist agenda, they have been silenced, marginalized, ridiculed, harassed, and/or persecuted; and the struggle for their rights independent of what is called the "Black liberation movement" has largely been subverted, trivialized, or simply ignored.[34]

These failings of Black nationalism stem from the fact that, as a politics of masculine protest, Black nationalist theory has been consumed with demands for the reclamation of Black manhood. From the issues of abolitionism and enfranchisement to the platforms of Black Communists and the Million Man March, manhood rights—defined as a (natural) right to male superiority in the public and private spheres—have figured prominently in the Black nationalist agenda. For instance, in 1830 a group of thirty-eight free Blacks met in Philadelphia to determine a course of action for their antislavery activism. Their conclusion: elevate Black manhood. "[O]ur forlorn and deplorable situation earnestly and loudly demands of us to devise and pursue all legal means for the speedy elevation of ourselves and our brethren to the scale and standing of men."[35] This sentiment would be echoed by Black male nationalists throughout the nineteenth and twentieth centuries. In fact, David Walker's fixation on the need for Black men to establish themselves as "men" among (white) men was prevalent throughout his 1829 *Appeal to the Colored Citizens of the World*, proving that his work was indeed a seminal piece of Black nationalist thought in more ways than one: "[T]he Americans," he insisted, "are waiting for us to prove to them ourselves, that we are MEN, before they will be willing to admit the fact."[36] And in certain passages of the *Appeal* Walker's commitment to this subject seems frantic, even desperate, as in this passage in which he strongly asserts that servitude is antithetical to manhood: "Are we MEN!!—I ask you, O my brethren! are we MEN? . . . What right then, have we to obey and call any other Master, but Himself?"[37]

Even W. E. B. Du Bois, who is known as an early champion of women's rights, was prone to masculinist imaging. In fact, in an insightful critique of *The Souls of Black Folk* Hazel Carby assesses its gendered language and composition and concludes: "There is, unfortunately, no simple correspondence between anyone's support for female equality and the ideological effect of the gendered structures of thought and feeling at work in any text one might write and publish."[38] Du Bois's association of race, nation, and manhood did not end with *Souls*. After the death of Bishop Henry McNeal Turner in 1915, Du Bois lamented the loss of a hero. And in his tribute to Turner's memory, he engages in the type of hero-worship R. W. Connell called the "production of exemplary masculinity."[39] This creative process is central to the maintenance of hegemonic masculinity, and judging by the nature of Du Bois's eulogy, a politics of hegemonic masculinity is central to the political ideal of Black nationalism. He immortalizes Turner in a manner reminiscent of the folk hero John Henry.[40] "In a sense Turner was the last of his clan: mighty men, physically and mentally, men who started at the bottom and hammered their way to the top by sheer brute strength."[41]

The preoccupation with the status of Black manhood was not the sole domain of nationalist men. Black women have also been known to stress the need for Black men to reclaim their manhood. In her 1833 "Address at the African Masonic Hall," Maria Stewart told her male audience in no uncertain terms that they must prove themselves worthy of manhood rights in order to receive them: "Talk, without effort, is nothing; you are abundantly capable, gentlemen, of making yourselves men of distinction; and this gross neglect, on your part causes my blood to boil within me." For Stewart, action speaks louder than words, and without (male) action there could be no results: "Here is the grand cause which hinders the rise and progress of people of color. It is their want of laudable ambition and requisite courage."[42] As a woman who defied gender conventions and appeared on the political scene during a time when the "cult of domesticity" bound genteel women to the home, Stewart was one of the first Black women to publicly advocate women's rights. Yet despite her burgeoning feminist views, she continued to reinforce patriarchal norms by daring Black men to fulfill their "manly" duties: "Had our men the requisite force and energy, they would soon convince [white Americans] by their efforts both in public and in private, that they are men, or things in the shape of men."[43]

More than a hundred years after Stewart colluded with the masculinist discourse of her male peers, Black women continued to uphold the idealized "traditional" roles that characterized nineteenth-century race/gender theory—particularly that which endorsed an aggressive expression of masculinity. "The Black Man in America has been quiet for so long that it seems almost unbelievable that he will ever make a decisive move toward his manhood and in that very process challenge the white man to be a human being," Louise Moore taunts in the Black militant newspaper *The Liberator*.[44] Like Maria Stewart's 1833 speech at the African Masonic Lodge, Moore's 1966 article "When Will the Real Black Man Stand Up?" uses provocation to bolster her point, showing that even among women, the reclamation of Black manhood has proven to be one of the most potent forces behind the conceptualization of Black nationalist thought. In the midst of a controversy surrounding the myth of the matriarchal Black family, Louise Moore embraced mainstream American gender ideals and challenged Black men to stand up and be accountable as men. "A mature leader will be he, that has thrown off the yoke of his family's oppression, the yoke of the white man's oppressive culture and who has risen above his own fear of death and feels within himself that he is a man who wants to join with all real men to make possible all things," she explains. At a time when the rehabilitation of "emasculated" Black manhood figured prominently on the Black political agenda, Moore did not hesitate to exploit the source of this perceived psychic dismemberment—the castrating Black bitch—to inspire Black male activism: "Will the real Black man stand up or will the Black woman have to make this revolution?" [45]

Therefore throughout the nineteenth and twentieth centuries, the proponents of Black nationalism have overwhelmingly placed a premium on maintaining standard gender conventions, or as Paul Gilroy notes: "The integrity of the race is . . . made interchangeable with the integrity of black masculinity, which must be regenerated at all costs."[46] The toll, more often than not, was exacted at the expense of those who were not Black, heterosexual, and/or male. At times, not even they would be spared. For many Black nationalist theorists and activists the re-masculation of Black men would be achieved, as Malcolm X declared, by any means necessary. And it was in Malcolm's memory that Eldridge Cleaver warned: "We shall have our manhood. We shall have it or the earth will be leveled by our attempts to gain it."[47]

Violent resistance, or the threat of violent resistance, has been a pivotal theme in masculinist Black nationalist discourse. Just as the hunger for male power and authority determined the direction of Black nationalism, the masculine values of competition and aggression would determine its method. The struggle to redeem Black manhood and a strong belief in the redemptive power of militancy in that struggle have shaped Black nationalist strategy and framed Black nationalist politics as a politics of violent resistance.

"The War Must Go On": Black Nationalism as a Politics of (Violent) Resistance

In the aftermath of World War I and a season of anti-Black violence that earned the historical title the "Red Summer" of 1919, Marcus Garvey thrilled his audience in Newport News, Virginia, by exposing the hypocrisy of white Americans who declared the wartime effort a victory for democracy abroad, when Black Americans could not enjoy their constitutional right to life and liberty at home. Being no stranger to pomp and circumstance, Garvey was a master of oratory. He was known, and is remembered by many, as a "demagogue," a leader who could exploit the emotional needs of the "masses." While this may be true, Garvey was also able to tap into the political awareness of many Black (im)migrants, exposing the contradictions between American democratic principles and America's undemocratic practices. Therefore when he demanded the extension of constitutional rights to all Black Americans in October 1919, his battle cry was met with cheers: "We new Negroes of America declare that we desire liberty or we will take death," he pronounced, appropriating the most celebrated (and dramatic) slogan of the American Revolution.[48] Yet despite the diehard lust for equality exhibited in this quote, Garvey's true passion was, apparently, equality between men. For his declaration of war was conceived not as a war to liberate all Black peoples, but as a domestic war to determine—unequivocally—the status of Black manhood. "The war must go on," he insisted, "the war will go on . . . to decide once and for all in the very near future whether black men are to be serfs and slaves or black men are to be free men."[49]

For Black nationalist leaders, the mission was well worth mortal sacrifice, for as Garvey attests, dying with dignity is preferable to living in emasculated shame. Garvey's words illustrate the militant imagery that has been a popular tool in androcentric Black nationalist discourse. For those who advocate gender domination in the name of racial equality, "The war must go on." The masculinist discourse of war provides Black nationalist rhetoricians with the vocabulary and symbolism to translate a politics of liberation into a politics of violent resistance; and with the invocation of violence, the quest to reclaim Black manhood is immediately transformed from an idle threat to a mortal proposition. "It'll be ballots, or it'll be bullets," Malcolm X announced in 1964. "It'll be liberty, or it will be death."[50] Under these do-or-die circumstances, Black nationalist politics becomes not only an example of performative masculinity, but the ultimate form of masculine protest.

A slave metaphor figures prominently in the masculinist discourse of violent resistance, as many Black nationalist theorists have used violence, or the threat of violence, to purge an emasculated sense of (male) Self. It is a homeopathic strategy[51] that has its roots in a historical and perduring shame about slavery, a shame that puts the burden of enslavement on the male slave.[52] (Even in those cases where Black nationalists discuss the enslavement of slave women, it is done in relation to its castrating effects on Black manhood.)[53] This is where the class/race/gender positionality of the nationalist subject is most apparent. From David Walker to LeRoi Jones, the distance between the reality of the free and that of the enslaved contributed to the arrogant/ignorant dictate of death before submission, suggesting, as bell hooks writes, that "the worst that can happen to a man is that he be made to assume the social status of a woman."[54] However, contrary to nationalists' assumptions, the cultural production of slaves suggests that—for better or worse—slave men were subject to "traditional" gender conventions.[55] While they internalized threats to their manhood, slave men were forced by circumstance to express their masculine identity in alternative ways. More often than not, the human instinct of self-preservation took precedence over a desperate attempt to establish their masculinity through violence.[56] Nevertheless, many nationalist theorists insist that one of the most destructive legacies of slavery is the inheritance of an emasculated "slave mentality."[57] They then conclude that the only way Black men can overcome this mentality and claim their gendered right to political power and patriarchal authority is through violent resistance.

In his esteemed work on *Black Religion and Black Radicalism*, the theologian Gayraud Wilmore puts forth this view, presenting the 1831 Nat Turner insurrection as a divinely inspired blow against the emasculation of Black manhood during slavery. In his celebration of violent resistance as the antidote for endangered Black masculinity (and in protest of William Styron's compromising representation of a nationalist hero), Wilmore wrote: "Nat Turner discovered his manhood by unveiling the God who liberates. His fanatical attempt to authenticate that manhood in blood was the inevitable consequence of the fanatical attempt of white men to deny it."[58]

The endorsement of violence as a weapon in the war against the personal/political castration of Black men constantly (re)appears throughout the oral and literary tradition of Black nationalist thought in the United States. In fact, it was the motivation behind one of the most provocative publications in the history of American Black nationalism, Henry Highland Garnet's *An Address to the Slaves of the United States of America* (1848).[59] Like most Black nationalists, Garnet strongly believed in divine retribution for the sins of white America. Yet he did not suspend this belief in hopes of judgment in the hereafter. Garnet—a Presbyterian minister—insisted the slavocracy pay for its crimes against "God and man" in the here and now. Like David Walker, he concluded that the enslaved should avenge the murder, brutality, and exploitation perpetrated by their enslavers. Yet Garnet did so by casting doubt upon the "manliness" of male slaves. Like most nineteenth- and twentieth-century Black nationalists, he did not recognize quotidian resistance, and he misinterpreted slave dissemblance as submission. In a polemic that reads like it could have been torn from the pages of a speech by Nation of Islam Minister Louis Farrakhan (at least, Farrakhan *circa* the late 1980s/early 1990s), Garnet challenges the manhood of slave men.

> You act as though, you were made for the special use of these devils. You act as though your daughters were born to pamper the lusts of your masters and overseers. And worse than all, you tamely submit while your lords tear your wives from your embraces and defile them before your eyes. In the name of God, we ask, are you men?[60]

According to Garnet's account, by failing to perform their most important male role—protecting their wives and daughters—slave men were rendered impotent to the will of their masters. Yet in his *Address* Garnet provided a means for his bonded brethren to erect their male status: the act of rebellion. Insisting that it was God's testament, he proclaimed: "Heaven would frown upon the men who would not resist such aggression, even to death."[61] This riotous revelation shocked Garnet's abolitionist peers, for moral suasion was the principal strategy of the antislavery movement in the 1840s. Nevertheless, he took his cultural cues from the ancestors[62] and his political lessons from the American Revolution and concluded that only through violence could Black men redeem their manhood. "However much you and all of us may desire it, there is not much hope of redemption without the shedding of blood. If you must bleed, let it all come at once—rather die freemen, than live to be the slaves."[63]

While Garnet believed the re-masculation of slave men was a matter of do or die, for some Black nationalists, it was kill or be killed. In David Walker's *Appeal* the message to slave insurgents was clear.

[I]f you commence, make sure to work—do not trifle, for they will not trifle with you—they want us for their slaves, and think nothing of murdering us in order to subject us to that wretched condition—therefore, if there is an attempt made by us, kill or be killed.[64]

Walker's command was fearless, but not unfounded. The boundary between slavery and freedom was secured by a constant threat of violence, and any attempt to cross that line could result in death. While Walker recognized the gravity of his proposal, he rationalized that it was a calculated risk. He deemed counter-violence a necessary evil in the crusade to fulfill both manly and Christian duty.

Look upon your mother, wife and children, and answer God Almighty; and believe this, that it is no more harm for you to kill a man, who is trying to kill you, than it is for you to take a drink of water when thirsty; in fact, the man who will stand still and let another murder him, is worse than an infidel, and, if he has common sense, ought not to be pitied.[65]

As this passage shows, violent resistance was not considered a sin, but a divinely ordained crusade among Black nationalists—even at the turn of the century. For many Black leaders, as lynching became a social/economic prescription for destabilized race relations, the desire to aggressively pursue manhood rights was suppressed by the will to live. Yet in an era dominated by the "accommodation politics" of Booker T. Washington, the threat of mob action did not intimidate all Black leaders. Bishop Henry McNeal Turner was proving himself a "fearless confrontationist in an age of compromise"[66] as another Black preacher assured his colleagues in 1889 that "the surest guarantee of respectability for Negroes was for every black man to purchase a gun and use it at the slightest provocation."[67]

What is most interesting about the aggressive stance assumed by these turn-of-the-century Black clergymen, particularly that taken by the latter, is its apparent contradiction of the gospel of the New Testament, the foundation of modern and postmodern Black Christian teachings and preaching. However, what these Black nationalist ministers and others demonstrated is an alternate reading of the New Testament that adapted the story of Jesus to address the needs of their Black congregations. It is the religious manifestation of Black cultural politics that James H. Cone termed "Black theology" in 1969, and it reflects a knowledge system—a standpoint—that is both pragmatic and radical. Modern problems call for modern solutions, or as Cone points out in *Black Theology and Black Power,* "we cannot solve ethical questions of the twentieth century by looking at what Jesus did in the first."[68] While this realization does not necessitate abandoning or avoiding the work and words of Christ, it does require a reorientation of the Christian en-visionary. For example, in his 1968 book *The Black Messiah,* Albert B. Cleage Jr., pastor of the Black nationalist church Shrine of the Black Madonna, demonstrates the revolutionary potential of New Testament doctrines by quoting a passage from the Gospel of Matthew, eleventh chapter, 34th verse: "Do not think that I have come to bring peace on earth; I have not come to bring peace, but a sword." Like his nationalist predecessors Cleage is resourceful, using the Bible as a conjure book in the struggle for Black liberation.[69] He unveils Jesus as a "troublemaker" and represents conflict as being as much a part of New Testament doctrine as compassion.[70] Christian righteousness, most often translated in terms of love and forgiveness, can also be expressed through resistance against injustice, Cleage argues. "The question is a very simple one. If we are afraid of conflict then anyone who is not afraid of conflict is our master." Therefore Cleage concludes, like Walker, Garnet, and Garvey before him, that violent times demand violent measures, for "[a]nyone who is willing to use violence can make anyone who is afraid of violence his slave."[71]

An extensive knowledge of the Bible has proven extremely adaptive to the masculinist discourse of Black nationalism. Yet it also reflects the (de)constructive/revisionist, Object-to-Subject positioning characteristic of the Black nationalist tradition. While the Bible is used as an interpretive tool to explain Black historical experiences, the slave metaphor is used as an analytical tool to describe the symbolic emasculation of Black men in America. The fact that the master/slave analogy continues to have currency in contemporary Black politics speaks to the sense of manly dispossession Black men have experienced, even as it condemns the slave for the condition of enslavement.

Conclusion: Problematizing Black Nationalism as a Liberation Politics

Whether explicit or implicit, a gendered code has underlined and undermined the very definition of empowerment in the race politics of Black nationalism. The preoccupation with manhood demonstrated in the oral and literary work of Black nationalists, from David Walker to Ice Cube, signifies that there has been a "conceptual and political failure of imagination"[72] at work in Black public life. That is, these Black men (and many Black women) have not even *conceived* a politics of liberation that is not dependent upon a masculinist ideal of nation that incorporates a subordination of the feminine. The desire to attain the power and privilege associated with hegemonic masculinity has haunted Black nationalists and limited Black nationalism's liberatory potential since its debut on the Black political scene in 1829. This covetous style of politicking is most evident in the cry for "manhood rights" or the right to male domination in the public and private spheres, and is witnessed in David Walker's *Appeal* in the early nineteenth century and at the Million Man March in the late twentieth century. In fact, the success of the Million Man March was evidence of the enduring lure of a gendered narrative of the Black American experience and of the continued power of mas(k)ulinity and masculinist politicking in U.S. Black nationalism. Yet any politics based in gendered rationale has the potential to—indeed will inevitably—both legitimate and replicate dominant hierarchical stratification in social, political, economic, and cultural relations.

Take, for example, the slave metaphor used by most Black nationalist ideologues to legitimate a politics of violent resistance to attain Black "manhood rights" in the public and private spheres. If Black nationalists advocate the use of violence to obtain patriarchal order, what is to say they will not also use violence to maintain that order? The theory and practice of "revolutionaries" in the Black Power and Hip-Hop movements provide the most explicit manifestations of verbal, physical, and/or sexual violence against men and women, Black and white, straight and gay. Whether it be Eldridge Cleaver's rape fantasy/reality or the fatal rivalry between the Panthers and the US Organization,[73] Ice Cube's "Cave Bitch" or Brand Nubian's "Punks Jump Up to Get Beat Down," Black nationalists' endorsement of violence was not restricted to dismantling the white power structure. That is because their macho "it's-a-dick-thing" politicking knows and respects no boundaries but its own. As an embodied-social politics it necessitates a strict policing of its race/gender and sexuality, even its generational and class, borders. And part of that policing includes violence, even if it involves violence against those within the "nation"—Black women and Black (especially gay) men.

Therefore it is extremely important, as bell hooks argues, to be "seduced by violence no more."[74] To do so involves calling into question the legitimacy of Black nationalism as a liberatory politics. For any political ideology that does not incorporate the liberation of *all* Black people cannot be legitimately considered a liberation politics. As an embodied-social politics, Black nationalism has proven itself to be an ideology and praxis concerned primarily with the liberation of Black heterosexual men. While its primary objective has always been self-determination, Black nationalism has been shaped in profound and unexpected ways by dominant society, particularly in terms of its framing as a politics of masculine protest. To be fair, Black nationalists' definitions of manhood and masculinity are at some times reflective of dominant culture and at others reflected in dominant culture.[75] Yet in the end, it makes little difference. The results are the same.

Because the "Negro Problem" is defined as a crisis of masculinity, whose "imagined solution," as Phillip Brian Harper notes, "is a proper affirmation of black male authority,"[76] Black nationalism continues to be handicapped by its own self-consciousness and short-sightedness. Insights provided by feminists of color concerning the interlocking nature of race, class, gender, and sexuality have yet to be acknowledged, much less embraced, by Black nationalists. And until this dynamic is recognized, Black men and women whose vision of liberation is circumscribed by a gendered discourse that aspires to the status quo will continue to be betrayed by their own contradictions.

NOTES

1. In another moving scene—one of the most memorable scenes of the film— Trip is punished for abandoning the army camp by public whipping. In a cinematic moment that is deliberately reminiscent of the institution of slavery (with the Irish sergeant standing in for his overseer counterpart), Trip takes his beating like a "man." He is defiant, unwilling to give his white superiors the satisfaction of witnessing his pain—with the exception of an extremely dramatic tear. Denzel Washington won an Academy Award, as Best Supporting Actor, for his portrayal of Trip.

2. *Glory*, dir. Edward Zwick, 2 hr. 2 min., Columbia TriStar, 1989, videocassette.

3. Gail Bederman, *Manliness & Civilization: A Cultural History of Gender and Race in the United States, 1880–1917* (Chicago: University of Chicago Press, 1995), 21.

4. Ibid.

5. It is interesting to note that Broderick's character, Colonel Shaw, who represents authority—or white power—in the film, is nevertheless depicted as effeminate; his bleeding-heart liberalism is juxtaposed to the brute masculinity of

Washington's portrayal of Trip, the fugitive slave who is involved in a constant struggle to claim his manhood. This race/gender construction is a familiar one among Black nationalists. For while white men are often conceived of by Black nationalists as all-powerful (hence, "The Man"), the model against which Black masculinity is positioned and judged lacking, at times this status is reversed and it is white men who are considered weak, effeminate—even "gay."

6. Even scholars of Black nationalist thought fall prey to masculinist appeals. Take, for example, Victor Ullman's position on the debate over who should be considered the "father" of Black nationalism, David Walker or Martin Delany. Delany is the premier Black nationalist, he argues in what appears to be an attack against David Walker's masculinity: "Delany was the first to demand—not appeal—for black freedom and equality for the very simplest of reasons—because 'I am a Man.'" Victor Ullman, *Martin R. Delany: The Beginnings of Black Nationalism* (Boston: Beacon Press, 1971), 516.

7. Women have also participated in the masculinist discourse of Black nationalism. However, because men have dominated the Black political arena they have also dominated Black politicking—and Black nationalism is no exception. Take, for instance, the early nineteenth century and the birth of Black nationalism. During the antebellum period, a privileged few among the northern Black (and predominantly male) elite were able to attend institutions of higher learning. Some of these men held ministerial positions in white religious denominations, while others led their own congregations in all-Black churches; and a significant number of free Blacks, the majority of them men, moved within the circles of the white abolitionist movement, which was growing increasingly militant. These centers of influence and power—the universities and seminaries, the churches, and the antislavery movement—contributed to the political development of a community that was in a precarious position in relation to white society, a position some described as "slaves to the community." And it was these male-dominated centers of influence and power that cultivated Black nationalism's premier theorists, from David Walker and Henry Highland Garnet to Alexander Crummell and W.E.B. Du Bois. Therefore, it should come as no surprise that Black nationalist politics is an androcentric and masculinist discourse.

8. Alfred Adler, *The Individual Psychology of Alfred Adler: A Systematic Presentation in Selections from His Writings* (New York: Basic Books, 1956); quoted in R. W. Connell, *Masculinities* (Berkeley: University of California Press, 1995), 16.

9. Anne McClintock, "'No Longer in a Future Heaven': Gender, Race and Nationalism," in *Dangerous Liaisons: Gender, Nation, and Postcolonial Perspectives*, ed. Anne McClintock, Aamir Mufti, and Ella Shohat (Minneapolis: University of Minnesota Press, 1997), 95. McClintock introduces the concept of a "politics of substitution" after quoting Algerian anticolonialist and revolutionary theorist Frantz Fanon's statement that "The fantasy of the native is precisely to occupy the master's place" (McClintock, 95).

10. Paul Gilroy, *The Black Atlantic: Modernity and Double Consciousness* (Cambridge: Harvard University Press, 1993), 85.

11. Ice Cube, "Horny Little Devil," *Death Certificate* (Priority Records, Inc., 1991). In "The Failure to Transform: Homophobia in the Black Community," Cheryl Clarke exposes the hypocrisy of Black "revolutionaries" who rationalized their homophobia in terms of homosexuality's role in the "genocide" of Black peoples. She quoted a flyer from the First National Plenary Conference on Self-Determination held in New York City in December 1981: "Revolutionary nationalists and genuine communists cannot uphold homosexuality in the leadership of the Black Liberation Movement nor uphold it as a correct practice. Homosexuality is a genocidal practice. . . . Homosexuality does not produce children. . . . Homosexuality does not birth new warriors for liberation. . . . The practice of homosexuality is an accelerating threat to our survival as a people and as a nation." Cheryl Clarke, "The Failure to Transform: Homophobia in the Black Community," in *Home Girls: A Black Feminist Anthology*, ed. Barbara Smith (New York: Kitchen Table/Woman of Color Press, 1983), 198–99. Not all nationalists assumed an anti-gay position. In 1970 Huey Newton published a letter in the Black Panther newspaper advising members to build coalitions with gay and lesbian brothers and sisters in the movement, although his tone was homophobic and sexist: "Whatever your personal opinions and insecurities about homosexuality and various liberation movements among homosexuals and women . . . we should try to unite with them in a revolutionary fashion. I say 'whatever your insecurities are' because, as we very well know sometimes our first instinct is to hit a homosexual in the mouth and want a woman to be quiet. We want to hit the homosexual because we're afraid we might be homosexual; and we want to hit the woman or shut her up because we are afraid that she may castrate us, or take the nuts we may not have to start with." "A Letter From Huey to Revolutionary Brothers and Sisters," *The Black Panther*, August 1970.

12. Gilroy, *Black Atlantic*, 85.

13. The signs and symbols of "manhood" sought by Black nationalist theorists are those associated with white men of power and privilege, men who are able to use their influence in ways that protect their interests—be those interests personal, familial, or community.

14. R. W. Connell explains the symbiotic relationship between masculine and feminine in *Masculinities*: "The phallus is master-signifier, and femininity is symbolically defined by lack" (Connell, 70). In the United States, this relationship is complicated by race and class, so that "femininity" in both the nineteenth and the twentieth century is most associated with middle-class and upper-middle-class white women whose ethnic background is Anglo-Saxon Protestant. Toni Cade Bambara's assessment of proper male and female behavior during the Black Power movement is a prime example: "if a woman is tough, she's a rough mamma, a strident bitch, a ballbreaker, a castrator. And if a man is at all sensitive, tender, spiritual, he's a faggot." Toni Cade Bambara, "On the Issue of Roles," in *The Black*

Woman: An Anthology, ed. Toni Cade Bambara (New York: Penguin Books USA Inc., 1970), 102.

15. Connell, *Masculinities*, 16.

16. This ideal of Victorian "manliness" was carried into the early twentieth century by Black intellectuals and activists, particularly those in the Black elite. In her 1998 book *Race Men* Hazel Carby notes the conscious masculine imaging of Alexander Crummell's protégé, W.E.B. Du Bois, at the turn of the century. According to Carby, Du Bois deliberately projected an image of manly civility through his demeanor and dress. Hazel Carby, *Race Men* (Cambridge: Harvard University Press, 1998), 21. This gendered styling can also be seen among Du Bois's peers in the "Talented Tenth," the artists, activists, and intellectuals of the Harlem Renaissance.

17. Alexander Crummell, "The Black Woman of the South," in *Destiny and Race: Selected Writings, 1840–1898*, ed. Wilson Jeremiah Moses (Amherst: University of Massachusetts Press, 1992), 214.

18. Ibid., 221.

19. Ibid., 215–16, italics in original.

20. Many young Black men and women who participated in the Black Power movement equated the political strategy of non-violent civil disobedience with an emasculated sensibility. "CIVIL RIGHTS POEM," written by Black Arts Movement leader and founder of the Congress of African People Amiri Baraka, is an example of the kind of attack leveled against civil rights organizations and leaders. In this poem, Roy Wilkins, leader of the NAACP, is labeled an "eternal faggot": "His spirit is a faggot / his projection / and image." As Phillip Brian Harper notes in *'Are We Not Men': Masculine Anxiety and the Problem of African-American Identity*, because of his liberal politics Wilkins is targeted as being less than a man—branded a feminized man, a "faggot." In fact, according to Harper, "so well understood was the identification between inadequacies of manhood and black consciousness in the Black Arts context that this poem needed never render explicit the grounds for its judgment of NAACP leader Roy Wilkins, for the perceived racial-political moderation of both him and his organization clearly bespoke his unforgivable 'faggotry.'" Phillip Brian Harper, *'Are We Not Men': Masculine Anxiety and the Problem of African-American Identity* (New York: Oxford University Press, 1996), 51.

21. hooks, *Outlaw Culture: Resisting Representations* (New York: Routledge, 1994), 110. In her essay about the perpetuation of rape culture within the Black community, titled "Seduced by Violence No More," hooks describes the cultural commodification of a Black male identity that is based on the abuse and exploitation of Black women, an identity she called "dick-thing" masculinity.

22. "Huey Newton Talks to the Movement about the Black Panther Party, Cultural Nationalism, SNCC, Liberals and White Revolutionaries," in *The Black Panthers Speak*, ed. Philip S. Foner (New York: Da Capo Press, 1995), 60.

23. Within the Black nationalist tradition, the political role of Black women has, historically, been defined in terms of their reproductive capabilities. In fact,

while the Black Panthers were promoting the sexualization of their female comrades with the theory and practice of "Pussy Power," many of their peers discouraged extramarital female sexual activity (at least in theory) and made official
policy out of exalting Black motherhood, arguing that it was women's duty to reproduce and raise warriors for the revolution. These Black Power advocates believed birth control and abortion to be a genocidal plot of "The Man." But as Toni
Cade Bambara noted in 1969, while many talked of propagation, there was no talk
of family planning—no plan to take care of women and their children. Therefore
she, as others, concluded: "Seems to me the Brother does us all a great disservice by
telling [women] to fight the man with the womb. Better to fight with the gun and
the mind." Toni Cade Bambara, "The Pill: Genocide or Liberation?" in *The Black
Woman: An Anthology* (New York: Penguin Books USA Inc., 1970), 167.

24. Eldridge Cleaver, "Pronunciamento," *The Black Panther*, December 21, 1968.

25. Again, not all Black Power activists encouraged promiscuity among Black
women. In fact, many conformed to the Victorian sexual ethic popular among
nineteenth-century Black nationalists. In the early years of the Congress of African
People (CAP), organized in 1970 and led by Amiri Baraka, gender roles in the liberation struggle corresponded with the "separate spheres" doctrine of the nineteenth century. For example in a pamphlet titled "Mwanamke Mwananchi (The
Nationalist Woman)," the women of the Committee for Unified Newark, the parent organization of CAP, argued that "[n]ature has made women submissive" and
that women's duties—inspiring her husband, educating her children, participating
in the "social development of the nation"—were confined to the private sphere.
They validated their position with a quote from Maulana (Ron) Karenga, leader
of the US Organization: "What makes a woman appealing is femininity and she
can't be feminine without being submissive." Mumininas of Committee for Unified Newark, *Mwanamke Mwananchi (The Nationalist Woman)* (Newark, N.J.: Ji-
had Productions, 1971).

26. bell hooks goes in search of an empowered female sexuality—or, as she
named it, "Power to the Pussy"—in her 1994 book *Outlaw Culture: Resisting Representations*.

27. Connell, *Masculinities*, 111. Connell observes implicit and explicit displays
of masculine protest among Australian men, all of whom are assumedly white and
most of whom are in their twenties, working-class and/or marginally employed.

28. Huey P. Newton, "Fear and Doubt," *The Black Panther*, 15 May 1967.

29. Newton, "Fear and Doubt."

30. Eldridge Cleaver, *Soul on Ice* (New York: Dell Publishing Co., Inc., 1968), 14.

31. Bederman, *Manliness and Civilization*, 8.

32. I must thank John L. Jackson Jr. and Martha S. Jones, co-organizers of the
October 1996 Black and Latino graduate student conference titled "passing: fluidity, certainty, ambiguity, fixity, identity," for their inventive and innovative conception of "MASKulinity." The use of "mask" as a descriptive in this context is

reflective of the discourse on the social construction of gender, that is, I use "mask" to describe the phenomenon of gender performance. If gender is socially constructed, not biologically determined, then it is a set of social expectations, a scripted role, to be performed by males and females. Masculinity and femininity are those roles. They are the masks we wear in interpersonal interactions, interactions that are figured by the overarching power relations of race, class, gender, and sexuality.

33. McClintock, "'No Longer in a Future Heaven,'" 89.

34. This is not to suggest that Black nationalists are the sole perpetrators of sexism and anti-gay beliefs and behaviors. Take, for example, the treatment of Ella Baker by the Southern Christian Leadership Conference or Bayard Rustin by the organizers of the March on Washington—both played a critical role in the mobilizing and organizing of these movements, yet both were shafted by the male leadership of the modern civil rights movement. And, according to V. P. Franklin, Martin Luther King avoided sharing a public platform with James Baldwin—on a television program and at the March on Washington—because of his homosexuality. V. P. Franklin, *Living Our Stories, Telling Our Truths: Autobiography and the Making of the African-American Intellectual Tradition* (New York: Scribner, 1995), 309–10.

35. Ullman, *Martin R. Delany*, 10.

36. David Walker, *Appeal to the Colored Citizens of the World, but in Particular, and Very Expressly, to Those of the United States of America* (New York: Hill and Wang, Inc., 1965), 27.

37. Ibid., 16.

38. Carby, *Race Men*, 12.

39. Connell, *Masculinities*, 214.

40. John Henry is one of the original Black American folk heroes, his manly presence was evoked by Black laborers in the nineteenth century, and well into the twentieth. The narrative songs of early-twentieth-century Black railroaders and agricultural workers bear witness to the masculine (con)figuration of John Henry: "If I could hammer / Like John Henry / If I could hammer / Like John Henry / Lawd, I'd be a man / Lawd, I'd be a man." Lawrence Levine, *Black Culture and Black Consciousness: Afro-American Folk Thought from Slavery to Freedom* (New York: Oxford University Press, 1977), 425.

41. Gayraud Wilmore, *Black Religion and Black Radicalism* (Garden City, N.Y.: Anchor Press/Doubleday & Company, Inc., 1973), 192.

42. Wilson Jeremiah Moses, ed., *Classical Black Nationalism: From the American Revolution to Marcus Garvey* (New York: New York University Press, 1996), 92.

43. Ibid., 96.

44. Louise Moore, "When Will the Real Black Man Stand Up?" *The Liberator*, May 1966.

45. Ibid.

46. Gilroy, *Black Atlantic,* 194.

47. Cleaver, *Soul on Ice,* 61.

48. Moses, *Classical Black Nationalism,* 246.

49. Ibid.

50. Malcolm X, "The Ballot or the Bullet," in *Malcolm X Speaks: Selected Speeches and Statements,* ed. George Breitman (New York: Grove Weidenfeld, 1965), 32.

51. The rationale of using violence as a counter-strategy to violence is extremely popular among Black nationalists. In a 1968 interview Huey Newton justified his philosophy of self-defense in exactly these terms: "Many people have spoken of violence or of our advocating violence. Well, we're not advocating violence. We're advocating that we defend ourselves from the aggression. That if America is armed, and if it's right for America to arm herself and even commit violence throughout the world, then it's right for black people to arm themselves." "In Defense of Self-Defense: An Exclusive Interview with Minister of Defense, Huey P. Newton," *The Black Panther,* 16 March 1968.

52. In *Black Culture and Black Consciousness* Lawrence Levine assesses the masculinist definition of "resistance" in traditional slave studies and its underlying implication about the lack of a "real" male presence within U.S. slave communities (i.e., equating violence with "manhood"). This may, in part, explain the pervasiveness of a masculinist agenda within Black nationalist thought and the deliberate predominance of men within the Black public sphere. Distorted portrayals of slave behavior (most specifically the over-characterization of slaves as childlike and submissive to account for the comparatively lower number of slave insurrections in British North America) and the relative scarcity of alternative representations have had a significant impact on Black nationalists' reconstructions of the history and legacy of slavery in the United States. This misrepresentation leads them, as Sterling Stuckey notes, to "exaggerate the degree of acquiescence to oppression by the Black masses." Sterling Stuckey, *Going Through the Storm: The Influence of African-American Art in History* (New York: Oxford University Press, 1994), 90.

53. W. E. B. Du Bois's discussion of white men's sexual exploitation of Black women in *Souls of Black Folk* provides a good example of this phallocentric discourse. Du Bois conceived the "Negro problem" in the post–Civil War era to be threefold. His was a burden of poverty, ignorance, and the "red stain of bastardy." Like his mentor Alexander Crummell, who described the degraded condition of Black women subject to the "lustration" of white men in "The Black Woman of the South," Du Bois believed this private shame had grave effects on public advancement. In *Race Men,* Hazel Carby argues that his race/gender politics led Du Bois to interpret the sexual exploitation of Black women in terms of Black male emasculation. For Du Bois, the "systematic legal defilement of Negro women" was a problem because it was evidence that, as a consequence of enslavement, Black men had been stripped of their right to dominate Black women. "This 'hereditary weight,'" Carby writes, "is the burden imposed on black men by history because they could

not control the sexual reproduction of black women. Under this weight of betrayal by black women, most black men stumbled, fell, and failed to come into the full flowering of black manhood" (Carby, 33).

54. hooks, bell, *Ain't I a Woman: black women and feminism* (Boston: South End Press, 1981), 20. An example of this characterization of slaves is found in a statement made by Eldridge Cleaver, as remembered by Huey Newton: "a slave who dies of natural causes will not balance two dead flies on the scales of eternity." "Huey Newton Talks to the Movement about the Black Panther Party, Cultural Nationalism, SNCC, Liberals and White Revolutionaries," in *The Black Panthers Speak*, ed. Philip S. Foner (New York: Da Capo Press, 1995), 62.

55. In *The Ideological Origins of Black Nationalism* Sterling Stuckey wrote of a "Hymn of Freedom" sung during an 1813 slave revolt off the coast of South Carolina. It is clear that these slave rebels had a sense of manliness as well as a sense of masculine duty to their wives and children: "Look to Heaven with manly trust / And swear by Him that's always just / That no white foe with impious hand / Shall slave your wives and daughters more / or rob them of their virtue dear / Be armed with valor firm and true / Their hopes are fixed on Heaven and you / That truth and justice will prevail / And every scheme of bondage fail." Sterling Stuckey, ed., *Ideological Origins of Black Nationalism* (Boston: Beacon Press, 1972), 4.

56. Although violent resistance against whites may not have been a viable option by which slave men might assert their masculinity, violent resistance against slave women was. As Eugene D. Genovese, bell hooks, and Deborah Gray White suggest, slave men could use tactics ranging from physical intimidation to sexual exploitation to reinforce their masculine status over slave women.

57. In his 1963 book *Blues People*, LeRoi Jones, who later changed his name to Amiri Baraka to signal his changing "radical" consciousness, defined "slave mentality" as "the most socially unfortunate psychic adjustments that the slave had made during the two hundred years of slavery." He writes: "two hundred years of bending to the will of the white man had to leave its mark. And that mark was indelibly on the very foundations of the new separate Black society." LeRoi Jones, *Blues People: The Negro Experience in White America and the Music that Developed from It* (New York: Morrow Quill Paperbacks, 1963), 57. The belief in a "slave mentality" was not restricted to Black nationalist theorists; many historians, Black and white, also bought into the idea that slavery left a lasting impression upon the manhood of the Black race. One of the most striking examples of this masculinist reading of the slave experience in an academic study is Eugene D. Genovese's essay "The Legacy of Slavery and the Roots of Black Nationalism," originally presented at the September 1966 Second Annual Socialist Scholars Conference. In his attempt to explain what he perceived to be the lack of a radical political tradition among Black Americans (as opposed to Afro-Caribbeans or Afro-Brazilians, for example), Genovese insists that the American slave system, which he believes was characterized by a paternalistic relationship between master and slave, pacified African

America and made its leaders accommodating to the will of white men: "Slavery and its aftermath emasculated the Black masses; they are today profoundly sick and shaking with convulsions." Therefore after the height of civil rights protests and at the beginning of the Black Power era, Genovese suggested that the reclamation of Black manhood was at the center of Black American politics. "Those who believe emasculation is the figment of the liberal imagination ought to read the words of any militant leader from David Walker to W.E.B. Du Bois, from Frederick Douglass to Martin Luther King, from Robert F. Williams to Malcolm X. The cry has been to assert manhood and renounce servility." Eugene D. Genovese, "The Legacy of Slavery and the Roots of Black Nationalism," in *For a New America: Essays in History and Politics from Studies on the Left, 1959–1967*, ed. James Weinstein and David W. Eakins (New York: Random House, 1970), 413–14.

58. Wilmore, *Black Religion*, 89.

59. Originally a speech given before the 1843 national Negro convention at Buffalo when Garnet was twenty-seven years old. Garnet published the *Address* in 1848 along with David Walker's *Appeal*.

60. Sterling Stuckey, *Slave Culture: Nationalist Theory and the Foundations of Black America* (New York: Oxford University Press, 1987), 155.

61. Stuckey, *Ideological Origins*, 168.

62. In an inspired argument for the presence of African cultural traits in (and the influence of slave culture on) Black nationalist thought, Sterling Stuckey claims that Garnet purposefully appealed to slaves' African sensibilities by invoking their ancestors when he wrote: "Awake, awake; millions of voices are calling you! Your dead fathers speak to you from their graves." Stuckey, *Slave Culture*, 155.

63. Henry Highland Garnet, "An Address to the Slaves of the United States," quoted in Herbert Aptheker, ed., *A Documentary History of the Negro People in the United States*, vol. 1 (New York: The Citadel Press), 231.

64. Walker, *Appeal*, 25.

65. Ibid., 26.

66. Wilson Jeremiah Moses, *The Golden Age of Black Nationalism, 1850–1925* (Hamden, Conn.: Archon Books, 1978), 202.

67. Ibid., 183. This statement was made by an unnamed Black preacher at the "colored" 1889 National Baptist Convention.

68. James H. Cone, *Black Theology & Black Power* (San Francisco: HarperSanFrancisco, 1969), 139.

69. For a more extensive explanation and illustration of the conjuring potential of the Bible see Theophus H. Smith, *Conjuring Culture: Biblical Formations of Black America* (New York: Oxford University Press, 1994).

70. Albert B. Cleage Jr., *The Black Messiah* (New York: Sheed and Ward, 1968), 214.

71. Ibid., 224.

72. Carby, *Race Men*, 10.

73. The feud between these two groups, which according to the source refer-enced began either because of ideological differences or because of recruitment from rival gangs, turned fatal in January 1969. On that date two Panthers, John Huggins and Alprentice "Bunchy" Carter, were murdered by US members at a UCLA Black Student Union meeting. The war of words that ensued was riddled with gendered and sexual language; in fact, this conflict was probably one of the reasons Black Panther leaders were forced to address issues of sexism and the sex-ual division of labor within the Party. After making public statements against the US Organization's "male chauvinism," leaders like Fred Hampton and Bobby Seale could not continue to condone such behavior within their own ranks.

74. hooks, *Outlaw Culture*, 109–13.

75. In *Manliness & Civilization*, Gail Bederman discusses how some white men during the late nineteenth century abandoned their "manliness," a gendered state characterized by moral character, self-mastery, and restraint, for an ideal of "mas-culinity," which at that time was defined in ways familiar to contemporary Ameri-cans—e.g., aggressive behavior and virility. According to Bederman, this shift in manhood ideal was influenced by the industrial revolution and, at times, shaped by popular perceptions of African and African-American men, who in certain contexts would be deemed primitive and savage. This idealization of the Black "masculine primitive," as Anthony Rotunda called it, is also observable in Norman Mailer's *The White Negro* (San Francisco: City Lights Books, 1957) and in liberal and conservative media accounts of the Black Panther Party during the late 1960s.

76. Harper, *"Are We Not Men,"* x.

About the Contributors

Elsa Barkley Brown is Associate Professor of history and women's studies at the University of Maryland. She is the co-editor of the two-volume *Major Problems in African American History* and the two-volume *Black Women in America: An Historical Encyclopedia*. Her award-winning articles on African American political culture have appeared in *Signs, History Workshop Journal, Feminist Studies, Sage, Public Culture*, and the *Journal of Urban History*.

David S. Cecelski is a historian and journalist who holds the Lehman Brady Joint Chair Professorship in Documentary and American Studies at Duke University and the University of North Carolina at Chapel Hill. He is the author of several books, including *The Waterman's Song: Slavery and Freedom in Maritime North Carolina*, and is co-editor (with Timothy Tyson) of *Democracy Betrayed: The Wilmington Race Riot of 1898 and Its Legacy*. His essay in this volume is adapted from an earlier version that appeared in *Democracy Betrayed*.

Charise Cheney is an assistant professor of ethnic studies at California Polytechnic State University. She received her doctorate in history from the University of Illinois, Urbana-Champaign, in 1999. She is currently working on a book titled *Brothers Gonna Work it Out: Masculinity and the Black Nationalist Tradition from Slave Spirituals to Rap Music*.

Greta de Jong is assistant professor of history at the University of Nevada, Reno and the author of *A Different Day: African American Struggles for Justice in Rural Louisiana, 1900-1970*.

Caroline Emmons is an Assistant Professor of History at Hampden-Sydney College. She is the author of a forthcoming article in the *Florida Historical Quarterly* on the efforts to equalize teachers' salaries in Florida. She is working on a manuscript about Ruby Hurley, Southeastern Field Secretary for the NAACP from 1951 to 1978. She would like to acknowledge the assistance of Hampden-Sydney College in helping her complete the research for this article, and Maxine Jones of Florida State University for her helpful suggestions. An earlier version of her essay on Harry Moore appeared in the *Journal of Negro History*.

Thavolia Glymph teaches African & African American Studies and history at Duke University. She is the co-editor of *Freedom: A Documentary History of Emancipation—The Wartime Genesis of Free Labor, Freedom: A Documentary History of Emancipation—The Destruction of Slavery*, and *Essays on the Postbellum Southern Economy*. She is currently working on a book titled *Emancipation and the Destruction of the Plantation Household*.

Adam Green is Assistant Professor of History and American Studies at New York University. He is currently working on two book projects— *Selling the Race: Culture and Community in Black Chicago, 1940– 1955* (University of Chicago Press), and a study of the Depression-era friendship of journalists Claude Barnett and Fay Jackson, as it relates to the black struggle for happiness.

Michael Honey teaches African American, labor and ethnic studies and American History at the University of Washington, Tacoma, and holds the Harry Bridges Chair in Labor Studies at the University of Washington. His prize-winning books include *Southern Labor and Black Civil Rights: Organizing Memphis Workers* and *Black Workers Remember: An Oral History of Segregation, Unionism, and the Freedom Struggle*.

Winston James teaches history at Columbia University. His books include *Inside Babylon: The Caribbean Diaspora in Britain*, with Clive Harris, *Holding Aloft the Banner of Ethiopia: Caribbean Radicalism in Early Twentieth Century America*, and *A Fierce Hatred of Injustice: Claude McKay's Jamaica and His Poetry of Rebellion*. He is presently working on a book titled *Claude McKay: The Making of a Black Bolshevik, 1889–1923*. An earlier version of his essay here was published in *Souls: A Critical Journal of Black Culture, Politics and Society*.

Brian Kelly is a Lecturer in the School of History at Queen's University Belfast in Ireland. His first book, *Race, Class, and Power in the Alabama Coalfields, 1908-1921*, received the H. L. Mitchell Award of the Southern Historical Association for a distinguished book on the southern working class in 2000–2001. He is currently working on two projects: a textbook on *African Americans and the Labor Movement,* and a monograph on *Black Elites, Black Workers, and the Labor Question in the Jim Crow South.*

Tracy E. K'Meyer is an Associate Professor of United States history at the University of Louisville, where she is also the director of the Oral History Center. Her first book was *Interracialism and Christian Community in the Postwar South: The Story of Koinonia Farm.* She is currently working on a book-length study of the civil rights movement in Louisville.

Paul Ortiz is Assistant Professor of Community Studies at the University of California, Santa Cruz. He is co-editor of *Remembering Jim Crow: African Americans Tell about Life in the Segregated South,* and author of *Like Water Covered the Sea: The African American Freedom Struggle in Florida, 1877–1920* (University of California Press, forthcoming). He has written on Latino farm worker organizing and is currently doing research on labor movements and anticolonialism in the Caribbean.

Charles M. Payne is the Sally Dalton Robinson Professor of African-American studies, history, and sociology at Duke University. His areas of research interest include urban education and social change. He is the author of *I've Got the Light of Freedom: The Organizing Tradition in the Mississippi Civil Rights Movement* and a co-author of *Debating the Civil Rights Movement.*

Wim Roefs is a Ph.D. candidate in the History Department of the University of South Carolina. His dissertation will be about editor John McCray and the South Carolina civil rights struggle in the 1940s and 1950s.

Scott A. Sandage is Associate Professor of United States cultural history at Carnegie Mellon University. He is the author of *Forgotten Men: Failure in American Culture.* An earlier version of his essay here received the 1993 Louis Pelzer Memorial Award from the Organization of American Historians and the 1992 Bryant Spann Memorial Prize from the Eugene V. Debs Foundation.

Ula Y. Taylor is an associate professor of history in the African American Studies Department at the University of California, Berkeley. Her articles on feminism and black nationalism have appeared in *The Black Scholar, Journal of Black Studies, Feminist Studies, Souls,* and *the Journal of Women's History.* She is the author of *The Veiled Garvey: The Life and Times of Amy Jacques Garvey.* Her current project explores the experiences of women in the Nation of Islam under the leadership of Elijah Muhammad.

Peter H. Wood teaches Colonial History and Native American History at Duke University. He is the author of a book on early South Carolina entitled *Black Majority Negroes in Colonial South Carolina from 1670 through the Stono Rebellion* and a survey of early African American history titled *Strange New Land.* He is the co-author of *Winslow Homer's Images of Blacks: The Civil War and Reconstruction Years* and a recent U.S. history survey text titled *Created Equal.* He has chaired the boards of the Highlander Education Center and the Africa News Service.

Nan Elizabeth Woodruff teaches at Pennsylvania State University. She is the author of *As Rare as Rain: Federal Relief in the Great Southern Drought of 1930-31* and *American Congo: The African American Freedom Struggle in the Delta.*

Permissions

Peter Wood, "Slave Labor Camps in Early America: Overcoming Denial and Discovering the Gulag." In *Inequality in America*, ed. Carla Pestana and Sharon Salinger. Copyright © 1999 by the Trustees of Dartmouth College, reprinted by permission of the University Press of New England.

David S. Cecelski, "Abraham Galloway: Wilmington's Lost Prophet and the Rise of Black Radicalism in the American South." In *Democracy Betrayed: The Wilmington Race Riot of 1898 and its Legacy*, ed. David S. Cecelski and Timothy B. Tyson. Copyright © 1998 by the University of North Carolina Press.

Elsa Barkley Brown, "Negotiating and Transforming the Public Sphere: African American Political Life in the Transition from Slavery to Freedom," *Public Culture* 7, no. 1 (fall 1994): 107-46. Copyright 1994. All rights reserved. Reprinted by permission of Duke University Press.

Ula Taylor, "Intellectual Pan-African Feminists: Amy Ashwood Garvey and Amy Jacques-Garvey," *Abafazi* 9, no. 1 (1998). Reprinted by permission.

Greta de Jong, "'With the Aid of God and the F.S.A.': The Louisiana Farmers' Union and the African American Freedom Struggle in the New Deal Era," *Journal of Social History* 43, no. 1. Reprinted by permission.

Winston James, "Being Red and Black in Jim Crow America: Notes on the Ideology and Travails of America's Socialist Pioneers, 1877-1930," *Souls* 1 (fall 1999): 45-65. Reprinted by permission of the author.

Caroline Emmons, "'A Bland, Scholarly, Teetotalling Sort of Man': Harry T. Moore and the Struggle for Black Equality in Florida," *Journal of Negro History* 82, no. 2 (spring 1997): 232-43. Reprinted by permission.

Scott Sandage, "A Marble House Divided: The Lincoln Memorial, the Civil Rights Movement and the Politics of Memory, 1939-1963," *Journal of American History* 80 (June 1993): 135-67. Reprinted by permission.

Index

Note: Page numbers followed by the letter *f* indicate figures.